PRACTICAL
PROBLEM
SOLVER

READER'S DIGEST

PRACTICAL PROBLEM SOLVER

Published by The Reader's Digest Association Limited
LONDON NEW YORK SYDNEY CAPE TOWN MONTREAL

CONTENTS

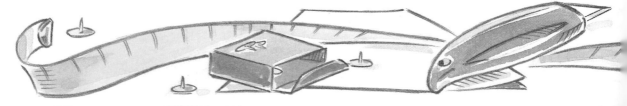

*Feature boxes on specialised
repairs and decorative
techniques include:*

An alphabetical selection of
easy-to-make household
products, craft accessories,
herbal remedies and delicious
dishes. Make your own
mouthwash, use up a glut of
courgettes or bring a shiny finish
to your car with a homemade
wax polish   this is the section
that fills in any gaps in your
essential home knowledge and
will let you rely more on yourself
and less on others.

CONTRIBUTORS

STAFF AND CONTRIBUTORS (AMERICAN EDITION)

Project editors
Jim Dwyer
Sally French

Art editors
Evelyn Bauer
Perri DeFino

Writers
Marty Anderson
Ann Arnott
Pauline M J Bradshaw
Therese Hoehlien Cerbie
Rita G Christopher
Thomas Christopher

Sarah Clayton
Donna Dannen
Kent Dannen
Gene Hamilton
Katie Hamilton
Signe Hammer
Lorna B Harris
Merle Henkenius
Penny Hinkle
John H Ingersoll
Peter H Johnson
Frank B Latham
George deLucenay Leon
Margaret Moore
Boyd Norton
Cinda Siler
Elizabeth Tener

Joseph Truini
Frank X Wamsley
Jeff Yablonka

Illustrators
Stephen Gardner
John Gist
Linda Gist
Ed Lipinski
Marianne E Markey
Ray Skibinski
Mario Stasolla
Victoria Vebell
Mary Wilshire

STAFF AND CONTRIBUTORS (BRITISH EDITION)

Project editors
Sandy Shepherd
Henrietta Wilkinson

Consultants
Pat Alburey
Adrian Bailey
Peter Bateman
Jane Bidder
Richard Bragg
Dr Barrie Brown
Dr P J K Burton
Ivor Carroll

Carolyn Chapman
Dr James Cox
Martin Davey
Simon Gilham
Bee Golding
Stan Greenberg
Cassandra Kent
Cameron McNeish
Sheena Meredith
Philip Swindells
Arlene Usden
Peter Vaines
Sharon Wickens
Tony Wilkins

Jim Williams
Professor David Williams
Peter Willis
Barbara Yardley

Illustrators
Richard Bonson
Mike Gray
Malcolm McGregor
Larry Rostant

PROBLEM SOLVER'S DICTIONARY

You may not find a cure for all the world's woes in the following A-Z, but it certainly contains plenty of inventive, down-to-earth suggestions to help you deal with the sorts of problems that bedevil day-to-day life.

Abdominal flab

• Proper posture can do wonders for the way your stomach looks. Stand up straight, put your shoulders back, and tuck in your abdomen and buttocks.

• Breathe deeply, from the diaphragm.

• Pull in your abdominal muscles and hold for several seconds. Make the exercise part of your routine; do it while you're brushing your teeth or sitting at your desk, or whenever you're stuck in traffic or waiting for a bus or train.

• If you don't have a bicycle, try this bicycle exercise. Lie on your back. Put your hands beneath your buttocks and bend both knees up to your chest. Extend one leg straight up towards the ceiling. As you bend it with a pedalling motion, extend the other. Repeat 10 to 20 times.

Caution Do not attempt this exercise if you suffer from back pain; consult your doctor about the exercises that will strengthen your abdominal muscles without damaging your back.

• Do bent-leg curl-ups as shown below. Lie on your back. Inhale and then, as you exhale, slowly curl your head and shoulders upwards and slide your hands up your thighs towards your knees. Pause. Inhale, and then exhale while uncurling down to a resting position. Repeat 10 times.

• While doing any exercise, contract your abdominal muscles to keep yourself in alignment. During an abdomen-toning supine exercise, keep the small of your back on the floor; otherwise your hip flexors will take on the abdomen's work.

Abrasive paper

• Run out of sandpaper? For smoothing down plaster walls after stripping wall-coverings, use a nylon scouring pad or unwoven fabric pad of the type used for cleaning kitchen utensils.

• A pumice stone, of the kind used on the skin, can be used dry to smooth wood, or dampened with water to smooth hard plastics.

• Metal-cleaning wadding is ideal for smoothing and polishing acrylic plastics.

• For fine-finishing decorative wood surfaces prior to varnishing, use fine steel wool. It is more effective than the finest abrasive paper. Always work with the grain of the wood to avoid scratches across the grain.

• Emery cloth is ideal for awkward spots, as it can be used in strips and pulled back and forth across the surface to be smoothed.

• Don't be tempted to keep old abrasive paper 'because it feels smoother'. The irregular surface of worn materials leads to serious scratching. Always use new paper.

• With a rough surface, start with coarse abrasive paper and gradually work down to the finer grades as the surface improves.

• When working with wood, wear a simple dust mask to keep the dust from your lungs. Some hardwood dusts are dangerous if inhaled.

Acne

A blemished skin is a great worry to many people and particularly to teenagers, who suffer the most from acne. But the good news is you can control acne, and it will eventually improve. Here are some simple and easy tips for keeping it at bay. Your spots may not respond to treatment immediately, but at least you can stop them from getting worse.

• Wash regularly with medicated soap and hot water. If this does not work, try antiseptic and keratolytic creams. Your chemist will advise you which to use.

• Try not to touch your face with your hands – you will leave more germs on it, and it has enough to cope with already.

• Don't squeeze or pick the spots or blackheads – you will make them worse, quite apart from damaging your skin structure and leaving scars.

• Drink 6-8 glasses of purified water daily. If sweets or fatty foods, such as chocolate, chips, cheese, nuts and fried food, make your spots worse, stop eating them. Fresh fruit, salads and raw vegetables are far better for your skin.

• Try to get sunlight on your face in short bursts and without burning your skin.

• Keep your hair short and wash it regularly. The oil on dirty hair that falls on your face can cause spots.

• If you have to use cosmetics, ask your chemist for a non-greasy make.

• If your spots turn into cysts, go and see your doctor. He may prescribe antibiotics, or a hormone or vitamin A preparation, which are necessary to prevent the cysts from turning into scars.

Adult children at home

• Talk to your adult son or daughter about how long they want to stay at home for – and why. Express your own views and reach a compromise.

• To reduce friction, write out a contract outlining rules for food, expenses, chores and sharing facilities (such as the cooker and washing machine). Wage-earners living at home should pay their own way as well as sharing household tasks – it will also prepare them for independence.

• Install a contributions box next to the telephone. If you're desperate to stop calls, buy a phone lock (see p.203).

• Coordinate social plans by encouraging everyone to use a family diary or bulletin board. (A parents' night out at the theatre might be a good time for an adult son or daughter to have friends

Bent-leg curl-up: this exercise fights flab by strengthening the abdomen.

around, for example.) Set aside one evening a week or month for the whole family to have dinner together or perhaps go out for a drink.

• Invest in large stackable, plastic containers (or vegetable racks) to store excess books and baggage until your child moves out. These containers are available from most hardware stores.

Aggressive pets

• An aggressive dog is always potentially dangerous. But if your dog misbehaves in a non-threatening manner around a new baby, the postman or anyone else, you may be able to modify its behaviour with positive reinforcement. You might try showering it with attention and treats when the disliked person is present. The dog may gradually begin to enjoy the person's presence.

• Does your bird peck at you when you're filling its water dish? Darken the cage by hanging a black cloth over it – this will subdue your bird instantly and allow you to remove and replace cage furniture at your leisure and comfort.

• If your cat tries to attack your bird, suspend the cage from the ceiling or place it on a pedestal.

• Spray an aggressive cat with a plant mister. Or smack the floor next to the animal with a rolled-up newspaper.

• Are you trying to stop a dogfight? Don't yell at the dogs; make a loud noise –

press your car horn, ring a bell, or beat on a frying pan. If this fails, douse the combatants with a hose or with buckets of water.

Airing cupboard

• To keep table linen from creasing, install a wooden or metal rod just beneath a low shelf and hang the linen on hangers padded with cardboard tubes, from finished rolls of kitchen towel.

• Fold and store bed or bath linen in sets, rather than by size. That way you can grab a complete set when you want it instead of having to pick through several stacks.

Airsickness

• If you suffer from this problem, reserve a seat over a wing, where you feel the least turbulence, in a non-smoking zone. Fly well rested and wear loose clothes. Eat light, easily digestible food before and during the flight, and try to avoid alcohol and cigarette smoke. As soon as you're seated, tilt the vent above you so that the air is directed towards your face.

• If your child is susceptible to airsickness, bring along his favourite games, toys and puzzles to distract him.

• Take anti-travel-sickness medicines (available from a chemist) ½ to 1 hour before departure. Some travel medicines may cause a dry mouth, others may make you drowsy.

• If you begin to feel dizzy or nauseous, recline your seat (unless the plane is taking off or coming in to land) and close your eyes or stare at a fixed point. Alternately tense and relax your body.

Air travel

• Book your ticket through a travel agent wherever possible. Insist that the agent checks all available flights and prices. Return scheduled flights are usually cheaper if you are able to stay over a weekend. Check whether there are senior citizen or child discounts.

• Charter flights are much cheaper than

scheduled flights, but you must be sure you can meet the conditions and limitations set by the charter company.

• If your flight is part of a package holiday, make sure that the tour operator is a member of ABTA.

• Do not book a ticket unless you are sure that you can travel at that time. Airline policies on postponement and refunds vary according to the type of ticket, but may not be generous. Do not book standby unless you are prepared to be disappointed.

• If possible, pay for your ticket with a credit card. This will usually give you free travel insurance.

• Read your ticket immediately. Check that the information is correct. Make a photocopy of your ticket or write down the number and keep it in a safe place. This will help you get reimbursed if your ticket is lost or stolen. If that happens, contact the airline or your travel agent immediately and put in a lost-ticket claim. Duplicate tickets are usually issued only subject to an indemnity if the original ticket is used.

• Before you leave home or work for the airport, call the airline or the check-in desk at the airport to find out if the flight has been delayed.

• Flight delays are more common on charter flights. If your scheduled flight is delayed, or the airline has overbooked and there is no seat for you, the airline should provide you with a refund on your ticket, in accordance with an EC directive, which depends on the length of the delay. For refunds for delays on package holidays, see your booking conditions. You can expect your airline to provide you with refreshments and accommodation in the case of substantial delays.

• Pack your luggage personally, lock your case or bag (preferably with a combination lock) and see it is checked in. Never pack any of the prohibited items shown on your ticket. Never carry anything for anyone else, unless you know them personally and have checked out the item fully.

• Be prepared for substantial security at airports. You may be subjected to a short body search.

• On international flights check out your duty-free allowances. Do not take more unless you are prepared to pay duty.

• Remember that smoking is not permitted on planes on most domestic flights and is forbidden in some terminals.

• You can fly at greatly reduced rates by delivering a package as an air courier. Some companies advertise for freelance couriers in newspapers or magazines. You can also check the Yellow Pages under 'Courier services', although some listed companies don't use freelancers.

• Even if you don't fly regularly, consider joining a frequent flyer programme. Some credit cards award a points system for 'air miles' travelled, which entitles you to free travel after you have accumulated a certain number of points. However, membership of this system is not automatic and has to be requested by the card holder.

Alarm clock

• An electronic timer can serve as a backup alarm clock for home or travel. You can get one that times up to 10 hours and, with three separate channels, can even work as a 'snooze alarm'.

• Ask a friend or relative to give you a morning wake-up call – and offer to return the favour.

• British Telecom provides an alarm call service. Dial 100 to book the call or series of calls. However, choose the time at which you make the booking carefully, because you are charged for the call or calls at the time of booking.

• Set an automatic timer to turn on all the lights, the radio and the TV in your bedroom for the time you want to get up.

• On the night before you have to get up early, set out a breakfast that needs little preparation – fruit, cereal and rolls, for example. Invest in an automatic coffee or tea machine with a timer to make your early morning drink.

Alcohol

If your alcoholic drink is too strong and there's no room in the glass for any more mixer, you can float one or two thin slices of cucumber on the surface;

they will help to absorb some of the harsh taste. Floating long slivers of cucumber in a punch bowl will mellow punch in the same way. See also TIPS ON TIPPLING, p.261.

A levels

How can you decide which A levels to do if, like most 16-year-olds, you don't yet have a clue what you want to do with the rest of your life? Contrary to what anxious school careers advisors and parents will tell you, your choice of A levels is perhaps not as crucial as you might think, although it is important. It is true that A levels limit the scope of what you study and can deny you later access to some occupations, but if you want to keep several longer term career options open, here are some steps you can take.

• Ask yourself what interests you most, feels important to you and stretches you in a fulfilling way. Answers to these questions will give you a clue about whether arts, sciences, life studies or art and design (or something else) should be the general direction you take. Don't be tempted simply to do the A levels that match your highest GCSE grades. Remember, the style of learning, the content and the format of the A-level examinations are very different.

• If you feel your A-level choices narrow your options, start a new subject or keep up with one or two secondary interests after you've embarked on the A-level course – for example, doing a new GCSE subject, such as an additional language, or joining a music club.

• If you are worried about how your choice will affect your access to degree or other further education courses, remember that many colleges and universities now offer integrated subjects such as urban studies, media studies or business studies. Many courses of this kind are a sound basis for moving into several occupations and applicants do not have to have a narrow range of A levels to qualify for them.

• Consider broadening your experience after school by taking time off from full-time education to gain work experience in a field that attracts you.

Allen keys

Are you lacking a set of Allen keys? You can still tighten or remove an Allen-head screw; just try different sizes of small, plain screwdrivers until you find one that fits across the opening.

Or, if the Allen screw protrudes above the work surface, use a hacksaw to cut a slot in the top; then use a standard screwdriver to tighten or remove it. Or grip the head of the screw with the jaws of a self-grip wrench or pair of pliers.

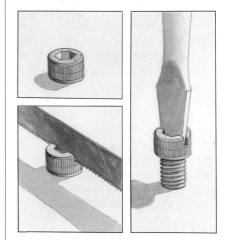

Allergies

Many people have physical reactions to allergens such as pollen, dust, foods, feathers, animal fur and medicines.

Hay fever This is the most common allergy. Its familiar symptoms are sneezing and a stuffy, runny nose. It's usually a fairly mild reaction to pollen and can be treated with over-the-counter preparations or prescription antihistamines.

See your doctor. He may prescribe medicines such as eyedrops, nasal spray or inhaler to damp down your body's reaction to pollen. In more severe cases he may prescribe steroid tablets or injections.

Anaphylactic shock This is the most severe form of allergic reaction. It can develop in minutes or even seconds after contact with an allergen, or it may appear half an hour or more later, or even progress suddenly from an apparently mild allergic reaction.

Honeybee venom is a potent allergen to some people.

The face, chest and back may become flushed, itchy and burning. The face, tongue and lips may swell and the lips turn bluish. Breathing is laboured and wheezing. The pulse becomes weak and rapid. Pale skin, dizziness, nausea and headache may follow. Finally, in very serious cases, the person may faint and lapse into a coma.

The casualty needs immediate medical assistance. Treat for shock and ensure that he has an open airway. If he becomes unconscious, place him in the recovery position. If breathing fails, start artificial respiration immediately (see p.167). Take him to a doctor or call an ambulance. See also ASTHMA, p.13.

Altitude adjustment

If you are planning a holiday walking in mountains, try to avoid altitude problems by taking it easy during your first day. Don't do aerobic exercise. Drink plenty of water but no alcohol. If you begin to feel unwell (headache, dizziness or nausea), go to bed and rest.

Serious mountain climbers need to take further precautions to help prevent acute mountain sickness (AMS). If you have a heart or lung condition, consult your doctor before you go. Even if you're in good health, ask about prescription drugs that will prevent the symptoms of AMS developing.

If your destination is higher than 8000ft/2400m, spend the first day at an intermediate level. Then proceed upwards at a daily rate of 500-1000ft/150-300m, resting often and drinking at least 4 pints/2.3 litres of water a day. If you're already used to living at a high altitude, you can probably ascend or descend as much as 5000ft/1500m with few problems.

Breathing pure oxygen will ease discomfort, as will descending to a lower level to rest. If you develop a headache or a nosebleed or feel dizzy or nauseous, immediately descend 2000-3000ft/600-900m. Make sure you get medical attention promptly.

American football jargon

Here's your guide to what the commentators are saying on television and radio:

Audible A play called at the line of scrimmage, nullifying the play that was called in the huddle.

Blitz A defensive play in which one or more linebackers rush the passer. It's a gamble, since the rushing linebackers leave holes in the defensive formation.

Bomb A very long forward pass.

Bullet An extremely forceful forward pass which travels in a straight line.

Bump and run A defensive manoeuvre in which a cornerback hits or bumps into a potential pass receiver as he leaves the line of scrimmage, hoping to upset his timing, and then runs with him. Only one such bump is allowed.

Clipping An illegal block in which an offensive player hits a defensive player from behind.

Completion A forward pass that's caught by an eligible receiver.

Conversion The scoring of an extra point after a touchdown, made by kicking the ball from a set position so that it clears the crossbar between the goalposts. In college ball only, a team can score a 2-point conversion by running or passing the ball into the end zone.

Fair catch An option of the receiver of a short kick. By raising his hand before catching the ball, he indicates he will not run with it; defenders may not tackle him.

False start A violation committed by an offensive player who, after having assumed a set position on the line of scrimmage, moves before the ball has been picked up.

Interference Preventing an opposing player from catching a pass by holding or pushing him intentionally; an illegal manoeuvre.

Line of scrimmage An imaginary line upon which the forward point of the ball rests; it separates the offensive and defensive forces.

Offside A 5-yard penalty called when a player has any part of his body beyond the line of scrimmage as the ball is put into play.

Onside kick A deceptive kickoff in which the ball skitters along the ground just far enough so that the kicking team may recover it.

Pocket An area protected by blockers behind the line of scrimmage, within which the quarterback sets up to throw a pass.

Reverse A play in which an offensive player running in one direction hands the ball to another moving in the opposite direction.

Sack To tackle the quarterback behind the line of scrimmage.

Safety A 2-point score awarded to the defence for placing the ball in the offence's own end area.

Shotgun An offensive formation, used primarily for passing, in which the quarterback stands several yards behind the centre to receive the ball passed back by the centre.

Snap The point where the ball is passed back from the line of scrimmage.

Two-minute warning An official timeout, called when 2 minutes of play remain in each half of a game, during which commercials and promotional spots are aired.

Anchor

If you are going canoeing or rowing, take along an old netball net, a net shopping bag or even a sturdy canvas bag. When you arrive at your anchorage, fill it with rocks and close the ends with cord or wire. Attach a rope to it to make a disposable anchor. When you need to, just lower the net to the bottom; when you've finished, simply throw away the stones.

Antiseptics

• Soap and warm water are your first line of defence against germs; always wash even minor grazes, burns and cuts thoroughly.

• Be sure to remove all foreign material, such as gravel, from grazes and cuts. If necessary, gently use a scrubbing brush.

• Before doing anything else, cool burns with cold water. *Do not apply* antiseptics to deep burns or blisters, but antiseptic ointment may be applied to small superficial burns to prevent them from becoming infected.

• If a wound is large, bleeding heavily or likely to require medical attention, do not apply antiseptic ointment.

• Non-prescription antiseptic creams are good for cuts and have the added advantage of preventing the dressing from sticking to the wound. Use them with caution, however: they can produce an allergic rash. If the wound isn't healing after a couple of days, you should see a doctor.

Ants

Ants enter houses in search of food, warmth and shelter. When they find food, they establish a trail that leads back to their nest outside. Follow the trail to the point of entry into the house and block it off with mastic sealer.

• Destroy and wipe up every ant you find. Or mix some boric-acid powder (which is lethal to ants) with icing sugar and leave it on their trails. They will eat this and take it back to their nests, where the poison will be spread.

• Traditional organic ant repellents, such as talcum powder, cream of tartar, powdered sulphur or oil of cloves, were once advised to be scattered at entry points, but there are now laws against their use.

• You could also use a proprietary ant

killer. There is a jelly bait which the workers take back to the nest; an insecticidal lacquer for wall and floor junctions; and a puffer pack of powder for blowing into nest entrances and into any cracks, crevices and wall cavities where ants are seen.

Aphids

• Wash aphids off houseplants under a gentle flow of tap water. Organic gardeners treat large infestations with soft soaps or derris dust.

• Interplant vegetables with plants such as onions, garlic and chives which are claimed to repel aphids.

Appetite control

• Avoid crash or fad diets. A sensible goal for a diet is a weight loss of 1-2 lb / 0.5-0.9 kg a week.

• Eat foods low in fat and sugar but high in complex carbohydrates (fruits, vegetables, grains and pulses). Animal fat readily turns to human fat.

• Don't skip a meal; eat regular small meals instead of infrequent big ones – you won't feel as hungry and your body will use more energy in digestion.

• Eat slowly, savouring each bite. It takes about 20 minutes for the feeling of fullness to register; wait that long before eating more.

• When you feel hungry between meals, have a sugarless cup of tea or coffee – caffeine inhibits the appetite.

• Exercise regularly. Not only does it burn up calories, but it can also make you feel temporarily less hungry.

• After about 3 weeks of dieting, you may stop losing weight altogether until your body accepts its new norm. The trick is

to get past this 3-week mark without regaining what you have lost. When you finally reach your ideal weight, maintain it for at least 3 weeks to set a new norm.

Appetite loss

In children

• If a toddler seems to have lost his appetite, he may just be growing more slowly than before. Don't force him to eat. Give him as much as he wants at mealtimes, but cut down on snacks between meals – he'll soon get hungry.

In teenagers and adults

• Check that you're getting the recommended daily dose of B vitamins, which help important enzymes to function.

• Cut out all caffeine (found in coffee, tea, chocolate and soft drinks), which is an appetite suppressant.

• Try eating faster; you may be able to beat the brain signal that says you're full 20 minutes after eating.

• See a doctor if symptoms persist – loss of appetite may be caused by illness.

• Prolonged appetite loss in a teenage girl, particularly if periods stop, could be anorexia nervosa, a serious disorder that requires a doctor's care.

In elderly people

• At about the age of 65, many people lose some sense of taste and smell, and their appetite suffers. Try stimulating it with a variety of strongly flavoured foods, such as curry or chilli con carne.

• Vary the texture, colour and temperature of your food; this may compensate for the lack of strong flavour.

• Savour each bite. Chewing slowly and moving the food around in the mouth before swallowing increases contact with the taste buds and, through the back of the mouth, with smell receptors in the nose.

Appointments

There is no such thing as being fashionably late for an appointment. If you are habitually late, you are guilty of wasting others' time and will certainly gain a bad reputation for it. Here are some habits that will help you become more punctual:

• Give yourself extra time – just in case you're delayed by weather, traffic or other circumstances.

• Keep only one diary; carry it between your home and workplace.

• Use a watch, a calculator or an electronic 'secretary' with a beeper to remind you when to leave.

• If possible, travel by scheduled public transport, such as a train, so that you'll have to depart at a set time.

Lateness in others

• Ask a chronically late person to call you just before he leaves.

• Avoid meeting him for scheduled events, such as films or concerts. If you must do so, plan to meet early, perhaps for a meal. Arrange to meet where it is convenient to wait.

• If your doctor or dentist is known to overbook patients, call first to see if he's running late.

Aspirin

Aspirin relieves pain and reduces inflammation. It also lowers high temperatures and fever. It is therefore useful to take aspirin if, for example, you have a cold, sore throat or inflamed joints.

The first wonder drug

Before there was aspirin, willow bark was used to ease pain. About 400 BC, Hippocrates, the 'father of medicine', advised chewing it to ease the pain of childbirth. For centuries people all over the world knew of, but did not understand, its power to treat aches and pains.

Then, in Germany in the 1820s, the magic chemical was isolated and named salicin. Later in the century, acetylsalicylic acid was developed, but no one knew what to do with it. Meanwhile, people still took a crude form of the drug that, they said, burned in their stomachs like fire ants. It was only when a young chemist at Bayer and Company tried acetylsalicylic acid on his arthritic father, with some success, that aspirin was born.

Why it was named aspirin is a subject of debate. One theory is that the word came from Spiraea, the plant genus from which salicin was actually isolated and to which the willow belongs. Aspirin tablets first appeared in shops at the turn of the century. Except for coatings and buffers, they have hardly changed since.

Aspirin also makes blood less likely to clot, thereby reducing the risk of a repeated heart attack or stroke. However, aspirin can irritate the stomach and cause ulcers and internal bleeding, so sufferers from ulcers and indigestion should avoid it. Paracetamol is less likely to cause an upset stomach but does not help to prevent heart attacks and strokes.

Caution Children under 12 should not be given aspirin to take when they have a virus because of the danger of Reye's syndrome, a rare but often fatal disease which has been linked to viral infections and aspirin. Paracetamol is considered a safer alternative if taken with care.

Asthma attack

• If someone is having an asthma attack, he will cough, wheeze and have difficulty breathing out; reassure him and try to keep him calm.

• To ease breathing, have him sit up and lean slightly forward, resting on his elbows. Or turn on the hot water in the bathroom and have him sit and breathe the moist air.

• Give him his prescribed medication and plenty of liquids, in order to prevent dehydration.

• If the medication doesn't bring immediate relief, take him – quickly but calmly – to the nearest hospital or contact his doctor.

Exercise as treatment Although exercise is usually recommended for asthmatics, if it is too strenuous it can trigger an attack – especially outdoors during cold weather or the allergy season.

• Indoor swimming is best for most asthmatics. Aerobic exercise is also good; a physically fit person gets more oxygen into his body – important during an asthma attack.

• An asthmatic should begin his exercises with a slow 15-minute warm-up and finish with an equally slow cool-down. See WARMING UP AND COOLING DOWN EXERCISES, p.224.

• To help keep his airways open, he should exercise in 1 to 2-minute spurts, breathing through his nose.

Athletics jargon

Anchor leg The last segment of a relay.

Bell In most of the world a bell is rung to denote the start of the last lap of a race. In North America a gun is fired.

Blocks In races up to 400m, starting blocks are normally used to enable runners to get away faster.

Break point In races from 600-1000m, run in lanes at the start, there is a point delineated after the first full bend at which the runners can cut into the inside. To cut in too early leads to disqualification.

Draw The order of starting, or lining up, in a race decided either by officials or by finishing position in a previous race.

Finishing line The finish is denoted by a line across the track. In some races there will also be a tape fixed at chest level. With automatic timing devices this tape is now rarely used.

False start Any athlete attempting to 'jump the gun' is decreed to have made a false start. Competitors are allowed one such transgression and are disqualified for a second; heptathlon and pentathlon athletes are allowed two.

Flyer A false start which has not been recalled by the starter.

Kick Strong injection of pace.

Lane The track is usually divided into lanes, within which athletes have to stay for the whole of some races (up to 400m) and for part of others (up to 800m, and sometimes 1000m).

Lap One complete circuit of the track. Thus a lap time would be for the last full circuit completed.

No-jump In jumping events, an attempt which has failed or was ruled illegal.

No-throw In throwing events, an attempt which has been ruled illegal.

PB Personal best – improving on an athlete's previous best performance.

Photo-finish Automatic timing device, activated by the starter's gun and stopped by a beam on the finish line, which records on film the finishing positions and times of the athletes.

Points Allocated for a performance, according to official scoring tables, for scoring multi-discipline events such as the decathlon and heptathlon.

Recall gun The starter or his assistant will fire a second shot if they consider there has been an infringement of the rules at the start of a race.

Stagger On a circular laned track, in races up to 800m and sometimes 1000m, it is necessary for the starting positions to be staggered in order to ensure that all the runners run the same distance.

Straight The section of the track approaching the finish line is called the home straight, and that on the other side is known as the back straight.

Take-off board A rectangular white board, usually wood, sunk into the runways of the long and triple jumps, from which jumps are made and measured. The athlete's foot must not overlap the far edge of the board.

Take-over zone In relays the designated area within which the baton must be passed. Failure to do so leads to disqualification.

Wind assistance For record purposes in the sprint, high hurdles and jumps, the wind component behind the athlete must not exceed 2m per second. A wind gauge set alongside the track or runway measures the strength of the wind, the direction of which can either aid or hamper the athlete.

Atomiser

• If the atomiser on your perfume bottle or plant spray gets clogged up, unscrew it from the bottle, lift it up and let the liquid inside drain out of the stem. Immerse the atomiser in water. Then pump it a few times, take it out of the water, and pump until no more water sprays out.

• Any small spray bottle, available in chemists or department stores, can be a short-term substitute for a perfume atomiser. But don't leave perfume in a plastic container for long: the plastic will interact chemically with the perfume and alter the scent.

Attics

• Short on cupboard space? Install a wooden rod or a metal rail between rafters, for hanging out-of-season

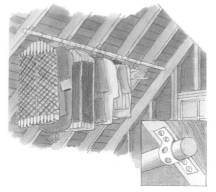

clothing. Drill through the rod and secure it with bolts. Or use pipe straps or pipe clamps to hold it against the rafters.

• Think hard – what's stored in your attic? If you can't remember, it's time to take stock of its contents. Stick up a list of the contents near the attic door or entrance, and update the information whenever you add or remove items.

• If your attic is unfinished, create a floor by nailing down two or more panels of hardboard to the ceiling joists. To support walking and storage, the panels should be at least ⅝in / 16mm thick (¾in / 19mm is even better) and span three joists. (If you want to turn your attic into an extra room, investigate local building regulations.)

• No electrical wiring in the attic? Battery-powered lights, found in most hardware shops, provide an easy means of illumination.

Avocados

• You can prevent a bowl of mashed avocado or guacamole from darkening by covering the surface closely with plastic food wrap.

• To keep sliced or cubed avocado from discolouring, sprinkle with lemon or lime juice. Coat larger pieces with softened butter, margarine or mayonnaise before refrigerating; they should keep for up to 24 hours.

• Avocados ripen almost twice as fast if sealed in a brown paper bag and stored in a warm (not hot) place, such as the airing cupboard. Even a cut avocado will ripen this way, but first cover its cut surfaces closely with plastic food wrap, as described above.

Awnings

Instead of an old-fashioned, pulley-operated awning, install a single piece of canvas attached to a wooden pole at the top and bottom. Secure the top above your window with brass hooks and attach the lower pole to the wall, as shown. Or you can create a natural awning by constructing a trellis above and out from your window and growing a flowering vine or ivy on it.

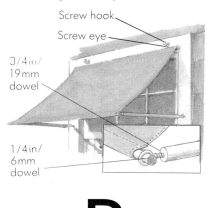

Screw hook
Screw eye
3/4in/ 19mm dowel
1/4in/ 6mm dowel

B

Babies' names

The name you choose for your child must last for ever (unless he or she changes it when adult). So consider the names carefully.

• Choose a name which can grow with the child and suit it as an adult.
• Write down the name to see how it balances with the surname.
• Consider how many other 'Sophies' and 'James's' you know. You might prefer to be more unusual.
• When drawing up a short list of middle names, check that the initials don't result in odd spellings. Include plainer middle names in case your child hates the more original first name.
• Think of possible nicknames and abbreviations.
• Imagine calling the name at the top of your voice to summon your child.
• Check that the name goes well with that of any brothers or sisters.

Baby cries

Keep calm: try to see your baby as a small person who is crying because he can't say what's wrong – and not because he's being intentionally difficult. If the following remedies don't work for you, ask your partner or friend to take over for a while. They might have more success.

• Feed him, change his nappy and check that he's not hot, cold or ill. If in doubt, ring the doctor.
• Crying babies are often tired. Rock him to sleep in your arms or in a portable baby seat (holding the handles firmly). If desperate, take him for a car ride (the motion can work wonders).
• Has he got colic? Lie him, tummy down, on your knee and rub his back towards his head with stroking movements. Try a bottle of cooled, boiled water. Keep a record of his diet (and yours, if you're breastfeeding) and consult the health visitor.
• Is he teething? Try a water-filled ring (cooled in the fridge); rub his gums with a clean finger or flannel; apply teething gel to his gums to soothe them.
• Sing. It soothes both him and you, even if your voice isn't up to scratch.
• Put on the vacuum cleaner or hair dryer. Try taping these sounds and playing them back to him. The mechanical noise often helps. Some stationers sell 'baby soother' tapes with the same kind of sound, but these are usually effective only if played from birth.
• Play finger/toe games, such as This Little Piggy Went to Market. Even if the baby's too young to understand, the smile on your face can be catching.
• Massage his arms and legs with baby lotion for reassurance.

Baby fitness

As infants develop basic coordination and reflexes in their first few months, parents can provide soothing and stimulating activities to help them. Try not to push your baby; his own movements will let you know what's good for him.

Even in your baby's first days, his eye-head and eye-hand coordination can be helped by brightly coloured mobiles and toys to look at, as well as friendly people to interact with. After the first month, you can foster body awareness and confidence simply by supporting your baby in different positions. Carefully support your child in the bath so that he will enjoy the water and start to become aware of the feeling of his muscles.

You can massage your baby. Use no more pressure than your hand's weight with the palm open. Stroke smoothly outwards in slightly circular motions; this relaxes tension, soothes cramps and allows your baby to develop a sense of his body.

To stretch and strengthen your baby's arms and legs, place him on his back; raise one arm smoothly above his head while bringing the other down by his side, then reverse. Always make sure your baby's head is well supported.

Starting with his legs straight, gently bend one knee towards his stomach, then straighten the leg again. Alternate legs – and let him participate as much as he wants to.

Backache

Prevention

• Avoid any sudden strain; exercise regularly to loosen up the back and strengthen its supporting abdominal muscles.
• If you sit for long periods, make sure your back is properly supported. Place a small roll in the arch of your lower spine (at belt height) to maintain its normal S-curve. (Stuff the inside of a paper towel roll with rags and strengthen it with masking tape.)
• When lifting, never bend down from the waist – lower and raise yourself at the knees. Keep your back straight and hold the object close to your body.
• Balance items you carry evenly on both sides of your body and hold them close – or use a knapsack.
• Sleep on your back if possible, with knees raised on a pillow. If you sleep on your side, a pillow between the knees is a big help.
• If you need a firm bed, place a bedboard between the mattress and the box

spring. (Cut a sheet of ¾in/19mm plywood 1in/25mm smaller all around than your mattress and sand its edges.)
Treatment
• Limit activity or stay in bed for 48 hours.
• Depending on which works better for you, apply either heat or a cold pack for 15 minutes at a time every couple of hours over a period of 2 days. (Keep an athlete's soft cold pack in the freezer or use a bag of frozen peas; both will mould easily to your back.)
• Taking aspirin or ibuprofen (found in Nurofen) will help to combat both the pain and inflammation.
• To minimise chronic minor back pain, tip your pelvis back, then forward, until you find the position of least pain, then maintain it.

Back exercises

Strengthening and stretching the muscles of your lower back will help prevent lower back strain. The following exercises progress from gentle to strenuous. *Do only what's comfortable for you; stop exercising the moment you feel pain.* If you've had back problems, consult your doctor before starting.
Pelvic tilt Lie on your back with both of

your knees bent. Keeping your spine against the floor, squeeze your buttock muscles as hard as you can, pull your stomach muscles in, flatten the small of your back to the floor, and hold for 5 seconds. Your pelvis will tilt slightly upwards of its own accord; don't try to raise it. Repeat 10 times.
Cat stretch Get down on your hands and knees. Then arch your upper back upwards, contract your stomach muscles, and let your head drop. Hold for 5 seconds. Follow this by raising your head and reversing the action, until you return to the starting position. Avoid pushing your pelvis forward to create a swayback. Repeat 5 to 10 times.
Hip roll Lie on your back, both arms out for support. Raise your knees towards your chest and, keeping them together, roll them gently from side to side, keeping your shoulders on the floor if you can. Roll 10 to 20 times.
Backward leg raises Lie flat on your stomach, resting your head on folded arms. Keeping your hips flat on the floor, slowly raise one leg from the hip until your foot is 6in/150mm above the floor. Repeat 5 to 10 times with each leg.
Single leg raises Lie on your back, knees bent, and place both hands under the lower part of your back. Press your

back into your hands, then straighten one leg and slowly raise it to the height of your bent knee. Hold in that position for 5 seconds, then slowly lower the leg to the floor. Repeat 5 to 10 times with each leg. While doing this, your lower back must always be pushing down against your hands.
Diagonal reach Start on your hands and knees. Slowly reach your right arm out in front of you; at the same time, reach your left leg straight out behind you. Stretch and hold for 5 seconds; then return to your original position. Then stretch your left arm and right leg. Repeat 10 times.

Back-packs

Cat stretch Arch your upper back upwards while contracting your stomach and letting your head drop. Hold for 5 seconds.

Then raise your head and reverse the action until you return to the kneeling position. Avoid pushing your pelvis forward.

To make a temporary backpack for carrying your lunch on a short walk, bringing home wayside treasures or transporting other light objects, just tie the waist of a long-sleeved sweatshirt or jersey with string. Knot the sleeve ends together to form a strap. Stuff your cargo inside, slip the strap over your shoulders, and you're on your way.

Backseat drivers

To deal with one of these pests:
• Use humour ('Hey, do you want to cause an accident?') or distraction ('Please add up the miles / kilometres to the turnoff').
• Turn up the volume on the radio or tape deck, without saying it's to drown out unwanted advice.
• Sing while you drive. You may even inspire your passenger to sing along with you.
• Take the other passengers aside before setting out and ask them to keep up an active conversation.

Bad breath

• Brush your teeth with a paste of bicarbonate of soda and water to keep your breath fresh. Bicarb neutralises the acids in which the bacteria that cause bad breath and tooth decay thrive. An antiseptic mouthwash will also help.
• Chew fresh parsley after eating a meal. This fragrant herb contains an antiseptic that kills bacteria in the mouth. It's effective against garlic and onions too, as are mint leaves and cloves. (Suck, don't chew, the cloves.)
• Use dental floss to dislodge decaying food particles. If your gums are red, swollen and sore, see your dentist.

Bags around the eyes

Despite the common belief that bags around the eyes result from heavy drinking, late nights or overwork, the condition is due to none of these things. Unfortunately it is hereditary, and in most cases develops in people with loose skin around their eyelids.

A cosmetic concealer stick can lighten the area under the eyes and reduce the effect. It should be applied carefully and gently smoothed into the skin. Women can hide loose skin on the upper eyelid by using one of the darker shades of eyeshadow applied across the deepest part of the lid.

People who have sinus problems or allergies can experience a slightly swollen area around the eye, but this is usually temporary.

Baking ingredients

Margarine or vegetable fat works as well as butter in most cakes and quick breads, although the finished product may look and taste different to one made with butter. Here are some other substitutes:
• If you're out of self-raising flour, replace it with plain flour sifted with baking powder. For 4oz/115g of self-raising flour, substitute 4oz/115g of plain flour plus 1 level teaspoon of baking powder.
• For 1oz/30g of chocolate, mix 3 level tablespoons unsweetened cocoa powder with 1 tablespoon softened butter, margarine or vegetable oil.
• For ½ pint/285ml whole milk use ¼ pint/150ml evaporated milk plus ¼ pint/150ml water
• To make up 1 teaspoon of baking powder, use ¼ teaspoon bicarbonate of soda, ½ teaspoon cream of tartar and ½ teaspoon ground rice. Or use ¼ teaspoon bicarbonate of soda plus 4fl oz/115ml yoghurt or sour cream (omit 4fl oz/115ml of liquid from the recipe).
• For 4oz/115g of granulated sugar use 4oz/115g honey or golden syrup.
• For 4oz/115g of dark brown sugar combine 3oz/85g white sugar and 2 tablespoons molasses or black treacle. Keep in mind, however, that syrup, honey and treacle will make your baking heavier.
• If you have some spare yolks in the refrigerator – for example, after having used the whites for a sorbet or meringue – use 2 yolks mixed with 1-2 tablespoons water, depending on the size of the yolks, as a substitute for a whole egg.

Ball

Don't just throw away your child's punctured beach ball. An inflatable vinyl ball can be repaired simply with a heated screwdriver.
• Inflate the ball slightly and plunge it into a bucket of water. Identify where the bubbles are coming from, take out the ball, dry it and mark the puncture holes with chalk.

Heat a screwdriver over a gas flame or with a blowtorch, and then rub it back and forth over the puncture. The vinyl will melt and close.

Leave to harden for 5 minutes, and then reinflate.

Ball cock

Is your toilet cistern overflowing? This may mean that the ball inside it is damaged and not rising enough, or that the float arm needs adjustment.
• Take the top off the cistern and look inside. If the ball is lower in the water than one-third of its diameter, it probably has a crack or hole in it. Unscrew it from the float arm and shake it, to hear if it contains water. If it does, buy a new one from a hardware shop or plumbers' supplier and screw it on.
• If the ball is not damaged, try adjusting the float arm by means of the screw adjuster, if there is one; if not, slightly bend the metal arm. Make sure that when the arm is adjusted the water level remains below the overflow pipe. Check by flushing the toilet and watching the cistern fill up.
• The valve itself may have collected deposits and need cleaning, or it may

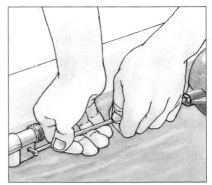

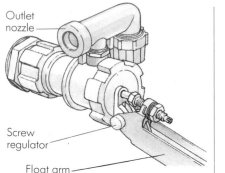

Outlet nozzle

Screw regulator

Float arm

need a new washer. Turn off the water supply. Then, using pliers, remove the split pin that attaches the arm to the valve. Unscrew the valve cap and take out the piston, valve washer and piston cap. Use wire wool to remove deposits from the piston. Check the valve washer. If it is severely corroded, replace it – a new one can be bought from a hardware shop.

Check the rubber washer on the other side of the valve casing. If it is worn, replace it.

Put the piston back together again and then smear it lightly with petroleum jelly, before inserting it back into the valve casing.

Ballpoint pen

• In cold weather, the inkflow in ballpoint pens slows down. Warm up a pen by rubbing it vigorously between your hands, or place it on a radiator for a few minutes.

• Sometimes air pockets separate portions of ink in the tube inside the pen. With some pens you can remove the ink tube and blow down it to force the globules together. This is easier if you have already warmed up the ink as above, however.

Bamboo furniture

To clean dust from the crevices of bamboo furniture, use the brush attachment of a vacuum cleaner.

Sponge dirty bamboo with a solution of warm water and mild detergent; rinse and wipe dry. Apply liquid wax occasionally to stop the bamboo from cracking.

Bandages

• Improvise an adhesive bandage by moistening a ball of cotton wool with diluted antiseptic and holding it in place with adhesive tape, masking tape or clear sticking tape.

• If you need an emergency dressing for a serious wound, use the cleanest material available: a sanitary towel, a clean handkerchief, a shirt, a T-shirt, a folded sheet or towel, or a washcloth. Fold the material to make a pad that covers the entire wound.

Hold the dressing in place with wide strips torn from a shirt or a sheet, or with a tie or folded scarf. Get medical treatment as soon as possible.

• Where there may be some delay in treating a deep cut, make a butterfly strip from sticking plaster (see below). Hold the cut closed while applying the strip and then cover it loosely.

• If anything, such as grass or gravel, is stuck in the wound, use a raised pad to avoid pressure on the object. See also CUTS AND ABRASIONS, p.59.

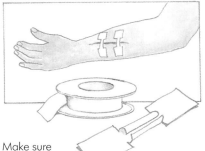

Make sure the edges of the cut align before applying the bandage.

Basketball jargon

Here's a guide to what the television commentators are saying:

Air ball A shot that misses the backboard, the basket and the rim.
Backcourt The half-court that is being defended; the defence's backcourt is the offence's forecourt.
Draw a foul To provoke a foul.
Dribble To bounce the ball on the floor; a player who stops dribbling and starts again has committed a double dribble.

Double-team To guard an offensive player with two defenders.
Dunk To put the ball into the basket with your hands above the rim.
Foul out To commit more than the allotted number of fouls (six in professional games, five in amateur basketball) and be forced to leave the game.
Free throw The reward for being fouled: an undefended shot at the basket from the foul line, worth 1 point if made.
Full-court press A defence in which the entire court is guarded.
Goaltending Interfering with the ball as it arcs downwards over the rim of the basket.
Hook A one-handed shot by a player who pivots to face the basket, lifting his arm over his head.
Lay-up A shot delivered by jumping up and tossing the ball lightly off the backboard or over the rim.
Loose-ball foul A personal foul committed while trying to gain control of the ball.
Pick An offensive manoeuvre in which a player, by standing still, blocks a defender.
Point guard A guard who directs his team's offence, usually from behind the offensive foul line.
Rebound To gain possession of a ball after a missed shot.
Slam dunk A dunk that is jammed hard into the basket.
Swish A shot that goes into the basket touching only the net.
Three-point play The result when a player is fouled while making a basket and therefore gains the right to a free throw. Also, a basket scored from outside the 3-point line; worth 3 points.
Trap A defensive manoeuvre in which the ball handler is quickly double-teamed in order to steal the ball or force a passing error.
Travelling Taking two or more steps without dribbling the ball.

Bathing on camping trips

Take along a waterproof vinyl bag for heating water by solar energy. Fill it in the morning, leave it in the sun, and you'll have warm water for a sponge bath by evening. The plastic bladder from a boxed wine dispenser works well, and it comes complete with tap. Or you could use an empty plastic bottle.

Bathtub rings

To avoid bathtub rings, don't use oily bath preparations; use a water softener if you live in a hard-water area; rinse the tub immediately after bathing.

To prevent scratching the surface of glassfibre baths, avoid abrasive cleaning powders. Instead wipe gently with a mild cream cleaner or a fine metal polish such as Brasso or T-Cut.

Bathwater slow to drain

If a bath is slow to empty, it's possible that grease or hair have accumulated in the waste pipe, or that something like a hair grip is blocking it.
• Pull the hair up from the plughole with a bent piece of wire or a paper clip.
• If the bath is still slow to empty, wait for the water to drain and then pour in a solution of washing soda (or borax) and boiling water.
• As a last resort, use a chemical cleaner. First let the water drain, then smear petroleum jelly over the metal rim of the plughole to protect it. Protecting your hands with gloves, pour the cleaner into the hole, following the manufacturer's instructions on the packaging.
• If the bath won't drain at all, place a sink plunger over the hole and pump it sharply a few times.

Batteries

• Remove batteries from items you seldom use. Bundle them together with a rubber band and store them in a plastic sandwich bag to keep moisture out. Don't allow them to touch metal objects during storage or they may lose their power. Keep them away from warm places – best of all, store them in the refrigerator. Let them warm to room temperature before using them.
• When using battery-operated equipment in freezing weather, keep the batteries warm in your pocket until you

need to use them.
• If you can avoid it, don't store or use old batteries with new ones. New batteries can put stress on old ones and cause them to leak acid.
• Do not top up a rechargeable battery after every use. Let it run right down first or it will not recharge fully, because the battery 'remembers' how much it was recharged and will work for only that amount of time.

Bedding plants

Instead of consigning all bedding plants to a fixed place in the garden, make them portable so that they can do double duty or more. Let them brighten a party on your patio one night and adorn your front steps the next morning.
• To save strain, choose containers that are strong but light, such as fibreglass pots; even a large wooden tub is easy to move if it's set on castors. Or use an old wooden wheelbarrow; its big wheel makes it both portable and decorative.
• To lighten the load of a large container, fill it to within 10in/250mm of the top with polystyrene chips or a similar lightweight foam-based packing material; sprinkle this with a 2in/50mm layer of cat litter for drainage, and top with potting soil.

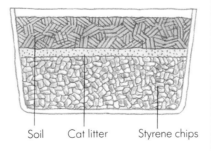

Soil   Cat litter   Styrene chips

Beds

Guests coming and you don't have enough beds in the house? If the sofa alone won't solve the problem, consider sleeping bags, air mattresses or pads of thick foam rubber. All are easy to store when not in use.

A futon – a cotton-filled, pliable mattress – is another alternative, although more expensive. You may consider it

worth the cost because it can be shaped into a low sofa for extra seating when it is not being used as a bed.

To make a double bed, place two air mattresses or futons side by side and hold them together with a fitted double sheet. (Foam rubber is not rigid enough.)

For more comfort and to prevent temporary beds from sliding during the night, place them on a thick rug.

For infants, a playpen will do. Or take a drawer from a chest of drawers and pad it, checking to see that there are no splinters in the wood. A third choice is a plastic laundry basket, also padded.

Bedsores

• An air mattress – or a thick sheepskin pad, fluffy side up, over a standard mattress – relieves pressure and prevents bedsores on heels, buttocks, elbows, head and shoulders. Pads or pillows at these points help too.
• Change a bedridden person's position every 2 hours.
• Rub in moisturising cream every day to help sustain skin tone.
• Three 3oz/85g servings of a protein, such as milk, egg or meat, taken daily will help to maintain muscle tissue and aid healing if bedsores develop.
• Bedsores are easier to prevent than to treat. If you notice any red spots on the skin, keep pressure off the area and consult a nurse or doctor.

Bedtime rituals

Most children love bedtime rituals. They ease the transition from play to sleep and provide a reassuring pattern.
• Help your child to wind down towards bedtime with a warm bath, bedtime stories, a lullaby, night-time prayers and similar activities.
• If you're away and a babysitter is in charge, make a list of your children's rituals for her to follow to make the children feel more secure.
• If your children want to see visiting guests, ask the guests if they would mind participating in the bedtime rituals, such as turning down the bedcovers or reading a little story.

Bedtime stories

• Make them a habit, even if you're tired. If pressed for time, read a chapter aloud while the children are having their evening meal.

• Choose a book you both like, to hold your interest and the child's. Read it imaginatively with different voices and expressions.

• Make up your own story. Insert your child's name into the text – it makes the story come alive.

• When reading to older children, let them watch your finger touch each word you read. It helps them with their own reading. Ask them to read the occasional word too.

• If you're going out and the babysitter will be reading the story, prepare a simple tale (with pictures cut out from glossy magazines) to show what Mummy and Daddy are doing, such as having dinner, or watching a film.

Bedwetting

• Try not to scold your child or make an issue out of bedwetting. Simply say 'Oh dear, I see you've wet yourself again'. Encourage older bedwetting children to help strip the bed, providing you don't accompany this with reprimands.

• Praise a child on dry nights. Make a star chart and reward a week of stars with a story or an extra 10 minutes staying-up time.

• Restrict fluids before your child goes to bed. Wake him up to visit the lavatory before you go to bed yourself.

• Protect the mattress with a shower curtain or incontinence sheet (available from chemists).

• If bedwetting suddenly starts in an older child, talk to him in case something is upsetting him.

• If none of these remedies work, see your doctor.

• If bedwetting persists in older children, use a buzzer alarm system, which wakes the child and reminds him to go to the toilet. The alarm is battery operated, connected to a special sheet, and is activated when moisture soaks into the sheet.

The evolution of the bed

For most of us, a bed is not only the place where our lives begin and end, but also the place where we spend about one-third of the time between those milestones.

Early beds were probably little more than pits lined with leaves, reeds or other natural cushions. Later, to keep out crawling insects and animals, latticed thongs were attached to an elevated wooden frame and topped with skins. The Egyptians went much further. Their beds were topped with a mat, linen sheets and woven blankets. A footboard even prevented sleepers from sliding down their beds, which were tilted upwards at the head. A separate hard headrest protected the coiffure.

It was not until about 3500 BC, in the royal palaces at Sumer in Babylon, that the bed was given its own room. Such luxury, however, was reserved for the master of the house. He occupied the bedroom while his wife, children, servants and guests slept elsewhere – on couches or the floor.

The Greeks were the first to use headboards, against which the wealthy laid embroidered silk pillows. The Romans invented the first true mattress: a sack stuffed with straw, wool or feathers. Water beds, developed in the early 19th century for hospital patients with bone fractures or bedsores, made a big splash in the 1960s and are still popular, along with bunk beds, platform beds and other variations. The divan bed became popular as living space grew smaller, because it could double as a sofa during the day. And now there are sofa-beds, which conceal a folding bed that can be pulled out and opened up when needed.

Beetles

• Furniture beetles may come into the house on firewood or in pieces of secondhand furniture. Make sure you keep your firewood outside and away from the house.

• May bugs (cockchafers) fly at night. Replace white outdoor bulbs with yellow ones so as not to attract them. Fit flyscreens to windows if they persist.

• Carpet beetles can damage natural fabrics. Thoroughly vacuum rugs, dark corners, wardrobes and under furniture, then remove and dispose of the vacuum bag. Clean pet bedding regularly and seal all floor cracks. Store clean clothes in pestproof bags or boxes, along with some mothballs or crystals.

• Garden beetles occasionally wander indoors, but are harmless.

• Beetles may drop in from a bird's nest in the loft or come in with the groceries. An aerosol for crawling insects will get rid of them, but try to find the source and eliminate it.

Bellows

Having trouble getting a campfire started? Use your lungs as a bellows. Blow through a hollow tent pole section. This will enable you to direct and concentrate the air where it is needed.

Hold the tent pole section with a sock, glove or flannel to protect your hands from the heat, and blow through a cupped hand to avoid direct contact with your lips. Blow gently – and *don't* breathe in through the tube.

Bereavement

Adjusting to the loss of someone you love takes time. Don't be afraid to show emotions; bottling up your grief could cause immense problems later on.

• Do not panic if you think you are losing your mind. Grief can cause erratic behaviour and many unusual feelings. Share them with someone – a reliable friend, your doctor or perhaps the local vicar (even if you have not been to church recently). Widows and widowers may like to contact an organisation such as Cruse-Bereavement Care (126 Sheen Rd, Richmond, Surrey TW9 1UR, Tel. 0181-332 7227) which has a network of voluntary counsellors. And bereaved parents can contact Compassionate Friends (53 North St, Bristol BS3 1EN, Tel. 0117-953 9639).

• Try not to drown your sorrows in drink or tranquillisers. They won't offer a long-lasting solution.

• Avoid making irreversible decisions during the first year. If you lived with the deceased person, consider renting your house rather than selling it. And instead of leaving your job, ask for time off.

• Don't force yourself to go through the deceased's personal possessions immediately.

• Stress weakens your immune system, so try to eat regularly, go to bed early and exercise.

• Try to think of others, too: friends, the surviving partner, or the deceased's children will also be feeling the loss, so will need support and counselling.

• Contact social services for advice on widow's benefits and find a solicitor to deal with the will (the Citizens Advice Bureau will suggest where to find legal help). Also contact employers, banks, credit card companies and building societies to inform them of the death.

Bicycle care

• To keep your bicycle running smoothly, make sure it is well oiled and check the brakes and gears regularly.

• Every 2 weeks or so, oil the bike with a proprietary brand of cycle oil. Oil the handlebar brake bearings and the front

and back pivot points and stirrup guides.

• Turn the bike upside-down and trickle oil into the ball races.

• On the front hub, turn the spring clip and drip oil into the oiling hole.

• Oil the chain by turning it slowly and dripping oil onto the links. Wipe off any surplus or it will stain the clothes that touch it.

• Release the brake cable and trickle oil between the cable and cover.

• Drip oil into the rear hub, in the oil holes in the plate of the gear wheel.

• Drip oil into the holes in the end caps of the pedals.

Bicycle riding

• Keep a whistle on a chain around your neck and use it instead of a horn; it's louder and shriller. Or buy a very loud horn if you can find one.

• Having trouble climbing hills? Maybe you're hunching over the handlebars; this constricts your breathing. Sit up tall instead.

• On wet roads brake lightly now and then to whisk water off your brakes – especially after you've gone through a puddle and before you start down a hill. Your brakes don't work as well in the wet because they can't grip the wheels.

• If you skid, don't try to move your wheel; keep it in whatever direction you're going. Similarly, on a loose surface, let the bike drift the way it wants.

• In the country, sharp curves often have loose gravel and holes. Brake to reduce speed *before* you get to a curve, not while you're on the loose surface. Keep as far to the left as possible to avoid cars that may move into your lane as they round the corner.

• Use a ski hat or a balaclava as a helmet liner in cold weather. For further warmth, push a folded section of newspaper up under your shirt to help block cold winds.

Bicycle safety

Cyclists are always vulnerable on the roads, especially in larger towns and cities, so it's worth taking extra safety precautions.

• Wear light-coloured clothing, preferably with a reflective belt, arm bands or jacket, and invest in a safety helmet, especially if you are riding on main roads or in cities.

• Paint your cycle with luminous paint, and make sure it carries effective lights and reflectors.

• Watch out for pedestrians who step into the road unexpectedly, for car doors which are suddenly opened onto the road, and for drivers who pull into or away from the kerb without indicating.

• Be sure to indicate clearly when you are turning left or right.

• Concentrate on the road ahead, and try to avoid riding over bumps or into potholes which make you lose control.

• Don't ride on the pavement – it's illegal and a danger to both pedestrians and yourself.

• Don't overtake vehicles in the face of oncoming traffic, or ride on the nearside of a vehicle. If you can't see the car indicating a left turn, you won't be able to take evasive action.

Bicycle tyre

Even if you don't have a repair kit, you can fix a tyre in no time with tyre levers (or kitchen spoons), some fine sandpaper, contact cement, talcum powder and a thin piece of rubber or soft plastic.

For patches, cut small squares of rubber from an old inner tube or swimming cap. Coat one side with contact cement and let it dry.

Remove the wheel and push in the tyre with your thumbs just enough to angle the levers, 5-7 in / 125-180mm apart, under its edge. Work them round, pulling the tyre edge over the rim.

Take the inner tube out of the tyre and look for the puncture by putting your ear to the tube to hear the air escaping. If you can't find the leak, inflate the tube and submerge it in water; bubbles will indicate the hole. Check inside the tyre for any sharp stones or debris.

Dry the tube and rough up the area around the hole with sandpaper. Coat it with contact cement and apply the patch, sticky side down. Finally, sprinkle talcum powder over the whole of the patched area so that the inner tube will not stick to the tyre wall.

If you inflate the tube a little, it will be easier to put back in the tyre. Begin re-mounting the tyre by first inserting the air valve into the rim, then work the tyre back onto the rim with your thumbs. (Even if this proves difficult, don't use the levers – they could puncture your newly repaired tube.)

When the tyre is back on the rim, inflate it and replace the wheel.

Bill paying

• Pay bills just before their due dates to avoid penalties. Do not rush to pay bills as they arrive; you may lose the use of your money and any interest that may accrue. Wait until you get a reminder, and then pay the bill immediately.
• If you find it difficult to keep track of regular payments, set up a direct debit order with your bank or building society, and they will pay the bills, automatically, on the correct day.
• After paying your bills, keep receipts that establish the purchase date for items under warranty.

Bird feeder

• Make a funnel to load a bird feeder by cutting off the bottom of a plastic milk or fruit-juice bottle. Unscrew its cap and hold it upside-down when you're ready to fill the feeder with seed.
• Fill a nylon-mesh bag, the kind onions or oranges are packaged in, with suet and pieces of bread. Hang it outdoors, but near a window, so that you can watch the birds feed.

• Tie a string around the top of a pine cone; roll the pine cone first in room-temperature bacon fat or peanut butter and then in birdseed or breadcrumbs.

Birds as pests

Birds can devastate a fruit or berry crop in seconds. If you don't want to go to the trouble of covering your trees or bushes with the netting that is normally used to thwart them, try one or more of these tactics:
• Let your cat wander loose among the trees or in the soft fruit patch, but tie a bell to its collar so that it won't get an opportunity to kill the birds.
• Put a stuffed animal – a teddy bear, for example – in the branches. Move it every few days; birds quickly get used to stationary objects.
• Plant a mature mulberry bush as a trap crop. Birds go for mulberries before they attack other fruits. Plant the bush well away from the house, however, since mulberries are messy.
• Birds' nests, droppings and feathers in the roof often harbour infestations of lice, mites and carpet beetles that invade the house. Have the roof checked every year to remove any nests.

Birth certificate

It is a good idea to keep your original birth certificate in a secure place, such as a safe-deposit box in a bank. Keep a copy in your home or office as you will need evidence of your age to take out insurance policies and pensions, and as proof of identity for official purposes such as a full passport.
• To get a copy, apply to the Registrar of Births and Deaths in the district where you were born, or to the central registrar. For a fee you can obtain a short certificate, indicating your name, sex, and date and place of birth. A copy of the full certificate, including details of your parents, is also available, but will cost you more.
• If you have changed your name, or your birth was not registered under your full name, you will need evidence of your name or change of name to get a new copy.
• If your birth is not registered in Britain because you were born elsewhere, check the local rules of the place of birth. If you are claiming to be a British citizen, your parents may have registered your birth with the local British consul or embassy where you were born.

Birthday superstitions

Many of the cherished rituals performed during children's birthday parties actually have their origins in ancient superstitions.
• Wishing on candles: the offering the ancient Greeks made to Artemis – the protector of the young and the goddess of the moon, the hunt and childbirth – was in the form of a round honey cake with a candle on top. German bakers, who invented the modern birthday cake during the Middle Ages, encircled the cake with lit candles. The custom was refined over the years, and the cake itself came to be decorated with one candle for each year of life. Some people add an extra candle 'to grow on'.

• Playing games: a birthday begins a new year, and games of power and skill – physical and mental – give the birthday child a chance to demonstrate increased strength and wisdom.
• Birthday bumps: swinging the child in the air and down again ensures good luck for the coming year. In some countries, guests give the birthday child whacks, punches or pinches – but all are given for good luck.
• Gifts to the guests: the small prizes embedded in a birthday cake – such as rings, coins or buttons – are tokens for telling fortunes in some families. Guests may also be given presents or little bags of treats.

Biscuits

• Very rich biscuit doughs, the kind made with a lot of butter or margarine, such as shortbread, and soft creamed doughs, are easier to handle if they are chilled for 30 minutes to an hour before being rolled out.

• Need to soften hard biscuits? Put them in an airtight tin or jar with a piece of fresh bread or a wedge of apple. Or wrap a wet paper towel in aluminium foil and place it in the tin on top of the biscuits.

• To keep newly baked biscuits crisp, cool them on wire racks and transfer at once to an airtight tin.

• When the children ask for homemade biscuits and you've run out of them, fake some in a jiffy by baking bits of marshmallow on digestive biscuits. Make them even better by adding some chocolate chips.

• Use the crumbs at the bottom of the biscuit tin as a tasty topping for ice cream or yoghurt.

Bites

If someone has been bitten by an animal or by another person, your first priority is to stop any severe bleeding. Then wash the wound thoroughly with soap and water. Rinse under running water for 5 minutes, then dry and cover with a sterile dressing and bandage securely.

Arrange for medical treatment as soon as possible, as anti-tetanus treatment may be required. Dog bites should be reported to the police. See also DOG AND CAT BITES, p.63; INSECT BITES, p.114; STINGS, p.194.

Blackheads

The best way of keeping your skin free of blackheads is to cleanse it regularly, both morning and night, and to try to follow a sensible diet, avoiding fatty food. Drinking 6-8 glasses of water a day will also improve the quality of your skin. However, despite your best efforts, pores can clog up, and blackheads form.

Do not attempt to squeeze them, as you will only worsen the situation, causing enlarged pores and scarring, and

possibly infecting the area. Blackheads should be removed by an experienced skincare therapist who has been trained to remove them gently without damaging the delicate tissue of your skin.

Black tie

An invitation saying 'black tie' used to mean formal evening dress, where rules were rigidly observed: men wore black dinner jackets and trousers, white dress shirts and black hand-tied bow ties; women wore long or short dresses in rich fabrics or the classic 'little black dress'.

Today's interpretation of 'black tie' formality is more relaxed, and personal style is acceptable: for men, colourful bow ties in rich fabrics, but still hand-tied, are perfectly correct – with or without a matching cummerbund – and women can wear trousers.

The conventional dinner jacket can quite easily be exchanged for a brocade or velvet one. For formal summer occasions, light-coloured linen suits as well as a white dinner jacket and black evening trousers are all acceptable dress.

Hiring an evening outfit makes financial sense especially if yours is a once-in-a-lifetime function, if your weight fluctuates or if you want to wear the most fashionable styles. Women's dress hire agencies hire out complete designer outfits for a fraction of the real cost. However, for men who have many

'black tie' engagements, buying a classic dinner jacket and trousers is a practical idea.

Hire shops sell off evening wear, and it is also worth hunting at charity shops and jumble sales; many outfits have hardly been worn and go for bargain prices. Look out for broken zips, damaged linings, and heavy perspiration stains (which are rarely successfully cleaned); moth holes and cigarette burns are also very expensive to repair.

For a good fit it is worth enquiring at your dry cleaners about alterations: sleeves can be shortened and hems expertly let down and taken up. Large sizes can be altered to several sizes smaller, but a small size can rarely be altered to a larger one.

Bleach spots

• If the garment is dark, disguise the spot by rubbing it with a fabric marker or paint that matches the fabric's colour. Cover coloured areas with a piece of cotton sheet and iron at a hot setting.

• Treat non-colourfast fabrics with a pre-wash dye remover. For white or pastel-coloured fabrics, treatments for colour-run accidents can effectively bleach the whole garment a uniform pale colour.

• Sew an appliqué over the spot.

• Dye the garment a darker colour or tie-dye it.

Blinds

• If a window blind tends to curl up at the bottom, you can usually weight it with a matched pair of magnets. Slip the magnets into the hem at each corner.

• A towel can make an adequate temporary blind – just secure it to the frame with tacks. Dark-coloured towels do the best job of blocking the sun's rays; lightweight white ones give a translucent glow.

• You can refurbish old blinds by carefully removing the worn fabric from the roller and using it as a pattern to cut a new piece. Use a staple gun or a length of double-sided tape to attach one end to the roller at the top; stitch a hem at the other end, to carry the weight-bar.

• To remove stains and smudges from a window blind, lay it on a flat surface and then carefully clean it with a soft rubber or dough-type wallpaper cleaner.

• If a blind won't stay down, easing the tension in the spring usually helps. Roll up the blind, remove it from its brackets and unroll it by hand. Then replace it in the brackets and roll it up again.

• If you are fitting a blind to a frame that is rounded or oddly shaped at the top, install the brackets at the base of the frame, and fit a small pulley at the top. Then run a cord through the pulley to raise and lower the blind.

Blisters

• Try to avoid any friction which might break the blister.

• Don't burst the blister yourself, unless the stretched skin is causing great discomfort. If you burst it you increase the risk of infection.

• If a blister does burst, keep it open to the air to dry out, but only in hygienic surroundings. Where it is likely that dirt will get in, cover it with a bandage or plaster.

• If a blister gets infected and inflamed, see a doctor.

• To prevent blisters, take care when cooking and ironing. Wear oven gloves whenever you lift a hot dish out of the oven and don't use a tea towel. Wear protective gloves whenever you're doing manual work. Don't wear badly fitting shoes and wear new shoes for short periods only. Don't go out into the sun without a protective cream.

Bloodstains

• Put a paste of water and cornflour or talcum powder on fresh spots; let dry and brush off. Or soak fresh or dried stains in a cool solution of biological liquid or powder detergent. Follow by washing in a biological detergent.

• To remove fresh blood from leather, sponge immediately with water, then wipe with a damp cloth that has been rubbed across a bar of soap. If the stain remains, take to a specialist cleaner.

• If you prick your finger while sewing and get blood on the fabric, quickly wet a long piece of white cotton thread with saliva and place it across the spot. The thread will absorb the blood.

Board games

• Bottle caps and coins make good counters or draughts. Use different coloured crayons, tabs of adhesive-backed paper, or coloured stick-on dots to indicate opposing sides.

Check your sweet tin: flat round mints or refreshers also work as draughts. Each player uses a different colour to distinguish the pieces. And when you take an opponent's piece, you can eat it.

• If you lose the dice, mark sugar cubes with a ballpoint pen; they won't last long in play, but they're easy to replace. Be sure the numbers on the opposite faces add up to seven.

• To make the simple board game of Fox

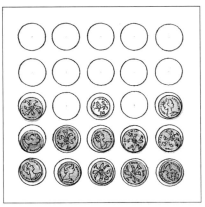

and Rabbits, draw 25 circles in 5 rows of 5 each on a cardboard square. Place 10 2p pieces (the rabbits) across the bottom 2 rows of circles and 1 on each end of the centre row. Put a 10p piece (the fox) in the middle of the centre row.

One player controls all the rabbits; the other controls the fox, who starts the game. A rabbit or the fox may move one circle up, down or across on each turn. To win, the rabbits must surround the fox, or the fox must capture all but one rabbit. The fox captures rabbits by jumping over them, as in draughts. The fox may make more than one jump in a turn if all the jumps are in a straight line.

Boating mishaps

Tarpaulin

• For a larger leak or a hole, first try plugging from the inside with pillows or a mattress. If that doesn't work, make a damage-control device with a tarpaulin and four lengths of rope as shown above. Tie a rope to each corner of the tarpaulin. Secure three of the corners on the damaged side of the boat and bring the fourth rope under the craft at the bow or stern and tie it on the other side.

• You may be able to plug a small leak in a boat temporarily with rags, cotton or towels. But it is better to use underwater epoxy glue, which is available at boating supply stores. Use fast-drying epoxy alone or with a small piece of fibreglass.

• You can also plug a large leak by running two ropes loosely around the hull and stuffing a mattress between them and the hull. Tighten the ropes to hold it in place – and make for shore!

• Sometimes the vibrations of high-speed power boats cause the powder in dry fire extinguishers to compact so tightly that they won't work, even when the pressure gauge indicates they are ready. To make sure your extinguisher will work when you need it, occasionally hit it lightly with your hand or against the side of the boat several times to loosen the powder.

Body bulges
Women

• Avoid tight-fitting undergarments: they can emphasise or even create bulges. You can minimise bulges with a one-piece garment, such as a slip or a 'body' which has a fitted top or built-in bra, or select loose-fitting underwear such as French knickers.

• Detract attention by playing up your best characteristics. Concentrate on flattering make-up and hairstyles – jewellery and scarves can make a great deal of difference.

Men

• A beer drinker's paunch looks worse in tight, brightly coloured pullovers and figure-hugging slim shirts. Buy jumpers, shirts and jackets several sizes too large and stick to dark colours.

Body odour

Every person has a distinctive smell, which is normal. It only becomes a problem when the smell is offensive. This happens when bacteria develop in the sweat that accumulates in areas where it cannot evaporate freely, such as the armpits, groin and feet. The best remedy is to bath or shower frequently and change and clean your clothes regularly.

• If you feel self-conscious about your smell, you could try a deodorant. This doesn't stop you from sweating, but disguises the smell.

• If you perspire heavily you could use an anti-perspirant, which dries out the sweat glands and reduces the amount of sweat they produce. Never use a deodorant or anti-perspirant on broken or inflamed skin.

• There is no need to use a vaginal deodorant, and indeed these can cause irritations. Daily washing with soap and water should be sufficient. However, if you find the smell offensive, or if there is a heavy discharge, see your doctor – you may have an infection.

• If your feet smell, it may be that the shoes you are wearing are not allowing sweat to evaporate. Avoid shoes made from or lined with synthetic materials. Wear socks or tights made from pure cotton. If it is possible, wash your feet several times a day and dry them thoroughly. You could also sprinkle foot powder or talc on your feet before putting on your socks and shoes. Try not to wear the same shoes every day.

Bookcases

• Plastic crates can be stacked to make a colourful set of shelves for a child's room. These crates can usually be found in DIY stores. With diligence and a bit of luck, you may even locate some old-fashioned wooden milk crates at a flea market or country antiques shop.

Some plastic crates are designed to interlock. If yours aren't, secure them with twist ties, strips of cloth or insulating tape. Try to choose a colour that matches the crates.

• For a quick, attractive bookshelf, lay planks of wood across bricks or concrete blocks.

Bookends

• To make a bookend in a minute, snip off the hook of a wire coat hanger with wire cutters and bend the hanger at a 90° angle. Slip one end of the folded hanger under the books.

• Draw a line down the middle of an unwanted 45 or LP record, just to one side of the label. Heat the record on both sides with a hair dryer along the line until it is soft enough to bend. Bend it at 90° and slip one end under the books.

Books

• To flatten wrinkled corners, put a sheet of paper on top of the straightened page and press with a warm iron.

• Mend torn pages with gummed tissue or glue rice paper over the tears. Sandwich newly repaired pages between sheets of wax paper so that they won't stick to other pages.

• Have you just spilled water on a book's pages? Put the book into a frost-free freezer. It will draw out the moisture and unstick the pages.

If this process leaves the pages of your books crinkled, try pressing them with a warm iron, as before.

• Clean leather bindings with saddle soap, neat's-foot oil or petroleum jelly. Apply sparingly and gently with your fingers or with a piece of felt, muslin or chamois leather. Wait several hours, then repeat.

• Protect your books with covers made from greaseproof paper or leftover wallpaper. Fold the paper inside the book cover, using diagonal folds at the corners. Seal with a moderately hot iron.

• Clean books with the dusting-brush attachment on your vacuum cleaner, or brush off the dust with a shaving brush or soft paintbrush.

• Books kept in a damp room will develop mould and mildew. If this has happened, wipe it off the bindings and pages with a clean soft cloth. If the pages are still mouldy, wipe them with a cloth dampened with alcohol, then fan out the pages to dry. Or sprinkle some cornflour onto the affected pages and brush it off after a few hours.

• Remind yourself of books to be returned to the library with a list of due dates stuck to the refrigerator door.

• If you lend a book to a friend, write 'Please return to (your name)' inside the front cover. Keep the book jacket, if it has one, and make a note of the borrower and the date. It will remind you to ask for the book after a reasonable time.

Boots

• To dry boots, stuff them with balls of newspaper and leave. Never place them in front of a radiator or fire, or in the sun, because the heat will crack the leather. When dry, rub with a leather conditioner such as saddle soap, then polish.

• Make your own boot trees with a couple of paper towel tubes tied together, or lengths of rolled-up newspaper. These will help to keep the boots upright and stop them from sagging and developing creases.

• Blow warm air on wet rubber boots with the blower attachment on your vacuum cleaner or a hair dryer.

• To remove salt stains, wipe the boots with a solution of 1 tablespoon of vinegar in ½ pint/285 ml of water.

• Buff rain spots off suede boots with a sponge or a stiff upholstery brush. Rub persistent marks gently with an emery board.

• Protect boots from the rain with a silicone or waterproofing shoe spray. Or rub on a light coat of floor wax after polishing them.

• When trying on new walking boots, kick the toes gently against a solid surface. If you can feel your toes against the end, take a half size bigger.

Bottle and jar caps

• Run hot water over a recalcitrant jar cap to expand it. Then, for additional grip, wrap a rubber band around the sides of the cap.

• To loosen the stopper from a decanter, wrap a hot, wet cloth around the neck of the bottle. If necessary, let a few drops of water trickle into the neck and around the stopper to dissolve whatever might be holding it tight.

• To remove a bottle cap without an opener, use locking-grip pliers or the strike-plate opening of a door frame (the plate that receives the latch). And remember that corkscrew handles are often bottle openers too.

• Or fit a coin between the lip of the cap and a hard, firm surface. Then hit the top of the bottle with your clenched fist.

Bottles

To clean a narrow-necked bottle, fill it with equal parts water and detergent or ammonia. Add some uncooked rice and swirl the solution around until the bottle is clean.

To get rid of cloudy marks on the inside of a glass bottle, pour in vinegar and some coarse sand. Every half hour for up to 5 or 6 hours, shake and swirl it around until the stain disappears.

Bra and slip straps

• To prevent straps showing at a neckline, sew small Velcro strips (hooks side up) to the top of each strap, and sew the corresponding strips to the shoulder seam inside the garment.

• Or carefully pin your strap to your garment with small brass safety pins.

Bracelet

• If you need a bracelet to go with a special outfit, wrap one in matching fabric or ribbon.

• Or you can make one by stapling together a strip of card, large enough to fit over your hand. Make a papier-mâché mix and mould it over the band. When dry, paint with emulsion and poster colours. Finish with a protective coat of clear varnish (see PAPIER-MACHE p. 408).

Brass

• To remove the tarnish from brass fittings, nameplates and other small objects, submerge them overnight in a solution of equal parts water and ammonia; then rub with extra-fine steel wool or a soft brush.

• For stubborn tarnish, rub with a paste of salt and vinegar or use a salted lemon rind. Toothpastes –both regular and gel – also work.

• If the brass is covered with lacquer, clean it with mild detergent and water, then rinse and dry. Avoid abrasives, which can wear through the lacquer.

• In all cases, rinse afterwards in clear water and buff dry with a soft cloth or chamois leather.

Bread baking

• To get dough to rise, you need a draught-free spot with a temperature of 24°-27°C/75°-80°F. Try putting the bowl of dough, lightly covered, in the airing cupboard, by the cooker or on top of the central heating boiler.

• A quick fix for bread burned in baking or reheating is to rub off the black spots with a kitchen grater. For severe burns, simply cut off the damaged part and eat the rest.

Breadcrumbs

• Instead of relying on shop-bought dry breadcrumbs, you can use crushed cornflakes, unsweetened bran cereal, or matzo meal. Or make crumbs from fresh or lightly toasted white bread; crush toasted slices with a rolling pin or an empty bottle, or whizz fresh, dry or toasted bread in an electric blender or food processor.

• Water biscuit or cheese cracker crumbs can also double as breadcrumbs but contain more sodium, so taste for saltiness as you prepare a recipe.

• Freshly made breadcrumbs will keep for a week or more in a tightly closed jar in the refrigerator, or in the freezer for up to 6 months.

• Really dry or toasted breadcrumbs will keep for weeks in a tightly covered jar in the larder or in a cool, dry, airy cupboard.

Breast-feeding

If full-time breast-feeding is impossible, the best substitute is expressed breast milk given from a bottle. The second best substitute is a commercially prepared formula.

A good time to introduce a bottle is when the baby is 4-6 weeks old. Some babies may take 2 weeks or longer to become comfortable with bottle-feeding.

Practise expressing your milk – manually or with a breast pump – before returning to work or other duties. In order to have adequate milk for regular bottle-feedings, you will need to express milk two or three times during the course of the day.

If you are away from home, take a vacuum bottle filled with ice cubes with you; empty out the ice when you want to store the milk. At home, store expressed milk in 5 fl oz/150ml plastic (not glass) bottles.

If you plan to use the milk within 48 hours, place it in the refrigerator. For longer storage, use the freezer; it should remain good for at least 3 months.

When you are ready to use the frozen milk, thaw it in the refrigerator for several hours, use a microwave oven or hold it under warm running water for a few minutes. Shake the bottle well before feeding.

Caution Thawing in a microwave oven may overheat the milk; test it before giving it to the baby.

Breast-feeding myths

Advice to nursing mothers has been rich and varied – and often contradictory – over the years. Here are some examples from various times and places:

If you eat peanuts, your milk will dry up (unless you are in Africa, where they say that peanuts increase the flow).

Some people insist that eating chocolate will stop your milk; others, that it will produce more.

In many places it has long been believed that drinking beer, or stout, will increase your milk supply; in Ireland, Guinness is said to help.

There are more examples: if you breastfeed in a car, the baby will get wind. If you rock while nursing, you'll shake up the milk. And if a mother becomes nervous, angry, frightened or sexually stimulated, her milk will turn sour. Others say no matter what happens, the mother will pass her own nature onto her baby in her milk.

Breathing exercises

Increasing the volume of oxygen in your lungs can help to relieve tension.

Diaphragm breathing Stand straight or lie flat on your back and place your hands flat against your diaphragm with your little fingers along your waistline. Inhale slowly and deeply through your nose, pulling the air down into your lungs. You will feel the bottom of your lungs fill and your ribcage expand. Exhale through your mouth. Repeat 5 times.

Y movement Stand, or lie flat on your back, arms crossed in front, with each palm resting on the opposite thigh. While inhaling deeply through your nose, slowly raise both arms above your head, uncrossing them and turning the palms to face each other. As your shoulders open and your lungs expand, your arms will separate slightly. Reverse the movement as you exhale, bringing your arms back down to cross in front of you. Repeat 3 times.

Brick and stone cleaning

• Brighten up dull brickwork by rubbing it with a piece of broken brick of matching colour and texture. Use the broken surface as the abrasive, and it will remove the face of the bricks being renovated, exposing a clean surface. The same treatment can be used for a grubby stone surface.

• You can also brighten brickwork or masonry by raking out weathered pointing to a depth of about ½in/13mm and replacing with new mortar.

• Where brickwork is stained with mortar droppings or cement-based paint, use a special cleaning fluid. This will dissolve the cement without affecting the masonry. Be sure to protect eyes and hands when working, as the material is acidic, and follow the instructions on the tin very carefully.

• A high pressure hose is often recommended for removing grime and algae from walls. But proceed with caution, for with the water jet moving at anything up to 250mph/400kph, you can force water into gaps and cracks around frames, increasing the risk of rot. And you will dislodge soft mortar from between brick or stone.

• For oil stains on brick paving, use a proprietary cleaner such as that used for cleaning car engines. Or spread cat litter over the patches, allow the litter to absorb the oil, then brush it off.

• For mould or algae growth on stone or brick, use a proprietary fungicide to kill off the growth. Follow the instructions on the pack very carefully.

Bruises

A small bruise requires no special treatment, but if bruising is extensive, remember RICE: Rest, Ice, Compression and Elevation.

R Rest the injured part.

I Place ice or a cold compress over the bruise to help control bleeding and swelling and relieve pain.

C Press your hand firmly over the injured area.

E Elevate the bruised area to a level just above the heart.

Brushes

• Whenever you vacuum or dust, carry a whisk broom or a small unused paintbrush with you – it will be useful for cleaning the hard-to-reach places.

• A soft-bristled baby's hairbrush is excellent for cleaning tapestries and the delicate fabric on lampshades.

Bulbs

• If you're the kind of serious gardener who plans for the long term, save money by harvesting the tubers, corms, bulbs or bulbils that your bulb plants produce. Bulbils are the tiny dark bulbs which are produced by tiger lilies and fire lilies in the angle between the leaf and the stem.

Pick the bulbils just after the flowers have faded and divide the tubers, corms and bulbs. Plant bulbils just below the surface in containers of potting soil, and divided bulbs in the ground at the usual depth. Be sure to space them well apart so that you won't have to thin them before they're established.

Bulbils will take a long time to flower – 3-4 years – but they will come true, even those from hybrid lilies.

• Don't think of bulbs solely as spring bloomers. Plant the traditional tulips, daffodils, snowdrops and grape hyacinths for that season, but also consider putting in gladioli and galtonia for summer, colchicums for autumn, and winter-flowering crocuses for the colder months. Pots of cyclamen, amaryllis and other bulbs can brighten your windowsill on gloomy winter days.

Bumper stickers

Before you put a bumper sticker on your car, make sure you'll be able to remove it – apply it over a layer of car wax. You will also find it much easier to peel off if you remove it within a month.

Remove an old bumper sticker from chrome by scraping off the top layer of paper or vinyl with a sharp knife or a craft knife. (Try not to scratch the surface.) The adhesive beneath should come off with white spirit. If the sticker is on a painted surface, test a tiny patch to make sure the white spirit doesn't dissolve the paint.

Burglar alarms

• Even if you don't have a dog, put up a 'Beware of the Dog' sign. Wire a recorded bark to your doorbell, or carry a small recorder with a taped bark to set off when you answer the door.
• Hang a dummy alarm bell outside your home.
• If you install an alarm system, ask your local crime prevention officer for a list of well-established suppliers in your area. A well-known supplier is likely to be cheaper and guarantee prompt service.
• Even if you can't afford an alarm system, paste security-system stickers on the windows. Instruct your children to tell no one that the system doesn't exist.
• Turn on outdoor lights, or wire infrared or sound-activated detectors to switch them on if intruders come within range.

Burglaries

• If you come home and see an open door or objects out of place, turn around at once and leave quietly. Notify the police from a neighbour's home.

Watch your home from a safe distance – don't try to stop the burglar when he leaves. Get a good description and write down the licence number of his vehicle. See WITNESSING A CRIME, p.234. Stay out of your home until the police arrive in case the burglar has accomplices.
• If you hear a burglar entering your home or prowling around, don't confront him or pretend to be asleep. Switch on the lights and make a lot of noise. If you are on your own, pretend that there is someone with you and call out loudly to them. Telephone the police as soon as you think it is safe to do so.
• If you confront a burglar face-to-face or wake up to discover one in your room, stay quiet and cooperate. Screaming may frighten or anger an already scared or irrational burglar into violence.
After a burglary The police need a full description of all stolen items. For that reason, it's wise to photograph and list all your valuables (including serial numbers) long before a crisis arises, and keep the inventory in a safe place. See also INSURANCE CLAIMS, p.114; SAFE-DEPOSIT BOXES, p.173; VALUABLES, p.219.

Burned cookware

• To clean burned food from pots or pans, wet the burn, sprinkle with salt and leave for 10 minutes. Scrub well.
• Or cover the burned area with a paste of bicarbonate of soda and water. Leave it on overnight, then scour. (Be aware, however, that bicarb and other alkaline substances will etch the surface of an aluminium pan if they are left on for more than an hour.)
• For stubborn burns, scrape off as much burned food as possible with a wooden spoon and fill the pot halfway with water. Add a strong detergent or scouring powder, boil for 10 minutes and leave overnight. Then scrub.

Burns

The seriousness of a burn depends on three things: how deep it is, how much of the body it covers, and the age and health of the victim.

Infants, children under the age of 5 and adults over 60 are especially vulnerable; a burn that might be only moderately harmful to a young adult could be fatal to a toddler with more sensitive skin.

First-degree burns are superficial; the skin becomes slightly reddened and swollen. The pain is similar to that of a sunburn.

Second-degree (intermediate) burns penetrate the first layer of skin and damage the second. The skin is red, mottled and blistered; pain is intense.

Third-degree (deep) burns damage all layers of the skin, usually leaving charred, black areas or dry, white ones. There may be extreme pain or, because of nerve damage, very little pain after the initial acute pain. Such burns are serious, as they are easily infected.

1 The golden rule is *cool it*. If clothing is on fire, put out the flames with water or other non-inflammable liquid, or smother them with a coat or blanket. Keep cooling the affected area for at least 10 minutes, or until the pain has eased. Don't try to remove anything that has stuck to the burn, such as clothing or fat.
2 Remove rings, watches and bracelets carefully before swelling starts.
3 Facial burns or soot in the nose or mouth indicates that the person has inhaled smoke. Check that the victim has no breathing problems.
4 Apply a loose, dry, lint-free, preferably sterile dressing to all burns. If the burns are extensive, wrap the person in a clean sheet. *Don't put anything else on the burn.* Get the person to a hospital.

If the burn is minor, apply a loose dressing, moistened only with cool water to help relieve the pain. Be careful not to break any blisters. If there's tar, grease or wax on the skin, cover with a loose, dry dressing, and take the person to a room where they can rest.

Burping a baby

If your baby needs burping but you need to move around and keep one of your hands free, try one of these walking-burping techniques. Remember to protect yourself with a cloth, or carry one with you to clean the child's face – he may bring up some milk when he burps.
• Set the baby on your hip, facing out, with one of your arms securely around his tummy. The slight pressure of your

arm plus the movement of your walking will help bring up the bubble.
• Strap on a baby carrier that attaches to your front and put the baby into it.
• If the baby is over 4 months old and can hold up his head, put him in a backpack carrier – the movement of your walking will help a burp develop.
• If you have time on your hands and your baby is windy, place him on your knee face down with his head looking down at the ground, and stroke and rub his back towards his head.

Business lunches

When initiating a business lunch, especially with someone you don't know, be sure to state the reason, even if it is only to share information and get to know each other. This will prevent misunderstandings and give both of you a chance to prepare.

The one who suggests the lunch should be ready to pay the bill. But if you're asked to lunch informally by someone who is obviously not on an expense account, offer to share the bill. No matter who had what, split it down the middle.

To pay the bill unobtrusively, speak with the waiter or head waiter privately before lunch to make sure the bill is given to you and not your guest. If you forget to settle this matter before lunch, excuse yourself to use the washroom and speak to the waiter on the way. You can even arrange to pay the bill while away from the table. (Paying by credit card is less obvious than by cash.)

If you entertain at one restaurant regularly, the staff will help make your

lunches smoother. Call in advance to make a reservation. Give your name and company, the day and time, the number of people and the table you'd like. After lunch, discreetly tip the waiter well. After doing this a few times, you'll find that you've bought and paid for especially good service.

Butter

• Margarine can replace butter in most recipes. Hard margarine is best used for shaped, rolled or dropped biscuits; soft margarine will make biscuits spread out more over the baking sheet.
• Vegetable oil can substitute for butter in all dishes, even in some baked foods, although the amounts will be different: ½oz/15g butter equals ¾ tablespoon vegetable oil; 6oz/175g butter equals 7fl oz/200ml vegetable oil.
• Butter won't burn as quickly in a sauté-pan if you add 1 teaspoon of corn oil or olive oil.

Buttons

Temporary measures
• When a button falls off, stay 'decent' with a safety pin hidden under the buttonhole until you can replace the button.
• Fasten a pretty brooch or pin in place of a missing button on a blouse.
• Fix the button to the fabric with the wire from a twist tie.

Permanent alternatives
• Use button-sized Velcro circles and squares. Position each piece with a pin, then stitch around the edges.
• Cut 'buttons' any size you desire from iron-on Velcro tape. Follow the manufacturer's directions for attaching them to the fabric.
• Buy press studs or hooks and eyes that

are anchored to tapes. Cut off as many fasteners as you need; stitch the tape edges to the fabric.

• Try grommets, or eyelets; they're sold in many finishes. Attach them with a grommeting tool or a hammer.

C

Cakes

• To find out if a cake is cooked, insert a wooden toothpick or a clean knife into its centre. If it comes out clean, the cake is ready. Or press the centre with your finger; the cake is cooked if the top springs back, leaving no imprint.

• Cakes risen with beaten egg whites – such as angel food, chiffon and sponge cakes – often fall while cooling. To minimise the chances, invert the tin as soon as it comes out of the oven and let the cake cool upside-down. Don't worry about it falling out of the tin; egg-white based cakes have to be loosened with a spatula or palette knife.

• When turning out sponge cakes, place a sheet of kitchen paper on top of the sponge, then invert it onto a wire rack. Immediately, turn the cake back onto another rack and remove the paper. This prevents the top of the sponge from being marked by the rack.

• Because microwaved cakes often come out of the oven sticky, uneven and unbrowned on top, only microwave cakes that will be frosted or those that have crumb toppings.

• To decorate a cake, turn a plastic bag into a piping bag. Spoon frosting into it and refrigerate, until the cake is ready. Snip off a bottom corner of the bag and pipe away.

• Use a paper doily as a stencil. Position it on top of the cake and sift icing sugar generously over it. Then carefully lift the doily.

• A cut cake will stay fresh longer if you place half an apple inside the cake tin. A cut apple also helps to moisten over-baked fruit cakes.

Calorie counting

No more than 30 per cent of your daily calories should come from fat. Study the labels of packaged foods and drinks and consult the nutritional analyses that accompany the recipes in some cookbooks. Then use this 9-4-4 formula to determine the sources of the calories:
1 gram fat is 9 calories;
1 gram carbohydrate is 4 calories;
1 gram protein is 4 calories.
Divide the calories-from-fat figure by the total number of calories to find out if it amounts to more than a third.

Camera filters

Do you need an ultraviolet filter to reduce haze in that scenic shot? You may already have the best one in your camera bag – a polariser. Normally used to darken blue skies, polarisers also cut down haze in distant scenes. On a single-lens reflex camera, rotate the polariser until you see the best effect.

A soft-focus filter adds a dreamy feeling and soft edges to portraits and scenic shots. As a substitute, lightly smear petroleum jelly on any ultraviolet or skylight filter. Wipe off the jelly later with a tissue.

Cameras

Protection from the elements Carry a supply of plastic bags in your camera pack. An inverted bag with the corners snipped off and the camera straps threaded through will give some protection against rain, snow or sand – especially sand, the cause of 90 per cent of the faults that can occur in cameras. Let the bag hang over the camera, open end down; slide it up to take a picture. For more waterproofing, tape the edges of the holes to the strap with vinyl tape.

A self-sealing food storage bag, used as pictured, will protect your camera from sand and dust particles.

Backlighting An effective way to shoot a portrait is by posing your subject with the light behind her – low or oblique sunlight in an outdoor setting, for example. This is called 'backlighting' or

1 Raise the plastic bag for picture-taking.

2 Slide it down to protect the camera.

'contrejour'. But – and here's the problem – where there is a strong light source behind your subject the camera's automatic exposure system overreacts and tends to register the subject more or less as a silhouette. Most cameras have either a backlight control switch, or provide sufficient flashlight to 'fill in' and bring more light to areas in shadow. Either way will retain the halo effect on the hair and give good facial detail. Consult your camera handbook.

Camp cooking

• A lightweight camping stove is faster, cleaner and easier to cook with than a fire; it also causes less wear and tear on the landscape. If you do use a fire, spread the coals out for low, easily controlled heat.

• You can buy sets of cooking pots that nest inside each other from shops which sell camping equipment.

• Supermarkets sell many freeze-dried

foods which are very useful as one-pot meals to cook at the tent door on a rainy day. Add macaroni, noodles or rice to packet or tinned soups for a satisfying camp meal. Other standbys, such as powdered milk drinks, instant potatoes, instant oatmeal, spaghetti or noodle snacks and instant puddings, are also useful.

• Other foods that won't spoil if left unrefrigerated for a few days are hard cheese, hard salami, smoked fish, dried meat, dried fruit, sliced carrots and celery, margarine and pitta bread.

• Pack the ingredients for meals in double plastic bags for extra protection. Use colour codes to distinguish breakfasts, lunches and dinners.

• Because water boils at lower temperatures in high altitudes (about 1°F per 500ft/150m), you must boil foods longer. Experiment with cooking times.

• Fumes from cooking with a stove inside a tent can cause headache, nausea, dizziness or even death from carbon monoxide. In bad weather set the stove just outside the inner tent door under the bell-end, while cooking from inside the tent. Some tents are designed with vestibules for this purpose.

Caution Always refuel a stove outside the tent and away from all open flames. And don't ever throw used fuel canisters into the fire.

Campfires

Romantic though they may be, camp fires are prohibited in many wilderness areas. Even where legal, they're dangerous and troublesome. If you must build an emergency fire, and a camp fireplace is available, use it.

Otherwise, clear away all organic material down to the bare dirt within a 3ft/1m radius. Assemble rocks into a circle that's slightly larger than the cooking utensils you intend to use.

Collect several dozen dry dead twigs and break them into kindling no more than 12in/300mm long. Use a pocket-knife to slice two fistfuls of very thin shavings. Then assemble the materials as shown. Light the shavings from the windward side and feed more shavings

Tinder   Pencil-thin kindling
1 in/25mm sticks

into the flame, one at a time, until the fire is vigorous. (If it is windy, try to shield the flame with a flat rock.) Build a pyramid of larger wood pieces around the tinder, as shown above.

Before you leave, be sure to return the rocks to their original locations, sooty side down. Douse the ashes with water until they are completely cold, then cover them with earth.

Carry all-weather matches in a waterproof tube and some old candle stubs or birthday candles. In wet weather a candle will help to sustain a flame.

Camping in rainy weather

• Wear a waterproof jacket and overtrousers.

• Rain gear works better and feels more comfortable when it fits loosely. Air spaces provide ventilation and allow your body to dry.

• Any camper who has endured the tedium of a rainy day knows that a paperback book can be important first aid for boredom. Travel-size board games (draughts, chess, backgammon, Scrabble) and a pack of cards are also lightweight, easy to carry protection against the dreary monotony of a soggy campsite. Writing letters will take your mind off the rain.

• Suspend a waterproof groundsheet over a picnic table on a rainy day to create an airy shelter for children's activities outside the cramped confines of a tent or caravan. Anchor the corners with wooden pegs.

Campsite lighting

If your torch fails, turn to these short-term substitutes:

• Car headlights can provide light for 10 to 15 minutes without the battery dying.

• Make a lantern from an open tin; punch a few holes for air and place a candle inside it, securing it to the bottom with melted wax. This lantern can be hung from a tree branch, from a forked branch planted into the ground outside your tent, or can be used to guide your way through the darkness. For a handle, punch holes in the side and thread a length of sturdy wire through them.

Create extra space on a wet camping trip by suspending a spare tarpaulin over a table and chairs.

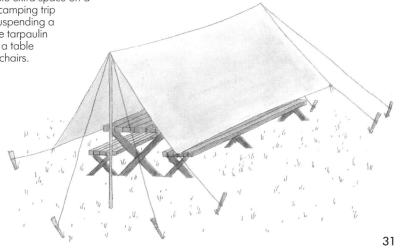

Campsite washing

Wear large rubber gloves over wool gloves to keep your hands warm and dry while drawing water or washing clothes or dishes in cold weather.

Laundry

• To dry socks, handkerchiefs, T-shirts, underwear and dishcloths, shut a car window on their edges and let them blow in the wind. Or tie wet clothes to a rucksack or drape a wet towel across it – they'll dry as you walk.

Dishwashing

• Let fire-blackened pot bottoms stay black; they'll heat faster and more evenly.

• Towelling nappies are lightweight and make good camping towels.

• Granular snow or sand stirred in greasy bowls and pans makes a good scouring powder.

• Thoroughly rinse cookware and dishes to avoid an upset stomach.

Cancer

There are many different types of cancer, more and more of which can be cured. See your doctor if you have any of these symptoms:

• coughing up blood
• persistent cough or hoarse voice
• passing blood in your urine
• blood in your bowel motions
• change in your bowel habit
• difficulty swallowing because of a blockage in your chest
• vaginal bleeding after intercourse
• vaginal bleeding after the menopause
• a breast lump
• lumps in the neck, groin or armpits
• pigmented moles that grow, bleed, itch or change
• unexplained weight loss or tiredness

Candles

• To make a candle burn longer and drip less, give it a light coat of clear varnish.

• Melting some wax into the holder and quickly jamming the candle onto it is the usual way to get a candle to fit snugly. A cleaner method is to wrap the base of the candle with string or strips of paper towel, making sure they can't be seen.

• To remove melted wax from candle holders easily, place the holders in the freezer for an hour or two, and then chip the frozen wax off.

Cane chairs

As a temporary measure, you can support the sagging seat of a cane chair by tacking a piece of plywood covered with some old towelling to the underside. Or brush water onto the chair seat to shrink and straighten the cane.

Can openers

• Open tinned liquids with the triangular punch end of a beer bottle opener; punch on both sides so that air can enter for easier pouring.

You can also use the triangular punch (with difficulty) all the way around a tin, but be careful – there will be lots of sharp edges.

• Puncture the tin with a sharp rock, a pocketknife, or a screwdriver; then work it open a little at a time with pliers or some other tool (not your hands).

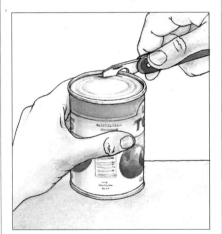

• Multipurpose camping knives often have can openers. Plunge the sharp point of the U-shaped tool inside the rim, hook the other end on the outer edge, then work it, up and down, around the can. (The tool is made for right-handed people; left-handed people will have difficulty.)

Caution Watch out for any metal scraps that may fall into the tin.

Car accelerators

If you ease up the accelerator, but the engine keeps racing, shift immediately into neutral and brake gently until you can pull off the road safely. If the accelerator is revving dangerously high, turn the ignition off (one click back of the key only).

Push the accelerator sharply to the floor, then let it go. If the pedal is still stuck, turn off the engine; do not drive any farther.

Then look under the bonnet to see if something is stuck against the throttle linkage; free it if possible. Perhaps the throttle return spring has broken; if so, and if it is accessible, temporarily repair it by shaping the end into a hook and reattaching it.

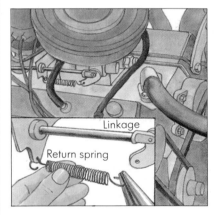

Linkage

Return spring

Car batteries

If your car battery is dead, jump leads and another car can get you driving again. But check your car handbook first: some cars with electronic engine-management systems are seriously damaged by jump-starting.

• Bring the two cars nose to nose, but not touching, and open up their bonnets. Start up the engine of the car which is working, and connect the positive (+) terminals of both batteries with the red lead. Then connect one end of the black, negative lead to a negative (–) terminal and the other to any unpainted metal part of the faulty car.

Switch on the ignition of the faulty car and start up the engine. When the car is

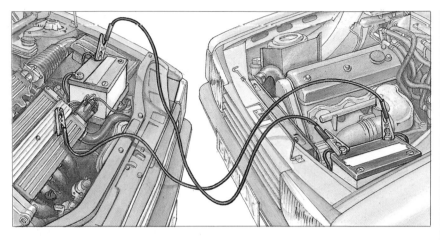

running smoothly, disconnect the two terminals. Drive the car for at least 30 minutes before parking, to allow the flat battery to recharge thoroughly.

Caution Be very careful in wet weather, and don't smoke or strike a match.

Car bonnets

If the bonnet of your car suddenly flies up, don't slam on the brakes; slow down carefully and pull off the road as soon as possible. Steer the car by sticking your head out the window, if it is open, or peering through the opening between the bonnet and the dashboard. (Prepare for this emergency in advance by opening your bonnet to see which is the better vantage point.)

If the bonnet latch is broken, and not just improperly closed, tie the bonnet shut with a piece of rope or a pair of tights and get it fixed immediately.

Car boot sales

If you are fed up with household clutter, why not get rid of some of it at a car boot sale? They are advertised in local newspapers and on posters stuck up in the street. If you can't find one near you, ring your council or local paper for any information they might have.

• Get advice from a friend who has done it before.

• Take a fold-up table or trestle table with you to display the goods on – your boot may not be big enough.

• Take a rug to spread out on the ground

in front of the car, and arrange your items with care – you'll sell them faster.

• Price the items for sale beforehand and keep the prices low – you aren't going to make a fortune, but you will get rid of the goods with some financial return. Be prepared for some haggling and expect to reduce some prices.

• Place collections of small items in a box and fix a price for the whole boxload.

• Wear a money belt, or hang a purse on a cord around your neck, for safekeeping. Take plenty of change with you.

• Ask a friend to come with you to help you deal with crowds, should they occur, and to keep you company in the quieter moments.

• Bring food and drink to keep you refreshed during the day.

• Take all unsold goods to a local charity shop afterwards.

Car brakes

If your brake warning light is on, check to see if the handbrake is fully released.

If the light comes on when you push the brake pedal, there may be something wrong with your car's main braking system. It could simply be that the brake pads are worn or the brake fluid level is low, or it could mean that the system is losing pressure. If it is, don't panic. You probably have enough braking power to slow and stop the car.

• Turn on the hazard lights, then head off the road to stop. Keep in mind that you may need more distance than usual for

braking; you may have to press the brake pedal harder and it may depress farther.

• Pump the brake pedal rapidly to build up pressure. If that doesn't work, use the handbrake or change down a gear so that engine drag slows the car. When in low gear and slowed to a virtual stop, pull onto the shoulder of the road and turn off the ignition.

• If none of these measures halts the car, you may have to sideswipe something – a kerb, a hedge, even a parked car – to stop it. Sound your horn and flash your lights to alert other drivers to your emergency.

Car doors

Sticking doors Before going to the expense of getting a sticking door realigned, try lubricating its hinges with an aerosol penetrating solvent (sold in motor accessory shops). This lubricant will also take the squeaks and groans out of the hinges.

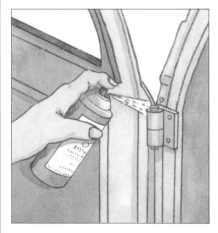

Weatherproofing Don't wait until the rain is dripping into your car and the windows are difficult to move up and down before taking care of the weatherproofing. Instead, prevent it from cracking and tearing by applying a spray vinyl-and-rubber protectant occasionally, when you wash the car.

Locked back doors If you can't open a back door from the inside, check the child-safety lock. Open the door from the outside and trip the lever inside the jamb to the open position.

Car drive belts

Does your car make a screaming noise as you drive? The drive belt, or the power-steering drive belt, may be slipping and need adjusting. It is probably also wearing out quickly and will soon break. You should replace it as soon as you can.

• With a spanner, loosen the mounting bolts on the generator or the power steering pump, depending on which belt needs replacing.

• Move the generator or pump towards the engine, and remove the old belt from the pulleys.

• Fit the new belt in position, making sure it sits in the grooves of the pulleys. If it won't fit, or you have to stretch it with effort to get it onto the pulleys, it is probably the wrong size.

• Move the generator or pump away from the engine and tighten up the mounting bolts. The belt should now feel tight when you press it along the length of its run between the pulleys.

• Carry spare belts in the boot.

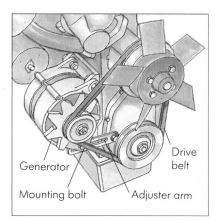

Generator

Drive belt

Mounting bolt

Adjuster arm

Career changes

• What do you really like doing best? You might be happier pursuing your hobby as a full-time career.

• Which activities do you find most fulfilling? Do they involve working alone or with others? Solving new problems or making systems work? Negotiating or giving orders? The answers may help you find the career that you are best suited for.

• Before leaving your company, ask the personnel department about jobs in other departments or divisions that you're qualified for.

• If you want to investigate other fields, try to continue the work you've been doing on a part-time, freelance or consultant basis.

• Many colleges have courses designed for mature students, including those who work full-time.

• If you're thinking about a new profession but you're not sure it's right for you, do volunteer work in the field to find out more about it.

Career development

• Make yourself visible to the people who count; identify the influential people in your department or division (they may not be the ones with the formal power) and look for opportunities to work with them, even if it means extra hours.

• When your boss is away, resist the temptation to sit back and relax; work at your normal pace or even harder. This will earn you a reputation as a self-motivated worker. If your boss gives you a job before he goes on leave, make a point of completing it before he returns. This will mean you can be trusted in the future.

• People with a wide network of contacts in the company have a better chance of promotion. Join in company social activities – organising social events or joining a charity drive, or company team sports – but don't overstretch yourself.

• Make your good work known to your senior colleagues by showing them any complimentary letters you receive from customers or clients. If appropriate, include a cover memo with a good word about your boss and/or department. You'll make your work group and yourself look good, and you'll reassure your boss that you're not trying to steal the limelight.

• Learn all you can about the business you're in. Don't limit your contribution to your own speciality.

• Take evening classes in subjects outside your own discipline.

Car engine overheats

If the needle on your temperature gauge moves to 'hot', or the coolant warning light flashes on while you are driving, your car engine is overheating. Stop the car as soon as possible and let the engine cool down for at least 15 minutes.

Never remove the radiator cap while the engine is hot. You could be badly scalded by the steam or hot water.

• When the engine is cool, check the level of coolant water. This can be seen easily in cars which have a plastic expansion tank. If your car does not have an expansion tank, cover your hand with a thick cloth or glove and slowly unscrew the cap on top of the radiator.

You can often simply top up the water level, by filling the expansion tank to the level marked on it, or the radiator to just below the cap. *Do not* use cold water to refill an overheated engine – it could damage the engine. Wait until the engine is cool.

• The water level could have dropped because there is a leak in the radiator or coolant hose. While the engine is cooling down, check for these. A coolant hose can be repaired temporarily with tape, and a leaking radiator can be sealed temporarily with chewing gum.

• Check the drive belts. Some cars have a generator drive belt that also drives the water pump and radiator fan. If this breaks or slips the engine will overheat. See also CAR DRIVE BELTS, left.

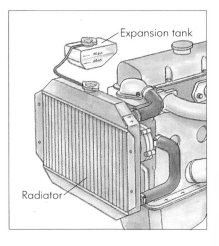

Expansion tank

Radiator

Car fires

In the engine compartment If you suspect a fire, pull off the road and turn off the ignition and lights; in so doing, you stop the flow of fuel and electricity, which may be enough to stop the fire.

Get everybody out of the car. If the fire is near the fuel tank, stay at least 500ft/150m away and warn approaching cars and pedestrians of the danger.

Call the fire brigade or emergency service (or ask a passing motorist to do so). Do not open the car's bonnet or try to fight even a small fire yourself.

In the passenger compartment Every car should ideally have a 2½lb/1.1kg dry-chemical fire extinguisher to fight small interior fires that might be caused by stray ash. Keep the extinguisher inside the car, either under the front seat or in the glove compartment. In the time it would take to retrieve the extinguisher from the boot, the fire could be out of control.

Car horns

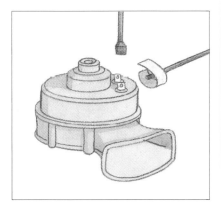

If your horn won't stop blowing:
• Switch off the engine, open the bonnet and locate the horn.
• Disconnect or cut the wires leading to the horn and tape the exposed metal ends.
• If you can't get at the horn wires and know where the fuse box is, pull out the relevant fuse.
• Or temporarily disconnect the earth lead wire from the battery; reconnect before starting up the car. Have the horn system repaired immediately.

Car jacks

Jack Board   Chock

It's best to jack up a car on level, firm ground. If you must do so on a slope, put large rocks or wedges on the downhill side of the tyres.

In an emergency you can use a hubcap or wheel trim to support a jack on soft ground. Many newer cars don't have hubcaps, however, and others have wheel covers made of plastic or thin metal that may be ruined by such use. (Still, a wheel trim may be a small price to pay to get back on the road.)

A better solution is to carry a couple of boards with you. Ask a timber yard for scraps of wood ¾in/19mm thick: one about 18in/450mm square to use as a base under the jack and another, about 6 × 8in/150 × 200mm, to use as a chock for the tyre diagonally opposite the one being changed, to prevent the car from rolling off the jack. (If you're caught without a chock on the road, you can use a brick or a rock.)

Car keys

Avoid locking yourself out of your car by taking a few simple precautions.
• Carry a spare key with you, or hide one on the exterior of your car. Magnetic key cases are available, which fit under a wing or door sill, or you could tape the spare key behind your bumper.
• If your car has self locking doors, get into the habit of always locking them from the outside using the key.
• If you lock yourself out, call the police, who will open the car for you.

Car lights

• If both headlights or both back lights fail to work, the cause is probably a dirty or blown fuse. Check your car handbook to see where the fuse box is – it is usually on the side or back of the engine compartment, or under the fascia inside the car. The fuses are colour coded and the fuse box cover usually gives details of the relevant circuit.

Unclip or pull the relevant fuse from its terminals. If the wire down the centre is broken, the fuse has blown and needs replacing. If not, the metal ends may need cleaning – use a nail file or small piece of sandpaper.
• If a replacement fuse blows again when you switch on the lights, it is short circuiting. Call your breakdown service or local garage for help.
• Always carry spare fuses.
• If one light goes out, the bulb probably needs to be replaced. Switch off the lights. Remove the lens cover screws or unclip the back of the light from inside the engine compartment (if it is a front light) or the boot (if it is a back light).

If there is rust or white corrosion inside the bulb holder, scrape it off with a nail file or piece of sandpaper.

If the bulb filament is broken or the glass is discoloured, fit a new bulb.
• Some cars have a light bulb for the number plate which matches the rear light bulb. In an emergency you can swap them round, but replace them as soon as possible.

Carpet beetles

• To prevent the larvae of carpet beetles from infesting your home, vacuum your carpets often.
• Seal all floor cracks and cracks in skirting boards with flexible wood filler.
• Check the loft for old birds' nests and remove them.
• Check the airing cupboard for signs of beetles or their larvae. If there are any, clean out and spray with mothproofing aerosol or carpet beetle killer.
• Place mothballs in stored clothes and bedding and spray with a mothproofing aerosol.
• If your carpets are infested, vacuum them thoroughly and throw away or burn the vacuum bag. Spray under the carpet and all other exposed furnishing fabrics with mothproofing aerosol or carpet beetle killer.

Carpets

• To ensure even carpet wear, rearrange your furniture occasionally, redirecting the flow of traffic. Use rugs in front of everyone's favourite chairs, and turn them around regularly.

• To revive any dents left by furniture legs, hold a steam iron about 6in/150mm above the spot until the fabric is moist. Then work the fibres back and forth with the edge of a large coin or the back of a comb. Prevent such dents by slightly shifting your furniture, and use coasters with smooth or rounded edges under chair feet.

• Prevent static shock by spraying carpets with a solution of 1 part liquid fabric softener to 5 parts water. The solution can also be applied with a sponge or cloth.

• To revive the colour of a rug, vacuum it first and then apply a solution of 1 part white vinegar to 3 parts boiling water using a sponge or cloth. Dampen only the nap and don't wet the backing. When the rug is dry, rub it lightly with dry bread crumbs, then vacuum.

• To make your own carpet shampoo for nylon or other synthetic-fibre rugs, add 1 tablespoon ammonia and a generous amount of mild detergent to a large bowl of warm water; mix vigorously, preferably with an egg beater, to make suds. Rub the suds lightly over the carpet, leave it to dry, then vacuum.

• Cornflour can also act as a carpet cleaner. Sprinkle it on, leave it for at least 2 hours and then vacuum.

• To deodorise a carpet, liberally apply bicarbonate of soda (4-5lb/1.8-2.3kg for a 9 × 12ft/2.7 × 3.7m rug). Leave it for at least 15 minutes (overnight for strong smells), then vacuum.

Carpet repairs

If burn marks or worn patches mar your carpet but you don't want to replace it, patch repairs can improve its appearance dramatically.

• To fix burn holes, trim away scorched fibres with a sharp craft knife to expose the backing. Cut matching tufts from a spare piece of carpet, or from an area of the carpet that is not normally visible. Spread an appropriate latex adhesive onto the backing and dab it onto the ends of the tufts, then press them into the hole onto the backing. Let it dry, then trim and brush the tufts to blend with the pile.

• To repair worn patches on carpets that have the pile woven into the backing, turn the carpet over and mark a square on the backing under the damaged area. Spread latex adhesive over the backing square, adding 1in/25mm extra all round, and rub it in. Place a piece of wood under the pile, and cut out the marked square from the backing side, with a sharp trimming knife.

Cut strips of hessian tape 2in/50mm longer than the sides of the square, and cover the hole with them.

Using the old square of carpet as a template, cut a new square from a spare piece or from an area that won't show the hole. Make sure the new piece matches the old one in pattern and direction of the pile.

Spread adhesive over the back and edges of the new piece, but make sure you don't get it on the tufts.

Press the new square into the hole onto the hessian strips and tap the edges with a hammer so that they lie flush with the rest of the carpet.

• With a foam-backed carpet, cut a patch from a piece of new carpet and position it so that it covers the mark and matches any pattern. Use a carpet or trimming knife and cut through both layers, fairly close to the edge of the new piece, but try to avoid cutting the underfelt. Lift away the trimmings and the damaged piece of carpet.

Fix strips of carpet tape, sticky side up, to the underneath of the carpet, across the gap. Carefully fit the new piece into the gap and gently hammer the edges flush with the rest of the carpet.

Carpet stains

Scrape off any solids. Blot up liquids quickly, dabbing lightly with a clean towel or paper towel.

• To remove greasy stains, apply a non-flammable dry-cleaning agent to the spot with a flannel; work from the edges towards the centre. Don't scrub, because you will damage the fibres: dab gently until the spot comes clean. (Always test any cleaning agent on an inconspicuous part of the carpet first, and let it dry before continuing.)

Coat less stubborn greasy stains on carpets with carbonated water. Use a hair dryer to speed up drying, then vacuum the carpet. Or sprinkle grease stains with bicarbonate of soda, cornflour or talcum powder. Leave for at least 6 hours, then vacuum.

• To remove water soluble stains, dab excess with white paper towel or a clean cloth. Spray with a proprietary brand of carpet shampoo, following the manufacturer's instructions and taking care not to saturate the carpet. Gently work the foam into the pile, dabbing and drying to check the results. Work the foam into the surrounding area so as not to leave a 'high-water mark' when the shampoo has dried. Vacuum when dry.

• To remove excrement, urine or vomit stains, try this: after scraping off the solids, apply a detergent solution (½ teaspoon biological washing powder per pint/570ml of water) and blot. Then use a solution of household borax (1 tablespoon per pint/570ml of water) and blot. Follow with a solution of equal parts white vinegar and water (but to be safe, it's best to test this solution on an inconspicuous place first, because vinegar can remove some dyes). Blot, flush with water, and blot again.

Carrots

Mix a packet of carrot seeds with a cup of unused ground coffee. Not only does the extra bulk make the tiny seeds easier to sow, but the coffee aroma is said by some gardeners to repel root maggots and other pests, too.

You can also add a few radish seeds to the blend. While the carrots may take 3 weeks to sprout, the radishes will be up in a matter of days to mark the rows. And when it's time for you to harvest the radishes, you'll be thinning the carrot seedlings and cultivating the soil at the same time.

Car security

• Etch your car's registration number, or some other number personal to you, onto the window tops (so that it can be seen if the door windows are lowered), wing mirrors and lights. Etching kits are available from motor accessory shops, or ask your local garage.

• Don't leave valuables visible in the car.

• Sharply turn the front wheels of the car to lock the steering wheel. Make sure the steering wheel is turned to the fully locked position. Set the gear lever in Park on an automatic-transmission car; on a manual, leave the car in gear. Engage the handbrake.

• Close all windows tightly, including the sunroof. Lock the car and pocket the key, even if you're only stepping away for a few minutes or you're parked in your own driveway.

• Vary your routines – don't park in the same place every day, for the same length of time. And park your car between others so that it will be more difficult for a thief to tow away.

• Avoid parking in a low-traffic, dimly lit area, such as the remote sections of a shopping centre, where a thief can work undetected.

• Always take valuables inside at night.

• Special locks, alarms and assorted disabling devices are among the many anti-theft devices available for cars today. Fit an alarm or ignition immobiliser, which prevents the engine from starting, and always use it. Fit a lockable fuel cap and lockable wheel nuts.

Carsickness

If you're prone to carsickness and are unable to buy travel sickness pills, these ideas may help. Get plenty of rest before you set out on a car trip. Eat a light, easy-to-digest meal about an hour before setting out, and wear comfortable, light clothing. To be on the safe side, carry waterproof plastic bags and a damp flannel or premoistened towelettes. Take along bland food and drinks: water biscuits or tea biscuits, bread, water, juice or fizzy drinks such as mineral water, ginger ale or soda. Sit in the front

seat and keep a window or the vent open. Stop every hour to get out of the car for some fresh air and exercise. If disaster seems imminent, open a window and breathe deeply. See also AIRSICKNESS p.9.

Car-starting problems

• Check the fuel gauge to make sure there's fuel in the tank.

• Try the headlights. If they seem dim or don't work at all, the battery may be either weak or dead. While this is a problem that usually occurs in winter, it can happen at any time of the year. See CAR BATTERIES, p.32.

If the battery is weak, but not dead, you may be able to start a car with manual transmission by push-starting it. Note that a car fitted with an electronic management system should never be push-started. Get a helper to push the car for you. Turn the ignition on, depress the clutch and put the car into second gear. Keep the clutch down and release the handbrake. Get your helper to start pushing and when the car has picked up speed, let out the clutch quickly and rev the engine when it catches.

• If nothing happens when you turn the key and the car has an automatic transmission, be sure the selector lever is firmly in Park or Neutral. Jiggle the lever in each position as you try to start the engine. If it then starts, you probably have a faulty safety switch; get someone out to look at the car.

• If you flood the engine trying to start the car (you'll smell petrol), wait 5 minutes; then hold the accelerator to the floor and turn on the ignition for 10 seconds. If this doesn't work the first time, wait at least 5 minutes and repeat the procedure. Never pump the pedal; you'll only flood the engine more.

Car stuck in snow or mud

If your car gets bogged down in snow or mud, don't accelerate to try to get it out. The tyres will just dig in further and make it more difficult for you to get the car out again.

• If the wheels cannot grip, prevent them

from spinning by using the fourth or fifth gear, then partly disengage the clutch, to get the car rolling.

• If this doesn't work, use the third and reverse gears alternately to rock the car back and forth until it rolls and the wheels grip.

• If the wheels have become firmly stuck, try to clear some space around the driving wheels. Find something inside the car – such as the floormats from the boot or the front seats, or an old coat – to put under the wheels. This will give the treads something to grip on.

Car warning lights

Oil-pressure light If your car's oil-pressure light stays on longer than a moment as you start up, or if it glows steadily as you drive, turn off the engine. This light is a warning that you may not have enough oil to lubricate the engine – a condition that can cause the engine to wear and do serious damage to it very quickly.

Check the oil level and add oil if it's needed. If the oil is at the correct level or the light stays on after you add oil, the problem probably lies with the light circuit. To be on the safe side, have the car towed to a garage.

Alternator light If the alternator light goes on while you're driving, the battery is expending more energy than it is receiving.

• Don't switch off the engine – you may not be able to restart it.

• Turn off any unnecessary electrical equipment and drive to a garage. In the meantime, keep an eye on the temperature gauge. If the car overheats, pull off the road to stop and get professional help. See also CAR BRAKES, p.33.

Car windscreen

• If both your windscreen wipers stop working, this is probably because a fuse has blown. Check your fuse box (see CAR LIGHTS, p.35), and replace the relevant fuse if necessary.

• If one blade fails, the nut that secures the arm has probably worked loose. Turn the wiper switch to the 'off' position and, with a screwdriver, lift the cap at the base of the arm. Tighten the nut with a spanner, then replace the cap.

• If the blades judder on the windscreen, the rubber may be worn and need replacing. As a temporary measure, switch off the ignition when the blades are upright, then twist the arm until the blades lie horizontally across the windscreen.

• If something hits your windscreen while you're driving and it shatters, immediately signal and pull over onto the side of the road. Then turn on your hazard lights. *Do not* try to knock out the windscreen while you're driving. You will probably get cut and glass may fly into your eyes.

If it is absolutely essential that you continue your journey soon, then place a cloth or newspaper over the dashboard, wrap your hand in thick cloth and knock out the glass with something heavy, or with your fist. Remove the remaining pieces with gloves or the cloth. Close the car windows and drive to a garage, wearing glasses or sunglasses if possible, to protect your eyes from stray bits of glass.

If you are not in a hurry, call a windscreen replacement service and wait for it to arrive.

Cats

• Cats are nocturnal and will pester you to be let outside at night (unless they live entirely indoors and have been neutered). To make sure you are able to sleep uninterrupted, fit a cat flap to a

door which gives access to the outside.

• To keep your cat from licking or biting at its wounds, isolate its head by securing a circular cardboard collar around its neck.

• In winter, cats like to snuggle up in a warm place, such as a car engine. You might save your pet's life by banging on the bonnet or pressing the horn before starting up.

• Run a damp cloth along your cat's coat to pick up shedding hair.

• To discourage your cat from jumping on beds, sofas and other pieces of furniture, squirt it gently with a water pistol each time you spot it in a place that's off-limits.

• A pine log or plank makes a good scratching post. For toys, try aluminium foil crushed into a ball, ping-pong balls, old knotted socks, paper bags, empty cotton reels and plastic pill bottles filled with rice. Avoid string, thread, wool and rubber bands – your cat may swallow them.

• A clean cardboard box can serve as a cat bed. Cut an opening into one side for easy access. Then for comfort and warmth, line the box with a pillow, blanket or towel.

• To help eliminate hair balls, add a teaspoon of liquid paraffin to their food three times a week for short-haired cats, and every day for long-haired cats.

• If you have trouble getting your cat to swallow a pill, coat it with butter first. If the medicine is liquid, use an eyedropper to squirt it down its throat.

Caterpillars

There are many varieties of caterpillars that can lay waste to plants in a short space of time. All can be dealt with in the same way.

• Examine your plants often, and remove egg clusters and caterpillars by hand regularly.

• If they become too much to deal with 'kindly', insecticides are the only means of getting rid of them. Approved 'organic' insecticides that kill caterpillars include derris. This is particularly appropriate for edible crops because the plants can be eaten two or three days after application. Other 'organic' pesticides include pyrethrum and the bacterium *Bacillus thuringiensis berliner*, which is harmful to caterpillars but not to other insects. It is available at a good garden centre or through British Organic Farmers or the Henry Doubleday Research Association (see PESTICIDES, p.152). Derris and pyrethrum are available as dusts to treat soil or leaves that may harbour caterpillars.

Dust infested plants as soon as you notice the grubs.

Ceilings

• Expanded polystyrene ceiling tiles offer a means of hiding a ceiling surface spoiled by fine cracks. But they have gone out of fashion – partly because of the added fire risk (despite the use of self-extinguishing grades of plastic), and partly because of the problems with cleaning and decorating.

• A better solution is to use a fairly heavy wall covering, such as blown vinyl. This will hide both fine cracks and any slight irregularities in the ceiling surface. Always choose a heavyweight paste for ease of hanging. The ready-mixed tubbed pastes are ideal.

• If you wish to decorate directly on to the ceiling, choose a paint specially formulated for this situation. The paint is designed to be elastic when dry, so it can accommodate any slight movement of the ceiling.

• If you use your loft for storage, don't overload it, and spread as much weight as possible around the edges. Overloading is a common cause of ceiling cracks.

• Stains that bleed through the ceiling plaster, perhaps because of a leak in the plumbing, can ruin new decoration if not dealt with. Use a special stain-blocking coating, available either in aerosol form or as a primer, to seal off the stained area. Then you can decorate over the top.

• If you don't have a special sealer for stains, use aluminium primer/sealer. The scale-like nature of this material will effectively isolate any stain so that it can't bleed through the new decoration.

• Give a room a period look by installing lightweight imitation timber beams. These reproductions can be very effective and are 'authentically' produced – even down to cracks, knots and signs of woodworm. Small beams may be stuck in place with a special adhesive. Larger beams have a ∪ section so that they can be sited over a timber batten screwed to the ceiling, then screwed in place. Special plugs are available to hide fixing holes. You can make up your own beams from distressed timbers which are then stained, but the extra weight of solid timber means that the beams must be securely anchored to existing ceiling joists.

• The best way to clean ceilings that have a highly textured finish is with a vacuum cleaner; use the dust-brush attachment to avoid damaging the surface. Sweeping the ceiling will also work, but use only a spotlessly clean soft-bristled floor brush.

• Here's how to remove dust from small areas, such as around light fixtures, that attract dust: remove the crusts from several slices of fresh white bread, roll the bread into a ball, and roll the ball along the dusty surface. Its stickiness will pick up the dust.

Cellulite

If the skin on your thighs, knees or buttocks looks dimpled – even if you aren't overweight – you have cellulite. Your best bet is a well-balanced diet and regular exercise – to reduce body fat and to tone the skin. (The more fat you have, the more dimpling there will be.)

Exercise Aerobic exercise is best, especially walking and swimming. Spot callisthenics may tone and shape problem thighs. Do ten repetitions with each leg for each exercise.

Selling cellulite

Purveyors of expensive 'solutions' to the cellulite problem sometimes say that the culprit is a different kind of fat from the stuff that is found elsewhere on your body. Or worse, that the condition is caused by 'toxic' fat – a sort of swamp of suet trapped in abnormal, chronically inflamed tissue through which blood and lymph fail to flow as they should.

In fact, cellulite is caused by normal fat laid down unevenly under thin skin. The chief cause is heredity, which determines whether – and where – normal fat is to be deposited.

There is no sure cure for the condition, and no proof that special creams, scrubbers or massage have any effect. Surgical liposuction may remove fat, but it may also create or worsen skin dimpling. If you have cellulite, you probably have it for life, although it is possible to improve the appearance of cellulite-dimpled skin.

Avoid 'cures' that promise to release nonexistent 'trapped toxins'. Saunas to sweat them out, electrical devices to loosen them, crash diets to melt them and body-wrapping tapes are all equally ineffective.

Diet Avoid crash diets; if you regain the weight, your skin may stretch, making cellulite worse. Instead, cut back on fatty, fried and salty foods and add fibre to your diet. Make sure you drink eight to ten glasses of water every day.

Chair substitutes

You're having a party, but you have more guests than chairs. Apart from asking your neighbour to lend you some chairs, what else can you do?

• For a children's party, make a picnic bench by nailing a 12 × 1in/300 × 25mm plank to two sawhorses or wooden crates. To prevent splinters, sand the board and cover it with a blanket or adhesive plastic. Or turn sturdy metal or plastic wastepaper

Flex foot, raise and lower top leg ten times. Repeat with foot pointed.

Flex foot; raise and lower bottom leg ten times. Repeat with foot pointed.

baskets over; pad each 'seat' with a towel or old cushion and decorate with crêpe paper.

• Floor cushions stacked two or three high can make a person feel like a rajah. They stand up to hard use if you cover them with nylon, densely woven cotton such as corduroy, or other upholstery-weight fabrics.

• Don't forget the garden. Patio or garden chairs can be brought indoors and dressed up with cushions.

• Use a coffee table for dining from, with colourful placemats adding a festive touch. Guests won't mind sitting on the floor (or on cushions) if you let them know your plans beforehand so that they can dress appropriately.

Chandelier cleaning

You don't have to take a chandelier or central light fixture apart to clean it. First, switch off the light and let it cool. Then cover the light sockets and bulbs with plastic sandwich bags and secure with rubber bands or twist ties. Cover half the chandelier with a plastic sheet and spread another sheet on the floor. Spray the uncovered half with window cleaner or a commercial chandelier cleaner and carefully wipe each piece clean. Repeat for the other half.

An easier way is to spray the chandelier liberally with a solution of 2 teaspoons surgical spirit in 1 pint/570ml water and then let it drip-dry.

Chapped lips

The skin on your lips is much more sensitive than the rest of your face, because it is actually just a membrane and is not naturally lubricated, unlike the rest of your skin. This means that it is prone to dryness, chapping and flaking in extremes of temperature, cold air, sun or wind.

Prevention

• Lipsticks usually smooth and lubricate as well as provide colour, while lip balms give colourless, quick relief from chapping. Many lipsticks and balms now contain ultraviolet light filters to protect against sunlight.

• Always cream your lips when you apply moisturiser to your face, morning and evening. At night, take off make-up with a moisturising and emollient cream or lotion and not soap, which tends to be drying. At night, apply a lip ointment or petroleum jelly.

• Even though licking your lips seems to provide relief, resist the temptation; when the moisture evaporates, your lips are likely to chap even more.

• Treat your lips gently – don't rub them, and try not to pick the peeling skin.

Charcoal starter

Try this ignition sleeve for barbecue charcoal lighting: first, punch holes around the lower edge of a clean 1 gallon / 4.5 litre metal tin with a screwdriver; then remove both ends of the tin. Punch two holes at the top and attach a handle of coat-hanger wire.

Set the sleeve in the barbecue and place one or two sheets of loosely folded

newspaper inside. Fill the sleeve with charcoal briquettes and light the newspaper through the punched holes at the bottom. When the coals are alight, lift the sleeve from the barbecue with tongs, leaving the burning coals behind. You can also use a 500g tin and surround it with briquettes; they'll light after the sleeve is lifted from the hot coals.

Or you can fill an empty, dry milk carton with briquettes and light it at the bottom. The briquettes will be alight by the time the carton burns away.

Cheese grater

Drum grater

• To avoid skinning your knuckles, use a hand-held cheese grater with a drum and turning crank.

• At a pinch you can use a strong four-pronged fork as a cheese grater; holding the cheese you just scrape away at it with the fork. Or place small cubes of Parmesan or other hard cheese in a blender or food processor and whizz for a few seconds.

• Brush a little cooking oil onto a grater before using it; that way, you'll find that cleaning it after use will be easier. Keep an old toothbrush next to the sink to scrub off any cheese that clogs the holes.

Chequebook balancing

Balance your chequebook as soon as your bank statement arrives and notify your bank of any errors.

• Compare each debit entry on the statement with the counterfoils in your chequebook and mark them off.

• Add up the cheques you have drawn but which have not yet gone through the bank, and subtract them from the bank statement total; add in any deposits that may have been made after the statement was drawn up.

• Deduct from your chequebook total all interest and service charges, direct debits and standing orders; add any interest and other receipts.

Your chequebook and bank statement should then balance. If they don't, take one total from the other and look at the difference. If the difference is 1 or 10 or 100 (or 9 or 99) you have probably made an error in addition; if the difference divides by 9 you have probably transposed a figure – that is, written £89 instead of £98. If it still won't balance, check that you have not missed out anything from your statement and recheck your arithmetic. See COMPUTATIONS, p.50.

Cheques

Although banks resist substitutes, anything you can write on and take to the bank can serve as a cheque: a blank sheet of paper, a napkin, even a coconut, will do as long it's dated, says 'Pay to the order of . . .', names a sterling amount, includes the bank's name and the account number, and is correctly signed. (In all probability, a bank will charge a 'special handling fee' for such a cheque.)

If you run out of cheques, the bank can give you blanks while you wait for a new chequebook.

Security Fill out cheques carefully. Write the amount of the cheque close against the £ sign; don't leave room between the figures. On the middle line, start writing at the far left; draw a line through any space after the word 'pounds' or 'pence'. When depositing a cheque, write 'for deposit only' with your endorsement.

Bounced cheques To make sure that none of your cheques ever bounce, arrange an overdraft reserve on your account. This permits you to draw more money on your account than you have in it – up to a limit set by your bank – if the need arises. But interest on this service is steep. A cheaper solution is to arrange for the automatic transfer of funds from

your savings to your current account.
Stopping payment Contact your bank or, better, go in person. Give the bank all the details about the cheque. You will probably be asked to sign the stop-payment order the same day. You must pay a charge for the cheque stopper.

Dating cheques Most banks don't execute cheques until the date written on them, and will always refer back to the payer before honouring a cheque that is more than 6 months old.

Chewing gum

• To remove chewing gum from a rug or carpet, harden it with an ice cube and scrape it off with a blunt knife. To avoid wetting the rug, put the ice in a plastic bag.

• To remove gum from hair, work a little cooking oil or peanut butter into the gum and hair, then pick or comb the gum out. Or harden the gum with ice and 'crack' if off the hair. Follow with an oil treatment.

• To remove chewing gum from fabric, apply Stain Devils Chewing Gum Remover, according to manufacturer's instructions. Dirty residue may need washing out with detergent, later.

Chicken breasts

• Don't give up if the recipe you want to prepare calls for pork or veal escalopes and your butcher or supermarket is out of them. Thin slices of chicken or turkey breast are equally delicious in virtually any pork or veal dish.

• Buying boneless chicken breasts is expensive. You can save money by

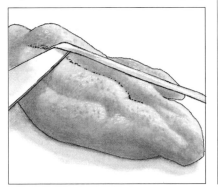

boning the breasts yourself. First, dry the chicken breasts with paper towels. Place them skin side down, on a cutting board. Using a small, sharp, pointed knife, carefully remove the bones by inserting the tip of the knife under the tips of the rib bones. Then, keeping the knife close to the bones, carefully cut away the flesh. Remove the white tendons from the flesh, if you wish, and then gently pull off the skin.

Use the breast whole, in thin slices or in strips. To make chicken escalopes, lay the breasts between two sheets of greaseproof paper or plastic food wrap and flatten them with a rolling pin. Make stock with the bones.

Chicken pox

• To relieve the irritating itch, apply calamine lotion to the affected areas. Some people find a gentle, unperfumed skin cream more soothing.

• Keep the rash clean and dry.

• Take paracetamol to ease fever.

• Drink plenty of liquids.

• Wear loose clothing and take frequent, cool baths or showers.

• To keep children from scratching, put mittens on their hands.

• Consult your doctor if you get chicken pox as an adult, particularly if you are pregnant or your symptoms are severe.

• Make sure that you get plenty of rest.

Child care

If you hire someone to look after your children during the day, consider these pointers:

• If you want a full-time nanny (who works in your own home), make sure that candidates have the NNEB child care qualification. If you would prefer a childminder (who takes children into her home), contact the National Childminding Association on 0181-464 6164 or ask your local authority for a list of registered minders in your area.

• Establish clearly the salary and hours and, for live-in nannies, days off, level of responsibility and duties. Write these out in detail and give the candidate a copy to consider, then make any changes agreed upon. This serves as an informal contract after both of you have signed it.

• Carefully check all references, by telephone if possible, and ask previous employers about the childminder's strong and weak points.

• Arrange a trial run: ask the prospective helper to spend an afternoon or a weekend with your child. Then observe your child's behaviour afterwards.

If he becomes grouchy, quarrelsome, disobedient, irritable or silent, keep searching for your Mary Poppins.

• Before settling the agreement, have a candid talk: will the childminder be happy with your child, requirements, family and neighbourhood? You won't want to start interviewing all over again in three months' time.

Children's chores

Start encouraging children to help around the house when they are young. Be patient, firm and fair – boys should wash up as much as girls.

• Ask the children to draw up a list of chores they could help you with such as folding pyjamas, clearing the table, drying cutlery (it can't be broken).

• Divide up these jobs so that each child has a set number of his own every week. Rotate the jobs monthly or weekly.

• Reward them by providing pocket money in return. Extra money might be earned for extra jobs. Make it fun by storing 'job descriptions' in a chore jar that children can dip into to choose extra tasks (such as feeding the cat).

• Help toddlers to join in the household chores by handing out a duster.

Children's crafts

Many household leftovers can be turned into toys by children.

Puppets Paint faces on worn socks for hand puppets; cut the fingers off old woollen gloves for finger puppets.

For a milk-carton puppet, cut off the carton top and slice the carton across the middle on three sides. Cut finger holes in the back. Make puppet hair with wool, draw on faces with felt-tips, and

Milk carton puppets

finally glue on paper cutouts as ears.

Space helmet Using a craft knife, cut off the bottom of a 1 gallon / 4.5 litre plastic bottle and cut a face hole in the side. Make a cardboard visor with openings for the eyes; attach it to the helmet with hair pins or paper clips or, better still, a staple gun. Decorate with pipe cleaners, paper cutouts, and twist ties wound around the bottle's neck.

Spaceship Cut one of the top flaps of a cardboard box into a T-shaped handle, with the stem coming out of the box; remove the other flaps from the top and cut them into the shape of tail fins. Glue the fins onto the outside of two sides of the box, but not the side with the handle; add buttons and bottle caps for a control panel inside the box, onto the side with the handle; attach paper cups or cardboard tubes from toilet paper or paper towels to the outside for rocket exhaust pipes.

Etchings Save the sheets of polystyrene that come with packaged meat and fish. Clean them thoroughly, and dry. Draw a picture on the polystyrene, leaving an indentation, then brush poster paint over the surface. Press a piece of paper onto the paint and lift it off. The drawing lines should remain white on the paper.

3-D animals Draw an animal's outline on dark paper and paint the space inside the outline with white glue. Stick on polystyrene packing beads, then spray-paint. Colour individual beads for features.

Children's friends

• Don't worry if your child is content with just one or two friends – we can't all be social butterflies. But if she's concerned, you can help by making your home an inviting place for young people to gather.

• If your child's 'best friend' is 'stolen' by a third child, help her realise that she shouldn't restrict her attachments, that she should get along with lots of people.

• Young children sometimes invent imaginary friends – it's not a sign of mental instability but an indication of an active imagination. Don't ridicule it in your child; play along with it.

• Even if you don't like the way your child behaves in the company of certain friends, don't criticise her. Consider inviting them into your home, feeding them, letting them stay the night, including them in family occasions. You will learn a lot about your child, and you will be able to show by example what kind of language and manners you find both appropriate and acceptable.

Children's parties

If you have qualms about giving a birthday party for an active 6-year-old, think about buying or hiring some of the vital party ingredients.

The place Rent a room in a church hall or synagogue, YMCA, sports centre, school or day-care centre. It will be more childproof than your home. In warm weather, have a picnic in a park.

The food Order some or all of the food – pizza, roast chicken, birthday cake – to be delivered, or have the whole party handled by a professional caterer.

Take the guests out. Many fast-food and family restaurants provide birthday meals, including a decorated cake and special attention for the birthday child.

The entertainment Take the children out to a film, the zoo, a park where they can play football or Frisbee, or a skating rink. Take them on a nature walk or bowling, fishing or swimming.

Invitations You can buy invitations, of course, but you and your child may enjoy making them together so that you

Please
come
to a party
for Evan.
April 5, 1-3
Evan's house.
R.S.V.P.

can build up anticipation for the party. One simple design is illustrated above.

If you're sending the invitations by post, make sure they fit your available envelopes. Or make fold-over invitations and seal them with stick-on dots (available at stationers shops in many colours). Use extra dots as 'balloons' next to each address.

Children's quarrels

• Try to ignore small squabbles. Only intervene if it becomes physical.
• Ask each child (if old enough) to give his or her version of the story. Try not to tell off just one participant – it takes two to fight. Ask them how *they* would stop their children quarrelling when they're parents themselves. And stick these suggestions on the fridge door or noticeboard for future use.
• Remove objects that could cause squabbles among younger children. If you know your child and a friend always fight over the same toy, remove it before the child visits.
• Make a game out of sharing for little ones. Hand them a toy and then gently take it back. Repeat until the child is happy to hand it over to you.
• If fighting breaks out in the car, pull over to a safe spot. Tell them you won't drive on until they promise to be quiet, as you can't concentrate on the road.
• If your children are constantly fighting, ask yourself why. Are you favouring one unconsciously? Are they happy at school? Are they hungry?
• Write out a list of house rules (such as, no playing with the ball near the window; Sally isn't allowed to touch William's modelling clay).

• If you're desperate, separate fighting children for half an hour. They'll soon want to play together.
• Tell them about your own childhood squabbles with your brothers or sisters. It doesn't make you so perfect.

Child swallows small object

A violent coughing fit and congested face and neck often signals that a child is choking on something.

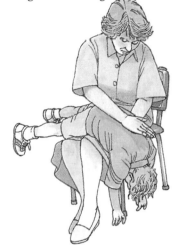

• Lay the child over your knees with his head down. With one hand supporting his chest, slap firmly between the shoulder blades with the heel of the other hand. Do this four or five times. This should dislodge the obstruction.

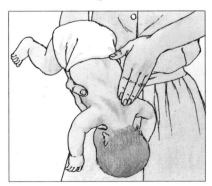

• Look inside a choking baby's mouth; if you can see the obstruction, remove it with your finger. If not, hold the baby upside-down with one hand supporting its chest. Slap the baby firmly between

the shoulder blades with the fingers of the other hand. Do this up to four times, using less force than with a child.
• Prevent a child from suffocating by keeping out of its reach all small objects, ribbons, string and cord, and don't feed children small pieces of food, especially nuts. Do not give them toys with small parts that come loose.

Chilli peppers

• Wear rubber gloves when handling jalapeño, serrano and other hot and mild peppers. Never rub your eyes while working with them; oils in the peppers can irritate and burn your skin and will certainly sting your eyes.
• To peel fresh chilli and sweet peppers, first roast them under a grill or on a long fork over a gas flame. Turn often until the skin is charred all over, then immediately seal in a plastic or brown paper bag for 15 minutes. The skin will then peel off easily when required.

Chimneys

• To reduce the possibility of having a chimney fire, ensure your chimney is cleaned at least once a year so that any build-up of material within the flue is removed. In the event of a chimney fire, extinguish the fire in the hearth using soapy water and call the fire brigade.
• Clean your wood-burning stove chimney at least twice a year. Whatever the type of fireplace, a build-up of materials (chiefly creosote) can pose a real danger of a chimney fire. Many hardware shops sell chimney brushes; be sure to get the right size for your flue. If you feel you cannot clean the chimney yourself, hire a professional chimney sweep.

Chipped porcelain

• If you want to conceal nicks and scratches in porcelain, use specially formulated porcelain paint to paint over them. First, scrub the damaged area thoroughly to remove all traces of soap and grease. Then wipe with nail polish remover and leave to dry before applying the paint.

• Always repair large chips and cracks in a porcelain fixture with a coloured epoxy resin designed for the job. When you can find it in the right shade, this does two things: it patches the surface and colours it to match the object.

First, scrub the area around the blemish with fine-grain sandpaper to remove all rust and soap deposits. Then, using a clean cloth, wipe with nail polish remover. Next, mix the resin and hardener and add the colour (which is usually provided with the epoxy) until it matches the object. Using a craft knife, fill the crack with the epoxy compound. Pour surgical spirit on your finger and – using a very light touch – smooth the surface taking care not to smear it.

Chocolate

If you have no cooking chocolate in the cupboard but you do have cocoa, and you need 1oz/25g of plain chocolate for baking – you don't have a problem. Just blend together 3 level tablespoons of unsweetened cocoa powder with 1 level tablespoon of soft margarine.

Chocolate stains

Blot or scrape off the excess chocolate. Apply a solution of biological washing powder or liquid in water, and blot with a clean towel. If the stain remains, dab white fabric with a bleach solution or soak coloured fabric in diluted biological detergent.

If the chocolate is on a carpet, remove the excess by hand and then spray or sponge with carpet shampoo, making sure you do not saturate the carpet. Dry excess moisture with a hair dryer or dab firmly with white paper towels or an absorbent hand towel.

Choking

A piece of food, a coin or a peanut stuck in the airway may cause choking. If a person cannot breathe, the brain will be starved of oxygen and, without prompt treatment the victim will fall unconscious and die within a few minutes.

Suspect choking if someone stops breathing, particularly during a meal. Before collapsing, a victim may feel embarrassed and get up to leave the room. Ask if she is OK. If she can speak, she is not choking.

If the victim cannot breathe:
• Call for help and an ambulance.
• If she is still conscious, encourage her to cough hard to expel the obstruction.

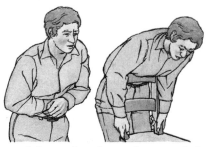

• Ask her to lean forward over a chair and give her firm blows on the centre of her back.
• If the victim is unconscious, feel inside her mouth with your finger to try to locate and remove the foreign body.

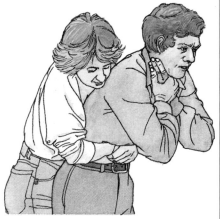

• Try the 'Heimlich Manoeuvre', or abdominal thrust. If the victim is conscious, stand behind her, put your arms around her waist and make a fist between her navel and her breastbone. Hold the fist with your other hand and

thrust it upwards and backwards. If necessary, repeat six or seven times before trying back blows again.
• If the victim is unconscious, try an abdominal thrust by lying her on the floor. Sit astride her and press upwards and inwards with your fist between the navel and the breastbone.

Chopsticks

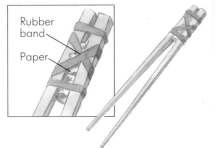

Rubber band

Paper

Do you find chopsticks unmanageable? Here's how to tame them: wind a rubber band around the square ends, as shown, and slip a small wad of folded paper between them. Then slip a loop of the rubber band round the chopsticks and below the paper. Now you've created a hinge.

Hold one chopstick between your thumb and middle finger and manipulate the other stick with your thumb and index finger. You can use this technique for unhinged chopsticks too!

Christmas trees

Choose a tree with pliable needles and branches; test its freshness by dropping it on the cut end – few needles should come off.

To prolong your tree's freshness, saw 1-2in/25-50mm off the bottom of the trunk and put the base in a bucket of water as soon as possible. (Warm water will clean the sap off the cut and let the tree drink better.) Then spray the branches with water – be sure they are dry before you put on the decorations. To help a tree absorb water better still, use a long drill bit to bore a hole up through the centre of the trunk. Pack the hole firmly with cotton balls; they'll help to conduct the water up the trunk.

Keep the tree in the coolest part of the room, away from sunlight, radiators, heaters and fireplaces. When refilling the stand, use cool water with a few aspirins added.

If you buy a live potted tree, wrap wet towels around the root ball before putting it into the bucket, and keep it moist. Protect the carpet, rug or floor from needles with a heavy plastic sheet. Keep the tree away from heat and draughts while it is indoors.

Chrome

• Clean chrome with any of the following: soda or mineral water, window cleaner, bicarbonate of soda, vinegar (cider or white) or lemon peel. Or use a solution of 1 part clear ammonia to 16 parts water.

• To remove insects from your car's bumper, rub with a soap-impregnated scouring pad moistened with cola. To remove rust spots, rub with crumpled aluminium foil.

Cigarette smoke

If you are allergic to cigarette smoke, don't provide ashtrays for visiting guests. Politely explain your problem, and don't be afraid to ban smoking in your house or office.

If you smoke or live with a smoker

• Buy special ashtrays that absorb smoke and stale smells, or invest in free-standing air purifiers. Better yet, install a permanent air ioniser or smoke filter and clean or replace its filtering mechanism regularly.

• Decorate your home with potpourri (see p.411) and houseplants (try the chlorophytum, or spider plant, said to be a natural air purifier).

For temporary tobacco smells

• Burn scented candles or incense; they will clear and perfume the air. Put solid room deodorisers near air vents or windows.

• When your guests have gone, open all the doors and windows and make sure you empty all ashtrays.

To combat smoke in the car

• Empty the ashtrays after each use.

Then put a layer of bicarbonate of soda in them to smother new butts and ashes. Or make the ashtrays unusable; fill them with boiled sweets and loose change for the parking meter.

Cleaning

• With all cleaning problems, test a cleaner out on a small area – preferably one that won't show – before applying it to the stained or dirty part of the object. The finishes, paints and colours on some objects react to certain cleaners. Always wear rubber gloves when cleaning.

• Dishwasher detergent works well on refrigerators, cookers, floors, walls and glass. Dissolve 2 fl oz / 60ml in 1 gallon / 4.5 litres of very hot water; wipe with a dry cloth afterwards.

• Remove crayon marks from painted walls by scrubbing with toothpaste or an ammonia-soaked cloth. Rinse and dry.

• Surgical spirit will clean the sealant around baths; it also shines chrome and glass. Liquid chlorine bleach (2 fl oz / 60ml to 1 gallon / 4.5 litres of water) will also clean sealant.

• Clean the toilet bowl while you're away by pouring in 2 fl oz / 60ml bleach and leaving it until you return. (Don't use bleach if you're already using a tank-held cleaner that's released when the toilet is flushed; the two may react chemically.) Or you could use a more environment-friendly cleaner such as vinegar or lemon juice.

• Use an old toothbrush mounted on a bamboo cane if you need extra length to reach into a dirty corner.

Clogged shower heads

If your shower has become erratic, spitting water in peculiar patterns, the openings in the shower head may well be clogged with mineral deposits.

Unscrew and take apart the entire shower head, keeping the pieces in order for easy reassembly. Soak the parts in vinegar overnight, then scrub off the encrusted minerals with steel wool or a wire brush. Poke open the small holes in the faceplate with a pin.

Clogged toilets

• If you think you can reach whatever is clogging your toilet, put on a rubber glove and try to fish it out. If necessary, reach in deeper with a bent wire coat hanger.

• Next, try a wc plunger. Push the plunger sharply into the bottom of the bowl to cover the outlet. Give it several tries. If water rushes out, victory! Before flushing, pour in a bucket of water to make certain the toilet drains.

• If the plunger fails, try a wc auger (see below), or snake – a tube enclosing a cable with a corkscrew on the end, which can be hired from tool hire shops. Put the corkscrew end into the outlet and crank the auger handle clockwise, forcing the cable around the bend of the trap as shown. When the tip bites into the blockage, continue cranking while pulling out the auger – the blockage should come with it. Or move the auger handle back and forth to break up the blockage. When the blockage is loosened, pour several buckets of water into the toilet to wash it through the pipe.

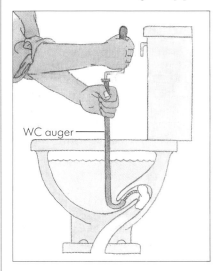

WC auger

Clogged waste pipe

First try using a plunger on the sink or bath plughole. If it fails, place a bucket underneath the bottle trap; use a spanner to remove the plug on the bottom of the trap (or remove the trap itself) and then try to dislodge the blockage

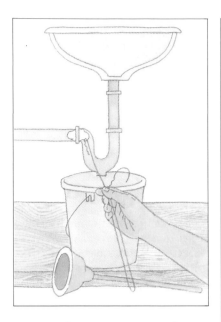

with your fingers or a wire coat hanger bent into a hook shape.

Caution Chemical drain cleaners are dangerous; they can burn your skin and damage the plumbing. If you use one and it fails to work, call a plumber – don't keep working on a drain with chemical cleaner in it.

Close-up photography

• A cluttered background can spoil a close-up photo. One solution is to use a piece of black velvet or other solid-colour fabric about 2 ft / 610 mm square. Flowers, in particular, will stand out against the dark background.

Another alternative is a small wall mirror, angled to reflect blue sky as a background for flowers. Make sure you check the exposure carefully since you

Mirror angled to reflect sky

have introduced a bright background. If you are using a single-lens reflex (SLR) camera, note the exposure for the flowers without the mirror behind them. Then set your camera to the manual mode, and use this exposure to shoot with the mirror in place. If your compact or zoom camera has them, try the back-light control or use the fill-in flash mode, but be careful not to catch a reflection from the mirror.

• Inexpensive, lightweight alternatives to macro lenses – which you use for close-up photography – are close-up filters that screw on to the front of a 35 mm camera lens. Several zoom lenses already have a macro mode as a built-in feature. The filters come in a range of magnifying powers, but magnification depends on the minimum focusing distance of the lens in use. They can be used in combination, so that a +1 coupled with a +2 will give a +3 magnification to further increase image size.

• When photographing flowers outdoors with a macro lens you will need a shield to prevent movement – the slightest breeze will blur the shot. Support a piece of card, or get someone to hold it to shield the flowers from wind, but be careful that the card doesn't appear in the picture.

Clothes moths

There are several species of clothes moths, the grubs of which eat wool, fur, hair and leather. There is little you can do to kill them off completely, but you can keep them at bay by vacuuming carpets and hangings regularly, dry-cleaning upholstery and spraying fabrics and the inside of cupboard doors with a mothproofing aerosol. This discourages moths from laying their eggs on the fabric. You can also put moth-balls and moth crystals in cupboards and drawers out of the reach of children.

Clothes shopping

The high prices you pay for your clothes are determined by fashion trends and a shop's overheads. Mark-ups can be as much as 100 per cent on designer labels.

Look for sales bargains and end-of-season ranges and samples, or try these alternatives:

• Discount shops may sell current designer fashions, usually with the label cut out. But you may not be able to return the item – check before buying it. The mark-up is around 70 per cent, but can be lower.

• Clothing manufacturers often have their own factory shops for selling 'seconds' and samples. Hosiery, silk scarves and knitwear with small faults can often go for a song. It's worth contacting the individual manufacturers to find out when they are open – many are at the weekends.

• Charity shops and secondhand clothes shops offer unexpected fashion bargains. But once purchased, clothes cannot always be exchanged, so always try items on in the shop and examine articles carefully before buying them.

Clutter

• Clear out magazines and newspapers often, keeping any magazines you really want in baskets. Place the recipes and articles you want to save in folders labelled by subject.

• Set out bedside baskets for reading material. Place dishes on dressing tables to collect loose change, other pocket items and jewellery.

• Provide stackable plastic boxes for records, videos, tapes and games in rooms where the family relaxes; insist that users return these notorious clutter culprits to their 'homes'.

• Take old medicines to your pharmacy for disposal. To keep bathroom shelves tidy, install boxes for extra supplies – and any items that won't fit in medicine cabinets.

• Outdoors, keep a plastic rubbish bin in the garage or back garden for play-things. Install pegboards with hooks in your garage or toolshed for gardening supplies and sports equipment.

• Above all, clear out your whole house. Room by room and in stages, go through all your possessions. Throw away, give away or sell anything that you don't use. See CAR BOOT SALES, p.33.

Coasters

Make your own coasters for furniture legs with the scrap ends of carpeting or cork samples from a flooring supplier. Textured carpet works best: it is cheaper and more durable than plush or velvet. Trace the shape from another coaster, then cut the new coaster to size.

Cockroaches

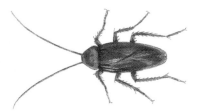

Cockroaches lay their eggs in little brown capsules that look like purses. Look for the egg cases in dark, damp, warm places: under sinks, behind stoves and refrigerators, even in curtain pleats and inside curtain rods. Scrub them away or vacuum them up afterwards, but be sure to discard the dust bag.

If you can find the source of infestation, spray with insecticide. However, do-it-yourself treatments may not be adequate. Call your local environmental health department or a commercial pest control service.

One effective commercial product is a bait that has hydramethylnon as the active ingredient, but it is for professional use only.

Coffee

• Instant coffees can taste and smell just like the real thing. The secret is to cover the cup or mug with a saucer after you've added the hot water, then let the brew steep for a full minute.
• To preserve its fresh flavour, always store ground coffee in the refrigerator or freezer.
• Freeze very strong leftover coffee in ice cube trays. When you want a cup, put a couple of cubes in a mug, top up with water, and heat in a microwave.
• Stretch 1lb/450g of coffee by adding

3oz/85g of roasted chicory; it increases the yield by about ten cups. If the pleasant bitterness of chicory suits your taste, add still more – up to 8oz/225g.
• Instead of decaffeinated coffee, try one of the coffee substitutes on the market. They are made from roasted grains, nuts, chicory or dandelion root. You can mellow their taste by adding a vanilla bean to the grounds.

Coffee grinders

• Grind only as many beans as you need each time you make coffee. For filter pots, including automatic coffee makers, grind them as fine as possible; for percolators, a coarse grind is better; for cafetières, a medium grind. Keep the grinder spotless, brushing out any stray bits of bean after each use.
• While electric grinders do the fastest job, an old-fashioned metal or heavy ceramic mortar and pestle still gives the finest grind and will never break down or wear out. But be prepared to work hard; the process is slow and tedious.
• Don't try grinding coffee beans in your blender or food processor; you'll more than likely dull the blades and possibly stall or burn out the motor.
• When you have only beans and no grinder, wrap the beans in a clean cloth, then pound them with a mallet or heavy weight. The cloth will probably not be usable afterwards.

Coffeepots

• Line a funnel or a strainer with a coffee filter paper (a white paper napkin or a double thickness of paper towel or muslin will do). Spoon in 2 level tablespoons of finely ground coffee for every 6fl oz/175ml of water, then set over a heatproof container and pour the boiling water through.

You could also use a jug or saucepan. First warm it with hot water and empty it; then spoon in the measured coffee. Pour in freshly boiled water, stir, cover, and allow to steep for about 4 minutes. Allow the grounds to settle, then strain through a fine tea strainer.
• Even if you don't own a long-handled

pot, you can still make Turkish coffee. For four small cups, heat 6fl oz/170ml water in a saucepan until lukewarm, and then add 2 heaped tablespoons of coffee and 1 of sugar (grind the coffee beans to a very fine powder; mocha is a good choice). Stir thoroughly, then heat the coffee until bubbles start to form around the edge. Remove from the heat and leave to settle for a few minutes, then heat again until froth forms on the surface. Serve immediately. Do *not* boil.

Coffee stains

To remove a coffee stain from washable fabric, try one of these methods.
• Soak in a warm biological detergent solution if the fabric is suitable, then wash as usual.
• Rub the stain with a bar of white household soap or a commercial stain remover and then launder.
• If the fabric is not washable, sponge the coffee stain with a laundry borax solution (1tbs/15ml to 18fl oz/500ml of water), then blot dry. If the stain remains, apply a 50-50 solution of glycerine and water, leave for an hour, then sponge with water.

Colds

• Take aspirin or paracetamol for cold-related aches and fever. Children under 12 should be given the correct dose of paracetamol (see ASPIRIN, p.13).
• Rest as much as possible. Sleep helps to recharge your immune system – and stops you from spreading your germs.
• Avoid strenuous exercise as your strength and endurance are low, and you might injure a muscle. Exercising with a fever makes the illness worse.
• Drink lots of fluids to replenish those

you've lost. In addition to water, drink plenty of citrus juices. Avoid fizzy soft drinks, coffee and tea; they contain caffeine, a diuretic that causes you to lose body fluids.
• Keep your temperature down. Do *not* wrap up in extra clothes and blankets and do not heat up the room excessively or sit in front of a hot fire. Babies in particular are vulnerable to overheating. Tepid sponging may cool and soothe children.
• To soothe a sore throat, gargle every 2 hours with a solution of ¼ teaspoon salt dissolved in ½ pint/285ml warm water.

Nasal congestion
• Saltwater nose drops may help relieve a stuffy nose. To make your own nose drops, boil ¼ pint/150ml water, let it cool, and dissolve ¼ teaspoon salt in it.
• If you prefer medicated nose drops or sprays, don't rely on them for any longer than 3 days; prolonged use can cause the 'rebound effect', which increases congestion.
• Steam inhalation may help. Fill a bowl with hot water and add a little menthol or Friar's Balsam. Be careful not to

expose children to danger of scalding if you use boiling water.
• Do not smoke, and ask friends and family not to smoke near you.

Cold-weather starting

If you're having trouble getting your car engine to turn over in cold weather, the problem is probably a weak battery. To forestall the problem, check your battery before cold weather sets in. At the same time, make certain that the clamps on the battery terminals are securely connected and the terminals are clean.

To clean battery terminals, first remove the clamps: loosen the bolts and twist the clamps back and forth – you may even have to tap them lightly with a hammer before they'll move. Scrub both the clamps and the terminals with a wire brush. Before you reattach the clamps, apply a thin coat of petroleum jelly at the connection to retard further corrosion.

If cold-weather starting is a constant headache, consider buying an engine heater (sold at motor accessory shops). You can choose from several types; all plug into a standard 240 volt electrical outlet.

Colic

Some colicky babies seem to cry less if they sleep in a very quiet environment and are handled extremely gently. Others are soothed by rocking or by monotonous sounds such as that of a vacuum cleaner or hair dryer.

A car ride is frequently effective treatment for a colicky baby. For times when this is impossible, some babies' accessory stores sell a small motorised

device that attaches to the cot and simulates the vibration of a moving car.

Try giving the baby a fennel or anise solution. Boil 4fl oz/115ml water for 10 minutes; add 1 teaspoon fennel tea or aniseed and ½ teaspoon sugar; reboil for 1 minute, then strain into a bottle. Leave to cool until tepid.

Collections

• Organise a shell, rock or pressed-flower collection around a theme such as colours, interesting shapes or geographic origin, for example. Such a collection of small objects disappears against a white background, so it is often a good idea to paint display shelves a dark colour or line them with dark paper before gluing on shells or the like.

Small wooden boxes – the kind that some nurseries sell bedding plants in – make attractive, if rustic, display frames. After cleaning and sanding smooth, rub the sides with a furniture oil and cover the inside with dark adhesive plastic.
• Look around the house to see if you already have the makings of a 'pop culture' collection that can grow in value: Star Wars figures, teddy bears, theme glasses or rock 'n' roll records. To add to your stock, check out flea markets and jumble sales.
• Stamps, coins and antiques often grow in value with time, but they're easier to buy than to sell. Dealers seldom pay more than half the retail value.

College or university applications

Before making an application for a place in the college or university, and the course of your choice, work through the following checklist.

• Obtain the up-to-date UCAS handbook and application form from your school, college or local careers office. If you have difficulty, contact UCAS (Universities and Colleges Admissions Service), PO BOX 28, Cheltenham, Gloucestershire GL50 3SA. The handbook lists the courses available and gives advice on completing the form. Make sure you understand the UCAS and clearing system, and pay particular attention to all deadlines. UCAS does not deal with applications for art and design, postgraduate or Open University courses.

• What do you hope to get out of going to college or university? Choose courses that will help you achieve your aims.

• Have you kept an open mind about where to go and what to do? Consider more courses and institutions than the eight you can actually apply for. Discuss your options with everyone who will listen, help and advise — but make up your own mind.

• Consider the content, quality and style of the course at different institutions. Send for their prospectuses, and try to visit them to see your department and talk to students there; or talk to other people who know the institutions.

• Draft your answers before completing the form. Photocopy the form and experiment with different presentations. Have you filled in the application form to your best advantage? Ask yourself whether you have shown that you are the right person for the course you have chosen. Write neatly using black ink or type (which will photocopy clearly). Never attach additional sheets, which could go astray; instead, cut out unnecessary detail.

• Are you prepared for the interview if one is necessary? Know yourself – your experience and achievements, your strengths and limitations – and how to describe yourself. Know about the course and the institution, and find out who is to interview you if you can.

• Have your own questions ready – it will show that you have a real interest in the course that you have chosen.

• On the day, arrive a little early to give yourself time to sit and adjust to the surroundings before facing the interviewer.

College or university fees

If you have not received a local authority grant and are having difficulty paying your college or university tuition fees, try both of the following.

• Check with the student affairs office in the college or university whether institutionally funded bursaries or other local sources of support are available.

• Get a copy of 'Pay Your Way as a Student', published by Hobsons and available from Biblios Publishers' Distribution Services Ltd, Star Road, Partridge Green, West Sussex RH13 8LD. Or get 'Students' Grants and Loans: A Brief Guide' free from the Department of Education and Employment, Publications Section, Tel. 0171-510 0150.

Colour in the home

The way colours are combined in a room sets the mood and also creates optical illusions capable of 'changing' room sizes and proportions. Light-coloured walls, floors and ceilings make dark, poky rooms feel larger and more spacious; dark colours in these areas make large, cold rooms feel cosier and more intimate.

Reds, oranges and yellows bring warmth to a scheme, whereas blues, greens and purples add coolness and tranquillity. To gain confidence and enjoy experimenting with colour, study the colour wheel or spectrum and learn some basic colour terms.

• 'Monochromatic' colour schemes use shades or tints of the same colour; they are the simplest schemes to start with and are very effective.

• 'Related' colours, such as blue, turquoise and green are naturally harmonious, as are red, orange and yellow. If an existing colour scheme needs more drama, consider adding other related colours.

• 'Complementary' colours from the opposite sides of the spectrum, such as red and green, orange and blue or violet and yellow, produce a complementary scheme that works best if one colour predominates and the other provides accents. Complementary colours are tricky to balance, so test them out first in small amounts, such as with cushions and ornaments.

Inspiration

• Take the colours of a favourite rug, vase, poster or painting, and use these as the basis for your colour scheme. Cut out squares of colour from a manufacturer's colour cards and play around with them to see what proportions of the various colours you find pleasing.

• Making a sample board is a good idea and can help you to match colours perfectly. Use A4 or A3 size stiff white or grey card and stick on the colour squares, pieces of fabric, floorcoverings, braids and fringes. Try and relate sample sizes to the amount of colour likely to be taken up in a room. For example, floorcoverings take up about ⅙ of a total room surface.

• Paints can be mixed to almost any shade you want. Some specialised paint shops can electronically match paint colours to fabric, carpets and tiles. Their results are far more reliable than using DIY tints, which are mixed into a basic colour and can give streaky uneven results.

• Home-dyeing sheets, towels, cushion covers and lightweight curtains can give stunning results. But dyeing to match existing colours is tricky. Try writing to the dye product manufacturers enclosing a snippet of fabric and the colour you want it to match.

Fabric dyes work best on wool, cotton, silk, nylon and viscose. Polyester and acrylic do not accept dyes, but blends containing them will tint a shade. Always try out the dye on a small sample of your fabric first.

• Professional dyeing for heavy lined curtains and loose covers is expensive but may be worth while, as these items are usually too bulky for domestic washing machines. But be prepared for some shrinkage to occur.

Colour run in washing

Have your whites turned a pale shade of grey, blue or pink? You have probably sorted your clothes wrongly and included coloured objects in the wash.

• Wash the clothes again in the hottest water that is safe for the fabric.

• If this doesn't work, soak whites in a proprietary colour-run remover, following the manufacturer's instructions. A colour-run remover, which can be used on coloured items in the washing machine, is also available.

• You may be able to remove accidental dyes from whites and other colours by gently bleaching them with 20 volume strength hydrogen peroxide. Mix 1 part to 6 parts water and soak for 30 minutes.

• *Never* mix whites with coloured items.

Compass direction

• If you have lost your way and you don't have a compass on you, your watch may be able to help you. Just point the hour hand in the direction of the sun; due south is a line equally dividing the smallest angle between the hour hand and 12 o'clock.

During the period of British summertime (between the last Sunday in March and the last Sunday in October), add one hour to the time actually showing on your watch and then divide the angle between that time and 12 o'clock.

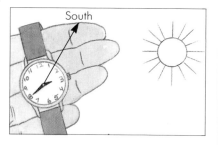
South

Compost bins

• A 50 gallon / 227 litre plastic or metal barrel or dustbin makes a good compost container. First, remove both ends to make an open cylinder. Then set it upright in a corner of the garden and raise it on bricks to allow air to circulate beneath. On the bottom, arrange a layer of crossing sticks or a similar base which will allow air in. There should also be a cover to keep the rain out. Fill the drum gradually with compost material. When the drum is full, let the compost age for 6

Garden debris

Kitchen waste

Crossed sticks

to 12 months, then lift it to release a pile of garden-ready humus.

• In a small garden or on a roof terrace, conceal your compost neatly in a large dustbin lined with a large black plastic bag. If the compost material is dry, such as autumn leaves, add a gallon of water and a sprinkling of ammonium sulphate. Seal tightly, keeping in any smells. The composting process should be complete in 3 to 4 months.

Compost material

• Use your kitchen leftovers to feed your plants. Fill a compost bin gradually with alternating 6in/150mm layers of kitchen waste (no meat scraps, grease or bones), garden debris (no weed seeds) and soil. Add a sprinkling of ammonium sulphate to each layer. (A little lime will also help, but don't add it if you're going to use the compost to top-dress acid-loving plants such as azaleas.) Let the mixture age for 3 to 6 months, dousing it regularly with a hose.

• Standard rural compost ingredients such as animal manure and spoiled hay may be hard to come by. Look around your town for suitable industrial by-products instead: shredded cardboard and newspaper, rotten vegetables from the greengrocer, mill wastes of wool and silk or hair clippings from the barbershop. All can be used on the compost heap.

However, a word of warning: don't use ashes from the barbecue, dog or cat droppings, or shredded magazines; they may contain sulphur oxides, organisms

or inks that are bad for plants. And avoid cooking oils or fats; they attract scavenging animals and will also slow down the composting process.

Computations

Are you stuck without your trusty calculator? Here are a few easy ways to double-check your arithmetic.

Addition A quick way to check your addition is to add up the digits in each number and then add up the digits in each sum; keep the process going until each number is reduced to a single digit. Then add together the single digits above the line; their total should equal the single digit in your sum.

Example: $9236+5347=14{,}583$	
$9+2+3+6=20;$	$2+0=2$
$5+3+4+7=19;\ 1+9=10;$	$1+0=1$
	3
$1+4+5+8+3=21;$	$2+1=3$

It's even easier if you 'cast out the 9s'. Eliminate all 9s and digits adding up to 9 – take this on trust, they don't affect the outcome.

Example: $9236+5347=14{,}538$	
$9\,2\,3\,6\ =2$	
$5\,3\,4\,7\ =1$	
$1\,4\,5\,3\,8=3$	

Subtraction To make sure you've subtracted correctly, add together the result and the number you subtracted – you should get the number you started with.

Multiplication Divide the answer by one of the numbers being multiplied. You should get the other number.

Division Multiply the answer by the number you divided by; if you come up with the number you originally divided, you have got it right.

Computers

When you can't get your personal computer to work properly, don't panic – the problem may be easy to remedy.

• Check all the cables and connections; one of them may have worked loose.

• Did you turn everything on? The screen? The printer?

• Did you put a disk in upside-down or

back to front? Exit from the program and start it up again.
• Did you skip a key step?
• Is a special-function key in the wrong position?
• If all else fails, refer to your user's manual.

Disks Treat your floppy disks with extreme care. Heat, fingerprints, magnetic sources (telephones, stereo speakers, televisions, motors), writing directly onto or clipping something to a disk – all these things and more can destroy its contents.

Fatigue If you find it tiring to work (or play) at a computer for long periods of time, check these points:
• Is the console placed too high, forcing your shoulders and upper arms into a strained position?
• Is your chair the right height? Does it provide good support for your back?
• Is there glare on the screen from the sun or room lighting, causing unnecessary eyestrain? (Wearing a visor may help if overhead lighting is bright.)

Concrete floors

Here's how to remove earth stains from a concrete floor. Spray the affected area with a garden hose and then liberally sprinkle scouring powder over the stain. Wait 20 to 30 minutes, then scrub with a stiff-bristled broom. Rinse and sweep up the residue.

For grease or oil stains, cover with a layer of powdered Fuller's earth and saturate the powder with paint thinner or petrol. Spread a sheet of plastic over the area and leave it to stand overnight.

The next day, sweep the powder away.
To make future cleaning easier, apply a liquid concrete sealer to the floor with a paint roller.

Constipation

Despite their popularity, laxatives and enemas are seldom the answer to constipation; in fact, they may even make the condition worse because many of them can be habit-forming. If you are often constipated, see your doctor
• Double your consumption of fibre-rich foods. But remember, not all fibre is the same. Wheat bran, wholewheat bread, cereal and pasta, brown rice and other whole-grain foods contain the kind of fibre that works against constipation. The fibre in beans, apples, broccoli and other fruits and vegetables helps less.
• To get your digestive system operating smoothly, drink 3-4 pints / 1.7-2.25 litres of water a day – at least a glassful with any whole-grain food. And take a daily half-hour walk, jog or swim.
• Whatever your normal pattern, don't ignore the urge to defecate; that in itself can cause constipation. So can the use of antacids, diuretics, hypertension medication or antidepressants.

Contact lenses

Many soaps leave an oily film on your hands that transfers to your lenses when you touch them. To check how oily your soap is, run a finger down a mirror after washing your hands. If your finger leaves a streak, use a different soap before handling your contact lenses.
Lost lens If your contact lens falls on the

floor, darken the room and sweep a torch or a small lamp slowly and methodically back and forth across the area. The lens will glint in the beam, even if it has fallen into a pile rug.

Contests

The chances of your winning a lottery, sweepstake or contest can be remote – as low as one in a million. There are a few ways, however, of bringing down the odds.
• If the rules permit, you can enter the contest several times. Send in each entry form separately, posting them on

Don't be duped

To protect yourself from being taken for a ride by con artists, remember a simple rule: if something sounds too good to be true, it probably is. Here are some common swindles:

Lucky winner: a telephone caller informs you that you've won an expensive prize, but he needs your credit card number to 'verify' your identity. On your next bill you discover that you've been charged several hundred pounds for the 'free' prize.

Not-so-free holiday: a letter offers you a free trip, but when you call for reservations, you learn that all the 'free' days are booked. For a small fee, however, your trip can still be arranged. By the time the charges have added up, you've taken an expensive holiday.

Make a million: a 'financial adviser' touts a surefire investment. But once you put up your money, the cash vanishes, along with the broker.

Something for nothing: but you have to visit a new holiday resort to pick up your prize. When you arrive, you get a high-pressure sales pitch to buy a holiday home.

different days and in different weeks.
• To increase your chances, enter contests that run for only a short time. The best time is summer, when a great many other potential contestants may be away on holiday.
• Follow the contest rules to the letter – and be especially sure that your entries are postmarked before the deadline.
• Watch for contests that allow you to send in a facsimile of the entry form. If you make yours on bright-coloured cardboard, you will improve your chances of having it drawn. Pleat or fold your entry into an intricate shape so that it stands apart from the others in the drum.
• Subscribe to one of the many newsletters that give tips and details on current contests.
• Stay away from any contest that offers a prize to everyone: the prize will be worthless.
• Read the text of the offer carefully. There may be a catch and the prize may not be quite what you think it is. If you feel there has been a misrepresentation of what was on offer, make a point of reporting it to your local Trading Standards Department.

Cookers

• If the reflector bowls on your cooker have turned brown or black, soak them in hot soapy water; if they're porcelain-coated, soak them in a solution of bicarbonate of soda and water. Then wipe with a clean cloth and a recommended cleaning product.
• To prevent a build-up of grease and burnt food, clean up spills and spatters as soon as the cooker top has cooled. Use a spatter shield for messy cooking such as frying or cover unused units with overturned foil pie plates.
• Flat cooking surfaces such as an Aga or ceramic hob require that the bases of all pots and pans be perfectly flat. To check that your pots are flat, rest a ruler across the bottom of an overturned pan. If you can see light at any point, the bottom isn't flat and cooking will be slow and uneven.
• If the flame is uneven on a gas burner,

some of the jets may be clogged. Clean the holes with a straightened paper clip, a pin or a pipe cleaner – do not use anything that could break off and get lodged in the jet, such as a toothpick.

Cooking oils

• To cut down on cholesterol, substitute virgin olive oil (which is cholesterol free) or polyunsaturated vegetable oils for saturated fats. Substitutes don't always work in baking, however.
• When buying soft tub margarine, choose one that lists corn, sunflower or soybean oil as the first ingredient. If the first ingredient is qualified as 'partially hydrogenated', or if palm or coconut oil is an ingredient, choose another brand.
• You can make French fries in the oven by brushing potato slices with a little olive oil and baking them at Gas Mark 6, 200°C / 400°F for about 20-30 minutes. Turn three times during cooking, brushing each time with a little more oil. The 'fries' will have considerably fewer grams of fat than the deep-fried kind.

Cookware

• Some common items can do double duty in the kitchen. A wok with a lid makes an efficient vegetable steamer. A plastic fruit basket or an old aluminium pie plate with holes punched in the bottom can both serve as a makeshift colander in an emergency.
• Used baked bean or tomato tins are perfect for baking banana bread, courgette bread (see p.391) or any other fruit loaf. And a swiss-roll tin can stand in as a roasting or baking sheet.
• If you're caught without a fish kettle, use a roasting tin. Put a cooling rack or an inverted oval plate under the fish and cover the top with foil. Or you could wrap the fish completely in foil and place it on the roasting tin. If the fish is too large for the tin, curve it or cut it in half. The join can be covered with thinly sliced cucumber or a garnish of parsley or watercress when serving.
• For minimum washing up, nothing beats baking in foil packets; they're ideal

for braised steak and for simply seasoned chicken breasts, meat loaf, fish and vegetables. Lay the ingredients on one half of a large piece of heavy-duty foil. Dot with butter or margarine, add herbs or seasoning of your choice, and fold over the foil. Seal the edges tightly, then fold over once more, leaving a little room for expansion, before placing it in the oven.
• Try a favourite campfire dinner at home. Place a beefburger, potato slices, a piece of carrot, a thin onion slice and a pat of butter on foil. Season, seal the foil and bake the contents for 45 minutes to 1 hour at 175°C / 350°F / Gas Mark 4 .

Cooling

• During a very hot summer, think about installing a ventilator fan in your loft. Under a blazing sun, the air in the loft can be as much as 15°C / 60°F hotter than the air outside – and some of that heat will radiate down through the house, raising the temperature indoors.
• Position portable or window fans in such a way that they blow the hot air out of your rooms. For cross-ventilation, open windows on opposite sides of a room and leave all internal doors open.
• Keep your home cool during a very hot spell by creating a through draught from the bottom to the top of the house. Hot air rises, so it is important to keep the windows open at all levels of your home. Leave the door to your loft open too – that way, hot air can escape through the air vents.

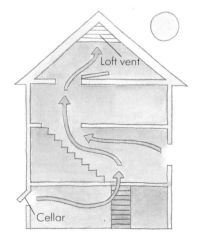

Loft vent

Cellar

• Use awnings, solar screening, roof overhangs or shutters to block out strong sunlight.

• Interior shades, venetian blinds, curtains and tinted glass are all helpful in reducing indoor heat, as long as they are drawn before the full sunlight enters a room; but they don't work as well as devices that keep sunlight from getting through the window in the first place. Heat trapped between the glass and interior shading will eventually start to circulate through the room.

Cork retriever

If a large piece of cork falls into a bottle of wine, your best option is to transfer the wine into a decanter or spare bottle. If this is not possible, use the following method to remove the piece of cork. Twist three pieces of stiff wire together at one end and make hooks at the other ends. Push this 'claw' into the bottle and grasp the cork with it. Tighten the grip by slipping a ring or nut down the wires, then draw out the cork.

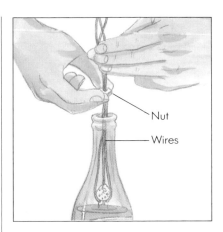

The art of keeping cool

If summers are becoming hotter in Britain as a result of global warming, it might be well worth our while to take a look at how people managed to keep cool in warmer parts of the world in the past.

In hot climates, families learned to build shelters that shielded the sun's rays and took advantage of cool breezes. Thatched huts, for example, kept out the sun overhead while filtering the wind through thinner wall weavings.

Several thousand years ago, Indians hung wet grass mats over openings at night so that breezes could flow through, cooling interiors by evaporation.

In African lands bordering the Sahara, in many Mediterranean areas and in the American southwest, people built with adobe, stone and stucco, which produced what is now called thermal lag. The roof and walls were thick enough to absorb and retain the day's heat, keeping interiors cool. At night, when the air cooled, the walls released their heat to warm the interior.

For many people, the best way to get relief from the heat was a trip to the mountains or the seashore. But the wealthy were sometimes able to buy comfort. Roman emperors, for example, imported snow from the Alps in summer, and Middle Eastern rulers had slaves fan them with palm fronds. And no less a consultant than Leonardo da Vinci was engaged by one Milanese duchess, who kept her boudoir cool with the inventor's foot-powered fan.

By the late 19th century, ornate but functional metallic sculptures concealing ice compartments, such as the one below, were used to combat high temperatures indoors.

This 19th-century cooling device consisted of a statue with an ice-filled urn that dripped cold water into a basin filled with plants and fish.

Corkscrew

• Have you lost your corkscrew? Use a large screw hook or eye instead, and use a mixing spoon or sturdy stick to pull a cork out. Or drive a plain screw into the cork and grip the head of the screw firmly with a pair of pliers. (This technique is not advisable with a good, rare wine, however.)

• To ease out a stubborn cork, dip a cloth in very hot water and wrap it around the neck of the bottle; it will expand the glass and free the cork.

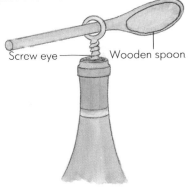

Screw eye — — Wooden spoon

Corns

Corns are commonly caused by shoes that don't fit properly, which squeeze or rub your feet. They can be extremely painful, but once the cause has been removed they should disappear. If you suffer from corns, here are several remedies to try to get rid of them.

• Wash your feet regularly and remove any rough skin with a pumice stone.

• Bathe your feet in a bowl of hot water with Epsom salts for 5-10 minutes every night and morning. Or soak them in a bowl of 2 parts warm water to 1 part vinegar for 5-10 minutes.

• Paint your corns with lemon juice or apply a poultice of crushed garlic, which can be fixed in place over the corn with a sticking plaster.

• Corn pads containing salicylic acid ointment are available from a chemist; these are left in place over the corn for some time and apart from getting rid of the corn, protect the tender area from chafing.

• If none of these methods work, see a chiropodist.

Couch grass

This inhabitant of wasteland frequently becomes a pest in gardens, choking flower beds and spoiling lawns.

• As soon as young couch grass shoots appear on a lawn, mow the area regularly, to keep down the grass and stop it from seeding.

• If you see young shoots in flower beds, use a selective weedkiller on them to avoid harming your perennials. Never hoe couch grass – this breaks up its rhizomes, and any broken bits you leave behind will multiply.

• If you are preparing ground for a lawn, remove all couch grass shoots and roots.

• If couch grass has established itself in a lawn, carefully dig out whole clumps with a fork. Lawn weedkillers do not kill it, and if you have to resort to poisons, use one such as Tumbleweed or Roundup, which contain glyphosate.

Once you have removed the dead growth and are sure that the active period of the treatment is over, reseed or returf the area.

Coughs

• To ease a cough that has developed from a cold, dissolve 1 tablespoon each of lemon juice and honey in a small glass of warm water and sip it.

• If you prefer something stronger, combine equal parts of lemon juice and honey. Take ½ to 1 teaspoon at bedtime. Either mixture will help to loosen irritating mucus.

• Make a soothing 'stew' by boiling quartered oranges and lemons in a little water and adding extra lemon juice and honey to taste. Take at bedtime.

• To soothe your throat so that you can sleep, take 1 teaspoon honey at bedtime; let it trickle slowly down your throat. See also COUGH DROPS and COUGH MIXTURE, p.391.

Council tax

You have to pay council tax on your home, but how much depends on the house and where you live.

• Check which band the house is in. The lowest band is A and the highest is H. These are governed by the value of the house.

• Find out the tax your local council applies to houses in that band. If two or more people live in the house, that is the tax you must pay.

• If only one person lives in the house, you can get a reduction of 25%. If the house is empty, then no tax may be payable, at least for the first 6 months.

• Some groups of people are also exempt from the tax. These include: students and those in hospital. They do not count at all. So a house with only students living in it is exempt from tax.

• Those on income support or with low earnings may get Council Tax Benefit to help them pay the tax.

• If you are paying too much tax, or think you may get benefit, ask your local council for help.

Courgettes

• Courgettes are very easily grown and suffer from few pests and diseases but they can be afflicted by mildew.

• Treat mildew with appropriate systemic fungicide. Courgettes do best if they are planted in the open when the danger of frost is over, and are not overwatered. See also COURGETTE BREAD, p.391.

• Just before the buds open into blossoms, they're delicious to eat sautéed in butter or dipped in batter and deep-fried.

Cracks in walls

• The most common wall crack appears in the joint between wall and ceiling. Most houses move very slightly on their foundations according to the season, as the ground beneath changes its water content and expands and contracts. This movement becomes evident at weak spots in the house. It is pointless

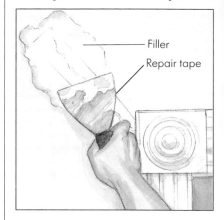
Filler
Repair tape

using fillers. The pressures involved just crack or compress them. So hide the crack with a coving, which also forms a decorative feature. The most effective is gypsum plaster coving, which is available from DIY shops and builders' merchants. Attractive plaster and plastic covings in shorter lengths can be easier to fix if you have no help.

• Fine hairline cracks are no problem. Use one of the powder or paste cellulose-based fillers, or a tubed interior sealant. The sealants are ideal around door frames, as they can deal better with the vibrations caused by doors being slammed.

• To fill a wall crack, rake out all loose and crumbling material with the point of a small trowel; dust with an old paintbrush, then dampen the crack with clean water, if using a water-based filler. Keep dry if tubed sealant is used. Take the sealant just proud of the surface, then, when it is dry, lightly sand it smooth to the level of the surrounding surface.

• A simple way of hiding large cracks is to use a repair tape or mesh. This is very thin and self-adhesive, and once in place can be skimmed over with a filler or, in some cases, just painted. The only disadvantage is that there is still a hole behind the repair.

• If you find a crack opens alarmingly and shows no signs of closing, check to see if there are similar cracks on the exterior walls. Settlement in some areas can be a real problem, and filling cracks would a waste of time. Call in a builder, or, if you need unbiased free advice, consult your local Planning Department. Ask them to send a planning officer or your local building control officer round.

• If walls are in generally poor condition, they can be resurfaced using plasterboard or timber panelling. These can be stuck directly to the wall with special wallboard adhesive or nailed to timber battens fixed to the wall.

Cramp

• Cramp is a muscular spasm which generally affects the legs, feet or hands. Many sufferers are those who use certain muscles all the time, such as sportsmen or gardeners.

• If you wake up with a painful cramp in your leg, try to flex first your toes and then your whole foot upwards, towards your knee. Or bend your knee, grab your toes, and flex them towards you while pushing back with your foot. If this gives only partial relief, massage your calf and the sole of your foot under the arch, pressing firmly.

• For a calf cramp, straighten your leg and flex your foot as far up as you can. Or put your toes on the floor and slowly lower your heel.

Prevention

• If you sleep on your back, use an open-ended box or a frame to keep the weight of the covers off your feet. If you sleep on your stomach, let your feet hang free over the end or the side of the bed.

• Drink lots of water (some people find tonic water is beneficial) and eat a balanced diet (see p.254).

• Do wall stretches nightly: stand 2-3 ft / .0.5-1 m from the wall and lean on your hands towards it, keeping your heels firmly on the floor; hold for 1 minute.

Cramps

• Whenever possible, always clamp work that is being drilled sawn or cut; this leaves both your hands free to manipulate the tools you are using. Many serious accidents are caused to hands that are holding work – from knives, chisels and even pieces of metal spinning when a drill-tip jams.

• A vice may be used as a simple means of holding work while gluing small projects. Protect work from metal jaws with scraps of softwood or rubber.

• A self-grip wrench will hold very small items. It can be locked on, then held in a vice, leaving both hands free.

• When gluing sheet materials in place, cover them with a number of bricks to ensure close surface contact while the glue sets.

• When repairing items like chairs, hold joints tight together with a strip of rubber taken from an old cycle inner tube. Use it like a large elastic band. This will exert considerable pressure with no risk of marking the wood.

Adjustable cramp

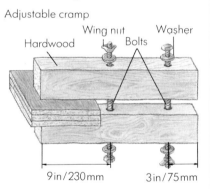

• You can make an adjustable cramp yourself quite easily. Cut two 16in/400mm lengths of 3 × 2in/75 × 50mm hardwood. Drill two • holes through each as shown – 3in/75mm from one end and 9in/230mm from the other – both a bit larger than the diameter of a 12in/300mm long coach bolt (available from a specialist DIY supplier). Insert two such bolts, one through each set of holes, using washers on both ends. Secure both with a wing nut. Position the open end of your cramp over the work you want to hold together and tighten the nuts.

Crank calls

• The most effective way to deal with a crank telephone call is to hang up, depriving the crank of any satisfaction he may derive from harassing you. Do not start a conversation with the caller or express any feelings. Instruct your children and babysitters to do the same. If the calls continue, leave the telephone off the hook for a while.

• If the crank calls persist or if they are threatening, record the time and date of each call. This may help the police apprehend the offender if you decide to make a formal complaint.

• Some crank calls can make you unwilling to answer the telephone. You could change your telephone number, go ex-directory or ask BT to trace the call. If you are on a digital exchange, dial 1471 after a call; you should be able to discover the last caller's number.

Cream

• For ½ pt / 285 ml double cream, substitute 6 fl oz / 175 ml whole milk and 3 fl oz / 85 ml melted unsalted butter. (Don't use in ice cream or mousse, however the butter will go lumpy. Use this substitute only in sauces.)

• If you're counting calories, replace 8 fl oz / 225 ml double cream (832 calories) with tinned evaporated skim milk (176 calories). An extra bonus: evaporated skim milk has far less cholesterol, too.

• Double cream will whip up better if it is well chilled beforehand. Chilling the bowl also helps.

Credit cards

• Keep the number of your credit cards to a minimum to curb impulse spending and to reduce the risk of losing them or having them stolen.

• Make sure that the credit card you're applying for is a credit and not a debit card, for which payments are taken directly and immediately from your bank account.

• Remember that a card's rate of interest doesn't necessarily indicate its true cost. You must also consider the cardholder fee and the grace period – if any – before interest is charged. Make sure you pay interest only on the amount left unpaid at the end of a billing cycle; on some cards, unless your bill is paid up, interest is charged from the date of the transaction.

Security

• Sign new credit cards as soon as they arrive. Cut up the old ones.

• Carry your credit cards separately from your wallet. Keep a record of their numbers and the telephone number of each company in a secure place.

• Avoid placing credit card orders from a telephone in a public area.

• Never sign a blank receipt.

• Destroy all carbons and void all incorrect receipts.

• Save all receipts to compare with your monthly statement.

Credit ratings

• If you are refused a loan or any kind of credit and suspect that this is because you have a poor credit rating, you should find out what the credit rating agency has said about you. If you write to the credit agency enclosing £1 they must provide you with a copy of your file showing all the information they have about you – in plain English.

• If you find that the information is wrong you should correct it at once. Write to the credit agency and ask them to amend their records. They must tell you what (if anything) they have done within 28 days. You cannot make them remove details that are true, however much you would like them to remain secret, but you can give your side of the story. Write a brief statement (it must not be more than 200 words) and insist that it is placed on your file. This statement must accompany every credit report they give about you.

Cricket jargon

All rounder A player good at batting, fielding and bowling.

Bails Two bars of wood placed on top of the three stumps to form the wicket.

Bouncer Fast, short-pitched ball aimed at the upper half of the batsman, also called a bumper.

Boundary Limit of the playing area marked by a white line, rope or fence. Also a hit which sends the ball across this line.

Bowled Dismissal of the batsman when the bowled ball knocks the bails off his wicket.

Bowling crease Painted line, 8 ft 8 in / 2.64 m in overall length extending on both sides of the wicket.

Bye A run scored from a ball which passes the batsman without touching his bat or body.

Carrying one's bat Applied to an opening batsman who remains unbeaten at the wicket throughout his side's complete innings.

Century One hundred runs scored by a batsman in an innings.

Crease Painted line within which the bowler must bowl and at which the opposing batsman stands.

Duck When a batsman fails to score.

Extra A run that is added to the total, but not credited to a batsman, as for a bye, leg-bye, wide and no-ball.

Follow-on A side which bats first and leads by a set number of runs after the first innings has the option of making the opposing team bat again before they do.

Full toss A bowled ball that arrives at the batsman without hitting the pitch beforehand.

Hat-trick Three wickets taken with three consecutive balls by the same bowler.

Inswinger A ball which moves in flight from off to leg stump.

Leg before wicket (LBW) When a bowled ball that would have otherwise hit the batsman's wicket strikes any part of his body or dress first; he is then dismissed from the field.

Leg-bye A run obtained from a bowled ball that has been deflected off any part of the batsman's body except his hands.

Maiden over An over from which no runs are scored.

Night-watchman A lower order batsman sent in to play out time when a wicket falls shortly before close of play.

No-ball An illegal delivery, for various reasons, for which a penalty of one run is awarded.

Over Period of play. Currently, an over in first-class cricket in Britain comprises six consecutive deliveries by one bowler from one end of the pitch.

Runner A member of the side who is allowed to run for a batsman who is injured during a match. He must be equipped in the same way as the batsman.

Run-out A way of dismissing a batsman during an attempt at making a run, when he fails to reach the crease.

Run-up The approach by the bowler to his delivery.

Seam The stitching around the circumference of the ball.

Sight-screen A movable screen, usually painted white, placed beyond the boundary behind the bowler to give the batsman a good view of the ball.

Single One run by a batsman.

Stumped A method of dismissal by the wicketkeeper, when a batsman is outside his crease.

Stumps Three small wooden posts, which when surmounted by the two bails comprise the wicket.

Wicket Made up of three wooden stumps with two wooden bails on the top. The wicket is 9 in / 230 mm wide and the top of the stumps 28 in / 710 mm above the ground. Two sets are used, placed 22 yds / 20.1 m apart.

Wide A ball bowled so high over or wide of the wicket, that in the opinion of the umpire it is out of reach of the batsman. A penalty of one run is invoked.

Yorker A ball delivered so that it pitches under the bat.

Croup

• A child with croup can breathe more easily sitting up.

• A humidifier or vaporiser may help. For temporary relief, turn on a hot shower and sit with the child in the steam-filled bathroom.

• If the child is having serious difficulty breathing, cannot swallow saliva, or is not relieved by the measures above, seek medical help right away.

Crutches

Crutches A crutch is at the right height if there's a three-finger-wide space between its top and the armpit when a person is standing normally.

The armpits and the shoulders shouldn't carry the weight – let the hands and the wrists do that. Keep your elbows slightly bent and rest your armpits on the crutches only briefly when swinging the uninjured leg forward.

Walking sticks A walking stick is the right height if the hand holding it is at hipbone level and the elbow is slightly bent. For the best support, hold the stick on the side opposite the injury or weakness – 6in/150mm to the right or left of the 'good' foot, as shown.

Emergency assistance
• Lay the arm on the good side of the injured person over your shoulder, grasp the wrist, and put your other arm around his waist.
• A broom can serve as a crutch.
• A thick stick, sturdy umbrella or croquet mallet makes a serviceable walking stick.

Cupboard clutter

• Use your cupboards for everyday things – not for long-term storage. If you haven't used an item for some time, get rid of it or store it in the attic.
• Coats take up space; put them on a coat rack near the door.
• Whenever you take a piece of clothing off a hanger, return the hanger to the rod, where it will be easy to find when needed.
• To conceal open shelves at the top of the cupboard, hang a decorative blind over the opening.
• To keep cupboards clean, dry and fresh smelling, try placing open, empty perfume bottles or unwrapped bars of soap in them. Or make moth-repellent sachets from dried lavender, whole peppercorns, orange peel or a 50-50 mixture of dried rosemary and mint. If you can't find sachet bags, make your own sachets out of baby socks or pieces cut from a clean stocking.

Cupboard doors

Do you want to hide unsightly or makeshift storage areas? Here are some ideas for decorative substitutes for cupboard doors.

• Build shelves on bedroom walls and cover them with matching curtains. Or position Japanese paper screens at one end of a long room to hide the shelves.
• Hang bamboo or wooden roll-up blinds from the ceiling to conceal a bedsit kitchen. Or suspend a blind at the end of a long corridor and stow the ironing board and vacuum cleaner behind it.

Cup stains

Remove stubborn coffee or tea stains from your china cups and mugs in one of the following ways. Then rinse thoroughly and dry.
• Scrub with salt or a paste of bicarbonate of soda and water or a 50-50 mixture of salt and white vinegar.
• Place in a denture-cleaning solution and soak overnight.
• Leave to stand overnight in a solution of 4fl oz/115ml household bleach in 3¼ pints/1.8 litres of water.

Curdling

• Has your cream sauce curdled? Strain it through a fine sieve or muslin.
• To save a Hollandaise sauce, add 2 tablespoons boiling water; beat with a wire whisk until smooth. Or set the pan in a bowl of iced water; whisk until smooth, then warm very gently over barely simmering water, whisking constantly.
• If your mayonnaise curdles, beat up an egg yolk in a separate bowl, and slowly add the curdled mayonnaise to it, beating it all the time.

Curfews

• Talk to your child about what time you both feel it's reasonable for him to be home by. Talk to other parents too about their curfew rules. And be flexible: just because you had to be home by 10pm doesn't mean your child should do the same. Some occasions might justify a later time to return home by.
• Set an alarm clock in your bedroom if you want to go to sleep. When your child comes back, he can switch it off.

• If your child returns considerably later than the agreed time, ask him why. There might be a good reason (such as transport problems). And tell him to telephone next time he's late so that you don't worry.

• Draw on your own childhood experiences. Describe a time when you were late and your parents were worried.

Curtains

• To determine how much fabric you'll need, measure the distance from the top of the window frame to where the hem will fall. Add 3 in / 75 mm at the top to which you sew curtain tape to hold hooks; or fold this amount to make a 1½ in / 38 mm pocket to hold a rod, if you are making café curtains. Add another 2-4 in / 50-100 mm for a hem (the heavier the fabric, the deeper the hem). For width, triple the distance you plan to cover with the drawn curtains.

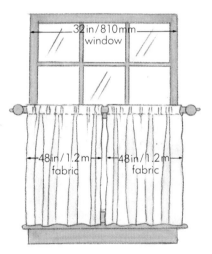

Customs

• There are no customs duties on goods imported from other EC countries, but there may be VAT or excise duties. Each traveller has a duty-free allowance (free of VAT and excises). Check your allowance with your travel agent before you go abroad.

•There are no customs checks on travellers between the United Kingdom and other EU countries: these are Austria, Belgium, Denmark, Finland, France,

Germany, Greece, Ireland, Italy, Luxembourg, Netherlands, Portugal, Spain and Sweden. Private travellers can import goods freely, so long as they are for private rather than commercial use.

• Goods imported from non-EC countries are subject to customs duty, VAT and excise duty. There are strict duty-free limits. Check with your travel agent before you go abroad.

• If you're taking valuables, such as jewellery, computers or camcorders, outside the EC, carry evidence of purchase with you.

• Be careful of 'duty-free' shops. Items bought in duty-free shops are only free of duty if they are within your personal travel allowance. Duty is payable above those limits. Consider, too, that goods in these shops may not be cheaper than similar goods bought in ordinary, non-duty-free shops.

• Although there used to be both a Green Channel (for those with nothing to declare) and a Red Channel (for those with goods to declare) at customs on arrival in the United Kingdom, this has changed since 1993. EC travellers now find only a Green Channel with a Red Spot to deal with dutiable goods.

• Customs officers can search you and your luggage if they suspect smuggling. If you object, ask for the senior duty officer. But officers can insist you answer their questions.

• If your luggage is searched, it is your task to repack it. But the property should not be damaged by a search. If it is, register your complaint with the customs officials at the time.

Cutlery

• Wash or rinse cutlery as soon as possible after you've used it. Foods with a high sulphide content such as eggs, fish and green vegetables, and salt and acidic foods, stain cutlery if they are left sticking to it.

• Dry cutlery as soon as it is washed, even if washed in a dishwasher. Some stainless steel will mark when air-dried and knife blades are particularly vulnerable to hard-water minerals, which corrode them.

• Don't store cutlery loose in a tray or drawer – you just increase the risk of scratches. Store similar sizes of knives, forks and spoons in their own compartments in a canteen or cutlery tray.

• Clean silver-plated cutlery by placing it on top of aluminium foil laid in a plastic bowl. Add a handful of washing soda and cover with hot water until clean. Rinse, dry and polish.

Utensils for disabled people Eating utensils which have been specially designed for disabled people include built-up cutlery for those who have difficulty gripping, and a rocking knife (as used for chopping herbs) for people who have the use of only one hand. For more information on these and other products, contact the Disabled Living Foundation, 380-384 Harrow Rd, London W9 2HU, Tel 0171-289 6111, or your local branch of Age Concern.

Substitute utensils At a pinch, a number of items can serve as eating utensils. Before using any item, clean it thoroughly.

• Substitutes for a knife include: a seashell edge, a nail file, a letter opener, the serrated edge of an aluminium foil box, a single-edge razor blade, scissors or even a sharp-edged rock.

Tableware facts

The earliest spoons were shaped from clay, carved out of wood and stone or utilised the natural shape of shells.

The forerunners of the earliest knives, dating back 35,000 years, were flints — stone chips with sharpened edges. They were used mainly to prepare the food rather than to eat with. As these flints were fixed to a handle, so the knife began to take shape.

The Romans invented the two-pronged fork, but eating with forks was still considered an affectation up to the 16th century. They were not in common use in Britain until about 1700.

- As a makeshift fork, use a sharpened twig, a skewer or your fingers.
- As a substitute spoon you could use a seashell, a small stone with a hollow, a tin lid or moulded aluminium foil.

Cuts and abrasions

The seriousness of a cut depends on how large it is, how deep it is, and how much it bleeds.

Although painful, small cuts and abrasions are seldom dangerous. Wash them gently with mild soap and water; cover with a large adhesive bandage or a substitute (see BANDAGES, p.18).

Severe bleeding With a deep cut, the first priority is to control bleeding.
- Apply firm pressure directly to the wound.
- Raise an injured arm or leg, unless it is fractured or dislocated, something is impaled in it, or you suspect spinal injury.
- If direct pressure and elevation don't stop the bleeding, find a point between the heart and the wound where a major artery crosses bone near the surface (you can feel a pulse). See below for the four main pressure points. Apply firm pressure to the artery *for no more than 10 minutes* to cut off the blood supply to the limbs.
- When bleeding has stopped or lessened considerably, place a clean cloth directly over the wound, completely covering it; put a clean bulky dressing on top. Wrap wide strips of cloth tightly over the dressing and on each side of the wound, and secure. Seek medical help.

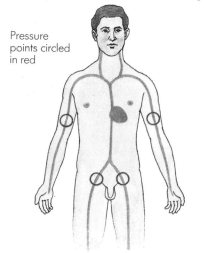

Pressure points circled in red

Cuttings

A hanging bag of soil makes a space-saving medium for rooting stem cuttings from begonias, dieffenbachias and other plants. Use one bag for each kind of cutting, as the different plants have different rates of rooting.

Mix enough peat and perlite or vermiculite (available at any garden centre) in equal parts to fill a large, strong transparent plastic bag. Moisten the mixture thoroughly and fill the bag with it. Poke small holes in the bottom of the bag for drainage.

Close the bag with stout cord and hang in an airy, well-lit place with a waterproof floor; a shaded corner of a balcony or patio, or a garage window is ideal. (In winter hang the bag over the draining board of a sink, perhaps in a utility room.)

Poke small holes into the sides of the bag and gently insert your stem cuttings. Spray the cuttings daily, letting water run down the stems to remoisten the rooting mixture. When the cuttings have rooted, slit the bag open with a knife.

Cutworms

The usual method of foiling cutworms is to place a bottomless tin or plastic cup around young plants. A disc of cardboard or felt with a slit cut in it to take the stem usually works as successfully and does not disturb the plant.

However, a better control is to wrap the stem of a seedling with aluminium

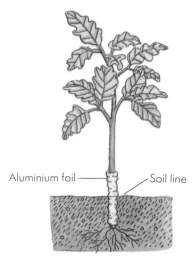

Aluminium foil — Soil line

foil before setting it out, but this must be done extremely carefully so that you don't damage the plant. Plant the seedling out with 2in/50mm of foil below the soil surface and 2in/50mm above. Wrap loosely so that the stem has room to grow.

D

Dampness

There are two main causes of damp in the home – structural faults and condensation. Sometimes it is difficult to decide which you've got. Structural damp can be caused by blocked gutters, a damaged or missing damp-proof course, porous brickwork absorbing too much moisture, or the general entry of rain around window and door frames. Condensation can be caused by too high a concentration of moisture in the air searching out a cold surface on which to condense.
- As a general rule, if you find damp patches on internal walls on a warm, rainy day, suspect structural problems. If they occur on very cold dry days, the problem is probably condensation.
- Structural problems may involve repair to guttering; the treatment of walls with a special waterproofing liquid which still allows the wall to 'breathe'; the insertion or repair of a

damp proof course, or the lowering of paths or soil away from the damp proof course by at least 6in/150mm. This ensures that rain can't splash above the damp proof course.

• To combat condensation effectively, extract the steam-laden air as it is produced by installing extractor fans in the kitchen and bathrooms. Choose a fan with ample capacity (given in cubic metres per hour). First calculate the volume of the room in cubic metres (length × width × height) and multiply this by the number of air changes needed in the room per hour (10-15 in a kitchen or toilet, and 15-20 in the bathroom). With this information, the salesperson in the shop will be able to offer you a fan of the correct size.

• A dehumidifier is an effective way of collecting moisture from the air, and in humid conditions it can collect 2-3 gallons/9-14 litres in 24 hours. Regular emptying is therefore necessary.

• Moisture-collecting silica-gel crystals can be used in drawers and small cupboards. But they are totally useless in larger areas when you consider what a dehumidifier can collect.

• To discourage condensation in built-in wardrobes, fit small ventilators in the doors to ensure a flow of air.

• Fit a small oil-filled radiator or airing cupboard heater in cupboards on external walls. Be sure to protect the heater from anything that may fall onto it, causing it to overheat. Some of these heaters are very economical and use no more electricity than a light bulb.

• To reduce condensation in a used bedroom, open windows at night while the heating is off. Even normal breathing produces considerable amounts of moisture vapour.

• Avoid using paraffin heaters indoors. They produce about 1 gallon/4.5 litres of water vapour for the equivalent amount of fuel burned.

Dandruff

Do flakes of skin constantly fall around the neck and shoulders of your clothes? You may have dandruff. The cause is unknown and unfortunately while the condition can't be cured, it can be controlled.

• If you have a mild case, use a gentle shampoo twice a week.

• If you have a severe case, use an anti-dandruff shampoo containing salicylic acid, tar or selenium (women who are pregnant or breast-feeding should avoid selenium).

• See a doctor if the condition persists after several weeks. It may in fact be due to eczema or dermatitis and he may recommend other treatment.

• Avoid using hair dyes, scented hair creams or any oily hair dressings.

Debt

Does more than 35 to 40 per cent of your annual gross income go to cover your debt? For example, if you earn £30,000, are you paying more than £12,000 on a mortgage, instalment loans and credit card purchases? If so, you should consider taking immediate steps to reduce your indebtedness.

• Stop the debt from growing – cut up your credit cards, or postpone your expensive holiday or the purchase of a new car.

• Cut back on open-ended lines of credit, such as bank credit cards or overdraft accounts, where the monthly payments vary according to the unpaid balance. Make all minimum payments on time, then add something extra to reduce the balance.

• Rather than spending windfalls, such as bonuses or tax refunds on a treat, put them towards paying off these open-ended accounts. If anything's left over, pay off as much as possible on other loans.

• Think about consolidating all your debts into one big loan. The interest rate on loans is usually lower than credit card rates.

• You might be able to pay off all your personal loans by increasing your mortgage. The interest rate on mortgages is much lower than credit card rates. Don't forget to include the costs of refinancing your mortgage or obtaining a home equity loan. (Ask your bank for the true costs of such financing.)

Decanter

• If the stopper is stuck in your decanter, wrap a hot, damp towel or dishcloth around the neck. Tap a wooden spoon gently against the sides of the stopper.

If this doesn't work, pour some olive oil around the stopper in the neck of the decanter and leave it in a warm place.

• Stains and deposits at the bottom of a decanter can be removed by half-filling the decanter with warm, soapy water and adding 2 tablespoons of uncooked rice. Swirl the mixture around several times over a period of 30 minutes. Then pour it out and stand the decanter upside-down to drain and dry.

Dehydration

Heat, overexertion, illness and long bouts of vomiting or diarrhoea can cause the loss of body fluids and salt. Infants, small children and the elderly should see a doctor.

• Prevention is the most effective measure. In hot weather or when doing extended heavy exercise, drink plenty of non-alcoholic drinks.

• If you suspect dehydration in a person, give him lots of water or juice, or in summer or after heavy exercise, give cool water with enough salt to make it taste slightly salty. If these measures don't help, seek medical advice. See also HEAT EXHAUSTION, p.105.

Dentist visits

Fear of the dentist is old-fashioned. With today's techniques and materials, dentistry need not be painful. Seek out a dentist who seems sensitive to your fears and who will explain exactly what he's going to do before he does it.

To conquer anxiety in the chair, breathe slowly and deeply and focus on something else, such as counting back from 100. Or try distraction – bring a cassette player with earphones to drown out the noise of the drill. If you tend to panic, work out a hand signal with your dentist which will let him know if you become anxious.

Try not to convey your anxiety to your

children. Ask your family doctor to recommend a dentist who specialises in preventing both tooth decay and fear of dentists.

Dentures

• If your new set of dentures becomes loose or keeps slipping, this may be because your gums have shrunk where teeth have been recently extracted. See your dentist so he can make minor adjustments.
• If your dentures begin to feel uncomfortable, ask your dentist to check the fit. They should be checked, anyway, every five years.
• Clean dentures every day with a medium toothbrush and denture paste. Rinse and keep brushing until they are absolutely clean. Don't rely on just soaking them – this merely bleaches them.
• Remove your dentures before you go to sleep and place them overnight in a glass of water to keep them fresh.

Deodorant

Some experts believe that it is the way we digest meat and dairy products that is responsible for offensive body odours, and the way to banish them is to improve the diet with the emphasis on fresh, natural foods with a vegetarian bias. But for most people, cleanliness is the key to freshness.
• Bath every day using a non-irritant soap.
• Women who are bothered by body odour could remove hair from their armpits regularly; hair tends to encourage smells to linger.
• A deodorant will help to discourage some of the bacteria that lead to body odour, whereas an anti-perspirant will have an astringent effect on the sweat glands, reducing moisture.
• If you have run out of deodorant, dab your armpits with cotton wool dampened with cider vinegar or a solution of bicarbonate of soda. After you have dried off from your bath or shower, dab a little under your arms; the moisture on your skin will help it to stick.

• If you have persistent body odour, try a different brand of soap. Some soaps contain chemicals that react with certain people's skin, producing an odour.
• If you are overweight you will sweat more. Try losing some weight.
• If you are prone to heavy perspiration, avoid highly spiced foods and alcohol – these make you sweat more. See also BODY ODOUR, p.25.

Depth gauge

• Wrap a small strip of masking or insulating tape around a drill bit so that the exposed part of the bit equals the desired depth of a hole. Or mark the bit with a wax crayon.
• Alternatively, use a block of wood as a gauge; position it beside the bit so that the chuck will butt against it when the desired depth is reached. Some modern drills have a rod for setting the depth.

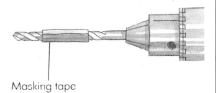

Masking tape

Diabetic emergencies

Insulin shock (too much insulin in the blood) starts very quickly. The symptoms are damp, pale, clammy skin; a strong, rapid pulse; sweating; dizziness; headache; hunger; aggressiveness; convulsions; fainting; or occasionally coma.
• Immediately give the person some sugar, honey, a boiled sweet, fruit juice or a sweet drink – make sure that it is sweetened with sugar, not a sugar substitute. Do not give an unconscious person anything; get him to a hospital quickly or call an ambulance.
Diabetic coma (not enough insulin in the blood) develops more slowly than insulin shock, over several hours or days. The symptoms are thirst, abdominal pain, vomiting, restlessness, confusion and a gradual lapsing into stupor and coma. The skin is dry, red and warm. There may be a sweetish smell of acetone, like nail polish remover, on the breath. Whether the person is conscious or not, take him to a doctor or call an ambulance.
• If you're not sure whether a conscious person is in the first stages of diabetic

Common sense about common scents

Perspiration is the way the body cools itself. Every 24 hours, millions of sweat glands all over the body produce 1-3 pints/0.5-1.7 litres of perspiration, which evaporates, taking away excess heat.

It's not perspiration that causes body odour – it's the action of bacteria fermenting in the sweat produced by glands in our armpits and groins. People didn't know this until fairly modern times, and so for centuries they tried to overpower their own smell by dousing themselves with perfumes.

The ancient Egyptians knew nothing of bacteria, but they understood all about countering the odours they caused. Apart from regularly anointing themselves with

perfumes and oils made from citrus fruits, spices and wood resins, they were fastidious about daily bathing. They also frequently removed their underarm hair – which offers bacteria an expanded surface on which to grow.

Later cultures, in their own efforts to smell sweet, copied the Egyptian formulas and added powder and bicarbonate of soda to the list of deodorants.

Around the turn of this century it became stylish in some circles for women to flaunt a slight aroma of the upper body. It was romantically called 'bouquet de corsage', and these ladies believed men found it attractive. Perhaps. But the fad soon passed.

coma or is going into insulin shock, ask them which it is. Most diabetics will know. If you're still in doubt, give the person some sugar and get help.

Diarrhoea

The cause may be a viral or bacterial infection, food poisoning or an inflammatory disease. Or it could be caused by stress, or simply an overindulgence in food or drink.

• An infant under 6 months old can quickly become dehydrated from diarrhoea; if it continues for more than half a day, you must call a doctor.

• If you are breast-feeding a child, the diarrhoea may be due to something you are eating, such as highly spiced foods, onions, tomatoes or rhubarb. Stop eating any possible irritants and see if the diarrhoea stops.

• Continue to feed a baby milk, especially breast milk, and let him drink plenty of sugar water or a flat soft drink. Feed this to him regularly, up to every 2 hours.

• When the condition stops, reintroduce easily digested solids such as puréed vegetables and starches. Gradually increase the amount and variety over the next few days.

• Give a child clear liquids and avoid solid foods. As the diarrhoea tapers off, move straight to solids, such as rice and potatoes, that don't contain any milk or dairy products.

• An adult should be treated in much the same way. If the diarrhoea persists for several days, however, and the person hasn't eaten and drunk enough to balance the loss of fluids and nutrients, dehydration becomes a threat.

• If thin, watery stools last longer than 3 days, contain blood or mucus, or are accompanied by fever, vomiting or severe abdominal pain, call a doctor.

• When travelling in a foreign country, avoid contamination from water and milk by always boiling them first, even water used to brush your teeth. Suspect even ice cubes. Add water-sterilising tablets (available from a chemist) to your water, or drink only recognised brands of bottled mineral water. In tropical or subtropical areas eat cooked

fruit and vegetables only, and try to avoid shellfish, raw fish and uncooked egg products such as mayonnaise. Carry anti-diarrhoeal tablets with you to settle stomach upsets.

Dimmer switches

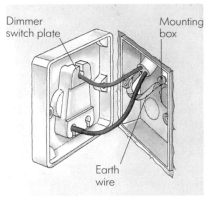

Dimmer switch plate   Mounting box

Earth wire

To replace a dimmer switch, first switch off the power to that circuit (see FUSE BOX, p.93) and remove the relevant fuse. Then pull off the dimmer knob and remove the cover plate screws and cover plate. Remove the screws fastening the switch to the box and pull the switch out, noting the wire connections. As in all switch loops, the switch should connect the black or red wires only. Undo the wires from the old switch leads and connect them to the new switch leads with wire nuts. Then fasten the new switch to the box and replace the cover plate. Finally, push the dimmer knob onto its shaft.

Dinner parties

For a dinner party with a different twist, try one of these ideas:

• Throw a theme party featuring food, drink, music and decor from a foreign country or a distant region of the United Kingdom. Or, for the sake of variety, turn it into an international buffet.

• Go co-op: ask each guest to prepare and serve one course at his or her home. You should be the one to coordinate the transportation of guests.

• Serve elaborate but substantial finger food, such as stuffed croissants or chicken croquettes with a savoury dip.

In summer, prepare a cold alternative, such as ceviche (raw, marinated fish) or cooked kebabs with a spicy dip.

• Have a potluck picnic: ask everyone to bring a favourite dish.

• Supply the grill and cold drinks and then ask each guest to bring one item for a barbecue.

Directions

You're lost in a strange place and you ask one of the residents for help, but the directions you get only confuse you further. It has happened to all of us, but how do you make sure it doesn't happen next time?

• Carry a map. It's easier to mark out a route than to describe it.

• State your destination clearly. If possible, write down the name and address. Ask the person to locate it on the map, and mark where you are. If you don't have a map, ask her to sketch the route.

• Write down all instructions, including landmarks, and repeat them. Don't be embarrassed to admit you don't understand a direction; ask for clarification.

Giving directions Remember that the person you're helping doesn't know the area.

• Be sure you understand where the person wants to go. If he speaks another language, use a map or get him to write down his destination.

• Use large, obvious landmarks as references rather than those that require familiarity with the place.

• Give an idea of distance as best you can, whether in miles or in the number of road turnings.

• Make sure that the person understands. Have him repeat your directions back to you.

• Draw a sketch.

Dishwashers

Has your dishwasher stopped working? The timer may just be at a normal pause in a cycle; wait a few minutes to see if the action resumes.

Make sure you've closed the door and set the timer dial and cycle selector properly. Check the fuse or circuit breaker. See if the water is turned off anywhere on the line.

On small, counter-top models, the electric lead may not be plugged in securely or the hot-water tap may be off. Check the door. Look for a kink in the hose.

Leaks Many leaks are caused by objects blocking the water inlet. Remove and reposition them.

• You may have used too much detergent, or your brand may generate excessive foam, forcing water out. Stop the machine and add a cup of vinegar to neutralise the foam. If that doesn't do the trick, remove the racks and bail out the water. Let the motor dry thoroughly before turning it on again.

Drainage problems A little water at the bottom of a dishwasher is normal. (It keeps the seals from drying out.) If there's a lot of water, be sure the strainer at the bottom isn't clogged and the rubber drain hose isn't bent. If the water drains through a waste disposer, check that it's empty.

Dirty glasses The most common cause of spots or film on glasses is hard-water deposits. Soak the spotted item in vinegar for a couple of minutes; if the film disappears, the problem is hard water. To prevent a recurrence, increase the amount of detergent, be sure the water temperature is 60°C/140°F, and use a rinse additive to help water to 'sheet' off. Or install a water-softener in your home.

• If the clouding can't be removed with vinegar, use less detergent, a lower water temperature and a rinse additive; switch off before the drying cycle.

Dizziness and fainting

Fear, anxiety, pain, the sight of blood or injury and a stuffy, overheated room can all cause dizziness and fainting.

• To prevent a dizzy person from fainting, make him sit down and loosen tight clothing at the neck. Place his head between his knees. If he has a heart problem, difficulty in breathing or any serious injury, lay him down with his feet elevated.

• If a person faints, try to prevent him from injuring himself in the fall. Then,

make sure that he is breathing. Lay the person on his back with his legs raised above the level of his head. If he doesn't revive quickly, seek medical help.

• Middle-aged and elderly people who faint should see a doctor right away; such an occurrence can be a sign of a serious medical problem.

Dog and cat bites

Although a dog bite may look more serious, a cat bite is more dangerous — there are more bacteria in a cat's mouth.

• Wash a dog or cat bite with soap and water, rinse under running water for at least 5 minutes, and cover with a dressing or a clean cloth. Try not to move the affected area until the bite has been treated by a doctor.

• Cats and dogs in Britain are free from rabies. But rabies exists in other European countries as well as elsewhere in the world, and it is fatal if you don't get instant treatment. Do not make a fuss of a dog or cat. If you are bitten or even accidentally scratched by a dog, cat or wild animal in a foreign country, treat as above and seek a local doctor at once – *don't* wait until you get home. See also BITES, p.23.

Dog baths

• Walk your dog before bathing it so that it won't go outside wet.

• If your dog dislikes baths, let it watch you take one yourself. But be prepared – it may jump in with you.

• To keep soap out of a dog's eyes, gently apply a thin layer of petroleum jelly over its eyebrows and around its eyes.

• To minimise soap film, add vinegar or lemon juice to the rinse water. Rinse your pet thoroughly.

• To prevent your dog from splattering you, wash its head last – a wet head makes the dog want to shake itself dry. Wrap the dog in a towel before lifting it out; this will also greatly reduce the water it shakes off. Towel your dog dry immediately after its bath.

• Use a blow dryer. Set it on warm, not hot, and hold it at least 6in/150mm away from your pet.

Dog chasing

Cyclists and joggers can take a few precautions to protect themselves against being chased by dogs.

• Carry a folding umbrella to shoot open in the animal's face.

• If you can't outdistance a pursuing dog on your bike, dismount and use the bike as a shield. If necessary, try squirting the dog in the eyes with your water bottle.

• Keep dog treats, such as biscuits, in your pocket. Throw one in the direction of an approaching dog – as far as you can.

• Carry a personal 'dog alarm'. This is a pocket-sized alarm which emits a high-pitched noise that arrests the dog's behaviour. It is an aerosol and is sold with refills.

• Speak to the dog in a commanding but calm tone.

• Draw the owner's attention to the fact that his dog is a nuisance and it is his responsibility to put the dog on a lead or train it not to chase people.

Dog hair

• To collect loose hairs, put your dog on an old sheet or towel before you brush it.

• To remove burrs, crush them with pliers or soak the tangles in vegetable oil, then just comb them out.

• To get rid of sticky substances such as tar, saturate the fur with vegetable oil. After 15 minutes apply dog shampoo; rinse immediately.

• Allow paint or gum to harden, then snip off the hair that holds it.

• To clean a dog brush, move a toothpick through the rows.

Dog leash

If you have to walk the dog and you can't find its leash, try using one of these substitutes:
• A rope or length of clothes line. Make sure you tie a secure bowline or other nonslip knot around the dog's collar. Make a loop for the handle and wrap it with insulating tape.
• A long leather belt. Push the end under the collar and then through the buckle.
• A pair of tights. Push one leg underneath the dog's collar and tie the feet together with a reef knot.

Dogs

If dogs are a nuisance:

• Keep rubbish bins tightly sealed to prevent dogs from tipping the waste into the street. If possible, never put rubbish out in unprotected plastic bags. Set bins or bags out as close to collection time as possible. Sprinkle pepper around your rubbish bins to deter persistent scavengers.
• Check to see if a dog has a tag identifying its owner. Or ask your neighbours where you can find the owner of a dog that barks incessantly or tramples gardens. Try to resolve the problem with the dog's owner before complaining to local authorities. A joint petition from neighbours is usually more successful than an individual one.

Doorbell

Has your doorbell stopped ringing? It probably needs new batteries. Fit long-life batteries, which should last for up to two years.
• If it still doesn't work, unscrew the covers of the bell and bell push and check the connections. Reconnect any loose wires.
• To check that the bell push isn't faulty, place the blade of an insulated screwdriver across the two terminals. If this makes the bell ring, the bell push could be corroded. Disconnect the wires and clean the contact points with sandpaper. Reconnect. If the bell still doesn't work, fit a new bell push.
• Why not save on batteries and hang a string of bells knotted onto coloured rope or string outside your front door?

Doorknobs

Most loose doorknobs can be tightened by securing the little grub screw in the handle. The screw is worked loose by the vibrations of constant use. Loosen the screw a little further; push the knob into close contact with the door rose, then tighten the screw.
• Some handles have a threaded spindle. In this case, loosen the grub screw and tighten the handle on the thread until the handle just turns easily without any looseness. Re-tighten the screw onto one of the flat sides of the spindle.

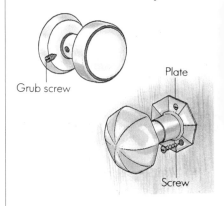

Grub screw

Plate

Screw

Doors

• When a door refuses to stay open, check the hinges. If one has shifted or a hinge screw has pulled loose, reset the hinge in its original position and tighten the screws. If a screw cannot be tightened because the hole has been stripped or enlarged, remove it, pack the hole with a sliver of wood dipped in PVA adhesive, reinsert the screw and tighten securely.
• To quieten a door that slams, stick a strip of foam rubber to the edge of the doorstop moulding. Peel-and-stick foam weatherstripping tape works well. A short length of foam rubber near the top and bottom of the frame will often suffice. You can also try a narrow strip of cork or leather.
• To keep a door from slamming against the wall when it opens, fit a rubber doorstop to the floor.
• Here's an easy-to-make door bumper for a child's room: put a rubber ball in a

---

Canine trivia

★ Some experts believe that a dog can be trained to understand as many as 400 words.
★ Dogs have better night vision than humans because of the arrangement of the rods at the back of their eyes and a membrane called the tapetum, which acts like a reflector. That's what causes the strange shine you see in a dog's eyes when it looks into a car's headlights.
★ The old saying that 1 dog year is equal to 7 human years is not true. A 1-year-old puppy is roughly equivalent in development to a 15-year-old human; a 2-year-old dog, to a 24-year-old human. Thereafter, as the dog ages, each year could be compared to 4 human years, so that its age at 10 approximates 56 human years. These calculations, however, vary from breed to breed.
★ A cold, wet nose says nothing about a dog's health.
★ The fastest dog is the greyhound. It can run at 35mph/56kph and cover as much as 18ft/5.5m in a single stride.
★ The tiniest dog, at about 4lb/1.8 kg, is the Chihuahua. The largest is the St Bernard; it can weigh up to 200 lb/90kg.
★ A dog's hearing is far more sensitive than a human's, particularly at higher frequencies. Dogs also use their ears to communicate, varying the position to signal fear, anger, and so forth.
★ Newborn puppies cannot see or hear, but they have an acute sense of smell, which leads them to their mother's milk.

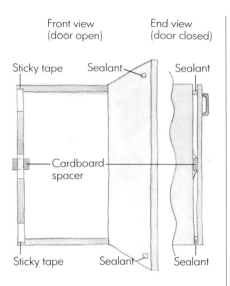

Front view (door open)

End view (door closed)

Sticky tape — Sealant — Sealant

Cardboard spacer

Sticky tape — Sealant — Sealant

sock and hang it from the inside doorknob.

• The self closing hinges on many kitchen cabinet doors make them slam shut. Muffle the noise with bumpers made of silicone rubber sealant.

Put two small blobs of sealant – each about the size of a pencil rubber – on the inside corners of each door, one at the top and the other at the bottom. Then place strips of sticky tape on the cabinet where the sealant makes contact. Smear each tape strip with a thin film of petroleum jelly to keep the sealant from sticking when the door is closed. And, to act as a spacer, tape a small piece of 1/8in / 3mm thick cardboard to the cabinet between the tape strips. Close the door, let the sealant dry overnight, then peel off the tape and cardboard.

Doorstep sales

• If someone calls at your door to sell you something, ask to see his pedlar's licence. If it is not shown, call the police. However, this does not apply to canvassers, such as double-glazing salesmen, who are soliciting agreement to a later visit by a salesman.
• Beware of buying from door-to-door salesmen. They are difficult to trace, and if the item you buy is faulty you have no means of recompense.
• If you agree to a contract away from the trader's premises, whether it is in your own home or elsewhere, and you have not specifically invited the trader there to do business, you are entitled to back out of the contract without penalty within seven days. The trader should tell you of this right, but you have it whether he does so or not. All you have to do is write to him telling him that you are cancelling the agreement. This holds, too, for sales on credit agreed off trade premises.

Down payments

To save money on a major purchase, pay for it outright or make the largest down payment you can afford. Because you'll need to borrow less, you'll pay less interest.

The savings may be greater than you realise. For example, if you buy a £12,000 car at 10.4 per cent and make a 10 per cent down payment, you'll pay £1818.36 interest over 3 years. But if you make a 50 per cent down payment (£6000), you will pay only £1010.10 interest over the same period – a saving of £808.26, or almost 45 per cent.

Few, if any, investments offer a higher rate of return than the interest you pay on a loan. Therefore, when making a major purchase, if you can withdraw money from your savings account without incurring a penalty, consider using it to make a larger down payment.

Drainage in the garden

• To test how well your garden soil drains, run the hose on the surface at different points around your garden. Then observe what the water does.

If it drains away immediately, your soil is too sandy for most plants; dig in some compost, or other organic matter, or apply a mulch when the soil is wet to help it retain water.

If the water stands for 30 minutes to 1 hour, the drainage is ideal for vegetables and flowers.

If it remains in the hole for several hours, your soil drains poorly. Either dig in some sand, manure or compost, or construct raised beds (see RAISED-BED PLANTING p.166) of improved soil.

Drains blocked

If your outside drain is smelly or overflows, it is blocked and needs cleaning. Kitchen waste that doesn't break down easily, such as grease or tea leaves, or leaves from nearby trees, can clog the grid or trap of a gully drain.

• Put on long rubber gloves and, using a trowel, scoop out any debris. Lift out the grid and wash it thoroughly in a bucket of hot water and detergent.
• If this doesn't solve the problem, the U-shaped trap below the grid is probably blocked. Wearing rubber gloves, remove the grid and use an empty tin to remove any debris in the bend of the trap. When the trap is clear, wash it with a hose at high pressure, or pour several buckets of water down it.
• It helps to prevent the problem if you clean the grid three or four times a year, to remove grease and potential blockages, and pour domestic bleach over it every couple of weeks.

Draughts

• Most draughts are caused by the pressure of the wind against the face of a house, seeking out gaps and cracks. Seal all window and door frames with draughtstrip, and fit covers to keyholes and letterboxes.
• Another form of draught is caused by the convection of air over a cold window pane. Warm air coming into contact with the glass is cooled and falls towards the floor to be replaced by more warm air above, causing draughts. Cure this by fitting double-glazing and well-fitting curtains.
• Draughts are also caused by the pull of a flue when a solid fuel fire is used in a fireplace. Very considerable amounts of air are required for efficient burning, and this may be pulled across the room from beneath a door. To prevent these draughts, give the fire its own air supply by fitting vents either side of the hearth. Or fit a modern fire grate which has its own underfloor air supply.
• You can kill the draught from under a door by fitting a threshold draught excluder to its base, then cutting a

slot in the top of the door. This ensures that air enters at ceiling level, where it will be warmed and no longer felt as a draught.

• An unused flue may be pulling up more air than necessary, causing draughts. Block off the flue with a sheet of fire-resistant board, but fit a small ventilator in the board so that there is enough air movement to keep the flue ventilated. Failure to do this is often the cause of damp patches on chimney breasts.

• Draughts coming up between floor-boards can be reduced by laying building paper under a carpet underlay and carpet. On an exposed timber floor, seal gaps between boards with papier mâché pressed between the boards and allowed to dry. Then sand and stain to match the floor.

• Never block off external air bricks to reduce draughts. They prevent the flooring timbers from developing dry rot.

Drawers

• When a drawer won't pull out, the chances are that something inside is projecting above the sides. Simply remove the drawer above, then empty and repack the sticking drawer.

• A loose nail in the drawer frame may also be the culprit; if so, hammer it down.

• When the bottom of a wooden drawer sags, turn over the drawer. If nails hold the bottom to the back, pull them out with pincers. Break the glue blocks from the bottom with a chisel and mallet.

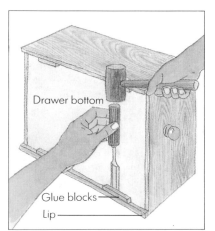

Drawer bottom

Glue blocks

Lip

Slide out the bottom and turn it upside-down. Then re-nail the bottom to the back and glue the blocks back in place.

• If the sagging bottom fits into a groove in the back of the drawer, you must dismantle the frame to fix it. Wrap a cloth around a mallet and tap apart the dovetail joints at the corners of the drawer. Slide the bottom out, scrape off the old glue, and reassemble the drawer with the bottom upside-down.

• Replace a split bottom with thin plywood, or mend it with a canvas strip and PVA adhesive.

• If a wooden drawer drags, sand its runners lightly and then rub them with a candle stub or a bar of soap, or dust with French chalk. Or if the wood has swollen in damp weather, lightly sand or plane the front lip of the drawer and along the tops of the sides and back.

• If a wooden drawer pulls out too far, the chances are that you need to re-attach or replace either the glue blocks that secure the drawer bottom, or the stop that is on top of the rail – below the drawer – at the front of the chest.

Drawstrings

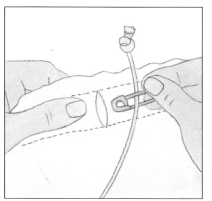

• If you lose a drawstring, substitute a shoelace, ribbon or fabric tubing; attach a safety pin to one end to help feed the replacement through the casing.

• Play it safe – tie the drawstrings together before washing.

• If the drawstring in a pair of pyjama bottoms frequently disappears into its casing, double-knot the tips. Or harden the tips with a few drops of epoxy resin for easy retrieval.

Drills and drilling

• Confused by drill bits? Don't be. The twist drill has the twist right to the end, with sharp cutting edges as part of the twist. It is used for cutting metal and wood. You can use it on plastics, but as a general rule work at a very low speed to avoid melting the plastic and clogging the bit.

The masonry drill has a special tungsten carbide tip welded into the twist part of the drill body, and it is this hardened piece that cuts into masonry. There are general-purpose masonry drills, but also tougher types better able to cope with the now popular hammer-action methods of drilling into hard masonry.

• When drilling masonry, always withdraw the tip about every 5 seconds to allow the tip to cool, keeping the drill running. Failure to do so can lead to overheating of the tip, causing irreparable damage.

• There are simple drill sharpening devices now available which connect to an electric drill and enable you to sharpen both twist and masonry drills.

• Always wear eye protection when drilling. And wear a simple dust mask when using hammer action on masonry.

• Drilling glazed surfaces such as ceramic tiles can be tricky. Mark the spot to be drilled with a cross formed of clear adhesive tape. This will hold the drill tip in place just long enough to make a start. Never use hammer action on tiles!

Dripping taps

Do your taps drip no matter how firmly you turn them off? This usually means that they need a new washer, but could also indicate a damaged valve seating.
Replacing the washer

• Turn off the water supply, at the stopcock.

• Turn your tap on and put in the plug to prevent anything from falling down the plughole.

• Unscrew the bell-shaped cover of the tap. If this is not easy to do, wrap a cloth around the cover and use a spanner. If

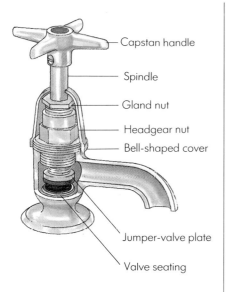

- Capstan handle
- Spindle
- Gland nut
- Headgear nut
- Bell-shaped cover
- Jumper-valve plate
- Valve seating

the tap has a shrouded head, lever off the top plate, undo the little screw on the top and lift off the handle. This exposes the hexagonal headgear nut.

- Use a spanner to undo the headgear nut. If it's stiff, pour a little penetrating oil around the joint, wait 10 minutes and then try again. Keep applying the oil until the joint loosens.
- The washer may be in the headgear unit or resting on the valve seating. If there is a small nut holding the washer in place, undo it with a spanner and then prise the washer off. Fit on the new washer. It must be the right size: if you're not sure, take the old one to a hardware shop to measure against a new one.
- Grease the threads of the tap and put it back together again. Turn on the tap and then turn on the water supply.

Repairing the valve seating
- When you've removed the headgear unit as above, take a look at the base of the tap. If it is rusted or worn, it needs renewing.

Buy a washer-and-seating set. This has a plastic seat which fits over the metal seat of the tap, and a washer-and-jumper unit which fits into the headgear. Reassemble the tap. The tap may drip for a few days because it takes a few days of use for the new seating to settle in place and fit tightly.

Driver's licence

If you lose your driver's licence, go to your post office and get form D1. Complete it and send it to the DVLC at Swansea, with a cheque for the relevant duplicate licence fee. You may drive until the duplicate licence reaches you.

Drowning

If you see a person in the water fully clothed, assume that he may be drowning and be prepared to help. Don't expect him to answer if you call out – he may be too weak to shout back.

- When you get to a drowning person, if he has stopped breathing, try to start mouth-to-mouth resuscitation (see below). Tread the water and hold the victim's head clear of the water in the crook of your arm. Try to lift the upper chest out of the water too. Remove any debris from his mouth with your index finger, tilt his head back and breathe into his mouth, holding your cheek against his nose to stop any air escaping.

When his chest rises, remove your mouth. Repeat the process each time the air has escaped, and try to move towards land between breaths.
- Once you reach shallow water or dry

Mouth-to-mouth artificial respiration

It is always worth trying artificial respiration on someone who has stopped breathing, even if you feel it might be too late. Give the first four breaths as soon as possible, then continue the steps below as long as you can, or until qualified medical help takes over.

1 Tilt the head backwards to open the airway, with one hand on the forehead and the other under the chin.

2 If still not breathing, pinch the nose and give four full breaths into the mouth. Then check whether the chest is rising and falling. If it is not, make sure there is no obstruction in the mouth and that the airway is free.

3 If the chest does rise and fall, continue breathing into the person's mouth at your normal rate (at around 15 breaths per minute).

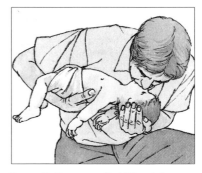

Resuscitating a small child or infant
Seal your lips around the child's *nose and mouth* and puff quickly and gently into his lungs – about 20 breaths per minute. Breathe very lightly indeed for small children. Check for a heartbeat after the first four puffs. If it is absent, try applying chest compression as a last resort if you have been trained how to do so.

land, continue artificial respiration. Give chest compression if you can't feel any pulse and have been trained to do so. Don't stop artificial respiration. Children, in particular, have been revived 40 minutes after breathing has ceased.

• The victim will probably bring up large amounts of water as you give artificial respiration. Turn his head to the side and clear his mouth frequently.

• Once the victim has started breathing, place him in the recovery position (see p.168). Treat any injuries you can and cover him with towels or blankets. Call an ambulance or get medical help as soon as possible.

Drug interactions

Anyone who takes more than one drug at a time – prescription or over-the-counter – or who drinks alcohol while taking medication may suffer adverse side effects from their interactions. The elderly are especially vulnerable. Here's how to help prevent this problem:

• Keep an updated list of all the drugs you take; go over it with your doctor whenever a new medication is suggested.

• Take samples of all your drugs along whenever you see a new doctor.

• If you develop new symptoms at any time, especially after starting a new drug, put all your drugs into a bag and take them to your doctor for a review of your prescriptions. The doctor can check the latest medical literature for information about interactions with other drugs, food and alcohol, as well as possible allergic reactions.

• Check that your chemist has a complete record of all the drugs you take, your allergies to foods and drugs, and your doctor's name and address. When a new medication is prescribed, this record will identify incompatible drugs.

Drunk drivers

• If you intend to drink alcohol at a party, arrange with your partner who will drive home, or catch a lift with someone else.

• If an intoxicated person is about to get behind the wheel of a car, reason firmly with him not to drive. If that doesn't work, take his car keys away and call a taxi for him, or find someone who will give him a ride home.

• If you're already on the road when you realise the driver is drunk, insist that he pulls over and lets someone else drive. If he refuses, ask him to let you out at the first opportunity and call the police. Give them your location, a description of the car and driver, and the car registration number. You may lose a friend, but you may also save a life.

• If you see a car being badly driven on the road in front of you, assume the driver is drunk and be prepared to take evasive action.

Dry-cleaning

• Always check that your garment is suitable for dry-cleaning by checking the fabric care label. Do not rely on the dry-cleaner to reject an item that should not be dry-cleaned.

• Dry-cleaning guarantees to remove all general grime and dirt, but may not remove some specific stains. If your clothes have a stain, always point it out in advance and tell the cleaner what it is, if you know. You may have to accept that they can only do their best.

• Before you leave the shop with your cleaned garments, always check that they are in fact clean and that any particular stain that the dry-cleaner has agreed to remove has gone. If you have to remove packaging to do so, don't be put off. If the item still has a stain, ask them to do it again.

• There will be some solvent smell initially in newly dry-cleaned clothes, but if your garment is damp or still has an excessive smell of solvent (or other resinous smell), complain and do not take it away. This is due to faulty processing, and the garment should be cleaned again.

• Do not take a cleaned garment inside a closed car – the solvent fumes may make you unfit to drive. Open a window. When you get home, remove the packaging and hang your clean clothes up for a short while in a place where there is fresh air.

Dry skin

All skins dehydrate with low humidity, whether it is very hot or very cold; some skins are inherently dry and even the greasiest of teenage skins dry out after the age of 45.

• The best solution is to apply a moisturiser one or more times each day, immediately after bathing, when the skin is still slightly damp. Dry skin that is not lubricated regularly may become itchy and break out in a rash.

• The best remedy is also the easiest to find: water. Drink 6 to 8 glasses a day and eat foods high in water content, such as fruits and leafy vegetables. Use a humidifier in winter.

• Bathe in mildly salted water (4 tablespoons of salt per tubful) to rehydrate your body, then apply a moisturising cream or lotion. Oatmeal added to bath water (without the salt) eases itchiness.

• For a moisturising facial, mash a banana, add a tablespoon of honey and smooth the mixture over your face. After 15 minutes rinse with warm water. Alternatively, mix up a beaten egg yolk with the honey and spread the yolk mix onto your face.

Dual careers

Do you and your working partner spend too little time together? If so:

• Go through your diaries and make dates in advance, such as going to see a film or having a romantic meal at home.

• Take up a new sport or hobby together. Discovering something new as a couple gives you more to talk about.

• Don't use the children as an excuse. Find a good babysitter – even during the day, so you can go for a walk alone.

• Make a specific time each day to ring each other from the office.

• Spend more nonworking hours together by delegating household chores which take up time. Give the babysitter extra money to wash dishes or do the ironing.

• Find out which shops will deliver.

• Encourage the children to help out, see CHILDREN'S CHORES, p.45.

Dustbins

If you want to prevent putting your back out, use your child's skateboard or a trolley to take full rubbish bags or dustbins out to the street.

Cleaning

• Wash dustbins with 4fl oz/115ml ammonia in 1 gallon/4.5 litres of water. To disinfect them, substitute 6fl oz/175ml bleach for the ammonia; leave them to stand for 5 minutes, then rinse.

• To fight mould and bacteria, sprinkle the base and sides of a dustbin with 4fl oz/115ml borax.

To prevent scavenging

• Stretch bungee (elasticated) cords across the lids, hooking them onto the bin handles.

• Strap or tie the bins to a sturdy post.

• Slip broom handles or stakes through the handles and drive them into the ground.

• Tie the dustbins together – they'll be harder to knock over.

• Put the bins in a box with a lid fastened by a padlock.

• Sprinkle pepper on the ground surrounding the bins to discourage cats.

Dusting

• Your aim is to pick up dust, not displace it. For dusters, spray discarded vests, nappies or old towels with silicone polish. Muslin moistened with diluted lemon oil also works fine. Avoid feather dusters; get the lamb's-wool variety.

• Starting at the top and working down, use slow, even strokes. If you'll be dusting for some time, wear a small face mask (available from DIY stores) to prevent a scratchy throat.

• Wear a multipocketed apron or carry a cleaning tray – a cheap, compartmented plastic box with a handle makes a good one – to keep supplies within reach. Include a bag for collecting debris.

• Treat an old sock with silicone polish and wear it as a glove to dust tables and chairs.

• Don't bother dusting knick-knacks one by one. Just soak them all together in a washing-up bowl with detergent. Then

Bamboo cane

Damp sock

use your hair dryer to blow them dry.

• To get at narrow spots behind radiators, between louvres or under the refrigerator, dampen an old sock, slip it over one end of a bamboo cane, and secure it with a rubber band.

• Wax your dustpan so that dust won't cling. Shake mops and dusters inside a plastic bin liner outdoors.

• Hard-to-dust things and places – pleated lampshades, carved furniture and crevices – are easy to clean if you blow the dust out with a hair dryer or the blow attachment of a vacuum cleaner. An empty squeeze bottle used as an air pump also does the trick.

• Use spectacle-cleaning tissues to dust small picture frames.

E

Ear popping

• Avoid travelling by air if you have a cold, flu or allergy; you may develop painful ear or sinus problems. If you must fly, take an oral decongestant an hour before takeoff and landing, or use a nasal spray before and during descent.

• If your ears start to pop or you get an earache, try to swallow, chew gum, suck on a boiled sweet, sip liquid or yawn. Don't sleep during takeoff and landing; you won't swallow often enough to keep your ears clear.

• For babies, nursing or sucking a bottle or dummy will help, especially during ascent and descent.

Ear problems

• If you've got something in your ear, don't probe it – you may drive the object deeper and damage the eardrum. Seek medical help.

• If it's an insect, put your head on one side and float it out by pouring warm olive or baby oil gently into the ear.

Earache

• For temporary relief, take paracetamol or aspirin and lie with your head raised and your ear resting on a hot-water bottle or hot compress. Give children under 12 a liquid painkiller such as Calpol. Keep any fever down with tepid sponging and cool drinks, and remove extra clothing and bedclothes.

• Call a doctor if your baby is crying constantly and rubbing its earlobe, if the ache is associated with a high fever; if a child is inconsolable despite regular doses of painkiller; if the ache continues after 4 to 8 hours' rest; if there is a discharge from the ear; or if the ear aches after flying, diving or a respiratory illness.

• If earache persists but your doctor finds that your ears are normal, see your dentist. Sometimes toothache is 'referred' to the ears.

Earwax

• Never probe your ear canal with anything smaller than a clean fingertip. If wax builds up, lie on your side and put a few drops of warm olive oil in your ear. Drain your ear after 15 minutes – the softened wax should work its way out.

Ringing in the ears

• Ask your doctor to check for earwax buildup.

• Eliminate caffeine and aspirin.

• Avoid loud noises.

• If the ringing persists for more than a week, see a doctor.

Water in the ear

• To get rid of water, gently clap the heel of your hand against the side of your head and tip it to the affected side. The water will drain out naturally.

Pierced ears

• To prevent infection, swab newly pierced earlobes with surgical spirit twice a day. Apply an over-the-counter antiseptic ointment with a cotton bud nightly.

• To avoid an allergic reaction, make sure the posts are gold or surgical steel.

Earrings

• To keep pierced earrings from flopping forward and to balance heavy ones, make an earring guard. Fold a small piece of transparent tape together so that the sticky side is covered. (You may want to cut it into a circle.) Or cut a circle from the plastic tab that seals a loaf of bread. Poke a pinhole through the centre of this tab; then insert the post of your earring through your earlobe and the tab. Secure it with the earring back.

• If you lose one earring, put the remaining one on a chain to wear as a pendant. Or turn it into a pin or a stickpin with parts sold in craft shops – you could even make a ring out of it.

• Avoid very heavy earrings for daily use as these can eventually distort your ear lobes. Many chunky, dramatic styles are actually made from lightweight materials which are much more comfortable to wear.

• Allergies to metal clip and earring backs are very common. Some people are allergic to every metal except gold. And hypo-allergenic coatings can also wear off after a time. One answer to prevent skin from contact with metal is to

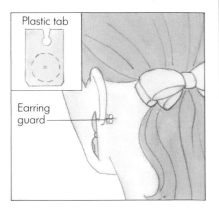

Plastic tab

Earring guard

slip special transparent plastic sleeves over the earring clip; a tiny self-adhesive sponge pad sticks onto the metal of the opposing part of the earring. Kits are available from jewellery counters of major department stores. Temporary earring shields can be made using clear sticky or masking tape.

Earthquakes

If you're indoors

• Stay indoors when tremors start.

• Get under a sturdy table, desk or bed, or stand in a doorway or an inside corner next to an interior wall.

• Keep away from windows, mirrors, glass, bookcases, light fittings, tall cabinets and fireplaces.

If you're outdoors

• Get into an open area; avoid buildings, walls, power lines and trees.

• If you're in a car, stop – but stay inside until the tremors stop. Avoid bridges and power lines.

Afterwards

• Be on guard for smaller aftershocks that can cause additional damage.

• Apply first aid to any injuries.

• Check the building for structural damage, fires and damage to utility lines and electric appliances. Open doors and cabinets carefully.

• If you smell gas, open all doors and windows, leave the house, and report the leak to the gas company.

• If electrical wires cause short circuits

or fittings have become loose, switch off the power (see ELECTRIC SHOCK, opposite).

• Until public water supplies are declared safe, boil all tap water for 10 minutes before use.

• If water pipes are damaged, switch off the water supply (see WATER LEAKS, p.227). Get emergency drinking water from the toilet tank (not the bowl), boiler or ice cube trays. Don't flush the toilet until you know that the sewer lines are intact.

Eggs

• Test eggs for freshness by placing them in a bowl of cold salted water. Discard any that float to the surface or turn their broad ends up – they're stale.

• Don't discard an egg just because its white is cloudy. Most likely it's the freshest egg of all, since 1 or 2-day-old eggs still retain a little carbon dioxide. The gas is harmless and tasteless.

• For a perfect poached egg, add a tablespoon of vinegar to the water. It helps to set the white.

• When you cook eggs in a microwave oven, prick the yolks first to keep them from bursting. And never microwave eggs in their shells – they'll explode and make a mess.

• When whisking egg whites and making meringues, whisk them up in a clean, grease-free, glass or porcelain bowl. Do not use bowls or whisks made of plastic – the plastic prevents the whites from whisking properly.

• Adding a pinch of salt, cream of tartar or ½ teaspoon of vinegar to egg whites will help to whisk them up stiffly.

Elastic

• To replace worn-out elastic on pyjama bottoms with a drawstring or cord, cut it 24in/610mm longer than the casing and knot both ends; brush clear nail polish or epoxy resin on the tips to prevent fraying. Pin one end to an open seam and feed the other through the casing. Then trim. (See DRAWSTRINGS, p.66.)

• To replace a waistband that has lost its stretch, snip open a seam across the

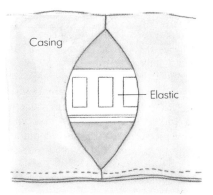

Casing

Elastic

casing and pull out the old elastic. Cut a piece of new elastic 1 in / 25 mm smaller than your waistline. (Use nonroll elastic with vertical ribs to prevent twisting.) Pin one end at the open seam and work the other through the casing with a safety pin. Smooth out the elastic; then overlap the ends by ½ in / 13 mm, sew them firmly together, and stitch up the seam.

Electrical appliance fires

• If flames are shooting out of an appliance, or if you see smoke or smell burning coming from one, immediately turn off the power supply at the mains, then pull out the plug, if safe to do so. If you are in any doubt as to whether you can safely and completely extinguish the fire, do not attempt to do so. Leave the room, close the door, leave the building and call the fire brigade from a neighbour's house.

• If smoke comes from your oven, check to see that there is no food inside. If not, switch the oven off and wait until it has cooled down, then try cleaning it. (A continuous-cleaning oven normally smokes a little.)

• If grilling creates smoke, food may be too close to the heat. Or fat may not be draining properly; if you use foil or a disposable grillpan, cut slashes in it to allow fat to drip into the pan below.

• If smoke comes out of the microwave, interrupt the cycle, sort out the problem, and restart the cycle.

• To be on the safe side, never leave an appliance plugged in when you are away from home.

Electric blankets

An extra low voltage electric underblanket is more efficient and comfortable than an electric overblanket. Because the heat is under you, little of it is lost to the air.

If you prefer non-electrical warmth, try an old-fashioned hot-water bottle, which does a good job of heating the bed before you climb into it. Flannelette sheets help, too; even without a hot-water bottle, they warm your skin more than smooth sheets do.

Electric fence

An electric fence keeps dogs, rabbits and other small animals off your property or out of your garden. Use one that conforms to BS6167 or 6369. Planning permission isn't normally required, but it shouldn't impede rights of way.

• Control weeds and prune away branches to prevent them from touching the wires and causing short-circuits. Keep weeds down with well-anchored plastic sheeting; herbicidal sprays may corrode the wires.

• Check the fence occasionally for cracked or broken insulators; they can cause a short-circuit, especially when fence posts are wet

Electricity

• If you have a mains electricity supply from an electricity company, the company has a statutory obligation to maintain the electricity it supplies you with to the proper voltage. If you get periods of low voltage, contact the company.

• Electricity companies do not have an absolute obligation to supply you with electricity. They may cut it off at any time, such as to make repairs or if you do not pay your bill. Compensation is not normally payable.

• Consider from time to time whether you could get your electricity cheaper by changing to another tarriff. The company will advise you on request.

• If you have a complaint about an electricity company, get in touch with the management. If you get no satisfaction

from them, complain to the Office of Electricity Regulation (OFFER), who have a consumer complaints panel. (See the phone book or back of bills for the address.)

Electric shock

• Never approach a victim of electric shock if there is any risk of being shocked yourself. If he is still touching the electric source, cut off the power – if this is a low-voltage source, such as the frayed lead of an iron or electric fire, switch it off at the plug; otherwise, switch off at the mains.

• If the person is still holding or touching the source, get a broom handle or other long length of dry wood, stand on a dry rubber mat or pile of newspapers and use the wood to move him away from the source.

• Once he is out of harm's way, douse burning clothes with a towel, blanket or fire blanket. If he is unconscious on the ground, check his breathing. If this has stopped, apply artificial respiration (see p.67) and, if necessary and you know how, chest compression. When he starts breathing, lay him in the recovery position (see p.168).

• Check the casualty for burns. Treat these with cold water and cover them with sterile dressings. Call an ambulance.

Electronic banking

• No matter how technically proficient you may be, before you make your first transaction at an automatic machine, ask a bank official for a full explanation of how it works.

• Memorise your personal identification number (PIN) as soon as you get it. Don't write your number on your banking card. If you don't trust your memory, keep a copy in a secret place at home.

• Follow the machine's instructions exactly. Wait until it has returned your bank card and given you the money and a printed receipt (if you have requested one) before walking away. Check the receipt to make sure that no mistake has been made.

- Record each transaction in your chequebook so that it is easy to balance your bank statement. If there are any inconsistencies, tell the bank at once. See also CHEQUEBOOK BALANCING p.40.
- Lost your bank card? If you tell the bank immediately, you will not be liable for later transactions made on the card.

Employee health insurance

To prevent surprise medical expenses when using private health care, learn how your company health insurance plan works. Find out the answers to these questions:

- What does your insurance policy cover? What about pregnancy? What coverage is available for dependants?
- How much do you have to pay for medical expenses, and when does your insurance plan take over?
- Do you have to pay the bill first and then reclaim the expense, or can it be sent to the insurer for direct payment?
- Does your company insurance policy cover the cost of a private or semi-private room?
- Does your company offer a plan that provides all services for one fee?
- Must you have a second opinion before undergoing surgery?

If you have special health benefit needs, check with your company's personnel or benefits department. You might be able to pick and choose among the benefits offered. And make your needs known to your employer; if enough people need certain coverage, your company might redesign its plan accordingly. See EVALUATING A COMPANY'S BENEFITS PACKAGE, p.245.

Employee tests

- A prospective employer may require you to take job-related tests to make certain that you have the skills needed to do a job. The most common tests include typing and dictation for secretarial positions, maths tests for accounting jobs, and various tests in computer programming languages.
- Applicants for some jobs may be asked

to undergo a physical examination, including the taking of blood and/or urine samples as a health check or, very occasionally, to test for drug abuse. Ask the company to explain its policy and procedures regarding blood and urine tests and tell you the precise method being used. Remember that it is unethical for an employer to test you for the HIV virus without your knowledge and agreement.

- If the results of a physical examination are used to decide whether or not you are offered the job, each part of the examination must be shown to be relevant to the successful performance of the job.
- No test should discriminate against any minority group.
- The chemicals in some foods and medications can show up positive on drug tests, so let your potential employer know if you fear this might happen.
- Increasing numbers of companies are using psychological tests of aptitude and personality as part of their selection procedure. For more senior jobs you may be asked to take part in a simulation test (for example, a group discussion or a management simulation game). Make sure that the company explains which tests it intends to use, which comparison groups you will be tested against, and how the test results will contribute to the decision to employ you. Any prospective employer who does not know the answers to these questions or will not answer is not worth working for. In spite of their increasing popularity with employers, most psychological tests have a limited role to play in selecting employees compared with interviews and application forms.

Employment agencies

Don't expect an employment agent to provide career counselling. His business is filling vacancies for clients, not helping individuals find the right vocation. Take the agent's assessment of your skills and potential with a grain of salt; he may even belittle you or mislead you

about the job market so that you'll take the job he has available. If this happens, try another agency.

To help an agency find the right job for you, write a letter stating:

- Your job objective, target industry, desired salary range and the geographical areas you'd consider working in.
- Your most important achievements in previous jobs, including hard facts such as increases in turnover or value of savings introduced.
- A description of your personality traits that make you ideal for the job, with examples.

You'll probably have to undergo an interview at the agency office and complete an application form. Have an up-to-date but brief cv available (see WRITING A CURRICULUM VITAE, p.245).

When you get a job offer, negotiate the salary on your own; to serve his client, the agent may try to convince you to take less money. And don't be afraid to turn down a job if it's not right for you; the agent won't drop you – on the contrary, he will assume that if you've received one offer, you'll get another. See also HEADHUNTERS, p.103; JOB HUNTING, p.117; JOB INTERVIEWS, p.117.

Empty-nesters

Despite the relief parents often feel when their children finally leave home, after a while many of them experience a sense of loss. Here are some survival strategies:

- Move into a smaller space; sell or store the excess furniture.
- Expand your environment. Convert a former child's room into a den, home office or workroom.
- Fill the void. Some young people who have left their homes in distant cities may need not only a place to live but a family to live with. You may gain a substitute son or daughter who will gladly do household or other tasks in exchange for rent. Draw up a written contract so that expectations are clear on both sides.
- Develop new relationships, volunteer to drive old age pensioners around or to work with children.

• Expand your horizons – don't just sit at home waiting for your children to pay a visit. Enrol in further education (see p.93), or take trips to beauty spots around the country that you've wanted to visit.

• Join a tennis or swimming club, go horse riding or aim to lower your golf handicap. Pick up the old pastimes and hobbies that you left to one side during the years of working and/or raising a family.

Evening wear

If you plan to go straight out from the office, dress with care in the morning.

Women

• Wear a simple dress or ensemble to work and bring accessories – earrings, bracelets, necklace – a pair of dressy shoes or an evening wrap, such as a brightly coloured shawl or silk blouse, to wear as a jacket. A length of black satin ribbon, 1½-3in/38-75mm wide, can serve as a last-minute evening belt or hair tie. The finishing touch: a silk tassel (you can buy one at a haberdashers or curtain shop) attached to the zip of a leather handbag.

• Carry with you a small handbag containing a change of underwear, lipstick

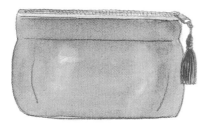

and a bottle of expensive perfume.

Men

• Wear a clean suit to work, bringing a clean shirt, fresh tie or even a silk handkerchief with you.

• If the event is being held at a hotel, take along an electric razor and some aftershave lotion.

Exams

• Look after your physical needs. Get a good night's sleep, avoiding the temptation to cram last-minute revision far into the night. Eat a carbohydrate-rich breakfast, or lunch if the exam is in the afternoon. Take some boiled sweets to suck on when your energy flags.

• Read all instructions twice before you begin. When reading the questions, underline key words such as 'not' and 'except'.

• Budget your time. Divide the total

number of questions by the allotted number of minutes to determine how long to spend on each question. If you find you're taking too long on one, leave it and go on to the next.

• If you can make an 'educated guess' between two or three choices on a multiple-choice question, do so; the odds favour you – even if the exam has a penalty for incorrect answers. But if you haven't a clue, don't guess wildly between five or six choices.

• Begin with the easiest essay questions. If you don't have time to complete an essay, try writing an outline adding the explanation 'Ran out of time'.

Exchanging currency

• Learn a country's official exchange rate before you go; check with a large bank or the business section of a newspaper. You'll usually get a better rate in the country itself, but take the equivalent of £100 with you – order it from your bank or exchange it in the airport – for immediate costs such as tipping, phone calls and taxi fares.

• In your host country, hotels, shops and independent bureaux de change generally offer the worst rates; airports and downtown banks, the best – although in some countries officially tolerated black markets offer the best of all. Travellers' cheques often get better rates than cash. If there is a difference of more than 5 per cent between the buy and sell rates, you are probably paying too much.

• You must show your passport during transactions, and you may be required to show your receipts when you exchange your currency back into sterling. Coins are usually not exchangeable.

• Be aware of bank hours and holidays in the country you're visiting. Banks at train stations and airports often have longer opening hours.

• The exchange rate on a credit card and Eurocheque withdrawal is based upon the rate in effect when the charge clears in Britain, not when you make the transaction.

• A pocket calculator is handy for converting prices when you shop.

Tuxedo rebellion

The year – 1886. The place – Tuxedo Park, New York.

As the story goes, tobacco tycoon Pierre Lorillard was bored with the formality of traditional tails. And so for the annual Autumn Ball, he had his tailor make him several tailless jackets in the mode of the British riding coat popular among fox hunters. It was a daring idea, but Pierre lost his nerve and donned the standard formal costume.

His son, Griswold, however, possessed the audacity that Pierre lacked. He and his friends astounded the cream of society by appearing in short dinner jackets. Tongues wagged for a while, but

the desire for change must have lurked beneath the staid surface of society – or perhaps the famous Lorillard name worked some magic – because others were soon wearing the tailless 'Tuxedo suits' that eventually became standard attire.

Accessories to the tuxedo also have their histories. A forerunner of the cummerbund, for instance, was worn in India as part of Hindu formal attire. The British liked the look and adopted the style for themselves. The pleats were worn facing up, probably because dress trousers lacked pockets and, after all, one needed a place to carry theatre tickets.

Exercise equipment

You don't have to own your own gym to work out. Improvise with household goods.

- 1lb/450g tins of vegetables or soup make good hand weights for arm exercises. So do hand-size bottles or cans of soft drink. (Don't open them immediately after use.) Holding the weight in each hand at your sides, alternately raise each arm to shoulder level.
- Squeeze a tennis ball or tightly rolled-up pair of socks in each hand to strengthen your grip.
- To stretch your calves, sit on the floor with your legs straight, loop a bath towel around the ball of one foot, and pull, resisting with your foot; repeat with the other foot.
- For ankle weights, fill socks with dry sand, dry rice, dried lentils or beans, or clean cat litter. Weigh them (start with 2lb/900g) and tie them shut, leaving

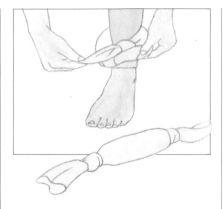

enough room in the toe to fasten the weight round your ankles.

Lie on your back, with one knee bent and the other leg straight, making sure your lower back is flat on the floor. Raise the straight leg as high as you can. Switch the position of both legs and repeat.

- Stand, holding a towel above your head, and pull on the ends so that you bend sideways at the waist. Repeat, bending the other way. Don't lean back or forward as you bend.
- Rest your ankle on the back of a chair at hip height, keeping the leg straight. Bend forward, getting your face as close to your knee and your hands as close to your ankle as possible; hold for 5 seconds. Repeat with the other leg.
- If you're not doing somersaults, a bath or beach towel on a rug or a folded cotton or wool blanket will work just fine as an exercise mat.
- Or exercise on a firm mattress, preferably one resting on a bedboard, a platform bed or the floor.

Exercising gently

If you're chair-bound

- Raise first one arm, then the other straight up over your head. With both arms overhead, reach for the sky with your right hand, then your left. Repeat five times on each side, then relax.
- Let your head fall forward. Slowly tilt it to the right, then to the left, and back to the front. Repeat in the reverse direction. Don't force the action, and *never* tilt your head back.
- Shrug your shoulders high, then let

them drop; repeat four times. Pull them back, then push them forward four times.

- With your feet firmly on the floor about 12in/300mm apart, hold your arms straight out in front of you. Bend forward as far as you can, stretching out your arms. Return to the starting position. Twist to the right and bend as far as you can, then to the left. Repeat.
- Hold the seat of your chair. Raise your right leg from the knee, wiggle your toes and move your foot in a circle, first one way, then the other. Return the right foot to the floor and repeat with the left leg.
- Raise one knee as high as you can, then let it drop and raise the other. Repeat this action as vigorously as you are able to, 'marching' in place ten times.

If you're bedridden

- Lie on your back on a firm mattress. Raise your head; with your chin close to your chest, turn your head slowly from side to side.
- Lie on your back with your arms comfortably at your sides. Raise your right arm, cross it over your face, then return it to your side. Repeat with your left arm, three to five times each.
- Lie on your left side, with your legs straight, your head resting on your left arm, and your right hand flat on the mattress at chest level. Bend your right knee and pull it up towards your chest. Hold it there, resting on the mattress, for 2 to 3 minutes. Then roll over and repeat the action with the left leg.

Exercising on the go

- Whenever possible, walk, jog or cycle to work. Carry your work shoes in a bag. (You can even carry a change of clothes in a small backpack.)
- If you take a bus or train, get off 1 mile/1.6km before your stop and walk the rest of the way.
- Use the stairs, not the lift or escalator.
- Walk a mile/1.6km before eating lunch.

While watching television

- Ride an exercise bike, bounce on a mini-trampoline, skip with a rope or run in place while watching your favourite programmes.

While on the telephone
• Use wrist and ankle weights to do leg lifts and arm raises while you're talking on the phone (see EXERCISE EQUIPMENT, opposite).

While doing housework
• Warm up with a light activity such as dusting or washing dishes, then proceed to vigorous vacuuming, sweeping or floor polishing for 20 to 30 minutes. Upbeat music may help to keep you moving.
• To pick up light items from the floor, stand with your feet apart, arms at your sides. Bend slowly from the waist until you reach the floor, flexing your knees if you have to. Count to ten before straightening slowly, lifting your head last.
• To dust a high shelf, stand with your feet apart and hold the duster in both hands, bending from side to side to wield it.

While at your desk
• While reading, put your foot through the handle of your handbag or briefcase; lift until your leg is horizontal. Repeat ten times without touching the floor. Then do it again with the other foot.
• While sitting, lean slightly forward, grip the sides of your chair and raise your knees alternately to your chest. See also OFFICE EXERCISES, p. 144.

Extension leads

Be careful when you choose an extension lead. Just because it happens to have a multiple socket end, don't think this means that it can carry more amperage than the outlet it's plugged into. A 3 amp plug carries 720 watts maximum.
• Be aware that the longer the lead, the greater the amperage drop. A 100 ft/30 m lead, for example, has to be heavier than a 10 ft/3 m lead performing the same task.
• If an extension lead feels warm, consider that a stern warning. Replace it with a heavier lead or unplug an appliance or two from the multiple socket.

Exterior sealants

• There are no substitutes for good-quality sealants to fill gaps around window and door frames. Putty and cement mortar, which were once used by many builders, should be raked out when they show signs of deteriorating; the cavities should be brushed clean, then filled with an exterior grade sealant.
• Where gaps are deep, use tubed sealant in a cartridge gun and force sealant deep into the holes. Bring the sealant a little higher than the surface, then smooth with a wet finger.
• Where gaps are shallow, use a mastic supplied in strip form. Merely peel off the protective strip and press the sealant in place, smoothing it with your finger.
• When you cut off the nozzle from a tube, keep it as a cap for the nozzle; merely reverse the cut-off piece and push it in the end of the nozzle.
• With awkward-to-reach holes, such as where waste pipes come from an external wall, use a modern expanding foam filler, supplied in pressurised cans. Direct the nozzle deep into the cavity and allow foam to fill the void. It will expand to many times its original volume, then set. It may then be trimmed with a knife. A serrated kitchen knife is ideal.
• If you find fine hairline gaps between putty and window or glazed door frames, but the putty is sound, clean out any dirt with the point of a knife; make sure the surface is dry, then seal the cracks with clear silicone rubber sealant of the type used for sealing around baths and basins. This is highly adhesive and will stick to the glass. And it will remain flexible even when set.
• Sealant will not normally stick to damp surfaces. If you encounter damp, dry the surface with a hot-air paint-stripper, using it rather like a powerful hair dryer. Keep it well back from the surface so you don't damage paintwork or crack glass.

Eye problems

Sties A sore lump on the edge of your eyelid is a sty. Apply a hot, wet compress several times a day to bring it to a head, then allow it to burst. Avoid squeezing. If it remains for several weeks, see a doctor.

Red eye A bright red blotch in the white of your eye is usually a harmless haemorrhage caused by coughing, choking or rubbing the eye. It should disappear by itself in about a week; if it occurs again soon or if you are bruising easily or experiencing headaches, see a doctor.

Pinkeye If one (or both) of your eyes is red, weepy and sticky, you may have pinkeye, or conjunctivitis. Apply an over-the-counter antiseptic eye ointment to the eye, or see your doctor who can prescribe an antibiotic ointment or drops.

The disease is contagious. Wash your hands before and after touching your eyes and keep your towels and flannels separate from those of the rest of the family. Women should throw out all their old eye makeup. (Replace with new products once the infection is over.) See a doctor if pain is severe.

If your eyes are red, itchy, weepy and feel sandy but are not sticky, you may have noncontagious pinkeye. This condition may be due to an allergy; use cold compresses to relieve the itching and avoid the allergen if possible. The condition may also be the result of chemical irritation; if so, use eye drops (available without prescription from a chemist), avoid chemicals and make sure you wear goggles while swimming in a chlorinated pool.

Burned eyes If you burn your eyes, wash them out with copious amounts of tap water or eye wash immediately. Then ask someone to put moist and preferably sterile pads over your eyes and secure with a bandage (at a pinch, you can use a wad of toilet roll, a handkerchief or any other clean soft cloth in place of a sterile pad). Then seek medical help right away.

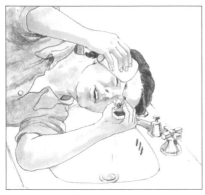

Foreign bodies in eyes
• Even an infinitesimal foreign object – a speck of soot or a grain of sand – can irritate your eye. If you refrain from rubbing it, your tears may wash the object away.
• If an object is on the white of the eye or under the lower lid, irrigate your eye gently with sterile water, if available; otherwise, use tap water. Tilt your head and pour from the inner corner of the eye so that the water drains down towards the outer corner and out. A small, irritating scratch may remain after the object has been removed.
• If the object doesn't wash out, it may be stuck to or embedded in the eye. Don't try to remove it; seek medical help.
• If the object is under the upper eyelid, grasp the lashes with your thumb and forefinger and fold them up over the tip of a cotton bud. If you can see the object, remove it with a moist, sterile cotton bud. Or you can try pulling the upper eyelid down over the lower one – the lower lid lashes should brush the foreign body off.
Change in vision If all or part of what you see suddenly appears hazy, blurry, wavy or distorted; if you see sudden flashes of light; if you experience a sudden partial or complete loss of vision, however brief, see your doctor or optician without delay. You may require urgent treatment.

Eyestrain
Prevention
• Do not position your computer screen under a bright fluorescent light or opposite a window.
• Install an antiglare screen; reduce blur by cleaning it often and tuning the display so that there is a high contrast between the words and background.
• When reading or writing, light should come from over your shoulder – the right shoulder if you're left-handed, the left shoulder if you're right-handed.
• Turn on a low light when watching television and sit directly in front of the screen, 6-7 ft / 1.8-2 m away.
• Wear polarised sunglasses in sunlight, particularly when sunbathing, boating, skiing or driving long distances.
Relief
• If your eyes feel tired and ache after prolonged close work, refresh them by refocusing on a distant object for several seconds.
• Whenever possible, rest your eyes for 15 minutes every hour or so.

F

Fabric care
• Read and follow all care labels. If you buy fabric, make a note of its content and use only those cleaning agents recommended as safe for it.
• Wash or clean all the pieces of a matched set together every time – the jacket and the trousers, all the living room loose covers, all the bedroom curtains and so on. Exceptions are sets in which one piece is a solid colour and the other a print.
• Bleach generally whitens and brightens a washable fabric, but check the label to see whether chlorine or a milder bleach is called for. Permanent-press white fabrics, for example, often yellow when exposed to a chlorine bleach.
• Always remove stains before washing or tell the dry cleaner where and what

the stains are. Light-coloured liquids such as ginger ale and perfume may leave no mark but in time or with heat may turn brown and stubborn. Blot up food spills on washable fabrics at once and sponge from the wrong side with soda water. Wash or dry-clean the article promptly.

Facial hair
Some people are bothered by their facial hair, particularly if it is dark or thick. There are several ways of removing it.
• You can neaten and shape unruly eyebrows by plucking out stray hairs with tweezers. Clean the skin area first and then pluck out the stray hairs one by one, pulling in the direction that they grow. Never pluck out hairs from above the eyebrows, but always from underneath them.
• Dark, but sparse, facial hair can be bleached with an appropriate cosmetic bleach, which is available from a chemist. Follow the manufacturer's instructions and always test the bleach on a small patch of skin first, in case you are allergic to it.
• Thicker facial hair can be removed with a proprietary facial depilatory cream. Do not use any other types of depilatory cream on your face because they are too harsh. Again, test the cream first on a small patch of skin, in case you are allergic to it. Never use the cream on your eyebrows or near your eyes.

Some men, particularly those with darker skins, find that shaving causes ingrown hair and bumps on the surface of their skin. Facial depilatory creams alleviate these problems and make shaving less painful.
• Facial strip wax can be used on chin, upper lip and eyebrow hairs. Smooth it on in the direction of the hair growth and wait for the time specified in the instructions before ripping it off. Never wax after a hot bath or shower, or over broken or inflamed skin, warts, moles or scars.
• Electrolysis is a more permanent way of removing unwanted hair. It involves passing an electric current through the hair follicle, which destroys the root, and

must be done by a professional electro-lysist. However, it is the most expensive and painful means of hair removal and is not always successful.

Family relationships

Keep the family close – even if grand-parents live quite a way away.
• Start a new photograph album at the beginning of each year. Add witty captions underneath. And include pictures sent by distant relatives.
• Keep a scrapbook of notes, photographs and birthday cards from aunts, uncles and other relatives to remind children of happy relationships.
• When youngsters leave home, give them a scrapbook to pass on to their own children.
• Draw up a family tree (the reference library might help you with sources).
• Write down stories (or record them on tape) to remind children about ancestors who have led unusual or interesting lives.

Fashions

• No matter what the latest fashion is, ignore it until you determine what basic lines and colours suit you. If you can't tell by spending some time in front of a mirror, ask a friend for an honest opinion.
• Experiment with colour. Hold fabric swatches next to your face to see which colours are most flattering. Don't be a slave to fashion – if this year's colours don't look good on you, don't wear them.
• To play it safe, choose classic styles for expensive items such as coats; go trendy with less costly separates and sportswear.
• An alternative to making a big commitment to this year's styles is to follow the fashions only with accessories: shoes, belt, bags and jewellery. Scarves in particular can give clothes a fashionable lift. You can make them out of any light-weight fabric, new or old, and tie them at your neck or waist, or use them as head-bands or shawls.
• For a budget fashion accessory, make a

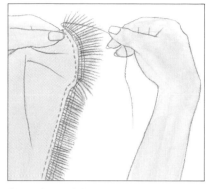

fringed scarf from a length of fabric. Loosen a thread at the edge of the fabric and pull it away along the scarf's end. For a longer fringe, remove more threads in the same way.

Fastening to external walls

Items that are fixed to external walls, such as one end of a garden clothes line or a gate post, need very strong fixings. Usually, special devices called Rawl bolts or expansion bolts are used on solid walls. These are made of metal and expand, exerting great pressure when a bolt is tightened into them. Various types are available, some with bolt heads and others with hooks or eyes. The holes involved are larger than those for wall plugs, so you may have to borrow a larger masonry drill or a hand-held star drill and a club hammer.

Fastening to interior walls

• Brick walls are the simplest to fix things to. If covered with plaster, remember that the plaster itself has no strength, so your fixing must go into the solid masonry beneath.
   Drill a hole with a masonry drill, having decided on the size of screw and wall plug you'll need. The three are related, and many plug packs incorporate a simple gauge to help you relate all three items. The hole should be slightly deeper than the length of plug and the plug should be a tight fit so that it doesn't turn in the hole as you screw.
• Walls made of concrete blocks are often fairly soft or have a coarse open

structure; use special wall plugs for fixing shelves.
• Many modern internal walls are constructed of plasterboard sheets nailed to timbers, or of special hollow partitioning consisting of two sheets of plasterboard separated by a honeycomb divider and supported internally with timbers. Plasterboard itself is not strong enough to take any form of screw, so a special hollow fixing device is needed to form an anchored wall plug into which the screw can be driven. There are various types, from those that are lost if the item fixed is removed, to those that are held in place by a special strip. Check this point when buying them.
• Where a very heavy cabinet is to be fixed to a hollow partition, use heavy-duty wall anchors. In addition, locate two convenient vertical timbers inside the wall and screw a horizontal batten to them on which you can rest the cabinet. You can locate the hidden timbers with a stud or timber-seeking tool. Usually this is a combination tool which will find metals and supporting timbers hidden in a surface. It indicates either by noise, by a light or by both.

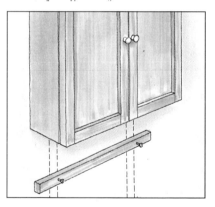

Fastening to metal

• When fixing to metal sheet, drill holes into the metal and use special self-tapping screws which cut their own thread in the prepared holes.
• An alternative to screws is the pop rivet, used with a pair of riveting pliers.
• For fixing items such as wing mirrors on car bodies, there are special fixing devices called Rawl nuts. When inserted

in a hole in the metal, the rubber body of the device expands behind the metal as the bolt is tightened, producing a cushioned and watertight fixing.

Fastening to wood

• Use woodscrews (either single-slot or cross-slot) to fix objects directly onto wood. The cross slot is safer when working with decorated surfaces, as the screwdriver cannot slide out of the slot and mark the surface.

• When screwing two pieces of wood together, always try to screw the thinner piece to the thicker one.

• Drill a clearance hole in the top piece to take the screw shank. Drill a smaller hole in the lower piece to give the screw thread a start. Then use a countersinking bit to countersink the top piece if the heads of the screws are to sit flush with the wood surface.

• When working with hardwoods, always drill holes into them first to prevent splitting.

• When working with chipboards, use special chipboard screws designed to get a better grip without splitting the material.

• When fixing into veneered chipboard, it helps to sink a wall plug into the edge of the board, locating the plug so that the expansion of the plug will be along the board, not across it.

• When screwing into the end grain of timber, you get a very weak anchorage. You can improve this by inserting a piece of dowel into the wood so that the screw enters this when driven home. Make a start-hole in the dowel in order to avoid splitting it.

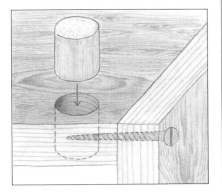

Faulty goods

• Avoid the problems by choosing and shopping carefully. Before buying larger items, do some research. Read such magazines as *Which?* in your local library. Many products are unsatisfactory because people purchase the wrong model or have unreasonable expectations. Remember that, while we all want a bargain, you will essentially get what you pay for. Always buy from a reputable shop.

• Before buying, always seek the advice of the trader as to the expected life of the item. If he seems not to know, go elsewhere. Before you buy, read the instructions and ensure there is a full guarantee.

• Remember that you must try out new goods straight away. If they are faulty, act immediately. If you delay you may lose your rights.

• If you have a legitimate complaint, go back to the shop where you bought the goods. The faulty goods should be replaced or you should be given back your money. Don't accept a repair unless the shop will lend you a replacement item while yours is away.

• If you get no satisfaction from the shop, try writing to the manufacturer identifying the problem and the shop. Enclose copies (but not the originals) of the purchase receipt and warranty. It may be easier simply to take advantage of the manufacturer's guarantee, anyway.

• Lastly, consult your local Citizens Advice Bureau or Trading Standards Department. See also REFUNDS, p.169; CONSUMER CAVEATS; p.243; and USEFUL ADDRESSES, p.422.

Fences

• The cheapest form of fencing is galvanised or plastic-coated netting supported on galvanised wires anchored to posts. The secret is to strain the wires really tight, and for this buy special wire-straining bolts which pull the wire taut as the nuts are tightened. The posts must be very well anchored.

• A fence of open palings is sufficient to divide off a garden and offers little resistance to the wind, so is unlikely to be damaged even in severe storms.

• A woven panel fence offers privacy, but has no great strength. So in exposed areas of high winds, it is best not to go above about 5ft/1.5m. The legal limit is 6ft/1.8m and then it is best to use slotted concrete posts into which the panels slide. In high winds the panels may be forced out, but without damaging the structure of the fence.

• Concrete posts are the most trouble-free, but if you want to use timber, select pre-treated posts which have been impregnated with preservative.

• To treat your own posts, make up a simple trough with two rows of bricks and a sheet of 500 gauge polythene. Fill the trough with preservative. Lower in the posts and weigh them down with bricks and leave to soak overnight. Superficial brush applications of preservative have very limited effect.

• Protect the tops of wooden posts with timber caps screwed or nailed in place. It is the ends of posts where the damp is most likely to soak in.

• Horizontal fence supports, called arris rails, often rot where the rail enters the post. You can buy special galvanised support brackets that screw to both rail and post, making a strong repair. The brackets can also be adapted to suit concrete posts (see p.180).

• Give your timber fencing an annual coating of wood preservative. More and more environmentally friendly preservatives are appearing in the shops; being water-based, they don't harm plant life.

• If you have trellis topping a fence, prevent roses from twining through the trellis because eventually they destroy the slats. Rather, tie them to the surface of the trellis.

Fertilising the organic way

• Mow regularly to keep grass clippings short. Leaving the clippings in place, as a mulch every third clipping not only saves the trouble of raking them but also returns nutrients to the soil.

• Prepare your lawn with a spray of biodegradable liquid detergent (5 fl oz/150 ml in 10 gallons/45.5 litres of water for every 1500 sq ft/140 m² of turf) to reduce surface tension in the soil and allow fertilisers to penetrate more effectively. Apply to dry ground.

• To rebuild garden soil naturally, plant a 'green manure'. Agricultural lupin, a legume that manufactures its own nitrogen fertiliser, is a good choice.

• Blood, fish and bone meal are good organic fertilisers that you mix into the topsoil before planting. They act slower than chemical fertilisers but last longer.

Old-time fertilisers

Before the development of today's powerful synthetic fertilisers, gardeners made do with what they found around the house and farm. Animal manure was widely used, as was human waste from privvies and potties, which was known as night soil. Large quantities of night soil were shipped out of the cities and into the surrounding countryside on canal barges.

Gardeners who lived near the coast harvested seaweed to dig directly into the soil; the high salt content killed weeds and hastened decomposition.

Until recently, guano (the accumulated droppings of sea-birds and bats) was imported from Peru, used as a fertiliser because of its high content of nitrogen and phosphorus.

Bones, too, have long been used, although bone meal of the past enriched the soil far more than today's.

Fever

Except in a very young or a very old person, a fever up to 38.5°C/101°F is not ordinarily serious; aspirin or paracetamol (see p.13) will usually bring it down to the normal 37°C/98.6°F. In the meantime, get plenty of rest in a warm, not hot, room and drink lots of fluids, such as fruit juice, non-fizzy soft drinks, water and broth. If body temperature rises higher than 39°C/102°F, get someone to sponge you, or sponge the patient, with tepid water, and consult a doctor.

Contact your doctor if a child is in pain or drowsy and unresponsive, or if the fever persists for more than a few days.

Files and rasps

Files and rasps are used for rubbing down wood or metal prior to fine-finishing – files are generally used for metalwork and rasps for woodwork.

• Avoid files sold without handles, because the shaft of a file can easily damage your hand while you're using the file.

• You can use a shaping tool instead of a wood rasp. This has a slotted blade which quickly cuts away the timber. The design of the blade makes it very safe to use.

• Another form of rasp is the coarse abrasive sheet made from tungsten carbide granules bonded to a metal sheet. Use it like a sanding block to shape wood.

• Always work a rasp towards the centre of the ends of a piece of timber. This will make sure that the wood does not split away at the corners.

Fingernails

• If you don't have an emery board, smooth a jagged nail against the side of a matchbox.

• Wear two coats of nail polish on weak nails to give protection, applying a new transparent top coat every day until the next manicure. It is better to touch up nails than to keep on using nail varnish remover.

• Clean very grubby nails by washing some clothes; or mix 1 tablespoon of detergent or soap with 1 teaspoon of hydrogen peroxide and apply to the nail with a cotton bud or cotton wool wrapped round an orange stick.

• To remove excess nail enamel neatly, use a cotton bud (or use cotton wool wrapped round an orange stick) dipped into nail varnish remover.

• Get rid of the smell of food on your fingers by rubbing them with dry mustard, then washing them in cold water.

• Remove stains with lemon juice, then rub gently with pumice; apply hand cream afterwards.

Fire damage

• Photograph or videotape all damage immediately after a fire to document the extent of the fire.

• If your home is not habitable, tell the police that you will be absent from it. Remove valuables and important documents where possible.

• If firemen have broken doors or windows, have them boarded up securely. Glaziers who operate a 24-hour emergency service are listed in the Yellow Pages and local Thomson Directory, or enquire at your local police station for contacts. Local councils may provide this service for their tenants. You will probably not be able to claim this expense against your insurance policy.

• If temporary repairs are necessary to prevent further damage, such as stopping rain coming through the roof, have these done immediately, and keep the bill for insurance purposes. Don't make any permanent repairs without sending the quotes first to your insurance company.

• Contact an insurance claim consultant or public adjuster to assist you with your insurance claim.

• Collect receipts for all costs related to your fire damage.

• If you are able to live in your home, do not reconnect the gas or electricity or turn on any water until the gas and electricity boards and a plumber have checked pipes and fittings.

• Move damaged household goods to a

safe place so that the insurance adjuster can inspect them.

• Use fans, blowers or dehumidifiers to dry out the house. If the weather is warm, keep windows open as much as possible to ventilate your home.

• Move all rugs and carpets (and their padding) outdoors to dry and get rid of smells. Or hire wet/dry vacuum cleaners from a cleaning or equipment hire company. If the task is too great, use a specialist cleaning company.

• Clean walls and ceilings with sugar soap or a mild detergent. Do not paint until they are thoroughly dry.

• Wipe down wood furniture and leave it to dry, before applying wood polish. Vacuum loose sooty residue from upholstery and all horizontal surfaces. Or use a specialist cleaning company.

• Don't let wet fabrics dry where they are. Move them to an undamaged room to dry at room temperature.

• Transfer art, books and other porous valuables to a freezer (if yours is too small, try a local frozen-food company) until you can hire specialists to restore them.

• Discard all food, drinks and medicines that have been exposed to high heat or otherwise damaged.

• When fridges and freezers have defrosted, wash them with an ammonia or vinegar solution before rinsing with clean water to remove any smell. Let them dry naturally.

• Send clothing to a dry cleaner who will give it specialist treatment; improper cleaning methods can fix the smell of smoke permanently.

Fire extinguishers

There are two different categories of fire – Class A and Class B – which depend on the materials that are burning. Class A fires involve solids, such as wood, cloth, paper, plastic and coal. Class B fires involve liquids, such as grease, fats, oil, paint and petrol.

Different types of extinguisher are needed to put out the different types of fire. You need to choose them according to the possible fire risks in your home. If you are unsure about the type of fire

blanket or extinguisher to buy, ask the advice of your local fire brigade.

• Fire blankets, which are made of a fire-retardant material, are best kept in the kitchen. There they can smother burning oil, chip-pan fires and a person's clothing which has caught alight. They must conform to British Standard BS 6575 and be at least 3 × 3 ft / 90 × 90 cm. Few can be used again after putting out a fire. Since many fires in the home begin in the kitchen, if you can't afford any other sort of extinguisher elsewhere in the house, this is where you should definitely have one.

• A multipurpose dry powder extinguisher is best for solids and liquids, but must not be used on chip pan fires. It can also be used on live electrical equipment. It knocks down flames and melts on burning solids to form a smothering skin.

• An aqueous film-forming foam (AFFF) extinguisher is equally good for Class A and Class B fires but must not be used on chip pan fires. It works by forming a film on the burning surface which extinguishes the flames and has a cooling effect.

• A Halon 1211 (also known as BCF) extinguisher is best for Class B fires except chip pan fires, and Class A fires in a small area. It is also effective on live electrical equipment and is ideal for use in cars. However, it does not cool fires efficiently and the flames may start up again. Also, its fumes can be harmful in confined spaces or when used on metal. Ventilate the area well after the fire has been put out.

• Water extinguishers are good for cooling burning material and will put out Class A fires, but they must not be used on live electrical equipment or on Class B fires.

• Carbon dioxide extinguishers smother flames by displacing the oxygen in the air, and are best for Class B fires except chip pan fires. They can also be used on live electrical appliances but must not be used on Class A fires. One disadvantage, however, is that they do not cool very well and the fire may start up again. The fumes can also be harmful in confined spaces.

Fireplace mess

• Keep a hearth brush with your poker and shovel to make it easier to sweep up little bits and pieces of bark, coal and firewood.

• Remove ashes from the fireplace as soon as they're cold to prevent them being spread throughout the rest of your home. With the damper closed, gently sweep up as much as possible into a dustpan. To make the job easier next time, spread aluminium foil beneath the grate; when the ashes are cold, simply gather up the foil and discard it.

• Vacuum the fireplace occasionally, using the crevice tool to clean out the corners. Wipe the andirons with a damp cloth or buff them with a metal cleaner.

Fireplaces

Fireplaces are inefficient because most of the heat rises up the chimney. In fact, the heated house air may go with it, making the house even colder than it would have been without the fire.

• Think of installing an enclosed wood-burning stove with an adjustable air vent over the fireplace opening; this gives the fire enough air to burn while controlling the loss of heated air. Close the air vent whenever the fireplace is not in use and before leaving the room.

• Raise efficiency another notch by putting in a cast-iron plate, many of which are decorated at the back of an open firebox. It reflects heat into the room.

Fires

If you decide to put out a small fire, get everyone else out of the house and then position yourself between the fire and your escape route. If after 2 minutes you can neither contain nor extinguish the flames, or if your extinguisher runs out, don't waste critical time. Close the doors and windows to confine the flames, gases and smoke, get out of the house, and call the fire brigade. Never try to extinguish a fire that has spread to other items in the room or if the room is filling with smoke.

Chip pan fires

• Don't touch the pan, and turn off the heat if you can.

• Wrap your hands in a tea towel to protect them and place a damp cloth, lid or fire blanket over the pan.

• Leave the pan for at least 30 minutes to cool sufficiently so that the fire doesn't start up again.

• *Never* use water or any kind of extinguisher, except a fire blanket, to douse a chip-pan fire.

Furniture fires

• If it's a small fire, use an AFFF (see opposite) or water extinguisher.

• If the fire is burning fiercely or producing a lot of smoke, get out and shut the door. Burning upholstered furniture can produce extremely poisonous fumes and the flames can spread very quickly.

Curtain fires

• If it's safe to do so, douse with an AFFF, water or multipurpose dry powder extinguisher. If you're in any doubt, leave the room quickly and close the door – fires in curtains spread very quickly.

• Once the fire is out, check the curtains to make sure they are not smouldering. When it is safe, pull down the curtains.

Paraffin-heater fires

• Leave the heater where it is. If possible disconnect any electrical appliances nearby. Use a water, AFFF, multi-purpose dry powder or halon 1211 extinguisher. After the flames are out, keep an eye on the heater – the heat of the metal may make the fire flare up again.

Gas-appliance fires

• Call the fire brigade immediately and tell them a gas fire has started.

• Turn off the gas supply at the main stop valve.

• When the gas has stopped flowing, extinguish other burning materials. *Do not* try to extinguish a gas fire until the gas supply has stopped flowing – this would risk an explosion.

Making an escape

• If you can, get out of the room where the fire has started. Close the door, and close all other doors behind you.

• Before opening a closed door, test it with the back of your hand for warmth. Do not open it if it feels hot or if smoke is

seeping out from under it, because this means there is fire on the other side.

• Get everyone out of the house, if they have not already vacated it. Don't try to find or pick up your valuables or any other possessions. Get out quickly, staying low if there's smoke – smoke can also kill.

• If you're in bed when the smoke alarm goes off, roll out and crawl to the door. If the door is not hot, proceed as above. If possible, cover your mouth and nose with a damp cloth.

• If your exit is blocked by fire, close the door nearest the smoke and fill in the gap along the bottom with towels or sheets to stop the smoke from seeping in. Open the window and try to attract someone's attention; tell them to call the fire brigade. If smoke is in the room, crouch down at floor level – this will make it easier to breathe. Wait for the fire brigade.

• If you are in immediate danger, drop bedding, a mattress or cushions onto the ground to soften your fall. Get out feet first, turn round and hang by your hands to the full length of your arms before dropping to the ground. If you must break a window, use a chair or drawer – anything but your hands.

Burning clothes

• Make the victim lie down quickly to prevent the flames from spreading up to his face.

• If cold water is available nearby, and an electrical fire is not involved and neither you nor the victim are near an electrical heater, use the water to douse the flames and cool the burns.

• If you would have to fetch water, or water would be dangerous, find another

way of smothering the flames – use a fire blanket, blanket or rug to wrap around the victim. Once the flames have died down, check that there is no smouldering material and then call an ambulance.

• If your clothes are on fire, get down to the floor immediately and roll your body over and back until the flames are out. Cover yourself with a blanket and call for an ambulance.

Fire safety

• Fit smoke alarms on each floor of your home and in rooms where a fire is likely to start, such as the sitting room or bedroom. Don't fit one in a kitchen as steam or cooking fumes may set it off.

• Be prepared for the event of a fire and plan your escape route. Draw a plan of your home (including stairs, windows, and doors) and plot two escape routes from each room. Study the plan with household members; assign someone to help children or the less agile.

• Display the fire emergency number near telephones.

• Make sure everyone who may need to use a window for escape is able to reach and unlock it, and reach the ground easily. Check the safety of a porch or garage roof that may provide an escape.

• Hold regular fire drills and designate a place to meet outside for a head count.

• Every month check that your fire blanket or extinguisher is in place and has not been used or damaged. Get your non-aerosol extinguishers serviced once a year by specialists, and replace aerosol extinguishers as suggested by the manufacturer.

• Always switch off electric blankets before getting into bed.

Fires in public places

• Note the location of the fire exits whenever you visit a public building, no matter how brief the visit.

• In the event of a fire, do not use the lift unless it is designated as a means of escape. If in doubt, consult the fire instructions displayed in the building.

• In hotels and motels, check the fire

safety instructions immediately after checking into your room. Familiarise yourself with the escape routes, fire exits and location of the fire alarm call points.

• Keep low to avoid the smoke.

Firewood

• For the hottest, cleanest fire, burn hardwoods rather than softwoods. Apple, beech, oak and silver birch produce the most heat. For a pleasing scent, throw a pine log or two onto the fire.

• Brittle frozen logs are the easiest to split. But don't use a frozen axe; the steel may crack.

• Use a forked branch as a prop if you have trouble keeping a log upright on the chopping block.

• If you have a lot of wood to split, save time and muscle by renting a power saw; they're available at low daily rates and do the job in a fraction of the time.

• If you don't have a woodshed, stack the split wood in layers alternating in direction. Store the wood bark side up so that it sheds rain.

• Save money by buying bark cuttings and warped boards from a timber yard.

• Tightly roll a stack of newspapers to log size and tie the roll with string. (Avoid colour pages; the ink may release chemicals.) These 'logs' may lack the romance of glowing embers, but they burn cleanly and last almost as long as hardwood.

Fireworks

Strict regulations control the public use of fireworks. Find out what they are from your local fire brigade and inform them, the police and a local first aid organi-

sation of the date and time of your fireworks display.

• You need enough space for your display – at least 60 × 50yds/55 × 45m. The spectators must be kept at least 27yds/25m away from the fireworks and separated from them by a strong rope or barrier. No more than three people should be allowed into the display area, and then only to set off the fireworks.

• Buy only labelled, top-quality fireworks; store in a cool, dry place, in a metal or wooden box well away from all flammable materials.

• Have fire extinguishers, buckets of water and sand ready nearby to put out any fires.

• Light fireworks outdoors, one at a time, in an open area, and light them at arm's length. Don't smoke while handling fireworks.

• Never ignite a firecracker indoors or in a tin or a bottle.

• Aim rockets and set off Roman candles or Catherine wheels away from people and houses.

• Never pick up a 'dud' for at least half an hour; it could explode at any moment.

• Don't use petrol or paraffin to light the bonfire. Once it is finished, make sure it has been put out completely.

• Don't let children collect spent firework cases when the display is over.

Waterworks As a summer alternative to fireworks, present a night-time display of colourful waterworks to amuse your children and their friends. Ask the youngsters to wear swimsuits and hand out flashlights covered with coloured cellophane. Turn on your sprinklers (if

locally permissible), then light up the water as it sprays in all directions; play recorded marches – or Tchaikovsky's 1812 Overture, which actually ends with cannon fire.

Fish bait

• When you are fishing, you can substitute cheese balls, bread balls or pieces of sausage meat for live bait. A bit of frayed aluminium foil makes a convincing minnow.

• Ensure a steady supply of bait by starting your own worm farm. Line a wooden box 2-3ft/610-910mm long with leaves and grass and fill it halfway with soil. Add another layer of dry grass and leaves and 1 pint/570ml or so of compost – coffee grounds and vegetables that rot quickly, chopped together. Top with a final layer of leaves and wet the mixture down before adding the worms. Feed the worms monthly with compost and sour milk and they'll multiply rapidly. If you keep maggots for a few days, they will turn into chrysalises, or casters, which are good as hookbait.

• Alternatively, place a large wet sack on a grassy area for a few days. Keep the sack moist. When you lift it there will be worms on the undersurface. Collect them quickly – they will burrow below the ground very fast.

• Garden worms can be collected in the early morning from grassy areas, particularly if there has been a heavy downpour in the night. Or you can collect them at night with a torch.

• Grubs and mealworms also make good bait. You can raise mealworms by filling a jar three-quarters full of flour mixed with sawdust. Put in the mealworms and punch tiny holes in the lid. Don't be surprised when you see that the mealworms, which are actually beetle larvae, have matured inside the jar into full-grown beetles. They will, in turn, produce more mealworms.

• Freeze unused minnows. But don't defrost them completely when you use them again or they'll be too soggy to stay on your hook.

• Other, less usual baits include sweetcorn kernels, for use in still waters and rivers, and fruit such as elderberries, redcurrants and blackcurrants and pieces of banana.

Fish cleaning

• Before cleaning a fish, wash it well under cold water and pat dry with paper towels.

• Using scissors, cut off the fins. If the fish are scaly, remove the scales with the back of a small knife or with a fish scaling knife. Hold the fish firmly by the tail, then scrape the knife from the tail end down to the head. To prevent the scales of larger fish flying all over the kitchen, place the fish inside a large polythene bag and scrape it in the bag.

• To remove the entrails of round fish, such as trout, salmon, mackerel and herring, insert the tip of a sharp-pointed knife at the tail end of the fish and slit it right along the belly up to the head, then simply pull out and discard the entrails.

• Rinse the fish once again under cold water and pat dry. Any fine black membrane that remains inside the fish can easily be removed by rubbing it with a little fine salt.

• Flat and round fish bought from most fishmongers will be cleaned already.

Fish filleting

• If you want to skin flat fish, such as plaice, sole and turbot, before filleting, it's best to pull the skin off from the tail and right down to the head in one go. Make a small cut across the skin at the tail end and lever up a flap of skin with the point of the knife. Then, holding the

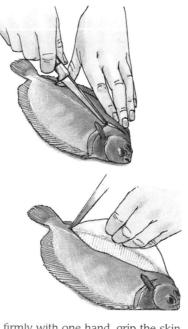

tail firmly with one hand, grip the skin with the other hand and pull it off down to the head. Repeat on the second side.

• To fillet flat fish, use a very sharp flexible filleting knife to make a deep cut right along the centre of one side of the fish, cutting right down to the bones. Then, keeping the knife close to the bones, work from the centre outwards to the fins and remove one fillet.

Remove the second fillet in the same way. Then turn the fish over and repeat on the other side.

• To remove the fillets from round fish, make a deep cut along the back of the fish to the bones. Carefully cut down one side of the fish, keeping the knife close to the bones. Repeat on the other side.

• To remove skin from filleted fish, lay the fillet out flat on a board with the skin side down. Using a sharp knife, separate a little of the flesh from the skin at the tail end. Then, holding the skin firmly with one hand, cut the flesh away from the skin using a gentle sawing action from side to side across the skin, taking care not to cut right through the skin.

Fishhook

• Do you need a fishhook? At a pinch, even a small pocketknife can become a hook for a large saltwater fish. Prop the blade partly open with a piece of wood and tie it in place. Use a smaller blade at the other end to form a barb.

• For smaller prey, try a safety pin, wire, bent nail or even a paper clip. Or you can carve a hook from bone or hardwood, binding on a thorn or sharp sliver of wood for a barb.

Fish stories: the ones that didn't get away

The average angler of today, with sophisticated tackle, special lures and all kinds of high-tech equipment, is a far cry from the old image of a person waiting patiently all day for a bite at the worm on the end of his line. Of course, fish still manage to get away, but some that have been caught are record-setters. In June 1937 a common sturgeon weighing 507 lb 8 oz/230 kg and measuring 9 ft/2.74 m long, was netted by accident in the mouth of the Severn; and in 1922 a Miss Ballantine caught the largest salmon ever in Britain in the River Tay in Scotland; it weighed in at an enormous 64 lb/29.05 kg.

Here are some more examples of British all-time monster catches.

Brown trout (cultivated) ....28 lb 1 oz/12.729 kg, Dever Springs, Hants, 1995
Carp ....55 lb 4 oz/25.061 kg, Mid-Northants Fishery, Northants, 1995
Catfish (Wels) ....57 lb 4 oz/25.968 kg, Withy Pool, Beds, 1995
Pike ....46 lb 13 oz/21.234 kg, Llandegfedd, Gwent, 1992
Porbeagle shark......................507 lb/230 kg, Dunnet Head, Highland, 1993
Rainbow trout (cultivated) ..36 lb 14 oz/16.740 kg, Dever Springs, Hants, 1995
Sea trout ....28 lb 5 oz/12.850 kg, River Test, Hants 1992
Tench ....14 lb 7 oz/6.548 kg, private lake, Herts, 1993

Fish poaching

• You don't need a poaching pan to poach fish; your roasting tin will do just as well. Place the fish on the rack, cover with water or stock, and barely simmer for 10 minutes per inch of thickness at the middle.

• To keep a poached fish from breaking as you transfer it from cooking pan to serving dish, cook it on muslin or greased aluminium foil. Cover the rack of the poacher or roasting pan, making sure enough material extends over the edge so that you can get a good grip. Hold the material taut as you lift the fish from the pan and slide or roll it onto a serving dish.

Fish stuffing

• To dress up a fish, stuff it with your own mixtures of chopped mushrooms, herbs, fennel or watercress, bread-crumbs or cheese. Prawns, crabmeat and lobster also make a good filling. If a big enough cavity is left after cleaning, simply stuff the fish and close with skewers or sew shut with heavy-duty thread or fine string.

• When stuffing a round fish such as trout, herring or mackerel, it is better to remove the bones first.

• To bone a herring or mackerel, lay the cleaned fish out flat on a board with the skin side uppermost. Press gently but firmly right along the backbone. Turn the fish over and insert your thumb under the fine bones at one side of the backbone. Run your thumb along under the bones right up to the tail. Repeat on the other side, then lift the bones completely out of the flesh. Cut off at the tail end with scissors.

• To remove the bones from trout and other fine-boned round fish, gently insert the point of a knife under the fine rib bones at the tail end, then carefully work the knife under the bones to free them from the flesh along both sides of the backbone. Then carefully cut around the backbone to free it from the fish, taking care not to cut through the skin. Cut the bones free at the tail and head ends with scissors.

Fish tanks

To keep tropical fish happy, it is important that you change about a third of the water in their tank every week. The simplest way is to make a siphon from an old hose or plastic tubing. Pinch the bottom tightly with your fingers and fill the tube with water from the tap; pinch the top closed and carry it to the tank. Insert one end in the tank and the other in a bucket a few feet or a metre or so below it. The water will flow automatically from the tank to the bucket. When you've removed enough water, refill the tank with water that has been sitting at room temperature for several hours.

To start the siphoning without filling the tube with water, suck sharply on the loose end of the tube before putting it in the bucket. But do this carefully, as it is easy to get a mouthful of fishy water by mistake.

Fitness building

Are you badly out of shape? Recuperating from an illness? Start rebuilding your fitness slowly by walking up and down your road for 2 minutes at a time. Walk 5 days a week, a little longer each time, until you can walk 15 minutes without stopping.

Gradually increase your speed until you can walk a mile/1.6km in 15 minutes. Start your workout by walking slowly until your body is warm; slow

down again towards the end to cool off. Finish with stretches for flexibility (see WARMING-UP AND COOLING-DOWN EXERCISES, p.224). Increase the distance until you're walking 3 miles/5km in less than 45 minutes. This should take about 12 weeks to achieve.

The goal Now you're ready to start jogging, aerobic dancing, rowing or cycling two to four times a week for 30 minutes or so. Or just keep walking; aim for 4-5 miles/6.5-8km at 4 mph/6.5kph – when you reach 20 miles/32km a week, you'll be in good shape.

Ultimately, your heart rate should increase to between 70 and 90 per cent of your maximum rate (calculated by subtracting your age from 220). If you're sedentary, aim to increase your heart rate to 60 per cent of your maximum.

Caution If you're over 35, overweight or have a family history of high blood pressure or heart disease, see a doctor before beginning any exercise.

If at any time you feel an irregular heartbeat or pain or pressure in your chest; if you're dizzy or light-headed or if you vomit during or after exercise; if, after finishing your workout, you can't get your breath back in less than a minute, stop and seek medical help.

To measure the distance you walk, wear a pedometer on your belt or waistband.

Fitness for the elderly

• If you're not exercising regularly, ask your doctor if it would be advisable. If he thinks you should exercise, choose an activity, such as walking, cycling or swimming, that won't cause stress to your joints or tendons – and don't start out too strenuously.

Check with your local Age Concern office or health club for classes in aerobics and callisthenics tailored for older bodies. Whatever exercise you select, in order to reduce the chances of injury, warm up and cool down gradually (p.224).

• If you have difficulty walking or are otherwise disabled, rent or buy exercise cassettes to guide you in less strenuous fitness routines. Or seek out an adult activities centre where a professional instructor leads special exercise sessions.

• To keep fit mentally, stay involved. Church, family and volunteer activities; crafts, puzzles and games; and especially a wide circle of friends – all contribute to sustained mental alertness. If you live alone, adopt a pet, preferably one that's easy to look after. If a dog is too much to handle, consider a cat instead or perhaps a bird or fish.

Fitness while travelling

On an aircraft
• Exercise in your seat (see OFFICE EXERCISES, p.144; EXERCISING GENTLY, p.74).
• Go for a walk up and down the aisles when they are not congested; take the opportunity to stretch and touch your toes.

On a driving trip
• Stop every 2 hours for a good stretch and a 15 minute walkabout.
• If you are stopping for a meal, walk about before sitting down to eat, or while waiting for your food to come.

At high altitudes
• On the first day just take a stroll; after that, do your usual exercises but reduce the time by 15 per cent for each

5000ft/1500m gain in elevation. If it's hot, don't exercise outdoors between 10am and 4pm.

At the hotel
• If there's no exercise room or pool, ask at the desk for a list of local health clubs or get a street map so that you can walk or jog in the area.
• To find an aerobics class, look under 'Health clubs and fitness centres' in the Yellow Pages.
• Is the weather too bad for outdoor exercise? Walk or jog in the hallway. Or stair walk: up for 1 minute, down for 30 seconds.

In your room
• Pack a skipping rope, exercise tape and cassette player.
• Run in place to the morning news or dance to radio music.
• Make sure you stretch for at least 10 minutes morning and night.

Fits

Your companion suddenly becomes rigid and then begins jerking violently – he is having a convulsion. What can you do to help?
• Assist him to the floor or the ground, away from potentially dangerous objects.
• Loosen restrictive clothing.
• Stand by to protect him from injury. Don't try to hold him down or place anything in his mouth. Most people neither bite nor swallow their tongues during a seizure, but they may break or choke on anything that's in their mouth (even objects as large as a small wallet).

A convulsion, whether epileptic or from some other cause, may last from one to several minutes. The victim may dribble or foam at the mouth; his lips and face may turn bluish. He may be rigid for a few seconds.
• After the convulsion is over, remove anything from his mouth. Then keep him resting comfortably on his side, in the recovery position (see p.168), with his head down. This will allow him to breathe easier and to prevent choking.
• A person with epilepsy will usually be able to continue normal activities after a short rest.

Flashing

Flashing is the seal between two adjoining surfaces – such as the joint between a chimney stack and the roof. It can be a weak spot in the defences against damp. Slight movement of a house on its foundations can damage flashings, so regular checking is advisable.

• Check for damage around the chimney stack, using binoculars if you don't have easy and safe access to the roof. If flashing has worked loose from the brickwork, dig out the old pointing and press the flashing tight into the gap, jamming it in place with wedges of lead.
• If flashing has cracked or shows signs of deterioration, clean off any debris, prime with special flashing primer, then apply a strip of self-adhesive flashing tape, pressing it well into place.
• Examine other flashing around dormer windows or where extensions, garages or porches butt up against the house. Repair as above.

Fleas

Attack fleas on two fronts: on your pet and in the house. For every one flea on the pet there will be hundreds of immature fleas in the carpets. Fleas like dark, dusty areas – under sofas and beds are favourite spots.

• Buy a product from your vet to treat the house. The safest and most effective contains a flea hormone – methoprene – that interrupts the life cycle of the flea. Spray the inside of your vacuum-cleaner with this, so that any fleas and larvae will be killed when they are vacuumed up. Respray the new bag when you change it.
• Spray every room that the pets have access to. Do this twice yearly. Concentrate your efforts around the skirting boards, and under low furniture, and then do a big zigzag from one end of the room to the other to treat the carpets. This spray is not too poisonous for humans, but keep children out of the treated room for half a day.
• An anti-flea spray to treat your animals is also available from your vet. This is toxic in large quantities so follow the

instructions on the can carefully. Spray pets outside to reduce the amount of spray you inhale.

• Fit a flea collar to your pet.

Flood damage

• Before dealing with the effects of flooding – whether from an act of nature, a burst pipe or an overflowing bath – be sure to switch off the electricity at the mains.

• Remove standing water with a submersible pump. (If the power is still off, hire a petrol-powered pump.) Then scrape all remaining debris into piles with a squeegee or a 4in/100mm wide strip of ½in/13mm plywood screwed to a broom handle. Shovel the piles of mud and debris into buckets and deposit them outside. If there's a lot of debris, shovel it out into a rubbish bin or wheelbarrow, or hire a skip.

• To dry out a room quickly, place fans at the windows. You can also dry out a room with portable paraffin heaters, which can be rented from a local equipment hire company.

• If trapped water has caused a ceiling to sag, punch drainage holes at the low points with an awl or a small screwdriver, and catch the water in a bucket placed underneath.

Floods

• If your home is susceptible to flooding, consult your local Building Control officer, through the local Planning Department. It may be possible to install land drains that would divert the water away before it affects your home. These are perforated pipes which are set in the ground with a gradual slope leading to a drainage area.

• Ask the local water board if there is a system for flood warnings, and be alert for them.

• Keep a supply of sandbags ready (you can make your own by filling plastic bags with sand or soil) and make sure you always have a stock of emergency supplies, including warm clothing, a portable stove, candles and matches, oil or gas lamps, and a signalling device, such as a torch.

• Photograph and list all your household belongings (see VALUABLES, p.219); keep this inventory safe.

Flood watch

• As soon as you hear of a flood warning, place sandbags outside outer doors to block gaps. If you have none, fill pillowcases or plastic bags or use rolled up carpets or blankets.

• Wash baths, sinks and jugs with household bleach, rinse away the bleach and fill with clean water for drinking.

• Switch off both the electric power and the gas at the mains.

During the flood

• Listen to a portable radio for information and instructions.

• Don't leave your home unless your life is in danger there.

• If the floodwaters rise to window level, sandbag the windowsills. Move your emergency supplies and, if there's time, valuables, to the top floor.

• If you are forced out onto the roof, make sure you are wearing warm clothing and take out sheets or rope to tie yourself to the chimney stack. Take your signalling device with you.

Afterwards

• Check your home for structural damage.

• If you smell gas, open all the doors and windows, leave and report the leak to the gas board.

• Throw out all food touched by floodwaters – it may be contaminated.

• Boil all drinking and cooking water for at least 10 minutes before use. See also FLOOD DAMAGE, left.

Floors

• To remove stains from vinyl flooring, use a detergent that contains ammonia. Scrub lightly with a plastic scouring pad. If that fails, rub lightly with extra-fine (No. 000) steel wool, then polish.

• If you spill nail polish on resilient flooring, allow it to dry until sticky, then peel it off. Clean up any residue with nail polish remover.

• Has chewing gum become stuck to the floor? Put an ice cube in a small cup and turn the cup upside-down over the gum. When the gum is brittle, gently prise it up with a butter knife. On a wood floor, wipe up any melted ice water quickly before it can damage the surface.

• Never clean a wood floor with water; it can cause warping, and even worse, wood rot. Instead, use a dry mop. If necessary, wrap the mop with a damp, soft cloth that's thoroughly wrung out.

Flower arranging

• You can make your own preservative to keep cut flowers fresh. To each 2 pints/1.1 litres of water add a drop of chlorine bleach.

• Before setting flowers in the water, remove 1-2in/25-50mm of stem by

making a diagonal cut with a sharp knife (scissors crush the stems). Wash bowls and vases with hot soapy water before using; fill them with lukewarm water.
• Keep flower arrangements out of direct sunlight; store them in a cool room (5-10°C / 40°-50°F) until ready to display. Although florists keep cut flowers in a cooler, the home refrigerator is not a good storage place, especially if it contains fruit; fruit releases ethylene gas, which will cause the flowers to age prematurely. See also TULIPS, p.216.

Flower drying

To keep your house full of flowers through the winter, dry your favourite blossoms in your microwave oven. Roses (including buds), geraniums, marigolds and zinnias dry well; impatiens and petunias don't.

Whatever you use, cut the flowers late in the morning, after the dew has dried. And be aware that your dried flowers will come out a couple of shades darker; red roses become almost black, pink or coral ones become red.
• Line a microwave-safe container with a bed of silica gel crystals (available at craft shops) and heat on High for 3 minutes to make sure the crystals are as dry as possible.
• Pour 1in / 25mm of warm crystals into a heavy glass container wide enough to accommodate the flowers you're drying.
• Snip each flower stem so that only 1in / 25mm remains attached to the flower, then push the stem into the crystals so that the blossom stands upright.
• Gradually pour the remaining warm crystals down the side of the glass until the blossom is completely covered.
• Microwave on High for 1 minute 45 seconds for rosebuds, or up to 4 or 5 minutes for large, fleshy blooms. Experiment first with imperfect blossoms to judge the precise timing of the drying process.
• Cool for 20 minutes, then gently pour off the crystals. Clean the flower petals carefully with a fine paintbrush, then mist lightly with an acrylic spray. Tape to florist's wire to make a new stem.

Flowerpots

• Look around the house for containers that would make good flowerpots. Pretty coffee mugs fit on a windowsill and make the perfect holder for herbs or small plants. Drill a drainage hole in the bottom with a carbon-tipped glass or masonry bit, or place an inch of gravel and some charcoal in the bottom of the container to keep the roots from becoming waterlogged.

Larger kitchen containers, such as ceramic milk jugs and the baking dish that sits abandoned at the back of the cupboard, are good choices, too.
• Cleaning a plastic flowerpot requires nothing more than a stiff brush and hot soapy water, but the stains and ingrained dirt on an old clay pot may prove more stubborn. Soak the pot in a solution of 4fl oz/115ml bleach per gallon / 4.5 litres of hot water for 5 minutes, then remove, rinse and scrub; repeat as necessary.
• If a pot has housed a diseased plant, sterilise it before you fill it up with a new plant. Soak it in boiling water or run it through a complete cycle in the dishwasher after first rinsing off any grit.

Fluff

Since clothes fluff easily catches onto other clothes, remove it before you put a garment in the cupboard.
• If you don't have a clothes brush, use a strip of masking or sticky tape wrapped around your hand, adhesive side out, or a damp sponge.
• You'll find that fluff is much easier to remove with a damp clothes brush than with a dry one.
• To remove fluff from velvet, a sponge powder puff works well; on wool use a dry synthetic sponge.

Fly swatter

Because flies are sensitive to air currents, a rolled-up newspaper is actually a poor substitute for a mesh fly swatter. Instead, put some surgical spirit into a plant mister and spray the fly. The stuff kills on contact – but be aware that

it may mark some finished surfaces.
• Or spray the fly with hairspray to immobilise its wings and then you can swat it. But don't do this near any good pieces of furniture.

Folding laundry

• To reduce creasing, remove clothes from the dryer and hang them up as soon as possible. Since most of the laundry is stored in or near the bedroom, do your sorting on the bed. If the seams or pockets on jeans or other sportswear are slightly damp and rucked, pull on them and flatten them with your fingers; then let them air-dry before putting them away. This can often save you ironing time.
• Fold towels lengthwise first so that you don't have to refold them when you hang them on the rack in the bathroom.
• Try this method for folding fitted sheets: (1) Fold in half, bringing the fitted ends together; at each corner align the fitted edges and fold one over the other. (2) Fold in half again, bringing one matched set of corners to the other; fold one set of corners over the other set. (3) Then fold as usual, smoothing the edges as you go.

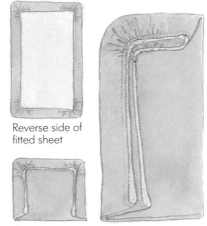

Reverse side of fitted sheet

Step 1   Step 2

Followed by someone

• If you think you are being followed, cross to the other side of the street and listen or glance back to see if the person crosses after you.

• If you decide you are being followed, go into a place where there are lots of other people – a pub, launderette or shop, for example. If you are not near shops, go to the first house that seems to be occupied. Ask to use the phone and call the police to give them a description of the person following you. If you did not see him properly, call the police anyway so that they can look out for a person acting suspiciously. Call a taxi to take you where you want to go.

• Don't use a phone box to call the police – you could be trapping yourself.

Food odours

• To rid a plastic container of food smells, freeze it or expose it to sunlight for several hours. Or drop a lemon wedge into it, close it, and let it stand until the smell disappears. (It may take a few days.)

• Freshen a lunchbox by moistening a piece of bread with white vinegar and leaving it in the closed box overnight.

• Eliminate lingering food smells in the kitchen by baking orange peelings at 175°C/350°F for several minutes.

• Fast cooking prevents the powerful aroma that brussels sprouts, cabbage and broccoli can leave. Put them in a pot of rapidly boiling water and return it quickly to the boil. A few drops of vinegar in the water helps, too.

Food processors

• Don't ignore your food processor because you can't face cleaning it. Check the instruction manual; the bowls of many models can be cleaned in the dishwasher, although 'top rack only' may be specified.

• The bowls of food processors have been known to crack right in the middle of processing. Don't remove the food; just tape the crack temporarily with several layers of masking tape, then finish processing. Replace the bowl at the first opportunity.

• To prevent leaks between an average size bowl and its cover, never fill it more than half.

• Nothing is wrong with your processor if food is left on top of the disc after slicing or shredding. It's normal.

• Avoid overprocessing foods: use the pulse button to chop. Check the food frequently to make sure that it's not getting mushy. Chill meat thoroughly before processing – this prevents it from being liquidised.

• If you have some pastry scraps, throw them into the processor along with some sesame seeds, honey, brown sugar or a zesty spice. Children and adults love biscuits made this way.

Food safety

• Bacteria lurk in the cracks and little knife nicks on your wooden chopping board. Use a brush to scrub the board vigorously with hot soapy water after each use. And don't let any meat, fish or poultry – raw or cooked – sit on the board for more than a few minutes. Plastic boards can be cleaned in the dishwasher.

• Before freezing uncooked poultry, remove it from the package, rinse well, and rewrap with your own plastic film or freezer paper; this reduces the bacteria accumulated between processing and purchase. It's also a good practice to rinse chicken under cold running water before you cook it.

• If you're grating lemon, lime or orange peel, scrub the fruits first under cold running water; they may have a residue of insecticide or wax.

• Store eggs in the fridge rather than in a basket, and don't keep them for longer than 2 weeks.

• Don't leave homemade custards or other milk-based dishes in the refrigerator for more than 2 days. Yoghurt is an exception.

• It's safer to thaw frozen foods, including the Christmas turkey, in the refrigerator than outside it, but you have to allow about 3 times as long for it to defrost.

• In hot weather, carry an insulated cooler in the boot of your car and then use it to make sure cold foods get from the supermarket to the kitchen without spoiling.

• Stow a dry ice pack in a lunchbox. Or freeze the sandwiches overnight before you pack them in an insulated lunchbox – they'll thaw nicely by the time lunch time arrives. See also PICNICS, p.155 and PERISHABLE FOOD STORAGE, p.257.

Food storage for campers

• Remove powdered foods from their original containers and repack small quantities in double plastic bags. Between the two bag layers, slip in an identification label and the mixing instructions.

• Transfer spices from large containers into clean prescription bottles or plastic film canisters; label the containers and lids.

• To protect eggs, carry them in a container filled with flour.

• To lighten your backpack, carry powdered egg, which is as nutritional as fresh egg and is easier to store. For the same reasons, take powdered instead of liquid milk and potatoes, and dried vegetables and fruit.

• A stream can serve as a refrigerator; put the food in well-anchored waterproof bags.

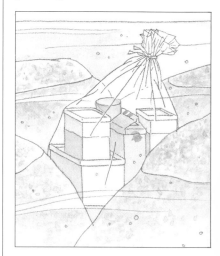

Football jargon

Booked When an offending player has his name and number taken down by the referee.

Caution A warning by the referee for

an offence committed during the match.

Centre-spot The marked point in the centre of the halfway line from where the kick-off takes place.

Corner flags Placed at the four places from where corner kicks are taken.

Corner kick This is awarded to the attacking team when the ball passes over the defender's goal line, having last been played by a defender.

Cross A pass played from near the touchline into midfield, usually the penalty or goal area.

Direct free kick A free kick from which a goal can be scored directly by the player taking the kick.

Extra time In knock-out cup matches, when a definite result is required, and the teams are level after the normal 90 minutes play, an extra 30 minutes is played.

Foul An infringement of the rules, usually in relation to the defending players.

Free kick Awarded to a team for a foul against them. Can be direct or indirect.

Goal Scored when the whole of the ball crosses the line between the goalposts and under the crossbar, under conditions covered by the laws of the game.

Goal area The small rectangular area extending 6yds/5.49m each side of the goalposts and into the field of play.

Goal-kick Awarded when the ball has passed over the goal line, but not into the goal, having last been played by a member of the attacking team.

Hand-ball An offence committed when a player (other than the goalkeeper) handles the ball, deliberately or accidentally, on the field of play.

Indirect free kick A free kick from which a goal cannot be scored unless it is touched by two or more players.

Injury time Time added to a game for stoppages, usually for injuries, incurred during the game's normal duration.

Kick-off This takes place at the beginning of a game, after half-time, and after a goal has been scored. The ball must initially be played forward by the side which kicks off.

Linesmen Two officials who operate on either touchline, who aid the referee in controlling the game.

Marking Keeping a player under close surveillance in order to discourage passes to him and to restrict his movements if he does receive the ball.

Offside When an attacking player within the defending team's half of the field is nearer to the opponents' goal line than a defender at the moment that an attacking ball is played through to him by a teammate.

Penalty Awarded by the referee when a defender fouls an opposing player, or deliberately handles the ball, within the penalty area.

Penalty area The rectangular area extending 18yds/16.46m to either side of the goalposts and into the field of play.

Red card Shown to a player after a serious offence, such as a deliberate foul to thwart a goal, or in place of a second yellow card. The player is then sent off.

Referee The official in charge of the game, who decides on infringements of the rules and the penalties thereby incurred.

Reverse pass When a player runs one way and passes the ball in the other direction.

Score draw When each side has scored and finished with the same number of goals.

Set-piece A pre-determined situation (such as a corner, free kick or throw-in) from which practised moves can be executed.

Selling a dummy Feinting to dribble or pass in one direction, and then going in another to beat an opponent.

Striker An opposing player who normally would stay upfield with the intention of scoring a goal.

Strip The playing gear of the players, usually consisting of the team's colours and the name of the club's sponsor.

Sweeper A player who stays behind the defensive line to literally 'sweep up' loose balls.

Through-ball A pass to a colleague running forward in an attempt to by-pass the opposing defence.

Throw-in When the ball leaves the field of play across one of the touchlines, it is returned to play by being thrown in by a member of the opposite team to the one that last touched it.

Touchline The line delineating either side of the pitch.

Volley The kicking of the ball when it has been passed in the air before it hits the ground.

Yellow card Shown to a player for an infringement of the rules, as a caution.

Foot odour

• Soak your feet two or three nights a week for 10 minutes in a foot tonic made from equal parts water, witch hazel and surgical spirit. Keep your toes separated to ensure penetration, and then dry them with a rough towel and an astringent powder or spray.

• Wash your feet every day and dust them with deodorant foot powder.

• Spray your shoes with an anti-odour product or try deodorising inner soles.

• Avoid wearing the same pair of shoes, tights or socks two days in a row. Wear cotton socks and tights to allow your feet to breathe.

• Air your feet as often as possible by wearing open sandals or walking bare foot around your home.

Foot problems

Athlete's foot

• Wash your feet every day and dry them carefully between the toes. Don't use the same towel for other parts of your body or share it with other members of your household.

• Change your socks and shoes every day, especially if you have sweaty feet. Wear socks made from natural fibres, to allow your feet to breathe, and wear sandals as much as possible.

• Apply a proprietary anti-fungal powder or cream between your toes and on reddish, scaly areas of your feet twice a day for a month. Sprinkle anti-fungal powder in socks and shoes daily.

• To prevent a recurrence, wear rubber or wooden sandals in public showers and changing-rooms; keep your feet dry and clean; dust the inside of your shoes with anti-fungal powder and change your socks twice a day.

Blisters

• If the blister is caused by wearing a

particular pair of shoes, avoid wearing them until the skin has healed. Break in new shoes gradually with short periods of wear.

• Leave blisters alone to break spontaneously. If they do break, expose them to the air as much as possible to dry out, except if there is danger of dirt getting onto them, when they should be covered with a plaster or bandage.

Bunions

• Stop wearing badly fitting shoes and wear only loose-fitting ones.

• Bathe your feet daily for 20 minutes in hot water with a tablespoon of Epsom salts dissolved in it. Or raise your feet and apply an ice pack, 10 minutes on, 10 minutes off, or run cold water over your feet for 2 minutes at a time, until the swelling and pain dissipate.

• Protect your bunions with felt pads, available from a chemist.

Calluses and corns

• Use a pumice stone to smooth off calluses immediately after bathing. Calluses are caused by badly fitting shoes and almost always disappear when well fitted shoes are worn.

• Don't cut corns away – rub them with an emery board or a pumice stone. Or bathe your feet in a hot-water solution of Epsom salts.

• Cover a stubborn corn with a 20 or 40 per cent salicylic acid plaster; after 4 or 5 days soak the foot in water and check to see if the corn has dissolved enough to lift off or scrape away. Repeat the treatment if necessary.

Caution If you're a diabetic or elderly, don't attempt to treat calluses and corns yourself – seek professional help.

Ingrown toenails

• Insert a piece of gauze soaked in surgical spirit under the corners of the nail, twice a day. Repeat daily until the ingrown toenail has healed. Consult a chiropodist or your doctor if it is not healing.

• Cut a V-shaped nick in the centre of the nail's top edge to reduce the pressure on the sides of the nail.

• To prevent ingrowing toenails, wear properly fitting shoes and cut or file toenails straight across rather than shaping them in a curve.

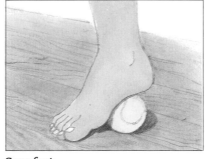

Sore feet

• Massage sore feet by rolling a tennis or golf ball along the soles. Or knead the feet, pulling each toe for 10 seconds, and run the knuckles of a fist along the midsoles.

• Soak weary feet in a basin of hot water to which you have added 2 tablespoons Epsom salts or a handful of plain salt. Or rub with ice cubes, towel-dry, and splash with cologne. Keep them raised whenever possible.

Footwear for sports

• Your old-fashioned trainers are still fine for boating as long as they have a nonslip tread.

• Try high-top basketball shoes for canoeing; they'll provide extra ankle support when you need it.

• Aerobic shoes are suitable for playing tennis in (they give support for quick side-to-side movements), but don't do aerobics in tennis or running shoes – they lack sufficient cushioning under the ball of the foot.

Fit

• Be sure your shoes have enough room for your toes to spread under your full weight; allow ½in/13mm between the end of your big toe and the tip of the shoe when you are standing on both feet.

• Shoes should be snug and supportive

Footwear favourites: the story of trainers

Although actor Dudley Moore (whose feet are two different sizes) bought 30 custom-made pairs in one day, and singer Mick Jagger got married in them, and comedian Woody Allen was spotted wearing them with a tuxedo, these modern miracles of comfort are really nothing new. When – as Indian lore has it – members of a Brazilian tribe dipped their feet into the liquid latex of rubber trees some 300 years ago, they created what were, in effect, the world's first trainers.

In the 1860s, the vulcanising process made it possible to manufacture rubber soles for shoes, but it wasn't until just before the turn of the century that the first canvas-and-rubber trainers appeared.

For years trainers (sneakers in America because of their noiselessness) were white or black, low or high cut, and maligned as unhealthy and informal. In 1962 the first modern running shoe, with a comfortable wide front, a rippled sole and a shock-absorbing wedge, was marketed.

Innovations followed: designer colours, new sole patterns, 'breathable' nylon uppers. Today, trainer technology has leapt ahead: one model is made so that the wearer can pump up the air cushions for custom-made comfort; another has a built-in microchip that measures speed, distance and calories burned; and yet another, when plugged into a computer, tracks long-term performance. Where will they go next?

in the heel, but not tight. If you have narrow heels, buy shoes with extra lacing holes towards the ankle or with high tops.

Forcing flowers

For a spring display in midwinter, you can force flowers from a few branches of forsythia, pussywillow or witch hazel.
• Any time after the first buds of the year appear, choose branches with the fattest buds (these are flower buds – the smaller ones produce only leaves). Cut the branches off with sharp pruning shears.
• Scrape the bark from the lower 3-4 in / 75-100mm of each branch and split the end lengthwise for 2-3 in / 50-75mm.
• Plunge the whole branch into a bathful of room-temperature water for a few hours.
• Arrange the branches in a vase or bowl of cold water and set it in a sunny room. Ideally, the temperature should be 16°-18°C / 60°-65°F. Spray the branches twice a week to protect the buds from drying out. They should bloom within 2 weeks or so.

You can also force apples, crab-apples, pears, dogwoods and lilacs, but they'll take 3 to 4 weeks to bloom. Don't cut these plants until 6 weeks before their normal flowering time.

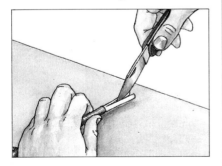

Foreign phrases

• Before visiting another country, it's best to learn the language; take a course, buy tapes or borrow them from the library. But if there isn't time, take along a phrase book and dictionary or at least learn a few basics such as 'Please',

'Thank you', 'Good day', 'Where is . . . and 'Help, I need a doctor'.

Don't be afraid to use these phrases; a few words can go a long way towards making friends and getting assistance. Gestures also help. Or carry a pocket-size electronic device that translates your phrases. To get the most from your sightseeing expeditions, however, consider hiring a guide.
• In a country that uses a different alphabet (Japan, for example), buy a map with both foreign and English place names. Before leaving your hotel, get someone to write your destination in the native language. Carry the name, address and telephone number of your hotel with you at all times (a printed matchbook or the hotel's business card is good for this). Keep a list of emergency telephone numbers handy, including the police, local tourist board and British embassy or consulate.

Fractures

Even a slight force can cause a broken bone. Fracture victims often feel the bone break or hear a snapping sound.

There may be intense pain and tenderness – especially when there is pressure on the area of the break – with swelling and discoloration; the limb may look deformed or oddly angled. But swelling and pain may not occur for some time and many fractures are impossible to detect without an X-ray. If any of these symptoms are present, however, assume there's a fracture and seek medical help.

While awaiting treatment
• Steady and support the injured limb.
• If an ankle or foot is fractured, carefully lifting the leg will help to reduce the swelling and therefore the pain.
• If bone has pierced the skin, cover the wound with a dry, clean dressing. See also Slings, p.186; Splints, p.191.

Freckles

• Most people now consider freckles an attractive asset. However, if you don't like your freckles, stay out of the sun; it darkens them, since freckles are

patches of melanin (a skin pigment) triggered off by sunlight. Don't put lemon juice on them; it just increases the skin's sensitivity to the sun.
• If you must go into the sun, use a sun cream with a high sun protection factor.
• Disguise your freckles with a beige foundation or translucent powder.

Free information

• For consumer information, first go to the reference section of your local public library. This will have trade directories, both local and national. Trade associations will be listed with their telephone numbers and they can give you further information.
• Government and local government organisations will usually provide free advice on their appropriate special areas. Local authorities often produce manuals which may be delivered to you or are available at your library.
• For local information, use the Yellow Pages or Thomson Directory and check your local newspaper.
• The Citizens Advice Bureau or local Trading Standards Department will be able to give you specific consumer advice or be able to refer you to an appropriate body.
• To learn more about a place you want to visit, contact the local Tourist Information Centre in or near that place. It will often be able to provide information on accommodation as well as tourist attractions. Read the travel pages of your national newspaper for information on holiday places and prices to these destinations.
• For facts on a foreign country, contact the embassy or tourist bureau of that country in London or in some large provincial centres.

Freelancing

Selling your art, writing, photography and other skills is difficult, but successful freelancing can be a rewarding full-time job, or it can supplement a more stable source of income.
• To help you break into the freelance market, ask your tutor, if you're still at

college, for names of commercial contacts; or join a writers', artists' or photographers' group; or consult the *Writers' and Artists' Yearbook* in your local library for the names of appropriate organisations to contact. Many will send you samples and freelancers' guidelines if you provide a stamped, self-addressed envelope big enough for the publication you've requested.

• The easiest areas to break into are local newspapers, free papers supported by advertising and regional magazines. Submit your work for no fee at first, then photocopy your published work to send to larger publications.

• Subscribe to magazines for writers, photographers or artists for tips and names to know.

• Once you've targeted a publication, submit several ideas for stories, photos or illustrations; you might even get an assignment and a cash advance.

• If you're trying to sell your artwork or photos, make an appointment to see the art director and take along a portfolio of your work.

• If you're trying to sell skills that don't fall into the categories mentioned, find appropriate companies to target in company and trade directories in your local library. Send your cv to them (see p.245), and a letter which explains how you could help them as a freelance rather than as a permanent member of staff.

• Be professional. Use appropriate business cards and headed paper. Do your best on every project and include a bill with each assigned submission. Be cordial but persistent when you follow up on projects you've had no word on or payments that are late.

Freezer smells

• To prevent food smells, wrap all foods in moisture-proof, vapour-proof, packaging materials, preferably marked for freezer use. Old bread wrappers, wax paper, margarine tubs or plastic supermarket bags are not as effective.

Cure

• Spread bicarbonate of soda or activated charcoal (available at chemists or hardware shops) on shallow foil plates and place them on the freezer shelves.

• Remove all food from the freezer and pack crumpled, slightly dampened newspapers on each shelf. Replace the newspapers every day until the smells disappear. (It may take 5 or 6 days.)

• When defrosting, clean and deodorise the freezer with a solution of 2 tablespoons bicarbonate of soda in 2 pints / 1 litre warm water. If you have a frost-free freezer, wash the interior with a bicarb solution at least once a month.

• To get rid of the smell of spoiled food after a freezer failure, place bowls filled with used or unused coffee grounds inside the freezer.

Frost

• Marrows, cucumbers, melons and courgettes planted before the end of May are vulnerable to frost damage. Invert large plant pots over them at night to protect them, and remove the pots during the day.

• Cover frames containing seedlings with mats or sacking. Do this at dusk and take the mats off the next day.

• If you wake to find that there was a frost you didn't expect, minimise the damage by spraying plants before the sun strikes their leaves.

• To protect tender seedlings from a late-spring cold snap, cover them with cloches, or miniature greenhouses. Just cut the bottoms off plastic bottles or jugs and build up a mound of soil around the

base of each container to hold it in place. On cold but sunny days, unscrew the caps for ventilation.

• If you know in advance that a frost is likely, build straw cones around your plants, fastened at the point by string, to protect them at night. Remove them during the day.

Frostbite

• Superficial frostbite can develop rapidly in a cold wind. The skin turns whitish or mottled, is painful and feels firm to the touch. Warm the affected part against the body and go indoors at once. If you're walking, get to a warm shelter right away and call for help.

• If flesh feels hard and cold, or the skin turns greyish blue or white, treat it as soon as possible. Warm the area with your hands until the circulation returns. If feet are frostbitten, take off the shoe and sock and cover the foot with a cotton handkerchief. Do not rub the skin or apply any direct heat or pressure to it.

• Fit padding between the fingers or toes and cover with a triangular bandage. Put the base of the bandage under the wrist of the hand or behind the heel of the foot and bring the point under and over the fingers, or the toes of the foot. Bring the two opposite points of the bandage over the third point and cross and tie at the ankle or wrist. Fasten firmly, but not so that circulation is slowed, with a knot. Fold the tip of the point over the knot and fasten. Raise the foot and keep it warm with a blanket or sleeping bag. Place blankets or a sleeping bag around the victim and feed him hot, sweet drinks.

Fruit flies

These tiny flies are attracted by fermenting or overripe fruits and vegetables, vinegar, fruit juices and yeasts. To trap them, insert a paper or metal funnel into the mouth of a jar baited with bits of overripe fruit. They'll fly into the jar but won't be able to find their way out. Outdoors, promptly collect fallen tomatoes and other fruit from the garden and keep rubbish bins tightly closed.

Fruit

• If you have a big bunch of bananas or a large quantity of other fruit that you're afraid may ripen all at once, place a few in a brown paper bag with holes made in it. The bag traps ethylene gas, making the fruit inside ripen almost twice as fast.

• Fully ripened fruit belongs in the refrigerator. Unripe fruit is best kept at room temperature in an open-weave basket that allows air to circulate.

• If fruit has become overripe, don't throw it away. Purée it in a blender or food processor with a little lemon juice and sugar and spoon the result over ice cream.

• Do not wash soft fruits unless absolutely necessary. Instead, wipe away dirt with a paper towel or brush it off with a pastry brush. However, if you do have to wash strawberries, they will retain more juice and absorb less water if you wash them before hulling. And always rinse the berries quickly in running water instead of soaking them.

Funnel

• A better substitute for a funnel than a rolled-up, taped piece of cardboard is an empty food tin – a 1 lb / 450 g one will do – with a hole punched near the joint between the bottom and the side. (Don't punch the hole in the centre of the tin as you'll have less control over the flow.) Hold the tin at an angle while you pour through it.

• Cut the bottom off a plastic soft drinks bottle and turn it upside-down.

Furniture polish or wax

• To avoid a build-up of polish or wax, apply it sparingly and no more than a few times a year. To prevent a build-up in the crevices of carved or decorative areas, put a small amount of polish or wax on a cloth before you wipe it onto the furniture.

• If a build-up does occur, you can remove it by wiping the furniture with a soft cloth dampened with a little methylated spirits; then apply fresh wax or polish.

Homemade polishes

• Use sunflower oil. If you prefer a lemon-scented polish, add 1 teaspoon of lemon oil for every 16 fl oz / 450 ml of sunflower oil.

• Mix 2 pints / 1.1 litres boiled linseed oil with 16 fl oz / 450 ml turpentine. (Store in a covered container.)

• Combine 1 part lemon oil and 3 parts olive oil.

Furniture stains

• To remove the white rings left by cups or glasses, rub the wood with a mild abrasive. First, try cigarette or cigar ashes moistened with a little cooking oil; apply with your finger. If that doesn't work, try successively stronger steps: use table salt and a drop of water; silver polish or car polish; and, finally, on teak, use fine glass paper and then oil.

• Erase superficial ink spots with oiled pumice or steel wool.

Further education

Leaving school does not mean losing your last chance of gaining qualifications. Throughout the country, Colleges of Further Education and local Adult Education Institutes offer a wide range of evening, day-release and weekend courses at GCSE and A level or a technical qualification. They include courses in languages, computing skills, secretarial and office skills and sports coaching. Many cater for hobbies and leisure pursuits. Some colleges build up close relationships with local employers and tailor courses to meet the needs and interests of local people. Larger colleges often offer crèche facilities for students with children.

Your local library and town hall will have details of courses, methods of application and fees. Public sector colleges are usually subsidised, and offer a relatively inexpensive method of continuing your education after leaving school and/or starting work. But, beware of some pitfalls. For popular subjects, class sizes can be large and consequently there is little individual attention given to students. Classes that fall below a minimum size because students drop out can suddenly be cancelled. If you have a very specialised interest, you may have to travel some distance to find a suitable class.

Fuse box

Make sure you know where the fuse box or consumer unit lies in your house. It may be under the stairs, in a hall cupboard or in a lobby. Keep the area around it clear of clutter and keep a working torch and spare fuse wire or cartridges handy.

The fuse box will be equipped with a mains disconnect switch that will take one of two forms, depending on the type of panel:

Miniature circuit breaker (MCB) This has no fuse. It can be shut off by flipping the mains disconnect switch. If it trips due to an overload, it can simply be reset by pushing a button. But try to rectify the cause first, or it will simply trip again.

Plug-in fuse box This type can be switched off without opening the cover. It contains a row of plugs, one for each circuit, colour-coded for rating: 5 amp (white) for lighting; 15 amp (blue) and 20 amp (yellow) for special circuits, such as the immersion heater; 30 amp (red) for ring (socket) circuits; 45 amp (green) for cookers. This fuse box may contain a wire or a cartridge. Always replace a cartridge with a cartridge, never with wire, and always with one of the correct rating.

Learn which fuses control which circuits and label them, or pin up a diagram.

Fuses

• Never replace a fuse with one of a higher rating, and never use a coin, a piece of aluminium foil or any other object in place of a fuse. Doing so could cause a fire.

• The power surge that occurs when starting up motorised equipment can cause a fuse to blow. If this is a persistent problem, install a time-delay fuse.

• If fuses blow regularly, call in an electrician. It may be time to rewire your home or at least older circuits.

G

Games for grown-ups

Badminton volleyball Play badminton over a volleyball net using volleyball rules.

Frisbee golf Use trees, poles and rocks as holes and designate tee-off spots. Throw a Frisbee and keep throwing it from where it lands until you land at a 'hole'. The person who takes the fewest throws to hit all holes is the winner. Assess a penalty point whenever the Frisbee lands on a spot from which it can't be thrown.

Word spell One person says a letter and the next person adds another letter to logically spell a word. Play continues around the room, with the object being not to complete a word; giving the last letter of any word costs you a point. For example, if the existing letters are *t* and *a*, add a *c*, perhaps (for tack), or an *i* (for tail). A *b* (tab) or *g* (tag) would complete the word and penalise you 1 point – 5 points and you're out. In case of a challenge, you must identify the word you have in mind or lose a point. The winner is the last person left.

Call my Bluff The player who is 'it' picks an obscure word from the dictionary, states it, and writes its definition on a card; the other players write what they think the word might mean. The cards are shuffled and the definitions read

aloud by the 'it' player; then each player guesses which definition is correct. The 'it' player keeps score, awarding 1 point for guessing correctly and 1 point for fooling someone with a false definition. He himself gets 5 points if no one guesses the word. The game continues until each player has been 'it'.

Gomuku This Japanese noughts and crosses game uses a grid of 19 horizontal and 19 vertical lines. One player places Xs, the other Os on the intersections of the lines. The first to place five letters in a row wins.

Garden hose

• You can temporarily plug a pinhole leak in a rubber hose by jamming a round wooden toothpick into the hole. Snap the toothpick off flush with the hose's outer skin. Then wrap the hose with insulating tape up to 2 in/50mm on either side of the leak. Stretch the tape tight over the hole but looser towards the ends, so that it can flex as the hose bends. As the wood absorbs water, it will swell to seal the hole.

• Never store a garden hose by hanging it over a nail or peg. The hose will sag and kink, and repeated kinking will crack the rubber, vinyl or plastic skin. Instead, mount an old wheel rim on the garage or toolshed wall and wrap the hose around it when not in use.

Gardening

You can get more plants out of your vegetable plot – and reduce pest damage at the same time – by interplanting a mixture of vegetables in a wide row. Choose plants that can be sown in the same season and, for the fun of it, follow a

theme. A salad row, for example, might consist of radishes, cress, red and green leaf lettuces, chicory, dill and parsley.

First, prepare a row at least 3 ft/1 m wide. Combine all the seeds in a small jar (a jam jar is ideal). Then punch a dozen or more holes in the lid and screw it on. Using the jar as a shaker, sprinkle seeds sparsely over the whole row. Scratch the surface lightly with a rake to cover the seeds, then water gently.

Thinning will be the only real chore and needs to be an on-going process. Widen the intervals between plants only as they actually need the room, since the less soil you leave bare, the less chance there is for weeds to invade. A thick blanket of foliage also shades the soil, acting much as a mulch would.

Be imaginative and choose other themes: a spaghetti sauce row, with tomato and onion seedlings, basil and garlic; or a soup row, with kale, carrots, leeks, turnips, beets and potatoes.

Garden pests

Although many pesticides are available for treating garden pests, some people prefer organic remedies.

• Aphids, mealy bugs and other soft-bodied insects can be removed with an insecticidal soap or a dusting of derris. Alternatively, wipe the affected areas gently with a clean, damp cloth or pick off the offenders by hand.

• Control onion fly maggots and bean weevils by scattering wood ashes around plants or on the foliage.

• Queen Anne's lace, fennel and sage attract beneficial insects such as hover flies, lacewings and parasitic wasps and flies. Sit back and let them do some pest-control work for you. See also entries under specific pests.

Garden produce

• To save mature green tomatoes from an early frost, pick them and set them on top of the refrigerator to ripen at room temperature. Or wrap them individually in newspaper and store in a cool spot.

• Keep bean weevils from ruining your kidney or butter beans when they are drying: just dip the freshly shelled beans in boiling water for 1 minute before you spread them out to dry.

• Instead of rapping your melons to check for ripeness, look for brown tendrils on the stem near the fruit and a yellow area instead of white where the fruit touches the ground. Both are signs that the melon is ready to pick.

• When you harvest courgettes and marrows leave a short stem on the vegetables to ensure that they stay succulent until cooking time.

• Test potatoes before you store them by rubbing the skin; if it rubs off easily, the potato is probably too young for storage.

• Don't wash or blanch freshly harvested peas before freezing them. Just shell them directly into a plastic freezer bag; they'll stay separated, allowing you to dip into them as you need them.

Garden tools

• An electric drill will keep your garden tools polished and sharp. Use a wire brush attachment to scour rust from neglected tools; a coarse disc can put an edge back on a nicked axe or mower blade much faster than a file and whetstone. Do it quickly, so that the high-speed sanding doesn't heat the steel and ruin its temper.

After polishing and sharpening your tools, keep blades and teeth bright with a coat of oil; dirty oil from your car or power mower is as effective as any and costs nothing.

• For jobs too big for a trowel but too small for a spade or shovel, use a hoe.

Make a seed drill by following a taut length of twine with a draw hoe blade.

• Use a wide putty knife for scraping earth from shovels and trowels. Use it also for delicate weeding between closely planted vegetables and for cultivating the soil in the crevices of a rock garden.

Garlic

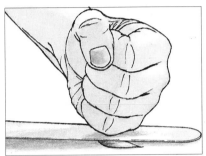

• Peel a garlic clove by placing the flat side of a knife over it and giving it a sharp rap with your hand or a utensil. The skin will come away easily.

• If you want a subtle garlic taste, chop the cloves with a knife. Or add unpeeled cloves of garlic to soups, stews and casseroles. Putting garlic through a press or mincing it in a food processor makes the flavour considerably stronger because more oil is released.

• If you don't have fresh garlic, substitute ¼ ½ teaspoon garlic salt for each clove and omit ½ teaspoon salt from the recipe.

• To tame your breath after a garlic-rich meal, munch fresh parsley.

Gas appliances

• Get your gas appliances checked every year by a professional installer, preferably registered with CORGI (the Confederation for the Registration of Gas Installers). In addition, you can take these steps at any time to ensure safety.

• Run the dust-brush attachment of your vacuum cleaner over the louvred access panel of the ventilator to remove accumulated dust and fluff particles. Ventilators and flues must not be blocked or obstructed, because the waste products formed by gas burning need to escape; if they do not they will build up and eventually poison you.

• If you have a gas fire fitted into a fireplace, get the chimney swept every year to clear it of any blockages. This must also be done before the gas fire is fitted.

• If you notice any sooty deposits or staining around a gas fire or heater, call a competent installer to check it.

• Buy second-hand gas appliances only if they have been certified for safety and the dealer gives you a written guarantee. Make sure there is a copy of the user's instructions with any cooker that you buy. Second-hand appliances should be installed only by a professional fitter – from British Gas or some other person registered with CORGI.

• *Never* fit gas appliances yourself.

Gas leaks

• If a strong smell of gas wakes you up or greets you at the door, open your doors and windows to let out the gas, check your cooker to see if the gas has been left on, and check water heaters to see if a pilot light has gone out. If not, turn off the gas supply at the meter (it is off when the ridged line on the lever's spindle lies in a horizontal position), and leave your home at once. Do not use your telephone or turn on any light fixture or appliance – an electric spark can cause an explosion. Don't light matches or smoke.

Call the gas board from a pay phone or a neighbour's home (the number can be found under GAS in the telephone book). Don't return home until a service representative says that it is safe for you to do so.

When you're sure the smell is gone, turn the gas supply lever to the 'ON' position. Carefully relight all pilot lights. If your cooker has pilotless ignition, turn on each burner to test it. If a pilot won't stay lit or the smell persists, call a professional fitter to service it.

Gatecrashers

• Try politeness first: ask the unwanted person to leave, explaining that he is intruding on a private party. If your intruder refuses, tell him to leave. If he still refuses, phone the police. When the police arrive, repeat your request in their presence. Only then can they act to remove your intruder.

• Avoid physical confrontation. Enlist the help of a guest in keeping the gate-crasher quiet and away from the rest of the party. If he is drunk, phone for a cab. If he insists on driving, immediately contact the police with the registration number, make of car and location.

Gifted children

• Gifted children can become bored and even disruptive if not stimulated enough. Talk to your child's teacher about broadening her curriculum.

• Contact one of the support groups such as Mensa (Mensa House, St John's Square, Wolverhampton, West Midlands WV2 4AH, Tel. 01902-772771), or The National Association for Gifted Children (Elder House, Milton Keynes MK9 1LR, Tel. 01908-673677). Each of these groups provides social activities for both parents and children.

• Tell your child you're proud of her. This helps to offset any jealousy from classmates. But stress that you love her for herself and not just her brains.

• Never use a gifted child's intelligence against her (such as saying 'How could someone as clever as you do something so stupid?').

• Emphasise that she doesn't have to do everything perfectly. (Gifted children can be very demanding of themselves.)

• Even though your child might sound like an adult, she's still a child who needs guidance.

• If you have other children, remember that each is special, and avoid making comparisons.

Gift wrap

• Aluminium foil is a good substitute for gift wrap; for a textured look, press it gently against a rough surface such as a stucco or brick wall.

• To premeasure a length of gift wrapping from a roll, wrap string around the package and use it as a guide.

• If your sheet of wrapping paper is a bit too short to cover your package, turn the

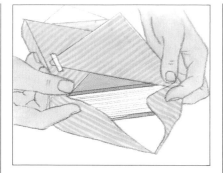

package at an angle and try wrapping it that way.

• Other interesting and attractive substitutes for gift wrapping include leftover wallpaper and fabric remnants, and magazine advertisement pages. The coloured comic pages from weekend newspapers, or even from discarded comics, make cheerful coverings for children's gift packages. You can also use plain brown wrapping paper for gifts, but tie them with bright ribbons of red, gold or yellow.

• Make your own printing block by cutting a simple design on a bar of soap or a halved potato. Then use it to decorate newspaper, paper bags or white shelving paper. Use an ink pad or pour out some paint on a paper plate or a clean plastic foam meat tray.

• Save wrapping paper. When you have a large object to cover, use different pieces of your stored paper to create a patchwork look.

Glass

• Never pick up broken glass with your bare hands – or approach it in your bare feet. Carefully sweep it into a dustpan, wrap it in newspaper, and throw it out.

• To pick up tiny slivers of glass, wipe all around the breakage area with a paper towel or cotton wool smeared with moist soap. Rinse with a water-soaked paper towel and wipe dry.

Glasses

• When buying a pair of reading glasses, whether over-the-counter or prescription, keep in mind that glass lenses are less likely to scratch than plastic, but

they will shatter more easily and weigh more. Shop around for tempered lenses that fit securely in the frame.

• If you lose the hinge screw that holds an earpiece to the frame, use a small safety pin or paper clip for a quick fix.

• Make your glasses fit more securely on your face by tightening the hinge screws with a jeweller's screwdriver, or use the tiny screwdriver that comes with a sewing machine, the point of a paring knife, or a letter opener.

• If a lens breaks cleanly, you can hold it together temporarily with a little transparent tape at the top and bottom of the crack.

• Clean lenses with soapy water or a drop of vinegar, vodka or surgical spirit. To prevent scratches, do not rub plastic lenses until you've rinsed off all the dirt.

• Do your glasses fog up when you come in from the cold? Before heading out on a chilly day, just rub a thin coat of soap on the lenses. Then polish them until clear – this technique provides instant waterproofing.

• Do the lenses tend to pop out of your half-moon glasses? In an emergency, put putty rubber, Plasticine or any other sticky substance in the corner of the lens to hold it in place.

• To secure a loose lens in a pair of full-frame glasses, tighten the set-screw near the hinge. See also MAGNIFYING GLASS, p.129.

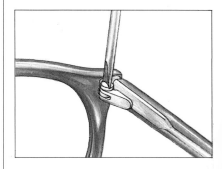

Glassware

• Use the bartender's method for speedy stemware washing. Holding the base, pump the glass vigorously in very hot soapy water, then quickly pump it in hot clear water (cooler water may shatter it); dry upside-down on a cotton towel.

• For extra-shiny, streakless glasses, add a little vinegar or borax to the final rinse water.

• If glasses have hard-water stains, rub them with a scouring pad dipped in vinegar.

• Never use hot water, harsh soaps, ammonia or washing soda on silver or gold-rimmed glasses.

• A well-lathered shaving brush cleans deeply etched or textured glass especially well.

• If eggs have dried on your patterned glass tableware, rub off the residue with a slice of lemon.

• Handle glass ovenware very carefully. Avoid hard knocks and sudden exposure to heat or cold and keep it away from water (even a moist kitchen top) while warm.

• If glass hob-safe cookware remains stained after washing, boil a solution of 1 part vinegar to 3 parts water in it for about 20 minutes.

Gloves

• Do you need gloves in a hurry? Slip a sock over your hand, move your thumb away from your index finger and cut through the material in that space. Remove the sock and stitch along the cut edge.

• Remove fresh spots from leather and suede gloves by rubbing them with stale bread.

• Clean white kid gloves with powdered starch or tailor's chalk. Apply with a piece of silk, then shake the loose powder off.

• For a stain on black kid, dab on indelible black marker, then rub in a few drops of olive oil.

• To dry out wet plastic or rubber gloves, hang them by their fingers or put them over propped-up wooden spoon handles.

• Instead of wearing plastic or rubber gloves while painting, apply liquid latex (available at hardware stores) over your hands, which dries to a flexible film; wash it off with the paint. To protect your hands during paint touch-ups, just coat your hands with hand cream.

Glue

• Replace the cap of a tube of glue with a cup hook or screw eye. Then you can hang the tube up for storage.

• A substitute glue for carpentry likely to be exposed to the weather is exterior gloss paint. Coat the surfaces to be joined, as you would with a standard glue. Condensed milk is also a good standby adhesive.

• When taking furniture to pieces, soften the old glue with warm distilled white vinegar. Drip it directly into the joints with an eye dropper.

• To unclog a tube which has become blocked up, don't try to poke through the hardened glue with a nail or pin. You may damage the tube. Instead, bore into the clogged nozzle with a small drill bit. (Soak the bit in lacquer thinner or nail-polish remover first and clean off all the glue afterwards.)

• Most white glues and carpenters' glues are water-based. To clear a nozzle, unscrew it and soak it in warm water. (Tape the bottle closed so that the glue won't harden.) Once the glue in the nozzle softens, clean it out with a wooden toothpick.

• Make yourself simple glue brushes using the barrel of a ballpoint pen and a length of coarse string. Feed the string through the barrel and fluff out the end to form the bristles of a brush. When that part of the string has been used, merely cut it off and pull through a fresh piece. This is ideal for PVA adhesive to be used by children.

Glued fingers

• If a superglue bonds your fingers together, don't panic. It will do no harm as long as you don't try to pull your fingers apart. Merely soak the hand in warm soapy water and use the handle of a teaspoon to slowly prise the fingers apart. Some of these adhesives come with a small bottle of release agent to speed up the operation, and they are generally soluble in water.

• If hands become contaminated with one of the many rubber-based adhesives, hand cleaners are available. Or use one of the solvents recommended by the suppliers of bitumen rubber-based paints and roofing compounds.

• If, after everything you've tried, the skin surfaces are still stuck together, seek medical aid.

For love of a glove

Power, wealth, nobility and even love – all these things and more were once symbolised by gloves. They seemingly carried the aura of the hands that wore them.

Not until early in the 17th century were gloves commonly worn by ordinary women – but fine ladies had begun to sport fancy gloves as early as the Middle Ages. Still warm from a soft hand, a glove would be given to a knight as a token of love. And off he would ride into battle, the intimate favour in his helmet, its mate with his mistress awaiting his return.

Dainty though it was, the feminine glove became a sign of strength to him – an amulet to ward off evil, an incentive for brave deeds and a reminder of the sweet reward that would be his should he survive.

His own armoured glove, or gauntlet, was a different matter entirely. There was nothing dainty about the gauntlet; it embodied strength, power and honour. It might be offered as a pledge in a court of law. And to 'throw down the gauntlet' at another man's feet was to challenge him to combat, often mortal combat. It was a meaning that lasted for centuries. Long after the knightly gauntlet had faded into history, perfumed dandies were challenging each other to duels at the drop of a kid glove as soft as any lady's of the time.

Golf jargon

Here's a guide to what the television commentators are saying:

Ace A hole in one.

Address To prepare to hit the ball.

Albatross To score 3 shots under par.

Approach shot A shot made from the fairway towards the green.

Back nine The last 9 holes of an 18-hole golf course.

Birdie To score 1 under par.

Blast A hard trap shot.

Blind hole A green that the golfer cannot see when driving or making an approach shot.

Bogey To score 1 over par.

Bunker A sand trap.

Carry The distance a ball stays in the air after being hit.

Chip A short, low approach shot.

Divot A piece of earth dislodged by the player's stroke.

Dogleg A fairway that bends.

Double bogey To score 2 over par.

Drive The first shot towards the green, generally from a tee.

Eagle To score 2 under par.

Fairway The area of well-mowed, hazard-free grass between the teeing-off area and the green.

Flagstick A marker on the green indicating the location and the number of the hole.

Gimme An easy putt conceded to an opponent.

Green The area of short, well-tended grass surrounding the hole.

Handicap The number of strokes that are deducted from the score of a weaker player when competing against a more skilful opponent.

Hazards The bunkers and water obstacles on the golf course.

Hook A ball that veers in midflight to the left for a right-handed golfer, to the right for a left-handed one.

Irons Clubs with bladelike metal heads, set at different angles.

Lie The position in which the ball stops after a stroke.

Links A golf course (from the Scottish word for the undulating land by the sea where the early courses were built).

Par The score an expert player in good weather is expected to make on a particular hole.

Putter The club used for making short, accurate shots on the green.

Rim To have a ball go around the edge of the hole and not drop in.

Shank To hit the ball poorly.

Slice The opposite of a hook.

Tee The peg used to raise the ball off the ground before it is driven, or teed off.

Trap shot A shot from a bunker.

Woods Clubs with hardwood heads, used for long shots.

Grants

Do you need money or equipment for a photography project, a community garden or theatre, or a youth recreation hall? Grants for an amazing variety of projects are available from government and community agencies, foundations, corporations and other organisations. Here are a few tips on getting the funds you need:

• Consult the many reference books available at your public library, including *A Guide to Major Trusts*, published by the Directory of Social Change.

• Once you have decided which grant to apply for, find out as much as you can about the organisation providing the funds. Call and ask for the trust or charity's brochure or an annual report. Try to make personal contact with someone at the organisation, especially if it's a local donor.

• Keep your grant proposal clear, simple and brief, with the most important information at the beginning. Explain how you're going to make the best possible use of the money. Include information on the support you already have for your project. Try to get endorsement letters from people well known in the community or in your field. Once you have submitted your proposal, ring and make an appointment to discuss it in person.

• If you're turned down, consider applying to the same donor again. It often takes three or four tries to gain approval.

• Apply for many grants. If you're lucky enough to be approved by two donors, decide which offer is better. Explain the situation to the other source – you may be able to receive two grants, either in succession or at the same time.

Grass

• Always be sure to buy seed that has been treated with bird repellent.

• For a coarse turf that is suitable for playing games on and for children to enjoy, choose a mixture of seed containing rye grass.

• For a more decorative lawn that will not receive hard wear, choose a mixture made from fine grasses only.

Grass stains

• Rub the stain with liquid detergent, or a pad soaked in methylated spirits, and rinse thoroughly. If the stain persists, try a commercial stain remover on it, a mild solution of hydrogen peroxide, or – if safe for the fabric – bleach.

• If you're in a hurry, dab the stain with a cotton bud soaked in water and a little methylated spirits. Be patient, it may take a few minutes for the stain to fade.

• Cover a permanent stain with an appliqué or a patch.

Gravy

• For extra flavour, when making gravy, stir a handful of diced carrots, celery and onions and a pinch of herbs into the pan juices. Allow to simmer for 20 minutes, then strain gravy into a serving jug. Or, if you don't have time to cut and chop, just add a stock cube. Turn the gravy into an epicurean treat with a splash of port, Madeira, sherry or white vermouth.

• Brown your flour in the oven before using it to make gravy. It adds colour.

• If gravy lacks body, stir in 2 level teaspoons of cornflour for every ½ pint / 285 ml of liquid. Cook and stir until the mixture bubbles, thickens and clears (about 3 minutes – no longer or the gravy will begin to thin).

• Remove fat from the surface of gravy with a bulb-type baster, or scoop it off with a large metal spoon. Pour the cooking juices into a jug, then stand the

jug in iced water for 20-30 minutes. The fat will rise to the surface and be much easier to remove. Or, time permitting, refrigerate the gravy overnight, then lift off the congealed fat. You can also blot up fat by placing several thicknesses of paper towels flat on the surface of the gravy. Repeat as needed.

• Freeze leftover gravy in ice-cube trays. Wrap the frozen cubes tightly in aluminium foil and reheat them as needed or add them to meaty soups.

Grease spots

• If you're in a hurry to remove a grease stain, apply shampoo to the stained fabric, then rinse and blow-dry.

• Absorb the grease from a fresh stain with cornflour or talcum powder. Leave on the spot for up to 12 hours, brush off, then wash the fabric.

• To remove grease stains from washable fabrics, wash in a detergent solution as hot as the fabric will bear. Use a commercial stain remover on carpets or on stubborn stains.

• Get rid of grease stains on white shoes with nail polish remover. (Be careful not to remove the shoe's finish.) For other colours, use a commercial shoe stain remover.

• Wash car oil from hands with laundry detergent and water. Swarfega Hand Cleanser works too, and can be rubbed into heavy grease marks on fabrics before washing. Rub away grease and tar on hands with cooking oil.

• To remove greasy heel marks from vinyl or linoleum floors, try silver polish or furniture wax.

Greeting cards

• To preserve a greeting card, coat it with a light film of hair spray.

• Use last year's Christmas cards to make this year's postcards. Tear a card apart and cut the front to postcard size. Glue it to a piece of white card if it is not thick enough. Draw a line down the middle of the back and write your message on the left side and the address on the right.

• If you find a card with just the right message but you don't like the picture, glue gift-wrapping paper or your favourite photo over the front.

• Make gift tags by cutting down last year's greeting cards, folding them and punching a hole in the corner for a ribbon. Use pinking shears to make an attractive edge.

• For an attractive greeting card, use a leaf as a stencil. Fix it to a sheet of stiff white paper or a note card with a dab of glue, then spray-paint. After the paint dries, just strip away the leaf.

Grey hair

• If you use a permanent tint to cover up grey hair, it is better to go one or two shades lighter than darker – it is less ageing.

• Since grey hair tends to be dry and wiry, use a conditioner every time you shampoo. Keep your hair well trimmed for manageability and to prevent split ends. For a more youthful look, avoid a rigid, overdone hairstyle.

• If you're just beginning to turn grey and would like to conceal it, use a semi-permanent colorant that matches your original hair colour and which washes out after around six washes.

• Your grey hair may look better than you think. Try to enjoy it rather than change it.

Grills

• To speed cooking, line a grill pan with heavy aluminium foil to reflect heat upwards. The foil also makes the cleaning easier.

• A wire cake rack can be used to replace a light camping grill. And oven shelves can also support pots over a campfire.

• Use an old Boy Scout trick to make a 'tennis racket' grill. Find a green forked stick and wire the ends of the fork together (or use long shavings from green wood). Use short green sticks to lace the meat into this circle before holding it over the campfire. If the meat is going to take a while to cook, use a pile of stones to prop the grill over the campfire.

• To prevent meat from sticking to grill racks brush them with oil.

Grommets

• Use two washers of the proper size to set the upper and lower parts of a grommet in a fabric hole. Put one washer on a solid surface – a block of wood or a brick will do – and centre the eyelet (the lower part of the grommet) on it. Push the eyelet through the hole and fit it to the upper half of the grommet. Position the other washer on top of the upper half and hammer it down.

• A sewing-machine buttonholer will reinforce a fabric hole, though not as securely as a grommet does.

• For temporary reinforcement, try sticking small strips of tape around the edges of a hole in fabric.

• You can recycle grommets from old plimsolls. Cut them off, then open them up with needle-nose pliers. Slip the grommet into the hole in the new fabric and then close it with a hammer.

Grout

• After regrouting, use a spray bottle to apply liquid water-repellent silicone, of the type used to seal exterior walls, to the dried grout lines; it helps to prevent

staining and makes the grout more water-resistant.

• Remove old grout with a bottle opener. Use the pointed end of the opener to scratch out the grout, taking care not to damage the tiles.

Guarantees and warranties

Before making a major purchase, always read the guarantee or warranty (the terms are interchangeable).

• Store all your warranties, along with proofs of purchase and dated receipts, in a separate file. If you misplace a warranty, call the shop where you bought the item and ask for a copy or get them to read the terms over the telephone.

• You needn't send in a warranty card to be covered by its provisions. (You won't be notified, however, if the manufacturer recalls the item.) Even if you lose the warranty, your merchandise is covered, as long as you have proof of purchase.

• Manufacturer's guarantees are legally enforceable, but cannot take away your other legal rights. Where the terms of the guarantee are such that it is going to cost you money, go back to the retailer first.

• If the manufacturer refuses to honour the guarantee, seek advice from the Citizens Advice Bureau.

Gum disease

• To prevent this major cause of tooth loss, clean your teeth after every meal and at bedtime with a soft, rounded, nylon-bristled brush; work up and down, keeping the bristles at an angle to the gum line. Start brushing at a different place every time you clean your teeth. Always use a fluoride toothpaste, because it will help to prevent tooth decay.

• If you can't brush your teeth after every meal, brush twice a day and preferably at night immediately before going to bed.

• Ask your dentist for advice about using dental floss to remove plaque and food particles from between your teeth.

• Massage your gums regularly with a toothbrush or a clean fingertip to stimulate blood flow.

• Eat a low-sugar diet.

• If your gums bleed, are swollen and sore, or contain pus, see a dentist immediately. See also DENTIST VISITS, p.60; TOOTHBRUSH, p.211.

Gutters

• Make a habit of clearing your gutters twice a year, in spring and autumn. If you don't, they may become clogged, with nesting birds or fallen leaves.

• Move debris from gutters with a garden trowel and stiff brush, transferring the material to a bucket suspended from an S hook on your ladder.

• With the worst of the debris removed, use a garden hose on jet to swill any remaining dirt in the direction of the downpipes. The flow of water will also help to check that the gutters are in good condition and that the fall will carry all the water away.

• If you find a blockage in a downpipe, don't push it down. Try pulling it up with a piece of hooked wire. If this fails, hire drain rods or other equipment from a local hire shop or contact a firm who specialise in clearing drains through the Yellow Pages.

• To keep gutters clear, you can fit special gutter guards made from wire netting, which clip onto the gutter. But keep an eye on them if there are trees nearby. Leaves can build up on top of the netting, directing water away from the gutter instead of into it.

• Protect the tops of downpipes with a metal or plastic balloon cage that fits inside the top of the pipe. This will prevent birds from trying to nest in the hollow where pipe and gutter meet – a very common cause of downpipe blockages.

Hacksaw

• If you don't have a hacksaw and need to cut a thin piece of metal, use the edge of a file or wood rasp to make a groove, then bend the metal back and forth until it breaks.

• Grind through hard metal with an abrasive wheel in your electric drill. **Caution** Make sure you wear eye protection and gloves.

Haemorrhoids

• Avoid constipation (see p.51); a high-fibre diet – rich in fresh fruits and vegetables as well as whole-grain or bran breads and cereals – and plenty of non-alcoholic liquids every day will soften the stool and eliminate the need to strain.

• Wash and dry yourself gently with soft tissues followed by baby wipes.

• To soothe the pain of a particularly severe attack, use an ice bag as a compress.

• Soak in a hot bath to relieve painful muscle spasms.

• Buy over-the-counter astringent suppositories to help soothe and shrink the haemorrhoids.

• See your doctor if you have any bleeding from the anus or if your bowel habit changes.

Hair

• Is there no time to shampoo your hair? Try putting an old, clean nylon stocking over your brush and run it through your hair to remove dust and oil. Rub along partings all over the scalp with cotton wool soaked in witch hazel, cologne or

skin tonic to help clean greasy roots.
• When you run out of your favourite conditioner, try one of these alternatives.

Use corn or olive oil warmed up in a cup standing in hot water. Comb it through your hair, and cover your hair with a plastic bath cap for half an hour. Rinse, shampoo and rinse again.

Or, beat 2 egg yolks, add 1 tablespoon rum, leave the mixture on your hair for half an hour, then rinse.

Or, try mayonnaise or natural yoghurt as a conditioner.
• For instant shampoos, try bubble bath or a delicate detergent.
• In the absence of hair-setting lotion, beer gives body and champagne gives crispness. Try tonic water; also, red wine for dark hair or white wine for blondes.
• A tablespoon of vinegar or lemon juice in the last rinse is good for greasy hair.
• Prevent sun and saltwater damage by applying a small amount of coconut oil, wheat-germ oil or petroleum jelly to hair ends.
• Make an aromatic hair spray from a lemon or, if you have dry hair, an orange. Boil 1 piece of fruit (quartered) in 1 pint/570ml of water until ½ pint/285ml remains; cool and strain. Keep in a spray bottle in the refrigerator.

Hairbrushes

To clean hairbrushes (and combs, too), soak them in warm water with a little detergent added to it. Rinse thoroughly, then leave to dry face-down on a towel. Comb through brush bristles to remove hair trapped in them.

Hair dryers

• If your hair dryer suddenly stops working, it may have simply overheated; wait a few minutes and try it again.
• In the absence of a hair dryer, put a net over your hair and sit in front of a fan.
• Or use a fan heater placed on a table. Cover your hair with a net and turn on the fan, setting it at low, or sit at a suitable distance so that you don't get burned.

Hairstyling

• If you want to curl or wave your hair, but you have no curlers, use narrow strips of cloth cut from an old shirt or clean rag, and knot them in the middle. Roll a section of damp hair around the knot and use the loose ends of the cloth to tie the curl in place, or secure it with a hair pin. For larger curls, cut a paper towel roll into four sections and roll the hair around them.
• To revive a perm or curly hairstyle, spray it with water using a plant spray and fluff up your hair with your fingers or a wide-toothed comb.
• For more body, spray flat beer on damp curly hair.
• Rub a little hairdressing cream or hair cream or gel into frizzy ends.

Halloween and fancy dress

Use household items and cast-off clothing to create Halloween or fancy-dress costumes that don't cost money.
• Transform old colanders, bowls and plastic containers into helmets and other hats. Cut a deflated football in half and spray-paint it silver for a robot's, spaceman's, Valkyrie's or knight's helmet. Turn thick work gloves into gauntlets by spraying them silver.
• Use shredded cellophane from gift baskets as a wig.
• A balaclava makes a good start for a lot of costumes; attach animal ears, wool or jewellery.
• Make white clown makeup by mixing 2 tablespoons of cornflour with 1 tablespoon of solid margarine or butter. Add some colour, if you like, with a few drops of food colouring.
• For facial decoration, cut stars, flowers or hearts from brightly coloured tissue paper. To make the glue, cook one large potato, with its skin, until it's soft, let it cool. Rub the cut-outs on the potato and then stick them on dry, clean skin.
• If you need extra padding for a costume, wear large tights and stuff them with cushions or rags.
• Try this for a fun outfit – turn yourself into a slice of pizza. Start with a piece of carpet foam underlay; cut it into a triangular shape as tall as you are. Spray it

---

Battling the bane of baldness

The Egyptians, in an attempt to stimulate hair growth, used to anoint their heads with fat from snakes or crocodiles.

In Greece, Hippocrates applied a mixture of opium, rose oil and unripe olives in an effort to reforest his pate. (The fringe of hair over the ears and around the back of a bald man's head is called the Hippocratic wreath even today.)

Romans who were too poor to buy wigs painted hair onto their scalps – evidence of the desperate measures people afflicted by baldness will take.

Through the ages, men have massaged their scalps with rum, vodka, red pepper, ginger, the boiled flesh of moles and even horse manure. But for all their ingenuity, their hair remained as sparse as ever. The most enduring, least expensive and least painful method of returning to a full head of hair is still to buy a toupee – a partial wig or a hair piece which is glued into place on the head.

orange onto the 'crust' at the base of the triangle (allow for plenty of crust, because you'll have to fold some of it over your shoulders). Then spray the rest of the triangle tomato-sauce red (or red and yellow if you like your pizza with cheese). Cut mushroom slices, green pepper strips and onion rings from plastic foam meat trays and paint them the appropriate colours. For pepperoni sausage, cut circles from a brown paper bag and paint them reddish-brown – they curl up just like the real thing. Glue the pieces on the pizza slice or, better still, attach them with Velcro glued to the slice and to the backs of the various pieces. Fold over the crust, cut a hole for your head, and staple the crust together at your shoulders.

Hands

• When you run out of hand cream, smooth on petroleum jelly or baby oil or lotion.
• Remove stains on your hands by rubbing them with lemon juice or lemon peel. Or mix a teaspoon of sugar into a tablespoon of warm olive oil, rub the mixture into your hands, wipe off and wash under warm water.
• While rearranging items in the freezer, wear oven gloves to protect your hands from the cold.
• Always dry hands carefully after washing them and then rub cream into them.
• Before ironing, massage hand cream into your hands and then pull on a pair of cotton gloves. The warmth will coax dry hands to absorb the cream.

Hanging laundry

• Have your clothespegs gone missing? Try clip-on earrings, tie clips, hair clips, paper clips or the pocket clasps of pens. (To avoid rust, put wax paper, plastic or cloth under metal clips.)
• If you need a clothespeg bag, use an empty hanging plant pot. Its drainage holes will keep rain from collecting and waterlogging the clothespegs. An onion or potato bag – the mesh kind – will do the same.
• To keep your hands warm on a winter day while you're hanging out the laundry, put a hot-water bottle in the clothes basket and squeeze it occasionally. Or wear cotton-lined rubber gloves.
• Hang shirts and trousers from the bottom hem to avoid visible peg marks when you wear them.

Hangovers

Prevention The best way to avoid a hangover is to avoid excessive amounts of alcohol.
• Just before you go out – and also while you're partying – line your stomach with milk and milk products.
• Fill up on bulky foods, such as bread and pasta, to slow the absorption of alcohol into the blood.
• Avoid red wine and such dark liquors as rum; they contain more impurities that intensify a hangover.
• Mix your drinks with fruit juice or plain water – carbonated water speeds the absorption of alcohol – or down a glass of water after every alcoholic drink.

Treatment
• Before going to bed, drink at least 1 pint/570ml of water or juice.
• The morning after, drink more water and juice. Avoid caffeine; it dehydrates the system. Eat easy-to-digest foods – cereal and milk, toast and fruit. (Skip eggs, which are difficult to digest.)
• Honey or a sweet drink may raise a low blood sugar level reduced after drinking alcohol.
• Paracetamol will ease a headache, but avoid aspirin, which may upset your stomach. For an upset stomach, try mint tea or an antacid.

Hatchets and axes

A sharp hatchet or axe is safer than a dull one; it cuts cleanly, whereas a dull one may ricochet off a log and onto your leg. Use a fine, flat file or a grinding wheel to sharpen the blade before each use, then clean and oil the metal before you store the hatchet with the blade covered in one of these ways.
• Make a wood or leather sheath and secure it against the blade with a heavy rubber band or strip of inner tube.
• Sink the blade into a sturdy block of softwood.
• Wrap a rag soaked in oil around the blade and tie it with string.
• Slice open a short scrap of garden hose and cover the cutting edge of the hatchet with it.

Hazardous waste

Leftover paint, household cleaner, insect spray and weed killer are all hazardous wastes. Flushing them down the drain can damage sewage treatment systems. And putting them out with the rubbish means that they are sent to the landfill, where they eventually seep into groundwater.

If you can't use up a potentially hazardous product, think of someone who can. Schools, neighbours or churches may be pleased to accept your extra paint, insect spray or cleaning solution.

Call your local environment health department, a recycling centre or an environmental agency to see if they organise collection drives. If they do, make sure the wastes are in sealed, watertight, labelled containers. If a container is rusting or leaking, put it in a larger, secure receptacle.

Headaches

• At the first sign of a headache, stop what you're doing and, if possible, lie down in a dark, quiet room with an ice bag or a cold pack on your forehead for 30 to 45 minutes.
• Relax. Ask someone to massage your neck, shoulders and upper back; take a long, leisurely hot bath; do relaxation

Rubbish disposal has always been a problem. The inhabitants of ancient Troy left their waste on the floors of their homes or dumped it in the streets. And as late as the mid-19th century, the British simply threw their rubbish out of the windows to pile up in the gutters below, despite various laws forbidding them to do so, and the fines they had to pay.

The ancient Greeks organised the first municipal dumps in the Western world, and Athens was the first city known to prohibit throwing refuse into its streets. In Britain, whenever rubbish became piled up so high that it threatened to block the streets, it was loaded onto horse-drawn carts and taken to the edge of town to be dumped on tips.

Today there are moves to make use of these tips, or landfill sites, by building on them. One of the problems, though, is the explosive methane gas that builds up in the dumps as the rubbish decomposes. However, there are methods of removing the gas, and housing estates and one of the largest shopping centres in Britain – Lakeside, at Thurrock in Essex – have been built on them.

Today, Britain produces 200 million tonnes of household waste a year – this amounts to an average of 44lb/20kg per household per week. Of this, 75-80 per cent is potentially recyclable, but in fact only between 2 and 10 per cent is recycled at present. In the meantime, the scarcity of landfill space has become critical.

exercises (see p.169, and STRESS, p.196).
• Take paracetamol (see HANGOVERS, opposite). To prevent a rebound headache, don't take too much or continue taking it after the pain has gone.
• As long as the pain persists, eat very lightly and abstain from alcoholic drinks.
• To identify and remove the cause of recurring headaches, keep a record of the date and time of each occurrence, what you were doing, what foods or beverages you had consumed and any recent change in habits.
• Even though most headaches are not serious, seek medical help if yours doesn't respond to simple self-treatment; if it includes a stiff neck or facial soreness; if it's accompanied by other symptoms or follows an accident or injury; or if it's piercing or localised. See MIGRAINE HEADACHES, p.133.

Headboards

If your bed doesn't have a headboard, you can make your own and hang it on the wall.
• Cut a piece of ½in/13mm medium-density fibre board (MDF) to size and smooth the edges. Paint or stain it, then hang it on the wall with heavy-duty picture wire or mount it with screws or toggle bolts. If you want to make the headboard more striking, dress it up by gluing on a geometric design in wood lath.
• To make a padded headboard, start with a shaped piece of ½in/13mm plywood or MDF, smoothing all edges. Cut a piece of polyurethane upholstery foam about ¾in/19mm thick to the exact size of your board, and hold it in place with double-sided carpet tape. Lay your fabric over the foam; turn the whole lot over, then carefully pull the fabric taut enough to round the edge of the foam. Staple the fabric in place. A decorative matching trim can be tacked in place

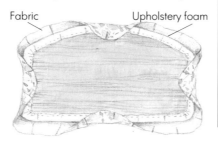

Fabric   Upholstery foam

around the perimeter. Trim off surplus fabric. If your bed has fixing screws set into the back frame, glue and screw two battens, about 2 × ½in/50 × 13mm, to the headboard, having cut two slots large enough to slide over the fixing screws. Position the battens to line up with the screws.
• For a still softer effect, mount a pair of café curtain rods, one above the other, behind the bed and stretch fabric between them. To create generous folds, sew enough widths of fabric together to form a panel three times wider than the length of the rods.
• Another attractive heading can be formed by fixing two pieces of curtain pole at right angles to the wall above the bed, and draping fabric across them to form a canopy. Or attach a single pole at right angles to the wall, in the centre above the bed and drape fabric on either side of it. Secure the fabric to the wall with loops of cord.
• To support the curtain poles at right angles to the wall, use socket brackets fixed to the wall with screws and Rawlplugs. When inserting the poles into the brackets, it is extremely important that the poles fit really tightly, or they will tend to droop under their own weight and the weight of the fabric draped across them.

Headhunters

A headhunter, or executive search specialist, is a recruiter, hired by companies to seek out candidates for high-level positions or specialised jobs. He finds people through research, contacts and discreet telephone calls.
Finding one
• Ask colleagues to recommend you to headhunters they know.
• Alternatively, use a directory of search consultancies to find headhunters who specialise in your field. When you have identified a headhunter working in your field, telephone and ask for an appointment. Send your brief CV (see WRITING A CURRICULUM VITAE, p.245) and a covering letter confirming your appointment.
Using one
• At your interview, be open about your

background and experience (don't lie about your salary or misrepresent yourself), and ask for an evaluation.

• Question the headhunter in depth about any companies to which he sends you. (But do your own independent research as well.)

• Discuss your career plans and aspirations. Ask for feedback on your cv.

Unsolicited calls

• If a headhunter calls you, ask for the firm's name, address and telephone number. Tell him you'll call back after you've considered his offer. Before you do, check out his firm.

• If the headhunter is vague concerning job information or asks a lot about your present firm and little about you, be suspicious – he may be trying to pump you for information about your employer.

• If he uses high-pressure sales tactics or seems unresponsive to your needs, don't work with him.

Head lice

If you or the school nurse finds lice in your child's hair, eradicate them with an over-the-counter preparation bought from a chemist.

Comb your child's hair every night, strand by strand, with a fine-toothed comb until you are sure there are no more lice and you have combed out all their eggs. To prevent a recurrence, tell the child not to share combs, hats or earphones with her friends at school.

Health farms

• Most health farms, or clinics, are set in their own grounds and include a wide range of facilities: a gymnasium, swimming pool, sauna and outdoor sports are all likely to be available. A week or fortnight in a health farm can help you to relax and improve your fitness, appearance and health, although the high level of individual attention that you receive means that health farms are generally expensive.

• Most health farms also have professional staff who are qualified to treat ailments such as back pain, liver disorders and sciatica, as well as advising on

anxiety and stress. Other therapies that are often on offer include massage, yoga, reflexology, aromatherapy and osteopathy. These options usually have to be paid for as extras.

• Most clinics serve a strict calorie controlled diet of mainly vegetarian meals, although some are more relaxed.

• *Healthy Breaks*, published by the British Tourist Authority, lists all Britain's health farms and their prices. If you cannot find or order a copy of the book locally, contact Discovery Books, 29 Hacketts Lane, Pyrford, Woking, Surrey GU22 8PP.

Hearing aids

Whatever the original cause of deafness, many sufferers can have partial hearing restored with the assistance of a small hearing aid. If you have difficulty hearing what's being said in a crowded room, consult your doctor; he may refer you to a specialist. Treatments can range from removing wax from your ears to taking a mould of your ear in order to fit an aid correctly.

• Modern electronic hearing aids work by transmitting sounds down a plastic tube from a tiny microphone and amplifier to an earpiece or a vibrator fitted into or behind the ear. The aids are powered by tiny batteries which last for several weeks at a time. Keep a couple of spare batteries for emergencies.

• A special device in the form of a low-voltage transmitter can be attached to the back of a television set to be used in conjunction with a hearing aid. This means the rest of the family can watch the television with the volume at a normal level. Ask your local television dealer or the RNID (below) for information.

• Clean your aid by wiping it with a damp cloth and occasionally rinsing it in a weak antiseptic solution. Clear a tube blocked with wax under hot, running water, and then empty the tube of any water drops by blowing through it.

• If your aid begins to whistle, check that the plastic tube has not cracked.

• If you would like to know more about deafness and the various treatments

available, contact the Royal National Institute for the Deaf (RNID), 19-23 Featherstone St, London EC1Y 8SL, Tel. 0171-296 8000. They produce several leaflets including *Aids to Daily Living* (useful day-to-day accessories for the hard-of-hearing), *NHS Hearing Aids Service* (which guides you through the process of getting a hearing aid through the NHS) and *Hearing Aids: questions and answers* (advice on choosing and caring for aids).

Hearing loss

• Safeguard your hearing – keep the noise down whenever possible and protect your ears. When close to or operating noisy power equipment, wear earplugs or anti-noise muffs.

• At a noisy concert or party, try to keep away from the loudspeakers. Most hearing loss after being exposed to a great deal of noise is temporary. Your normal hearing will return within a short time. If it does not, consult your doctor.

• Check any medicine you take. Too much aspirin can cause ringing in the ears, as can some antibiotics whose names end in -mycin. Talk to your doctor about the problem.

Heart attack

A victim of a heart attack may collapse and fall into unconsciousness.

• Check the victim's breathing and his pulse. If necessary, apply artificial respiration (see p.67).

• If he is conscious, breathing normally and his pulse is going, place him in a comfortable position and loosen clothing at his neck, chest and waist. Try and get him to breathe deeply. If he is unconscious, place him in the recovery position (see p.168).

• Call an ambulance immediately. Keep people who may be crowding over him away, and comfort him. Take his pulse regularly, at 10-minute intervals, and record how long you take it for, until an ambulance arrives.

• Warnings of a heart attack include: pain in the chest, sometimes down the left arm and up the left side of the neck; progressive shortness of breath, sometimes accompanied by wheezing; unexplained coughing; swollen feet or ankles, exaggerated in the evening or after activity. If any of these signs are detected, consult a doctor.

Heartburn

A burning sensation in the chest after eating is a form of indigestion, felt when the acid contents of the stomach are forced back into the food pipe.

• It should not be confused with having a heart attack, which is caused by a reduction in the blood supply to the heart. This leaves the victim with severe pains in the chest, sometimes spreading down one or both arms, dizziness and shortness of breath.

• Occasional heartburn is quite normal and is mainly caused by eating too quickly, by eating spicy foods or by swallowing a gassy drink. It can be relieved by taking antacids, obtainable from chemists in tablet or liquid form.

• Sufferers should avoid spicy food and dressings, alcohol, aspirin, garlic, onions, chocolate and coffee. Eat smaller meals, eat them slowly and sit upright at the table. If the symptoms persist, consult your doctor.

Heat exhaustion

When you overexert yourself or wear heavy clothing in hot, humid weather, you run the risk of heat exhaustion. Among its symptoms are cold, clammy, pale skin; heavy perspiration; dizziness, nausea and headache; rapid breathing and pulse; and faintness that may lead to unconsciousness.

If you see someone with these symptoms, make him sit or lie down in a cool spot immediately. Loosen his clothing and remove extra layers. Fan his skin. If he's alert, get him to drink up to 1 pint/ 570ml of water; if he's groggy, don't force him to drink fluids – you could cause choking.

Heatstroke If the condition doesn't improve within 30 minutes, there is risk of heatstroke. Its symptoms are hot,

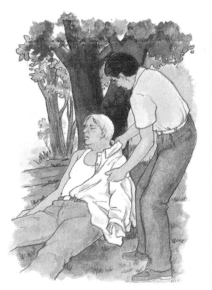

dry, flushed skin; deep, then shallow breathing; a rapid, strong pulse, followed by a rapid, weak pulse; dilated pupils; unconsciousness; twitching muscles; and convulsions.

If you suspect heatstroke, cool down the victim as fast as you can. Take extreme measures: soak towels and sheets in cold water and wrap them around his body. If ice is available, put it in plastic bags and place under his armpits, behind each knee, in the groin, on the wrists and ankles and on the sides of the neck. When the victim's temperature drops to 38°C/100°F, wrap him in a dry sheet. If it rises again, repeat the cooling process.

Call an ambulance or rush the victim, wrapped in wet cloths, to a hospital. If you can't get him to hospital, immerse him in the coldest water possible. Stay with him to prevent drowning.

Hedges

There's no instant cure for an overgrown hedge. It takes hard pruning and a few growing seasons to bring it under control. But there are ways to do the job while keeping the hedge healthy.

• If the hedge is too dense, cut it back to the main stems on one side only. Let the hedge recover and put forth new growth for a year. Then cut back the other side.

• If the hedge has become too tall, cut back every second shrub to within a few inches of the ground. A thicket of new

shoots should sprout around the severed trunks. Then cut back the remaining shrubs the following year.

• Don't prune a hedge into a vase shape, wider at the top than at the bottom. The lower part will be shaded, and the foliage will fall off while the upper growth spreads. The result will be a leggy hedge. Instead, prune so that the base is broader than the top.

Note Privet, yew, holly, berberis, forsythia, roses and spiraeas respond well to hard pruning.

Hems

• Instead of sewing a hem, use iron-on fusible tape. Turn up the hem, press it, and trim the edge, then insert the tape about ¼in/6mm from the hem's top edge. 'Baste' it with light touches of a warm dry iron; to secure, press the hem with a steam iron (use the Wool setting).

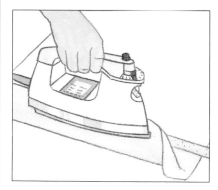

• A temporary solution for a drooping hem is to hold it in place with a length of double-sided masking tape or some other sticky tape.

• When lengthening a garment, sponge away the old hemline crease with equal parts of white vinegar and water. If the crease leaves a dark line, try a suitable stain remover. A white line is permanent; hide it under lace, or trim.

• Instead of pinning up a hem, use paper clips – they won't prick your fingers. And for easy measuring, notch a piece of cardboard at the desired hem width; place the turned-up hem in the notch and move it along as you sew or pin.

Herbs

• For a quick bouquet garni for soups, stews or sauces, use a tea infuser instead of the usual muslin bag. Fill with dried parsley, dried thyme and a crumbled bay leaf (the traditional mix). Or try celery seed, fennel seed and dried basil, marjoram or tarragon. Taste the dish often as it cooks and remove the herbs when the taste is right.

• You could also make a fresh herb bouquet garni by tying the following together with fine string – a sprig of parsley, thyme, rosemary and a bay leaf.

• When you're substituting dried herbs for fresh, use less as a rule of thumb: 1 teaspoon of dried herbs replaces 1 tablespoon of fresh herbs.

• Crumble dried herbs between your fingers to release their flavour.

• If you are short of tarragon, use parsley or chervil instead – but increase the quantity by about 50 per cent. If you're out of thyme, use marjoram, oregano or a bay leaf.

• Thyme on your hands? Dry whole plants upside-down in perforated paper bags; then use them to make herb wreaths or sachets. Or tie the dried bunches with ribbon and hang them from hooks for a country kitchen atmosphere. See also FLOWERS, p.303.

Dried herb and flower wreath

Hiccups

If all your standard remedies for hiccups don't seem to be having an effect, give one of these a try:

• Breathe in and out of a paper bag to allow carbon dioxide to build up in your body. *Do not* use a plastic bag – this could be fatal.

• Lie down with your head tilted as far back as possible and your mouth open.

• Ask someone to gently press the protruding skin directly in front of your ear canals while you drink a glass of cold water.

• Suck ice or drop a cold key or spoon down your back, inside your clothes.

• Ask someone to surprise you by unexpectedly slapping your back.

Hiking boots

• In an emergency you can make a hiking boot water-resistant by dripping candle wax onto the welt where the sole joins the upper. But to do the job properly, use boot wax.

Set the boots and the tin of wax in the hot sun until they are warm, or you can warm them with an electric hair dryer. Then apply the wax evenly and rub it in with your bare hands; put an extra-thick application all around the welts. Warm the boots again until the leather has completely absorbed the wax. Repeat the procedure, then remove any excess wax with a dry cloth. If the boots are likely to be exposed to moisture often, reapply boot wax frequently. (A small amount can be carried in a 35mm film canister.)

• To make boots warmer, use insoles.

Hinges

• For a quick repair, nail a short piece of leather belt over a broken hinge – it's flexible and surprisingly strong. Apply boot dubbin to keep the leather from drying and cracking.

• Replace a damaged or lost hinge pin with a snug-fitting nail or a machine screw. Coat the replacement pin with lubricating oil.

• Here's an easy way to silence a

Oil can
Pin
Felt washer

squeaky gate hinge. Cut a washer out of felt and saturate it with light oil. Then remove the hinge pin, push it through the washer and reinsert it. Add more oil if the squeak returns.

• Hinge screws often pull loose and lose their holding power. To repair them, whittle down a wooden stick to fit tightly into the screw hole. Coat it with glue and jam it into the hole. When the glue is dry, cut the stick off flush with the hole, and then drive in the screw. As an alternative, jam several toothpicks into the hole and cut off the excess; you don't need glue in this case.

Hire purchase and credit

Hire purchase and shop credit are two different ways of paying for an item in instalments. Hire purchase is now generally used only for buying cars, and it differs from shop credit in that the car still belongs to the vendor until the instalments are fully paid.

• As a rule of thumb, never buy anything on credit which has a value that won't outlast the payments.

• Work out how much you will actually pay – including interest and any service charges.

• Find out in advance what penalties the contract specifies in case you miss a payment. (It may be that the entire balance then becomes due.)

• Beware of added features you don't really need or want, such as insurance to protect the loan.

See also CREDIT CARDS, p.55; DEBT, p.60; DOWN PAYMENTS, p.65; HOME EQUITY LOANS, opposite.

Holes in knitwear

• Are you repairing a knitted garment? Place the unravelling part over the bristles of a brush – they will hold the knit and prevent it from stretching.

• To repair holes in a sweater, place a piece of muslin or net on the wrong side of it, then darn right through its holes.

• For a quick repair when your sweater snags, pull the loose loops to the inside and secure them with a hair pin or paper clip until you can get home and restitch them.

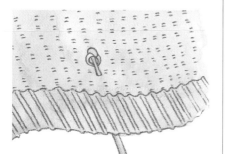

Use a crochet hook or bent paper clip to draw snagged stitches inside a sweater.

Holes in pockets

• For an emergency repair on an inside pocket, fold the torn edge under and secure it with safety pins or staples.

• If a patch (exterior) pocket gives way, attach it with double-sided sticky tape. (Don't put anything in the pocket until you can make repairs.) Or, if you can fold under the loose section, fasten it from the inside with safety pins.

• For a permanent repair, instead of stitching, insert iron-on tape between the two seam allowances of an inside pocket or between a garment and its patch pocket; press with a warm dry iron to fix the tape in place.

Home equity loans

A kind of second mortgage, this is the least expensive way to borrow money because you are using your home as collateral. For the same reason, it is also among the most dangerous of loans.

• A home equity loan can be used to finance school fees or an addition to your home, but don't use it to back a risky investment – if you can't meet the payments, you can lose your home.

• Before signing up for such a loan, ask your banker or lender these questions:

– What is the annual percentage rate and what is it based on?

– How often and how much can the interest rate change annually and over the life of the loan?

– Are there charges when you've paid off the loan? (Some banks absorb these.)

– What other fees will add significantly to the actual cost of the loan?

– Is there a conversion clause that allows you to change from a variable to a fixed-rate loan to protect against high inflation?

– Are there penalties for early payment?

Homeowner's insurance

• How much insurance do you need for your home? If you do not insure it for its full value, you will risk having your claim reduced by 'averaging', which means that you will recover only a proportion of your claim. Where the cost of rebuilding your house goes up so that it is no longer fully insured, the insurance company can exercise its discretion to decide how much of your claim they will pay. So play safe and keep your house insurance under review.

• Although separate coverage is available, your best bet is a homeowner's package that covers theft, liability, fire and other perils. (Particularly valuable possessions may require a separate policy.) Include inflation protection in your policy, as well as coverage for living expenses if your home becomes uninhabitable because of fire or flood. And don't forget to increase your coverage for any major improvements you make.

• To save money, shop around and look for special deals – some companies offer discounts if smoke detectors and alarm systems are fitted.

• To find a company that pays claims fairly quickly, call local contractors, roofers and carpet cleaners. Ask who pays them promptly – and without quibbling.

• Work out how much your home is worth in terms of rebuilding and refurnishing it – not including the original price or the amount of the mortgage. Enlist the assistance of a reputable surveyor or builder, not an estate agent.

• Make a detailed list of your possessions (see VALUABLES, p.219), then get a replacement-cost endorsement on your policy so that you'll be reimbursed at full value if your possessions are lost. See also INSURANCE CLAIMS, p.114.

Home pollution

Modern houses are so well sealed that they may keep pollutants trapped inside. Radon gas, formaldehyde, tobacco smoke, bacteria, fungi, pollen and combustion by-products such as soot and carbon monoxide can cause illness – even death – if they are present in high concentrations. The danger is greatly reduced or eliminated with good ventilation (which older, leakier houses encourage naturally).

• Install a small exhaust fan over a gas oven. Kitchen, bath, laundry and attic fans help, too. Do not, however, install a large exhaust fan upstairs if you have a conventional gas burner, oil furnace or boiler with a chimney downstairs. The fan could suck air down the chimney and bring dangerous combustion products into the house.

• Get all pipe leaks from boilers, fuel-burning cookers and space heaters repaired as soon as you notice them.

• Don't heat a closed space with an unvented device such as a paraffin heater.

• If you discover that you have asbestos insulation in walls, ceilings, cookers or boilers, don't touch it. Call a professional in to remove it.

Home study

Full-time education is not the only way to obtain better qualifications. Nor is it necessarily the best way for people who need to stay close to home or are unable

or unwilling to break into their working time. Studying at home is an alternative.
• Many universities and colleges offering degree and professional qualification courses now provide the opportunity for students to study at home. Of course, correspondence courses have been around for a long time, particularly for occupations such as accountancy, where continuous work experience is seen as important. But the arrival of video, CD ROMS, on-line computing links via a modem and other emerging technologies mean that so-called 'distance learning' is quickly becoming an attractive option for employers and employees alike.

The advantages of distance learning are that tuition fees are much lower; you can learn at your own pace; and you can go on working while learning.
• Most schools offering correspondence and distance-learning courses advertise in the national press. But before you enrol, do make sure you have the right course for the qualification that you are trying to obtain. If you are unsure, check with a professional body.
• Schools offering professional training courses also vary in quality. But they will be known to the relevant professional association or institution. Similarly, schools offering preparation for basic qualifications such as GCSE or A level will be known to the examining bodies. Before enrolling on a course, check its credentials with your professional body or the relevant examining body. You are also advised to question the school carefully about its previous results. Beware of schools that give vague answers or make exaggerated claims about success rates.
• Only recognised universities or polytechnics may grant valid degrees. The Open University is the best known and most experienced distance-learning university in Britain, but several other universities and polytechnics now offer distance-learning undergraduate and postgraduate degree courses. Details of these can be found in local libraries. Details of Open University courses can be obtained from the Open University, Milton Keynes, Bucks.

Horseradish

Make your own fresh horseradish sauce – it will be far better than anything you can buy at the supermarket.
• To make the sauce, just scrub and peel the roots and purée them in a blender or food processor. Don't be tempted to put your nose over the blender to smell the horseradish – the aroma is so strong that it will make your eyes water! Add 1-2 tablespoons of white vinegar for every 1oz/30g of horseradish. Season with salt and add a little sugar. Keep in a covered jar in the refrigerator. Make a creamy sauce by adding as much purée as suits your own personal taste to ¼ pint/150ml whipped cream.
• You can grow your own horseradish. But beware: the plant is very invasive. To keep it from taking over your garden, enclose its bed with bricks or sheet metal to a depth of at least 12in/300mm, or grow horseradish in a tub.

Hospital stays

• If you have a choice of hospitals, consider your own needs. A large teaching hospital usually provides state-of-the-art care, but for simpler procedures you may feel more comfortable and get more individual attention in a smaller district general hospital. Before making your decision, get the advice of your doctor and any family members or friends who have received treatment at the hospitals you're considering.
• Take with you:
    a change of nightwear
    dressing gown
    slippers
    toothbrush
    toothpaste
    soap
    shampoo
    razor
    flannel
    bath and hand towels
    talcum powder
    mirror
    hairbrush and/or comb
    tampons/sanitary towels
    paper tissues
    fruit juice

• Take a small amount of money to buy newspapers or to use the phone, but do not take more than you need. If you have to take valuable items such as jewellery, ask the staff to deposit them in the hospital safe.
• In preparation for getting up and about and coming home you may be able to keep a small amount of personal clothing in the hospital. However, space is usually very limited and the staff may prefer you to leave outdoor clothes at home until you need them.
• Mark all personal property, including clothes, with your name.
• Bring with you any medicines that you are taking – both those prescribed by your doctor and over-the-counter medicines from a chemist.
• Tell family and friends which ward you will be in. They should usually address letters and cards to: you, the name or number of your ward, the hospital name and the hospital address.
• Unless you are in a hospital with personal telephones, family and friends will be able to phone the ward but not you. Take money for the call box and phone them.
• If you are entitled to sickness benefit, ask the nurse in charge for a medical certificate dated from the day you entered the hospital. Fill it in and send it to your employer. Delay can result in loss of benefit. Take your National Insurance number with you so that you can complete the form.
• Take books, magazines and knitting to fill in time if necessary.
• Tell the ward staff if you require a special diet.
• Be sure that you understand what is going to happen to you. Do not be afraid to ask questions, and expect honest replies. Whenever possible, the hospital must obtain your informed consent before you have an operation, treatment or tests.

Hotels and motels

• When making reservations or checking in, ask if your age, employment situation, professional affiliation, motoring association membership or credit card scheme qualifies you for a preferred rate. (If not, ask what does.) At big city hotels, enquire about seasonal savings and weekend discounts.

• For low rates in city centres, check into a YMCA/YWCA. Youth hostels round the whole of Britain generally offer good rates, too. See YOUTH HOSTELS, p.236.

• Consider bed-and-breakfast alternatives; many guidebooks describe the ever-growing options, from a room with a shared bath in a private home to a nicely appointed suite with a private bath in a grander, less intimate hotel.

• Are you travelling abroad? For information on unusual accommodation in places such as castles, villas, farmhouses and canal boats, contact the country's tourist board in London or a reputable travel agent.

• House swapping is a possibility for a longer trip; put an ad in the classified section of the newspaper of your intended destination. Or take advantage of listings from the tourist board or travel agencies.

Hotel reservations

• Avoid spending telephone time on hold: call for reservations early in the morning or late at night.

• Hotels aren't legally bound to honour reservations, but in case of overbooking, they must obtain comparable lodging for you elsewhere, and they must pay for your transport there. To protect yourself when making reservations, always get a confirmation number and write it down.

• Ask about the cancellation policy. You may find that you can be charged for late cancellations.

• If you've booked a room for a week and paid only a night's deposit, it's all right to leave after the first night if you're not satisfied.

Hot-water bottles

• Make a bed warmer by filling a screw-top glass jar with hot water; then tighten the lid and wrap it in a towel.

• Store rubber hot-water bottles open, upside-down, to prevent mildew.

House guests

• When inviting guests to your home, let them know what time you expect them to arrive and to leave. Mention in your invitation any activities, such as tennis or swimming, that call for special clothes.

• If someone has a reputation for staying longer than scheduled, arrange an activity for the day after the agreed departure time and inform the guest of your other plans.

• Check to see if your guests have food and drink preferences or allergies.

The role of the guest

• Bring a small gift – wine, flowers or a homemade cake. Or bring toys to leave behind for your hosts' children.

• Adjust to the schedule of the house. If you're an early riser, try to remain in your room until your hosts are up and about. If you must have a cup of coffee, move quietly around the kitchen.

• Instead of asking if and how you can help, simply observe. Work out what needs to be done and do it. A good guest pitches in by helping to clean up after meals, emptying the kitchen bin and occasionally buying the groceries.

• Offer to bring or buy one night's dinner. If you plan to visit for three nights or longer (usually not a good idea), take your hosts out or cook for them, but give them enough warning so that they won't already have made plans for that meal.

• Keep the guest room neat and clean even when the door is closed. On the last day of your stay, remove and fold your soiled linen and remake the bed with just the blanket so that the guest room looks presentable after you leave.

• Ask permission before using the telephone and offer to re-imburse your host.

• Don't overstay your welcome.

Houseplants

You don't need expensive and temperamental houseplants to add greenery to your home. Many of the vegetables you bring home from the supermarket will sprout and brighten a windowsill. And children love to watch them grow.

• Cut the top 1-2in/25-50mm off a beetroot, parsnip, swede or turnip, and completely trim off the green parts. Line an earthenware ashtray or other low container with pebbles and fill it with water. Set the flat cut end of the vegetable on the pebbles. Over the next few days, change the water whenever it gets cloudy. The resultant forest of foliage will last for a month or more.

• Slice the leaf crown and 1in/25mm of flesh off the top of a pineapple. Set it in moist sand and keep it watered. When roots form, plant it in potting soil that has some peat moss mixed in, and you have a bromeliad that should flourish for years.

• To germinate apple, orange, lemon or grapefruit seeds, sow them in small trays of seed compost and keep well watered. When they're a few inches or several centimetres tall, transplant them to larger pots and watch them grow into lush (but probably fruitless) trees. Kiwi fruits, loquats, pomegranates and such tropical fruits as papayas, lychees and mangoes can also be started this way.

• You can easily turn a carrot into a hanging display of fernlike feathery foliage. Just cut 1-2in/25-50mm off the top of an extra-large carrot. Hollow out the centre, leaving the outer wall intact. With a stout needle, run a thread through the wall of this 'basket'. Hang it, leaves down, in a sunny window. Fill it with water and keep it filled – if it dries out, it will shrivel. Before long, delicate foliage will emerge and all but hide the carrot.

• That old standby, the indoor tree grown from an avocado stone, usually turns into a slender stem weighed down by a little pompom of leaves. This is because it's not pruned back hard enough. Don't be afraid to start again occasionally; cut the plant back to a 3-4in/75-100mm stem. You'll force new root growth and get a bushier, healthier plant.

Plant care on holiday Create a reservoir for plants if you are planning to be away for more than a week. Force a length of tights up through the pot drainage hole and into the soil. Fill a margarine tub with water and cover it. Punch a hole in the lid and thread the other end of the tights through it into the water. Set the plant on top of the tub.

Light for house plants The key to success in indoor gardening is finding the appropriate plants for the available light. Consult a reliable houseplant guide to find out the specific light needs of each of your plants.

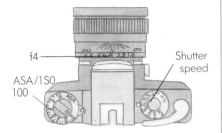

f4
ASA/ISO 100
Shutter speed

• Professionals use a light meter to match the plant to the location; you can substitute a 35mm camera with a built-in light meter and adjustable f-stops and shutter speeds.

Set the camera's ASA/ISO dial to 100 and the aperture ring to f4. Focus on a white matt card at least 12in/300mm square, in the spot where you plan to keep the plant. Move closer, taking care not to block the light, until the card fills the viewfinder. Then adjust the shutter speed until the correct exposure is indicated. The reading on the shutter equals the intensity of the light: strong light, 125 to 500; medium light, 60 to 125; low light, 30 to 60. Strong light is suitable for cacti, succulents and most fleshy flowering plants; medium light is ideal for most flowering plants and foliage plants; but ferns, aspidistras and similar plants need low light levels.

• Use artificial lighting where natural daylight is insufficient; not only will it improve your plant's growth and condition, but it can also look very dramatic.

Houseplant pests

Control spider mites and aphids with derris dust or malathion; use permethrin or insecticidal soap for whitefly; and a systemic insecticide for mealy bugs. Alternatively, wipe the affected parts gently with a damp cloth or try to remove the invaders by hand. Sooty mould is best dealt with in this way. Try to scrape off scale insects, but if they are resistant, wipe the leaf gently with a cotton wool swab which has been moistened with methylated spirit.

Old wives' tales suggest spraying them with liquid detergent or dishwashing liquid in water, but this can injure leaves in very hot weather.

Houseplant polish

Although excellent houseplant polishes are available, the leaves of many houseplants can be kept clean and shiny by a regular, gentle wiping with a damp cloth. Rinse the cloth often and don't let beads of moisture remain on the surface of the leaves. Remember to clean both sides of the leaf.

Humidifiers

• To add moisture to the air in your home, place pans of clean water on top of your radiators or other heat sources.
• For a temporary infusion of moisture, shower with the bathroom door ajar.

Hurricanes and high winds

The warning
• Fill your car's petrol tank.
• Make sure you have adequate emergency food supplies, containers of water, a radio, a torch, extra batteries, candles and a first-aid kit stocked with the family's special medicines.
• Cover small windows with masking tape; nail plywood or shutters over large

Are your houseplants killers?

At first it may seem merely annoying when your cat chews at the houseplants. But be warned: for the animal it could be fatal.

Most people know that oleanders are poisonous, but so are some innocent-looking favourites: caladiums, dieffenbachias, monsteras, philodendrons and even English ivy.

Not only cats, but also toddlers, can be attracted to houseplants — especially those with flowers or berries. Other hazardous flowers include angel's-trumpets (*Datura suaveolens*), every part of which is toxic, birds-of-paradise and lantanas, which bear berries that are poisonous while they are green.

Two plants popular at Christmas time also pose hazards. Mistletoe and the winter or Jerusalem cherry (*Solanum pseudocapsicum*) have berries that look invitingly edible — but don't eat them! And keep these plants well out of the reach of pets and children.

Many of the spring bulbs we raise on windowsills are also toxic: daffodil, narcissus, hyacinth and amaryllis bulbs may look like onions to a child, but are dangerous if eaten.

If you have any doubt about a plant's toxicity, ask your florist or nursery owner for its botanical name. Then call the Poisons Unit at your nearest hospital to find out if it's safe. The National Poisons Information Service has centres at hospitals in London, Cardiff, Edinburgh, Belfast and Dublin.

panes and doors. Wedge sliding glass doors shut.
• Bring all loose, heavy outdoor objects inside or anchor them down.
• If you have a boat, moor it securely or bring it onto land and fill it with water to weigh it down.
• Stay indoors, away from windows and glass doors.
• Leave low-lying areas that may be caught by high tides and waves.
• Stay tuned for weather bulletins.

Evacuation
Some low-lying coastal areas in Britain are prone to flooding and you may be advised to evacuate them.
• Take food, water, warm clothing, blankets, a first-aid kit, a battery-operated radio and important papers, such as birth certificates and insurance policies.
• Lock all doors and windows. Switch off gas, water and electricity if told to do so by the authorities.

The aftermath
• Don't be fooled by the calm in the eye of the hurricane; the powerful winds will return after it passes. Listen for the official all-clear and for other emergency information before venturing out or going home.
• Avoid loose or dangling wires; report them to the electricity company, the police or the fire brigade.
• If the power has been switched off, make sure that refrigerated and frozen food has not spoiled (see FUSE BOX, p.93).

Hypertension
Get your blood pressure checked by your doctor or nurse every 3 to 5 years. Avoid raising your blood pressure – it leads to heart attacks and strokes. Here are some tips:
• Stop smoking. It will decrease your risk of heart attack and strokes.
• Take regular physical exercise unless your doctor advises against it.
• Maintain a normal weight by eating a well-balanced diet and exercising often.
• Limit your salt intake. Avoid salty foods and do not add salt to your meals.
• Cut down your alcohol intake to less

than 10 units per week. (One unit is a measure of spirits, a glass of wine or a half pint of beer or lager.)
• Get a pet. Caring for, playing with, talking to and even watching pets can reduce stress and blood pressure.

Hypothermia
If you're out in the cold and one of your companions begins to shiver violently and then becomes lethargic and drowsy, move the person to shelter out of the wind and rain. Remove his wet clothes and replace them with dry ones. Cover him with blankets or get him into a sleeping bag. Call for medical help, but do not leave the victim alone.

Watch the victim's breathing and be ready to give artificial respiration (p.67) if necessary.

If he's fairly alert, feed him sweets or chocolate and, if available, warm, sweet, non-alcoholic liquids. See also FROSTBITE, p.92.

Ice cream
• Ice cream retains its texture and quality best at – 18°C / 0°F; put a thermometer in your freezer and adjust the setting accordingly.
• Ice cream picks up freezer smells easily, so store the carton in a sealed plastic bag.
• To soften ice cream quickly for serving, put the carton in a microwave on Defrost for 40 seconds.

Ice cream cones
• Before you scoop ice cream into a cone, drop a jelly baby in the bottom; it helps to prevent drips from coming through.
• With a bit of ingenuity, you can serve up an ice cream treat without relying on readymade cones. Here are some ideas: Make an ice cream sandwich by putting

The origins of ice cream
No one really invented ice cream – it just evolved. The Chinese were enjoying a mixture of snow and fruit juice 3000 years ago. History records that iced drinks were served in King Solomon's time. 'Milk and honey' mentioned in the Bible was probably early ice cream.

Later, the Roman Emperor Nero is said to have had snow retrieved from the mountains and served with fruits, juices and honey. At the end of the 13th century Marco Polo returned from the Far East with a recipe resembling today's sorbet. Most historians believe it was probably this recipe that evolved into ice cream in Italy some time during the 16th century.

Ice cream was first served to the general public in the late 1600s at Café Procope in Paris (the café, like the dessert, is still there). And it was a favourite dish of Charles II in the 17th century, although his chef was sworn to keep the recipe secret. Almost 200 years passed before it was really made available to all; in the late 19th century, street vendors sold ice cream known as hokey-pokey.

The first wrapped ice-cream bricks in Britain were made by Thomas Wall in 1922, and the following year 'Stop Me and Buy One' tricycles were seen on the streets.

If an ice cream vendor at the 1904 World's Fair in St Louis, Missouri, hadn't run out of bowls, we might never have seen the birth of the ice cream cone. It seems he had some Middle Eastern waffles to hand, and when he folded them into cornucopia shapes and filled them with ice cream, he started a fad that's still going strong.

a scoop between two large biscuits or splitting a trifle sponge in half and filling it.

• Hollow out a fairy cake to make a little edible bowl.

• Slice the tops off oranges, scoop out the flesh, then fill with ice cream. (Purée the flesh to make orange juice.)

• Make brandy snap cups by moulding just-baked brandy snaps over an orange or up-turned glass, instead of rolling them around a wooden spoon handle. Remove from the orange or glass as soon as they cool.

Ice cubes

• Do you need extra ice cubes for a party? Freeze water in clean plastic egg cartons, then transfer the ice to sandwich bags and store it in the freezer.

The iceman cometh

The almost mythical iceman was a familiar neighbourhood figure during the early part of this century. On hot summer days, as his horsedrawn wagon came dripping down the street, he was trailed by children who knew him by name and were often treated to slivers of ice.

Sporting a rubber apron glistening with ice crystals, the iceman stopped at house after house, where cards or slates in the windows told him how much to deliver.

This muscular man carried ice into each home, and if someone ordered a heavy block – say, 75-100lb/34-45kg – he slung it over his back. Sometimes a block was so big that its sides had to be chipped off so that it would fit inside the tin-lined icebox.

The electric refrigerator, introduced in 1916, eventually put the iceman out of business. But the 'icebox' lives on as the freezer compartment of a modern refrigerator.

• You won't get bubbles in your ice cubes if you use bottled, still mineral water, or if you boil tap water, cool and then freeze it.

• A freezer works best when it's full, so fill up the empty spaces. Giant ice cubes, made by filling bread tins or plastic bags with water, do the job. They're great for picnics, too; just pop them into a plastic bag in the cooler.

Ice hockey jargon

Here's a guide to what the TV commentators are saying.

Blue lines The two 12in/300mm wide lines drawn 60ft/18m from and parallel to the goal lines, dividing the rink into offensive, defensive and neutral zones.

Body check To block an opponent by hitting him above the knees from the side or front – a legal manoeuvre, provided that no more than two strides are taken first.

Butt end To jab an opponent with the butt of the stick; an offence.

Centre ice The neutral zone between the blue lines.

Crease The 4×8 ft/1.2×2.4m area in front of the net where the goalie stands; an attacking player is allowed to skate here only when he has possession of the puck.

Face-off A formal competition for the puck; the referee drops it inside a face-off circle, between the sticks of two selected opponents.

Glove save When a goalie blocks the puck with his glove and so prevents a goal from being scored.

Goalie The goalkeeper.

Goal lines The red lines that extend across the width of the ice, behind which the goals are centred.

Hat trick When one player scores 3 goals in a game.

High stick To hit a man with the stick held above shoulder level (4ft/1.2m in college play); an offence.

Icing Shooting the puck from your defensive zone across the opponent's goal line; if an attacking player touches it first, a face-off ensues (unless your team is shorthanded).

Kill a penalty To use up the time while your team is shorthanded without giving up a goal.

Offside A penalty that is incurred when one of the attacking team crosses the blue line into the offensive zone before the puck does; a face-off then occurs.

Penalty The punishment for an offence. The guilty player must leave the ice and wait in the penalty box for a set period of time (up to 5 minutes for a major infraction such as fighting), causing his team to be shorthanded.

Power play A concentrated attack on the goal when the defending team is shorthanded.

Shorthanded The status of a team when one of its six players is in the penalty box and it must play without him.

Slapshot A shot in which the puck is hit hard towards the goal, usually from some distance.

Spear To jab an opponent with the blade end of the stick; an offence.

Icy paths

• Use sand, sifted ashes or cat litter to improve a slippery surface.

• Spread rock salt before snow or sleet falls; this helps to keep ice from bonding to a concrete surface.

• Keep a path relatively dry and ice-free by digging shallow trenches along both sides. They'll trap rainwater and melting snow.

• On an icy walk, tilt your body slightly forward and set your feet down flat. Short steps also improve stability. If you fall, don't tense up; go limp and try to roll as you land.

Illness away from home

• If you are planning a holiday abroad, get all the required inoculations and request copies of all your prescriptions.

• Pack a first-aid kit with bandages, disinfectant, antibiotic ointment, diarrhoea medicine, motion sickness pills and aspirin (see p.13) or paracetamol.

• Carry a short medical history in your wallet and wear a tag indicating any life-threatening allergies or conditions such as diabetes.

• The pamphlet *The Traveller's Guide to Health*, available from your doctor's surgery or travel agent, includes information about immunisations, anti-malarial tablets and getting medical help abroad.
• If you are visiting another EC country, get an application form from a post office for a form E111, which may allow you to obtain free medical treatment should you need it.
• Ask your travel agent about special insurance that will help you get a doctor, a prescription, money or transport home. Carry your insurance certificate, your agent's name and phone number and several claim forms.
• If you get sick abroad, British embassies and consulates can usually give you a list of English-speaking doctors.

Income tax returns

To help keep your tax return problem-free, take these steps.
• Double-check your arithmetic – one error is one too many (see COMPUTATIONS, p.50).
• Fill in all the boxes. If necessary, write 'none' or 'N/A' (not applicable) in the relevant box.
• Make sure you haven't omitted any sources of income. Attach the appropriate copies of your P60 form to your return. The Inland Revenue cross-checks your figures with those provided by your employer, your bank and other sources.
• Make sure you have the same figures on the return and on the supporting schedules.
• Remember to sign and date your return.
• Submit your return on time even if you can't pay the taxes or you will be subject to late-payment penalties and interest. See also INCOME TAX COUNTDOWN, p.242.

Incontinence

When adults have trouble controlling urination, they should discuss the matter with their doctor. In most cases incontinence can be successfully regulated or cured.
• The first step is a medical diagnosis of the underlying cause. If the pelvic and bladder muscles are weak, they can be strengthened with a regimen of simple exercises or biofeedback methods. If the prostate has become enlarged, surgery may restore proper bladder function. Medicines and physiotherapy may also help to regulate the bladder.
• For incontinence that can't be managed medically, absorbent pads, lined underwear, collecting bags and catheters are available.
• Many District Health Authorities employ incontinence advisers who may be able to help. The Disabled Living Foundation, 380-384 Harrow Road, London W9 2HU, Tel. 0171-289 6111, may also be able to advise you.

Indigestion

• To relieve an attack of indigestion, drink a cupful of peppermint tea. Steep ½oz/15g of fresh peppermint leaves in 1 pint/570ml of boiled water for 20 minutes.
• Instead of a commercial antacid, try 1 teaspoon bicarbonate of soda in a glass of water (not recommended for those who must restrict their intake of sodium).
Caution A heart attack (see p.104) may be mistaken for indigestion. If you are in doubt, seek medical help.
Prevention
• Stop smoking and don't chew gum. Cut out aspirin, alcohol, caffeine and carbonated drinks. Decline foods that don't agree with you.
• Make time for stress-free meals. Try eating four or five small meals a day slowly instead of wolfing down two or three large ones.
• Relax, sitting up, for 15 to 30 minutes after every meal.
• Sleep with the head of your bed slightly elevated or with a pillow.

Influenza

• For achiness, fever or a headache, take some aspirin (see p.13) or paracetamol.
• Drink at least 8fl oz/225ml of fluids every 2 hours to prevent dehydration from fever. Dilute apple juice or flat ginger ale with water. Avoid citrus fruit juices if you feel nauseous and milk if you are vomiting or have diarrhoea.
Don't starve a fever. Eat small, bland meals – cottage cheese, yoghurt, bananas, dry toast, baked or boiled potatoes. Don't worry if you're not hungry for 3 or 4 days, but when your appetite returns, get back onto a balanced diet as soon as you can (see THE BALANCED DIET, p.254).
• If you have a sore throat (see p.190), gargle with salt water or suck lozenges.
• For a runny nose, sip hot tea sweetened with a bit of honey and take a decongestant if you wish.
• For a dry cough, use a humidifier (p.110) and suck cough drops (see COUGHS, p.54).
• Stay in bed – or at the very least reduce physical activity – as long as you can (at least until your temperature returns to normal); resuming your regular activities too soon will encourage a relapse.
• Don't drive; flu impairs reaction time almost six times as much as moderate alcohol intake.
• Make sure that you see a doctor if you're over 65; if you have a chronic disease; if you feel especially ill or the fever lasts more than 4 days; or if your fever is accompanied by a stiff neck, severe headaches, irritability and confusion. See also COLDS, p.47.

Informal attire

• A woman who gets an invitation for an evening party that says 'informal' should wear a cocktail dress; a man, a dark suit.
• If the invitation says 'casual' or is for a daytime event, and you're unsure what to wear, call your host and ask. If the answer is vague, ask what he is planning to wear.

Ink stains

• For ballpoint pen and felt-tip marks on fabric, act quickly. Press a cotton-wool pad underneath the fabric, then dab the mark with a cotton-wool bud dipped in methylated spirits, before washing it. As a last resort use chlorine bleach, if the fabric is bleachable.

• It's worth contacting the manufacturer for advice about pen stains. For delicate fabrics or heavy staining, professional cleaning is advisable.

From liquid ink

• If the ink is still wet, pour salt on the stain and brush it off after a few minutes; repeat if necessary.

• Sponge fabric or rub it under cold water until most of the ink has been flushed through. Wash as usual.

• On carpets, squirt with soda water then blot with paper towels. Sponge with a detergent solution and blot.

In-laws

• Work out ways of deflecting potential conflicts. As soon as you become an in-law, make a few discreet enquiries on matters such as what you should call your son's or daughter's new in-laws; where holidays will be celebrated; who will help after a grandchild is born; and whether attendance at family weddings is expected.

• Some relationships are permanent. Your son remains the grandson of his father's parents, no matter how many times you divorce and remarry. The same is true of aunts, uncles and cousins. Don't discourage such family relationships, however you feel about your former in-laws. They can enrich the lives of your children.

Insect bites

• To relieve the itch of a mosquito or other insect bite, apply an ice pack or ice cube for 10 minutes. Let the skin dry, then smooth on an over-the-counter hydrocortisone or antihistamine cream.

• If the bite is especially itchy, swollen or uncomfortable, or if you have many bites, take antihistamine tablets. But if you have to drive or operate machinery, make sure you use tablets which do not cause drowsiness.

• Some people have a physical reaction to insect venom that at its most extreme takes the form of anaphylactic shock (see ALLERGIES, p.10). If the victim's breath is laboured, he is dizzy and his skin burns, call a doctor immediately.

Insect repellents

• Natural substitutes for commercial repellents include oil of citronella, available from a chemist, or at health food or camping goods stores. Mix it with vegetable or baby oil – a few drops to about 1oz/25ml of oil.

• To make yourself less attractive to insects, wear light-coloured clothing and don't wear perfume or cologne.

Insomnia

• Cut back on smoking, chocolate, caffeine and alcohol, especially in the late afternoon and evening.

• Avoid heavy meals close to bedtime – a snack of hot milk and biscuits may be helpful – and all meals in the middle of the night.

• Do not exercise strenuously just before going to bed.

• Spend less time in bed. Get up at the same time every morning, but go to bed half an hour later; if necessary, keep pushing back your bedtime until you can doze off readily.

• Don't sleep late in the morning or take naps during the day.

• Turn your alarm clock towards the wall so that you don't keep checking the time on its dial; if it is a radio alarm, leave the music on playing very low.

Insulation

• Seal the cracks at the bottoms of doors by filling socks three-quarters full of sand or cat litter, knotting the tops and laying them along the bottom of the doors. Decorate them as mice or dogs.

Sand-filled sock

• If you don't have double-glazing, insulate windows in winter by taping clear plastic – even plastic film – to the frames. If you play a hair dryer over plastic film, this will shrink it slightly and smooth out any sagging wrinkles. See also DRAUGHTS, p.65.

Insurance claims

• List everything covered by your contents and buildings insurance policies. Photograph each item, mark it with invisible ink, note its serial number and keep the sales slip to show its cost and date of purchase. In case of loss, phone your insurer right away, then follow up with a letter. If the loss is the result of a burglary, report it immediately to the police to validate your claim.

• After a fire, make a detailed description of the damage done to your home; the insurance company's loss adjuster will prepare his own list. Get bids for repairs from several reputable contractors. If your home is uninhabitable and your clothing is beyond repair, save any receipts for lodging and new clothing and you can be reimbursed. See also HOMEOWNER'S INSURANCE, p.107.

• Be sure to disclose any pre-existing conditions on your health and life insurance applications; the policy may be invalidated if you make a claim for treatment of a condition you haven't previously reported.

• To get the best settlement on a motor insurance claim, keep all receipts for maintenance; take periodic photographs of the car to show its condition before the accident.

• Keep the information on how to make claims with all your policies.

Insurance costs

When you renew your annual policies, shop around to get the best deal.

Car insurance

• Decrease your collision and comprehensive coverage on less valuable cars by raising the excess.

• Ask about discounts for an accident-free and clean driving licence; no-claim bonus and mature driver's bonus; and if you insure your home with the same company.

• Insure your children on the family policy. If your son or daughter uses the car for less than 10 per cent of its total use, or is in the armed services, ask about an 'occasional driver' discount.

Life insurance

• Look for a policy which gives a high level of cover for a low premium.

• A cheap form of term life insurance (which pays a lump sum at the end of the policy) is the mortgage protection insurance which accompanies a repayment mortgage. The sum you are insured for decreases as the size of your loan falls.

• Find out if the insurer offers a non-smoker's discount on life insurance policies. See also HOMEOWNER'S INSURANCE, p.107; LIFE INSURANCE, p.124.

Interior decoration

Do you feel that your rooms lack interest or that your walls are too bare? Stamp your personality on them with some of these ideas.

• Create a stunning picture with a 4ft/1.2m square of abstract printed furnishing fabric stapled to a simple wood frame. A bold printed silk scarf or shawl also works well.

• Framing kits are an inexpensive, glamorous way to display posters and photographs. Or create your own postcard gallery: a collection of Oriental, Dutch or Impressionist paintings, for example, in matching frames and mounts, makes a dramatic display when grouped together on a wall.

• Let the room's use suggest appropriate decorations. In a hallway, for example, you could use hats or canes. In a living room, musical instruments, historic newspapers or antique embroidery tools might work. In the dining room, display doilies, baskets or napkin rings. In the kitchen hang decorative pots, a spice rack or a shelf of glass preserving jars. Hang maps to locate places that are in the news in the playroom and add interest to a child's bedroom with colourful kites, framed pages from books or a bookcase filled with dolls, model aeroplanes or stuffed animals.

Ironing

• When doing the week's ironing, start with the items that require the coolest setting and set the iron accordingly. Work up to those which need a hot iron.

• Move the iron in the direction of the weave of the cloth so that you don't stretch the fabric.

• To prevent a shine, iron dark fabrics, viscose and acetates on the wrong side.

• If you're travelling and don't have an iron, hang your newly-unpacked clothes in the bathroom and run hot water in the shower. Close the door and let the steam smooth out the creases. This works especially well with wool.

• If you have an iron but no board, cover a worktop with newspapers and then a towel or blanket. Or place a towel over the corner of the bed. Then lay a tea towel or sheet over the area, to prevent fluff sticking to the iron.

• Place a piece of aluminium foil, shiny side up, between the ironing board and cover pad; it will reflect heat for a faster job.

• If you want to avoid fabric shine on acrylic garments, iron them on the reverse side. Do the same with velvet to prevent crushing, pressing it through a double layer of cloth. Pieces of embroidery should be pressed on the reverse too – it makes the pattern stand out.

• To iron an unruly ribbon, pull the ribbon through under the iron.

Itching

• For quick relief, rub calamine lotion or witch hazel on the itchy area.

• If skin is not broken, apply a cooling lotion made from 4fl oz/115ml water, 4fl oz/115ml surgical spirit and 3-4 drops oil of peppermint. Store in a tightly capped bottle and shake well before using.

• For all-over relief, crumble 2oz/60g uncooked oatmeal into lukewarm bath water as it flows from the tap. Be careful getting in and out of the tub – it will be extremely slippery. Soak for 15 to 20 minutes and then gently pat yourself dry so that a thin coating of oatmeal remains on your skin.

• For itchy, dry or chapped skin, a mineral oil bath (2-3fl oz/60-85ml per tub of lukewarm water) or a salt bath (2-4oz/60-115g per tub) works wonders. (Mineral oil or salt will also make the tub slippery, so be careful getting in and out.)

This is the way we pressed our clothes

Ironing is still a chore, but today's lightweight, thermostatically controlled irons make the task a lot easier than it used to be.

In ancient Greece, where crisp clothing was a sign of status (and permanent-press fabrics did not exist), a heated rod resembling a rolling pin was used to put pleats into linen robes. The Romans fought creases as fiercely as they fought their foes – they hammered them out with a flat metal mallet, usually wielded by slaves.

By the 10th century, the iron had evolved into a mushroom-shaped glass object that the Vikings rolled back and forth on dampened fabric. Europeans in the 15th and 16th centuries used either a flatiron heated over a fire or, in wealthier homes, a hot box iron containing coals or a hot brick. Gas-heated irons were introduced in the 19th century, but they sometimes leaked or exploded, setting a house on fire.

The first electric iron was patented in 1882, followed by ones that were temperature controlled. But the real breakthroughs in the war against creases came in 1926, when the steam iron hit the market, and in the 1960s, when easy-care permanent-press fabrics were introduced.

These days, cordless irons make the chore safer, and steam presses make ironing trousers and jackets quicker and more efficient.

J

Jam setting

• To set well, jam needs the right balance of pectin and acid. Lemons provide the acid, but different types of fruit have various levels of pectin.

Pectin-rich fruits include apples, gooseberries, blackcurrants, redcurrants and damsons. Combine fruits with differing pectin contents, such as strawberries (low in pectin) and redcurrants, or apples and blackberries (also low).

• Test the jam for setting point when it reaches 105°C / 220°F (use a sugar thermometer to test the temperature). Dip a wooden spoon into the jam, lift it out horizontally and keep it in this position to cool. Then tilt the spoon and let the jam fall off it. If small drops run together on the edge of the spoon to form larger drops that then fall cleanly off the spoon, the jam has boiled long enough.

Or, drop a small spoonful of the hot

jam onto a cold plate. If it forms a skin on the surface as it cools, which wrinkles when you press it, the jam is at setting point and is ready to pot.

• If the potted jam is runny and won't set, don't reboil it – you will only ruin its flavour. Dissolve gelatine in warm water, warm the jam – simply so that you can mix it with the warm gelatine – and stir it into the gelatine solution. (Use 5-6 teaspoons of gelatine for 2½-3 lb / 1.1-1.4 kg of jam.) Pot it again and refrigerate when cool. Use it within a few weeks or it may become mouldy.

Jellyfish stings

If you're stung by a jellyfish on holiday, take the following steps.

• Quickly rinse your skin with large amounts of clean fresh or sea water, followed by surgical spirit (vodka or other spirits will do) or vinegar. Or you can apply moist sea or beach sand for 20 minutes. Or rub with fresh pawpaw or meat tenderiser.

• Remove any bits of tentacle stuck to your skin with tweezers or gloved hands, not your bare fingers.

• Cover the affected area with over-the-counter hydrocortisone cream three to four times a day until the redness disappears.

• To reduce swelling, take oral antihistamines; to relieve pain, take paracetamol (not aspirin – it promotes bleeding, which is a problem with these stings).

• If dizziness, nausea, vomiting or other signs of shock develop, get medical help right away.

Jet lag

• Alternate a 'feast day' (high-protein breakfast and lunch, high-carbohydrate dinner) with a 'fast day' (soup and salad) for 3 days before departure; during those days don't drink any liquids containing caffeine except between 3 and 5pm. On the flight day eat sparingly and drink caffeine-laden liquids only in the morning if you're flying west, and between 6 and 9pm if you're headed east.

• Preadjust your bedtime. If flying east, go to sleep an hour earlier each day for each time zone you're crossing; if flying west, move your bedtime later in the same fashion.

• When flying east over several time zones, try to take a morning flight instead of an overnight one. On arrival your 'body time' will be set at midafternoon; local time will be early evening. Eat dinner and go to bed late by local time. The next morning you'll feel rested.

• Flying west is easier. In fact, you may avoid jet lag altogether if you take a late flight, stay awake during the trip, then go

to bed as soon as you reach your destination.

• Drink lots of fluids before and during the flight, but avoid alcohol.

• Go outside into sunlight as soon as possible after arriving. Take a brisk walk or jog; moderate exercise may help your body adjust faster. See also FITNESS WHILE TRAVELLING, p.85.

Jewellery allergies

• To prevent your ears from becoming inflamed when you have them pierced, make sure a stainless-steel needle is used. Wear only stainless-steel earrings

---

A few golden nuggets

To produce 1 troy ounce of gold (about 31 g) nearly 2½ tonnes of rock are needed. In fact, its rarity is such that refineries who process the gold-bearing rock clean their roofs and chimneys periodically to recover any specks that might have accumulated.

It is a malleable substance that can be hammered into gold leaf and wire – as little as 1 oz / 31 g can be made to cover an area 1400 sq ft / 130 m² or pulled into an extremely fine wire 50 miles / 80 km long. It won't tarnish or corrode, and coins recovered from sunken ships are often as shiny as new, even after centuries beneath the sea.

Pure gold (24 carat) is so soft that it must be mixed with another metal to make it durable enough for pieces of jewellery. It turns reddish when mixed with copper, bluish when mixed with iron and forms white gold when platinum or zinc and nickel are added.

During astronaut Edward White's historic space walk, a gold-plated cord was his lifeline; and today gold wire and tubing are vital components of space exploration.

---

until your earlobes have healed up.

• If you have a reaction to a ring, earrings or metal spectacle frames, clean them with surgical spirit, then use clear nail polish to coat the parts that touch the skin. Reapply the polish when it wears off. Another way to lessen irritation is to apply a proprietary hydrocortisone cream to your skin before you put on the jewellery or frames.

• Nickel, a component in some jewellery metals, causes an allergic reaction in some people; if you suspect you're one of them, wear pure copper or nonmetal jewellery.

• Don't wear tight-fitting metal watch straps or bracelets. Wrap a handkerchief or other fabric under a watch or bracelet especially during humid weather when you may perspire.

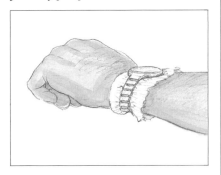

Job burnout

Are you fed up with your job? Perhaps overwork, stress or just plain boredom are making you think of moving on. An alternative to going through the trouble of finding, applying for and getting a better job is to develop the one you have.

• Redefine your job. Write up a realistic job description and discuss it with your boss, stressing that you want to adjust your duties so that you can be more productive.

• Develop and sell a new project. Write a memo to your boss explaining why your idea is worthwhile, what kind of help you would need and how long it would take. Even if the project doesn't work out, you'll have done something different, and you'll probably be remembered for your earnest attempts.

• Develop a life outside work – take up a hobby or do volunteer work. If necessary, take some time off to gain a new perspective on your situation.

• If you're still frustrated, perhaps it's time to find a better setting for your skills or make a career change (see p.34).

Job hunting

• A good careers adviser can be a great help. Choose one who has excellent references and charges by the appointment or, better still, find one that is free.

• Invest in an answering service or machine so that you can receive messages from prospective employers.

• Inform friends, business associates, acquaintances and former employers that you're job hunting. See also NET-WORKING, p.140.

Researching a prospect

• If you come across an interesting job through your network or the press, research the firm thoroughly. Read newspaper and magazine articles about it. Study the last couple of annual reports (available from Companies House). Go to your local reference library and look up the firm in the latest edition of *Key British Enterprises* (the standard authority on companies), published by Dun and Bradstreet.

• If possible, talk to people who work for the firm. Find out its position in the industry, what its main problems are, and what it's like to work for. Does it promote from within? Does it educate employees, or help them to advance?

• Visit the company if it is practical to do so. Do the employees look enthusiastic? Do they talk positively about their work?

• Write a letter to whomever is in a position to hire you and use headed notepaper, if possible; it looks impressive. Indicate your knowledge of the company, state how you could contribute to it, and request an interview. Say that you'll follow up by phone in about a week. Then do so.

If you have a job

• Ask agents or prospective employers to call you at home or leave only their first name if they call you at work.

• Arrange interviews for before or after work or during your lunch hour.

Job interviews

• Prepare a customised cv (see p.245) for each interview, tailoring your stated objectives to suit the job. (It's easier to customise a cv if it's on a computer disk.)

• Create two basic cvs – a chronological one, if you're working through agencies, and a functional one, organised around your skills and experience, if you've had a number of jobs or are returning to work after several years.

Preparation

• Choose four or five highlights from current and past jobs that show your accomplishments and work style. Create a success story for each one to help answer such questions as 'What are your major accomplishments?' or 'What is your relevant experience?'

• Rehearse the interview with a friend or family member. Anticipate likely questions and practise telling your success stories without rambling. Ask for feedback.

• Give yourself an extra hour or so to dress and get to the interview. If your hands tend to be clammy, use anti-perspirant on your palms.

The interview

• Look the interviewer directly in the eye and follow her lead in shaking hands.

• Remember that you are making a choice as much as she is. Ask any questions necessary to decide if this is a job you really want.

Jogging

• Before you buy a new pair of running shoes, check the soles of your worn-out pair. If the outer edge of the heel is worn, your running style is to roll your feet outwards; if the inner edge is worn, you roll your feet inwards. Take the old pair to the store and ask a salesperson what kind of shoe suits your style best.

• If your cotton socks are lined with towelling, wear them inside out to reduce friction and help prevent blisters. Smearing petroleum jelly on your feet before running also helps; rub it on your inner thighs to keep your legs from chafing, and your nipples to prevent them from becoming sore.

The jeopardies of jogging

Every form of exercise has its risks, but jogging may be the only one in which buzzards pose a health hazard. According to a letter to the New England Journal of Medicine, 12 joggers in Switzerland were attacked by European buzzards in a 2 year period. Such behaviour seems to be a threat only during the breeding season, when the birds protect their nestlings – but there are plenty of less dramatic, year-round dangers that joggers face. Consult a doctor before you start jogging, and take the following precautions to avoid injuries:

Wear running shoes with thick, flexible soles or use shoe inserts (orthotics), especially if you have flat feet or high arches.

Run on a resilient surface, such as grass, wood, or asphalt, to prevent shinsplints – an inflammation of the tissues in the front of the lower legs. Replace your shoes with new ones every 500-800 miles/800-1290 km.

Strengthen the muscles in the calves and in the front and back of the thighs to prevent runner's knee, a painful stiffening of the area around the kneecap. One exercise that does this involves jumping on and off a step with alternate legs.

Stretch the muscles and tendons in the backs of the legs to prevent Achilles' tendonitis, an excruciating inflammation of the heel cord.

And finally avoid excessive running, which can lead to the development of stress fractures, slight cracks that form in the bones of the foot or lower leg.

• If you find jogging too jarring, try walking briskly – it gives comparable benefits. Start moderately: walk a mile in 15 to 20 minutes five times a week. Gradually increase your distance and time over the next few weeks. See FITNESS BUILDING, p.84.

Juice extracting

When you don't have a lemon squeezer or juice extractor try these methods for extracting juice. They will work better if you knead and soften the citrus first.
• Insert a large fork into the centre of a cut orange or lemon, then squeeze the fruit against the fork to extract the juice.
• Gently squeeze cut citrus fruit over an inverted cup, using a saucer to catch the juice. Use an old, valueless cup. (A demitasse cup works best for lemons.)

Jury service

If you are summoned for jury service, you can only be excused in special circumstances. Valid reasons for exemption include illness, pregnancy, blindness or deafness, or domestic or business difficulties. Write to the Clerk of the Court as soon as you receive the summons, giving your reasons.
• Members of certain professions, such as magistrates, coroners, barristers and solicitors, prison officers, police officers, clergy and ministers of religion are ineligible. Doctors, dentists, nurses, midwives, MPS, peers and members of the armed forces may refuse.
• If you have been convicted of a criminal offence within the previous 10 years you are disqualified.
• If you have not lived in the UK, Channel Islands or Isle of Man for at least 5 years since the age of 13, you are ineligible.
• If you have served on a jury (except a coroner's jury) within the previous 2 years you can refuse.
• As a juror, you are not paid but may claim certain daily allowances such as subsistence, travel and loss of earnings.

K

Ketchup

• Don't just bang on the bottom of a stubborn ketchup bottle. Run the blade of a table knife around the inside of the neck; then tip the bottle and watch the sauce flow.
• When you've finished a bottle of ketchup, make use of the residue: add a little water or vinegar and shake, then use the liquid to flavour soups, stews or salad dressings.

Kettle scale

• Mix up a solution of one part malt vinegar to one part water and pour enough into your kettle to just cover the element. Bring to the boil and leave overnight. Then rinse out.
• Or, boil water in the kettle and then add 13 teaspoons/75g citric acid granules. Leave for 20 minutes, then rinse.
• Or, use a chemical descaler. Read the manufacturer's instructions first.

Keys

• Carry two sets of car and house keys just in case one set gets locked inside. Keep a third set at home in something that can't be locked.
• Colour code the faces of your keys so that you'll know instantly which lock each one opens.
• If a duplicate key is difficult to insert or remove, try filing down its rough edges with an emery board.
• To straighten a bent key, put it on the face of a club hammer and tap it lightly with a mallet.
• When a house key is hard to turn, squeeze a little powdered graphite into the lock and spread it around by jiggling the key back and forth. If you don't have any powdered graphite, scrape the point of a soft-lead pencil over the teeth of the key and insert it into the lock. Don't ever use oil – it will gum up the lock.

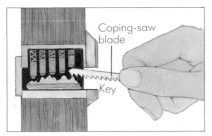

Catch the key with the teeth of the blade, then pull it out, keeping the blade parallel to the top of the keyhole.

• If a key breaks in a lock, you may be able to extract it with a pair of needle-nose pliers or a fine, stiff wire. An alternative method is to insert a coping-saw blade into the lock as shown.
• If you've lost the key to a locked drawer, first see if the drawer above is unlocked; if it is, remove it to get into the locked drawer below. If this approach is impossible, minimise damage by taking off the back of the desk or chest.
• Copy the manufacturer's code number imprinted on a new car key or its attached tag and keep it in a safe, handy place so that the car dealer can make a duplicate key for you. If you lose the code, your car dealer may have a record.

Knee problems

If God had intended humans to be perfect, goes an old saying, he wouldn't have given us knees. Despite the fact that the knee is the body's biggest, heaviest and best-protected joint, it is injured more often than any other. Many injuries can be prevented by taking these precautions.
• If you're overweight, slim down to reduce stress on the joint, especially if you engage in such activities as jogging or tennis.
• If you sit in one place for long periods, change the position of your legs often. Whenever possible, stand up and stretch your legs or take a short walk.
• Avoid climbing stairs or bending your knees any more than is necessary. When working on something below waist level, sit on a stool or on the floor.
• Avoid wearing high-heeled shoes or those with thin, poorly cushioned soles.
• When gardening, kneel on a piece of

foam rubber or an old cushion; shift your weight frequently from one knee to the other.
• Relieve wear and tear on your knees whenever you exercise. Use a resilient surface for walking, jogging, playing tennis or doing any kind of aerobics. Avoid cycling in high gears.
• To strengthen your knee muscles, do a set of knee curls daily. Lie on your stomach on an exercise bench or a bed so that your lower legs extend over the edge. Turn one foot inwards to an angle of about 45°, slowly bend your knee to a 90° angle, and lift your upper leg as high as you can. Hold this position for 10 seconds, then lower your leg slowly and let it straighten. Repeat ten times with each leg.
• Never ignore any knee injury, however slight it may seem. See a doctor as soon as possible after you have damaged your knee. Meanwhile, follow the RICE rule: Rest, Ice, Compression and Elevation.

Knitting

• If you don't have thick knitting needles, a pair of chopsticks or wooden dowels will do just as well. Just sharpen the tips in a pencil sharpener and smooth them off with an emery board or abrasive paper.
• Similarly, you can renew the blunted tips of wooden knitting needles with a pencil sharpener or by rubbing them with fine abrasive paper or an emery board.
• If you don't have a stitch holder, use a long twist tie instead.
• To keep a ball of wool from rolling about while you work, put it in a clean tin with a plastic lid; poke a hole in the lid, smooth any rough edges and draw the wool through.
• For row markers, attach the little plastic tabs used to close wrapped bread or use twist ties, firmly secured.
• Instead of wool, knit or crochet with a strip of fabric cut from an old T-shirt. Starting at the hem, cut the T-shirt horizontally into a continuous 1in/25mm wide strip. Tug on the strip and the cut edges will curl under neatly.

Knives

• To keep knives sharp, always use a wood or polypropylene chopping board. Never use knives to cut string or paper, and keep them in a knife block or magnetic knife rack.
• If you don't have a knife sharpener, the unglazed bottom of a mug will do. Hold the knife blade at a low angle and draw it backwards and forwards across the unglazed surface to sharpen the length of the blade.

L

Ladders

• Spray-paint the top two steps of a step-ladder bright orange or red as a visual reminder to keep off them. Always allow at least three rungs of ladder above gutter level as a handhold.
• Never climb a ladder with your hands full. Wear a tool belt into which tools and accessories can be stuffed, leaving your hands free to hold the ladder rungs.
• Before climbing an extension ladder, jump up and down lightly on the bottom rung a few times to make certain that the legs are firmly planted.
• On muddy or frozen ground, drive two 4 × 2in/100 × 50mm stakes into the ground behind the ladder, as shown. Then tie ropes around the second rung from the bottom, knot them tightly and

secure them to the stakes. If the ground is soft, stand the ladder on a piece of wood, then lash it to the stakes.

• When working high on a ladder against the house, lash the ladder through an open window so that it can't move. Tie one end of a rope to a rung about two-thirds of the way up, and the other end to a radiator or other solid object inside. Or use a 4 × 2 in/100 × 50mm length of wood long enough to bridge the inside of the window.

• Although PVC guttering is strong enough to take the weight of a ladder, it is slippery. So insert ring bolts about 3 ft/1 m apart into the fascia board (the board to which the gutter is screwed). Then, when the ladder is in use, run a piece of rope around a ladder rung and through the nearest ring bolt.

• As a safety precaution, always keep your hips within the vertical rails of the ladder.

• If you have to put up an extension ladder on your own, extend it on the ground, then rest the base of the ladder in the angle between the wall and ground. Now lift the other end of the ladder; stand under it and move your hands along the rungs, hand over hand, until the ladder is vertical. Lift the foot of the ladder away from the wall.

• The correct angle for a ladder is 12 in/300mm away from the vertical for every 4 ft/1.2 m up (a 1:4 angle).

Lamps

• Leave the converting and repairing of old or antique lamp fittings to the experts. There can be problems with flexes, switches and light holders that no longer meet current British Standard safety standards.

• Clip-on spotlamps and builder's inspection lamps fixed to a shelf can provide useful extra reading and working light. As bulbs and shades can become very hot to touch, these fittings are not recommended for bedhead reading lights or children's rooms.

• If a light bulb shatters, turn off the switch or unplug the cord, press a wad of putty or plasticine over the sharp edges, and twist the stub with it.

Lampshades

The following ideas for sprucing up tired lampshades are well worth trying. However, remember to fit a 40 watt bulb with any decorative, homemade shade and to keep the shade away from immediate contact with the light source.

• Cut out a 1¼ in/32mm diameter circle from the centre of a cotton handkerchief or brightly coloured square. Blanket stitch the raw edges. Remove the existing pendant shade from the holder, place the fabric over it, and refit.

• For lightly soiled card drum and coolie shades, try spattering the surfaces with a toothbrush or sponging them, using emulsion paint, fabric or shoe paints, in colours that match your room. (Practise these techniques on newspaper first.)

• For a country cottage look, glue on dried flowers or leaves.

• Create silhouettes of recognisable shapes or free-floating patterns by gluing pasta shapes, rice or paper stars inside the shade.

• Custom decorate a flat-surfaced shade with stencils. Or glue a colourful old map around the outside of a shade and varnish it when dry.

• Plastic, nylon and glass shades can be hand-washed in warm soapy water. Dry cleaners can no longer dryclean fabric shades, so vacuum them regularly using a dust brush attachment.

• When buying a brightly coloured shade, check the effect in the shop when the light is switched on. White linings reflect light best – you don't necessarily want a red light given off by an unlined red shade.

• Re-pleat a shade by simply gathering every two or three pleats with a decorative stitch or tassel.

Landlords

• Always check the property you're going to rent before you move in. Make sure everything is in good order. If it is not, ask the landlord to make the necessary repairs.

• If a Tenancy Agreement form is drawn up between you and your landlord, read it carefully before signing it, and in particular check details that cover matters such as repairs, payment of council tax and permission to sub-let.

• If you accept the conditions of the agreement and then break any of them later, the landlord may be able to sue you for damages and obtain an order for your eviction.

• The landlord or his agent may reserve the right to examine the property to make sure that it is being kept in good condition. This must be done at reasonable times and always with a prior warning to you of the visits. If the visits become too frequent, without any good reason, the landlord may be guilty of harassment.

• If you pay rent weekly, you must have a rent book with the name and address of the landlord and his agent, and the rent and rates due. If you pay cash, make sure you get a receipt.

• Pay the rent promptly. If you don't pay it within 21 days of the due date, the landlord can seek a court order for your eviction. But if by the time the case is brought to court you have paid up the arrears, an eviction notice cannot be served.

• You must leave the premises in good condition, but you're not liable for the sort of wear and tear that results from normal use. The landlord is required to repair the exterior structure of the property and to maintain the heating, plumbing, gas and electrical fittings. But you must report faults and repair minor ones, such as a blown light bulb or a detached door handle.

• When leaving you must give 4 weeks' notice in writing if you pay rent weekly or monthly, or 3 months if you pay quarterly. However, you can simply leave by moving out and returning the keys to the landlord. If the landlord accepts them, he has agreed to your leaving.

Laryngitis

• Rest your voice; whisper instead of using your voice box. Carry a pencil and paper to replace conversation.

• Give up smoking.

• Eat mild, easily swallowed foods; drink plenty of non-alcoholic liquids.

• Stay in a humid atmosphere. Use a humidifier or inhale steam – sit in the bathroom with the door closed and the hot shower on, or fill a bowl with boiling water, lean over it with a towel over your head and breathe in the steam.

• If the hoarseness lasts for longer than 3 weeks or you have difficulty breathing, you should call your doctor. See also SORE THROATS, p.190.

Latchkey children

This is not an ideal situation for school-children – particularly if they are under 16. Remember that you could be legally prosecuted for neglect if they come to harm. And you should never leave a child alone with a heating appliance such as an electric fire switched on.

• Consider other options, such as paying a local childminder to take the child in until you return, or asking the school if your child can stay on late. Some schools run after-school clubs. If yours does not, suggest that one is started.

• If you have to leave your child alone, prepare her by:

– Playing a 'What would you do if . . . ?' quiz, to check that she can cope with unforeseen problems (such as 'What would you do if someone knocked on the front door?').

– Letting your child lock and unlock the door when you go out together. Leave her alone for short periods, ensuring she locks the door behind you.

– Giving her small tasks to accomplish while you're out, so that she gets used to being independent.

• If your child has to be on her own until you get home, leave out plenty of food and refreshment so that she doesn't have to use the cooker.

• Always write down a contact number for you, a neighbour or relative and the doctor.

• Ring home every day to check that she's returned safely from school. If it's not possible for you to do this, arrange for someone else to do so.

• When you return, make time to talk to her about the day's events.

Lawn patches

When you dig a flowerbed or vegetable patch from scratch, use the upended turf to patch up bare or damaged spots in your lawn. Such homegrown turf may not be as flawless as the commercial product, but it will match your lawn, making mends invisible.

• Strip the turf from the new planting area by cutting it into 12in/300mm squares with a sharp spade and turning it over right in place. With an old butcher knife or machete, shave most of the soil from the roots so that the pieces of turf are no more than 2in/50mm thick.

• Prepare bare spots for patching by loosening the soil to a depth of 4in/100mm. Remove half the soil to ensure the turf is even with the lawn.

• If the bare patch in the lawn was caused by a spillage of herbicide or petrol, remove and replace all the loosened soil. If a dog was the cause of the damage, neutralise the soil with a handful of gypsum.

• Cut the turf pieces to size and fit them into the gap, sifting compost into the cracks to protect the roots from drying out. Water well.

Lawns

• A lawn looks best when it forms a sweeping, unified background to trees, shrubs and other features of the landscape. If you stud it with island beds of flowers and shrubs, it loses much of its aesthetic appeal.

• Aerate your lawn often, not just once a year, by wearing spiked shoes, such as golf shoes, as you mow it.

• Don't mow too short. Blades of grass are the turf's leaves, converting sunlight into food; if you leave them a little long, you'll reduce the need for fertiliser.

• If you have a large, high-powered rotary mower, another adjustment can save hours of labour in the autumn leaf fall. Tape a piece of cardboard over the exit chute to block it; then mow the newly fallen leaves instead of raking them. They'll be pulverised, sifting back into the turf to serve as organic fertiliser. However, this is a good idea only if there is a light sprinkling of leaves.

• Who says you have to grow grass? For a part of the garden that is usually only seen and not used, consider ground covers such as ajuga, euonymus, ivy, pachysandra, thyme or vinca. Not only are these creeping plants ornamental, but they also don't need regular mowing. See also GRASS, p.98.

Lawyers

• If you qualify, free legal advice is available through the Legal Aid and Green Form schemes (see LEGAL AID AND ADVICE, p.123). Some lawyers will also undertake initial interviews for a low fee.

• You can buy do-it-yourself legal kits that supposedly contain everything you need to draft a will or buy and sell your home. If you decide to use these, it is a good idea to have a lawyer look at the completed papers. (Because it will take less time, this will cost much less than having the lawyer prepare all the papers. And if you need guidance, it will be clear where the problems are.)

• When instructing a lawyer, ask for an estimate of fees, what services the fee will cover, and when payment must be made. If you think the fee too high, or you cannot afford it, don't be afraid to negotiate for a lower rate or more time to pay – or shop around for a lawyer whose fee rate is more appropriate. Fee rates vary and some lawyers will agree fixed sums.

Learning disabilities

Some children of average or above-average intelligence have difficulty learning and retaining information in the traditional fashion. Some early warning signs are hyperactivity; inability to concentrate; problems with discipline and changes in routine; lack of coordination; memory problems; and difficulties in speaking, reading and writing.

• If your child exhibits any of these 'symptoms', contact your family doctor to be sure there's no medical cause. If there isn't, ask your child's school to test him and to inform you about the results. If he has a learning disability, request the school to provide a special educational programme for him. You may question or appeal any plans that do not meet with your approval.

• If you feel the need for more help or support, ask your school administration about appropriate local parents' groups or contact the Rathbone C I (1st Floor, The Excalibur Building, 77 Whitworth Street, Manchester MI 6EZ, Tel. 0161-236 5358), the

---

Famous people with learning difficulties

Leonardo da Vinci. Some believe the mirror writing in the notes of this great Italian painter was a code; others say it was a symptom of dyslexia.

Hans Christian Andersen. The manuscripts of this writer contain amazing variations in spelling.

Thomas A. Edison. This brilliant inventor was taught by his mother after schools were unsuccessful.

Albert Einstein. This genius didn't talk until he was 4 or read until he was 9.

Woodrow Wilson. A notable American president who could not read until he was 11. His relatives considered him 'backward' and 'dull'.

Auguste Rodin. 'I have an idiot for a son,' the sculptor's father once said. He did poorly in spelling and arithmetic – but his most enduring work is 'The Thinker'.

Winston Churchill. A duplicate of his original application, sent anonymously to his old school, was rejected as not up to the school's standards.

British Dyslexia Association (98 London Road, Reading RG1 5AU, Tel. 01734-668271/2) or the Association of Workers for Children with Emotional and Behavioural Difficulties (28 High Street, Brigstock, Kettering, Northants WN14 3HA, Tel. 01536-373044).

Leather

Making garments

• For skirts, trousers and vests, buy 2-3oz / 60-85g leather or suede. It's easy to machine-sew with a leather-stitching needle and heavy-duty cotton or polyester thread.

For sturdy outdoor garments, belts and handbags, buy 4-10oz / 115-275g leather and rent a professional machine to sew up the pieces. Or punch holes along the edges with an awl and then lace the pieces together with thongs, using one of the methods shown below.

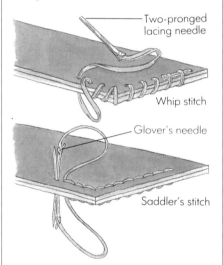

Two-pronged lacing needle

Whip stitch

Glover's needle

Saddler's stitch

• Before cutting leather or suede, check the hides for scars so that you can avoid them in laying out your pattern. If you find thin spots, reinforce them with fusible tape.

• Stroke suede to find the direction of the nap, mark the directions on the wrong side with a felt pen, then cut the pattern pieces so that the nap all goes one way. If you don't do this, the adjoining pieces won't match.

• Instead of basting seams on a leather garment, 'pin' them with paper clips 3in / 75mm apart, and then stitch them

---

removing the paper clips as you go. After you've finished stitching, brush a little latex adhesive onto the underside of the seam allowances and onto the adjacent leather. Let the glue dry, then press the seam allowances flat with your fingers; flatten these further by tapping along the leather lightly with a wooden mallet or special leatherwork hammer.

Maintenance

• If a leather coat gets wet, hang it on a padded hanger – not a hook – and let it dry away from direct heat. Creases will generally hang out overnight, but if they don't, press on the wrong side with a dry iron set on Low, using heavy wrapping paper as a pressing cloth.

• Clean small spots on smooth, glossy leather with a damp sponge.

• Erase scuff marks with wax shoe polish of the right colour. On suede use a wire suede brush, a damp towelling cloth or a sponge.

• When restitching leather gloves or slippers, use dental floss instead of thread. It lasts longer.

• To clean a combination bag, such as canvas and leather, clean the non-leather portion first. Make suds with washing-up liquid and rub them into the material with a sponge or soft cloth (use only suds – don't immerse the sponge). Work on heavily soiled spots with a soft brush, such as a nail brush. To rinse, dampen a sponge in warm water and rub the surface until the suds are gone. Use saddle soap to clean the leather portions, then apply a neutral shoe wax or a wax the same colour as the leather.

Leaves

Sending leaves to the rubbish dump is time-consuming and a waste of a valuable resource. Instead, stack the leaves in an inconspicuous corner of the garden, wet them down and trample them. Over the winter they will settle further, compacting into a tight, solid mass. The following autumn or spring, break the mass up into small chunks with a garden fork and spread it among shrubs, flowers and vegetables. It will serve as a mulch for at least one season, then decompose to fertilise and condition the soil.

Leaving a job

Be very careful not to alienate your boss when you leave. You may need his reference later on.

• Give at least 2 weeks' notice, although 3 or 4 may be required if you have been with the company for some years. Your contract will specify the minimum time that you must give. If you're in the middle of an important project, ask your new boss if you can stay until it's finished. Whether the answer is yes or no, your commitment to your old employer will be respected.

• Your letter of resignation is part of your permanent personnel file. Keep it simple and factual. If you're leaving because you are unhappy, don't put this or your reasons in the letter.

• Offer to train your replacement. If no one has started before you go, leave a list of things the new person should know. Make copies for your boss, your successor and any relevant colleagues.

• Tell your most important contacts you're leaving and give them the name of your replacement.

Leftovers

• Don't throw out stale bread and rolls. Use them for breadcrumbs, melba toast and croutons to serve with soups and salads, or for good old-fashioned bread puddings and bread and butter puddings.

• Freeze leftover cooked fish until you want to use it in a salad. Thaw, flake and toss with onions, salad vegetables and a dressing.

• Keep a special bag in the freezer for leftover vegetables. When you have enough for soup, thaw and purée in the blender with vegetable, chicken or beef stock.

• Or turn leftover vegetables into a salad. Toss with a vinaigrette dressing or mix with chopped onions, mayonnaise and herbs before mounding onto lettuce leaves.

• For a terrific sandwich filling, mince up beef scraps and mix them with mayonnaise or cream cheese; or spice it up with mustard, horseradish or pickle.

Legal aid and advice

• Do you need legal assistance but cannot afford it? Initial free legal help is available through your local Citizens Advice Bureau (Head Office: Myddleton House, 115-123 Pentonville Rd, London N1 9LZ, Tel. 0171-833 2181). In some areas there are also Neighbourhood Law Centres and Legal Advice Centres. Some may even help you to pursue a claim in court. Your local library can give you addresses, or you can contact the Legal Aid Board 29-37 Red Lion St, London WC1R 4PP, Tel. 0171-813 5300. See also WHERE TO COMPLAIN, p.243.

• Or go to your local solicitor. If you do not have a regular solicitor, choose one who displays the legal aid sign outside his offices.

• Many solicitors offer up to half an hour's advice and initial consultation for a small flat fee if you request it specifically (although they are not obliged to do so by law). Alternatively, they may provide advice on the inexpensive Green Form scheme. However, not all solicitors offer advice on this scheme, so if seeking help, enquire first.

• Your solicitor will advise you whether you are entitled to legal aid in a civil or criminal matter. Help is available for court work (other than divorce and libel cases) through the Legal Aid scheme. In practice you will not get legal aid in a civil matter unless your income and capital are both very low, or you receive income-related social security benefits, and your case is a reasonably good one. Remember that if you do not qualify for legal aid, legal charges can be very expensive. See LAWYERS, p.121.

• If you are arrested and need legal advice at a police station, you are entitled to a phone call to contact your solicitor. Alternatively, there is a rota of 'duty solicitors', who will visit you in the police station and give free advice. In criminal cases, if you are not represented, a court may decide to appoint a solicitor from the duty rota for you, if it thinks you need advice.

• If you are the victim of a crime and have suffered loss as a result, it is possible for the criminal court to order an offender to pay you compensation. Make it clear to the police or other enforcement agency that you want such an order or attend the court and ask for it yourself.

Lemons and limes

• You can substitute ½ teaspoon vinegar (any kind) for 1 teaspoon lemon or lime juice in a recipe.

• To get just a few drops of juice from a lemon or lime, prick one end with a fork or toothpick and squeeze. The fruit can be refrigerated and used again.

Letters

The art of letter writing, as practised by previous generations, is rare in today's electronic world. But there are some occasions when only a letter, note or card will do. When you must write, keep these tips in mind:

Personal

• Don't write only about yourself and your family. Ask questions, even rhetorical ones. Even if you don't expect a reply, at least express interest in the recipient's welfare and activities.

• Avoid dwelling on dreary topics such as a minor personal illness.

• Choose plain white cards for letters of sympathy. Don't be mawkish, but do say that your thoughts are with the bereaved and then recall a fond personal memory of the deceased. Offer specific help, if possible – babysitting or shopping, for example.

• Wait 24 hours before posting an emotion-packed letter – whether written in love or anger. Read it over and then decide if you still want to send it.

Business

• If you're writing to a company, address your letter to a specific person. Call the headquarters and ask who's in charge of the department you want to reach.

• Letters of complaint should be straightforward, factual and polite. Expressing too much indignation will merely antagonise the reader. If possible, work a touch of humour into the letter; it can be effective in getting results. See also LETTERS FOR VARIOUS OCCASIONS, p.284.

Lettuce

• Revive a wilted lettuce by rinsing it upside-down under a cold tap for a few seconds. Shake off excess water and put the lettuce into a large polythene bag. Tie up the bag tightly, trapping as much air as you can inside, then refrigerate for 1-2 hours, or overnight.

• Always make sure lettuce leaves are absolutely dry before tossing them with dressing; it won't cling to moist leaves.

• If you don't have a salad spinner, put washed lettuce leaves into a clean tea towel, gather up the four corners and spin round at arm's length.

• Use your fingers to tear lettuce into bite-size pieces; a knife can bruise the edges and destroy any vitamins.

• Use extra lettuce leaves as a hot vegetable. Braised, sautéed or stir-fried, they make a surprisingly good side dish.

Levelling

• Level a picture or mirror by holding a half-full glass of water against the top edge. The water surface will be level even if the glass itself is tilted.

• For long-distance levelling, make yourself a water leveller. Use a length of transparent plastic tubing attached at one end to the neck of an upside-down plastic bottle, with its bottom cut off, as shown. Fix the bottle at the right height to a ladder. Pour water into the bottle until it reaches the desired height at both ends; mark the spot on the tube. No matter how far apart the bottle and the end of the tube are, or how irregular the ground in between, the two will be at the same height when the water is aligned with the mark on the tube.

Liability

• Try to find an umbrella insurance policy that gives you additional coverage if an accident occurs on your property.

• Inspect your property regularly for hazards such as broken railings or deeply cracked pavingstones. Fix them as soon as you can; meanwhile, do your best to warn others of the danger.

• If you have an 'attractive nuisance', such as a swimming pool, put up warning signs and a fence and secure it with a locked gate.

• In winter, clear ice and snow from pavements and driveways as soon as possible (see ICY PATHS, p.112). If you have guests, warn them that the paths may be slippery.

• Keep family pets inside or within a fenced-in area.

• If, despite your efforts, a guest has too much to drink, call a taxi or make him stay until he sobers up.

Life insurance

Do you have enough life insurance for your family to live comfortably if you die prematurely?

• They will require a large enough lump sum to pay for the funeral and replace a company car, if you drive one.

• Ensure there is adequate provision for day to day living. Work out your average annual budget to see how much your family would need. Don't include mortgage payments, as they are probably covered by their own insurance policy.

• List all other financial resources your survivors can use, including your current assets – cash, securities, pension, Social Security benefits and so forth – as well as their own income.

• Consider taking out a family income benefit policy (which provides a regular tax-free income) if you think a lump sum (term) policy may not be enough.

Life jacket

• Anything buoyant – a polystyrene box, or even an empty, tightly sealed plastic bottle – can help someone stay afloat.

• If your trousers are made of a natural fibre – cotton or wool – take them off and knot the bottoms of the legs. Holding the waistband, swing the trousers over your head and down onto the water. Then tuck the air-filled legs under your armpits to serve as a buoy.

Caution Do not remove your clothes in icy water.

Inflating trousers as a buoy gives a temporary rest from treading water.

Lifts

Holding a lift button in or pushing it repeatedly may satisfy you but does nothing at all for the lift. Its electronic circuitry can register only the first call.

• The same is true when a lift misses your floor. Modern lifts have load sensors that cause them to bypass floors once they've reached load capacity. Be patient; the lift will stop on its return.

• Newer lifts have devices that are sensitive to pranks. If someone pushes all the buttons on his way out of the lift, the newer models will automatically cancel the calls. Just re-press the number of your floor to get moving again.

Light bulbs

• When replacing a screw-in, outdoor light bulb, coat the threads with a silicone spray polish before screwing in, to make it easier to remove next time.

• The commonest light bulb has a tungsten element which glows white-hot, giving light in all directions.

• Reflector lamps have a silvered inside which throws light forward in a beam.

• A crown silvered bulb is used to give a well-defined spotlight beam.

• A parabolic aluminised deflector is often used outdoors because it can withstand sudden temperature changes.

• A tungsten halogen lamp has about twice the life of an ordinary bulb, and gives about 25 per cent more light for the wattage.

• Fluorescent tubes are filled with a mixture of powder and gas which glows when current flows through the tube. They do not produce as much heat as a normal light bulb and are more cost-effective. They require special fittings.

• Energy-saving light bulbs work on the same principle as a fluorescent tube, but do not require special fittings. They run four times longer on a single unit of electricity than a conventional bulb, and last seven times longer.

Lighting

Add drama to a drab room by 'painting' it with light.

• Warm up a cold, white or pale green or blue room with colour-tinted bulbs. Pale pink, peach and cream add a subtle warming glow.

• For an element of surprise, vary the light sources throughout the room. Mount small fixtures under a row of wall cabinets, inside a china cabinet, on top of a bookshelf, and so forth. Bounce light both upwards and downwards.

• Varying lighting intensity in a room adds interest: a 25 watt bulb here and there provides a subtle touch. Dimmer-switches are a flexible way to control lighting mood and atmosphere at different times, but cannot be used to control domestic fluorescent fittings (see p.62).

• Focusing a floor spotlamp or uplighter on a leafy plant transforms a blank wall into a fascinating patterned screen of light and shade.

• Prevent glare from an overhanging pendant shade by fitting a crown-silvered bulb.

• In a child's bedroom, fix self-adhesive metallic foil stars to the ceiling. Illuminated decorative plugs can also double as tiny night lights.

• Picture lights add a generally warm background glow and can also highlight works of art.

Lightning

Lightning tends to strike the tallest object in the area, then arcs off to the side. If you get caught in a lightning storm and nothing nearby is taller than you, get to a low spot, squat down (preferably on something dry), and make yourself compact; hug your knees and tuck in your head (most fatalities occur when lightning strikes the head and exits through the feet or arms). Stay clear of hills, trees, fences, barns, cars and other conductors.

If you're playing golf, stop and go home. If you're in your car, stay there; don't touch any metal parts. Lightning will arc across the metal shell, but you'll be safe inside.

Often you'll get advance warning of a strike. If your skin begins to tingle and your hair stands on end, stoop down immediately. If someone near you is struck, keep her warm and dry and try to revive her breathing as soon as possible.

Lightning lore

Lightning can and does strike the same place twice – at least. The higher the structure, the more likely it is to be hit. Statistically, an average home on moderately flat terrain in a moderately active thunderstorm region might be hit once in 100 years. But a structure 1200ft/366m high might be struck 20 times each year.

To work out how many miles away a thunderstorm is, count the seconds between a lightning flash and the ensuing thunderclap, then divide by five.

Lightning helps to fertilise the soil. It converts nitrogen into an oxide, which, coupled with rainwater, forms a weak nitric acid (a compound of hydrogen, nitrogen and oxygen). Added to the minerals in the soil, this acid forms plant-nourishing nitrates.

Lipstick stains

Before washing a smeared garment with extra detergent, try one of these treatments:

• Rub in a 50/50 solution of glycerine and water, then rinse the stained area with water only.

• Rub the stain with a bar of white household soap.

• Apply a little neat liquid detergent.

• If the garment is white, soak it in lemon juice; if it's coloured, dilute the lemon juice by half with water.

• Place the stained area over a towel and sponge on a mixture of detergent and water.

Litter for cats

• Instead of commercial cat litter, you can use sand, wood shavings or peat. Don't use peat for long-haired cats, however; it sticks to their coats.

• To deodorise any type of litter, mix 1 part bicarbonate of soda into 3 parts litter; cover the bottom of the cat tray with a layer of bicarbonate of soda.

• Use cut-up plastic bin liners as litter box liners.

• Better still, make a 'pillowcase' for your cat tray: slip the whole box into a heavy-duty rubbish bag (or two thin ones – claws can punch tiny holes) and pour the litter on to the surface of the bag. When it's time to dispose of the contents, simply turn the bag inside-out over the litter and lift it out of the tray.

Locks

• All outside doors should be fitted with a good-quality lock which conforms to British Standard 3621 (look for the kite-mark) which guarantees that a lock has been approved by the British Standards Institution. Their tests include resistance to picking and drilling. The lock should have a 5-lever mechanism which gives up to 1000 key variations.

• If your outside door has a window in or near it, fit a deadlock to the door; this doesn't click shut but is operated by a key. Make sure you don't leave the key in the door or a burglar will simply walk off with your possessions.

• Sliding patio doors should be fitted with key-operated locking bolts mounted at the top and bottom at opposite corners. Fit special anti-lift devices so that sliding doors can't be lifted from their tracks. To prevent a sliding glass door from being opened, place a pipe or stick in the bottom track as shown.

• If you have basement windows, protect them by securing window bars or a metal grille into the brickwork.

On cars

• Do not try to force a frozen car lock open – the key may break off. Check the lock on the passenger side. It may not

have been affected by the frosty spell.

• Or heat the key with a match or lighter, then insert it into the lock. Repeat until the lock thaws.

Loft ventilation

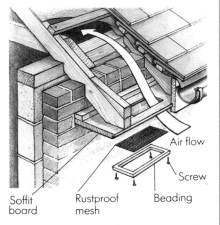

Air flow
Screw
Soffit board
Rustproof mesh
Beading

Lack of air flow in a loft space can lead to problems with condensation, which in turn can damage the timbers and the loft contents if not checked.

• Line the loft floor with building paper (under the layers of insulation). This will prevent moist air from percolating through the ceiling plaster. Also add a draught strip around the hatch opening.

• The loft space can be ventilated in a number of ways. Special vents are available for insertion into the soffits (the boards immediately under the fascia boards supporting the gutters). Or special tile vents can be found at a builders' merchants; these can be used to replace existing roof tiles – though the ideal time for this is during building or renovation of a roof. Ridge vents are also available.

• Ventilation bricks can be inserted in end gable walls if this is more convenient. Add fine perforated zinc or other metal mesh to keep out wasps looking for nesting sites.

• You can make your own vents by cutting holes in the soffit boards with a jigsaw, then covering the opening with a fine rustproof mesh. Add a simple quadrant beading to secure the mesh and make the job look neater.

• Ensure that all vents are kept free of debris such as fallen leaves.

Long-distance parents

Even though you and your child may live far apart – perhaps because of schooling or divorce – you can still maintain a bond between you.

• Phone regularly to keep abreast of news (such as what tests are coming up at school) and general chat. Talk about what you've been doing too, rather than bombarding your child with questions about his activities. Call at set times so that your child is prepared. Remember that not all children can talk easily on the phone, so write down a list of topics in case the conversation gets stuck.

• Send cards and newspaper or magazine cuttings in the post. Children love receiving letters and these small gestures show they're still in your thoughts.

• Visit each other as often as possible. Let him share your daily routine – you don't have to organise a whirlwind day of activity. Develop a set of rituals that only the two of you share, such as eating at a favourite restaurant, strolling in the park or going swimming.

• Keep a set of clothes and possessions at your house so he feels he belongs. Put his name on the bedroom door (Martin's room, for example) and start a 'treasure box' of knick-knacks (such as polished stones or souvenirs). Re-examining these treasures when your child sees you may give him a sense of continuity in your relationship.

Loose covers

• Save yourself the trouble and cost of matching up different pieces when making a loose cover for a sofa or chair; choose a solid-colour fabric or one with a small overall pattern. Avoid stripes, checks, large patterns and fabrics with a one-way nap.

• Don't use your old sheets as loose covers; get new ones with a factory finish that will protect them from soil and stains. After washing, apply a fabric protector.

• Buy everything you need at the same time so that you can be sure the sheets come from the same dye lot and match perfectly.

• Hide worn upholstery under a bed-spread, quilt, sheet or shawl. For a more finished effect, drape the fabric over the frame, tuck it into the inside crevices and pin it in place with a safety pin. At the outside corners, cut quarter circles to remove the excess cloth; stitch down the cut edge, then attach ties, grommets, Velcro or tape with plastic press-studs to pull the remaining cloth tight. Wrap loose cushions separately.

Lopsided houseplants

All plants grow towards the light. If you have one on a windowsill, keep it growing straight upwards by turning it 90° every 4 or 5 days.

Lost child

Getting lost can be a terrifying experience for both you and your child. You can prepare for it by:
• Teaching a standard routine, such as 'If you get lost in the street, stand where you are until we find you. Don't go into a shop, where it will be harder to track you down and don't talk to anyone unless it's a policeman.'
• Teach the child that if she gets lost in a shop, she should approach someone in shop uniform standing behind a counter. Always warn a child against going off with anyone else even if they promise to find Mummy and Daddy.
• Ensure your child knows her phone number and address. Or write the details down and slip them in an inner pocket in the child's jacket or coat. Practise using a payphone with your child so that she knows how to ring home.
• When going to a busy place, such as a shopping centre or the zoo, agree on a rendezvous in case your child gets lost.

Lost friends and relatives

To find friends or family you have lost contact with, try one of these methods:
• Call directory enquiries and ask for your friend's number in the city where you think your friend might be living. If there is a long list of subscribers by that name, call all of the numbers and explain that you're looking for the John Smith who grew up in, say, Manchester in the 1950s and attended Kelvin High School. Most people will help.
• Phone directories, or electoral rolls, both of which are available in libraries, may help you find a lost friend.
• College or university administrations will forward a letter to a former student.
• Professional bodies, such as the British Medical Association (Tel. 0171-387 4499), keep directories of all people currently in practice. Trade unions keep registers, too. If you know your friend's trade, call the union's headquarters.
• Contact the Salvation Army's family-tracing service on 0171-383 2772.

Lost in the wilds

• The first impulse of any lost person is to keep moving. Wrong! The best strategy is usually to stay put and signal for help. Find a way to give consecutive signals – shouts, whistle blasts or smoke columns, for example – to serve as an SOS. On a sunny day, use a mirror to flash signals, but if you don't have a mirror, use a knife blade, a piece of glass or any reflective surface. The International Distress Signal is six flashes or blasts per minute, followed by a minute's pause.
• If you must find your way out of where you are, first sit down and get your bearings. Try to remember the last spot where you knew where you were. Then try to recall distinctive landmarks between that spot and where you are now. Ask yourself: which way do the streams run? The roads? In which direction am I likely to find help?

Choose a direction and stay on course by using a compass (see p.50) or by walking from landmark to landmark. Within your line of sight, find two landmarks a good distance apart in the direction you wish to go, before you reach the first, look for a third one that lies beyond the second.

As you set out, glance behind yourself to keep track of how things look in case you have to backtrack. Build small cairns with stones or leave twigs set in the ground. If you stop to rest, sit or lie down facing the direction you've chosen. If you take a nap, scratch an arrow in the dirt to remind yourself which direction you're following.

Lost luggage or property

• If you leave something on a train, contact your nearest station enquiry office. They will tell you where to go to contact the lost property office. If you discover your loss immediately, they may be able to get staff to collect your property off the train before it reaches its destination and return it. British Rail levies a charge on lost property.
• If you leave something on a bus, contact the local depot or enquiry office of the company concerned, giving details. They will advise you
• If you lose something elsewhere, contact anyone who may have seen it and report details to your local police station.
• If you find something on a train or bus, hand it in to staff immediately. If, however, it looks suspicious, don't handle it, but inform staff straight away. If you find something elsewhere, hand it in to the nearest police station and get a receipt. If it is not claimed within three months the police will give it back to you.
• If your luggage is lost in transit when flying, file a Property Irregularity report at the baggage service desk immediately. You will need a signed copy for insurance purposes. Give an address where you can be contacted within a day or two. International convention limits an airline's liability, but most travel insurances have a clause which, if luggage is still missing after 12 hours, allows for a certain sum to be spent on essential items. If your bag isn't located within 3 days, the chances are that it will never turn up. Even so, hold on to your claim form, baggage check and ticket receipt for at least 6 months; you are entitled to compensation, but it may take some time to get it.
• Baggage loss is inevitable sometimes, but following a few simple rules reduces the risk. Use a suitcase, trunk or box that will not break open easily and do not overfill it.

• Lock your case with a combination lock. Put your name, destination address and phone number inside and outside the case, together with flight details (do not put your home address on the outside of the case – it invites burglars).

• Remove tags from other flights.

• If you are making a connecting flight, try to use the same carrier.

• Check in early – last-minute arrivals often mean lost baggage.

• Check the terms of your home contents insurance. It often covers you for items lost away from home, but it may not be worth while to claim for small losses. If you buy your tickets with a credit card, baggage insurance may be included automatically.

Lost pets

• Have your name, address and telephone number engraved on a tag and make sure your pet wears it on its collar at all times.

• Keep a clear colour photograph of your pet and a list of its distinguishing marks.

• If your pet is missing, search the neighbourhood and call the local police stations, animal shelters and vet surger-

ies. You can also put up notices with a photo and description, and check the lost-and-found section of the local newspaper. If your pet is a thoroughbred, contact local pedigree clubs; they may have their own rescue committees.

• If you find a pet with a collar but no address, contact the police and local animal shelters in case the owner has notified them, and check local newspapers for notices. Insert a notice of your own, describing the pet but leaving out a detail that only the owner will know.

• The latest in pet identification is a microchip implant under the skin of your pet, which contains a number unique to your animal. This number is put on a national register along with your details, so that even if your pet loses its collar, it can be identified and returned to you. The process is painless for the pet and could save time for everyone involved.

At present, all police stations and dogs' homes possess the apparatus necessary to scan the microchip and reveal the number. A growing number of vet surgeries also have scanners, so if your pet is found collarless, there is a good chance it will be returned to you.

Low-fat diet

• Aim to reduce your fat intake to less than 30 per cent of your daily calorie consumption (see p.30).

• Do not eliminate fat completely from your diet – fats contain fatty acids and vitamins A, D, E and K which are essential for good health.

• Eat small amounts of mainly unsaturated fats, such as fish oils, olive oil, sunflower oil, rape-seed oil and margarine.

• Avoid saturated fats such as fat meat, red meat, hard cheese, cream, butter and unskimmed milk.

• Choose fish and white meat such as chicken in preference to red meat.

• Choose cottage cheese or even medium-fat types, such as Brie, Camembert or Edam in preference to hard cheeses such as Cheddar.

• Use low-fat spreads instead of butter, but only in small quantities.

• Stop deep frying. When cooking, use as

little fat as possible. Use sunflower oil only when frying.

• Avoid egg yolks and any foods which are made with them.

• Avoid high-fat snacks such as crisps, peanuts, chocolate, biscuits, pastries and cakes.

Low-salt diet

Excess salt (sodium chloride) in your diet can lead to high blood pressure, heart attacks, strokes and kidney disease.

• Do not add extra salt to food on the table – use a salt substitute.

• Use little or no added salt when cooking. Food without added salt contains all the sodium you need.

• If you have high blood pressure or a heart condition, check with your doctor or chemist before using a salt substitute. Some contain potassium chloride, which may be unsuitable.

• Beware of tinned or dehydrated soups, almost all of which are heavily dosed with salt. Instead, make your own chicken, beef, vegetable or fish stock and freeze it for use in soups. A few cups of stock that have been boiled down to a concentrate and then frozen in an ice cube tray make handy stock cubes.

• Substitute lemon juice, vinegar, wine, aromatic bitters, herbs and spices for salt (dill and parsley, especially, have a vaguely 'salty' flavour). Experiment with your own herbal blends in the kitchen as well as at the table. Throw out salt cellars and use pepper mills to grind whole mustard seeds or black peppercorns over soups and salads. See also SALT SUBSTITUTES, p.175.

Lubricating oil

• Try liquid paraffin in place of oil – but not in your car's engine. Cooking oils also do, short-term, for squeaky doors but soon turn rancid.

• For lubricating parts underwater – such as in a toilet cistern – petroleum jelly is long-lasting.

• To remove rust or corrosion, use vinegar or lemon juice instead of penetrating oil.

M

Magazine subscriptions

• If you haven't received the most recent issue of a magazine you subscribe to, or if someone has given you a subscription to a magazine you already receive, write to the magazine's subscription department.

• If you're moving, notify every magazine you subscribe to at least 4 weeks in advance. Most have a change-of-address form in the publication which you can use, or send the address label from a recent issue.

• An annual subscription to a favourite magazine makes an excellent birthday or Christmas present, especially for an elderly relative.

Magnets

The attracting and repelling properties of a magnet are fascinating to children. Demonstrate them by laying two bar magnets end to end; the like poles will repel each other and the unlike poles attract each other.

You can get your child to make their own magnet using two bar magnets and a steel bar. Lay the bar horizontally, and hold the magnets by their tips, one in each hand, with two ends (north and south) that attract, pointing downwards. Stroke the bar simultaneously with the magnets, working outwards in opposite directions, from the centre of the bar. Stroking magnetises the bar by realigning its atoms to create its own north and south poles.

Magnifying glass

• Turn a wine glass or goblet on its side and hold it over the object or words you want to enlarge. Rotate the glass slightly, to bring things into focus.

• Poke a small hole in a piece of paper and bring it up to your eye; things will appear larger.

Mail

• When you must send a letter or a parcel by express mail, ask the post office assistant for the cost by DataPost as well as by Special Delivery. DataPost promises next-day delivery to most locations, but it is expensive. If your deadline is not critical, consider sending your item by Special Delivery. It usually takes a day for the item to reach its destination, but the charges are much cheaper.

• If you are sending important documents or valuable items in the post, send them by Registered Post. At least they will be insured if they are lost in transit. The post office is legally liable for loss, damage or delay only if the items are registered.

• If a letter or parcel is lost or damaged, ask your local post office for an Enquiry form. Fill it in, take a copy, and send it to the local head postmaster. If you don't get a satisfactory reply, send it to the postal regional director. You can also raise a grievance with the local Post Office Advisory Committee (you should find the address in the front of your telephone directory) and also with the Independent Post Office Users' National Council, 6 Hercules Rd, London SE1 7DN, Tel. 0171-928 9458.

• The post office will refund the cost of stamps that have been damaged before being used.

• Before you go on holiday, type addresses for postcards on gummed labels. You'll be more likely to send the promised cards.

• A cigar box is perfect for sending small items. It is worth asking tobacconists if they have an old one they are prepared to give you at no cost, or ask friends who smoke to keep their empty cigarette packets for you. See also POSTAL SERVICES, p.160.

Postmen of the past

Postal systems developed in the early civilisations of Egypt and the Middle East. As early as 1580 BC the ancient Egyptians had established a messenger service. More than a thousand years later, the Persians set up the first efficient communications system in the ancient world. They constructed a road system, with relay stations at regular intervals, to speed the delivery of letters throughout their extensive empire, which stretched from India to the shores of the Mediterranean. The Greek historian Herodotus claimed that nothing mortal travelled as fast as the Persian messenger on horseback.

It wasn't until 1783 that the stage coach was started in Britain. It was prompted by the slowness of sending postboys on horseback. On August 2, the first stage left Bristol at 4pm and arrived in London early the next morning, a journey that previously took 3 days. The coaches travelled at night, at a speed of 8-9mph/12-14kph. The service was so successful that it was soon extended to include deliveries to all the major towns throughout England and Scotland.

At that time, postage was paid by the person who received the item, and it varied according to the distance the item travelled. In 1840 the Penny Post was instituted, allegedly after its creator Rowland Hill saw an old woman refuse a letter from her son because she couldn't afford the charge — a shilling. That year saw the production of Britain's first postage stamp — the now much collected Penny Black.

Horses aren't the only animals people have enlisted to deliver mail. During the 19th century cows hauled mail wagons in some German towns. In Texas, New Mexico and Arizona, camels were used. In Scandinavia, reindeer pulled mail sleighs. And the Belgian city of Liège even tried cats, but they proved to be unreliable.

Mail-order buying

• Be wary of imitations of brand-name products. What you see in a catalogue may look better than what you get. If it's an unfamiliar brand, read the description carefully and study the illustration closely. If it's a name you know, be sure you know the model number you want.
• Order by phone – especially if there's a freephone number (0800). Your order will get into the system faster, and you'll be able to ask questions about the merchandise and delivery dates. (Be sure to get the name of the person you talk to.)
• Ask about the return policy before you order. You should have the right to a full refund as long as you have not damaged the product.
• Use a credit card whenever possible. You'll have a separate record of your order, and if there's a problem, the credit card company won't require you to pay until the matter is settled, provided you notify it of the dispute.
• Sometimes orders simply don't turn up. Under a code of practice the company is obliged to get the goods to you within 28 days. If the mail-order company becomes insolvent before you receive the goods, you can claim against the newspaper or magazine where you saw the advertisement.
• To protect yourself in case of disagreements, keep a copy of your order, noting the date it was placed and the name of the company representative, the original advertisement, cancelled cheques or credit slips and all correspondence with the advertiser.

Male menopause

Men don't go through the physical changes of menopause, but many experience some kind of psychological crisis in their 40s or 50s. The awareness that there are goals yet to be reached and pleasures yet to be enjoyed – and that time will, indeed, run out – can lead to anxiety, depression, self-doubt and marital discord.

If you're having such feelings, remember that they are perfectly normal and that they, too, will pass.

Here, nevertheless, are a few tips to help you get through difficult times.
• Keep in mind that the trappings of youth don't make you look younger, just faintly ridiculous.
• Remember that leaving your wife for a younger woman can be a mistake, and it's not really dealing with the cause of your unhappiness.
• Don't worry about sex. You may not be 17 any more, but your body still works; problems in the bedroom are often the result of worrying about them. Consult your doctor to be safe.
• If you dislike your job, don't just sit around complaining. Either leave or don't – then get on with your life (see CAREER CHANGES, p.34).
• Get involved in volunteer work. Find out how you can help with a local voluntary organisation, such as helping adults to read and write, helping to run a youth group or becoming a special constable or magistrate. Look in the Yellow Pages under 'Charitable & benevolent organisations' for an institution that could use your talents.
• Jog, walk or join a gym so that you get at least 30 minutes of heart-pumping exercise at least three times a week (with your doctor's permission, of course). You'll look better, feel better and probably add years to your life into the bargain.

Map protector

• If you are a keen walker, you might find it worthwhile to buy a transparent plastic map protector – it will keep your map dry on even the wettest outings. Sturdy examples with a zip top are available from most camping and walking equipment outlets.
• Or you can make your own with two sheets of heavy duty transparent plastic, each the same size, secured around three sides with insulating tape. Leave one side open so you can insert whichever map you need.
• If you regularly visit the same area, cover the relevant Ordnance Survey map with a piece of adhesive transparent plastic film, as if it were a children's exercise book, to keep it clean and dry.

Marking stick

Make your own marking stick using an old wooden ruler and a mole grip.

Insert a small wood screw through the 1in/25mm mark on the ruler. Then, if you want to mark a parallel line 3in/75mm from the edge of your work, for example, set the pliers at the 4in/100mm line. Hold the nose of the pliers against the edge of the work with one hand; hold the end of the ruler with the other. Keeping the ruler square with the edge, pull it evenly towards you across the work surface, so that the screw scratches a line.

Matches

• Starting a fire without matches is hard work, so carry reserves. If you must do so, however, first gather some dry tinder, such as the inner lining of an old birds' nest, fluff from clothing, bits of rope end or some dry, dead wood. Form the tinder into a sheltered nest.

Hold the striking edge of a matchbox or a dry hard stone as close to the tinder as possible. Strike it downwards with the back of a knife blade or a small piece of steel to send sparks into the centre of the tinder. Fan the smouldering tinder into a flame; add fuel gradually, starting with small, dry twigs.
• On a sunny day use a magnifying glass, a camera or binocular lens, or a pair of strong reading glasses, to focus the sun's rays on the tinder.
• When lighting a fire in windy or rainy weather, use a candle to save matches.
• To waterproof windproof matches, dip them in melted candle or paraffin wax.
• If you're short on paper matches, you

can double your supply. Insert the point of a sharp knife in the base of each match and slowly pull the halves apart.
• Store your matches in a film canister along with the striking pad from the matchbox. This will keep them dry.

Maternity leave

If you have worked for your employer for 6 months or more, you are entitled to 18 weeks of statutory maternity pay (SMP) even if you don't plan to return to work after the birth. This starts 11 weeks before the birth at the earliest.
• To claim SMP, inform your employer at least 3 weeks before you stop working. You may need a maternity certificate (form MAT B1, available from your midwife or doctor) as proof of pregnancy.
• Your job must be kept open for you for up to 29 weeks after the birth if you have worked there for 2 years full-time or 5 years part-time, and you told your employers you were returning to work.

Maths in your head

• A quick way to do calculations is to drop the os at the ends of numbers, then replace them for your final answer. For example, to add 120 and 90, get the sum of 12 and 9 and then add one 0.
• Similarly, to break down complex problems, start with the big numbers. To multiply 6 × 348, for example, first multiply 6 × 300 (1800), then 6 × 40 (240). Add the two to get 2040 and then add on the result of 6 × 8 (48) for a total of 2088.
• Change kilometres to miles by dropping the last digit and multiplying by 6: thus, 72 kilometres is approximately 42 miles. Most of today's cars have both scales on their speedometer, however.
• To multiply by 9, assign each finger a number, beginning with the little finger of your left hand (1) and ending with the right-hand little finger (10). Then, to multiply 3 × 9, for example, turn down the number-three finger, making a space on your left hand. Count the fingers to the left of the space (2); then count the fingers to the right (7). The answer: 27. See COMPUTATIONS, p.50.

Mattresses

• To keep a mattress from sliding around on its foundation, put a nonslip rubber mat between the two.
• To even out the wear, turn a new mattress over and reverse it end to end every 3 weeks for 3 months – and every couple of months thereafter.
• Don't use the handles on the mattress to lift it. They're not designed to take the full weight but only to move the mattress around while it's on its base.
• Air a mattress in the sun occasionally to keep it fresh and clean smelling.

Mealworms

If a packet of flour, nuts, cereal or birdseed is seriously infested with mealworms, discard it immediately. (If you've just bought the infested product, go back to the shop where you bought it and ask for a refund.)

To guard against infestation, keep dry foodstuffs in tightly closed containers. It's best if these have clear lids because then if mealworms do hatch in them they can be seen without removing the lid.

If infested food is found in the kitchen cupboards, clear them out, vacuum and scrub them, and remove and replace shelf paper.

Measuring

• If there's no one to help you measure a long stretch with a tape measure, use the hook on the tape end, secure the end of the tape with masking tape, or anchor it with a brick or a heavy wood block.
• To find the circumference of a cylindrical object when you don't have a flexible tape measure, try this simple trick. Cut a strip of paper and wrap it around the object. Mark the spot where the paper overlaps. Then lay the strip out flat and measure it with a ruler.
• Here's how to divide a board into equal parts lengthwise. Lay a ruler diagonally across the width of the board so that the beginning (0) is at the left edge. Then adjust the other end of the ruler until the

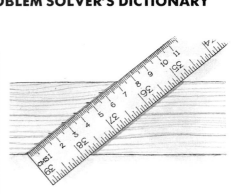

right edge of the board aligns with the number of parts desired. Mark off each of the inch/cm graduations.
• To lay out an exact 90° angle, use the 3-4-5 ratio. From a common point, stretch out two long strings roughly at right angles to each other. Mark one string at 3 ft from the common point and the other at 4 ft. Stretch a tape measure from the 3 ft mark on one string to the 4 ft mark on the other and adjust the strings until the distance between the two marks is exactly 5 ft. The angle between the two strings will be 90°. (This method also works for metres, yards or indeed for any unit of length.)
• For fast, approximate measuring, use your own body. On an average size man, the top joint of the index finger is about 1 in/25 mm long, the fist is about 4 in/100 mm wide, and the span from the tip of the thumb to the tip of the little finger on an outstretched hand is about 9 in/230 mm. A shoe is about 1 ft/300 mm long.

Measuring jug

• Use a clean milk bottle or carton if you have no measuring jug handy.
• If you don't have a milk bottle or carton, use a measuring spoon or kitchen tablespoon: 10 tablespoons equal ¼ pint/150 ml so it follows that 20 tablespoons equal ½ pint/285 ml and 40 tablespoons equal 1 pint/570 ml.

Medication schedule

• Make up a week-by-week chart: write the days of the week down the short side of a large piece of paper, the hours of the day across the long side; fill in the dosages in the appropriate hours. Hang the chart near or inside your medicine cabinet and check off each marked box as soon as you take the medicine.

• Label the compartments of an ice cube tray for all your waking hours. Each morning place pills, or small slips of paper representing liquid medicines, in their appropriate compartments. Discard the slips after taking the medicine.

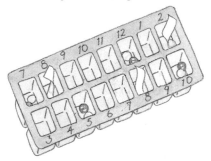

• If you're away from home, wear a digital watch set to beep every hour. Carry your medicine(s) and schedule in your pocket or bag. When the beeper sounds, check your schedule and take your medicine.

• To prevent confusion, write the name of each medicine in bold, bright letters on the biggest self-sticking label that will fit on the container. If possible, use a different coloured label for each of your morning, afternoon and evening medicines.

Meetings

• When it comes to meetings, keep in mind that less is more. Any meeting will be shorter and more productive if you invite only those people who are directly involved in the matters under discussion.

• Whenever possible, schedule a meeting in the morning, when people are more alert. But avoid 'first thing in the morning' sessions. The day before or after a weekend or holiday is also a bad time.

• A few days before the meeting, put your agenda in writing and distribute it to all the participants. Tell them how much time will be devoted to each topic, and allow extra time at the end just in case some topics run over.

• To stay on schedule, refer to the agenda as the meeting progresses. If

someone gets long-winded, wait until he takes a breath and say, 'I'm afraid we've run out of time on this topic, so let's summarise'.

• To keep participants on their toes, ask each one to give a brief presentation.

• To draw out a creative but shy person, tell her in advance that you'd like her ideas on a particular topic, then call on her. Or go around the table, asking each person in turn for a comment.

Memory

• To remember the name of a person you've just been introduced to, first make sure that you've heard it properly. (Ask to have it repeated or spelled out if you're not sure you have understood.) Then call the person by name in your conversation and again when you say goodbye.

• If you find it hard to keep the names of your friends' children straight, jot them down next to the friends' names in your address book. Do the same with business contacts you don't deal with often.

• Establish a place for putting such easily misplaced items as gloves and keys. Much of what people think is bad memory is just bad organisation.

• Keep a pad and pencil handy near your telephone and in your handbag, pocket and car. If you write something down,

you won't have to worry about remembering it. Make a habit of going over your list at a set time every day – say, right after breakfast.

• Don't be afraid to talk to yourself. If the telephone rings while you're on your way out, put your car keys down and say out loud, 'OK, keys, I'm putting you on the kitchen table'. It might sound silly, but it will also help to fix their location in your mind.

• Use the same technique if you have medicine to take daily. Before you swallow your pill, say out loud, 'I'm taking my pill now', and you won't wonder in an hour whether you've taken it or not.

• Give your memory a regular workout by playing quiz games that demand quick recall or card games (such as bridge) that require keeping track of the cards played.

• To remember the main topics of a talk you're to give, associate each one with a room in your house. As you give your talk, picture yourself moving from one room to the next.

Memory loss

Although older people are quite often forgetful, ageing itself may not be the cause. Memory can also be affected by medications, illness (particularly

---

Develop that memory!

'Richard of York gave battle in vain,' answered the boy when the teacher asked him to name all seven colours of the rainbow. Actually, he was simply using a device to aid his memory: his response contained the first letter of each colour.

Do you want a quick way to recall the planets in order? Take the first letter of every word in this sentence: Most Volcanoes Expel Mulberry Jam Sandwiches Under Normal Pressure. If the phrase itself takes some remembering, just try and visualise the scene it describes.

A mnemonic – the word is taken

from the Greek for mindful – is a device such as a formula or rhyme which helps you to remember. Make up a sentence using the first letters on your shopping list, for example:

Elephants Love Cold Showers, for a list of eggs, lettuce, cheese and sugar. Or for a series of errands at the dry-cleaners, the market, the post office and the florist, try Don't Make Porridge On the Floor.

And remember how to pronounce mnemonics, think of the title of this article. It's a mnemonic for Drop The M.

Alzheimer's disease), alcohol, depression, stress or isolation. If you or an older relative become increasingly forgetful, go to a doctor to see if there is a physical cause and if it can be remedied.

You can make life easier for someone whose memory is failing by organising the household:
• Label cupboard doors and drawer fronts with lists of their contents.
• Paint hot-water taps with red nail polish.
• Hang a list of emergency numbers in large type by the phone. Or buy a phone with a memory.
• Place an oversize hook next to the door for keys.
• Put up a big wall calendar and mark it with reminders of important dates.
• Talk about forthcoming events just before they occur.

Menopause

For many women the 'change of life' is a brief, relatively painless event. Some, however, experience several years of symptoms such as hot flushes, vaginal dryness, emotional upheaval and mental depression.

If you're having such difficulties, be honest with your family and friends. Tell them what you're experiencing; they can't be supportive if they don't understand the problem. It might be especially helpful to discuss what you're feeling with an older woman.
• Stay cool during hot flushes – in winter, lower the central heating thermostat and wear easy-to-remove layers of loose, cotton clothing.
• For night-time hot flushes, buy absorbent cotton sheets and nightclothes. Keep a spare nightgown and a Thermos of iced water at the ready on your bedside table.
• Keep two athlete's cold packs in the freezer; hold them against your cheeks when a hot flush begins.
• After checking with a doctor, start doing some regular aerobic and relaxation exercises.
• Ask your doctor about the pros and cons of hormone replacement therapy (HRT). See also OSTEOPOROSIS, p.145.

Menstrual cramps

• At the first sign of cramps, take ibuprofen: it works better than aspirin-based tablets. Some women get prompt relief with ibuprofen; others may find they need take it for 4-5 days.
• Instead of going to bed when you feel the pain, get some exercise – take a walk, ride a bicycle or do a few minutes of yoga.
• Give yourself a heat treatment: a warm bath or a hot-water bottle on your lower back or your abdomen.
• Some women get relief by taking B complex vitamins, vitamins C and E, zinc, calcium and magnesium. Check with your doctor.
• Get a lower-back massage. Or ask a friend to apply acupressure: rub the midback, 1in/25mm to the right of the spine, for 3-4 minutes. (You may get 3-6 hours of relief.) If you're alone, press on a point two thumb widths above the wrist joint on your inner arm, in line with your middle finger.
• Eat a low-fat, low-salt diet with plenty of fibre. See also PMT, p.159.

Mice

• Block up your mouseholes! Gaps around pipes, broken air-bricks and ill-fitting doors will all let mice through.
• Kill them with kindness, with a bait of mousekiller. Some brands send them to sleep before they die.
• If mice persist, call your local Environmental Health officer or a pest control company.
• If you use standard snap traps, don't fall for the old cartoon cliché of baiting them with cheese. Use small pieces of peanut butter, nut chocolate or cooked bacon instead; mice seem particularly fond of them.

Microwave ovens

• Find the hot and cold spots by spreading a layer of trimmed white bread slices edge to edge over the microwave floor. Set on High and watch the browning process through the glass door.
• To test whether a cooking dish is microwave safe, place it in the oven on Low next to a glass of water; if the water warms up, you know the oven is working. Turn onto High for 1 minute: if the dish still feels cool, it's safe to use; if it's hot, don't use it in the microwave.
• To get full cooking power, wipe out the oven after each use – especially around the door seal – using a mild detergent or bicarbonate of soda solution. Soften stubborn grime with steam by boiling a cup of water in the oven; then clean with a plastic (not steel wool) scrubbing pad.
• To give microwaved meat an appetising browned look, brush it first with soy sauce mixed with a little water.
• To get rid of lingering, stale food smells, place a thick slice of lemon on a paper towel and microwave it on High for 1-1½ minutes; leave it in the oven overnight.
• If greasy residue or food inside the oven catches fire, keep the door closed, turn the oven off and disconnect the appliance at the plug, or turn off the power at the mains (see p.80).
• If you're worried about high electricity or gas bills, economise by preheating food in a microwave on High before completing the cooking in a regular oven. See also MICROWAVE DO'S AND DON'TS, p.257.

Migraine headaches

The warning: flashes of light, dizziness and nausea. The affliction: an intense, throbbing pain on one side of your head.
• If you sense the warning stage, take any medicine you have and drink a cup of hot coffee (not decaffeinated).
• When pain strikes, pour cold water over your head, take a cold shower or use an ice or cold pack.
• Lie down in a dark, quiet place and imagine a beautiful scene. Listen to soothing music. (To develop a 'relaxation response,' do this for 30 minutes twice a week for 5 weeks, whether you have a headache or not.)
• Give yourself (or ask someone to give you) a gentle scalp, neck and shoulder massage.
Prevention
• Try to discover and eliminate the cause

of your migraines by keeping a diary (see HEADACHES, p.102). Common culprits are red wine, hot dogs, bacon, pork, salami, yeast, chocolate, cheese and cigarettes.

• Maintain a routine: get up at the same time each day, eat regular meals and exercise daily.

• Wear sunglasses in the sun and avoid looking directly at bright lights. See also PAIN RELIEF, p.148.

• See your doctor for preventive treatment if migraine is frequent or severe.

Mildew

To prevent mildew, try to keep things as clean and dry as possible.

Basements
• Close the windows and use a dehumidifier to reduce moisture.

• Check the drainage around the outside of the house and seal up all cracks so that moisture can't get in. See also DAMPNESS, p.59.

Bathrooms
• Use an old toothbrush to scrub the mildew from grout. For stubborn stains, cover with a paste of scouring powder that contains bleach and leave it for several hours; scrub and rinse off. Or use a proprietary mould killer.

• After using the shower, keep the shower door or curtain open while you wipe down the walls and leave them to dry. Then close the curtain or door so that it, too, can dry.

• To clean a fibreglass shower cubicle, gently scour the walls with bicarbonate of soda on a damp sponge, then rinse and dry.

• If your shower curtain is mildewed, just soak it in the bath in a solution of 1 part domestic bleach to 4 parts water. Rinse thoroughly, and then machine-wash if possible.

Books
• Put a piece of charcoal or silica gel in a closed bookcase to absorb moisture.

• For damp pages, sprinkle cornflour throughout the book; brush it off several hours later, after the moisture has been absorbed. If the pages are mildewed, brush the cornflour off outdoors to keep mildew spores out of the house.

Clothes If mildew has set into a fabric it can be impossible to remove. However, if it has recently affected clothes, you can try to wash it out. To treat mildew stains on a washable fabric, try bleaching the fabric (if it's white) or use a heavy-duty detergent containing oxygen bleach if the fabric will tolerate it. Machine-wash the clothes in the hottest water recommended for the fabric your clothes are made of.

Cupboards
• To increase air circulation, keep the door ajar. Consider replacing a solid door with a louvred one.

• Keep items susceptible to mildew, such as shoes and luggage, on wire racks or perforated shelves so that air can circulate around them.

Mattresses
• If possible, take a mattress outside and brush off the mildew; if not, vacuum it and throw away the bag. Lay the mattress in the sun for several hours until thoroughly dry; if drying indoors, use a fan.

• Platform beds often mildew. Buy one with slats, or drill a few holes in the platform to allow air to circulate around the mattress.

Refrigerators
• Wipe interior walls regularly with bicarbonate of soda to keep them clean.

• If your refrigerator has a pan underneath it, clean this regularly and sprinkle it with some bicarbonate of soda.

Milk

• If you're out of milk and need some for baking, try using the same amount of fruit juice. It works surprisingly well for many quick breads and cakes. Or use yoghurt (add ½ teaspoon bicarbonate of soda per 8fl oz/225ml). If you use skimmed milk, add 2 teaspoons of vegetable oil or melted butter per 8fl oz/225ml.

• Milk in cartons picks up refrigerator smells. Close the carton flaps tightly or transfer the milk to a covered jug.

• If milk starts to go sour, salvage it for use in cake mixtures and scones. Sour milk also makes a good substitute for buttermilk in recipes which require it.

Mincer

• Clear clogged holes in a meat mincer by rapping the grinder plate several times against the edge of the worktop.

• If your mincer is very greasy, run a piece of bread through it, then wash it.

Mirrors

• Never spray cleaner directly on a mirror – the drips could seep onto the silver backing and damage it. Instead, spray the cleaner on a clean soft cloth or paper towel and wipe the mirror.

The mystique of mirrors

The Greek mythological character of Narcissus became transfixed by his own image in a pool of still water, and reflections have lost none of their fascination since. But mirrors serve more than vanity. They've inspired both superstition and ingenuity throughout history.

Silver is used in mirrors because it reflects about 95 per cent of the light that falls on it. Its neutral colour accurately reflects skin tones and makeup hues.

The Chinese hung mirrors on their front doors so that evil spirits, seeing their horrendous reflections, would be frightened away.

Legend has it that the Greek mathematician Archimedes once used huge angled mirrors to save his native city of Syracuse, reflecting the sun onto an attacking fleet of Roman ships – they burned in the intense heat.

In wealthy Venetian homes during the 16th century, homeowners encouraged servants to be careful by telling them that breaking a mirror would result in 7 years' bad luck – and they had the power to make the curse come true.

• Make your own cleaner. Fill a spray bottle with water and a little vinegar, surgical spirit or ammonia. Avoid strong ammonia solutions and abrasives, both of which can damage mirrors.

• To hide a scratch in the silver backing of a mirror, turn it over. Cover the spot with a piece of foil, shiny side next to the glass, and then lacquer it.

Misleading ads

• Be wary of exaggerated claims in advertisements. If it sounds too good to be true, the chances are that it is!

• Question claims that a product is ahead of its time. Be suspicious of 'scientific studies' and 'testimonials'.

• Don't assume that the publication in which the advertisement appears has checked or is vouching for the advertiser. This is rarely the case.

• If you have any doubts, don't buy.

• If you find material in an advertisement that you discover is untrue or misleading, report it to both your local Trading Standards Department and the Advertising Standards Authority in London. The latter organisation will also deal with issues of poor taste in advertising.

Moles

• Sink a milk bottle into the mole run so that the neck is just above soil level. The sound of air passing across the open neck causes the moles discomfort. So too do dried eucalyptus leaves, which you can buy from a herbalist and push into the mole runs.

• Moles can damage roots as they tunnel through the garden. Protect plants by lining planting holes with fine-gauge wire mesh.

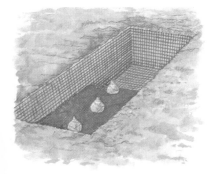

Moonlighting

Do you need a second job to make ends meet? You'll have more enthusiasm for moonlighting if your part-time job is built on your hobbies or interests.

• Try to find work you can do in your own time, perhaps even at home. Some possibilities: selling, fund-raising or conducting surveys over the phone; babysitting; selling cosmetics or home products; tutoring or giving lessons; teaching a course at a community college or trade school; selling property; proofreading; word processing on your home computer; bookkeeping for a local company; grooming or walking pets; growing plants; running a bed-and-breakfast guesthouse.

• Check with your employer first. If there's no conflict of interest, you're not legally or ethically obliged to tell your boss about your outside activities – but he'll probably appreciate your honesty. And some firms forbid employees to freelance, particularly for competitors.

Mops and brooms

• Always clean a dry dust mop before you store it. To avoid making a dust cloud, put a damp paper bag over the head of the mop before shaking it. Wash a very dirty mop in soapy water and rinse. Or, if the head is removable, toss it into the washer. Hang to dry in an airy place.

• Rinse and squeeze a wet mop after each use. Store with the head up; a string mop can be hung head down if its strings are well off the floor. Keep the door to the storage cupboard open slightly until the mop is dry. For best results, hang a sponge mop outside in the shade to dry, a cotton string one in the sun.

• Never store a wet mop in a bucket; it may develop mildew or become smelly. If this happens to a cotton string mop, soak it for a few minutes in a weak bleach solution (4 fl oz/115 ml chlorine bleach in 1 gallon/4.5 litres of water). Rinse several times and let dry.

• Trim a cotton mop occasionally with a pair of strong scissors.

• To spruce up an old, frayed bristle broom, soak the bristles in warm water for a few minutes, then wrap several heavy rubber bands tightly around them until the broom is dry.

• When you store a broom, hang it so that there's no pressure on the bristles. You don't need a special broom and mop holder; just screw a hook into the tops of the handles and hang them inside the cupboard door.

• To prevent a mop or broom handle from scratching or denting furniture as you clean under it, wrap the lower part of the handle with ribbon or a soft cloth.

Mortar repairs

• If the mortar used for pointing brickwork is attacked by frost, it may become crumbly. Dig out all loose material to a depth of about ½ in/13 mm, then re-point. You can buy bagged mortar mixes to which water is added.

• Use the minimum of water to form a mix which just compresses in your hand and has the consistency of sand pies. Then dampen the gap to be filled with clean water a short time before work starts. This way, the mortar will not mark the face of the brickwork. Surplus mortar can be brushed away.

• Should you get cement mortar on the brickwork, it can be removed by brushing with a special solvent. This is acidic, so be sure to protect your eyes and hands with a mask and gloves. It can also be used for cleaning your bricklaying tools.

• To keep the dampness out of pointing, coat the wall with a silicone-based water-repellent. This will allow the wall to breathe but will prevent water from penetrating it.

Mortgage arrears

You always paid your mortgage on time but suddenly you can't – perhaps you've fallen ill or lost your job. Tell your lender the situation. Try to renegotiate your mortgage to reduce the monthly payments – by extending the payment period, for example. (If you're regularly behind with your payments, however, your lender may not be so understanding.) Ask your lender how long you have to make your mortgage payments before repossession begins.

If your mortgage is called in, your home may be sold at auction and the proceeds used to pay off the amount outstanding on the mortgage plus any incurred costs. You may get nothing. It may be better, therefore, if repossession is a real threat, to sell your home (if possible), pay off the lender, and put the remaining amount into an interest-bearing savings account.

Mosquitoes and midges

• Check such innocent breeding places as flower vases and birdbaths.
• If you're camping in a mosquito-infested area, you may want to invest in a midge net hat and mitts, available at camping and outdoor supply shops. They are made from fine cotton mesh treated with an insect repellent.
• Mosquito repellent applied to exposed skin should be renewed every two hours.
• Slow-burning mosquito coils, which release insecticidal vapour as they burn, are effective in confined spaces such as a room, tent or caravan.
• Burn some dry cattle or sheep dung on a fire. This keeps midges and mosquitoes away.
• Dose yourself with Vitamin B, as found in brewer's yeast. This makes your skin exude a scent which insects don't like.

Mothball odour

• To rid clothes of the smell of mothballs, hang them outdoors on a windy day. To prevent a garment from blowing away, hang it on two hangers with the hooks facing in opposite directions; secure the hangers with clothes pegs.
• Let the clothes air for a few hours, then tumble them in a warm dryer for 15 minutes.
• Keep pot pourri sachets or empty perfume bottles in drawers or cupboards to scent the clothes.

Mothball substitutes

• Try hanging bunches of fresh or dry bay leaves in your cupboards and drawers. They're nonpoisonous but moths dislike the smell and so keep away from it.
• Use muslin bags, clean baby socks or nylon stockings to make moth-repellent sachets. Fill with any combination of the following: orange peel, dried lavender, cloves, whole peppercorns or a mix of equal parts dried mint and rosemary.

Mothproofing

• Keep moths away from stored clothes. Wash the clothes first, or have them dry-cleaned, then seal in polythene bags with adhesive tape. Before you seal woollen clothes, spray them with a moth killer – but be sure to air them before wearing them.
• Keep moths away from drawers by sprinkling moth-repellent crystals on the bottoms, or use herbal sachets (see above). Hang an insecticidal strip in cupboards to kill adult moths.
• If you find clothes with moth larvae or eggs, take them out of the cupboard and iron them, if possible. The heat will kill the moths.
• Vacuum infested carpets and spray with moth killer. Throw away the bag. If possible, lift up the carpets and sprinkle moth-repellent crystals on the floor and between any cracks in the boards.
• Protect upholstered furniture with a moth-proofer spray.

Moustaches

• To help you decide which style of moustache suits your face, have a black-and-white photograph taken, get several large prints made, and draw various styles of facial hair with a felt-tip marker. Be aware, however, that nature will also have a say – your whiskers will grow the way they want to, so make the most of your own attributes.
• Since wet hair stretches, always trim your moustache when it's dry.
• To give your moustache a neat, flat appearance, cut the top hairs shorter than those at the bottom.
• To shape your moustache more easily, apply moustache wax or a little hair-styling mousse.
• Remove after-meal crumbs from your moustache with a toothbrush. A firm-bristled toothbrush also works well for grooming beards.

Mouth ulcers

Mouth ulcers are painful and a nuisance, since they can last for up to 9 or 10 days. They are caused by a viral infection, by biting your tongue or by dentures that don't fit properly. If they recur or persist for 2 or 3 weeks, see your doctor.
• Treat mouth ulcers with a mouthwash, (p.406) or suck glycerine pastilles. Or rub glycerine onto the ulcers with a clean finger, to soothe the soreness.
• Take one or two soluble aspirin (paracetamol for children younger than 12) to relieve the pain.
• If you think the soreness may be caused by a jagged tooth or ill-fitting dentures, see your dentist.

Moving heavy objects

The key to moving something heavy by yourself is to use more brain than brawn. First make sure the item – including any protruding parts – will fit through openings and around corners. Then give careful thought to how you can do the job with the least strain. Once you decide on a strategy, be patient; going slowly may take time, but it may also prevent injury. If necessary, find a helper. Here are some tips:
• In general, pushing is easier and more effective than pulling.
• Make a big box lighter by removing all or some of its contents.
• If you are throwing the object out, or if it

is fairly easy to reassemble, take it apart carefully and move it piece by piece.

• When pushing something across the floor, put old newspapers, a blanket or a piece of cardboard under it. You'll protect the floor and the object will slide more easily.

• To move a large object, such as a refrigerator, get behind it, lean it towards you, and walk it slowly from side to side.

• To carry a box on your back, wrap a strap around it: a belt, large towel or blanket will do. Or make a loop of strong rope. Put one length around the box and hook the other around one bottom corner so that it passes under the box. Put your hands in the free ends of the loop.

Furniture

• To move a couch or anything else with legs, lay it on its back or side and slide it as much as you can.

• Take the drawers out of a desk or dresser.

• Heavy kitchen appliances, such as fridge freezers, dishwashers and washing machines, will slide across a vinyl floor more easily if you spray a little washing-up liquid on the floor first.

• To move a bulky chair, turn it so you can put the seat on your head and then slowly stand upright with the back of the chair on your back (see below). Balance the chair on your head. It is easiest to put the chair down with someone's help, but if you are alone, do it slowly and steadily, bending at the knees.

Stairs

• To get an object down a flight of stairs, use two boards as a ramp; slowly slide the object down the boards as you back down between them.

• Or lay the object on a quilt or heavy blanket; control the descent with your shoulder as you back down, lifting the leading edge of the 'skid' slightly with both hands.

Trolleys

• To get a trolley under a heavy object by yourself, put the trolley against the wall, then walk or slide the object to it; the wall will keep the trolley from scooting away.

• Improvise a trolley with a child's toy cart, a skateboard or roller skates. Or invest in a low-loading trolley.

• Or instead of a trolley, use lengths of piping or poles. Roll the object over them, and as those in the rear become free, move them to the front.

Mugging

• If you think you're about to be mugged, stay calm and consider your options: acquiescence, running, stalling for time, talking your way out, screaming or – as a last resort   resisting.

• If resistance appears to be your only choice, don't be squeamish about it – hurt your attacker any way that you can. Kick his groin or knee. Form your fingers into a 'V' shape and poke them into his eyes (a handful of keys or the teeth of a comb can also do a lot of damage to the attacker's eyes). Bite.

• If grabbed from behind, seize hold of your attacker's little fingers and force them back as hard as you can. Rake your heel down the inside of his leg. Screw your heel into his foot or stamp on your attacker's toes. But don't get too involved in the battle. All you want is a chance to get away.

Prevention

• If you live in a flat, put just your first initial and surname on the letterbox or door buzzer; if you live alone, add a fictitious sharer's name. If a threatening stranger follows you into the entrance, push all the buzzers to call neighbours. Don't enter a lift with him.

• Lock all your windows and outside doors when night falls.

• Install a peephole (see p.151). Ask meter readers and repairmen for their identity cards before letting them in; if you still have any doubt, call their place of business to double-check they are who they say.

• Travel with a companion and steer clear of dark, empty buildings, poorly lit streets and dangerous districts.

• Walk confidently at a steady pace, close to the kerb and facing traffic. If you think someone is following you, cross the street. If the suspicious person does the same, walk quickly to a busy, well-lit area or go to an occupied house or shop and phone the police. Avoid delay by having your keys in your hand when approaching your home or car.

• Drive with your car doors locked. If you see an incident, don't get out to help but drive on to the nearest place where it is safe for you to report it by telephone. If you are being followed in your car, drive to a garage or police station and sound your horn or flash the lights until you attract attention.

• If your car breaks down, stay in it and wait for help. Let friends and family know your route and proposed times of departure and arrival. If strangers approach, roll down your windows slightly and ask them to call the police. Wait inside until help arrives.

• Park in a well-lit area; look around before getting out and check inside before getting in. See also RAPE, p.167.

Mulching

To make black plastic sheeting even more effective as a mulch in your vegetable garden, paint it with a coat of aluminium paint. This shiny coating reflects sunlight away from the soil and onto the plants' foliage. It keeps the soil as much as 3°C / 6°F cooler, even in the heat of the summer, and promotes stronger growth. (In trials, it has increased the yield of marrow plants by 60 per cent.) It also repels aphids and thrips.

A coat of red paint has a similar effect on tomatoes, boosting their yield by up to 20 per cent over plants covered with ordinary black plastic. White plastic is good for potatoes and sweet peppers, while green plastic is best for early spring crops.

Mushrooms

• Keep mushrooms from becoming mouldy or mushy during storage by leaving them unwashed. Wrap them loosely in paper towels, refrigerate in paper bags and use quickly.
• Slicing mushrooms is easy if you use an egg slicer. Place the mushroom downwards so that the slicer cuts the rounded side of the cap. The fresher the mushrooms are, the firmer they are, and the better this method works.
• A rule of thumb when using tinned mushrooms: a 6oz/175g tin equals 4oz/115g of fresh mushrooms.
• Keep dried mushrooms in the store cupboard. You can buy them at larger supermarkets, and are excellent for adding to last-minute meals (see p.406).

Musical instruments

Homemade musical instruments can be fun and easy for children to construct. They can make them with their friends and organise a little rainy-day band. Who knows? It may be their ticket to fame and fortune.
• Use your old yoghurt pots to make a shaker, a rhythm instrument used in

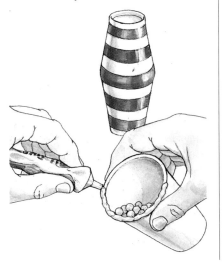

Latin American music. You will need two cartons, 4oz/225g coffee beans or dried peas and some modelling cement (such as found in model kits) for each one. Place the beans in one carton, and then apply modelling cement around the rim of both. Then put the two together and hold them in place until the glue is dried. Decorate your finished shaker with strips of coloured tape, hiding the central join.
• For a simple rubber-band zither, use four 1in/25mm nails, a 6in/150mm length of 6 × 1in/150 × 25mm wood with a hole cut in the centre, and a metal pie dish. Drive one of the nails into the centre of one side of the wood, about 1in/25mm from the edge, and then hammer the remaining three nails along the other side. String three rubber bands of different thicknesses from each of the three nails to the single nail. Then put the instrument on top of the inverted pie dish to give it a resonating chamber and pluck at the bands with your fingertips.
• Make a double bass – the kind you see in jazz bands – from an old metal wash tub, a broom handle and some sturdy string or fishing line. Turn the tub upside-down and punch a hole in the centre of its base. Push a small bolt through the hole and secure it on the inside with a nut, using washers at both the top and bottom. Tie one end of the string to the top of the bolt.

Make a notch at one end of the broomstick and a groove at the other about 1in/25mm from the end. Fit the notched end over the edge of the tub, then tie the free end of the string around the groove. As you hold the broom handle upright, the string should be fairly taut. Now put one foot on the edge of the tub and pluck away, varying the tone by moving the broom handle to change the tension on the twine. As you get better at producing a sound, experiment with changing the pitch by pulling the string taut at various places along the broomstick.
• Line up eight wine glasses, each containing different amounts of water. Use a teaspoon to tap the rims of the glasses, and adjust the water levels until you are happy with the notes you have got.

• Play the jug. A large earthenware one looks best and gives the most resonant tone, but you can also use a large glass soda bottle or even a sauce bottle.

Hold the jug straight up and pucker your lips against the rim; arch your upper lip slightly over the rim. Then blow gently across the top of the jug, adjusting your lips until you get a sound. One note is all you can play – the jug is a rhythm instrument. To change the note, add or remove water.
• Even the youngest children can join in. Just hand them a couple of spoons and let them drum along on a table top or metal biscuit tin. It will help them develop a sense of rhythm.

With practice, your group will be able to play real tunes, but you're probably better off letting a keyboard or guitar carry the melody and using these instruments as accompaniment. See also XYLOPHONE, p.236.

Mussels

• To clean mussels, scrub with a stiff brush, then pull off the beards or remove them with a sharp knife or kitchen shears. Place the mussels in very cold water and rub the shells together to remove any remaining debris. Or scrub with a vegetable brush. Rinse in several changes of cold water.
• If a shell isn't tightly closed, test to see if the mussel is alive. Tap the shell on a firm surface: it should close immediately. Discard any mussels that stay open, have cracked shells or float.
• Mussels clean themselves out to some extent if you soak them in cold water with 2 tablespoons flour, 2 hours before cooking them.
• If you want to serve the cooking liquor as soup, strain it through a muslin-lined sieve to remove any grit. See also SHELLFISH, p.180.

Mutilated money

• If your puppy chews up a £20 note or you wash and tumble dry one left in your pocket, your bank should redeem it if it's in fairly good shape. Even if it's badly mauled, take all the scraps along to your bank. If the note can be identified (if the bits you have show the number) or if you have more than half of the note, the bank will probably replace it immediately. You will have to sign a declaration to say what happened.

• If a wad of notes gets burned or mutilated, wrap the remains in cotton or polystyrene chips so that they don't disintegrate further, and take them to your bank. They will send them to the Bank of England, where specialists will try to identify the numbers. They will test the paper and look for the silver strips.

• If you have a few corroded or charred coins, take them to a bank for redemption. The bank will send them to the mint for assessment and cleaning.

Nail biting

• When you're tempted to nibble at your nails or cuticles, keep your hands busy – and not in your mouth. Doodle on paper, knead a pencil rubber or finger some worry beads.

• Give yourself a weekly manicure; the neat appearance may deter you from biting your nails.

• Promise yourself a treat if you can grow one nail without biting it.

• Paint an anti-biting preparation onto your nails. These are available from chemists, and their bitter taste reminds you to stop nibbling.

• If your small child also bites his nails, try giving him a small manicure set – it might encourage him to stop. Make sure you trim his fingernails after each bathtime, and reward the days when he doesn't bite them with a gold star or small treat.

Nailing

Nails come in all shapes and sizes. Be sure to select the right one for the job.

• Round wire nails are mainly used for rough carpentry work, where it doesn't matter if the head shows. If you are going to use round nails near the edge of a piece of wood, drill a small guide hole for the nail to avoid splitting the wood.

• Another way to prevent a nail from splitting wood is to blunt the point of the nail with a hammer. The flat surface will cut through the wood fibres rather than driving a wedge through them.

• Always avoid running a line of nails along the same wood grain. The combined effect will probably split the wood along that line.

• Use oval nails where you want to sink the nails in. Use the thin section of the nail along the wood grain to prevent splitting the wood. Then use a nail punch to sink the head without bruising the wood surface.

• Use panel pins for fine work. You need a pin hammer to sink them safely.

• Use tacks with large heads for holding any sheet material. A larger version is the clout nail, used for materials such as roofing felt.

• For outdoor jobs such as fencing, try to use rustless nails – either galvanised or alloy ones. These will last longer, and won't cause rust stains on the wood.

Nail punch

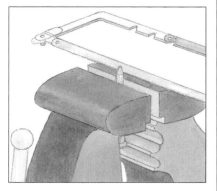

For a homemade nail punch, lock a 2in/50mm nail in a vice (without crushing the head), point up. Using a hacksaw, cut the tip off at an exact 90°

angle; then smooth the cut surface with a metal file. You now have an instant nail punch that does a good job of embedding 1in/25mm finishing nails, since the shaft diameter matches the finishing nailhead.

To drive smaller finishing nails, reduce the diameter of the cut end with a metal file and emery paper.

Neckache

• If you feel an ache coming on, shrug your shoulders several times.

• Take a hot shower, letting the spray hit the back of your neck for 10 to 15 minutes.

• While reading or watching TV before bedtime, rest your neck against a cushion.

• Using your fingertips, knead the back of your neck from the earlobes down to the shoulders; lightly massage the vertebrae. Finish off with brisk chopping movements, using the little-finger side of your flat, stiff hands – but not too hard.

• Exercise your neck. Stand or sit upright with your arms relaxed, or lie flat on your back with your knees bent. Slowly turn your head to the right as far as you can without feeling strain or pain; hold for 5 seconds, then turn to the left. Repeat the exercise five times.

Necklaces

• To prevent metal costume jewellery from tarnishing, store a piece of white chalk with it.

• To avoid tangled necklaces, hang them from adhesive-backed plastic hooks on your dressing-table mirror or from a tie rack on the inside of the cupboard door.

• Using soft fabric, make a small drawstring bag to keep pearls from being damaged by other jewellery.

• To clean nonplastic costume jewellery, immerse it in surgical spirit for 5 minutes. Then rinse in warm water and dry with a lint-free cloth. Soak rhinestone pieces in washing-up liquid for 15 minutes; rinse in warm water and dry with a flannel. Do the same for metal jewellery, but dilute the detergent with warm water.

Needle and thread

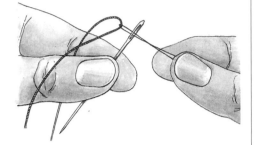

- Bend a piece of fine wire, such as fuse wire, to make a needle threader. Push the cotton through and insert it into the eye of the needle.
- To make threading a needle easier, cut the thread diagonally.
- For emergency sewing if you run out of thread, use dental floss or, on heavy clothing, fine twine.
- If you can't quite match the colour of a fabric, buy thread a shade lighter than the cloth. Or unravel the edge of the fabric you're about to mend.
- There's no need for a needle and thread with iron-on bonding web; use ¼in/6mm tape for tacking, ¾in/19mm tape for hemming (see p.105). If you change your mind about using the tape, iron it to reheat it and peel it off.

Needlecraft

- Knit a country classic – a rag rug – from pieces of old fabric cut lengthwise into thin strips. Sew the ends together and press the edges in for a neater look. Use a simple knit stitch and needles that are about ½in/13mm in diameter.
- To make a patchwork quilt in double-quick time, arrange your patches on panels of fusible web (sold by the yard/metre in fabric shops) and iron them down. Peel the paper backing from the web panels and iron them onto a bedsheet. Use the zigzag stitch on your sewing machine to conceal the patches' raw edges. Add filler and backing and quilt as usual.

Neighbours

Neighbours can also be the best of friends. Here are some tips on building good relationships.
- If your neighbours are willing, exchange home phone numbers and find out how to reach them at work in case of emergency.
- Invite your neighbours over occasionally. Make sure they know the layout of your house or flat and make an effort to learn theirs. Such knowledge could be important in a crisis.
- When a new family moves in, welcome them with a basket of fruit or some homemade biscuits and a list of nearby shops and plumbers, electricians and handymen, whom you would recommend. Offer to collect post and newspapers and to keep an eye on their home while they're on holiday. Be friendly, but don't make a nuisance of yourself; some people prefer to keep their distance from their close neighbours.

- Organise an annual party for your neighbours. Have everyone bring something – food, drinks or entertainment. Make an effort to chat with neighbours you don't know well.
- Noisy neighbours who disturb your sleep regularly can be reported to your local authority. New legislation allows for fines and sometimes confiscation of sound equipment when people are found to be creating more than 35 decibels between 11pm and 7am.

Networking

This is the modern term for the phrase 'It's not what you know, but who you know'. Whether you're trying to find a job, change careers or get a promotion, the fundamental principle still applies – you need help to achieve your goal. Here are some tips:
- Ask friends, neighbours, relatives and former colleagues if they know anyone who works in the field you're interested in. If so, write or phone the person to request a brief interview (be sure to mention the name of your contact). If she's too busy to meet you, invite her to lunch.
- When you meet, don't simply announce that you're networking or looking for a job. Instead, ask about her work, her company, her career path to

---

A patchwork of emotion

A kindly, elderly lady reminisced as she passed work-worn fingers over a quilt she had pieced together while her family was growing up: 'It took me more than 20 years, nearly 25, I reckon . . . in the evenings after supper when the children were all put to bed. My whole life is in that quilt. It scares me sometimes when I look at it.

'All my joys and all my sorrows are stitched into those little pieces. When I was proud of the boys and when I was downright provoked and angry with them. When the girls annoyed me or when they gave me a warm feeling around my heart. And John, too. He was stitched into that quilt and all the 30 years we were married. Sometimes I loved him and sometimes I sat there hating him as I pieced the patches together. So they are all in that quilt, my hopes and fears, my joys and sorrows, my loves and hates.

'I tremble sometimes when I remember what that quilt knows about me.'
(Taken from *The Standard Book of Quilt Making and Collecting*, by Marguerite Ickis.)

date and her plans for the future.
• Avoid getting too personal. Your attitude should make it clear that your interest is in business.
• Mention your skills in passing, but don't sell yourself. Bring a cv (see p.245) in case it's requested.
• At the end of the conversation, ask for the name of another person you could contact. Always follow up with a thank-you note.
• Remember that whenever a person recommends you, she is putting her own reputation on the line. Try not to abuse the privilege, and always offer to return the favour.

New baby

Don't announce your pregnancy immediately – a child will expect the baby to arrive at once rather than in 9 months' time. Here are several ways of forestalling or reducing jealousy among siblings before a new baby arrives.
• Talk about 'our' baby, so that brothers and sisters think of the newcomer as belonging to them too.
• Allow older children to help prepare for the new arrival, by choosing names and clothes, for example, and helping to get the nursery ready.
• Before you confront your children with the new baby, let them welcome their mother. They'll have missed her.
• Make a scrapbook of baby pictures cut out from magazines to show what

babies are like. Include the 'downside', such as images of babies crying and changing nappies, as well as the nicer side. Point out that although a new baby will need a lot of caring for at first, he'll become more independent – just as older children do.
• Ask your partner to bring in your children to meet the baby soon after he's born. Buy a small present for them beforehand: it might balance all the gifts that others will shower on the new arrival.

New pet

• Puppies and kittens should be bought or removed from their mothers at 6 to 8 weeks of age. Under 6 weeks they are too young to leave their mothers, and after 12 weeks you have missed the very important 'sensitive' period in their life when good lifetime habits can be initiated and the animal will learn to respond to human contact.
• When you're picking up a puppy or kitten that you've bought from a breeder, take a soft piece of fabric with you. Rub it on the fur of the animal's mother and siblings to pick up their scent and put it in your new pet's bed.
• If your pet cries at night, it may still miss its mother. Wrap a ticking clock in a towel and put it in the animal's bed. Or put a well-wrapped hot-water bottle in its bed for it to cuddle up against.
• If possible buy two puppies at the same time; they'll have each other for comfort and company.

Newspaper cuttings

• To prevent yellowing, dissolve a milk of magnesia tablet in 2 pints/1 litre of soda water. Let the mixture stand overnight. Stir well and soak your cutting in the solution for an hour; blot with a paper towel and place on a clean cake rack or grill to dry.
• If cuttings have been stored in a damp place, remove mildew by drying them in the sun. (On a rainy day, try the low setting on a hair dryer or an electric fan.) Then sprinkle cornflour onto them to absorb what moisture remains.

Nicotine stains

• Are your fingers stained with nicotine from cigarettes? Rub lemon juice onto them, or gently scrub the skin with a pumice stone. Then smooth on some hand cream.
• Has the nicotine from heavy smokers marked your walls and ceiling? Scrub the surfaces lightly with a soft brush and diluted washing-up liquid. Do the ceiling before washing the walls. If it is not possible to shift the discoloration, you may have to cover the surfaces with aluminium sealer and then paint the room again.

Night blindness

Avoid bumping into the furniture when you step into a dark room. Wait a minute or so to let your eyes adjust to the dark. Then focus your gaze slightly off-centre – the light receptors in your eyes are concentrated on the sides of the retina, so peripheral vision is better than direct vision in dim light.

Noise

• If you're regularly awakened by early morning traffic, dustmen or barking dogs, make use of 'white' noise – a low, constant sound that screens the din but isn't loud enough to keep you awake. Playing a radio softly may block out troublesome noise. A fan sometimes does the trick in summer, while an electric heater or humidifier is effective in winter. Or make a cassette tape of chirping crickets, running water or other soothing sounds.
• For 'white' noise in your garden, install a splashing fountain.
• If noise regularly disturbs your sleep, or causes vibrations or damage to your property, complain to the police. If it still continues, go to your local council and ask it to serve a noise-abatement notice. Or ask the Environmental Health Officer from your local authority to investigate the sound and advise you on the action you can take.
• You can also ask the local magistrate's court to issue a summons against the

offender. Gather evidence from neighbours and visitors who have been bothered by the noise, and any proof that it has affected your health – you may have had to ask your doctor for sleeping pills, for example.

• If you work in a place where you must shout to be heard 3ft/1m away, the noise around you may be causing permanent hearing loss. Wear ear defenders or earplugs.

• Don't listen to headphones or speakers at over 100 decibels, which is about the loudness of a car horn. See also HEARING LOSS, p.104.

Noisy pipes

Modern copper pipes are much more prone to noise than the old lead ones. Some of these alarming bumps and thumps are more easily sorted out than you might imagine – maybe these clues will help:

• A thumping noise that occurs when a tap or washing machine turns off rapidly is caused by a shock wave moving through the water in the pipe. Modern ceramic disc taps are more prone to cause this than the older screw down taps. To cure it, have a special unit fitted which contains a cushion of air or a special piston, both of which absorb the shock and kill the noise. The unit can be bought at a plumber's merchant.

• A hammering noise that occurs after water has been run is caused by the ball valve in the cold water cistern bouncing up and down on the water as fresh water flows in, thus opening and closing the valve rapidly. Cure it by fixing a piece of stiff galvanised wire to a clean yoghurt pot as a handle. Attach this to the ball valve arm so that the pot is suspended just below water level. It will pull the ball valve arm down, preventing the vibration that causes the noise.

• A clicking noise, often heard when a central heating system is heating up or cooling down, is caused by the pipes rubbing against wood as they expand and contract. If you can gain access to the pipes, slip heavy-gauge polythene sheeting between pipe and timber, or apply graphite to the wood.

Nonstick cookware

To remove grease build-up and stains from a nonstick pan, mix up one of these solutions: 3 tablespoons nonchlorine bleach and 1 teaspoon washing-up liquid in ½ pint/285ml water; or 3 tablespoons dishwasher powder in ½ pint/285ml water. Put whichever solution you choose into the pan and simmer for 20 minutes; then wash, rinse and dry the pan. Finally, prove the pan's cooking surface with a fine film of oil (see p.412).

Nosebleeds

• Sit down, lean forward and firmly pinch the fleshy part of your nostrils shut for 10 minutes.

• If the bleeding doesn't stop, hold an ice pack or cold compress to the bridge of your nose while continuing to pinch the nostrils.

• Do not speak, swallow or spit. Let any blood dribble out into a tissue or bowl.

• If bleeding does not stop after 30 minutes, or recurs, seek medical help.

Nursing and residential homes

There is an important difference between the two: a home which advertises itself as a nursing home for the elderly should offer skilled nursing care and be run by a qualified doctor or nurse. A residential home is for an elderly person who is not ill or frail.

How to find one Your social services department will have a list of nursing homes, although there are very few places available on the NHS. Local authorities provide a certain number of places in residential homes, although these are usually allocated according to need. Social services and voluntary organisations such as Age Concern can put you in touch with private homes. Also ask for word-of-mouth recommendations.

• Draw up a shortlist and visit as many as possible together with your elderly parent or the person who is going to stay there. Your first reactions will probably be negative, but in time both of you are likely to see which of the homes will be most suitable.

• Ask yourselves the following questions and take time to discuss them all with your elderly dependant.

1 Do the staff and residents seem friendly to you?

2 What is the staff-resident ratio? For full-time care, this should be one staff member for every three to five residents.

3 Are there double rooms for couples?

4 Do residents have their own bathrooms?

5 Are there aids for the disabled?

6 What social activities are provided?

7 How much independence can the residents have (for example, can they keep their own pension books)?

8 Is the home near family?

9 What is the weekly menu like?

10 What arrangements are made for religious worship?

11 Can a trial stay be arranged?

12 Can you visit regularly?

How to pay The local authority subsidises most residents in its own homes, although the amount depends on private means. Residents in private homes might be entitled to Income Support. To find out, contact social services and your local branch of voluntary organisations such as Age Concern and Help the Aged.

Dealing with your guilt

• Feelings of guilt may keep you from placing a family member in a nursing home long after the move is needed. Remember that even love and care can run to excess; if keeping your ageing relative at home causes severe depriva-

A place for the aged

In the modern world, the accumulated experience of the elderly is often undervalued – society's constant search for new technology makes old ways obsolete.

Old people in some non industrialised societies have been more respected than their counterparts in the rest of the world. Aged Hottentots in Africa, for example, were long valued for the advice they could offer to the active food producers in the group. In Bali the oldest people enjoyed the highest rank as they were living repositories of information; their knowledge of religion, social customs and history earned them unquestioned control over the community.

The Yakut nomads of Siberia, on the other hand, were not so generous to the aged. Living on the edge of starvation, people tended to neglect those who could not produce anything for the group, and those who were too weak or frail to contribute were left to die.

In the Western World, the idea of pensions from governments and former employers was started by the Germans, who initiated old-age pensions as early as 1883.

tion and ruins your family life, it is not good for either of you.
• Perhaps the most difficult problem will be bringing up the subject in the first place. But it is imperative to face this emotional situation honestly.
• Another key step is to come to terms with any revulsion you yourself feel for nursing or residential homes. Visit several homes in your area, and try to focus on how well they keep their patients functioning.
• Listen to your relative's concerns; he will be more reassured if you let him air

his fears. His major worry is likely to be abandonment. You must be very firm about the nursing or residential home being part of your continuing care – not the end of it.
• An important consideration is proximity to family members. Frequent visits will be the best way to reassure your relative that your love and concern are as strong as they always were. See also RETIREMENT HOUSING OPTIONS, p.247.

Nutcrackers

If you need a nutcracker in a hurry:
• Wrap a nut in a paper towel and pound it with a rock, hammer, mallet or wooden rolling pin.
• Squeeze the nut with a wrench, a pair of pliers or a vice.

Nuts

• Edible wild nuts include beechnuts, acorns, hazelnuts, walnuts and sweet chestnuts. Sweet chestnuts, which are abundant everywhere chestnuts grow, are easy to gather from the ground in autumn. Hazelnuts are less plentiful because squirrels and jays gather them quickly when they are at their best.
• Mature nuts usually fall by themselves; if necessary, gently shake the tree or bush. Gather no more than you need – leave some for the wild animals.
• Wear strong boots to crush chestnut husks underfoot and split them, and wear thick gloves to protect your hands from the prickles when extracting the nuts from the husks.
• Dry nuts for about 21 days in a shady place, safe from animals. To prolong the

life of dried nuts, store them in a covered container in the freezer, or for short-term storage, keep them in an airtight container in a cool, dark place. Nuts in the shell keep longer than shelled ones.
• Nuts will crack more easily and won't break up as much if you heat them in a covered glass dish of water in a microwave oven for 2 minutes. Drain, cool and then crack open.
• Acorns are very bitter and are really only edible after leaching. Crack them open and dry the kernels thoroughly. Boil them in water for 2 hours. Let them soak for 3 or 4 days, with occasional changes of water. Then roast them.
• Roast chestnuts in an oven – first slitting the skins so that they don't explode when ready – or cook them on a shovel over a fire. Serve the cooked nuts as a vegetable, with brussels sprouts and sage, or as a dessert, puréed and sweetened, with cream and meringues.
• To remove the skins from nuts such as almonds and pistachios, place the nuts in a saucepan with water, bring to the boil, then drain and remove the skins. Rub off the skin with your fingers while the nuts are still warm.
• Roast shelled hazelnuts in the oven, or toast them under the grill, turning regularly to loosen the skins – these can then be rubbed off in a teatowel.
• Sprinkle flaked almonds with water, then coat them with icing sugar. Roast them in a warm oven until golden brown to make a delicious ice cream topping.

Walnut   Sweet chestnut

Hazelnut

Nuts and bolts

- To keep a nut from working loose, slip a locking washer over the bolt before applying the nut or attach a second 'jam' nut tight up to the original one.
- If you are sure you won't need to undo the nut again, deform the exposed threads with pliers or a cold chisel. Or coat them with silicone rubber sealant, epoxy glue or a proprietary nut-locking compound after tightening the nut.
- The best way to remove a rusted or 'frozen' nut is with penetrating oil, sold at hardware shops. Let the solution seep in and then, using a spanner large enough to give good leverage, work off the nut with a series of short, sharp jerks rather than an extended pull. See also LUBRICATING OIL, p.128.
- Or heat the nut with a blowtorch or even a few kitchen matches. It may expand enough to break the rust.
- To prevent nuts from rusting and freezing to bolts in the first place, coat them in petroleum jelly before use. Then they will always come apart.
- If you find that there's no way to remove a nut, destroy it. Hold a cold chisel against the nut and give it a few hefty blows with a hammer.
- Here's how to shorten a bolt with a hacksaw without ruining the threads: first, screw a nut well up the shaft of the bolt. Then, before putting the bolt in a vice, put a spring-type clothespeg on it to protect the threads from the steel jaws. Finally, after sawing the bolt off to the desired length, unscrew the nut to restore the threads.

O

Obscene telephone calls

- Hang up immediately – don't get drawn into a conversation with the caller or give him your name.
- If you are often bothered by calls, ring 0800 666700 for a recorded advice message or BT Customer Liaison. You

should also report the calls to the police.
- If you have an answering machine, switch it on.
- If calls persist, you can change your telephone number (for a small charge) and then go ex-directory; alternatively, arrange for BT to trace the calls, which they can do very quickly.

Office exercises

Exercising at your desk or computer terminal will help you to relieve tension. Whenever time permits, try one or more of the following.
- Inhale deeply through your nose and then exhale through your mouth. Repeat six times.
- Raise your arms high above your head; stretch one hand towards the ceiling, then the other, and then both together; relax. Repeat twice.
- Clasp your hands behind your head to keep it still and press back your neck muscle to loosen and stretch it. Hold for 10 seconds and relax. Repeat five times.
- With your arms by your sides, push your shoulders back as if to make your shoulder blades meet; hold for 5 seconds and relax. Now push your shoulders forward; hold for 5 seconds and relax. Repeat three times.
- Hold your arms straight out at the sides, with your palms up, and slowly rotate them in small circles; do 20 forwards, then 20 backwards.
- For your hands, wrists and fingers, hold both arms straight out in front with the palms down. Keeping your fingers straight, gently bend your hands back at the wrists as far as you can, then bring them forward. Now spread your fingers as wide as you can; hold for 5 seconds, then make a tight fist.

Office politics

- The best way to deal with office rumour is to listen with interest but never pass on what you hear. That way you can benefit from inside information without getting a reputation as a gossip. In fact, people will be more likely to confide in you if they feel it will go no further.
- To prevent colleagues from stealing

credit for your ideas, put them in writing; send a copy to your boss.
- If you dislike a colleague, never let it show. The ability to get along with co-workers – including those you don't care for – is a measure of your professionalism.
- Though flattery may get you somewhere, in the long run it usually backfires. If someone is shallow enough to reward an employee for buttering him up, he probably won't last long – and neither will you if you become his yes-man.

Office romance

Depending on how you look at it, the office may be the best or the worst place to find someone special. On the one hand, it's an ideal setting in which to get to know someone well. On the other hand, mixing business and pleasure can jeopardise your job, your relationship or both.
- Before getting too involved with a colleague, weigh up the risks carefully – a relationship with the boss is especially dangerous. If you do decide to go out together, keep your behaviour at work strictly professional – don't call each other by pet names, don't display affection publicly, and don't spend hours chatting on the phone or in the corridors. And don't discuss your romance with other colleagues.
- No matter how discreet you both try to be, sooner or later teasing or gossip is bound to begin. If you're not prepared to accept this, don't start a relationship.
- Bear in mind that romances often go sour, and if this one does, you and your co-worker will still have to face each other every day.
- Also bear in mind that if you get married, your company may forbid you to work in the same department.

Oily skin

- To reduce the amount of oil your skin produces, avoid spicy foods, reduce oils and fats in your diet, cut out fatty sweets such as chocolate and toffee, and drink 6 to 8 glasses of water daily.

• For a facial refresher, fill a spray bottle with tepid water and 1 teaspoon of salt, then spray the solution on your face. Blot dry with a towel. For a quick steam, heat a wet towel in the microwave and form a tent over your face.

• Here's a quick facial mask. Mix 3 tablespoons each of mineral water and fuller's earth or powdered clay (from chemists or health food shops), and apply to your face. After 20 minutes, rinse with warm water. Or try a paste of warm water and oatmeal for 10 minutes.

• If you're out of astringent, mix cider vinegar or lemon juice with a little cool water, cover your hair and close your eyes, and splash some on your face. Wipe with cotton wool. During the summer, freeze the solution in an ice cube tray; run a cube over your face when you feel hot.

• Carry cotton-wool pads soaked in an astringent solution in a waterproof container, and wipe your face with them during the day.

• To remove makeup, mix a teaspoon of powdered skim milk with warm water; apply with cotton wool, wipe with tissues and blot dry.

• Try not to dry out your skin too much. The condition you are trying to relieve is the very thing that will keep your skin looking younger.

Older drivers

• If you're worried about your driving ability, contact a local driving school. Most will arrange for an instructor to take you out and go through procedures which may have been affected by slowed reflexes or limited vision, and point out any bad habits you may have developed. Or you may prefer to take the Advanced Driving Test; a pass can help to keep your insurance costs down.

• Steer clear of potentially dangerous situations. Devise alternative routes to shopping centres and doctors' surgeries which avoid busy roads and junctions. If you are thinking of replacing your car, buy a white, beige or yellow one so that other drivers can see you more easily.

• If you've stopped driving, look for alternatives: explore bus routes and scout out dependable taxi services. Many churches, senior citizen centres and clinics provide transport for older people. Contact your local branch of Age Concern for recommended pickup services.

One-day sales

It is unwise to buy from heavily advertised one-day sales. The goods sold are notoriously poor value. Don't be fooled by the extravagant descriptions. If something goes wrong with the goods, it will not be easy to track down the people who sold them to you.

Onion cutting

• If you have a microwave, here is an easy way of preparing onions for cutting. Trim off the ends of the onions – don't peel them. Place them on kitchen paper in the bottom of the oven and microwave on High for a minute. You will be able to remove the skin more easily and won't cry when you chop them up.

• Alternatively, leave the root end and cut off the top end only. Then peel back the skin over the root end and hold onto it as you cut the onion. The milky juice at the root end is thought to be the cause of tears.

• If you want to chop and dice an onion finely, cut the onion in half and place one half cut side down on the chopping board. Hold the onion with your fingers. Make a series of horizontal cuts towards the root but not through it. Then cut it vertically from the top end towards but not through the root. Finally, cut the onion diagonally. Continue chopping for finer pieces.

Only child

• Only doesn't have to mean lonely. Make sure that an only child has plenty of opportunities to play with others. Ask friends and relatives who have children to come over often and make sure your child spends time with them. Make young friends feel like part of the family; put an extra bed in your child's room to encourage friends to stay the night.

• One parent at a time rather than both should discipline or criticise an only child; if both gang up on him it tends to make him feel he's one against the world and to envy children who have siblings to side with. You and your partner should take turns at the unpleasant chore. (Praise, on the other hand, is reinforced when both parents join in.)

• Make time for silly behaviour now and then: a pillow or water pistol fight can be fun for everyone.

Osteoporosis

Just ingesting calcium may not prevent bones from growing thinner during and after menopause. Men are less prone to osteoporosis than women but they should also follow these suggestions.

• Dairy products, sardines, salmon, broccoli, spring greens and kale are excellent calcium sources (see THE BALANCED DIET, p.254). If your diet doesn't fulfil your needs, take a calcium supplement.

• To absorb calcium, you need 400 units of vitamin D daily; about 2 pints/1 litre of milk or 30 to 60 minutes in strong sun will do the job. It's best to avoid calcium supplements containing vitamin D, which can be toxic in high doses.

• Discuss hormone replacement therapy (HRT) with your doctor. Apart from preventing osteoporosis, it may reduce your risk of heart disease as well as relieving hot flushes, emotional instability and vaginal dryness.

• Weight-bearing exercise – walking,

jogging, dancing, tennis – for half an hour three times a week prevents loss of bone mass and may increase it. Before starting an exercise programme, however, check with your doctor; then, if she approves, begin slowly and build up gradually (see FITNESS BUILDING, p.84).

• Prevent falls and possible broken bones by 'trip-proofing' your home. Stabilise loose rugs by putting them on non-slip rubber 'mats', provide adequate lighting on stairways and install grab bars in the bathroom. It might also be a good idea to invest in a non-slip mat for the bath or shower.

Outdoor cooking

• You can turn an old metal wheelbarrow into a mobile barbecue. Punch ½in/13mm holes in the bottom and sides of the wheelbarrow, line it with a layer of stones and cover with charcoal. An old oven shelf can also double up as a grill (don't use refrigerator shelves; they might contain cadmium, which is poisonous).

• Season a new small iron hibachi (a portable, charcoal-burning grill) to prevent rust. First, check that there are no wooden parts. Then rub all surfaces with vegetable oil and put the hibachi on a baking sheet in a 120°C/250°F oven. Leave it to bake for half an hour, then turn off the heat and let the oven cool down. Remove the hibachi and wipe off any excess fat.

• If you want to know whether the coals are hot enough to barbecue meat, the fire is ready when the coals turn white.

• To prevent flare-ups when you barbecue, make a drip pan to catch any dripping fat from aluminium foil. Place this on top of the coals under the meat.

• Another way to prevent flare-ups is to spread the outer leaves from a head of lettuce on the hot coals before you barbecue fatty meat. The lettuce will blacken but won't ignite.

• Keep a water spray handy – the sort used to spray indoor plants – and use it to douse flames.

• Don't forget that you can barbecue vegetables as well as meat. Wrap onions, corn on the cob, or sliced or whole potatoes (all dotted with butter or margarine or brushed with barbecue sauce) in heavy-duty foil. Grill onions and corn over medium coals for 30 minutes, turning often; place foil-wrapped potatoes directly on the coals for 45 minutes, turning once. Put chunks of courgette or aubergine on skewers, brush with oil, and grill for 10 minutes over medium coals, turning often.

• Flies hate basil, so keep a pot of the herb close to the dining table: just crush a few leaves to release the oils. And you'll also have fresh basil leaves to chop into your salad.

Ovens

• If your electric oven isn't working, check to see that all the controls are set properly. If they are, see if a fuse has blown or a circuit breaker has tripped (see FUSE BOX, p.93).

• Never use a commercial oven cleaner in a self or continuous-cleaning oven. If you accidentally apply one, clean the oven thoroughly before using it again: apply full-strength white vinegar to the oven surfaces with a sponge, then rinse with warm water. Next, for a self-cleaning oven, run a full self-clean cycle. For a continuous-cleaning oven, heat the oven to 200°C/400°F for 1 hour. Rinse either type with warm water after it has cooled.

• Keep your oven as clean as possible by covering roasting tins with foil to contain splashing fat. Stand dishes that are likely to spill over during baking on a baking tray. Always use a tray at the bottom of the oven to catch drips – unless your oven has heating elements on the bottom.

• For an oven that is not self-cleaning, spread a thin paste of bicarbonate of soda and water on the oven floor and sides. It will absorb fat and splashed food and will come off easily when you next clean the oven.

Oven thermometer

You can check your oven's temperature with this simple test. After preheating it, lay a sheet of plain white paper on the centre rack and leave it for five minutes. The paper's colour will tell you the oven's temperature:

pale biscuit, 150°C/300°F or less;
light brown, 180°- 200°C/350°-400°F;
golden brown, 200°-230°C/400°-450°F;
dark brown, 230°- 260°C/450°-500°F;
black, over 260°C/500°F.

To determine the temperature in a wood-burning oven by the same method, let the fire burn for 20 minutes to preheat the oven.

Overdose

If someone has taken a drug overdose, get medical help immediately. The symptoms include breathlessness, vomiting, contraction or excessive dilation of the pupils, sweating, hallucinations, dizziness, incoherence and unconsciousness.

• If the person is still conscious ask him what he has taken and when. Get as much information from him as you can as quickly as possible – he may lose consciousness at any moment.

• *Don't* try to make the person vomit – it may be harmful.

• *Don't* give him black coffee or make him walk about to keep him awake. He should be kept as still as possible.

• If the casualty loses consciousness, lie him in the recovery position (see p.168).

• If he stops breathing, give him artificial respiration (p.67), and if his pulse has stopped and you are trained in it, start chest compression.

• Dial 999 and call for an ambulance.

• If the person has vomited, collect a sample and put it in a bag or a clean jam jar. Put any pills, pill bottles or containers that may help to identify the drug in a bag, too, and give them to the ambulance personnel.

Overheated engine

Overheating can ruin a car engine very quickly, so if the temperature gauge starts edging up near the HOT or red section, take immediate action to cool the engine down again.

• Turn on the heater to maximum and switch the blower fan on (it draws off engine heat). If you stop for a minute or more in traffic or at lights, shift into Neutral and rev the engine at a fast idle speed.

• If this doesn't stop the temperature rise, get off the road at your first opportunity. Raise the bonnet (but be careful – the bonnet and underbonnet areas are hot) and see if there is something obviously wrong, such as a snapped fan belt or water pump belt, a broken fan, a coolant leak, or insects or other debris covering the radiator.

• If there are no obvious reasons for overheating, wait an hour for the engine to cool, take off the radiator cap and check the coolant level in the radiator. If the water level is low, let the engine idle while you top it up with coolant (plain water will do). As soon as possible, have the system drained and inspected for radiator cracks or other flaws before it is filled with the appropriate coolant mixture (water and anti-freeze solution). See also RADIATOR HOSE, p.165.

Over-indulgence

Are you worried you may eat or drink too much at a party? Here are some survival strategies:

• Never go to a party hungry. Eat a light, carbohydrate-rich snack such as salad and pasta or a sandwich made with whole-grain bread beforehand so that you won't be tempted to overeat while you are out.

• At a buffet, put only one course on your plate at a time, beginning with the salad. You may be full before the dessert is served.

• Eat slowly, putting your fork down between each small mouthful.

• If you are offered a drink, ask for just a little alcohol in a tall glass of water or fruit juice; find out if there is alcohol-free beer or wine, or drink soda water with a twist of lemon.

• When your alcoholic drink is half finished, top up the glass with ice.

Overspending

Compulsive spenders are often the last to recognise that they have a problem, but if you are regularly overdrawn at the bank, or your total debt is more than 20 per cent of your annual take-home pay, here are some useful actions you can take to control your spending.

• If you shop mainly as a social exercise, look for new friends who play cards or golf, or join a choir or art class.

• When you feel an urge to go on a spending spree, telephone frugal friends and ask them to talk you out of it.

• Go on a 'spending diet' for a month. Shun department stores and shopping centres; switch off the TV when the ads are run; avoid glossy 'consumer' magazines and catalogues. Then count all the cash you've saved.

• Cut up your credit cards and close your bank account. Carry only small amounts of cash on you at any one time.

• When shopping is absolutely necessary, make a list of the things you need and buy only the items that appear on it.

• Once you've got your spending under control, open a savings account and deposit 15 to 20 per cent of your pay into it every month; restrict yourself to withdrawing the accrued interest.

Oysters

• Don't worry about eating oysters when there's no 'R' in the name of the month. They're edible all year round (but in summer they're more palatable cooked than raw).

• You can tell if an oyster is fresh because its shell is firmly closed or if open will snap shut when tapped. If it stays open, make sure there is a clean, sea-sweet smell and clear liquid before eating.

• A 'drunken' oyster is much easier to open than a sober one. Carbon dioxide does the trick; after 5 minutes in carbonated water, its muscles relax and the shell is easy to open.

• If you don't have a knife, put the oysters on hot rocks close to the fire – they'll open up immediately. Or wrap them in wet seaweed and lay them on hot coals for a minute or two.

• Cook opened oysters quickly over a low heat so that they don't become tough. The best way is to poach them gently in hot milk or sauce, just until the edges curl.

• If you're grilling oysters in their shells, steady them by sitting them in rock salt or propping them up with crumpled aluminium foil.

P

Packing clothes

• To reduce wrinkles, fold your garments in tissue paper or wrap them in plastic bags. Wrap several shirts or blouses around a piece of cardboard.

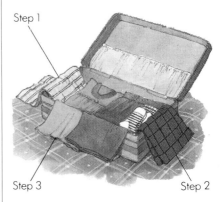

Step 1

Step 3   Step 2

• Or place one end of a long garment face down against an inside wall of the suitcase and let the other end hang out. Then lay several shorter items on top of it and fold the end over. Alternate the layers so that the garments cushion one another.

• Tuck small items, such as socks and handkerchiefs, into collars and along fold lines.

• Don't fold clothes that are going into a duffle bag; roll them.

• In a three-section suitcase put the heaviest items in the middle.

• Make sure that heavy items are always at the bottom of the bag when the luggage is upright. Don't overfill it.

• Put the delicate clothes into a hanging bag first. Centre garments on hangers and bring their sleeves slightly to the front.

• Use a dry cleaner's garment bag as a hanging bag in an emergency. Use a child's book bag or a rucksack for personal bits and pieces. On short trips a picnic basket is handy for carrying frequently used items.

Pain relief

If you are in pain go and see your doctor to have the cause identified. He will either prescribe painkillers of some sort or suggest ways of alleviating the pain. But sometimes it is necessary to live with pain, until the source is healed. Here are some other remedies:

• Laugh. A hearty laugh causes the release of endorphins, the body's natural pain relievers.

• Tension and stress tend to intensify pain. Take up meditation, get a massage or do relaxation exercises (see STRESS, p.196), but don't strain the painful part of your body.

• Explore hypnotherapy; it teaches you how to screen out pain with pleasant images. It's worth giving it a try. See also ASPIRIN, p.13.

Paintbrushes

• Use new brushes first with primer or undercoat so that loose bristles are worked out on coats that can be lightly rubbed down. Then, when a brush has matured, use it for fine finishing coats. This does not apply to artificial filament brushes made for use with water-based paints. Their bristles are permanently locked into the ferrule so do not work loose during use.

• If you take a short break while painting, or want to store the brushes or rollers overnight for use the next day, there's no need to clean them. Just load with paint and wrap the wet bristles or roller in plastic food wrap or kitchen foil.

• Soak a paintbrush that's stiff with dried emulsion in a 50/50 solution of vinegar and water for 10 minutes.

• To protect cleaned brushes for long-term storage, wrap the bristles in brown paper and secure with a rubber band or tape. Store brushes flat or hang them by their handles.

• After cleaning a brush, slip a small elastic band over the bristle tips to keep them in shape as the brush dries.

• To paint awkward objects, such as wrought-iron fences and narrow pipes, make a painting glove. Put a plastic bag over your hand and cover it with an old towel. Secure with a rubber band around your wrist, but don't make the band too tight. To discard the plastic bag cleanly, simply turn it inside-out and throw it away.

• Don't throw away an old paintbrush with ruined bristles. Snip about 1in/25mm off the tip and use the brush for dusting. Or cut the bristles to stubble – about ¾in/19mm long – for a handy scrubbing brush.

• Brushes which have been left with paint in the bristles and have become hard can be softened with a brush-restoring fluid and then cleaned in the normal way. But such brushes are best kept for rougher jobs, such as applying primers.

Painter's tray

Do you need a tray for a roller?

• Try a shallow baking tin lined with aluminium foil for easy cleaning. Or use a foil baking tin.

• Line a shallow cardboard box with a plastic rubbish bag held in place with an elastic band.

• Use a rectangular washing-up bowl, preferably one without ridges.

Painting

• If you need a dust sheet, make one from canvas or heavyweight cloth, not plastic; it will absorb paint that might otherwise be trailed through the house on shoes. If you must use plastic, cover it with old newspapers.

• Before painting a window frame, rub a stub of candle wax onto the glass next to the woodwork. Afterwards, scrape the dried paint off with a putty knife.

• If you use tape to mask a painted area, remember to remove it before the paint dries. If you forget, cut along the edge of the tape with a craft knife; otherwise you'll peel off the fresh paint.

• Because skin forms on the surface of paint, seal the tin tightly when you have finished using it and store it upside-down. When you re-open it, the skin will be at the bottom of the tin.

• Mask adjacent surfaces while painting trim or moulding with an old metal venetian blind slat. A piece of sheet metal or thin cardboard, on a ruler coated with masking tape, also works.

Paint pads

These consist of a mohair surface mounted on a pad of foam, bonded to a variety of shapes of handle. They are often called pad brushes. They give a very even but thin coat of paint, and cause less spattering than a roller.

• Use pads instead of a paint roller or brush for smooth and lightly textured surfaces. Do not use on rough-textured surfaces, because these can snag the mohair and damage the pads.

• Be sure to thoroughly clean pad brushes in water immediately after use. Dried paint will quickly ruin them.

Paint roller

• Be sure to choose the right type of roller for the job in hand. Use a foam roller for general painting where a high-quality finish is not required. For fine finishes choose a mohair roller. For textured surfaces, use a shaggy imitation sheepskin or nylon roller. For exterior walls, choose a special exterior-grade loose-pile nylon roller which can stand up to rough surfaces.

• If a roller is coated with emulsion paint and you plan to use it the next day, don't bother to clean it. Wrap the roller in plastic food wrap.

• For getting into awkward spots such as behind radiators, look out for miniature rollers designed specially for the job.

• Textured surfaces are fashionable. There are special textured paint rollers available, with sleeves designed to produce a variety of patterns.

Paint solvent

Solvents such as paint thinner, white spirit and methylated spirits can easily be reused. Pour the used solvent into a large jar and cap it tightly. In a couple of days, when the paint solids and resins have settled to the bottom, carefully pour the clean solvent into another container and save it for your next job.

Paint stains

• To make cleaning up easier after painting, apply a thin layer of petroleum jelly to your hands and face before painting.

• To remove dried emulsion paint from clothing, soak the garment in a solution of warm water and detergent for about 2 hours. Then brush the stain gently

with a toothbrush. Repeat if necessary.

• If you cannot shift the marks on a paint-spattered carpet, carefully snip off the stained fibres.

Parked cars

If you are parking your car in a large car park, try and find a space next to, or near, a memorable landmark such as a tree, large building or lamp post. It can also be helpful to jot down the location on a slip of paper, but don't write 'next to the big van' – it may be gone when you return. Don't forget that at night a well-lit car is easier to find than one in the shadows.

Child safety Toddlers have been known to release a handbrake, operate automatic windows, put a car in gear and even start one. Never leave a child alone in a parked vehicle, even for a moment.

Summer dangers On a day that reaches 30°C/85°F, the temperature inside a closed car can rise to 38°C/100°F in as little as 10 minutes, presenting a serious hazard to objects, children and pets left inside.

• Cassette tapes and camera film may deteriorate. Remove them if it's hot or if you will be parked for more than a few hours.

• Perishable foods will start to deteriorate within an hour, and milk-based foodstuffs and dishes can spoil even faster. See also FOOD SAFETY, p.88.

• To keep interior fabrics from fading, cover the front windscreen with cardboard shades. The side windows can be shielded with louvres or stick-on blinds, which are easy to install and can reduce the temperature by as much as 17°C/30°F. There are also covers for sunroofs.

• Never leave your pet in a parked car in warm weather – even in the shade with

the windows open. The animal can die from the combination of heat and stress.

• If your plastic-covered seats get too hot for bare legs, drape them with fabric.

Part-time jobs

• Consider turning one of your skills into a part-time business. Are you a good baker? You might supply cakes to a local restaurant. If you're good at fixing things, you might find work doing odd jobs.

• If you know someone else who is also looking for part-time work, see if the two of you might be able to split a full-time job. See also MOONLIGHTING, p.135; TEMPORARY EMPLOYMENT, p.205.

Party decorations

• For a special birthday or anniversary, decorate the room with enlargements of old photos of the guest of honour.

• If the food you're preparing has a foreign theme, ask a travel agency, the local consulate or the tourist board of the appropriate country for posters and spread them as a tablecloth. Add little national flags to flower arrangements. Make the flower arrangements in the national colours, where possible.

• If you forget to buy decorations, a plate of colourful fruits or unusual vegetables can make any table look festive.

• For a children's party, how about an arrangement of stuffed animals or toys down the middle of the table? (The arrangement won't last long, of course.)

• For help or ideas, look under 'Party goods' and 'Party planners and organisers' in the Yellow Pages.

Party guests

• Keep three lists: an A list of fascinating people, a B list of good listeners who can also converse easily and a C list of people to whom you are personally or socially obliged to return hospitality. Then, when you plan a party, draw from all three lists to balance personalities and interests. Bring together old friends but always invite someone new to keep things interesting.

• If there is a guest of honour, tailor the guest list to her likes and dislikes.

• If you're entertaining a newcomer, try to have at least one other person present whom she knows and invite guests who share common interests with her. Give everyone some information about the newcomer so that they will have points of departure for conversation.

• Never invite a roomful of people who share the same occupation unless you are planning an evening given over to shop talk.

• At a small dinner party, arrange the seating for complementary personalities and interests. Place people with opposing views next to each other for lively conversation (but only if you're sure they'll restrain themselves).

• A host has the right to stand firm against people trying to bring uninvited friends or children. If they say 'I can't come unless I bring my child' (or 'my poodle', for that matter), feel free to tell them that you'll miss them but you hope they can come next time.

Passports

• British Visitor's Passports no longer exist, but forms for a full European passport are available at Post Offices. You need to complete the form and submit it with personal details and two recent photographs signed by someone who knows you well, such as your doctor, lawyer or clergyman. Apply at least two months before you intend to travel.

• If you need a work visa, or are visiting other countries, you will need a full passport. This can be obtained from regional Passport Offices. Post Offices have forms and details. Apply in good time by post for a passport or renewal. In the summer this may take some weeks. Emergency personal applications can be made, but you will have to travel to the office and be prepared to wait. Take a completed form, photos and personal evidence with you.

• If you need a visa, get this well in advance from the consulate of the country concerned, usually based at the embassy in London.

• Passports are valuable on the black market. Always keep yours safe. If your hotel or an official wishes to retain it, get a receipt for it.

• Make photocopies of your passport in case of loss or theft. Leave one at home and keep others in your luggage, plus spare photos.

• If you lose your passport at home, report it to the police; if you're abroad, go to the nearest British consulate, embassy or high commission.

Pastry

• To stop pastry from becoming tough, keep it as cool as possible. Work with cold fat, on a cool surface, such as marble. If your hands get hot, run them under cold water. Better still, try to touch the pastry as little as possible with your hands. Rub in fat with your fingertips only, or cut it in with a knife.

• Work quickly when making pastry – overworked dough becomes elastic, difficult to roll and shrinks during cooking.

• Always refrigerate pastry for at least 30 minutes after combining the ingredients. Wrap it well in plastic food wrap or greaseproof paper. If dough is not properly wrapped it dries out and cracks at the edges when it is rolled out.

• If the dough is too dry, add a little more water.

• If the dough is too moist, chill it and then work in more flour.

• Never let dough made in a food processor form a ball. As soon as it clumps together, take it out of the bowl and knead it with the heel of your hand. It becomes quickly overworked.

• Always work on a lightly floured surface to stop the pastry from sticking to it, and dust the rolling pin with flour for the same reason.

• To line a deep pie dish, cut a piece of pastry to fit the base. Then roll out a strip of pastry the depth of the dish sides and press it around the sides. Moisten the joining edges with cold water and press them together. Then lightly brush flour over the joins to absorb the excess moisture. Don't blind bake pastry in a deep dish – the sides will just collapse.

• Bake pastry blind to keep it crisp when a moist filling is added, or if the filling needs little or no baking. Weigh it down with dried haricot or kidney beans or uncooked rice on a piece of greaseproof paper. See also ALUMINIUM FOIL, p.286.

• A basic recipe for shortcrust pastry is 8oz/225g plain flour, 4oz/115g fat, ½ teaspoon of salt and 2-3 tablespoons of cold water.

• Add zest to a sweet tart with sugar, grated lemon or orange rind or crushed nuts. You could also add ground nuts or spices, reducing the amount of flour by the weight of ground nuts.

• Make a savoury tart even tastier by adding dried herbs or a little grated cheese to the dough.

Pattern cutting

• If you can't find a tracing wheel to transfer a pattern with, look in your kitchen – a pastry wheel works as well.

• Protect the cutting surface beneath the pattern with felt, a sheet of cardboard, a magazine or thick newspapers. You can also pin the fabric to this layer to prevent it from slipping as you trace the pattern onto it.

• To strengthen pattern pieces that you may want to preserve for future use, iron fusible interfacing onto the edges. Store them, rolled up, in cardboard tubes.

• Create your own pattern. Take apart a favourite but worn-out garment by unpicking the seams and iron each piece carefully. Use the pieces as templates for cutting new fabric.

Peeling paint

• When paint peels, it is a symptom of problems beneath the paint film. On areas such as windowsills, which may have open-grain wood, the cause may be air or moisture trapped under the paint film. Warmth from the sun expands the air or moisture, forcing off the paint in the process. To prevent this in future, strip off the paint to the bare wood, then use a modern microporous paint. This can 'breathe', so any moisture or air trapped beneath it will be able to escape but rain will not be able to penetrate.

• If only a small area of paint has peeled

and the rest is sound, rub the peeled area lightly with fine glasspaper to remove all loose material. Feather the edges of the patch as much as possible with the glasspaper. Touch up the bare surfaces with primer and when dry paint them with an undercoat that matches the surrounding colour. Then apply the top coat, blending it in with the surrounding paintwork.

• A flaking ceiling in an older home usually points to the use of distemper at some time, to which emulsion won't stick. Using a paint roller, dampen the ceiling with clean water. Then scrape off the old coatings using a flexible scraper in one hand and an old dustpan in the other. Keeping the surface wet will reduce the amount of dust. When the ceiling is as clean as you can get it, seal the surface with a stabilising solution. Then repaint with emulsion.

• Paint may also peel because the surface beneath it is too smooth. Clean the old glazed surface with a strong solution of sugar soap in water. Wash it off, allow it to dry and then repaint.

• Another cause of peeling is dirt or grease on the surface before it was painted. Be sure to clean unpainted surfaces well, especially in kitchens, before any new paint is applied.

Peepholes

Don't depend on a door chain when checking to see who's at the door; some aren't strong enough to prevent a forced entry. The safest way to find out who's outside is with a peephole, or door viewer.

Although you can simply install a swinging cover over a hole in the door, you're better off with a wide-angle

peephole that gives you a 180° view of the exterior. Make sure that you install it at a convenient height for the shortest adult in the family.

• If you don't want to make a hole in your front door, you can mount a mirror above or beside the door (or on a nearby window frame) at an angle that reflects a visitor's image and in a position where it cannot be tampered with or obscured.

Peer pressure

Although we experience peer pressure throughout our lives, it is particularly difficult to cope with during childhood and adolescence. It's not easy for a teenager to say 'No!' to drugs, alcohol, petty theft or other dangerous group activities. But you can help.

• Encourage your child to mix with friends who share your family's values and standards. Once he is part of a particular peer group, he may be less influenced by others.

• Don't argue over things that are superficial and harmless. If your son wants an outrageous haircut to be like the others, let him. Save your energies for more important issues.

• Try to remember what you went through when you were young. Tell your child about your experiences, even if they're embarrassing.

• Keep in touch with the parents of your child's friends so you can work together to set standards.

• Tell your child he can use you as an excuse if he doesn't want to go along

with any of the group's activities.

• Remember that some circumstances, such as divorce or death, can be so stressful that your child is more susceptible to peer pressure at these times. It will help to discuss problems with him and encourage him to talk about these issues with his own friends.

Pencil and paper

If you have to take down a phone number, address or message and can't find a pencil or paper, try one of the following:

• Write with lipstick, eyeliner, nail polish or a spent match on paper napkins, newspaper, bus or tube tickets or shopping receipts.

• Try 'braille': use a pin to poke tiny holes in a piece of paper to form letters or numbers.

• If you have a pen but no paper, write the number on the back or palm of your hand.

• Trace the number on a dirty or frosty windowpane until you find a pencil to write it down. Or wet your finger and dip it in dust or dirt to use as 'ink'.

• If you're near a telephone, call your answering machine at home and leave a message with the number that you need to remember.

• Try singing a phone number or address to a familiar tune. Sing it over and over in your head until it is definitely stuck in your memory. See also MEMORY, p.132.

Pencil sharpener

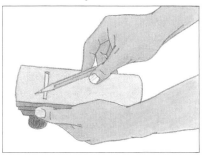

• When you can't find your pencil sharpener use a wood plane, if you have one, or a sharp knife. Pull the pencil against the blade, turning it as you pull.

• To hone the point of the lead itself, rub it across sandpaper, an emery board or the friction strip of a matchbox.

• Try a potato peeler.

• If you're desperate, break the pencil in two. You may be left with a usable, if jagged, edge.

• Glue a small plastic pencil sharpener to the bottom edge of your desk or telephone table. That way, you can sharpen a pencil one-handed, leaving the other hand free for the phone, and you won't lose the sharpener.

Perfume

• Be careful of 'nose fatigue'. If you've been wearing the same perfume or aftershave lotion for a long time, you may not smell it as easily as others do. If the scent is obvious to you 30 minutes after application, you've probably overdone it; dab surgical spirit or a paste of bicarbonate of soda and water on the perfumed area, and then wash it off.

• For a light scent, spray your perfume ir front of you and then walk through it.

• To make your fragrance last longer, apply it after your shower or bath, while your skin is still damp.

• To co-ordinate scents, spray a little perfume onto your bath powder, close the container tightly and allow it to dry.

• If you lose the stopper for your perfume bottle try the eraser on the end of a pencil.

• Never leave perfume or aftershave lotion in direct sunlight; keep it in the refrigerator or a cool dark place to help prevent evaporation and deterioration.

Permanent press

• To prevent creases, wash permanent-press garments in warm water and rinse in cold water. Place a dry towel with the wet clothes in a half-filled tumble dryer. Hang or fold the clothes once dry.

• Ideally, permanent press garments should be hand washed and allowed to drip-dry in the garden or over a bath, hanging from a rustproof hanger.

• If white garments turn yellow, use a washing powder containing oxygen bleach and as hot a cycle as the fabric can bear. Or soak overnight in a solution of hydrogen peroxide (1 part 20-volume strength to 6 parts water), then rewash. Only use chlorine bleach if the fabric is suitable.

• You may not have to iron creases caused by sitting. Go over the crease in your trousers or skirt with a flannel or sponge moistened in warm water, and then hang the garment up to dry.

Pesticides

Many pesticides can be harmful to humans and pets as well as to insects other than those you're targeting. But there are ways of using them that minimise harm, and there are other types of pesticide which are selective or less harmful.

• Treat plants with pesticide only when they are affected, and only those individual plants on which pest damage is evident. Don't treat a whole bed of plants just because one plant is infested.

• Use a pesticide that does as little harm as possible. The label will tell you what it kills. Follow the instructions closely.

• Treat houseplants outside.

• When using chemicals, protect your hands with rubber gloves. Keep a set of gloves, a watering can, a spray bottle and mixing stick specially for use with pesticides. Rinse them thoroughly with clean water after applying the pesticide.

• If you have to use a pesticide that is harmful to bees, apply it in the evening, when the bees are back in their hives.

• If there is the slightest breeze, don't use sprays or dusts. Apply dusts first thing in the morning when they can stick to the dew.

Organic pesticides You can reduce the danger of pesticides by using so-called organic pesticides. Traditional remedies are not advised, since government regulations prohibit the use of substances that have not been approved by the Ministry of Agriculture, Fisheries and Food. There are some substances, however, such as those usually used as disinfectants (like boric acid), which can be used in homemade remedies. 'Organic' pesticides which are government approved include: insecticidal soap, which controls aphids, white fly, red spider mite, scale insects and mealy bugs; quassia, which controls aphids, some caterpillars, sawfly and leaf miners; copper fungicide (Bordeaux and Burgundy mixture), which controls mildew and blights; dispersible sulphur, which controls fungi and rust; derris, which kills caterpillars and similar leaf-eaters; and pyrethrum, which kills most insects, including ladybirds and bees. Derris and pyrethrum are not selective, so use them as a last resort.

Organic pest control

• Remove caterpillars, leatherjackets, slugs and snails by hand, and destroy them. Squash cutworms with a trowel.

• Whitefly are attracted to the colour yellow – hang up a strip of yellow card smeared with petroleum jelly.

• Encourage natural predators. Ladybirds feed on a number of pests, such as aphids, mealybugs and scale insects. Birds eat grubs, caterpillars, slugs and aphids, but protect plants vulnerable to birds with netting. Beetles, centipedes, frogs, hedgehogs, hoverflies and lacewings are all natural predators.

• Grow a mixture of different plants. This encourages a greater number of predators than monocultures do.

• If you would like more information, get in touch with the Henry Doubleday Research Association, National Centre for Organic Gardening, Ryton Gardens, Ryton-on-Dunsmore, Coventry CV8 3LG, Tel. 01203-303517; or contact British Organic Farmers/ The Organic Growers Association, 86 Colston St, Bristol BS1 5BB, Tel. 0117-929 9666.

Pet allergies

• Are you allergic to animals? Brush your pet out of doors, or ask someone else to do it for you.

• The animal should be wiped down daily with a damp towel, and its living quarters or box thoroughly cleaned. If you must do these things yourself, wear a dust mask and wash your hands after you have finished.

• Make your bedroom a pet-free sanctuary. You might also consider having an air filter installed in there.

• Don't keep a cat's litter box in your bathroom (urine contains allergens), and if possible put the litter tray into a hooded box.

• If your allergy to cats or dogs gets the better of you but you can't live without a pet, consider a bird, fish in a tank or a bowl, or a terrarium with frogs, toads, lizards or snakes.

Pet odours

• In many cases, regular bathing with a pet shampoo formulated to reduce smells will do the trick.

• Tartar buildup can cause bad breath. Take your dog or cat to the vet regularly for dental cleaning.

• Ear infections, anal gland infections and dermatitis can also produce bad smells; check with your vet.

• The problem may be hormonal – the smell may have been designed by nature for sexual attraction. Neutering the animal is the only solution.

• If carpeting or upholstery smells after a pet 'accident', sprinkle it with bicarbonate of soda or cornflour and leave it for several hours. Brush off the excess, then vacuum. If that fails, try one of the new bacteria-enzyme solutions available at your vet's surgery or pet shops. But note that they can only be used on water-safe fabrics.

• The sight of other cats in your garden may be causing your tom to spray. Close the curtains when you go out or spot an interloper.

• If your cat tends to spray the furniture, protect the upholstery with a finishing spray so that it won't absorb the smell. If he favours one spot, attach a matching piece of fabric that you can detach and clean. However, recurrent spraying may be a sign of a medical problem; check with your vet, who may also be able to suggest effective ways of training your cat to stop spraying.

• If possible, keep all pet paraphernalia – beds, toys, litter boxes – in rooms with hard floors and hard-surfaced furnishings. Upholstery and carpeting absorb odours.

• A cat will pick up the scent of other animals when it stays at the vet or a cat home. This may cause your other cats to attack it when it returns home. Put some kind of natural fragrance (such as vanilla essence) on all of your pets for several days to prevent this.

Petrol

• The fuel gauge reads Empty and you think there's a service station within a few miles. Here's how to conserve fuel by coasting. Turn on the hazard lights and move into the slow lane or onto the shoulder of the road. If your car is an automatic, slowly accelerate to 30mph/48kph, then shift into Neutral and coast until your speed reaches 10mph/16kph. Then repeat the process. With a manual transmission, coast downhill whenever you can, but don't let the car slow to the point where you must shift into a lower gear.

• If your engine is sputtering to a stop, turn on the hazard lights and try to coast off the road to a safe spot. Leave the lights on and use a distress signal, such as a raised bonnet or a white cloth on the aerial, then call or wait for help.

• Keep an empty fuel container in the boot in case you run out of fuel and can walk to a service station. Never carry petrol in it in the car: the risk of fire or explosion is too great.

• Carry a siphon pump or some rubber hose so that another motorist can give you some petrol. But check what grade of petrol it is – leaded fuel will damage a car fitted with a catalytic converter.

• After running out of petrol, your refuelled car may be difficult to restart. Press down the accelerator once, then release it. Turn the ignition without pumping the accelerator; you may have to run the starter motor for 15 seconds or more. If the first attempt fails, wait for two minutes and try again. If a third attempt fails, call for help.

Pewter

• Don't store old pewter in oak furniture, which is particularly acid; pewter corrodes easily in acid conditions.

• Remove corrosion from old pewter by rubbing it gently with fine steel wool dipped in linseed, olive or vegetable oil.

• If you like your pewter to have a soft glow rather than a bright shine, wash it in soapy water and buff with a soft cloth.

Phobias

• All phobias represent a fear of losing control. To conquer yours, don't flee from it or the situation that brings on an anxiety attack. Accept it and control it; watch it happen and rate its intensity on a scale of 1 to 10.

• If you feel an attack coming on in a public place, try to act as though you're not anxious at all. Breathe normally but more slowly; focus intently on something specific, such as a window display or the directions printed on a package.

• Develop a ritual that gives you the illusion of being in control. If you're afraid to fly, for example, always carry a good-luck charm and sit in the same seat on the plane.

• Find a sympathetic person, preferably a recovered phobic, to help rid you of your phobia.

• Get an audiotape designed to counter your fears through self-hypnosis or relaxation. Do relaxation exercises (see STRESS, p.196).

Photo albums

If your photos are fading, your album itself may be the culprit. Cheap albums have high-acid paper that eventually disintegrates and gives off harmful fumes; the effect is increased if plastic sleeves enclose the page. Moreover, the adhesive that holds the pictures to the page can also cause fading.

• Keep important pictures in sealed polyethylene bags (don't use other kinds of plastic), with a small bag of moisture-absorbing silica gel (like the one that came packed with your new camera) in each. Store colour prints in a dark place; light accelerates fading, as do heat and humidity. Protect slides in the same way.

• Where you store pictures is important, too. Avoid attics (too hot) and basements (too damp). A cupboard in the middle of the house is the best.

Photo film

• If you keep a supply of film at home, you can extend its shelf life by keeping it in the refrigerator. Putting it in the freezer extends the expiry date by a year, but this only applies to medium-speed films, up to ISO 200. Fast films of 400 to 1000 ISO or above are not affected by freezing.

• If film gets jammed in your camera, you can rescue the pictures already on the roll by making a 'darkroom' with a dark-coloured jacket or coat. Put the garment on back-to-front so that your hands stick through the ends of the sleeves. Then turn it inside-out and lay it on a table in front of you without removing your hands. Place the camera inside and have someone pile clothing or pillows around the edges to further block the light. Open the camera, remove the film, and rewind it by hand.

If you are indoors you can also open the camera under a duvet or the bed-clothes or in an understairs cupboard.

Photo flash

The two major problems with flash pictures are 'bleaching' where the face is too pale because the flash is too close, and 'red-eye', where the retina of the eye has reflected the flash. To avoid the first, check your camera handbook for flash distances.

• When taking a portrait by flash, ask your subject not to look directly at the camera or, better still, to look first at a bright light before looking back at the camera (the light closes the pupil and prevents the reflection).

• You can also reduce red-eye by increasing the light in the room, by switching on more lights or by drawing back curtains.

• These problems are unlikely to arise with single-lens reflex cameras where the flash gun is mounted on the camera's 'hot shoe'. With a swivel-head gun you can 'bounce' the flash off the ceiling, or fit a diffuser lens to soften the light.

Photographing the family

If your family pictures are all forced smiles and stiff poses, try these tips to improve them.

• Avoid poses. Everyone is uncomfortable in front of a camera. To make sure your subjects look relaxed, photograph them while they're active. At a family gathering or Sunday lunch, sneak up on someone cooking sausages or setting the table. If he stiffens, ask him to describe what he's doing. Take his mind off the camera.

• Use a zoom lens. A camera at close range can be intimidating. A zoom lens lets you stand back while focusing in for a tight portrait.

• Watch the details. It takes only a second to check for cluttered or distracting backgrounds.

• Beware of light. Bright sunlight is harsh and causes squinting and ugly shadows. Shade is softer and more flattering to skin tones.

• Take two or three quick shots of the same person. Professionals know that it's rare to get a perfect picture on the first try. Shooting several pictures increases your odds of capturing the peak of action or the perfect smile. So always have plenty of film handy.

• To keep full-length shots from looking amateurish, include the whole figure; be careful not to cut off the subject's feet.

• Don't forget that your camera has two framing positions – horizontal, or landscape, and vertical, or portrait. Try to vary the framing of your pictures. A family group would probably need horizontal framing, a full-length figure or a head and shoulder shot would fit best into a vertical frame. Experiment and look for the most pleasing arrangement.

• Turn your snapshots into postcards by gluing them to index cards with latex glue; trim with scissors, a razor blade or a craft knife. Your friends and family will love finding pictures of themselves in the post.

Photographing snow and sand

Being highly sensitive to light, your camera's metering system may react to the very bright reflected light in snow and beach scenes. What happens is that the meter automatically 'stops down' the lens aperture, and produces a dark, under-exposed picture.

• When taking a figure against snow or sand, move in as close as you can and fill the viewfinder with the subject.

• If you're using a camera with manual and automatic facilities, and you want some of the background, a useful rule-of-thumb exposure guide is to shoot on manual mode, with a shutter speed of 1/250th a second, at f 11 for ISO 100 film.

• Alternatively, use your camera's exposure compensation or backlight control (refer to the handbook).

Pickpockets

• Carry cash and credit cards in separate wallets and pockets. If possible, divide your cash between your wallet and pocket.

• Keep your wallet in an inside jacket pocket or the front pocket of your trousers.

• Keeping your hands in your pockets keeps a thief's hands out.

• Don't keep a purse or handbag in your hand: it can easily be knocked away or snatched. Get a bag with a shoulder strap and wear it with the outside flap or pocket towards your body. An open-top handbag invites trouble.

• Carry your house keys in your pocket, not in your handbag.

• Make a list of the identification numbers of your credit cards, driver's licence, cheque cards and so on, as well as the numbers to call in case of theft.

Keep one copy at home and another in a locked drawer at work.

• Never flash money or jewellery in public – when buying a newspaper or at a bus stop, for example.

• When shopping, be especially alert at the entrances to shops, on escalators and in lifts, in bargain or demonstration areas, or in any place where large crowds gather. Also be on the lookout at the checkout counter, where you might lay down your purse and parcels.

• Before using a cash machine, take a good look around. If you see someone suspicious, go elsewhere. While using one, stand close so that no one knows the extent of your transaction or can read your PIN number. And when you leave, walk a short way in the wrong direction, then reverse yourself to see if you're being followed. If you are, run to the nearest spot with people and telephone the police.

Common scams Pickpockets often work with accomplices who create distractions while the thief robs the 'mark'. Here are some common ruses.

• 'Watch out for pickpockets!' Be wary when you hear someone shout this; your natural response, to reach for your money, alerts the pickpocket to its location.

• The accident. Perhaps someone's foot slips getting off the bus in front of you, or perhaps she drops packages in a crowded lobby; in either case, the momentary confusion is all the pickpocket needs.

• The fight. An argument breaks out and people jostle each other getting out of the way; when it's all over, you're the loser.

• 'Oh, I'm sorry!' Someone rushing through an airport or train station bumps into you or spills food on you, then stops to help you up or brush you off; then he rushes off again – with your wallet.

Picnics

• If you are planning a picnic but have no coolbox or bag, make your own by lining your picnic basket or box with cold beverages; and then pack the food in the centre. But remember that the cold cans are no substitute for ice; only use this trick if you have a short distance to travel and your food is unlikely to spoil.

• A clean shower curtain makes a good picnic cloth, because spills are easy to wipe up.

• Carry your food to the picnic site in sturdy cardboard boxes; once you get there, remove the contents, turn the boxes upside-down and cover them with a shower curtain or waterproof cloth to create a miniature table.

• To keep ants out of food, use aluminium foil or plastic film. Or pack food in containers with lids that you can close after each serving. You could also buy dome-shaped nets to cover plates and bowls.

• If you are worried about food poisoning, avoid egg salad, potato salad and fish and pasta dishes, especially on hot days. Instead, make sandwiches out of luncheon meats, tinned meats or cheese. And spread the bread with mustard (a fairly good preservative because of its acid content), butter or margarine instead of mayonnaise.

• If it is a very hot day indeed, freeze puddings, yoghurt and sandwiches without salad. Then pack them into a coolbox, if you have one, with ice packs (or cubes in a plastic bag); by the time you're ready to eat, the food should be defrosted. See also FOOD SAFETY, p.88.

Picture frames

• On a rainy day let your children make their own frames for portraits of friends or family. Mount each photograph on stiff cardboard with double-sided adhesive tape, leaving a ¼in/6mm margin all around. For a frame, glue wooden pencils to the margins.

• To make random frames look like a set, spray-paint them all one colour or use coordinated mounts.

• Reinforce a wobbly frame with a staple gun; drive two staples across the back of each mitred joint.

• Scour junk shops and jumble sales for framed pictures. You may not like the

---

Pioneers of modern photography

As early as the 10th century AD, Arab scientists discovered that light filtering through a small hole into a dark room would project an upside-down image of the scene. This basic principle of photography was used by astronomers to study an eclipse of the sun without hurting their eyes.

Four centuries later, the Italians refined this idea by developing a picture box they called a camera obscura (meaning 'dark room'), which was painted black on three of the inside walls and white on the fourth. An image of the scene outside the box was projected onto the white wall through a pinhole opposite. Later, more sophisticated versions of the camera obscura had a glass lens fitted over the hole to sharpen the image.

In the 1820s, the principle of the camera obscura was combined with advances in optics and chemistry to produce the earliest photograph. Frenchman Joseph Niépce fixed an image onto a pewter plate covered with a light-sensitive material after an exposure of eight hours. His ideas were developed by Louis Daguerre, whose 'daguerrotype' was much used for portraiture. It was left to the Englishman Henry Fox Talbot to find a way of making positive prints from a negative image, so pioneering modern photography.

pictures themselves, but the frames might be attractive. Just remove the old picture and then clean and paint or wax the frames before reusing.

Pie crust

• If the edges of a pie crust are browning too quickly, fold narrow strips of aluminium foil over them. Another trick is to trim the edge off a foil pie plate that's a little larger than the pie you're baking. Place this collar over your pie crust and bake.

• The liquid in fruit pies can make the crust soggy. Prevent the problem by brushing the bottom crust with beaten egg white or melted butter and letting it air-dry for 10 to 15 minutes before filling. Set the pie on a very hot baking sheet in a preheated Gas Mark 6, 200°C/400°F oven and bake for 10 minutes; then reduce the heat to the specified temperature and continue baking.

• When baking several pies together, keep pie crusts from baking unevenly by leaving ample space between the pies and make sure they are at least 2 in/50 mm from the oven walls. Never block airflow by covering the baking rack with aluminium foil. Place pies on baking trays to prevent any overflowing juices from dripping onto the pies below.

• Always preheat the oven to the correct temperature before putting pies in the oven to bake.

• For flakier crusts, keep everything cold. Use iced water and well-chilled fat for mixing. Chill the dough before rolling it out (a marble slab is best for rolling because it stays cool). If you have hot hands and find that your dough always becomes oily when rubbing in fat, use two knives or a pastry blender to cut fat into flour – not your warm fingers.

Pigeons

Get tough with pigeons that perch on your balcony, roof or windowsill. Forget scare tactics such as plastic windmills, noisemakers and cut-out cats, owls or hawks – they don't work with these urban pests.

• Screen the birds out of wall recesses and window ledges with fine-mesh chicken wire sold at hardware and garden shops.

• Sheets of plastic with plastic spikes at narrow intervals are available in hardware shops for use on flat roofs or window ledges. It is impossible for the pigeons to perch on them or find a comfortable foothold.

• Run a strand of wire across a ledge at about half the height of a pigeon's breast. This will halve the amount of space the birds can use and will encourage them to move on.

Pills

• A pill that sticks in your throat may be caught in the tiny fleshy pocket between the upper throat and the larynx. To prevent this from happening, drink a full glass of water each time you have to take a pill.

• Coat pills with butter or margarine to help them slip down. Or if your doctor approves, crush them and mix them into yoghurt, custard or ice cream.

• If your child is having difficulty swallowing a pill, coat it with a bit of banana or hide it in a bite-size piece of fruit. Or have her eat a few bites of banana immediately after taking the pill. See also MEDICATION SCHEDULE, p.131.

Pimples

• Clear up a single blemish quickly with an over-the-counter benzoyl peroxide gel (5 per cent concentration).

• To treat bigger breakouts, wash your face gently with warm water and a mild soap; rinse thoroughly and pat dry.

Pigeons in peace and war

An airmail messenger service started long before the aeroplane. Some 2500 years ago, Cyrus the Great of Persia used homing pigeons to carry messages. Guided by an uncanny ability to find their way (which a modern ornithologist called 'one of the classic puzzles in all of biology'), they have played an important role in history ever since.

In the first Olympic games, in 776 BC, a victorious athlete sent news of his triumph to his father by tying a purple ribbon to a pigeon's foot. Romans later used pigeons to relay the results of gladiatorial contests – and possibly to place bets before word of the results arrived by foot. Caesar conquered Gaul with the help of these small, sturdy avians, who can fly as far as 600 miles/960 km without food or water.

During the World War I Battle of the Argonne Forest, a pigeon named Cher Ami lost an eye and a leg while carrying a message that saved an American unit from being fired on by its own troops. The intrepid bird was awarded the Distinguished Service Medal, and its body was later stuffed and displayed at the Smithsonian Institution in Washington D.C.

In World War II the pigeon G.I. Joe flew 20 miles/32 km in 20 minutes and saved a British battalion, despite being shot through the wing. This feathered hero won a medal from the Lord Mayor of London.

The French army still keeps a pigeon corps in case communications are disrupted by nuclear holocaust. The birds can deliver a message some 500-600 miles/800-960 km in a day.

Apply a benzoyl peroxide gel once a day (start with 2.5 per cent). If after 2 weeks you see no improvement, apply it twice a day or use a 5 per cent concentration.
• When shopping for new skin products, look for water or glycerine-based moisturisers, sun lotions and foundations that won't clog your pores. Check the labels for any compound with lanolin and avoid these. If you're in doubt, test a product by dabbing it on a piece of clean brown paper or other parcel paper; wait 24 hours and check for an oily ring. If it appears, avoid the product.

Prevention If you are subject to skin blemishes, here are some hints:
• Do not touch your face or allow objects that gather grease and dirt, such as the telephone, to touch it.
• Wash your hair regularly and keep nails short and scrupulously clean.
• Avoid foods containing iodine (iodised salt, asparagus, kelp and shellfish, for example) or hormones (such as beef, liver and kidneys).
• Prevent flare-ups by learning to relax (see STRESS, p.196). Exercise also reduces stress, but make sure you take a shower soon afterwards to prevent the salt on your skin from causing a fresh batch of breakouts.
• Eat a healthy, balanced diet, with plenty of fruit and raw vegetables, and drink at least eight glasses of water a day. Cut out sugary, fried and fatty foods and sweet, fizzy drinks or alcohol.

Pipes

The most common cause of pipe damage is winter freezing. Wherever possible, locate the area of frozen pipe while it is still frozen. You can then repair it before you have water everywhere when the ice thaws.
• It's a good idea to keep some pipe repair tapes with your emergency repair tool kit (they are available from hardware shops). Simply wrap the two tapes around the damaged area; once in place they are strong enough to resist even mains pressure.
• An epoxy-based repair paste can be used to make repairs. It is best used together with a length of glass-fibre

bandage to add strength. But be warned! Plumbers don't like this kind of repair if they are called in later to make a more permanent job of it, because the hardened paste is difficult to remove.
• Where a small part of copper pipe is damaged, buy a special repair sleeve. Cut away the damaged area, then slip the sleeve in place and tighten the special compression fitting to make a neat and permanent repair.

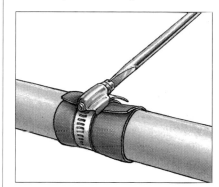

• As an emergency repair use a strip of old cycle inner tube, held in place with a jubilee clip. Tighten the clip until the rubber is pressed very firmly against the damaged area.
• When a pipe has been repaired, take care how you thaw out the pipe. You could use a hair dryer, keeping your electrical flex well away from anything wet. But hot cloths are safer, soaked in very hot water and then wrapped around the frozen area. Never use a blowtorch, especially in confined spaces such as in the loft – you could very easily start a fire with a stray spark.

Planing wood

• If your plane isn't working as smoothly as it should, it may be that sticky wood resin has collected on the sole. Remove it with paint thinner. To keep the resin from collecting in the first place, apply paste wax regularly to the sole.
• To prevent the edge of your work from splintering, clamp a section of scrap board to it and plane the two pieces at the same time.
• Always plane with the grain, not against it. To determine which way that is, look at the edge of the wood; the

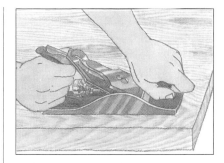

grain's pattern will be angled, not straight. 'With the grain' means in the direction of this pattern.
• To make a perfect square edge, attach a guide to the sole of the plane. Choose a piece of wood at least as long as the plane and position it flush with the edge of the plane iron so that it forms a square that can ride along the face of the work. Clamp it in place or drill two holes through the sole and screw it on.

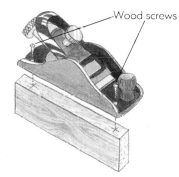

Wood screws

Plant markers

Instead of marking rows with the traditional empty seed packets on stakes, make far more durable labels out of plastic picnic knives. Use the plain white kind; their blades offer a good flat surface for inscriptions. Record the plant variety and planting date with an indelible marker; then push the knife, handle downwards, into the soil at the head of the row.

TOMATO-ROMA 15-4

Plants in winter

• Houseplants make good Christmas gifts but many require special care. Spray azaleas and winter cherries often with tepid water for extra humidity; cyclamens need a moist atmosphere, but water them from the bottom to avoid rotting the corm; and place poinsettias in a sunny window and water well.

• Protect autumn-planted evergreen shrubs from being withered by drying east winds. Drape a sheet of thin polythene, supported by two or three bamboo canes, round the young plants.

Plasterboard repair

• If a hollow plasterboard partition is damaged, cut a rectangular hole in the board slightly larger than the damaged area. Cut a piece of hardboard slightly larger again and make a small hole in the centre of it. Thread a length of cord through the hole and knot it at the back.

Apply liberal blobs of adhesive to the edges and corners of the hardboard's rough surface, then feed it diagonally through the hole. Pull it into contact with the back of the plasterboard. Hold it in place until it is firmly stuck.

When it is completely dry, cut off the cord and fill with repair plaster. When it has set, sand until smooth and repaint.

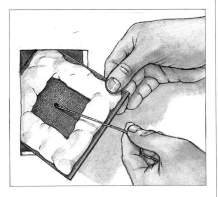

Playground equipment

• Children can jump and slide on a large, wet sheet of thick polythene available from DIY stores. Spread it on a slope and leave a garden hose running at the top corner. Move the sheet every hour to prevent too much damage to your lawn.

• A section from a big log makes a fine play horse. So does a section of large concrete water pipe.

• For maximum fun as well as good drainage, build a bottomless sandpit. Make a frame of 10 × 2 in / 250 × 50mm planks; reinforce the joints by driving stakes on both sides of each corner. Within the frame dig a pit 2 ft / 610mm deep and fill with play sand. Cover with plastic or canvas when not in use to keep pets, insects and water out.

Pleats and creases

• Before washing pleated clothes, turn them inside out; set your washing machine to its 'delicates' cycle.

• To drip-dry a garment quickly, roll it up lengthwise in a towel and squeeze out the excess water from one end to the other; then hang to dry.

Ironing

• To hold pleats in place while ironing them, pin the tops and the bottoms of the pleats to the ironing board. Do not iron over the pins.

• For sharp creases, turn pleated garments inside-out and iron them from top to bottom over a damp cloth. For longer-lasting pleats, lightly spray the edges with starch before ironing.

• To prevent pleats underneath from marking the fabric on top, insert strips of brown paper and fasten them under the folds with paper clips. Make sure you do not snag the fabric.

• Iron pleats in delicate fabrics through a double thickness pressing cloth.

• In an emergency, you can press pleats by keeping the garment under your mattress overnight. (Remember that the sides of the garment will also be creased.)

• To pleat curtains without ironing them, fold them while they're wet and hang them from trouser hangers.

Plumb bob

• Use a child's wooden spinning top as a plumb bob. Suspend it point down on a string; add weight by dropping a few metal washers over the string.

• Or make a plumb bob from an empty tin. Mark dead centre on the bottom; puncture it and insert a nail through the hole as your marker. Poke two holes exactly opposite each other in the top of the tin, just under the rim, and form a short yoke with a piece of string. Fill the tin with sand or gravel and suspend it from a string.

Plunger

If you can't find your plunger, try one of these remedies to unclog your sink:

• Bail the water out, then pour lots of boiling water down the drain.

• Put a bucket under the U-bend and remove the screw-on plug at the bottom of the bend. Poke a piece of flexible wire down the sink and wiggle it around to loosen the blockage. Then shove a hose down the drain as far as it will go, attach it to a mains tap and turn the water on full blast for just a second or two. Bail out the sink if it fills up with water and repeat.

• Block the overflow hole with a rag,

then cup your palm over the clogged drain and create suction by arching and flattening your palm up and down until the sink clears.

Plywood

Plywood is available in a number of grades. Be sure to choose the right one for the job in hand. Some have one finished side, others have two, and some have none, if the plywood is hidden.

• For rough work, shuttering plywood is adequate and cheap. For external use always choose weather-proof plywood, or marine ply. If in doubt, consult your local supplier.

• Store plywood flat to prevent warping. If you must store it on its edge, rest it on wooden blocks so that the bottom edge won't absorb moisture.

• To keep all edges from absorbing moisture, rub them with a stub of candle wax.

• When cutting plywood with a hand-saw, place the finished side face up so that any splintering will occur on the rough underside. If you're using a circular saw or jigsaw, place the finished side face down.

• To prevent splintering, cover the cutting line with masking tape, then mark the line on the tape.

• Or score the cutting line with a craft knife – just deep enough to penetrate the top veneer. Then make the cut; any splinters will break off cleanly at the scored line.

• Finish plywood edges with veneer tape. Or use adhesive plastic.

• Plywood occasionally blisters as the top veneer peels away from the core layer. To fix this, slit the blister with a single-edge razor blade and squirt a little glue inside. Spread the glue under the blister with a toothpick. Then cover the area with wax paper and weight it down overnight with large books.

• Don't toss out a sheet of plywood just because it's warped. First try moistening the concave side, then lay the sheet flat with weights on top. If that doesn't work, save it to use in small pieces.

PMT

• If you suffer from premenstrual tension, or PMT, keep a symptoms diary for 2 to 3 months; record when your periods begin and end, how you feel (bloated? headachy?) and what foods you crave. Report your findings to your doctor.

• To combat mood swings, irritability and fatigue, eat a low-fat, high-fibre diet (see p.12). Include four helpings of wholegrain breads and cereals a day and plenty of leafy green vegetables and fresh fruits; replace fatty red meat with fish and poultry.

• See your doctor, who may try to balance out your hormonal levels by prescribing progesterone, to be taken during the second half of your menstrual cycle.

• Try taking Vitamin B6 and Oil of Evening Primrose during the last fortnight of your menstrual cycle. They help to reduce headaches and irritability.

• Do aerobic exercise – take a brisk walk, dance or skip with a rope – for 20 minutes every day or for 30 minutes four times a week. See also MENSTRUAL CRAMPS, p.133.

Poaching eggs

• If you don't have a poaching pan use a deep frying-pan. Fill it with water to a depth of 3 in / 75 mm, add 3 tablespoons of vinegar to every 2 pints / 1 litre of water, and bring to the boil.

Break the eggs into the boiling water, then lower the heat to a simmer. With a spoon in each hand, quickly scoop up the whites over and round the yolks. Cook for about 4 minutes or until the whites are set.

Remove the eggs and place them in a bowl of warm water, if you're going to eat them hot. If you're eating them cold in a salad, place them in cold water. Trim the ragged whites with a knife or kitchen scissors. Drain on paper towels before serving.

Poisoned pet

Drooling, panting, vomiting, persistent diarrhoea, burns on the mouth, lack of coordination, convulsions and coma are all signs of poisoning.

• Try to determine what your pet has swallowed. The container's label may list an antidote.

• Call your vet immediately. If you can't reach him, call a veterinary hospital.

• Let your pet drink as much water as it wants. However, don't give it anything by mouth if it's unconscious or convulsing.

• When you go to the vet, take the toxic substance and any packaging that has a label. If you don't know what the animal has swallowed, take any suspect material – loose pills, solvents, pesticides. If your pet has vomited, take a sample.

Poisons

The symptoms of oral poisoning may be burns or stains around the mouth, abnormal breathing, foaming at the mouth, pain in the mouth, throat or stomach, nausea, vomiting, diarrhoea convulsions and shock.

Call a doctor or an ambulance immediately. You may be asked the size, weight and age of the victim; if you can, also give the name of the substance swallowed, how much and when, and whether the person has vomited.

On the skin If a dry chemical, such as an alkali, gets on your skin, brush it off thoroughly, remove all contaminated clothing, jewellery and shoes, then flood the exposed flesh with a gentle stream of cold water for at least 10 minutes. Then wash the skin with soap and water. Go to a doctor or to a hospital.

In the eye If a chemical or caustic agent gets into an eye, immediately flood it with cold water for 20 minutes. Run the water from the inside corner of the eye towards the outside, holding the lid open (see EYE PROBLEMS, p.75). If only one eye is affected, be careful not to let the water run into the other eye. If both eyes are affected, flood both by pouring water straight down onto the bridge of the nose. After washing, cover both eyes (even if only one is affected) with moist pads and get medical help as soon as possible.

Food poisoning Prolonged vomiting and diarrhoea 2 to 18 hours after eating generally indicate food poisoning. The symptoms continue until the digestive system is empty, usually not longer than 24 hours after eating. The victim may feel ill for another 24 hours. If he develops a fever over 38.3°C/101°F, if vomiting and diarrhoea persist for 48 hours, or if at any point he becomes unresponsive or has a seizure, seek medical help.

Carbon monoxide Headache, dizziness, nausea and drowsiness are the first signs of carbon monoxide poisoning. Get yourself or the victim outside into fresh air, or open all doors and windows and turn off the source of the fumes. If the victim remains groggy, call an ambulance.

Popcorn

• If your popcorn won't pop, the kernels may have dried out. Soak them in water for about 5 minutes, then drain and try again. Or freeze them for a day or so.
• In fact, the freezer is the ideal place to store popcorn – and you don't need to thaw the kernels before putting them in the pan. The additional moisture actually improves their performance.
• Unbuttered popcorn has fewer calories than most snack foods. Try sprinkling it with crushed herbs or spices.

Positive reinforcement

To get the response you want from children, partners and pets, adopt the praise and reward approach.
• Compliment your child regularly for good behaviour. It might only be a small point, such as washing hands before a meal, but it stops you criticising a difficult child all the time.
• Reward particularly good behaviour. Rewards might involve putting stickers up on charts: the accumulation of 10 stickers might earn, for example, a new book, a small packet of sweets, ten minutes extra staying-up time before bed, or special activities, such as a trip to the cinema or zoo.
• Try out this approach with your partner too. If she has agreed to take on an unpleasant chore or to do you a special favour, show your appreciation. Slip a thank-you note under her pillow or into her briefcase, or buy surprise theatre tickets.
• Test positive reinforcement on your friends and office colleagues by making them a cup of coffee or simply complimenting them.
• Praise and treat your pets when they do what you want (it's a good idea to keep dog biscuits in the house to reward a good dog) as well as reprimanding them for bad behaviour.
• Don't forget yourself! If you're having trouble finishing a project or sticking to an exercise programme or diet, promise yourself rewards for goals that you meet, such as a new jacket or jumper, or a dinner out.

Postal services

The Post Office no longer has a monopoly on postal services. For ordinary letters, however, it still provides the simplest and best service.
• If you value speed over cost, there are private courier organisations that will guarantee faster delivery than the Post Office. See your Yellow Pages.
• If you, the sender, and the recipient have a fax machine, it is cheaper to send a fax of up to three pages than to send a letter. You may be able to access a fax through local 'copy shops', but this will cost considerably more.
• Parcels deliveries are a very competitive area. Shop around the carriers for the cheapest price and best service offered. Security organisations are best for confidential and high-value material.
• If you have a complaint about the Post Office service, contact the Post Office Users' National Council. The current local address can be obtained from any post office.

Potato blight

Potato blight is a devastating disease that blackens the foliage of potato plants and causes the tubers to rot. It appears during the summer without warning, although always at times of warmth and high humidity. When this combination of conditions occurs, it is prudent to spray potatoes with Bordeaux Mixture, to arrest an attack. If dark brown patches start to appear on the foliage before spraying takes place, still apply the Bordeaux Mixture. Much of the crop can be saved, although it is unlikely that the potatoes will keep well.

Potatoes

• When catering for a crowd and you plan to boil potatoes, peel the potatoes in advance and keep them in a large bowl covered with cold water. Change the water daily, keep in a cool place.
• Deep fry fine potato peelings until crispy to make a delicious snack.
• Try stuffing halved baked potatoes, which have had the flesh removed, with cheese, meat, fish or vegetables. If you wish, mash the cooked potato and mix it with your chosen filling. Spoon it back into the potato skin, sprinkle with cheese and brown under a hot grill. Always eat the skin of a baked potato, as it provides a good amount of fibre.
• When you scoop out the cooked potato with a spoon, leave a little next to the skin so that the skin won't burn or tear when recooked.

Power cut

With advance warning, you can do a lot to ease the problems of sudden power loss. Even without warning, a power cut need not be a disaster.
Be prepared Stock up on torches and batteries, including at least one high-power model. Have a transistor radio on hand to keep you entertained.

• Make sure you have plenty of candles (in holders to minimise the danger) and perhaps some oil lamps and a camp stove. Don't keep fuel in the lamps or stove, but have it nearby.

• If you have a fireplace or wood-burning stove, be sure you have enough fuel in stock. If you depend on electric heat, invest in a safe paraffin heater and be sure it can be properly vented.

• Maintain an emergency supply of tinned and dry foods. Replace them regularly.

• If you cook with electricity, have a substitute cooker on hand – such as a charcoal grill or camping stove – but make sure you have adequate ventilation whenever you use it.

When a power cut occurs

• If you receive advance warning of a cut, do a big shop and fill up the car's petrol tank.

• Make sure your oil lamps or lanterns work properly. Place both the lamps and candles throughout the house, making sure they're in the open on surfaces which won't burn. For safety, place each on a piece of foil.

• Take enough food for immediate needs out of your fridge and freezer – fresh food from the refrigerator for today, frozen food from the freezer for tomorrow. Then leave both appliances closed for the duration of the cut.

• Switch off all air conditioners, ovens, microwaves, computers, television sets and other domestic appliances.

Pregnancy exercises

• During pregnancy your joints become looser and your centre of gravity moves forward, so avoid strenuous activities such as running, squash and skipping.

• Always do exercises that are specially designed for pregnant women. With your doctor's or midwife's approval, you can do stretching and conditioning exercises throughout your pregnancy if you don't have complications.

• Swimming, walking and stationary cycling are all good exercises if you don't do them too strenuously. Avoid any sport that could lead to a blow on your abdomen. Sexual intercourse is

fine as long as there is no bleeding or pain.

• You can jog if you are accustomed to it, but watch out for back strain. Drink plenty of water and don't get overheated or overtired.

• Here's a pelvic exercise to strengthen your abdominal and back muscles. Lie flat on your back, knees bent, feet comfortably apart. Rest your hands on your lower abdomen. Inhale and press your lower back against the floor. As you exhale, gently pull in with your abdominal muscles, squeeze your buttocks, and raise your pelvis from the waist, all the while keeping your upper back on the floor. Return to the flat position, inhale and repeat the exercise up to ten times. You can also do bent-leg curl-ups (see ABDOMINAL FLAB, p.8).

• After the fourth month add this cat-stretch exercise to your routine. Kneel with your buttocks resting on your heels, your torso folded over your knees, your forehead resting on the floor, and your arms stretched out in front of you. Inhale. Then exhale, raising your hips into the air and sliding your chest and arms forward as you do so. Gently press your chest down, keeping your hips still. Resume the original position. Repeat five times.

• This exercise to tone your pelvic muscles can be done as long as you're comfortable. Sit on the floor, legs crossed, back straight (against a wall if you like), and hands draped loosely over your knees. Close your eyes, relax your jaw, and tighten the vaginal muscles deep inside your pelvis. Hold for 5 seconds; release. Repeat five to ten times. Do 30 to 40 repetitions per day. If you are not able to sit as suggested, you can do this exercise while queuing in the bank or at a bus stop, sitting at a desk or lying down in bed.

• If you experience swelling in your legs and ankles due to water retention and increased weight, avoid high-heeled shoes and don't cross your legs when you sit. To counter the condition, do ankle circles. Lie on your back with your knees bent; raise one leg perpendicular to the floor, the knee slightly bent; rotate your ankle five times in each direction. Repeat with the other leg.

Keep your legs raised off the floor as much as you can throughout the day, by placing them on a chair or stool. Try to keep them positioned slightly above heart level for at least 2 hours a day.

Pregnancy tests

There are two types of home test kits, and both use urine samples. One, which claims to work within a day of a missed menstrual period, turns a dipstick blue if a hormone secreted after conception is present in the urine. With the other, done 9 days after a missed period, a dark brown ring appears in the test tube if the results are positive. Most doctors prefer the first test because its results are easier to interpret.

Both tests can be affected by heat, cold, vibrations and foreign materials. So, whichever test you choose, repeat it a few days later. Few tests are absolutely reliable before 2 weeks after the period is due.

Press studs

• An easy way to position a metal press stud is to fix the ball half to the overlapping edge of the garment with a dab of fabric glue. Rub the end of the ball with a pencil and press it down onto the opposing piece of fabric to mark where the centre of the socket half should be on the garment. Dab glue on the spot

Cat-stretch exercise: exhale as you slide forward from the starting position. Then gently press your chest down.

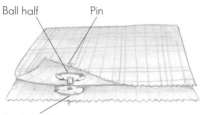

Ball half   Pin

Socket half

and press the socket to it. When the glue dries, sew on the press studs.
• If your press stud comes off and you're without needle and thread, hold the opening closed with a safety pin, paper clip or sticky tape.
• If you are dressmaking for a small child, or for an elderly relative with arthritic hands, use Velcro 'buttons' the size of a 10p piece instead of press studs. They're much easier to undo. Stitch the top and bottom of the Velcro circles in place and disguise with a button.

Price labels

If you can't get a price label off, peel away as much paper as you can, and then soften the residue. On china, enamel and glass, apply white spirit or methylated spirits; on plastic or painted surfaces, a hot rag or hair dryer; on metals, nail varnish remover; on fruits and vegetables, vegetable oil. Scrape off the softened residue with a dull knife, a coin, a letter opener or your fingernail.

Privacy

Don't feel guilty if you regularly require some time alone to relax and refresh yourself, even if there are jobs to be done. Everyone needs some time alone.
• Keep hours that are slightly different from those of the rest of your family. Get up earlier to recharge your energy, perhaps by doing a couple of exercises, or stay up a little later at night.
• Invest in an answering machine and turn it on when you don't want to be disturbed, even though you're at home.
• Set aside your own private area in the house as a sanctuary. This might be part of the study or a spare bedroom.
• Put aside a certain time in the week when the rest of the family isn't allowed

to bother you. It might be half an hour on Sunday morning so that you can listen to the radio in peace. If necessary, put up a 'Do not disturb' sign on the door.
• Go for a long walk. Or if you'd rather be alone in a crowd, go to a concert, a film or a museum.
• Learn to respect other people's privacy, too. Knock before opening a door, especially your children's bedrooms; don't open others' post or read their diaries or listen in on their phone conversations. See also QUIET TIME, p.164.

Prostate enlargement

In his twenties, a man's walnut-size prostate gland around his urethra can begin to grow, sometimes enlarging to the size of a lemon and obstructing the urinary tract. Symptoms include a frequent urge to urinate and a diminished stream of urine. See your doctor if you suffer these symptoms. A minor operation may be required.

Pruning shears

• Your pruning shears will cut more efficiently if you clean the blades after each gardening session with a toothbrush dipped in paraffin, then wipe with a light lubricating oil.
• To restore the cutting edge, take the shears apart by unscrewing the pivot nut and removing the pivot bolt. Sharpen by stroking a medium-grit oilstone along the cutting edge of the blade. Move from the pivot end to the tip, matching the original bevel as closely as possible. Never hone the inside face of the blade, except to remove the burr left by sharpening. Then repeat the process with a fine-grit stone. Reassemble the shears carefully.

Public speaking

Are you nervous about giving a speech? Most people are. Here are some ways to cope with the anxiety:
• Be well prepared but don't try to memorise your speech. Whether you read it (ten double-spaced typewritten pages equal about 20 minutes of speech) or

make notes and speak off the cuff, rehearse your speech once or twice.
• Grab the audience's attention by opening with a joke, a moving personal story or a relevant anecdote. Don't make it too controversial; if you antagonise your audience right away, you may never win them back.
• Organise your speech by asking yourself, 'If I could leave my audience with one main idea, what would it be?' Then focus on that idea, supporting it with no more than four secondary points. All your facts and anecdotes should relate to at least one of these points.
• When you arrive at the place, make sure that the sound system is working properly.
• Take advantage of your pumping adrenalin. Use the energy and excitement to help project your ideas forcefully. But calm yourself with a few deep breaths before you start speaking.
• Oddly enough, if you acknowledge your nervousness to the audience, there's a good chance that you will defuse it.
• Don't worry about being boring. Focus instead on the importance of what you're saying. You're there to communicate ideas – not to be judged on your performance.
• Watch your posture. If you stand straight, you'll automatically feel and look more self-assured.
• A comforting fact – most audiences report that they notice little anxiety in speakers. So don't compound your anxiety by thinking everyone can see your trembling legs.

Puffiness

• If your hands are puffy, hold them over your head for a couple of minutes, repeat at least three or four times a day. Lift swollen feet and keep them raised for a minimum of 15 minutes.
• If too much sun causes your lips to swell, use a sunblock (SPF 15) specifically designed for lips.

Around the eyes
• Since many moisturisers plump up the skin, apply them sparingly around your

eyes or try using a special eye cream.
• The cause of your puffiness may be water retention (see p.228); cut down on salt and eat more bananas and grapefruit, which are natural diuretics. Raise the head of your bed or sleep on two pillows to keep your head elevated.
• Apply soothing compresses of cold milk, cucumber slices, borage tea, or a mild astringent over your eyes for 15 minutes at the end of each day.
• Throw away your frosted eyeshadow – it accentuates puffiness.

Pumpkins

Most people use pumpkins to make Jack o'lanterns for Halloween, although they can also be eaten as sweet pumpkin pie.

• To make a lantern, take a large round pumpkin (or swede) with a flat bottom. Draw a face on one side, placing the mouth high enough so a candle inside won't be seen. Then cut a circular lid around the stem at the top (the hole must be large enough for your hand to pass through), and remove it. Cut away the stringy material on the inside of the lid, and then remove the seeds and membrane from inside the pumpkin. Cut out the face with a sharp knife. Place a candle in a holder inside the pumpkin, light it and replace the lid. Put it on a window sill away from curtains or other flammable material.

Punch

Liven up a party with a spicy rum punch, which can be drunk hot or cold. Mix 1 part of lemon or lime juice with 2 parts of sugar and 3 parts of rum, and then flavour to taste with Grenadine or Angostura bitters.

• If serving hot, top up a tall glass of punch with hot water. If serving cold, fill a glass with ice and then dilute the punch with 4 parts soda water.
• Don't forget your guests who are driving. Make them an alcohol-free punch which is just as delicious. See p.380.

Punch bag

• For a lightweight punch bag, put a football or volleyball into the waist section of a pair of sturdy nylon tights and knot the waist. Using the legs, tie it to a hook or beam.
• For a heavyweight bag, stuff a duffle bag or heavy-duty laundry bag with rags or laundry and hang it securely from a beam or firmly mounted ceiling hook. Or use a tightly rolled foam mattress.

Quackery

• Be wary of exaggerated claims – a guaranteed, fast, easy, painless miracle cure that sounds too good to be true probably is.
• Question claims that a product is ahead of its time or that the medical establishment is trying to suppress it or persecute its promoters.
• Think twice about travelling to a foreign country for an expensive 'cure'.
• Suspect unspecified 'scientific studies' and testimonials by 'satisfied users'.
• Don't assume that an advertisement in a reputable publication is an endorse-ment; most publications don't screen their advertisements.
• If you have questions about dubious drugs and medical devices that are sent to you by mail order, ask your doctor, the self-help group or society for a particular disease, or the local trading standards department.
• Anyone can call himself 'doctor', obtain an elegant diploma and hang it on his wall, or print impressive looking letters after his name. Only take notice of qualifications if you know what they mean. Check unfamiliar or suspicious credentials.

Quarantining pets

• Many countries (including Australia, Ireland and the United States) require animals to be quarantined for 2 to 6 months before entering the country. This experience can be very stressful for a pet. If your pet is old or sickly, consult a vet as to whether it will be able to cope with quarantine. If possible, leave the animal at home with a trusted friend.
• If you must take your pet with you, contact the relevant consulate or embassy well in advance to reserve a space in a quarantine facility. Try to arrange for one that will be near you and allows visits. Find out who to contact in case problems arise.
• If allowed, provide your pet with a toy and something that has familiar scents on it – a blanket or a pillowcase stuffed with old clothing from each family member.
• When your pet is released, take it to a vet for a checkup. Find out what it has been eating. An abrupt change in food could make the animal sick – the vet may suggest a transitional diet.

Quarrels

If you're about to quarrel with someone close to you, try one of these releases:
• Stop and count how many deep breaths you can take in 3 minutes.
• Call someone and talk about your feelings. Don't involve the outsider in the argument, but talking to him will help to relieve the tension and may give you a

different perspective on the problem.
• Escape to a quiet room, even the bathroom, for at least 15 minutes, with an apple and a magazine. Chewing and reading often relieve tension.
• Write down your feelings or let out your frustration through singing, painting or a musical instrument, if you play one.
• If you still want to fight, take vigorous physical activity – put on an exercise tape, beat up a pillow, go for a fast walk, kick a ball round the garden or hit a tennis ball against a wall. See also CHILDREN'S QUARRELS, p.43.

Quartz

Natural quartz crystals are usually clear, although some may be covered with a layer of rust. To see the real beauty inside, you can soak the crystals for a few days in oxalic acid or, at a pinch, rust remover. Wear rubber gloves when using oxalic acid.

Questionnaires

Many questionnaires ask for more information than you're legally obliged to give. Here's what you do and don't have to answer:
• You don't have to answer the questions about income, age and housing on warranty cards. This is just market research. In fact, you don't even have to send in the card – all you need for your guarantee is proof of purchase (see GUARANTEES AND WARRANTIES, p.100).
• If you don't want unsolicited telephone calls, don't give your number.
• Telephone surveys are just another form of market research. If you have neither the time nor the inclination to answer a multitude of questions, say so, firmly, at the start of the call.
• When you apply for a mortgage, a scholarship, credit, insurance or a bank loan, however, you should be prepared to answer all the questions about your health and finances. If there's a personal question you're not comfortable answering, consult a solicitor.
• On job applications you must answer questions about past employment truthfully. But you don't have to answer

questions about race, religion, sexual orientation or national origin. Nor need you answer personal questions that don't relate to your ability to carry out the job. These include marital status or future marriage plans, number of children, age or date of birth, weight, handicaps (unless they would affect job performance), the person with whom you live, home ownership or rental status and outstanding debts.
• Never give anyone you don't know information that might make you or your home more vulnerable to crime. Beware unsolicited telephone calls from people claiming to be security companies and asking questions about your home.
• Remember that, although you are not legally obliged to answer many of the questions, some people may not be prepared to deal with you (that is, employ you, or give you credit) unless you are prepared to volunteer the requested information, and they will usually be within their rights not to do so. Use your discretion. It is not always wise to stick to your strict legal rights unless you feel strongly about them. In such a case, explain politely why you don't feel you can give the information.

Quicksand and bogs

If you ever get caught in quicksand or a bog, don't panic. The way of surviving both is the same – spread the weight of your body over as wide an area as possible, and move only very slowly.
• Fall onto your back as gently as you

can, spread your arms, and try to float. If you're carrying a walking stick, manoeuvre it under you as you fall.
• Extremely slowly, try to get your feet back to the surface.
• Grab any nearby vegetation on solid ground and use it to pull yourself along, or 'swim' a very slow backwards breaststroke to safety. Don't hurry, as any quick, jerky movements will suck you down deeper; if you need to rest, lie flat and still with your arms and legs spread wide.

Quiet time

• Noise pollution, once mostly an urban problem, has become a major source of stress in modern life, no matter where you live. To help protect your health and sanity, set aside an hour or so – evening is probably best – when there will be no electronic amplification allowed in the house: no stereo, no TV, no radio, no video games, no toy fire engines. Unplug the phone or install an answering machine to intercept the outside world. You and your family will feel better for it, and perhaps you'll learn to talk to one another.
• For some quiet time on the way to work, walk or get off the bus a stop or two early. Or sit on the bus and read an entertaining book; you'll be less aware of noise if you're absorbed. If you drive, stop for a quiet cup of coffee before going in to work.
• To discourage an overly friendly passenger on public transportation, carry a personal stereo and put on the headphones. No one will know if you turn the tape on. Or just wear earplugs. See also NOISE, p.141; STRESS, p.196.

Quiz shows

• To get on your favourite quiz show, keep an eye out for addresses screened at the end of shows asking for contestants to apply. Alternatively, write to the television company concerned. If the show is independently produced, they will give you the address of the production company. Some shows simply select from the studio audience on the night. If so, keep applying for show tickets.

• The first thing potential contestants are usually asked to do is to fill in a questionnaire. Mention anything that makes you unusual or different.

• If you are asked to go further, you will usually be invited to the production unit for a screen test. Expect this to be at your own expense. You may be asked to do a written test. It is likely that you'll do a mock version of the show. Do whatever is needed to make you look more eye-catching and interesting than other potential candidates, but it is not wise to appear to be too clever.

• Once selected, watch the show as often as you can, get the rules down pat, and work out a strategy for winning. Then practise: sit under a bright lamp to simulate the studio lights and ask your family to take pictures of you while you rehearse so that you'll get over being camera shy.

• Weeks or months before the screening, you may be invited to return to the studio, again at your own expense. Some shows are recorded only in late spring or early summer – a convenient time for a contestant to plan a holiday to coincide with the recording.

• On the final screening of the show, you are likely to get at least a consolation prize, but accept that you may be out of pocket. Any prizes won are not subject to UK taxation.

Quotation marks

Here's how to use these helpful punctuation marks:

• When you write, use quotation marks to enclose a cited speaker's or writer's exact words; use them to set off the titles of short works, such as stories, magazine articles, poems and songs, as well as words and phrases used in a special or unusual way (irony and jargon).

• British printing generally uses single quotation marks for speech, but double quotation marks for a quotation within a quotation. For example: John said, 'I wonder who wrote "To be great is to be misunderstood."? Rachel thinks it was Emerson.' If the first and second quota-

tions end together, put a double quotation mark, then a single quotation mark after the final punctuation: John said, 'I wonder who wrote "To be great is to be misunderstood."'? Do just the reverse at the start of the quotation – single followed by double quotation marks – if the first and second quotations begin together.

• If the punctuation is part of the quoted matter, it goes inside the quotation marks.

• If a quotation has more than one paragraph, begin each paragraph with quotation marks but use them to close only the final one.

Rabbits

• Shiny moving objects in your garden will frighten rabbits away. Hang aluminium pie plates or pieces of kitchen foil from lines across your garden.

• Or make a homemade rabbit repellent in your blender. Purée two peeled cloves of garlic and three chilli peppers in 12 fl oz / 340 ml of water for 2 minutes. Steep the mixture for 24 hours, strain, and add 1 tablespoon of washing-up liquid. Dilute with 3 pints / 1.7 litres of water and spray the plants that attract rabbits.

• Put up a 2 ft / 610 mm high fence of 1½ in / 38 mm chicken wire. Plant the posts deeply and make sure the bottom of the wire extends at least 6 in / 150 mm below the soil line.

• Surround your vegetable garden with a double row of onions; rabbits hate the smell and won't cross the rows.

Radiator hose

A leaking radiator hose will cause your car to lose coolant and the engine to overheat. But you can usually fix the leak temporarily so that you can drive to a garage.

• Let the engine cool thoroughly. The coolant is probably well above boiling

point, and opening the radiator or expansion tank cap prematurely will release a scalding geyser.

• When the cap is cool to the touch (20 to 30 minutes), place a thick cloth over it and turn it counterclockwise until you hit a stop – about a quarter of a turn – and then let go. This will allow the remaining pressure to be released, and the cloth will catch any steam and hot coolant that escapes.

• If the leak is at the hose connection, retightening the clamp may solve the problem easily. If not, look for the leak in the hose and patch it, using insulating tape or even tied rags.

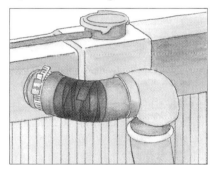

• Then start the engine and fill the radiator with plain water. Replace the radiator or expansion tank cap, but tighten it only to the first stop so that pressure won't build up.

• Put the heater on High (see OVER-HEATED ENGINE, p.147) and drive at moderate speed to a garage, where you can get the leak repaired permanently.

Replacing a hose

You may find that the clamp is stuck to the hose (or the hose to the hose neck) by scale or rust. Don't try to pry it loose – you could damage the connection at either end, causing another leak.

• Put some penetrating oil on the clamp.

• If it's a squeeze or spring-type clamp, squeeze and wiggle it with pliers. It should come loose.

• For a screw-type clamp, insert the tip of a screwdriver beneath the clamp and gently work it around.

• If the hose is stuck to the hose neck, twist it from left to right until it is released. If that doesn't work, cut the hose off beyond the hose neck, slit the rest of the hose lengthwise, and peel it off.

Radiators

• If a central heating radiator fails to warm up, there may be air trapped inside it. Use the special square socket radiator bleed key to loosen the vent and allow air to escape. Hold a cloth under the vent to catch any water as the air is cleared and then retighten the vent.

• Another cause of cold or unevenly heated radiators is sludge collecting in the base of the radiator. The radiator will have to be removed and cleaned out, but it is a sign that the whole system needs flushing through with clean water, and that a special anticorrosion fluid should be added to prevent future problems. This fluid is added to the small feed and expansion tank in the loft.

• Pinholes in steel radiators are a sign of internal damage. An isolated pinhole can often be sealed by the addition of a special radiator sealing fluid run into the system. But the trouble suggests that all the radiators may be affected by internal corrosion and that the whole system may need flushing through with a radiator-sealing fluid.

• White paint on radiators often tends to discolour with the heat. The answer is to use a special radiator paint which contains pigments better able to withstand heat without discolouring.

Radioactivity

If you're worried about radioactivity in your area, you can monitor it by planting hardy tradescantia (*Tradescantia virginiana*). The stamen hairs on these sensitive wild flowers change from blue to pink when exposed to a minute amount of radiation.

Radio aerial

• Is your car radio aerial broken? You can make a substitute from a wire coat hanger. Using pliers, unwind part of the coiled joint beneath the hook. Then cut off the hook, straighten the hanger, and jam the coiled end into the hollow aerial base.

• If the reception on your car radio is getting weak or ceases but the exterior portion of the aerial is not broken, it could be one of three problems: a defective aerial, a bad aerial connection or a broken radio. To find out which, use this test. Pull the aerial cable plug out of the jack in the back of the receiver. (If it's not accessible from under the dashboard, remove the moulding, take out some of the screws and pull the radio forward.) Then insert a straightened hanger or a 2-3 ft / 610-910 mm piece of wire through the centre of the aerial hole and lean it against the outer edge of the hole. If the radio begins to pick up AM stations, however poorly, the problem is in the antenna, its mounting, or the connection. If there's no improvement, the problem is with the radio.

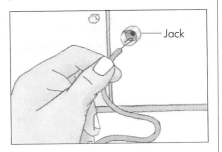

Jack

Raincoats

• In an emergency you can transform a plastic rubbish bag into a poncho. Cut a hole in the bottom for your head and openings in the sides for your arms. Make a hood from a smaller plastic bag.

• Remove spots from PVC and oilskin raincoats with bicarbonate of soda or scouring powder; rub on with a moistened cloth and rinse well.

• To make a water-repellent finish last longer, hand-wash rainwear instead of dry-cleaning it. (If the label says 'dry-clean only', don't attempt to wash it instead.) You'll know it's time to renew the finish when even a light rain soaks through the shoulders. This usually happens after a couple of dry-cleanings.

Rain when driving

• Slow down and leave double the usual distance between you and the vehicle in front. Tyre grip is reduced on wet road surfaces and the car will travel farther before stopping when you brake.

• In heavy rain, switch on your dipped headlights.

• Take care when overtaking large vehicles, because the spray from their wheels can obscure your vision.

• Take care on bends, even after a light shower. The moisture combined with the oil on the road surface can make roads very slippery.

Raised-bed planting

If your raised vegetable beds are infested with slugs and snails, it may be because you've surrounded the beds with boards or stones – ideal havens for the pests. Build your beds the Chinese way instead:

• Using stakes and string, divide your garden into 5 ft / 1.5 m wide beds separated by 24 in / 610 mm wide paths.

• Turn or rotavate the soil inside the beds to the depth of about 12 in / 300 mm, removing all stones and roots. Work in plenty of compost, manure, peat and sand so that the beds rise above the surrounding ground.

• Rake the beds flat and smooth and shape their sides. Do not frame them with boards or stones. Dig narrow trenches between them and the paths to catch water that runs off.

• You can remove the string from around the beds, but leave the stakes in place. They will prevent the hose from dragging across your vegetable plants as you water.

• Unlike a conventional garden, these raised beds won't need annual tilling. All you will need to do is to add a layer of compost and, if necessary, a dressing of lime every autumn and turn it over with a small fork.

Rakes

• Avoid painful accidents when working with a rake – always rest it against a support, with the head *up*, even if you will be using it again in a few minutes.
• A little wire mesh or chicken wire over the head of a garden rake keeps stones from bouncing over the top. Push the rake tines through the wire or mesh and pull it back over the head. Tack or staple it about 12 in / 300mm up the handle.

Rape

If you are raped, do not touch anything, change your clothes or wash immediately afterwards. Call the police, someone you trust – a close friend, a family member, your doctor or the Rape Crisis Centre (Tel. 0171-837 1600) and ask to be taken to a hospital. The hospital staff will provide medical assistance and a doctor will collect evidence that can be used in a court if the rapist is prosecuted.

If you are threatened with rape and there are people nearby, screaming, fighting back or running may improve your chances of escape. Other than that, it's impossible to make specific recommendations. A woman must assess her own situation – the circumstances and each offender's reactions will be different. See also MUGGING, p.137.

Rats

Every householder has a legal duty to keep his premises free from rats.
• Lay ready-to-lay proprietary baits. Or bait several traps but don't set them. Just leave them out for a few days, replenishing the bait as needed, until the rats get used to them as a food source. Then set them.
• Secure dustbin lids and preferably keep bins on a rack off the ground and 2ft / 610mm away from walls.
• Plug cracks and holes in outside walls with wads of steel wool, then permanently seal with wire mesh or heavy-gauge sheet metal.
• If you're still plagued by rats, call your Environmental Health department or a pest control company.

Razor bumps and nicks

• To prevent razor cuts and marks, shower before shaving or steam your face over a basin of hot running water before applying shaving cream, to open up the pores. Shave in the same direction as the hair grows, using a light touch and long strokes; avoid going over the same area more than twice.
• Rinse a nick with cold water, then press hard. If the bleeding persists, hold a small piece of tissue paper to the cut until it sticks. Remove when dry. For deep cuts apply an antibiotic ointment or cream.
• To loosen ingrown hairs that can cause bumps, clean your face with a loofah sponge. If you have just one or two such hairs, pluck them out with a sterilised needle or tweezers; if you have more, consider using a depilatory cream.
• If you have run out of shaving cream, use soap or baby oil instead.

Reaching things

• Extend your reach with a pair of barbecue tongs if you can't reach something.
• Push and pull objects out of tight spots with a bamboo cane, radiator brush or straightened wire coat hanger. To pick up light items, wrap sticky tape around the end, sticky side out.
• If a match won't reach the wick in a hurricane lamp, light a taper.

Reading

• If you haven't enough time for the reading you'd like to do, scan the first and last paragraphs of an article or the first and last pages of a book's first chapter to decide if it's worth your while to read what's in between.
• Set time limits on your reading material and sort it accordingly: a high-priority pile for newspapers and news magazines that become useless quickly; a medium-priority pile for material that should be read for your job or your investments; a low-priority pile for material that can wait, such as cookbooks, novels or travel magazines.
• Don't try to read everything – sometimes it's enough to know that you have an article on file in case you need specific information in the future.
• Make an appointment with yourself to do your reading; if necessary, get up half an hour earlier, go to bed half an hour later, or plan to read during your quiet

---

Stubble trouble

The quest for a clean-shaven face has driven men to experiment with many kinds of razors.

Prehistoric men shaved with clam shells, shark's teeth, sharpened pieces of flint or knives.

In the 4th century BC, wealthy Egyptians smoothed their faces with gold and copper razors – items that have been found in their tombs by archaeologists.

A widely used straight, or 'cut-throat', razor – a long steel blade that folded into a handle – was made in Sheffield in the 18th century. Although it offered an incomparably close shave, it could be hazardous when wielded by anything less than a skilled hand.

The first crude 'safety razor' – a blade set into a wooden casing so that it couldn't slice the shaver's skin – was manufactured in 1762.

In America during the early 1900s, King Camp Gillette collaborated with the inventor William Nickerson to design a safety razor with disposable blades. It first went on sale in 1903, and despite a wide array of improvements, its basic design has changed very little since.

In 1928, Joseph Schick patented an electric razor that provided the first dry shave. Today men and women can choose from a variety of high-tech models, including those with rotary blades and micro-screens.

time, as on a bus or train. See p.164.

• If you're looking for something other than a best-seller, ask your librarian for advice; she may ask about your interests or refer you to one of several guides to the classics.

• Don't throw away all those paperback books; set up an exchange at work. If you find you don't like a book you borrowed, there's no need to feel guilty – you haven't spent anything; just return it for another.

• If your child resists 'good' books, consult a children's librarian or a sympathetic, well-informed bookseller. She may be able to interest him in books you don't know about.

Scanning for speed

• Let your eyes follow your hand as it brushes down each page. Practise focusing on a whole line rather than one word at a time.

• Run your fingertip or a bookmark under every line as you read it, to focus your attention and prevent your mind from wandering.

• As you scan, mark the passages you'd like to return to with a pencil or a highlighter. Or jot down the page numbers on a piece of paper and slip it into the back of the book.

Record keeping

Is the tax return season a nightmare for you? If you keep good records, you'll find everything in order when you need it.

• Find out what you can deduct; check with an accountant or tax lawyer.

• Then buy a calendar with detachable pages. Every night jot down any tax-deductible travel, entertainment and meal costs; note the time, date and place, and the nature of the business conducted. It is a wise move to save all receipts, no matter what the amount, for at least 3 years.

• Keep all your receipts in large envelopes organised by category: telephone bills, office supplies and so forth.

• Pay all your bills by cheque. When you balance your bank statement, place the receipts for deductible expenses in the appropriate envelopes.

• Keep a separate envelope for records

of any share sales or other capital gains.

• Keep a record of the figures you submit on your income tax return form, in case you need to refer to them during the year. See also INCOME TAX RETURNS, p.113.

Recovery position

Treat any unconscious casualties who are breathing, except those with suspected spinal or neck injuries, by placing them in the recovery, or unconscious, position as quickly as possible.

• If the victim is breathing, clear the airway in his mouth with your finger, and clean up any blood or mucus.

• Kneel beside victim. Tilt his head back, lift his chin to open airway. Straighten both legs. Place nearer arm at right angles to body, elbow bent, palm of hand uppermost.

• Bring arm farthest from you over victim's chest. Place hand, with palm outwards, against his nearer cheek and hold it there.

• With your other hand, pull up his knee, keeping his foot flat on ground. Roll him towards you, supporting his head and stopping him rolling too far with your knees.

• Again tilt the victim's head back, to keep airway clear. Adjust his hand so that his head is well supported. Adjust his uppermost leg to keep thigh and knee at right angles. Never put coat or pillows under his head. Call for medical help, or get someone else to do so. While waiting, check victim's breathing and pulse regularly.

• If victim is not breathing, administer artificial respiration (see p. 67). If there is still no pulse, and if you have been trained to do so, give chest compression.

Redundancy

Redundancy is almost always shocking but can be an opportunity as well as a disaster. Keep in mind that you have several priorities: to handle the immediate crisis, to re-evaluate your career and to make plans for your future.

• Press for redundancy pay – some employers offer as much as 2 weeks' pay for each year of service.

• Losing a job can feel like losing someone close to you. Allow yourself to feel depressed and angry. Tell your family what you're experiencing and ask them for extra moral support during this difficult time.

• Don't panic. If you can afford to take a holiday, do so – it may give you a new perspective. If you can't, treat yourself to something for your house or garden, or escape to the cinema.

• Then get busy. Examine what (if anything) went wrong in your job — be honest, but don't torture yourself. Did you hang on too long when you knew things were going badly? Was there poor chemistry between you and your boss or your colleagues? Were you less than fully committed to your job?

• Investigate any offers or suggestions of redeployment your company makes and make use of any career counselling services it offers. Fruitful new ideas may emerge. See also JOB HUNTING, p.117.

References

• If you didn't get along well with your former boss, ask someone else with whom you've worked for a reference – preferably someone with a managerial title.

• If you know that a former employer had reservations about certain aspects of your work, tell her that you've improved in those areas. She might be willing to think again and give you a recommendation based on your strengths.

• If you've never held a paid job, ask a former teacher or supervisor you worked with in a work placement or a voluntary unpaid job for a reference.

• To avoid alienating a referee, always call first and ask if she would be willing to recommend you. Follow up with a thank-you note.

Reflecting light

When you are photographing someone, part of the face may be in shadow, particularly if she is sitting by a window. Here are some tips for reflecting light onto the dark side of the sitter's face.

• Use a square of white card, a mirror, or kitchen foil glued to cardboard to 'bounce' the light onto areas in shadow. A projector screen makes an excellent reflector of light. Remember to keep any reflector off-camera so that it won't appear in the picture.

Refrigerators

• If your refrigerator or freezer stops working, check for a loose plug, a tripped circuit breaker or blown fuse, or a temperature control accidentally turned off. If these are all working, test the socket by plugging in a lamp. If it lights, the problem is in the appliance or its cord; if not, the socket or house wiring is at fault. Until you can get it fixed, plug the unit into another socket, but be sure any extension cord you use is rated the same amperage as the unit.

• Water on the floor suggests the drain tray is placed incorrectly or is cracked and needs replacing. Or maybe the drain tube, if there is one, is clogged; if so, use a meat baster to flush hot water through the tube and unclog it.

Cooling problems

• Make sure the temperature control is turned on. If it is, change it to a colder setting; and then wait 24 hours to see if it needs adjusting further.

• Check that the door is sealed tightly. If the seal is damaged, replace it. If it's in good condition, the refrigerator is probably incorrectly positioned on the floor; adjust the levelling legs or rollers.

• Check the condenser coils at the base or the back of the refrigerator; if dust has collected on them, the unit won't cool properly. Clean the coils regularly with the brush or crevice attachment on your vacuum cleaner.

Refunds

• If you discover that you have bought faulty goods, act quickly to return the goods and get your money back. Do not delay longer than is reasonably necessary. With food you are entitled to some delay, since it is not until you come to eat it that you will discover that it is faulty.

• Do not consume food from containers that are obviously faulty or try to mend any object that is defective.

• You have the right to claim compensation for up to 6 years from the date of purchase of the faulty goods.

• If the defect can be fixed, the trader must foot the repair bill. You can have the object repaired anywhere and you are not obliged to hand it back to the manufacturer for repair.

• If goods cannot be repaired you can ask the trader for a partial refund, which should be the difference between the value of the defective goods and the amount you originally paid for it.

• If you have the right to have your money refunded, you have the right to insist on receiving it in cash.

• If you accept a credit note as a refund you can only spend it in the same shop that issued it.

• Contact your local trading standards office or Citizens Advice Bureau if you have no satisfaction claiming a refund.

Mail order purchases

• If you have not received the goods nor a reply-paid postcard and offer of a refund within 28 days of sending your money, notify the advertising department of the newspaper or magazine in which the advertisement appeared. They will investigate the advertiser. If it was a 'display' advertisement, the publisher can arrange for a refund.

• Lodge your claim for a refund within three months of the date of the advertisement appearing in a daily or weekly newspaper. If it appeared in any other publication, put in your claim within 2 months of sending the money. You will need proof of payment and of when it was made, to whom and for what.

• You are entitled to get your money back if the goods bear no relation to the description in the advertisement.

• If the quality of the object makes it unsuitable for its purpose, you have the right to demand a replacement or a refund.

• You are entitled to receive your money back in full if you send back the goods undamaged within 7 days of receiving them. Try to keep the packaging intact.

Relaxation

Taking a few minutes to relax each day can ease insomnia, reduce heart disease, stress, dependence on smoking and tranquillisers, and generally improve your sense of well-being. Set aside 10-15 minutes at the start and end of each day to concentrate on deep breathing or relaxing your muscles. For all these exercises, loosen your clothing, take off your shoes and lie on your back, with your head, neck and back aligned.

Diaphragmatic breathing This is the

natural way to breathe, but we often use our rib muscles instead, for short, shallow breaths. Diaphragmatic breathing is based on the contraction and relaxation of the diaphragm. By contrast, chest breathing promotes tension and is appropriate for getting the body ready for action but is not appropriate for relaxing.

• Place your hands on your abdomen. Slowly fill and empty your lungs. If you are breathing properly it should feel as if air is filling your abdomen and your hands should rise and fall as you breathe.

Slow breathing

• Breathe in and out very slowly, counting from 10 to 1 for each breathing cycle. Start at 10 and breathe in, counting 9, 8 and 7. Pause at 6 and 5. Breathe out and count 4, 3, 2 and 1. Relax any muscles that you feel are tense.

Muscle relaxation This exercise successively tenses and relaxes groups of muscles.

• Lie with your feet about 18in/460mm apart, palms turned upwards and held 6in/150mm away from your body. Raise your eyebrows and tense your forehead muscles. Count to 5, then relax. Repeat. Follow the same procedure by tightening and relaxing each of these muscle groups. Squeeze your eyes shut and then open them wide; open your mouth and eyes wide; purse your lips; tighten your chin; clench and relax your jaw muscles; raise your shoulder and tense your neck and shoulder muscles; raise one arm, clench your fist and tense the muscles, then do the same with the other arm; tighten your stomach muscles; lift one leg slightly off the floor and push the foot against an imaginary obstacle, then drop; repeat with the other leg.

Then lie still for several minutes, completely relaxed, and try to feel as if you are floating.

Restaurants

• If you are going to take children out to eat, shop around for a restaurant that offers a reduced price children's meal service. Some restaurants also offer a teenage menu. Remember, however, that most children will not like unusual foods, and actually prefer fast food establishments.

• When making a table reservation, always ask specifically for a particular table that you like. Give the number or description. If you want to smoke, you must ask for a table in a smoking area.

• If you fail to turn up when you have booked a table, the restaurant may be entitled to demand compensation for loss of custom.

• If your table isn't ready when you arrive, you may get it faster by being a slight pest. Rather than going to the bar to wait, stay put and keep asking when it will be ready.

• If you don't like the table you are taken to, ask for another one. If the restaurant is crowded, a tip may help.

• You will often find that country pubs offer better value for money than plush town restaurants. Ask friends for a recommendation.

• To get a waiter's attention, wave your hand or say 'waiter' as he goes past. Never be loud, rude or abrasive – you are likely to be ignored.

• If you think service is likely to be slow, it is worth suggesting from the start that you have limited time. If the bill is slow arriving, stand up and start to make obvious preparations to leave.

• If you do not get what you ordered, say so straight away and insist on getting the right thing. If this will take time, insist that other food is kept properly warm until everything is ready.

• If the waiter spills food or drink on you, you are entitled to dry-cleaning costs and expenses. Mention this immediately and get the waiter's name.

• If you have cause to complain, mention the matter to the waiter politely. If you do not get satisfaction, ask to see the manager or owner. Never shout or lose your temper.

• Look at the menu to see if there is a service charge. If the menu does not mention it, it cannot legally appear on the bill. Cross it off and don't pay it. If there is a service charge, you are not expected to tip as well. In other cases 10 per cent is a reasonable expectation, but

do not tip unless you have had satisfactory service.

• If your coat disappears from a restaurant cloakroom, ask for the cost of it. Exclusion notices are likely to be legally ineffective. You may need to get legal advice if the restaurant refuses to pay.

• If you get food poisoning after eating in a restaurant, report the matter to the local authority Environmental Health Department. In serious cases it might pay you to get legal advice.

Retirement

Are you considering early retirement? Experts estimate that you'll need 60 to 70 per cent of your current income to live fairly well. Here's how to work out your potential assets. See also READY FOR RETIREMENT, p.246.

• Check with your company's pension plan administrator to find out how early retirement would affect your pension.

• Also check with the Department of Social Security. Their rules are constantly being adjusted. However, at the time of writing, you will receive full benefits if you retire at the age of 60 (for women) or 65 (for men), providing you have a full contribution record. Write to the DSS in Newcastle for a Pensions Forecast which will tell you how much pension you will receive and what additional National Insurance Contributions you can make if you want to retire early.

• See how your investments could be rearranged to provide income instead of long-term growth.

• Work out how much money you would have if you cashed in your capital assets and add the amount to your savings. Then add in the money you would save if you kept just enough life insurance to allow your dependants to maintain their standard of living and to pay any estate duty, any leftover debts and your funeral expenses.

• Do you think you could live comfortably on the results?

Delaying retirement When you reach retirement age you do not have to draw your state pension. You can defer it for a maximum of five years. You will receive a bigger pension that way, but it might be better for you to draw your pension regularly and invest it elsewhere.

You do not have to retire from your job to receive your state pension. But if you are working, it may put you into a higher tax bracket and this might be a good reason for deferral.

Rice

• To stop grains of rice from sticking together, add a few drops of cooking oil or a teaspoon of butter or margarine to the cooking water.

• For snowy white rice, add a few drops of lemon juice or vinegar to the cooking water.

• Rinse uncooked rice in a sieve under a cold running tap before cooking; this removes excess starch, so preventing the rice from becoming sticky.

• Everyone has their favourite way of cooking rice, but here are two very successful methods:

Place the rice in a saucepan. Add ½ pint / 285 ml of water or stock for every 4 oz / 115 g of rice to be cooked. Bring to the boil, cover with a tightly fitting lid and simmer for 20-25 minutes until the rice is tender and the water or stock is absorbed. If necessary, add a little more liquid if the rice is not cooked before the liquid disappears.

Or simply cook the rice in a large amount of boiling salted water until tender. Drain thoroughly and serve, or keep warm in a sieve over a little boiling water.

Ring stuck on your finger

• Don't try more than a couple of times to pull the ring off your finger. If you inflame the knuckle it will swell and make the ring more difficult to remove. Simply moistening your finger in your mouth should do the trick.

• Drip some olive oil around the ring, massage some petroleum jelly into your skin, or rub soap around the ring and wet it slightly. Then try to ease it off.

• If your finger or knuckle has swollen, soak it in iced water to reduce the swelling, or put an ice pack around it.

Roller blinds

• Vacuum or brush the blind fabric when the blind is fully pulled down, to remove dust. Use your vacuum's crevice tool to keep the springs free from fluff.

• If the fabric is suitable, clean it with a foam upholstery cleaner on a flat surface. Hang the blind while it is still damp and don't roll it up until absolutely dry or it may lose its shape.

• When a blind won't roll up, it probably needs to be retensioned. Pull it down halfway, take it off the brackets and roll it up fully by hand. Place it back on the brackets and pull it down. If the tension is still not sufficient to roll up the blind fully, repeat the process until the tension is correct.

Roof gardens

Before starting a garden on the roof of your flat, or the roof of an extension, check the local building regulations about the construction of roof gardens. If you have any doubt, consult the local authority's building regulations officer. If you rent your home, make sure you consult your landlord before doing anything.

• Lay a thick sheet of plastic on the roof to protect it from seepage and plant roots. Then construct a box frame of 4 × 2 in / 100 × 50 mm wood and set it on top of the plastic. Reinforce the corners with angle irons.

• Fill the frame with well-rotted garden compost, if you can get hold of some. Perlite can be added to the mixture to improve its structure. (Beware of peat moss, which becomes very heavy when wet.)

• Water thoroughly and add 5 lb / 2.3 kg of fertiliser per 100 sq ft / 9.3 m². Water again lightly, then set out the plants and sow the seeds. (Herbs, vegetables such as onions, radishes, lettuce, green beans and peas, and strawberries and dwarf varieties of tomatoes thrive in roof gardens.)

• Keep the surface of the 'soil' evenly moist until germination, then increase watering daily. Feed with a soluble fertiliser every fourth or fifth watering.

Roof leaks

• A common cause of water in the loft during winter months is rain driven in by the wind, usually due to a lack of felting under the tiles or slates. To prevent further penetration, use building paper. This is bitumen-impregnated, and so is waterproof. Pin the building paper in horizontal strips to the rafters, starting at the top and working down. Allow a good 6 in / 150 mm overlap between the strips and seal the joints with waterproof clear adhesive tape. Use brass drawing pins to fix the paper in place. Slip the end of the building paper out under the eaves so that any water collected is directed out of the house.

• Treat a felt or asphalt flat roof which develops cracks with brush-on liquid rubber. You can apply the rubber with an old, large paintbrush or a small broom. Clean the roof of any loose dirt or chippings beforehand.

• Repair fine cracks in the felt with a bituminous sealant, which fits into an applicator gun.

Roofs

Never work on a roof unless you are happy with heights and have the right equipment.

• You need a ladder which extends high enough to give at least three clear rungs above gutter level, so you always have a handhold. And the ladder must be secured so that it can't slide or slip in any direction.

• To work on the roof, hire a special roof ladder which is designed to hook securely over the ridge. Do not move off the ladder yourself; always get down and move the ladder, however inconvenient it may seem at the time.

• Whenever possible, have a helper to pass up materials for use on the roof. Never balance or wedge materials on a sloping roof. If they fall, they could cause serious accidents.

• If working as a helper, always wear a safety helmet. This can be hired at the same time as the roof ladder.

• If you stand a ladder on a flat roof area, always place a piece of rough board underneath the ladder base. This will protect the flat roof coating. But also make sure you anchor the ladder so that it can't slide off the wood.

Rose propagation

To start a new rose bush from your favourite variety, snip a perfect rose along with 12 in/300mm of stem that has at least five leaf-clusters. Put the stem in water immediately and leave it there for an hour or longer (up to 2 days if you want to enjoy the bloom).

Prepare a bed of soil in a sheltered, shaded spot. Dig to a depth of 18 in/460mm and add 1 part builder's sand to each part of soil.

To prepare the cutting for rooting, snip off the blossom and cut off the top of the stem at an angle just above a bud. Cut off the bottom of the stem at an angle just below the bottom leaf cluster. Strip off all but the topmost leaves, then dust the bottom of the cutting with powdered rooting hormone (available from most garden centres).

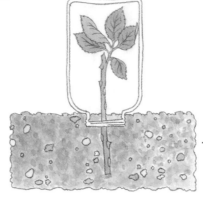

Plant this almost-bare stick in the prepared soil to a point just below the second leaf scar from the top. Press down the soil around the cutting, water well and cover with an inverted preserving jar. Lift the jar each day and wipe away any condensation on the inside.

The appearance of a second new leaf means that the cutting has started to root. Let it grow undisturbed for 8 or 9 months before transplanting; remove the jar as soon as the cutting has rooted.

Rubbers

Are pencil rubbers always impossible to find when you need them?
• Twist a rubber band round your finger to erase pencil marks. Or roll some putty, Blu-Tack or soft white bread into a ball.
• Cover errors on coloured paper – hand-lettered invitations and school projects, for example – with a dab of the acrylic paint used for model airplanes, if you have some. Choose matt paint and mix the colours until you have an exact match for the paper.

Rugs

• To keep a rug in place on a polished floor and stop it from sliding around, put a rubber mat under it.
• To make a small rug lie flat, paint some lacquer on the underside. When dry, wipe with a mild solution of laundry starch; leave to dry before using.
• Prevent rag rugs from curling up at the edges by rinsing them in a mild solution of starch and water.
• To wash cotton colourfast rugs, place them in the bath with warm soapy water and scrub with a broom. Use a long-handled plunger to stir the water.

• Wool rugs are best cleaned with a sponge and soapy water. Test the back first, in case the colours run. If they do, take the rug to a specialist cleaner.

Rulers and tapes

• For all cutting jobs, always choose a ruler with a metal edge inset, to avoid damaging the ruler itself.
• Do not use old dressmaking tapes when accurate measuring is needed, because they are likely to have stretched. Use a steel tape instead.
• Choose a steel tape with both imperial and metric markings on the same side. This offers you a simple visible conversion table from one system to the other. Merely read across the tape.
• Apart from a standard 10ft/3m tape, it is a good idea to have a longer surveyor's tape for room, house and garden measurements.
• A steel rule stuck to the workbench with strong glue is useful for small measuring jobs – it won't move as you use it and it will never get mislaid!

Runaways

• Little runaways, who tend to be newly independent infant and primary school-children, usually head for the fields behind the house or to a friend's house, and they generally make it home by suppertime or bedtime. In fact, you may miss what is a dramatic occasion for them, and think they're just visiting one of their friends.
• An older runaway presents a more serious problem. You, the parents, may have little or no warning, especially if communication has become difficult during the turbulent teenage years. Watch for signs of discontent: loss of interest in schoolwork, withdrawal, depression and unexplained bursts of anger. And pay special attention to your teenager when there is a major change in the family: death, remarriage, impending divorce, discovery of sexual abuse or a move to another town. Runaways are often accompanied by a friend who has no serious intention of staying away but has gone along for the thrills.

Roses of the past

Myths about roses abounded in ancient Greece and Rome. One was that roses were originally white until Venus, the goddess of love, pricked her foot on a rose thorn as she hurried to save her imperilled lover. A drop of her sacred blood fell on the white blossom, dying it red forever.

The rose gave its name to the Catholic cycle of prayer known as the rosary, meaning 'a rose garden'. Rose petals may have formed the first rosary 'beads'.

The long 15th-century conflict between the royal houses of York and Lancaster is known as the Wars of the Roses because the men of York supposedly wore a white rose in battle while Lancastrians wore a red one. In fact, Lancaster adopted the red rose after the wars were over.

• How well do you know your teenager? Do you know her closest friend(s)? Are her friends welcome in the house? Do you spend time with your child, talking to her about issues that affect her – boyfriends, premarital sex, drugs, school? If you feel that there may be a problem communicating with your child, look for help before a crisis arises. Talk to someone you can trust (a family friend, counsellor, doctor or vicar, perhaps).

• Nowadays, there are real dangers for children who run away. Report a missing child to the police as soon as you can, providing them with photographs and a description of what she is likely to be wearing. Ring her friends; ask them to tell her to call home if they know where she is.

• A number of nationwide organisations maintain hotlines offering help; through them parents and runaway children can exchange messages and arrange transport home. Among them are Childline (Tel 0800 iiii) and the Children's Society, Edward Rudolf House, 69-85 Margery Street, London WC1X 0JL (Tel. 0171-837 4299).

Rust

All bright metal objects are at risk from rust in our damp climate. Prevention is always better than cure, so try some simple measures to reduce the risk.

• Protect bright metalwork in the short term with an aerosol of protective oil. Spray lightly, but remember that the oil does evaporate fairly quickly.

• Protect surfaces that are not usually touched with a coating of car grease. The grease keeps air and moisture away from the surface – both of which cause rusting.

• Keep a jam jar with a little oil in it on your workbench, and insert a roll of felt or thick fabric. If you use this to lightly wipe tools after use, it will keep the metal bright.

• Outdoor articles such as garden furniture and gates can be protected by using a special rust-inhibiting paint. This needs no primer or undercoat, and it can be applied straight onto lightly rusted surfaces as long as all loose material has

been thoroughly removed first with an emery cloth.

• Protect rusted surfaces on items such as wheelbarrows with cold galvanising paint. This zinc-rich paint forms an ideal base for a decorative finish.

Cars

• Most new cars have extensive rust-proofing. Beware if your dealer tries to sell you more. It's rarely needed.

• To protect your car from the ravages of road salt in icy or snowy weather, wash the underbody, particularly under the wings and wheel arches, with a powerful hose to remove the dirt.

• To keep water out, make sure the access holes in the sides of doors and in the rocker panels are firmly plugged.

• Chips and scratches let moisture in under the paint surface. Fix them immediately. Scrape away loose paint and rust with the corner of a craft knife, then wipe the spot with rust converter (a product that combines a rust inhibitor with a primer). Wash the surface with a mild detergent, rinse well and dry thoroughly. Then, using an artist's brush, apply the primer that is recommended for your car's model and colour. Leave to dry, then apply the correct paint. Don't be worried if the colour doesn't match exactly – that's a minor problem compared to rust damage.

Rust stains

Non-washable garments must be dry-cleaned, but washable fabrics with rust stains can be treated in one of several ways:

• Rub a paste of salt and vinegar into the stain; leave it to stand for 30 minutes, then wash as usual.

• Soak the rust stain in lemon juice, then dry the garment in the sun to bleach it; rinse thoroughly.

• Work a paste of cream of tartar and hot water into the stain; leave it to set, then wash as usual.

• Boil five stalks of rhubarb (cut into ½in/13mm pieces) in 1 pint/570ml of water until soft; pour the hot liquid over the stain. Wash as usual.

• Use a commercial rust stain remover if these suggestions fail to shift the marks.

S

Safe-deposit boxes

• Keep all valuable or hard-to-replace documents in a safe-deposit box: birth, adoption, marriage, divorce and death certificates; property deeds; vehicle registration documents; stock, bond or savings certificates; a copy of your will; a household inventory; and all insurance policies. Keep a list of the box's contents at home.

• You can deposit your own box with your bank on payment of a fee and they will look after it for you. You keep the key – the bank will not have one. Some banks offer special safety deposit facilities where you rent one of their boxes in a purpose-built vault. But this costs a lot more. You have one key and the bank has another – both are needed to open the box. If you lose your key you may have to pay a hefty fee to have the lock drilled open – but the bank will need positive proof that it is your box.

• Check your householder's policy to see if it covers the contents of your safe-deposit box, or ask the bank if it offers insurance.

• When a box renter dies, the bank will only allow the box to be opened by a person who proves that he has proper authority, which will usually be the executor or administrator of the estate. A copy of the death certificate and proof of identity is required. See also GETTING ORGANISED, p.238; VALUABLES, p.219.

Safes

When looking for a temporary place to hide cash, jewellery, or other small valuables, avoid the obvious.

• Put them in a frozen vegetable bag in the freezer or in a cream carton or the cavity of a green pepper in the refrigerator. (Avoid the foods thieves are likely to sample, such as ice cream or fruit.)

• Wrap them in plastic and store in a vacuum cleaner bag.

• Buy a dummy wall plug socket, which has a drawer, and fit it into the wall or skirting board at ground level.

• Keep important papers in detergent boxes stored under the sink or in the laundry room.

Safety gates

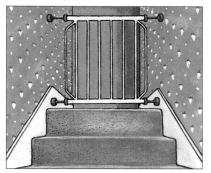

A standard adjustable child gate which can be used in hallways and doorways of varying widths.

• If you don't like the look and inconvenience of safety gates in your home, hang split stable doors between rooms instead; close the bottom section whenever you want to restrict your toddler's travels.

• You can replace a solid door with a door with a safety glass panel in the top half in your child's room. That way you'll be able to see what the child is up to, even though her getaway will be thoroughly blocked. Just make sure that the lock is on the outside.

• When a friend brings a crawler or toddler to visit your normally child-free home, you can improvise temporary safety gates from mattresses or tables turned on their sides.

Saffron

Substitute the petals of pot marigolds for expensive saffron. They have a similar pungent flavour and the same yellow colour. Let the flower heads air-dry or dry them in a microwave (see p.87), then grind them into a fine powder with a mortar and pestle. Use in pastries, risottos, fish stews and the classic Spanish paella, adding just a pinch more than you would of saffron.

Sagging verandah

With the help of a car jack, install a temporary brace for the sagging verandah of a seaside chalet until you have time to make proper repairs. Place the jack on a concrete building block and hook it securely under the header joist. Make sure the jack remains absolutely upright as you raise the verandah until the floor is level (stand clear in case the jack slips). Then cut a 4 × 4 in / 100 × 100mm post to fit between the bottom of the joist and another concrete block. Put the post in place and remove the jack.

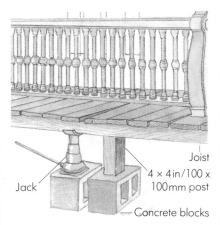

Joist

4 × 4 in / 100 × 100mm post

Jack

Concrete blocks

Salary increases

Before you ask for an increase in salary give some thought to your tactics.

• Try to determine what your job is worth. Ask friends in similar positions what they earn. Check the job advertisements in newspapers and magazines, and consult any professional organisations you belong to. Make allowances for factors that could affect your salary: your geographical location,

your education (an advanced degree may be worth more money), the number of people you supervise and the budget or work for which you are responsible (salary is usually commensurate with responsibility).

• Always ask for slightly more money than you think you can get. You'll allow your employers to feel they've saved money by giving you slightly less, and you'll probably end up being offered more or less what you wanted. You may even get what you ask for.

• Time your request wisely. Obviously your chances are better after you've had some kind of success or when the company is doing well; certainly not when it's doing poorly. (Although, surprisingly, many people have received big increases during shake-ups, when a company was anxious to keep things stabilised and didn't want to lose valuable employees.) If a performance review shows that your work has improved, take it as an opportunity to ask for extra compensation.

• Sometimes it is better to take on a new project and wait to ask for a rise until after you've completed it successfully.

• If a rise is less than you want, ask for a review in 6 months time. If possible, set goals which, when met, will entitle you to the increase.

Sales receipts

If you've lost the sales receipt for merchandise you want to return, don't despair.

• If the price sticker is intact, it will sometimes be accepted in lieu of a receipt.

• If you have a credit account with a shop, they will probably let you return the item in exchange for credit.

• Shops where you don't have a credit account will usually give a credit voucher for the amount to be spent at that shop only.

• Exchanging an unwanted gift can be a problem, but if you keep the container and packing material, they might help you convince the shop manager to refund the purchase price, or at least to exchange it for something you would prefer to have.

Salt solidified

• If the salt in your salt cellar gets too moist it sets in a clump. Put some grains of rice in with the salt to absorb moisture.

• If the salt has set too solidly for the rice trick to work, remove the cap from your salt cellar and scrape out the salt onto a baking tray lined with kitchen foil. Place it in a warm oven for 5 minutes to dry it out. Meanwhile, wash out the salt cellar and dry it thoroughly. Then pour the salt back into it, with a few grains of rice.

Salt substitutes

• Try this blend of herbs: 1 teaspoon garlic powder and 1 teaspoon each dried basil, oregano and celery salt. Use a mortar and pestle to grind them together; transfer to a salt cellar. Add a few grains of rice to keep the mixture dry.

• For a spicier salt replacement, use 1 teaspoon each ground cloves, black pepper and crushed coriander seed mixed together with 2 teaspoons paprika and 1 tablespoon rosemary.

Sanding

• Use fine glasspaper to roughen painted wood before applying new enamel or varnish. Sand between coats, too.

• To sand chair rungs and table legs, cut a strip of glasspaper and apply masking tape to the back as reinforcement. Then pull the paper back and forth around the rung, as if you were shining shoes.

• For carvings and turnings, fold the sandpaper and fit the folded edge into the curve so that the grit smooths both faces at the same time. Use fine steel

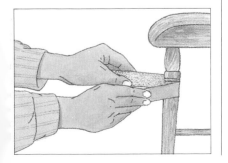

wool (No. 000) to get all the way into deep crevices.

• When you sand, wear rubber gloves or rubber thimbles – the kind designed for office use – to protect your skin and keep oily fingerprints off the wood.

• To clean off very fine dust from a smoothed surface, buy a tack (or tacky rag) from your local decorating shop. This is a special resin-impregnated duster which will pick up the fine dust without leaving the wood surface sticky to the touch. It will also ensure that painted surfaces do not appear gritty when new paint is applied. See also ABRASIVE PAPER, p.8.

Sandwiches

Sandwich fillings can be simple and nutritious – such as hard-boiled eggs, lettuce, sliced cucumber and tomatoes. Or they can be rich and elaborate – such as chicken, avocado, chives and mayonnaise, or anchovy, cream cheese and tomato. Whichever you prefer, don't skimp on the filling. A generously filled sandwich is always more appealing than a skimpy one.

• Choose firm, good-quality bread for sandwiches. For parties and teas, make dainty and elegant sandwiches, with the crusts removed. For all other occasions, suit yourself. Slice the bread as thin or as thick as you like – crusts and all. (Keeping the crusts prevents the bread slices from drying out and curling at the edges.) If you like contrasting flavours or textures, you could try combining two different kinds of bread of the same size in one sandwich.

• Sandwiches made in advance can be kept fresh by storing them covered with non-toxic plastic film or in an airtight plastic bag, in the refrigerator. To prevent bread from becoming soggy, spread it with softened butter or margarine rather than salad dressing or mayonnaise. (Alternatively, spread the mayonnaise or dressing between the layers of ingredients rather than directly onto the bread.)

• It is a good idea to keep moist ingredients – such as tomato and cucumber slices, lettuce and pickles – in separate

containers or bags, and add them to the sandwiches at the last minute.

• For children's parties, make small sandwiches of thinly sliced white bread. Use biscuit cutters to cut them into round, oval or other unusual shapes. Butter them lightly and spread them with a variety of tasty fillings – cream cheese, Marmite, ham, honey, jam, peanut butter or sardines.

• To make a quick sandwich spread, you can always use peanut butter – it goes well with many different ingredients. Try the following combinations on bread, toast or biscuits. Mix together 2 tablespoons each of peanut butter, drained crushed pineapple and shredded coconut. Or mix 2 tablespoons each of peanut butter and mashed banana, with a few drops of lemon juice. (Incidentally, the calorie count for these two spreads is 40 and 50 per tablespoon respectively.)

Club sandwich For a substantial snack in a hurry, make a club sandwich. You can have a hefty triple-decker for four people ready in 20 minutes. Just toast 12 slices of bread and remove the crusts. Butter 4 slices on both sides and the remaining 8 on one side only. Cover 4 of the partly buttered slices with a slice of tomato and top with crisply fried bacon (2 rashers for each sandwich). Put the 4 slices buttered on both sides on top of this, and cover them with lettuce and thin slices of cooked chicken or turkey.

Spoon mayonnaise over the chicken or turkey slices, and cover with the last 4 slices of toast. Then press the piled-up sandwiches firmly together and quarter them. Spear each quarter with a cocktail stick and serve. For the finishing touch, don't forget to add a stuffed olive to the top of each stick.

Sanitation in the wild

• Don't bury leftover food at your campsite. Wild animals will just dig it up and perhaps bother the next camper in the vicinity. Take empty tins, bottles and food scraps with you when you leave.

• Make sure you bury human faeces at least 4-12 in / 100-300mm deep. Save the overlying soil to hide the hole. In areas of little soil, follow local recommendations for shallow burial and cover waste with whatever soil is available. In rocky terrain, remove a rock, use the depression beneath it as a toilet, then place the rock on top again. Don't move rocks from one spot to another, though, as this creates unsightly pits in the ground.

• For a latrine that will be used by more than one person and will have to decompose more waste, lengthen rather than deepen the hole.

• Be sure toilet areas are at least 100ft/30m from watercourses, footpaths and campsites.

• Use biodegradable, chemical and dye-free toilet paper. Or burn toilet paper after use.

• Improvise a toothbrush by chewing the end of a green twig. Bicarbonate of soda, salt or ash can all serve as substitutes for toothpaste.

Sauces

• If a Hollandaise sauce curdles, take it off the heat and beat in 1 tablespoon of cold water, a little at a time, until the sauce becomes smooth. Alternatively, stir an ice cube into the warm sauce. If this doesn't work, beat an egg yolk in a clean pan over a low heat until it thickens. Then gradually beat in the curdled sauce until smooth.

• Rescue a lumpy sauce or gravy by whisking it hard in the saucepan. If this fails, whizz the sauce in a blender, or rub it through a sieve.

• A custard sauce curdles if allowed to boil or cooked over a high heat too fast. Immediately put the saucepan into just enough cold water to cover the base. Then stir in 2 teaspoons of cornflour for every 1 pint/570ml of custard. Alternatively, pour the custard through a sieve into a clean bowl and cool it quickly by placing the bowl in cold water.

• Save a sauce that is too sweet by adding a little lemon juice.

• Prevent sauce from burning or setting at the bottom by whisking it rapidly in a figure-of-eight motion.

• Simmer sauces if you want to reduce them – never boil them or they may curdle or cloud.

• If you need to leave a white sauce standing, coat the surface while still warm with a lump of butter to prevent a skin from forming.

Saving money

• Treat your savings as a necessity like food and clothing. Aim to build a readily available emergency cash reserve – enough to cover such essentials as food, mortgage and car payments, and household bills for at least 3 months.

• Instead of relying on your self-discipline, arrange with your bank or building society to automatically transfer a specific amount every month from your current account to an interest-bearing deposit account.

• If you get 26 pay cheques a year, use 24 of them – two a month – for the family budget; put the two extra pay cheques into your savings account.

• Or use the loose change system to help with the grandchildren. At the end of each day, put all your coppers and 5p pieces in a jar, and then deposit them in a building society savings account in their name every couple of months or so. Or change the coins for notes at the bank, and let their parents have the money to put towards shoes, clothes or school uniforms.

• Try not to supervise your children's saving and spending too strictly. Letting them learn lessons with small amounts will help them later in life.

Savings bonds and certificates

Are you looking for a safe, worry-free investment vehicle? If you don't need to get your hands on the money for a few years, consider National Savings Income Bonds or National Savings Certificates – both are available from Post Offices.

• Income bonds cost £1000 each, and the minimum you can hold is £2000. Income bonds pay a monthly income at a variable interest rate.

• National Savings Certificates run for five years – the longer you keep the Certificates, the higher the interest rate

paid. The interest is added to the value of the Certificates. Minimum purchase must be £100. After that, you can buy up to £10 000's worth.

• If you pay the interest from your Income Bonds directly into a National Savings Investment account, it will earn further (taxable) interest.

• Keep a record of the serial numbers, issue dates and amounts of each Bond or Certificate. If they are lost, stolen or destroyed, write for Savings Certificate replacements to Savings Certificates, National Savings, Durham DH99 1NS, and for Income Bond replacements to Income Bonds, National Savings, Blackpool FY3 9YP. You must include your name, address and holder's number with your request.

Scale insects

Scale insects look like tiny brown scales. They live by clinging to the leaves and stems of plants.

• Get rid of a scale insect infestation by spraying plants with insecticidal soap.

• A more spur of the moment but time-consuming treatment is to scrape them off with a piece of cardboard or a thin piece of wood.

Scissors

• If you have no scissors to hand, simply fold a sheet of paper in half backwards and forwards, and then strengthen the crease with your thumb. Hold the halved paper firmly and draw a ruler or paper-knife along the crease.

• Make decorative ribbon curls by holding a strip of ribbon firmly between your thumb and the scissor blade. Keeping your thumb and the scissors in place, pull the ribbon between them, under pressure, until it curls.

• Never cut paper with your haircutting or dressmaking scissors; it dulls the keen edge needed to cut hair or fabric.

• If your scissor blades are binding, adjust the screw.

• Left-handed people should look out for scissors designed especially for left handers – they are much more comfortable to use.

Screwdriver

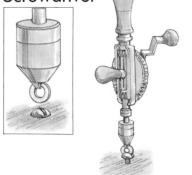

Here are some alternatives for those occasions when you lack a screwdriver.
• Tighten a steel washer into the chuck of a hand drill or brace and insert the edge into the screw slot. (This is also a good idea when you want to exert some extra leverage on a screw.) You can use a variable-speed power drill, too.
• Check penknives around the house. Some may have a screwdriver blade.
• A nail file can tighten a tiny screw – in spectacles, for example.
• If you do have screwdrivers available, always choose one that fits the screw slot comfortably. Remember that the old Phillips screws have now been replaced by Supadriv screws, which have a more sophisticated slot design.
• If you file a screwdriver tip, remember that the tip should be filed square, never to a point or wedge-shape. This ensures that the tip doesn't jump out of the slot when pressure is applied.
• To increase the leverage when removing a difficult screw, clamp a self-grip wrench to the blade of the screwdriver, then use the wrench as a lever.
• Invest in a set of jeweller's screwdrivers. They will prove invaluable for tiny screws.

Screws

• Attempts to remove a tight screw can often ruin the slot. If the head is above the surface, use a hacksaw to cut a new groove at a right angle to the original slot. Exert pressure evenly, not jerkily, with a screwdriver to ease out the screw.

• Or remove the screw by gripping the head with locking-grip pliers.
• Where a slot is ruined and you can't get a grip on the screw head, guess the size of screw shank and select a twist drill of the same size. Insert this into a power drill and use it to drill the head of the screw. Eventually the head will drop away. Remove any fitting, then turn out the screw shank with a mole grip. But be warned; there are some modern case-hardened screws which cannot be drilled out in this way.
• If a screw has rusted in place, try applying the tip of a hot soldering iron to the head. The heat will expand the screw head and may loosen the rust. Or try easing oil around the screw.

Sea-life stings

• If you don't know what has stung you, ask lifeguards or local people what is native to the area and treat your sting accordingly.
• Sea urchin spines can penetrate sandals and flippers. If one breaks your skin, it will probably cause redness, swelling and burning pain. Pull out any visible spines with tweezers. Wash with soap and water, then apply a hot-water compress and an antiseptic ointment or warm olive oil. If you feel intense pain, see a doctor.
• Treat a sea anemone sting like a jellyfish sting (see p.116).

Sea sickness

There's no cure for sea sickness once it strikes, but there are measures you can take to prevent it from happening or to relieve it.
• Take travel sickness pills half an hour before you start your journey. Check with your doctor or chemist that any medication you are already taking is compatible.
• Don't drink alcohol and don't travel on an empty stomach. Eat bland, easily digestible food.
• Try to keep yourself occupied by talking, playing games or listening to music.
• Go up on deck if possible. Fresh cool air and wind help to reduce nausea.

• Try eating crystallised ginger it settles the stomach.
• You can buy wrist bands with a little knob that presses on a point on the inside of the wrist just above the hand. These are said to be based on Chinese methods of treating illness by using pressure points. They are available from chemists.

Secondhand goods

• Before buying something secondhand look in magazines or newspapers which advertise secondhand goods to see how much similar objects are worth.
• Test out any electrical goods before buying them to check that they work.
• Even if you've made sure that the goods you are buying do work, have a dealer in those goods, or someone who specialises in repairing them, check that you haven't missed anything which might be potentially dangerous.
• Search any wooden objects or furniture carefully for signs of woodworm.
• Check upholstered furniture for fabric moth larvae and carpets and rugs for carpet beetle. It's best not to buy affected goods, however tempting the bargain, unless you know you can treat them quickly without introducing an infestation into your home.
• Test-drive a secondhand car and check carefully for rust, balanced suspension, worn tyres, up-to-date MoT certificate and obvious crash damage (see INSPECTING A USED CAR, p.276).
• Think hard about the honesty of the deal. If the goods are stolen and are traced back to you they may be seized from you without any compensation.
• Goods must be fit to sell and suitable for the purpose for which they are sold. If you inadvertently buy faulty secondhand goods, you have the right to a refund or compensation. See also FAULTY GOODS, p.78; REFUNDS, p.169.

Security blankets

It's natural for a small child to develop a close attachment to a special, cuddly object – even when it's worn and ugly. Don't take it away or substitute a newer, cleaner version (although it's wise to get a duplicate in case the original gets lost). Security blankets are often a substitute for thumb sucking, and generally prove easier to give up.

• If this precious object is accidentally left behind, say on holiday, explain that a holiday is a special time and that the blanket will be waiting when you return. Find a substitute to give some comfort: make a puppet out of a clean sock, or give your child something which smells comfortingly of you. See also BEDTIME RITUALS, p.19.

Seed germination

• For fast germination of pea and bean seeds, soak them in water overnight before planting. To speed the process even more, add a drop or two of detergent; it reduces the water's surface tension, helping it to penetrate the seed's coat. An easy way to soak seeds is to empty each seed packet into the individual cups of a plastic egg box, then fill each with the detergent solution.

Seed planting

Ensure proper spacing and eliminate the need for thinning seedlings with a homemade seed tape. An added bonus of this method is that the seeds will sprout faster.

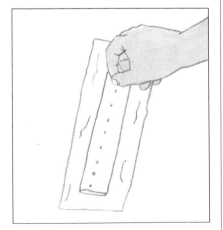

• Lay a strip of damp kitchen paper on top of a strip of plastic film, then set out the seeds on the paper at the intervals recommended on the seed packet.

Cover the seeds with another strip of damp kitchen paper, roll up the paper and plastic film together and put the roll into a plastic bag. Store this in a warm place (the top of the refrigerator is ideal).

As soon as roots begin to emerge, take the tape to the garden and unroll it onto a well-tilled bed, peeling the plastic away. Cover the seed strip with a fine layer of soil or sand and water thoroughly but gently. Don't worry about the paper – it acts as a mulch, preventing dehydration, and will soon dissolve to reveal a perfectly spaced row of young seedlings.

Self-adhesive hooks

To remove a self-adhesive hook from a tile, drip vinegar behind it. Scrape off any residue with your fingernail or a dull knife. On a painted or plastic surface soften stubborn residue with a warm rag or hair dryer. On unpainted surfaces use surgical spirit, methylated spirits, cleaning solvent, lacquer thinner, hair spray or nail-polish remover; test first on an inconspicuous area.

Sensitive skin

If your skin is easily irritated by the elements, cosmetic ingredients, chemicals in synthetic fabrics or by shaving, consider these sensible precautions.

• Stay away from alkaline soaps, facial masks, grainy cleansers, alcohol-based astringents and cosmetics, acetone products such as nail-polish remover, and anything with fragrance.

• Bathe in tepid or cool water, using mild unscented soap. Pat your skin dry, don't rub, then apply a moisturiser containing urea or lactic acid to your damp skin.

• 'Breathable' natural fabrics, such as cotton, linen and wool are the best choice for clothing, but if you prefer synthetics, launder them several times before wearing to remove potential irritants.

• Give extra protection to your hands when washing dishes or clothes by wearing a pair of cotton liners inside your rubber gloves.

• Don't assume products labelled 'for sensitive skin' are necessarily safe for you. Test a new line on a small area of your inner arm daily for a week; if your skin reacts in any way, look for another product.

Separating photographs

When two photographs, negatives or slides are stuck together, the only safe method of separating them is to use steam. It may take some time, so don't try to pull them apart or use anything like dental floss to separate them. Any sort of force is likely to damage the image.

Septic tank

Is the grass greener over your septic tank than the surrounding area? Worse still, are your drains backing up or smelling foul? If so, call a cleaning service and have your tank pumped out immediately.

If it's too late and your system backs up, whatever you empty or flush down a drain will back up into your lowest plumbing fixtures. (Don't add water – it will only make matters worse.) Your bathroom drains may seem clear, but if you use them, you'll cause an awful mess in any ground-floor sinks.

If the cleaning service can't come at once, a plumber may be able to dig down and break up the layer of semi-solid scum blocking the tank's inlet pipe, giving you what will probably be temporary restricted use of the plumbing.

Prevention

• If possible, measure the level of solid waste in your septic tank regularly by removing its cover and probing with a long pole. A dark stain on the pole's end deeper than 12-18in / 300-450mm means the tank needs pumping out. Generally, it should be emptied every 2 to 5 years (depending on the size of your tank and your family's plumbing demands), but have it checked in the first year.

• Keep all chemicals, including drain cleaners and commercial tank-cleaning compounds, out of your septic system.

• Instead of chemical bowl cleaners, add a gallon of vinegar to the water in the toilet bowl; let it sit for a few hours, then flush it away.

• To keep the decomposition process active, flush an ounce of dry yeast down the drain monthly.

• Don't pour liquid fat or grease down the kitchen drain.

• Never introduce cigarette ends, facial tissues, newspaper, paper towels, sanitary towels or any kind of wrapping material into your septic system.

Sex education

• Allow your child to bring up the subject of sex, and answer any questions briefly but factually. If you feel embarrassed, try not to let it show – it will make it harder for your child to ask questions in the future.

• Listen carefully to their questions. If your child asks where she came from, she might simply want to know the name of the hospital.

• Younger children can learn about sex through TV documentaries or books about animals being born. Perhaps you could visit a local farm to see the new spring lambs. For older children, use television plots or books to initiate personal chats about reproduction.

• As children grow older you can begin to communicate your own attitudes and values. Children need help in coping with their sexual feelings. Don't be scared of telling teenagers about your own problems at that age. If it is really difficult to talk frankly, write a letter describing the risks and responsibilities involving sexual behaviour. Or you can obtain literature from the education department of the Family Planning Association, 27-35 Mortimer Street, London WIN 7RJ, Tel. 0171-636 7866.

Sexual harassment

On the street

• People who shout obscenities, whisper unwanted endearments or make obscene gestures may be capable of physical violence. The best response is to ignore them completely and keep moving to a safe, well-lit place. If the offender pursues you, call the police.

• If you are constantly harassed at a particular building site, contact the contractor or the company constructing the building and put in a complaint.

At work

• Confront the harasser. Appeal to his or her professionalism and make it clear that you object to the advances. If they continue, send your tormentor a letter by recorded delivery, expressing your feelings and mentioning that such behaviour is against the law and that you may make an official complaint.

• Keep a dated, written record of all incidents. Save all notes, letters and your recorded postal delivery receipts.

• If necessary, file a written complaint with your employer. Most firms have a recognised grievance procedure with 'in-house' Equal Opportunities officers whose priority is to see you immediately. If the problem can't be solved in-house, and sometimes it can't, then your complaint may have to go to an Industrial Tribunal. This has to be within 3 months of the complaint being made.

• The main legal statute covering sexual harassment is the Sex Discrimination Act of 1974. This is further reinforced by EC legislation which deals with verbal and physical conduct.

• If you're a union member, your representative may handle the problem for you, but there can be divided loyalty if he also represents the person complained about. If so, contact the Central Office of Industrial Tribunals, 93 Ebury Street, London SW1 8RE, Tel. 0171-730 9161, and the Equal Opportunities Commission, Overseas House, Quay Street, Manchester M3 3HN, Tel. 0161-833 9244.

In a block of flats

• If a building employee is harassing you, send a letter of complaint to the landlord, the caretaker and the managing agent; keep a copy. If nothing is done or if one of the above is the problem, contact the local police.

• Document your case meticulously; write down exactly who said what to whom and when, and keep a note of any witnesses that were present while you were being harassed.

• Talk to your neighbours; if it is happening to others, perhaps you can take action as a group and give each other moral support. See also RAPE, p.167.

Shaded garden

If your garden lacks sunshine, don't give up on colour. Just think in terms of foliage rather than flowers. Here are some suggestions.

• Hostas – hardy perennials of the lily family – bear leaves in muted shades of blue, gold, green and white, with many interesting variegated forms. They thrive in a damp woodland setting. Many have attractive flowers and a few are sweetly scented.

• Vivid ground covers include the ornamental white dead nettles (*Lamium album*) with silver and green foliage and the variegated grasslike lily *Liriope muscari* 'Variegata', with leaves that are striped with green and white.

• Periwinkles, or vincas, are excellent shade plants, growing in quite damp conditions but being equally tolerant of drought once well established. Most have blue starry flowers, but there are some with mauve and white blossoms. The common kinds have green foliage, but there are some lovely variegated varieties as well.

Shaded lawns

The right choice of grass seed and a little extra care are all it takes to keep a shaded lawn full and green.

• Plant chewing fescue or creeping red fescue.

• To fill in bare spots, overseed with a fast-growing ryegrass. But you'll have to reseed it every spring, since rye won't last from year to year in the shade.

• Thin trees rather than remove them. A tree surgeon can remove 40 per cent of a tree's canopy without harming it. The extra light will benefit the grass underneath.

• Raise your mower blade to a height of 1½in/38mm before mowing a shaded part of the lawn; you'll leave more leaf surface.

• Water no more than once or twice a

week – and water thoroughly. Wetting just the surface of the soil encourages tree roots to grow upwards, where they compete with grass for water and nutrients. See also GRASS, p.98; LAWNS, p.121.

Sharing a home

• Choosing a flatmate or a lodger needs some care. When you interview a stranger, make sure you have a friend with you at the time whose judgment you trust. Chat about smoking, neatness, television, music and your social activities to make sure your habits and tastes are reasonably compatible.

• When you move in with a new flatmate, work out rules for bathroom times, overnight guests and dinner parties, TV and stereo noise, division of expenses including household costs and bills, housekeeping chores and refrigerator use, and how to keep the house secure.

• Arrange for itemised telephone bills, if possible. This will save endless haggling over the bill when it comes and avoid bad feeling.

• If you live with more than one person, put up a list of weekly household duties for each. The refrigerator door is a good place for the list.

• Develop an agreed method of airing problems and don't let annoyances fester. Humour can go a long way towards smoothing things out.

Sharks

If you are going on a seaside holiday somewhere where there are sharks, check with local inhabitants whether there is any danger of a shark attack before you go in the water. If there are lifeguards on the beach, ask them too.

• Stay out of the water if you have an open cut or scratch; sharks are thought to be attracted to blood.

• Avoid swimming near sewage outlets away from the shore; sharks are more likely to congregate there.

• Swim with at least one other person to keep watch for danger, and don't swim too far out to sea.

Sheet metal

If you need to cut a piece of sheet metal, perhaps to make a bracket for a broken arris rail (see p.78), try these methods.

• Use a hacksaw. Put the sheet on a flat bench or table with the saw line slightly overlapping the table edge. Position the blade at a 45° angle and keep the teeth in constant contact with the metal. Support a large sheet on another table or bench or ask someone to hold it. Wear work gloves – cut metal is sharp.

• Use a cold chisel to cut a small piece. Lock the metal in a vice with the cutting line level with the top of the jaw. Hold the chisel against the edge of the metal at a 45° angle to the jaw top and hammer it along the length of the piece. The waste piece will curl away.

• You can also slice a large piece of sheet metal with a cold chisel. Lay the metal on a hardwood bench or table with the cut line even with the edge; then clamp a length of straight steel or hardwood on top. Hold the chisel at a 45° angle to the bench or table edge and hammer along the length of the metal. The scrap should peel down towards the floor.

Shellfish

• Scrubbed mussels and clams will purge themselves of grit or sand if left for an hour or so in cold salted water with a sprinkling of oatmeal or flour.

• To open oysters, clams and scallops, use a strong thin knife with a blunt rounded tip, preferably an oyster knife. Oyster knives can be bought from good fishmongers or kitchen supply shops. Hold the shell in a cloth in the palm of

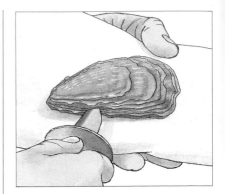

one hand and force the blade between the two parts. Run the blade around the inner edge of the shell to sever both muscles, then twist the knife to prise open the oyster.

• Mussels will open quite easily when cooked in the steam from their own juices, or with a little liquid or white wine. Place mussels in a saucepan, add a glass of white wine, cover the pan and place over a high heat for 4-5 minutes. Shake the pan frequently. When removing the cooked mussels, discard any that do not open. See also MUSSELS, p.138.

Shelves

• The most useful material for shelving is veneered chipboard, most commonly available with wood or smooth white plastic finishes. This material is not strong, so shelves do need support at about 16in / 400mm intervals. For extra support if they are to hold heavy items such as books, run a batten along the wall at the back of each shelf. Or make it stronger by gluing a hardwood strip, the same thickness as the shelf, to the shelf's front edge.

• To make a removable shelf, mount folding brackets on the wall. Pull them down and place a board on top when needed.

• Build a set of shelves from boards and paint tins. Paint the tins or cover them with matching wrapping or wallpaper.

• Clay flowerpots work well for medium-weight loads. They look especially nice if you top each 'column' of pots with a potted plant.

• For a colourful look, use glass blocks or large jars as shelf supports, filling the jars with marbles or some other bright objects.

• Hang shelves with rope from a beam or hooks attached to the ceiling or wall. Drill pairs of holes at the ends of the shelving boards and at all support points, 1 in / 25 mm from the edges. Knot the end of a length of rope for each hole and slip a washer onto it; then feed the ropes up through the holes in the shelf and knot them again on top. Measure up for the next shelf and repeat the process. Just be sure that when you hang the shelves the ropes are firmly anchored; they may have to bear a lot of weight.

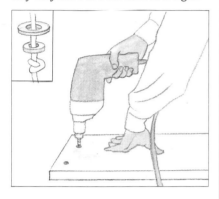

Shiny clothing

• If the knees or elbows on worsted-garments become shiny from wear, try steaming them. Hang them in the bathroom while running a hot bath. Make sure you close the bathroom door.

• To prevent a sheen appearing, press heavy cotton, wool, acetate, rayon, linen, permanent-press and dark fabrics on the wrong side. Or use a damp cloth.

• To get a high sheen on polished cotton, add half an envelope of plain gelatine to the last rinse.

Shoe heels

• Touch up scuffed heels quickly with a waterproof felt-tip pen. On white heels, white toothpaste acts as a temporary finish. For more permanent camouflage, shoe repair shops and haberdashery counters sell special heel paints in a wide range of colours.

• Protect and shine up wooden heels with polyurethane varnish. If they're

badly scratched, sand and stain with furniture finish. You can also fill badly pitted heels with plastic wood.

• Ask your local shoe repair shop about the full range of shoe repairs they can do. Heel shapes and heights can be changed, linings renewed, and holes and splits patched unobtrusively. For details of specialist shoe repairers in your area, contact The Society of Master Shoe Repairers Ltd, St Crispin's House, 21 Station Road, Desborough, Northants NN14 2SA, Tel. 01536-760374.

Shoehorn

If you need an emergency shoehorn, use a tablespoon, a soupspoon or a rubber spatula instead. Or use the narrow end of a silk tie or an old telephone card.

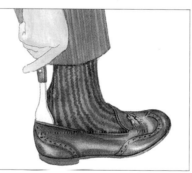

Shoelaces

• Have your spare shoelaces disappeared? Use a length of string, wool or twine instead. For women's shoes, ribbon makes a pretty substitute, especially if it's lace or satin.

• Here's how to retie a broken shoelace. Remove the lace, join the two pieces together with a reef knot, and estimate where the knot will fall in the laced shoe. Put the knot there and lace from that point outwards in both directions.

Shoe polish

• At a pinch, you can shine your leather shoes with floor wax or spray-on window cleaner.

• If you have run out of polish for dark brown and black shoes and boots use spray-on furniture polish.

• Rub real patent leather with milk – this really brings up the shine. Use spray-on glass cleaner for plastic patent. A thin film of petroleum jelly works well too.

• For a high shine, squeeze a few drops of lighter fluid into your solid boot wax – it will spread more easily and penetrate better. Or rub lemon juice into the leather after it's polished, then buff.

• If you don't have a soft cloth to buff shoes with, use cotton wool or kitchen paper.

• To clean suede shoes, scrape off mud and remove excess dust with a vacuum cleaner attachment. Use a special suede cleaner or shampoo and follow the manufacturer's instructions. If the pile on suede shoes has flattened, hold the shoes near the steam from a kettle, and then brush the skin gently to raise the pile. Leave to dry

• You can dye light suede shoes bright colours and black with dyes that are specially formulated for suede. Light leather shoes can also be dyed, but dye colours are limited to black, brown and navy. If you want to change dark coloured leather to light colours, use shoe paints. These can also be used for plastic and fabric shoes, and come in a wide range of colours, but are not suitable for suede.

• Use a cotton bud to get polish in that space between the uppers and the soles.

• Cover spots on black suede by sponging a little black coffee on them; on white suede, use chalk.

• Take spots off the white rubber on trainers with steel wool dipped in detergent.

• If your polish gets hard, heat it in the oven or add a few drops of turpentine or white spirit to soften it.

• To keep your hands clean while polishing shoes, wear old gloves or cut the pockets out of old trousers and use them as mittens.

Shoes

• Are your leather shoe soles lethally slippery? Sand them with coarse grade glasspaper, scratch them deeply with a fork or stick two strips of masking tape across them in the form of a cross.

• If you need a temporary patch on a hole in your shoe sole, clean the area and cover with a piece of carpet tape or an inner tube patch.

• Insoles can be excellent for improving the comfort and fit of shoes and boots. Different insole styles and materials range from thermal, quilted and fur fabric types for warmth, to long-lasting leather insoles and even remedial examples for back pain relief.

• Most insoles are impregnated with a special anti-bacteria formula. Fitting specially treated insoles inside sports shoes and trainers is a good idea. You can also keep insoles fresh by spraying them with a deodorant spray for shoes.

• Spray-on water and stain repellents are essential for delicate suede, leather and fabric footwear. But remember, these protective finishes must be resprayed every time shoes are cleaned. Avoid homemade stain remover remedies – they may turn delicate fashion leathers dark and make the surface feel sticky.

• To prevent leather shoes from cracking after they've become wet, apply a liberal coating of saddle soap while they're still damp. Dry away from the heat, then remove any excess saddle soap.

• Soften dried leather shoes by wetting the outside with warm water and rubbing the leather with castor oil, glycerine or paraffin.

Magic slippers

Since the earliest times, various peoples have regarded shoes as symbols of fertility and prosperity. In ancient Egypt, Palestine and Assyria, for example, the seller of land gave a sandal to the buyer as a gesture of goodwill and a seal of purchase.

In India, an old shoe placed upside-down on the roof assured a couple good fortune.

Childless Chinese women borrowed shoes from the shrine of the mother goddess to help them become pregnant.

For good luck, the Scots threw a shoe after a sailor departing for his first voyage or after anyone starting a new venture.

In Anglo-Saxon weddings the father of the bride transferred his authority to the groom by handing him one of his daughter's shoes – it was this ritual that gave rise to the modern-day custom of attaching old shoes to the bridal carriage.

Shopping addiction

Don't think that compulsive shopping is something to be laughed off. It's not. A steady flow of credit card bills can put you in serious debt more quickly than you can imagine. If you're not a compulsive shopper but still feel that you should pull the reins in, try these tips.

• Don't ever shop without a list – and stick to it.

• Avoid sales; the temptation to overbuy is too great.

• Keep a small notebook where you list everything you buy, even the morning paper. You'll find it harder to spend if you know you must write each purchase down.

• If you find yourself buying things you neither need nor can afford, talk to your bank manager or a financial adviser from the Citizens' Advice Bureau about getting a realistic budget. See also YOUR ANNUAL BUDGET PLANNER, p.241.

Shopping lists

Follow this suggestion in order to speed up your weekly household shop – and you may well save money too, as it should curb any tendencies towards impulse buying.

• Make a list of the items you buy regularly; arrange them in the order in which they're set out in the supermarket. If the fresh produce area is normally your first stop, for example, list the fruits and vegetables you routinely buy, such as apples, oranges, carrots and lettuce; then leave some blanks for less frequently purchased goods.

Make lots of photocopies of the list and always keep one on the refrigerator door; mark items as soon as you run out of them.

When you go to the supermarket, make sure you remember to take the list with you. That way, your shopping is organised as soon as you walk in.

Shower curtains and doors

• Make your plastic shower curtain more pliable by dipping it in warm water to which you have added a few drops of oil.

• Protect your new shower curtain by hanging the old one behind it to take the soaking. Wash both frequently to prevent mildew.

• To remove mildew (see p.134) from cotton duck shower curtains, use a solution of chlorine bleach and water.

• To remove water and soap marks from glass shower doors, rub with a sponge dampened with vinegar. Or gently scrape with a craft knife.

• If the shower doors don't slide smoothly, first clean the tracks with a brush and dull knife or screwdriver; use a cotton swab or toothbrush to reach nooks and crannies. Then wash with ammonia or a strong detergent solution. After the tracks dry, spray with a silicone lubricant. (But protect the bathtub – the spray will make it slippery.)

Shyness

Shyness can be embarrassing in social situations, but keep in mind that you are not alone in feeling shy. Many people experience it, since most of us are a mixture of shyness and confidence. There are steps you can take to overcome shyness, however.

• Make a note of every time you feel shy, including who was involved, what your thoughts and feelings were, and how you behaved. Look at your notes after a while to see if there is a pattern you can identify. Do certain people make you feel shy, or certain subjects or situations? Why do you think you are reacting to them in this way?

• If you feel shy in front of figures of authority, tell yourself you are as worthwhile a person as they are – they just do a different job.

• If you want to ask a question, tell yourself you are not a fool. Your question is worth asking, and you have a right to be informed.

• If you feel shy because you think people won't accept you or won't like you, remind yourself that this is probably not true, and doesn't really matter anyway.

• Look people in the eye and try to speak with greater confidence.

• Think about how you would like to behave in certain situations, and then try to carry it out.

• Think about the questions you may be asked at a social gathering, and plan your answers. Plan, too, some questions that you can ask to get the conversation going.

• Find someone who looks as shy as you feel and try to strike up a conversation with her. You'll soon forget your own feelings of shyness. See also SMALL TALK, p.186.

Sibling rivalry

• After a new baby arrives, give each older child some private time with you every day, away from the others. Use this time to focus on each one's strengths and accomplishments.

• Never compare one child with another and don't have favourites.

• Be fair. Make them take turns over who decides which programme to watch, or who sits beside the windows of the car.

• To encourage affection between siblings, arrange for them to enjoy things in common, such as building a make-believe house in the garden. Shared experiences help build a friendship that can withstand occasional angry flare-ups.

• Encourage older children to use their experience to help younger ones. Commend their cooperation.

Sieves and colanders

• Improvise a makeshift strainer for liquids from the legs of a clean pair of tights, or a stocking. Stretch the fabric across the bottom of a wide-necked funnel, hold it in place and pour.

• Punch holes in the bottom of a foil plate if you don't have a colander to hand.

• Use a fine sieve to smooth out the lumps in icing sugar; just push it through the holes with a metal spoon. The same remedy works for lumpy custard, white sauce or gravy.

Silencer noise

A small hole in your silencer probably won't do any damage, but the noise is offensive and probably illegal. Worse, poisonous carbon monoxide can seep into your car. Get the leak fixed as soon as possible.

Temporary repairs to small holes (under $1/8$ in / 3 mm wide) in the silencer or exhaust pipe can be made with exhaust paste (available at motor accessory shops). For larger holes (up to 1 in / 25 mm) you can buy inexpensive heat-resistant 'bandages'. At a pinch you may be able to cover the hole temporarily by slicing open a tin and holding it in place with wire or clamps, but such a patch probably won't last more than 50 miles / 80 km.

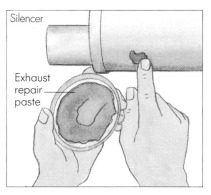

Silencer

Exhaust repair paste

Silk flowers

• To get more blooms for your money and to have greater flexibility in your arrangements, buy stems with more than one flower. Cut off the blossoms

and make a stem for each by twisting wire onto the cut end and covering it with florist's green tape.

• To clean, dust each blossom with a soft brush, or use the low setting on your hair dryer, or wipe with a damp cloth.

• For a more thorough cleaning, disassemble the arrangement and swish each flower in warm water and mild detergent. Rinse well and stand in tall vases or jars to dry. Or have the flowers dry-cleaned.

• To give your flowers a simulated fragrance, hide a perfume sample card in the arrangement.

Silver

With proper care, you can prevent your silver tarnishing, pitting or scratching. Be especially gentle with silver plate, as the plating wears off easily. Whenever possible, wash silver tableware by hand with a mild detergent.

• If you want to put it in the dishwasher, make sure the silver contains no other metal which might tarnish, and dry immediately with a chamois leather or soft towel. Dishwasher powder can pit silver, however.

• Don't leave silver overnight with food on it. If you can't wash it right away, at least rinse off all the food.

• If you don't have specially treated cloth bags or a silver chest for storage, thoroughly dry each piece, then wrap it in acid-free tissue paper.

• Never let rubber come in contact with silver – it causes it to tarnish.

• Don't let egg, fruit juice, olives, perfume, toilet water, salad dressing, salt, sulphur or vinegar stay on silver for any length of time – they cause stains and corrosion.

• Clean silver salt cellar lids frequently to keep them from corroding. To remove any corrosion caused by salt, soak the cellar for 5 minutes in a solution of hot vinegar and salt, and then wash and dry.

• If you put cut flowers in silver bowls, change the water often to prevent deposits at the water line. Remove the flowers as soon as they begin to wilt.

• If you keep fruit in a silver container, use a liner.

• If you run out of silver polish, place the silver in a bowl of hot water with a strip of aluminium foil and a teacup of washing soda. Leave for half an hour or so, until clean. Rinse and buff with a soft cloth.

• Polish silver with a gentle circular motion without too much pressure. Use a soft brush to get into hard-to-reach cracks.

• Use a pipe cleaner with silver polish on it to clean between fork prongs. Or put some polish on a string and pull it back and forth between the prongs.

• To remove minor scratches, rub a cream silver polish on with a soft cloth and polish with a chamois cloth.

Silverfish

These silvery insects may be found when you remove a book from a bookshelf or shift a pile of papers. They live on the starch in paper and the glue in bookbindings. Their presence may also indicate damp in your house.

• Reduce the condensation, if any, in the room; if there is condensation it will damage the books. Check for rising damp and leaky plumbing.

• Remove books from shelves and spray the shelves with an insecticide for crawling insects. Then flick through the pages to check for infestation and to air the books thoroughly.

Skewers

• If you've prepared the ingredients for shish kebab but can't find your skewers, cut new ones from unpainted wire coat hangers. Or look in the toolbox for some heavy-gauge wire. Or slice the food into small pieces and stir-fry it instead. (Just be sure to cook the meat – especially pork and chicken – longer than the vegetables.)

• If you use a single-pronged skewer, you may find that when you turn it the food doesn't turn with it. Solve the problem by using two-pronged skewers. Or simply thread the ingredients onto two skewers instead of one.

• When camping, improvise skewers by peeling the bark off thin green twigs and sharpening the ends.

• Use skewers to speed up the cooking time of baked potatoes. Clean the potatoes as usual and then push a skewer through each one lengthways. Or cook several potatoes on one long skewer.

Skidding

Don't slam on the brakes – it only makes the skid worse. Instead, take your foot off the accelerator and turn the wheel gently in the direction of the skid. When the front wheels start to grip the road surface, begin to steer again (but be prepared to counter another skid in the opposite direction). Very gently apply light accelerator pressure.

Ski goggles

To keep lenses from misting up, try one of these tricks.

• Spray the inside with shaving cream or furniture polish, then wipe clean.

• Wet the inside with a 50-50 mixture of liquid detergent and water; wipe dry.

• Rub the inside with a cut raw potato.

• Spread a thin layer of toothpaste inside the lenses, then wipe it off.

• For a quick demisting, spit into the lenses and rub the spittle around.

Ski story

Remnants of skis more than 4000 years old have been found in Sweden, and rock carvings of hunters on skis found in Norway can be dated as far back as 2000 BC. The first skis were made from the bones of large animals and strapped to the feet with leather thongs. Later skis were made from wooden boards.

In the 10th century, Norwegian tax collectors used skis to reach outlying districts (or perhaps to catch up with recalcitrant taxpayers). By the 12th century Norway had ski troops armed with bows and arrows, and by the 15th century Sweden, Finland, Russia and Poland had followed suit.

It wasn't until the 19th century that skis were used for fun. The Norwegians took the lead, racing one another down snowy hills – often trying not to spill the mug of beer they held in one hand! But the actual sport of downhill skiing was invented by an Austrian, Mathias Zdarsky, in 1896. The first skis and bindings to assist the turning that is needed for downhill skiing were developed by an Englishman, E.C. Richardson.

The world's first Alpine ski race was initiated by Sir Arnold Lunn, and was held in 1911 at Montana, Switzerland. In these early competitions, all the skiers raced down a wide course together, with the first past the post winning the race. This method was soon replaced by the safer one of timing each contestant at 1 minute intervals.

The largest ski resorts in Britain are found at Aviemore, in Scotland, but since snowfall is not that predictable or heavy in Britain, most British skiers go to the Continent. However, dry ski slopes are popular here as a training and practice ground for skiing on snow.

Skiing

• You don't need an expensive ski rack to carry your skis to dry or snow slopes. If your car has a standard roof rack, you can fasten skis to it with three bungee cords, one at each end and one in the middle. Hook the cords to one side of the rack, then circle them completely around the skis and hook to the other side. To keep the skis from scratching the car roof, tape kitchen sponges on the underside at each end.

• Remove your boot liners and dry them before storing boots at the end of the season. Wash the outsides of the boots, replace the dry liners, and fasten the boots before you put them away (fastening helps them keep their shape). Mice and spiders like to nest in ski boots, so stuff yours with plenty of tightly packed, wadded-up newspaper.

Conditioning exercises A few weeks before the ski season starts, use these exercises to get in shape:

• Chair sit. Press your back against a wall and lower yourself down as though sitting on a chair. Hold the position for 15 seconds. Repeat six times a day.

• Knee stretch. With your feet together, bend your knees to a half crouch. Hold this position for 30 seconds. Repeat several times a day. See also STRENGTH-ENING EXERCISES, p.196.

Skipping rope

A brisk 10-minute workout with a skipping rope can be as good an exercise as a 30-minute jog. You can use a length of clothesline (about 10ft/3m will do – measure it by stepping on the middle; the ends should come to about mid-chest).

For handles, tie a knot in each end of the rope and wrap plastic insulating tape 4-5in/100-125mm in front of each knot. At a pinch (but only if you skipped as a child and remember how), you can jump with a phantom rope – no rope at all.

Always skip on a carpet or mat, and always wear cushioned aerobic or jogging shoes with good arch support. Start with the rope hanging to the floor behind you, your arms angled out 6-10in/150-250mm from your hips. Twirl the rope forward from the elbows. Start skipping with your feet together; as you gain in skill, try alternate-foot jumps. Your feet should come only a few inches off the floor. For variation, lift your knees high in front or kick up high behind.

Skip for 30 seconds, then rest for 30 seconds. Do this ten times. Gradually increase the skip and rest times to 60 seconds each, for a total of 20 minutes, then gradually lengthen the total time until your heart rate is in your aerobic target range for 20 minutes. See also FIT-NESS BUILDING, p.84.

Sledges and toboggans

Occasionally in Britain the snowfall is heavy enough to make it possible to go tobogganing. Here are some ideas for homemade sledges.

• Flatten some large corrugated cardboard boxes to sit on. For a toboggan (which seats several people), use a refrigerator-sized box.

• Or you can slide down a hill on a tray, a dustbin lid (without handles) or the inner tube of a car tyre.

• You may have an inflatable plastic lilo which has been punctured and is sitting in the loft waiting for you to throw it away; uninflated, it will make a perfectly good sledge.

• Sheets of sturdy plastic, such as an old shower curtain, will also make good sledges.

• Unless the snow is very deep and the area is free from rocks and tree stumps, make sure you use a firm base for your sledge, to avoid injury.

Sleeping bag

If you have two blankets, you can improvise a sleeping bag. Fold one in thirds lengthwise and pin the free edge with large safety pins. Then fold up 3-4in/75-100mm at the bottom and pin it. Lay it on the other blanket, as shown, and fold the second blanket over the first, pinning the edges together. Tuck the bottom under.

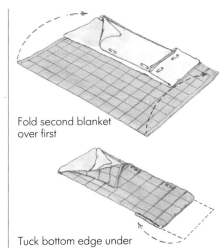

Fold second blanket over first

Tuck bottom edge under

Slides

• You can scan your slides more easily if you store them in plastic viewpacks instead of boxes. Viewpacks are plastic transparent sheets with pockets to hold each slide. The 35mm packs usually take 24 slides per sheet; the more expensive kind have a dust cover. They can often be hung in a filing cabinet like suspension files.

• For safe storage, slides should be kept in a cool, dry place – not the attic or the cellar. Heat and humidity are the enemies of colour dyes in slides and prints.

• Clean dusty slides without scratching by using a soft camel-hair brush, the kind that's used to clean camera lenses. Dust lightly and gently, starting from the centre of the slide.

Sliding glass doors

• To prevent children and guests from walking into closed doors, stick on two rows of transfers about 3ft/1m above the floor.

• To stop birds from flying into the glass, hang chimes outside the door.

• To insulate glass doors, buy a roll of special reflective film. This is applied wet, and squeegeed into position, where it forms a perfectly clear but reflective surface. It also acts as a safety measure, further increasing the impact resistance of the glass.

• Add security to the door by fitting a special sliding door bolt to each frame. This will prevent the door from being moved or lifted from its frame.

Slings

• Loop a towel or long scarf around an injured arm; pin or tie the ends securely around the victim's neck.
• Put a fairly tight jacket on the victim, leaving the injured arm out of its sleeve. Then button or zip the jacket around the arm, elevating the hand 3in/75mm above the elbow.
• Put an oversize, long-sleeved shirt, jacket or cardigan on the victim; support the injured arm by pulling up the bottom of the garment as shown and buttoning it at the top.

Slips

• If your full slip has become worn at the top, cut it in half, sew elastic into the waist and create a new half-slip.
• At a pinch, you can improvise a full slip, albeit a short one, by pinning it to the bottom of your bra.
• If your white slip is a dingy grey and bleach doesn't whiten it, darken it. Soak it in cold, strong, black tea until it's a shade darker than you want. Rinse in cold water and leave it to dry.
• Prevent nylon slips from going grey with correct washing – use the right temperature and quantity of detergent, and always separate all whites from coloured clothes.
• If your slip constantly rides up, sew felt or trim around the inside hem to give it weight. Or wear it inside-out. See also STATIC ELECTRICITY, p.193.

Slugs and snails

• Spread a circle of ash or grit around seedlings. Slugs and snails don't like them and will keep away.
• Sprinkle salt on slugs to kill them. Stage an evening raid in the garden, salt cellar in hand; sprinkle each slug once, then again in 5 minutes.
• Slugs and snails can be easily captured in an empty half grapefruit inverted on the soil. Leave it overnight and they will have congregated inside. See also GARDEN PESTS, p.94.

Small claims court

Do you have a small legal claim that isn't worth the time and expense of a lawyer? In a small claims court you can act as your own lawyer and collect sums of up to £3000. The following procedures apply to English small claims courts – those in Scotland are slightly different.
• You can issue a complaint in any county court, but the case is likely to be transferred to the defendant's local county court if the claim is defended.
• Get details and a 'plaint form' from your local county court office. Its address should be in the telephone book. Complete this and submit it with a small fee.
• Once you've filed the complaint, the court clerk will write to the defendant. Check that you have the right address.
• If you are claiming a debt, you can ask the court to award judgment without a hearing, unless the defendant files a defence. If damages are claimed, or a defence is filed, a hearing will be needed. The clerk will assign a date.
• If there is a hearing, the clerk will ask that it be referred to arbitration, rather than go before a judge in court. This is an informal hearing, chaired by a district judge, sitting as an arbitrator, where your case will be heard quickly and with a minimum of formality. The winner cannot recover the cost of legal representation, but awards may be made to cover loss of earnings and experts' fees.
• If there is a hearing, prepare your case beforehand. You need to take all relevant evidence with you, such as receipts, letters and legal agreements. If items are damaged, bring them or take photographs. If witnesses can help, ask them to attend. If they can't, ask if a written statement will be accepted.
• At the arbitration hearing, the arbitrator will explain the procedure. As the plaintiff, you may be asked to start. Explain your case, and the evidence to prove it, briefly and clearly. Do not provide information not directly relevant to the points in dispute. If asked questions, answer them directly and honestly. If you can't remember something, say so. Do not be bullied into agreeing with something that is not true. When the defendant states the defence, you may ask any relevant questions and note the answers. Do not repeat yourself.
• If you win your case and the defendant does not pay the amount due, when ordered, the court will advise on steps to enforce the decision. Decisions cannot be enforced if the defendant has no resources to pay. Check this before your case proceeds.

Small talk

If you get tongue-tied at parties and in other social situations, try these tips to make chit-chat easier:
• Start with a compliment – it gets the ball rolling on a pleasant note.
• Ask the other person about her hobbies rather than discussing your own interests.
• Enquire how the other person knows the host.
• Ask the other person's opinion of something. Try not to be too controversial – sport, films, books and celebrities are generally safe bets.
• Cultivate an inoffensive exit line, such as 'I'm just going to put down my drink. Perhaps we'll meet up later on', or 'I must see how my children are getting on upstairs'.

Smoke detectors

• The best location for a home smoke detector is on or near a ceiling close to the sleeping area, away from corners, windows and doors. The top of a stair-well is also good.

• Never paint your smoke detector. Twice a year (perhaps at the same time you change your clocks for daylight saving time), dust or vacuum it and change the battery.

• If cooking causes false alarms, put a shower cap over the detector while you're in the kitchen. It's obtrusive enough that you'll remember to take it off right after you've finished cooking.

Smoking

Stopping smoking isn't easy, but it may be one of the most rewarding things you ever do. If you've failed before, the following suggestions may help you.

• Investigate your options – from 'cold turkey' and nicotine chewing gum to acupuncture (in which a small needle is left in your ear), videotapes and self-help group programmes. Nicotine patches are available through the NHS and work by releasing small amounts of nicotine into the system through the skin.

• Be prepared for withdrawal symptoms. Anxiety, restlessness, irritability, lethargy, impatience, confusion and lack of concentration are common. So are coughing, headaches, insomnia and appetite swings. Take a brisk walk or do aerobic exercises to make you forget about your withdrawal symptoms and to burn energy.

• Join forces with another smoker who wants to stop and give each other moral support.

• Enlist a former smoker to help you through the rough times and focus you on the benefits of stopping.

• Get rid of all ashtrays, matches and lighters. Spend more time in places where you can't smoke.

• Get your teeth cleaned by a dental hygienist; resolve to keep them free of nicotine stains.

• Keep your mouth and hands busy. Chew sugarless gum, nibble raw vegetables and fruits, drink liquids through a straw; play with worry beads or an 'executive toy'.

• Put the money you used to spend on cigarettes in a special bank account; use the proceeds to reward yourself for every week you succeed.

• If you fail, try again. Many smokers need three or four tries.

Snakebites

Take the following steps if you think someone has been bitten by a poisonous snake:

• Carefully lay the casualty down on the ground and place him in the recovery position (see p.168).

• Wash the bite with soap and water; wipe away from the wound. Don't put ice on it.

• Immobilise the bitten limb with a splint (see p.191), and keep it at or below heart level.

• If the casualty becomes unconscious, place him in the recovery position and make sure his airway is clear (see p.168).

• If breath becomes laboured or fails, apply artificial respiration (see p.67).

• Seek medical aid or get the casualty to a hospital. Remember, you will need to give a detailed description of the snake to help identify the appropriate serum.

• Only one of Britain's three native snakes are poisonous – the adder. Its bite is rarely fatal, however.

Snoring

• Caused by a loss of muscle tension in the jaw and tongue, snoring can sometimes be prevented by raising the head of your bed on bricks or concrete blocks (extra pillows won't work).

• Don't take anything that might relax the muscles in your air passage, including alcohol, tranquillisers, sleeping pills and antihistamines.

• If you snore only when sleeping on your back, sew or tape a large marble or a tennis ball to the back of your pyjama

---

'A little night music'

The novelist Anthony Burgess once noted 'Laugh and the whole world laughs with you; snore and you sleep alone.'

Almost half the adult population snores occasionally; a quarter are habitual snorers. Problem snoring is more common in men, but women and children snore too.

Notable snorers from the past include Winston Churchill, George IV and several US presidents, all known to be nocturnal nuisances.

The highest measured snore level was recorded in 1987 at the University of British Columbia in Vancouver, Canada. Forty-year-old Mark Thompson Hebbard was monitored by a decibel meter placed 24in/610mm above his head, and reached a level of 90 decibels. (The noise level set by Vancouver traffic bylaws is 80 decibels.)

While snorers have tried everything from surgery to self-hypnosis to jaw-clamping chin straps, a dependable cure has yet to be found.

top. Or add a pocket in which to put such an object.

• Try strengthening the jaw and tongue muscles with these exercises. Grip a pencil between your teeth for 10 minutes before going to sleep; firmly press your tongue against your lower teeth for 2 minutes; and press your jaw with your hand while resisting, forcing your jaw to press back.

• If you or your sleeping partner stops breathing for long periods in between snoring loudly, consult a doctor.

Snorkelling masks

• To prevent your mask from clouding up, spit in it; rub the spittle around and rinse the mask.

• To clear the snorkel tube of water as you ascend after a breath-held dive, tilt your head well back and exhale just as your mask breaks the surface of the water. Keep exhaling as you roll your head forward to continue snorkelling.

• If your breathing tube fills with water, don't breathe in. Wait until the top of the tube is above the surface, then blow the water out.

Snow blindness

Skiers and people who go out walking in the snow risk the corneas of their eyes being damaged by ultraviolet rays reflected off the snow.

• Whenever you're out in the snow – even on cloudy or foggy days – wear specially coated sunglasses (preferably with side shields) that keep out ultraviolet rays.

• Alternatively, make yourself a pair of 'Eskimo-style' snow glasses. Cut a strip of cardboard about 12 in / 300 mm long and bend it lengthways. Cut two slits along the fold for your eyes, and a notch for your nose. Attach a piece of elastic, string or ribbon to each side of the strip. Bend it to fit your face and tie behind your head. Don't try to flatten the cardboard on your face – it will provide more shade for your eyes if it is at an angle.

• If you want to go out into the snow but have no protective glasses, blacken your cheeks, nose and the area around your eyes with soot, if possible. The darkened area helps to deflect the ultraviolet rays.

• If your eyes start to feel irritated and gritty 3 to 5 hours after being out in the snow without protection, or if you're having difficulty detecting variations in the level of the ground, you may be suffering from snow blindness. In this case, you should stay out of the sun for a few days to avoid any further damage.

• If your eyes hurt so much that you don't want to open them, cover them with cold compresses and rest in a dark room. Ask someone to get medical help – you should have your eyes checked out by a doctor or optician as soon as possible. To prevent infection, don't rub your eyes. With prompt treatment, you should recover within a few days.

Snowed-in car

If you're ever trapped in a blizzard, stay in your car and wait for help.

• Before the snow gets too deep, clear a space around the exhaust to let carbon monoxide escape when you run the engine and heater.

• Get whatever you need from the boot into the passenger compartment; look for a tool, such as a jack handle or an umbrella, to clear an air passage if snow buries the car.

• Keep warm. Put on all available clothing and cover yourself with blankets; for more insulation, stuff newspaper inside clothing. Wear a hat, or wrap your head with a scarf; you lose heat more quickly from your head than from the rest of your body. To conserve fuel, run the heater for no more than 10 minutes per hour. (Open a window slightly on the side away from drifting snow to let carbon monoxide escape.)

• Stay awake. Don't drink alcohol; it causes drowsiness and cools the body, making you more susceptible to hypothermia. Be active – stretch, flex your muscles, wiggle your fingers and toes.

• Limit your use of the radio and lights to conserve battery power.

• If other cars are snowbound near you, join forces to sing songs or play quizzes. More people in a car will keep it warmer, boost everyone's morale and encourage you to stay awake.

Snow shovelling

• Just before a snowfall, spread a little sand, rock salt or cat litter on steps, paths and driveways to prevent snow from sticking (see ICY PATHS, p.112).

• Don't lift snow; push it. If you must lift, bend your knees and keep your lower back straight. Carry the loaded shovel close to your body.

• Start shovelling as soon as 1-2 in / 25-50 mm of snow falls on the ground and never let more than 2 in / 50 mm accumulate.

• To avoid pulling a back or shoulder muscle, warm up indoors with a few minutes of light callisthenics and stretching exercises (see p.197).

• Use a small snow shovel or fill only half of a large one. For hard-packed snow use a garden shovel.
• To keep snow from sticking to a shovel, cover it with two thick coats of car wax.

Cold facts about igloos

For most of us, snow is snow, but to the Inuit, or Eskimo, snow is so important that their language contains more than a dozen words to describe its various forms. Few Inuit build igloos these days, but those that still go hunting build them as temporary homes while they are away from their settlements.

Perhaps the most useful form of ice is a solid sheet, created when snow from a single storm freezes. This is the only kind suitable for building an igloo. The Inuit clear away the soft snow on top of the ice sheet and draw the outline of the house – a circle measuring 9-15ft/2.7-4.6m.

Standing inside this circle the housebuilder cuts blocks of ice and places them along the outline in spiralling rows upwards, pressing them together to ensure a snug fit. Meanwhile his assistant plasters any cracks on the exterior with fine, soft snow. After an entrance has been made, an air vent in the ceiling and a window of clear, freshwater ice to admit light are added.

Socks

• If holes always appear in the same place on your socks, check your feet for rough spots – pumicing them may save your socks. Check your shoes, too.
• If your socks won't stay up, you may be drying them on too hot a setting, which damages the elastic fibres.
• Where do socks disappear to so mysteriously? We don't know, but here are a few ways to cope. Before washing, put all your socks in a string bag with a zip or tie the pairs together. Or buy socks of the same style and colour in quantity – you may even get a discount. Then you'll never have to worry about pairing them up.
• If several people in your household wear socks that look alike, mark the toes with small coloured stitches or initial them with indelible ink.
• Athletes are less likely to get blisters if they wear high-quality socks made of high-bulk synthetics like Orlon and polypropylene. They cushion the foot and draw perspiration away from the skin. Or buy socks specially designed for your sport. Aerobic socks are padded at the heel, the ball of the foot and the toes; ski socks along the shin.

Soft focus

• To add a misty, soft-focus quality to a photograph, shoot the picture through a nylon stocking, or one leg from a pair of nylon tights, stretched tightly over the lens with a rubber band.
• Or simply breathe on the lens just before taking the picture.
• You could also spread petroleum jelly onto the filter. Wipe it off afterwards with a soft tissue.

Soft drink can

If the ring-pull tab on a can breaks off and you don't have an opener, don't despair. Because the hole in the can's top is scored, you can open it by lining up the tip of a spoon with the hole and pressing down with your thumb. If you don't have a spoon, use a screwdriver or house key. See also CAN OPENERS, p.32.

Soil erosion

Use plants to stop soil erosion. They're cheaper and longer-lasting than a retaining wall.
• Plant tough, rapidly colonising plants like Creeping Jenny (*Lysimachia nummularia*) and Ornamental Dead Nettle (*Lamium galeobdolon*). These spread quickly and form a rooted carpet which holds the soil together. Until they are well established, it is necessary to remove any weeds that appear by hand.

Steep slopes Wattle the ground. Take pencil-thick, 12-36in/300-910mm cuttings of willow, alder, honeysuckle, forsythia, ivy or any other easy-to-root plant and tie them in bundles about 6in/150mm in diameter, alternating tips and cut ends. Lay the bundles flat in shallow trenches dug across the slope wherever there is evidence of runoff. Cover with no more than 1in/25mm of soil and place rocks around the cuttings to hold them in place. When they sprout, they will form a soil-holding thicket.

Soil testing

The type of soil in your garden determines how much water and fertiliser you should apply and even what kinds of plants you can grow. Plants which are rooted in sandy, or light, soil need plenty of water and nutrients; those in heavy clay may well be killed by overwatering.

In order to find out what kind of soil

Clay
Silt
Sand

you have, try this simple test on it.
• Fill a coffee jar two-thirds full of water. Add soil from your garden until the water level rises to the jar's lip. Screw on the cap and shake vigorously. Set the jar down and watch the particles settle. The larger sand grains will fall to the bottom of the jar almost immediately; finer silt particles will take a while longer; and tiny clay particles will settle only after several hours.

Now 'read' the layers. Equal layers of sand, silt and clay indicate loamy soil – ideal for plants. A thick layer of sand means light soil, which you could improve by digging in manure or compost. A thick layer of clay shows heavy soil. To improve it, dig in sand and organic matter.

Sore throats

• Avoid irritation – if you smoke, take the opportunity to stop.
• To numb the pain, make this icy honey-lemon drink: squeeze the juice of one lemon into 4fl oz/115ml of water and mix in plenty of honey or sugar; add lots of ice, stir well, and sip through a straw. Other soothers: gargle with ½ teaspoon of salt in 8fl oz/225ml of water three times a day, or suck specially prepared throat lozenges.
• Keep the mucous membranes moist by drinking plenty of non-alcoholic liquids.
• Take aspirin or paracetamol (see p.13) to relieve pain.
• See a doctor if you have a fever of 38.5°C/101°F or higher for more than a day or two, if the pain persists for more than a week, or if you have difficulty swallowing or breathing. See also PAIN RELIEF, p.148.

Soundproofing

• Any room can be soundproofed using materials such as cork wall tiles, acoustic ceiling tiles, thick carpet and underlay. Upholstered furniture and heavy curtains will all help to keep the sound inside a particular room.
• Be sure to place equipment such as hi-fi speakers and television sets well away from shared walls.
• Encourage music buffs to use headphones. This ensure that noise doesn't affect other people.
• Noise coming through a shared bedroom wall can be dampened by fitted wardrobes. The hanging clothes will tend to absorb sound.
• If double glazing is required to reduce noise, arrange for the extra pane of glass to be at least 3in/75mm away from the existing one. And choose glass of a different weight, otherwise the surfaces could vibrate in sympathy. Remember that opening a window will immediately kill the insulative effect.
• Noise from a busy road can be minimised by brick walls or by a shelter of bushes or trees – anything to help reduce the sound waves reaching the house. See also NOISE, p.141.

Sour cream

• Use plain low-fat yoghurt in dip recipes that call for sour cream. To thicken the yoghurt, spoon it onto a piece of muslin and suspend it over a bowl in the refrigerator overnight to drain off the whey.
• For a less calorie-laden baked potato topping, purée low-fat cottage cheese or ricotta in a blender to smooth out the lumps, then stir in chives or chopped parsley. Or use low-fat yoghurt mixed with chopped basil, Parmesan cheese and freshly ground pepper.

Soy sauce

• Dilute soy sauce with an equal quantity of water to lower its high sodium content. Or buy reduced-sodium soy sauce, like shoyu.
• There are two main types of soy sauce – light soy sauce and dark soy sauce. Light soy is lighter in colour and much saltier than dark soy sauce, which is slightly thicker and stronger.
• As a substitute for soy sauce when cooking, try using 3 parts teriyaki sauce to 1 part water.

Spades, shovels and scoops

• Plenty of garden tools are handy for breaking up the soil – a hoe, cultivator, pick-axe, metal rake, tiller, edger or pitchfork – but not much good for moving earth into a wheelbarrow. That takes a spade. If you don't have one, lay out a square of canvas or heavy plastic; then once the soil is loose, use a hoe or edger to heave the earth onto the square. Pull up the four corners and empty the soil into the wheelbarrow.
• You can make a shovel from a round 4½ gallon/20 litre can. Remove the top and cut out the bottom with tin snips, a jigsaw or a hacksaw. With the same tool, slice the can, top to bottom, into quarters, each a potential shovel. With screws and washers, fasten one of the quarters to a broomstick or dowel. For support, fasten most of the metal to the stick and bend the cut edges over like hems. If the shovel bends with too much weight, you'll still have three more.
• Another simple snow shovel can be made by cutting a square of hardboard and threading it through the tines of a garden fork. For preference, choose an

oil-tempered hardboard which is not affected by damp.

• To make a small scoop for quick jobs, like cleaning the steps of snow, cut the bottom out of a 4 pint/2.3 litre plastic milk container, then cut out the side beneath the handle. Now you have a durable scoop that's easy to hold.

Spelling

• Everyone knows the old rhyme 'I before E, except after C', but even this rule has its exceptions. A good example is the sentence 'Sheik, seize the weird

Flummoxed by spelling

Even champions have been stumped by the words on this list. Try holding a spelling bee at home to see how many of these tricky, hard-to-spell words will baffle your family as well.

afflatus	incandescence
atelier	lavender
baccalaureate	meringue
badinage	minuscule
cedilla	miscible
codicil	misogyny
conchology	mnemonic
dentifrice	persiflage
encomium	quietus
esoteric	ratiocination
exorcism	sarcophagus
haemorrhage	xenophobe
ichthyology	xylophone

words either and neither at your leisure'.

• Ask a skilled speller to check what you've written; see if there's a pattern to your misspelling.

• Use mnemonic aids to remember difficult words (see p.132), such as: there's an end in friend; the principal may be your chief school pal; but a principle is a rule.

• Play word games and hold family spelling bees to help your children improve their spelling.

• But note: some scholars believe that good spelling isn't a measure of intelligence and application but rather an innate neuromuscular skill – that is, it can't be acquired. If, after trial and many errors, you still can't spell, the problem may be in your genes. If so, keep a dictionary always to hand: at home, on your desk, in your computer, in your briefcase or handbag.

• If you don't have a dictionary and you need to look up a word, try finding it in the index of a book, an encyclopaedia, or even the Yellow Pages.

Spiders

• You don't have to kill a spider when you see it. Spiders in Britain are harmless to human beings. Remove a spider from a bath with a cardboard tube – it will crawl into the tube, because spiders like the dark, particularly if you splash it with a little water.

• Spiders are among a gardener's best friends. If you see a large spider on your wall, don't harm it; capture the creature in a wide-mouthed jar or yoghurt pot. Then release it in the garden, where it will make a meal of flies, aphids and other such pests.

Splinters

• Use a magnifying glass to help you find a small splinter. Then remove the splinter with tweezers and cleanse the area with soap and water.

• If the splinter resists, soak the wounded area in warm water and dry; then dab on some glue and gently press on a bit of gauze. When it's dry, peel it off; the splinter should come with it.

Splints

Almost anything can serve as a splint. The lighter it is the better, as long as it can keep the fractured limb immobile at the joints both above and below the fracture.

• A magazine works well; wrap it around the limb and secure it with cloth strips, tape or rubber bands. A thick newspaper will also do.

• Other usable objects include pieces of timber, plywood or stiff cardboard; broom handles, umbrellas or ski poles – even such soft items as a folded blanket. Using a roll of bandage or wide strips of cloth, fasten the splint snugly (but not so tightly that you cut off circulation) in several places above and below the fracture. Or wrap continuously upwards from the end of the affected limb.

• If none of these is available, secure a fractured arm to the victim's chest, and a broken leg to the uninjured one. In all cases, get the casualty to a doctor or hospital as quickly as possible. See also FRACTURES, p.91; SLINGS, p.186.

Spring fever

Does the end of winter leave you feeling lazy, listless and depressed? Here are some ways to cure the blues and put you in the frame of mind to make the most of the new season.

• Get plenty of extra rest and make a special effort to eat a low-fat, high-fibre diet (see LOW-FAT DIET, p.128; THE BALANCED DIET, p.254).

• Change out of your winter clothing. Spring's lighter fabrics and colours may give you just the psychological lift you need.

• Alter your daily routine. Get up earlier than usual, take a different route to work, discover new places to buy lunch.

• Instead of saving your holidays for summer, use one or two days now to do something out of the ordinary that you don't usually have time for.

• Brighten up your environment. Wash the windows, repaint a room, buy something new for your home.

• Start to work on your garden. Plant seeds indoors, lay out vegetable beds, and begin tilling the soil as soon as it's dry enough.

• Find excuses for getting outdoors. Make time to walk to work, watch the sun go down, count the stars at night.

Squaring a corner

Try one of these methods to check that an object is square:

• To check a bookshelf or cabinet, measure diagonally from the upper left-hand corner to the lower right-hand one, then from the upper right corner to the lower left. If the work is square, the two measurements will be exactly the same.

• Place a large book on the corner of the object, or in the corner of something you are making. The edges of the book will be exactly parallel to the two sides they touch if the work is square.

• Use a level and plumb bob (see p.158). Make sure the top of the work is exactly level, then hang the plumb bob from the top. A visual check should tell you whether the side is perpendicular to the top.

• Use maths – the 3-4-5 ratio – to check for an exact 90° angle; see also MEASURING, p.131.

Squeaking floorboards

• Sprinkle talcum powder or powdered graphite between the squeaking boards for a temporary end to the noise.

• Rearrange your furniture in order to change the traffic pattern in the room.

• To silence a squeak from floors above, drill pilot holes and drive screws through the floorboards into the joist.

• If the floor is accessible from below,

drive thin wood shims between the underside of the squeaking boards and the top of the joist.

Squeegee

Squeegees are ideal for cleaning large expanses of glass; some come with a sponge fitted as well.

• If the blade is nicked or damaged, reverse it. If it cannot be removed, smooth the edges with some fine sandpaper.

• An old rubber dish-draining mat makes an excellent squeegee when the real thing is not available. Cut off the end

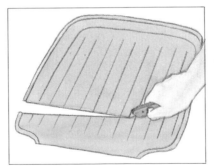

several inches back from the lip so that you can hold it comfortably.

• A good alternative for cleaning car windows is a section of windscreen wiper blade. Cut a wiper down to the right size and then hold it with a large bulldog clip.

• Mop up any rinsing water from window glass or glazed ceramic tiles with balls of crumpled up newspaper – it leaves a good shine, too.

Squirrels

• To deter these acrobatic interlopers, attach your bird feeder to a 6ft/1.8m pole. First slip a 12in/300mm length of 4in/100mm plastic pipe over the pole, then suspend it from the bottom of the feeder. Squirrels won't be able to scale it or climb inside. But keep the feeder away from trees, or they'll find a way to leap down onto it.

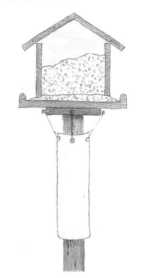

• Or hang the bird feeder from a long wire strung between two poles. Cut the bottoms off eight plastic bottles and string the wire through the bottles, four on each side of the feeder. They'll spin under the squirrels' feet, making the would-be thieves fall to the ground.

• Another trick is to surround the feeder with large mesh wire which allows small birds to enter, but not squirrels.

• Block up all holes under the eaves to keep squirrels out of the roof – they have been known to gnaw electric wiring and plastic pipes.

Staining wood

• To change the colour of wood, you can either use a wood dye or stain, or a stain-varnish that combines the stain with a finishing coat. The only disadvantage of the stain-varnish is that as extra coats are applied, so the colour darkens.

• For a lighter colour, use a wood bleach to lighten the existing colour, then either re-stain the wood or use clear varnish.

• Where old stain has soaked into the wood, use a fine abrasive in a drum sander or orbital sander to strip the wood down to a clean surface. Take care with veneered surfaces – you don't have much wood to take off.

• When applying a stain, always do a small test area first. Colours never look quite the same when dry.

• If a water stain has been used, you will find that the water slightly raises the grain of the wood. When the wood is dry, smooth it with fine glasspaper, working only with the grain of the wood.

Stairs

• To put a slip-resistant surface on concrete steps, mix silver sand into masonry paint, or use PVA adhesive and silver sand, and coat the treads with it. Stir often as you work.

• On uncarpeted stairs, apply a nonslip plastic strip about 1 in/25 mm from the front edge of each tread.

• When carrying a large object, such as a basket of laundry, it's safest to back down the stairs; drag the load after you with one hand and hold the banister with the other.

• To silence squeaky stairs, screw treads to the top edge of the risers. Be sure to bore pilot holes first.

• If a staircase has very little headroom, install a small mirror on the front of the low spot. When people see their reflection, they'll duck.

Stammering

About 4 per cent of the population stammers, and four times as many men stammer as women. Stammering is not inherited, but it can run in families. It is sometimes triggered by bereavement, trauma or insecurities in childhood. Stammering can be alleviated, with the guidance of a speech therapist, self-help tapes and support groups.

• Don't show your child that you're anxious about his stammer. This will only make him feel he's doing something wrong and will aggravate the problem.

• See your doctor, who will refer the child to a speech therapist.

• Encourage your child to sing and act. These activities often boost children's confidence and provide relief from the strain of stammering.

• For further information consult support groups such as the Association for Stammerers, c/o The Finsbury Centre, Pine Street, London EC1R OJH.

Stamps

• If your postage stamps get stuck together, place them in the freezer for an hour or two. They'll usually come apart and be usable.

• To remove a stamp from an envelope for collecting purposes, put it in the freezer overnight; then take it out and slide a knife under the stamp.

• Or cut off the corner of the envelope with the stamp and float it – don't immerse it – in lukewarm water until the paper comes off. Or lay the stamp face upwards on damp blotting paper or newspaper. It should peel off within a few minutes. Dry the stamp face downwards on blotting paper, then flatten it between the pages of a book. Or lay thin paper over the stamp and run a moderately hot iron over it.

Caution Never remove an antique stamp from its envelope or paper backing; it might be ruined as a collector's item. The postmark can be as rare and valuable as the stamp itself.

Staples

• If you don't have a working stapler, fasten papers at the corners with a dab of latex glue or small squares of double-sided tape.

• Alternatively, fold over the corners of a sheaf of papers three times, tear or cut the fold down to its inner edge but not all the way through, and fold back one half of the fold.

• If you're missing a staple gun, tap heavy-duty staples into woodwork or upholstery with a tack hammer.

• To remove stubborn staples from a wall or bulletin board, try needle-nosed pliers, tweezers or a nail clipper.

Static electricity

• Take the crackle out of your carpet with a mixture of 1 part liquid fabric softener and 5 parts water. Put it in a spray bottle, mist the carpet, and leave to dry.

• To fight static electricity in clothing, add fabric softener to the final rinse. If a clinging slip is the problem, starch it.

• If you're already dressed, rub your tights with a thin film of hand cream.

Staying awake

• Get up and move around; talk to other people.

• Splash your face with cold water. Open the windows and let in some fresh air.

• Drink beverages that contain caffeine and eat high-protein foods. Stay away from potato crisps, chocolates, sweet and savoury biscuits, cake and sweets; far from being a 'quick energy fix', these high-carbohydrate foods will make you sleepier.

• Chew on a peppermint or a piece of lemon; your body may rouse itself to the irritation.

• If it's absolutely necessary to stay up for a couple of days, it may work to take a nap during the first 24 hours; a nap on the second day, however, will probably leave you feeling groggy.

• If you feel drowsy while driving, stop and have a few minutes of fresh air and exercise. Open the windows and let the fresh air blow on your face. Sing along with the music on the radio or talk back to the disc jockey.

• If you have to change from one work shift to another, keep the same daily routine, regardless of what the clock says; eat breakfast before you go to work, break for lunch in the middle of your shift, and have dinner at the end of your work 'day'.

Stereo systems

• If your tapes don't sound as good as they used to, it's probably time to clean the playback heads on your cassette player. (A once-a-month cleaning is wise.) Although you can use surgical spirit on a cotton swab, it's best to buy a special cleaner from an electronics supply shop.

• To clean the stylus on your turntable, put a little surgical spirit on a fine camel-hair brush and move it gently along the cartridge from back to front – never sideways or front to back.

Speakers

• If a speaker stops working, make sure that all the connections are secure. If it's still dead, detach the jack or lead that goes into it from the back of the amplifier or receiver and connect it to the working speaker (after removing its own con-nection). If it continues to work, the silent speaker needs to be repaired. If the second speaker ceases to work, the problem is in the lead or the amplifier; to find out which, reconnect the speakers and reverse the jacks or leads on the back of the amplifier. If the dead speaker now works, your amplifier needs repair; if it doesn't work, replace the jack or lead.

• If one speaker has stopped working when you're using the turntable, check the stylus. One of the two wires trans-mitting the channels from the record may have become disconnected. If so, you will need a new cartridge. See also TAPES AND CDS, p.203.

Turntables

• Does your turntable hum? Check whether the earth wire (a thin black or

Right speaker Left speaker

green wire) is securely attached to the earthing post on the back of the receiver or amplifier.

• Try moving the turntable away from the speakers and other stereo com-ponents; it may be picking up vibrations. Or place it on a piece of foam rubber.

Stings

Insect stings – even multiple stings – are seldom very serious in Britain. The only notable exception (most often caused by a bee or wasp sting) is allergic shock (see ALLERGIES, p.10).

• To relieve pain and swelling, apply a cold compress, ice bag or surgical spirit. Calamine lotion may help to soothe the irritation. If the pain or swelling does not go after 24 hours, go and see a doctor.

• Remove the sting by gently scraping it with the dull edge of a knife blade or with a credit card – do not use tweezers. See also INSECT BITES, p.114.

Stitch in the side

• Breathe deeply in and out to oxygenate your blood and get the cramped muscle working.

• Dig your fingers into the muscle at the point where you feel pain – usually just at the bottom of the rib cage – then mas-sage the spot by digging and rubbing.

• If the stitch was caused by fatigue, rest is the best cure.

• Mineral depletion is often the problem. Prevent a recurrence by eating a banana or orange and some salt in the morning (for potassium and sodium). Pay atten-tion to your calcium intake; it helps to regulate muscle contractions. Drink lots of water.

Stitch removal

• To unpick a chain-stitch seam, cut through a single loop and you can unravel the whole line of stitching.

• The quickest way to remove a conven-tional machine stitch is with a stitch remover – or at a pinch, a craft knife – but be extremely careful not to cut the fabric. The slow but sure way of remov-ing stitches without cutting the fabric is to snip the individual stitches with tiny sharp-pointed scissors.

• Overlocked, or serged, seams look complicated, especially those using four

---

For want of a nap, much can be lost

The French emperor Napoleon, who slept on average less than four hours per night, believed that only fools and invalids required more sleep. But then history taught him a lesson.

When the little colony of Haiti rebelled against French rule in 1802, Napoleon dispatched a large army to quell the local uprisings. Though they were greatly outnumbered, the rebels feigned attacks night after night, depriving the French soldiers of their sleep. The tired soldiers eventually withdrew and Haiti became a sovereign state.

For most people, lack of sleep has far less devastating conse-quences, but sleep deprivation can result in some serious side effects nonetheless.

After only 24 hours without sleep, most people start to feel irritable. After about two or three sleepless nights their memory and judgment will start to deteriorate and ordinary everyday mental and physical tasks will become difficult to perform. If you manage to stay awake for long enough, you may even hallucinate or display other signs of mental illness.

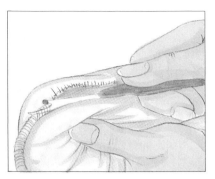

or five threads in ladders of chains and loops. But you can cut them simply by running a stitch remover along the edge of the fabric under the outer row of loops. They will then pull out easily.

Stolen car

• Thieves often repaint cars and change the vehicle registration number so that owners can't identify them. Foil them by having the registration number, or some number personal to you, etched onto all the windows. Put the number at the top of the windows so that it can be seen if the door windows are lowered. A thief is less likely to steal a car on which all the windows would have to be replaced.
• Don't keep your registration document in the car, but in a safe place at home. You will need this record of the year, make and model of your car, as well as the chassis and engine numbers, to report a theft. Keep a copy of the registration document elsewhere as an added precaution.

Stomachache

Stomach pain most commonly results from eating or drinking too much. But it does have many other causes, such as constipation, stress, ulcers, food poisoning and periods.
• Rest for 24 hours and drink small amounts of liquid, but don't eat anything until the next 24 hours, and then only bland, easily digestible foods in small helpings.
• Taking antacid tablets may relieve the pain within 48 hours.
• If the pain gets worse after 4 hours, or goes on for more than 2 days, or if there

is blood in your vomit or stools, or if you have shooting pains in your shoulders and arms, see a doctor. Also consult a doctor if you have stomachaches often.

Stopcock jammed

In a plumbing emergency you will need to turn off your mains water supply quickly – make sure you know where your stopcock is. It is usually sited where the water supply enters your home – in a cellar or airing cupboard, under the kitchen sink or in a larder.
• Twice a year check that your stopcock works. Turn on a kitchen tap and close the stopcock fully. If water still flows through the tap, the stopcock washer probably needs replacing. Get a plumber to do this.

If the stopcock is hard to turn, drip some penetrating oil onto the shank. By opening and closing the stopcock fully twice a year you reduce the chance of it jamming. After opening it fully, turn it one quarter of the way towards the closed position.
• If the stopcock is jammed and you need to stop the flow of water, turn off the outdoor stopcock in front of your house. This is usually under a metal cover in the pavement or just inside your garden. If you have no key to turn it off, remove the cover, reach down and turn the tap by hand or with pliers.

Storage space

• In one section of your cupboard install two rods, one 3-4 ft/1-1.2 m above the other. Use them for hanging short items such as shirts and skirts.
• Suspend shower curtain hooks from the rods to hold belts, bags and scarves.
• Place storage boxes in the wasted space at the bottom of a wardrobe. Make your own from old drawers; add hinged hardboard tops to keep out the dust. Or use the space to hold tiered shoe racks.
• Storage boxes also work well under the bed. And they will be far easier to pull in and out if you fit casters to each corner of the bottom of the boxes.
• Store items that you or your children

use all the time in clear plastic boxes or wire baskets on cupboard shelves.
• Attach hooks, towel racks or shoe bags to the cupboard walls or doors for miscellaneous items.
• In children's cupboards, place rods within their reach and use the upper space to store out-of-season clothing. To encourage neatness, use plastic storage bins or label boxes with pictures of what's supposed to go in them.
• Make a child's cupboard from an old chest with a hinged top, turned onto one end. Screw short legs to whichever end will be the bottom. Stand the chest up and put a rod across the inside and a knob on the 'door'. For safety, remove all locking devices; use a magnetic catch to keep the door closed.
• If you have a cupboard under the stairs, you can create quite a bit of additional storage space by installing a small shelf under each of the steps. Support each one with angle brackets screwed to the back of each step. You can use the

shelves for storing small frequently used articles such as polish, paintbrushes, torches, light bulbs, nails or plugs and fuses.
• If you have a holiday home, use metal storage compartments to keep out mice and other pests. Or line wooden compartments with aluminium sheeting or foil.
• Suspend a net across the ceiling of your garage to store items like tents and paddling pools.
• In the dining room turn a windowsill into a bar and build a storage chest under it.

• In the attic build triangular storage units to fit under the eaves.

• If your living room chimney breast sticks out into the room, you could build a set of floor-to-ceiling bookshelves or cabinets in the alcoves on both sides of the fireplace.

Strains and sprains

Both strains (injury to muscles) and sprains (injury to joints) hurt, and will swell up; a sprain will also show signs of bruising.

• To treat either injury, follow the RICE procedure. *Rest* the part. Apply an *Ice* bag or cold compress for at least 30 minutes. Apply a *Compression* bandage to control the swelling. And *Elevate* the injured part. See also FRACTURES, p.91; PAIN RELIEF, p.148.

Strengthening exercises

• For arms and shoulders, do hip raises. Lie on the floor on one side. Raise your upper body, supporting it with your arm. Push your hip up to straighten your body, then bend your elbow as you lower yourself to the floor. Repeat three to six times on each side. Never lock your elbows while doing this exercise.

• Or do modified push-ups. Stand 3-4ft/1-1.2m away from a strong desk or table – preferably one that has a rounded edge. Lean forward and support your weight with your hands on the edge, keeping your arms straight. Then bend your arms, keeping your body straight until your chin or chest touches the desk edge. Push back to the

starting position and repeat five to 20 times.

• For legs, try semi-squats. Stand with hands on hips 6in/150mm in front of and facing a chair. Bend your knees slowly, keeping your back straight, until the inside of your knees just touch the front edge of the chair (or as low as you can without pain), raising your arms straight in front as you bend. Rise to the starting position. Repeat five times; work up to 30 or more rapid repetitions. As you get stronger, remove the chair.

• For the calves, jump, first with feet together, then hop on alternate legs, then step forward on alternate legs as if walking. Repeat each exercise with each leg five times; work up to 25 times.

• To build up endurance for hiking, walk with a weighted backpack, increasing the weight as you become stronger. Foodstuffs such as potatoes or sugar work well, as do bags of dry pet food.

Stress

Stress can leave you feeling tense, restless, anxious or irritable.

• Clear your mind. Sit comfortably away from noise and distractions, close your eyes and focus on a peaceful thought, a tranquil setting or a neutral word. Try to recall, minute by minute, the finest hour of the happiest day of the best holiday you ever had. Or just listen to yourself breathe for 5 to 10 minutes.

• Set aside at least 30 minutes a day for relaxation – listen to soft music, read, write, think or dream.

• Breathe deeply for a few minutes several times a day or whenever you

begin to feel tense. Clasp your hands over your abdomen and inhale slowly and deeply through your nose, extending your abdomen as far out as it will go. Hold your breath for several seconds then exhale slowly through your mouth. See also BREATHING EXERCISES, p.27; RELAXATION, p.169.

• Loosen up tense muscles by doing stretching exercises (opposite).

Stretchers

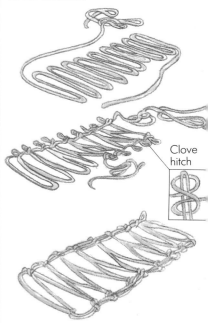

Clove hitch

Only move a seriously injured person if they are in immediate danger – away from a burning car, for example. If you have to move them, make an emergency stretcher from a blanket, or use one of the following ideas.

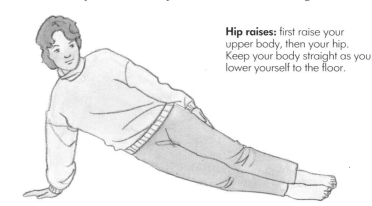

Hip raises: first raise your upper body, then your hip. Keep your body straight as you lower yourself to the floor.

• Place approximately 150ft/45m of rope on the ground and make 16 loops about as long and as wide as the person to be carried. Work the rope ends down the sides as shown, using a clove hitch to tie the loops together; thread what's left of the rope ends through the closed loops, then tighten all the loops.
• Button or zip up a coat or several jackets. Turn them inside-out and run two poles (or broom handles, pipes or oars) through the sleeves.
Caution Before using a makeshift stretcher, test it with an uninjured person of similar weight. It may need more padding or support.

Stretching exercises

To reduce muscle tension and feel more relaxed, try these stretching exercises. Do each one slowly and stop when you feel tension in the muscle – but before you feel any pain. Hold a position, but never bounce; you could injure a muscle.
• For your arms, shoulders and back, kneel down, bend over and rest your forehead on one forearm on the floor. Reach forward with your other arm, grab a sofa leg or other firm object, and pull, feeling the tension in your arms, shoulders, upper back and sides. Hold for 15 seconds and release. Repeat with the other arm.
• To stretch arms and shoulders, stand upright, raise your arms straight above your head, with your wrists intertwined and your palms together, so that the right palm faces right and the left palm faces left. Inhale as you stretch your arms up and back. Hold for 5 seconds, then lower your arms and relax. Repeat up to ten times.
• For your sides, stand with your feet a shoulder's width apart. Raise one arm straight above your head, palm in. Rest the palm of your other hand against your thigh. Bend sideways from the waist, sliding your hand down your thigh and bringing your raised arm over your head, but keeping it straight, until you feel a pull from hip to shoulder. Hold for a count of five. Straighten. Alternate five times on each side.

Groin muscles: support your legs against a wall as you spread them apart.

• Stretch your hamstrings by standing with your feet a shoulder's width apart and your knees slightly bent. Bend forward slowly, letting your arms and head dangle; keep your stomach pulled in. Stop when you feel tension in your back or in the backs of your thighs and knees. Hold and count to 30, letting yourself relax. Imagine that the backs of your legs are turning to soft butter.
• To work on your calves, stand about 3ft/1m from a wall and place your hands flat on the wall, arms straight. Bend your elbows and lean towards the wall, keeping your back and legs straight, until you feel tension in your calf muscles. Hold for 20 seconds, then push upright. Repeat three times. The goal is to hold this position for 1 minute with your head against the wall.
• To stretch your groin, lie flat on your back with your buttocks about 4in/100mm away from the wall, and your legs raised, the heels resting against the wall. Slowly spread your legs, letting your heels slide apart and down the wall until you feel a stretch in your groin and inner thighs. Hold for 30 seconds; then relax and pull your legs together. Repeat twice.

String

• To loosen a knot, twist the string while pushing towards the knot from both sides. If necessary, ask someone to open the knot with a pencil tip or nail while you push.
• Keep string neat by putting it in a dispenser. Make your own from a tin or jar with a lid; punch a hole in the lid for the string to feed through. Or use a watering can or teapot, pulling the string through the spout from the centre of the ball.
• Wrap short lengths of string around a fishing reel. Or use a cardboard tube with a notch cut in one edge to secure the loose end.

Stringing beads

• For heavy beads use fine fishing line or extra strong thread.
• If you're using string, dab clear nail polish on one end to stop it from fraying as you push it through the beads. Let it dry before starting to string.
• To keep the whole strand from coming apart if the string breaks, tie knots between the beads.
• To keep beads of varying sizes in order while restringing, stick them to a strip of tape. Or lay them in the fold of an open book or magazine.

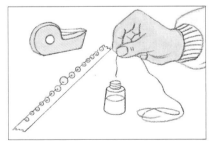

Studs

• If you have no studs for your dress shirt, and you're desperate, use brass or gold paper fasteners; you could even paint the round part with black liquid shoe polish or a felt-tip pen, but make sure it is completely dry before putting the fasteners into the shirt.

• Or use attractive buttons instead of studs. Take a strip of fabric the same colour as your shirt, lay it inside your shirt under the closed front and mark the buttonholes onto it. Sew the buttons onto the strip, slip it under your shirt when you put it on, and button up.

Sties

These painful swellings on the eyelid usually last for no more than a week, and generally fade away on their own.
• To treat a sty, dip cotton wool in very hot water and apply it to the swelling for 10-15 minutes. Do this every 2 or 3 hours. Make sure your hands are clean before treatment and wash them thoroughly afterwards. You could also apply a proprietary ointment to the sty.

The sty should burst after a few days, and when it does, wash the area well. If after 3 days it has not burst and is very painful, see your doctor.
• To help prevent the spread of sties, use your own flannel and towel and don't let anyone else use them.

Sudden infant death syndrome

This syndrome, also known as 'cot death', causes the sudden and unexpected death of about one baby in every six hundred. It usually happens between the ages of 1 and 5 months. The cause is still unknown, but reduce the risk to your child by taking a few precautions.
• Do not lay your baby down to sleep face down. Lie her on her back or side. You can stop her from rolling over onto her front by placing her lower arm forwards. Babies are not likely to choke if they sleep on their backs.
• Do not allow your baby to overheat. Keep the room temperature comfortable but not too warm. Do not wrap the baby in too many layers of clothes or blankets, and use lightweight blankets instead of a duvet or baby nest.
• Do not expose your baby to tobacco smoke. Many cot deaths are thought to be caused by passive smoking, so ask any visitors to smoke outside.

Sunburn

• For quick relief, take a cool oatmeal bath (see ITCHING, p.115), then smooth on a thin layer of a soothing moisturising lotion – do not use oil in any form. Apply cool compresses made of crushed ice, or a packet of frozen peas for 10 to 15 minutes several times a day.
• To prevent dehydration, drink lots of non-alcoholic liquids.
• To relieve general discomfort, take aspirin or paracetamol (see p.13).
• Wear loose clothes and cover up. Don't expose the affected area to the sun before all the symptoms have gone.
Caution If you feel intense pain or if you have blisters, swelling or fever, do not apply any creams or lotions to the skin. See a doctor as soon as possible.

Sundials

The advantage of using a sundial to tell the time is that it doesn't have to be wound up or plugged in. But the drawback is that it can't be used at night or on cloudy days.

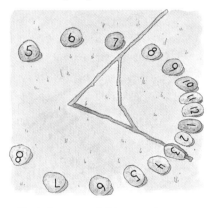

To help your children make a very basic sundial, plant a straight or forked stick firmly into the ground at high noon; tilt it slightly northwards (in the northern hemisphere) so that you get a shadow. Put a rock or start a line of pebbles at the tip of the shadow. Then set an alarm clock for each hour; when it rings, place another rock at the shadow's tip or continue the line of pebbles to the tip.

Repeat until sundown, and then start again at sunrise until you've completed the full circle.

Sunglasses

• Wear polarised lenses for maximum protection from the glare from water or snow. However, motorists may find that wearing polarised sunglasses reveals the stress patterns in a toughened windscreen, which can be distracting.
• The darkness of the lens does not necessarily indicate that it has ultra-violet absorbing properties. A dark lens may cut out a percentage of visible light but let through UV rays, while a more translucent lens may block all UV rays but let through all visible light. Check with your optician to make sure you get the right sunglasses for your needs.
• Inferior sunglasses often contain flaws which can interfere with your vision and may not control the effect of UV rays. To test the quality of the lens, hold the glasses at arm's length. Look through each lens singly at a slender vertical object, such as the edge of a window frame, a door post or lamppost. Rotate the lens slightly. If the vertical image appears to remain still, the lens is of acceptable quality. If the image seems to move or change shape, the quality is poor.
• When deciding which colour lens to choose, remember that greys and browns distort colour values the least.

Sunscreens

Sunscreens should be used regularly from early childhood to prevent skin damage, such as altered texture, wrinkling, discoloration, pronounced blood vessels and skin cancer.
• Here's a formula for judging their effectiveness. Determine how many minutes it takes your skin to begin to burn when unprotected. Multiply that number by the sun protection factor (SPF) printed on every commercial lotion. Divide the result by 60 to find how many hours of protection you can expect. If you would normally burn in 30 minutes, for example, an SPF 8 lotion should protect you for about 4 hours.
• The SPF number is an indication of protection against ultra violet B rays, but it does not tell you the product's ability to

protect against UVA, the radiation that penetrates deeply into the skin and which has been shown to encourage premature ageing. Products are now labelled with a star system to show UVA protection levels. First decide on the SPF you need for UVB, and then compare star-labelled products to find the best UVA protectors. But sunscreens should also be waterproof, non-stinging and give broad-spectrum protection (not just against UVA and UVB rays).
• If you burn very easily or must be out in the sun for a long time, consult your pharmacist; she may recommend a complete sunblock such as zinc oxide.
• Also take into account the sun's intensity; the higher in the sky it is, the more direct the rays are. You need a higher SPF number at midday than you do in the morning or evening, and a higher number in the tropics than farther north.
• Even a sunscreen labelled 'waterproof' will come off while swimming. Remember to reapply it.
• Never use a sunscreen that is more than a year old – check the expiry date, if there is one, or throw it away if you are in any doubt.
• Don't rely on 'natural' lotions such as sesame oil, cocoa butter or mixtures of vinegar and olive oil. They're not effective. See also BURNS, p.28.

Support groups

You no longer have to be alone with your problems; for almost every difficult personal situation, physical affliction, fear and addiction, there is a mutual help or support group. By joining one, you'll gain the understanding of others who have gone through similar experiences and get practical help in dealing with your problem.
Finding one
• Some of the larger organisations are listed by subject in the Yellow Pages and phone directory. The names of many more are available from local churches, doctors and community health councils. Your local library may also have directories of associations and their phone numbers and addresses.
• You could start your own group – but

first contact the national 'parent' organisation for advice. Recruit members who'll help you to set one up from the start; don't try to do it all yourself.

Survival in the wild

• When you're walking to safety, your first 5 to 7 minutes of rest do more good than the next 15 minutes. So several short rest stops are better than one long one.
• Save strength when climbing a steep slope by zigzagging back and forth rather than charging straight up. Go around barriers such as thickets and bogs; don't just barge through them.
• Snow is an excellent insulator, but don't sit or sleep directly on it. It will melt, wetting your clothes. Even a thin piece of plastic or some bark will increase your comfort. Best of all, use a small square of foam to sit on. This insulates your body from the cold earth. Use a full-length foam mat to sleep on – you can buy them in camping supply shops.
• Insect repellent from a bottle (not from an aerosol can) may provide heat if you try burning it in a small, flat container. Use a matchstick or large splinter as a wick.
• If your hands and feet are cold, put on a hat. If you keep your head from losing heat, more warming blood will flow to your extremities.
• Dressing too warmly in cold weather can make you colder if you sweat. Loose or open clothes allow water vapour to escape and may be warmer than tight-fitting jumpers and jackets.

Swearing

• Never be tempted to swear at work – even if your colleagues do so. It's unprofessional. At home, it's also a bad example for the children. If necessary, think of a witty substitute: W.C. Fields reportedly coined the phrase 'Godfrey Daniel'.
• If you're talking to someone whose swearing offends you, look mildly shocked or troubled. If that doesn't work, laugh it off by saying 'I really don't

know if my ears can take that language'.
• If your child uses bad language, explain that swear words are often used by inarticulate people who can't express their meanings more precisely. If he continues, don't institute swear boxes – they sometimes focus more attention on the problem.

Sweaters

• Cotton sweaters absorb a lot of water when washed, which makes them heavy and results in their being easily pulled out of shape if improperly hung or handled. You can hasten drying by turning them inside-out and putting them in the tumble dryer on Low for 15 minutes, but no more. Then spread flat on a towel to air-dry.
• Never wash a wool sweater in very hot water, or put it in the tumble dryer unless your dryer has a low-heat setting for cool; it can shrink beyond recognition.
• If your cotton or synthetic sweater is out of shape, dampen it and put it in the dryer for a few minutes. If only the cuffs have stretched, soak them in hot water and dry with a hair dryer set on Hot.
• You can speed up the drying of any sweater by putting colourfast paper inside it before spreading it flat. Or put the sweater on a towel, place another towel on top, roll everything up, and carefully walk on the roll with bare feet to extract excess water.
• To keep a sweater from getting baggy, mark the shape with pins on a towel before you wash it. Then place the washed sweater within the outline for drying.
• Never dry a sweater over a shower curtain rod or on a hanger. Don't pull on the bottom to even the front and back. Just straighten the seams and carefully smooth out any wrinkles.
• 'Shave' off those annoying balls of matted wool with a razor or electric shaver, or wipe them off with a dry sponge.
• Give an old sweater new life by dyeing it a new colour or by sewing pompoms, or lace around the neck and cuffs. Cover any holes with appliqué, or stitch a design onto it using tapestry wools.

Swimming emergencies

• If you get tired far from shore, don't panic. Float on your back. If there are people around, wave one arm slowly from side to side to attract attention. Start for shore when you regain strength. Don't push yourself; float when you need to rest.

• If you're tangled in weeds, relax, gently shake your arms or legs, and move slowly away – with the current. If you're stuck, roll the weeds down your arm or leg like a sock.

• Let heavy surf help you get to shore. As a wave approaches from behind, turn your body sideways to it, so that you can watch its progress while you tread water. Try to ride with the wave's upward movement. If the wave breaks on you, hold your breath until it passes over; then either resume a back float or ride behind it towards the shore.

• Body surf on smaller waves. Start swimming as one approaches. As it catches you, straighten your body, thrust your arms out in front, and hold your head up with your chin thrust forward. Ride the wave, kicking to keep up with it. Rest when the crest passes.

• If you get caught in an undertow, take a deep breath, relax, and let it carry you under and out. You'll bob up in time to breathe again. Body surf back to shore.

• If you get caught in a rip tide (a current moving out to sea), let it carry you out. As soon as it slows down, swim sideways (rip tides are usually only about 20ft/6m wide). Then swim towards the shore, moving at a wide angle away from the tide.

• Above all, don't panic. The most important thing is to conserve your strength for as long as you possibly can.

Rescuing others

• Never get close enough to a panicked swimmer for him to be able to grab you. Instead, reach out with a long stick or your leg while maintaining a firm hold on dry land. Or throw the victim a coil of rope or something that floats, ideally a lifebuoy.

• If the person in trouble is beyond reaching or throwing distance, try to go out with a floating support, such as a canoe or rowing boat. As you get near the victim, turn the boat and approach stern first. Let them hold on to the stern as you row to safety.

• Only as a last resort should you attempt a swimming rescue – and then only if you are a very good swimmer. If you have a shirt or towel, swim to the victim while holding it in your teeth. When you are just beyond arm's reach, take the shirt in one hand and flip the other end to the victim. Tow him to shore.

• If all else fails, grasp his hair, collar or chin. If he grabs you, try to break his hold. Or take a deep breath and sink with him – he'll let go. Kick away before trying again. See DROWNING, p.67.

Swimsuits

It's easy to make your own bikini. All you need are three large scarves and a little ingenuity. A sewing machine helps, too, or at least a needle and thread; but at a pinch, you could probably make do with small safety pins.

The bottom Fold two scarves in half to form triangles. Then fold back the tips (the bottom of the V) by about 2in/50mm and sew them down. Sew both folded sections together to form the crotch. Tie the loose ends at the sides, as shown.

The top Fold the remaining scarf into a triangle, then fold it over a few times until you have a wide band. Place the band against your back, then tie the two ends together in front tightly enough to

---

The world's smallest bathing suit

In 1946 French couturier Jacques Heim created 'the world's smallest bathing suit' – two tiny cloth triangles joined at the hips and topped by a narrow bra. That same year the United States announced that it would begin peacetime nuclear testing by dropping an atomic bomb on a small atoll in the Pacific known as Bikini.

Both events, though unrelated, inspired French manufacturer Louis Réard, who had copied Heim's design, to name his creation the bikini, hoping its impact on the fashion world would be as explosive as an atomic bomb.

To begin with, women were thrown off beaches for wearing bikinis. But these days they have become so acceptable that no one blinks an eye at them. In fact, the early bikini is considered over-modest in comparison with its successors. The 1970s saw the appearance of the Tanga bikini, which consisted of a high-cut triangle at the front and one at the back that disappeared into the buttock cleavage, and the thong bikini, which covered nothing of the behind at all. These days, many beach belles bathe topless, while others adopt the nostalgic 1950s trend and wear a bikini that closely resembles the original version.

support your bust; adjust as required.
• If the scarf is long enough, you can make a halter top. Put the scarf around your neck, cross it over your bust, then tie the ends at the back.

To ensure that the bottom half of your bikini lies flat, twist the front ends of the scarf upwards and the back ends down.

Switch selling

You see a bargain price advertised for a specific product and you go into the shop to buy it. There you discover that the advertised item is out of stock, but the shop just happens to have a slightly more expensive version. This is called switch selling. Unless the advertisement has advertised that there is only a limited stock, it may be illegal under the Consumer Protection Act 1987, but look for the disclaimer.
• Report any examples of switch selling you encounter to your local Trading Standards Department.
• Switch selling is also done by building contractors, who provide a low estimate for work to be done, and in the middle of the job discover that important and costly details have been left out.
• Never commit yourself to a building estimate until you have a written quotation from several contractors detailing the work to be done, and listing the materials to be used and supplied by the contractor. Make sure that there is an upper limit on the amount of over-run, too. Ask each contractor for the names

of people in the nearby area for whom he has done similar work, and then call them and check his work has proved satisfactory.

Table linen

• Stored table linen will discolour if all the dirt – especially oily food stains – isn't removed first with proper laundering. Use hot soft water and adequate detergent to make sure all stains are removed completely.
• Sun-drying helps to rid linen of musty smells. See also AIRING CUPBOARD p.9.
• If your linen has discoloured, a mild solution of chlorine bleach and water will work wonders to brighten it. But do check the care label first.
• To remove candle wax which has dripped onto a tablecloth, place a white paper tissue, folded four times, over the spot and press with a warm iron. Repeat with a clean tissue if necessary.

• Instead of ironing linen napkins, just smooth them out, still wet from the washing machine, onto a table or work-top. They'll dry crisp and neat. Spread a damp tablecloth out to dry over a table with a plastic or Formica surface.

Table manners

• If you can't get at your food with a knife or fork without making a mess – when eating spare ribs, corn on the cob or shellfish, for example – use your fingers. Otherwise, when in doubt, follow your host's example or consider the formality of the situation.
• If you've bitten into something that can't be swallowed – such as meat gristle, a pip or a fishbone – remove it from your mouth the way it came in (generally with your fork) and put it on the side of the plate.
• If you find hair in your soup at a dinner party, or an insect in your salad, either remove the interloper and eat your food, or leave it untouched – but refrain from commenting on it.
• If you find an unacceptable object in food you order in a restaurant, send it back immediately.

Minding your manners

'Refrain from falling upon the dish like a swine while eating, snorting disgustingly, and smacking the lips', cautioned one 13th-century book on etiquette.

Another warned, 'A number of people gnaw a bone and then put it back in the dish – this is a serious offence.' (The proper way to discard a bone, as all refined people knew, was to throw it onto the floor.)

Scratching while at the table was pointedly frowned upon, although fleas and lice were rife. 'Thou must not put either thy finger into thine ears or thy hands to thy head. The man who is eating must not be cleaning by scraping with his fingers at any foul part,' wrote the Italian Fra Bonvincino da Riva in 1290, in

The Fifty Courtesies for the Table.

Other writers on etiquette in the Middle Ages frowned on the common practice of blowing one's nose into a tablecloth or coat sleeve. They also advised their readers not to blow their noses into their fingers while seated at the table.

The proprieties put forward by medieval makers of manners differ sharply from today's codes of conduct. Among the worst offences in modern times are talking with a mouth full of food and waving a fork or spoon in the air for emphasis. And one more point to remember: it's considered rude to look down on a person whose manners are less than perfect.

• If ashtrays are on the table, you can assume it's all right to smoke; otherwise, ask if anyone minds. Never smoke while others are eating, only between courses and only if no one objects.

Tables

• If the sides of your drop-leaf table rattle against the legs, put a small adhesive bandage or corn plaster at each point of contact. (If the repairs you make are visible, paint them to match the wood.)
• For a toddler's birthday party, use a long coffee table and short stools. If necessary, put books under each table leg to make it higher, and then cover it with a waterproof tablecloth.
• Large, old leather or metal trunks can make interesting coffee or occasional tables, placed either in the centre of the room or next to a sofa end.
• Create a dining table out of two stained or painted trestles which support an old flat-fronted door.
• Shade your garden table with a big outdoor umbrella. Drill a hole in the centre of the tabletop, put the umbrella through it, and secure the bottom in a weighted umbrella stand.
• A sturdy table with a badly damaged surface can be brought back to life with a colourful collage, created with cutouts from colour magazines or old prints. Cover the collage with seethrough adhesive-backed plastic before use, or buy a sheet of clear plastic or Perspex with rounded edges as a top.
• Or place a sheet of heavy, toughened Perspex on top of a matched set of sturdy pedestals such as inverted urns, clay flowerpots or heavy baskets.

Talcum powder

Cornflour makes a good substitute for talcum powder, as does rice powder, which is especially good for use in place of a face powder.
• Sprinkle talcum powder inside shoes if you are not wearing socks or tights in summer. It absorbs moisture.
• Pat some talcum powder on your skin before slipping on anything tight – it prevents the fabric from sticking to your skin, especially after a bath.

Tangled flexes

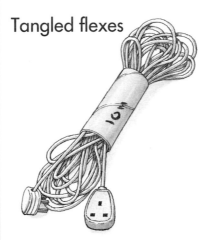

• To keep lengths of unused extension lead and detachable appliance flexes neat, fold each one separately, slip it through an empty toilet paper roll and label it. You can also keep folded flexes in napkin rings or cardboard tubes.
• Or hang your extension leads from a tie rack.
• When putting away appliances that have a flex permanently attached to them, avoid making kinks in the flex by bending it. Hold a coiled flex together with a twist tie or a large rubber band.
• Keep kitchen worktops tidy and safe by using curly, or coiled, leads for kettles. Other appliances, such as toasters and coffee-makers, may have flex-storage lugs on the underside; otherwise cut the flex down to the length required.
• Rather than having unmanageably long flexes, keep them fairly short. Use an extension cable when using items such as power tools and mowers.
• To be safe, insert a residual current circuit breaker (RCCB) into the circuit. This will trip should the flex be damaged in any way.

Tape

• If you're having trouble finding the end of a roll of sticky tape, just slide a credit card along the roll until it catches. A knife will also work.
• If tape is difficult to peel off a roll, put a drop of paint thinner on the end and wait 30 seconds.
• To mark the end of a roll, insert a paper clip under the sticky side of the tape, or fold a short piece of tape under.
• Do you need several short pieces of tape that are the same length? Use a craft knife to cut into the roll through several layers of tape at regular intervals. Then peel off one piece at a time.

Tapes and CDs

• Don't touch audio or video tapes with your fingers; you'll leave grease marks and particles of grit on them.
• Don't keep tapes on top of televisions, amplifiers, speakers or VCRs. All these machines generate magnetic fields that could erase the recordings.
• In the car keep tapes off a hot dashboard; they'll get brittle.

• If you bring a videotape in from the cold, let it warm to room temperature before you play it. This gives condensed moisture on the tape a chance to evaporate. VCRS are sensitive to moisture, and even a small amount can do damage.

• To make sure you get the best sound quality from your CDS, regularly clean the discs themselves with a special cleaning kit available from most music outlets. Clean the inside of your CD player with a cleaning disc only.

Tape splicing

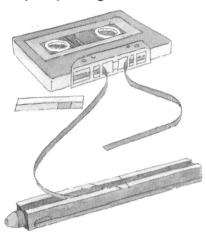

• The most foolproof way to edit or repair a cassette tape is with an inexpensive kit sold in electronics supply shops; it includes picks for retrieval, splicing tape and a rewinding device. But if you find that the tape is badly tangled in the cassette, don't force it; seek professional help.

• Splicing videotapes is not recommended; even professionals won't try it. So use an ounce of prevention: make a copy of valuable tapes and play only the copy. 'Exercise' the master tape twice a year by running it fast forward through the player, then rewinding it.

Taxis and minicabs

Taxis and minicabs (or private hire cars) are different. The local authority plate on the front and back of the car should say which it is.

• Minicabs cannot pick you up on the street. If one does stop for you on the road, do not take it. It is illegal and may not be safe.

• Minicabs have to be booked. Some do not have a meter; in such cases always agree a price in advance of travel. They also vary in standard and are not necessarily cheaper than a taxi.

• Taxis can be pre-booked, and doing this will ensure that you get one. Remember that taxis tend to disappear when you need one most. To ensure that you won't be stranded at the last moment, book a black cab a few days ahead; call a few hours before your departure to confirm the reservation.

• If you want a taxi on the street, look for a busy road where there is plenty of traffic. Go to the side of the street where there is the least traffic – you are more likely to get one that is free.

• When a crowd of people are trying to hail taxis in one spot, walk up the road away from them and then try to flag one down. Stand where the taxi can pull in easily.

• It may be quicker to walk to a hotel, restaurant or station where there is likely to be a taxi dropping people off. At a taxi rank, always take the front cab.

• Smoking is prohibited in most taxis. The driver is also likely to be upset if you leave a mess.

• Always make a note of the taxi number as you enter. It may prove useful in case of loss, theft or other problems, should you have to contact the taxi company or the police.

• Taxis work on a meter within their authorised area. Make sure the meter is restarted as you enter the taxi. There is a starter fare and you will be charged a supplement for extra passengers and a lot of luggage. Some authorities permit taxis to charge premium fares late at night and on bank holidays.

• Outside their authorised area (usually a local authority district) taxis are permitted to charge what they like and will not use the meter. For an out-of-district run always agree a price in advance. If it is excessive, wait for the next cab.

• Some authorities lay down out-of-district charges, which drivers are not permitted to exceed. These will usually be displayed in places such as airports.

• Taxi drivers will expect a tip of around 10 per cent and are likely to be impolite if you do not give one. You are not legally obliged to pay it, however. A promise of an additional tip in advance may get you somewhere faster.

Teachers

• A bad or unsympathetic teacher can spoil school for a child. So don't dismiss your child if he complains about his teacher. Remember that children can exaggerate and that teachers can also have bad days. But if the problem continues, talk to either the teacher or the head teacher.

• See the situation from the teacher's point of view. Does your child pay attention? Does he talk in class, write sloppily, bully others, always arrive late? If so, talk to your child and ask him how he'd cope with a pupil if he were the teacher.

• Chat about your own school experiences. Your child might be more likely to confide in you if you had similar problems as a child.

Teething

Babies start teething from about 6 months onwards. It causes them a great deal of discomfort, which makes them niggly and tearful. Various remedies to relieve the pain can make your life – and theirs – more bearable.

• Let the baby chew on something cold, such as a water-filled teething ring chilled in the fridge.

• Or dip your finger in ice-cold water and massage the baby's gums.

• Give him something to chew on, such as a rusk, carrot or apple.

• If none of these work, rub a little teething gel on your baby's gums. If necessary, give him a little pain reliever, following the maker's directions.

Telephone calls

• Are people in your household making too many calls while you're out? Fit a locking device that allows just a few key numbers to be called.

• If someone rings you by mistake and asks who you are or what number he has dialled, don't tell him – you never know who it is or what he really wants. Instead, ask what number he was trying to reach and tell him his mistake. See also CRANK CALLS, p.55.

• If you have a call waiting service and another call comes in, out of courtesy to the first caller, tell the second you'll call him back unless it's an emergency.

• If you enjoy long phone chats but worry about wasting time, keep some handiwork near the telephone.

• If you have a toddler who loves to dial the phone but doesn't know the meaning of 'expensive long-distance call', hold the handset down with a rubber band.

• Save the price of a stamp or long-distance call by using 0800 and 'free-fone' services whenever possible. Many businesses maintain these numbers to take orders and handle questions and complaints. When placing an order, make sure you have your credit card number and product information to hand. Make a written record of the order, including the name of the person you talked to, the date that you ordered the product, the quantity ordered and the estimated delivery date.

Telephones

• If your telephone doesn't work, make sure that all the cords are properly connected: at the wall socket, on the telephone and between the handset and the phone. If the phone is a plug-in type, test it by switching it with a working phone in your house, or borrow one from your neighbour; if the instrument then works, call the telephone company for service on the line.

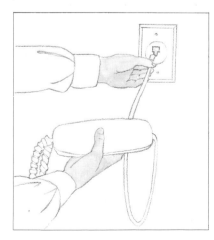

• Whenever someone is ill at home, wipe the mouthpiece, receiver and handset with surgical spirit.

• To avoid electrical shock, never use the telephone while you're in the bath, shower or swimming pool.

• If you find it difficult to read the numbers on your push-button telephone, write larger numbers on white masking tape or address labels and stick them on the buttons.

Telephone sales calls

• Telephone sales calls can be a nuisance which there is no easy way of avoiding. Don't be fooled into thinking it is a company conducting market research. Never agree to see 'someone who is in your district' without first finding out what it is that they want to sell you – and making sure that you are interested in it.

• It is unwise ever to use words that might suggest that you have agreed to buy something. If you are interested, ask them to send you their sales literature by post. Make it clear that you are not agreeing to anything at this stage. Do not agree to let a representative call at your home until you have seen the sales literature.

• There is a telephone sales Code of Practice, which requires callers to identify immediately the company that they represent and ask if you are willing to listen to them. They should not speak to children in the house who answer the telephone. If the caller does not abide by the code, tell them you will report it to the telephone company. Automatically report any such caller who is rude or abusive.

• If you are not interested, say 'I am not interested' or 'No thank you' in a loud voice and put the telephone down. You don't have to wait until they have finished their sales pitch. Repeat calls are uncommon.

Telephoning for services

How do you select a repair service, contractor or other company from all the listings in the Yellow Pages?

• Most people simply ask how much a company charges and how soon someone can come. Then they take whatever they get. Instead, try to determine the company's experience and professionalism. Does the owner do the work or is it done by employees? How are the employees trained? How long has the company been in business? Is it a member of a local trade association? Is it insured in case a worker is injured on the job? Did the owner learn his trade on his own or did he have professional schooling? Is the company licensed? (If so, get the licence number.) What is its policy if you're dissatisfied? Finally ask, 'Why should I do business with you?'

• After weeding out unqualified and unprofessional companies, ask about price and availability – then make your decision. When the repairman arrives, get a written estimate to back up all verbal claims.

Television addiction

Here are some tips on kicking the square-eyed habit.

• Don't switch aimlessly from channel to channel. Select specific programmes to watch, and as soon as they're over turn off your television.

• Store the television in a cupboard or back room and bring it out only when there's something special to watch.

• To help judge the quality of your viewing time, write yourself a brief report on each programme as soon as it's over. Say what it was about, what you learned from it, and what satisfaction it gave you. Be honest. Then read the reports weekly and write down what else you could have been doing with your time.

• Instead of watching your football team on television, attend home games in person. You'll be reminded that television makes much of life seem secondhand.

• Don't use television as a babysitter. Help your children select television pro-

grammes they want to watch and don't give in when they beg for more.
• Suggest other forms of entertainment when children plead boredom. Play cards or board games with them until they get used to the idea of generating their own fun.

Televisions

• Has your aerial blown down or out of alignment? Try improvising an indoor aerial with a wire coathanger. Pull the hanger into a diamond shape and place the end of the hook in the central hole of the aerial socket. You may need to move both the television and the makeshift aerial around to find the best reception, but it will get you through the evening.
• Do you see 'snow' on your television when you play a video tape? Using drawing pins or glue, stick a sheet of aluminium foil to the shelf between your VCR and your television to reduce interference.
• For clearer viewing, spray the television screen at least once a week with window or spectacle cleaner; dry with a soft tissue or paper towel.

Temper tantrums

The most important thing to remember is to keep tantrums in perspective. However embarrassing and upsetting the situation, temper tantrums are part of growing up.
• They are quite normal and are most frequent between the ages of two and four. At this time, most children indulge in fits of uncontrolled rage, and seem unable to respond to reason. It signals the child's realisation that he or she are separate to their mother, and is able to express personal likes and dislikes. Most children outgrow these outbursts by the age of five.
• Keep calm – getting angry with the child will only make things worse. If you see a tantrum developing, try talking to the child. A good cuddle won't do any harm, either.
• If it's too late to stop the tantrum, try ignoring it and tell your child you'll talk about the problem when she calms

down. If you're at home, pick up a magazine to read or continue with the housework, but stay within sight. If you're shopping, pick up your child and, if possible, continue around the shop. If not, take her home without creating a scene. The less attention you pay to her, the less effective the tantrum.
• Try anticipating scenes that cause tantrums. If they happen when your child's hungry, serve her meals earlier. If they occur when she's tired, increase her daily nap or do something quiet, such as colouring, rather than going out.
• One of the most frightening forms of temper tantrum is when your child holds her breath for too long. A firm slap on the back and gentle shake will get the child breathing again.
• Don't create problems for yourself. If she hates wearing that red coat, allow her to wear the blue one every now and then. Tantrums often stem from children wanting more control, so let her make some decisions. Save arguments for bigger problems, such as insisting she takes important medication.

Temporary accommodation

Who do you turn to if you find yourself homeless, or your house has been repossessed?
• You should be able to get free advice and assistance from your local housing authority under any circumstances. If your situation is caused by an emergency such as a fire or flood, you have dependants or you are pregnant, you are entitled to temporary accommodation.
• If you are evicted because of rent arrears, the council may consider you 'intentionally homeless' and refuse to rehouse you. They must find storage space for your possessions, however, although they can charge for it. Appeal to your MP if the council won't help.
• Or contact Shelter (88 Old Street, London EC1V 9HU, Tel. 0171-253 0202) or the Salvation Army (101 Queen Victoria Street, London EC4P 4EP, Tel. 0171-236 5222). Both of these organisations run hostels for homeless people, all over Britain.

Temporary employment

• Most towns and cities have employment agencies that specialise in temporary jobs, from clerical work to manual labour. Some agencies provide training in skills such as word processing.
• Think seasonally. Hotels and restaurants hire extra employees during peak tourist periods. Farms need help at harvest time; department stores need extra staff at peak holiday periods and during sales.
• Start looking at businesses with high employee turnover – fast food places, telemarketing services, taxi companies. See also MOONLIGHTING, p.135; PART-TIME JOBS, p.149.
• Local councils often need temporary staff to fill in during someone's maternity or holiday leave.

Tenants' rights

• What are your rights if you live in a rented house or flat? Issues such as security of tenure, maintenance and repairs and sub-letting are all governed by complex regulations.
• A series of housing booklets about private rented accommodation is put out by the Department of the Environment. They are available, free of charge, by telephoning the Environment offices on 071-276 3534 or 071-276 3403.
• If you are having problems with your landlord, or need clarification of any rental agreement you may be asked to sign, contact your local Citizens Advice Bureau. See also LANDLORDS, p.120.
• If you feel your rent is too high, ask the local Rent Office to come and fix a fair rate. But don't forget that they can also raise the rent if they feel it is too low.
• Most council or housing association tenants have security of tenure as long as they fulfil the conditions of their tenancy agreement. If you get into rent arrears, contact the housing department about paying the arrears off on a weekly basis.
• Council tenants can generally exchange their home for a larger or smaller property in another district if they have a good reason for doing so.

This does depend on the councils involved and the availability of properties, however.

• If you plan to make home improvements to your council property, inform the council beforehand. The council is not entitled to raise your rent because of your own work.

Tennis elbow

Anyone working strenuously at some repetitive action can develop this painful and debilitating condition. Tennis elbow is caused by strain and overuse of the forearm muscles, inflaming the tendon that anchors the muscles to the bottom of the upper arm bone.

• Regular massage, painkilling tablets and a support around the elbow may well ease the condition. But by far the best treatment is rest, keeping the elbow strapped with ice packs.

• If the pain persists (it can last for months), consult your doctor. Options include osteopathic treatments involving deep friction massage, physiotherapy with exercises, manipulation and short-wave ultra-sound treatment.

Tennis jargon

Here's a guide to what the television commentators are picking up on during Wimbledon week:

Ace A winning serve that is not touched by the opponent.

Advantage The first point scored after deuce.

Approach shot A ball hit deep into the opponent's court, giving the hitter a chance to rush the net.

Backspin The effect on the ball when a hitter's stroke makes it rotate in the opposite direction of its flight, causing it to bounce high, backwards or to stop suddenly.

Baseline The line marking the end of the court, behind which a player must stand to serve.

Baseline strategy A plan in which the player avoids the forecourt, staying close to the baseline.

Chip A short, slicing return, often aimed at an opponent's feet; a deceptive shot

frequently used in a game of doubles.

Chop A sharp spin given to the ball by slicing down and under it with the racket.

Crosscourt shot A ball that is hit diagonally across the net from one side of the court to the other.

Deuce A score where both players are just one point short of the usual winning total. As a result, either player has to win two consecutive points to take the game.

Double fault A point lost by the server for failing to get both his first and second serves into the correct service court.

Down-the-line shot A ball hit along the sideline deep into the corner of the opponent's court.

Dropshot A softly hit ball, often with backspin, that falls just beyond the net.

Fault A service that fails to clear the net or that lands outside the proper service court.

Foot fault A fault called when the server's foot touches or goes beyond the baseline while serving.

Forecourt The section of the court nearest the net.

Let A serve which hits the net but still bounces into the proper service court – the ball is served again.

Lob A ball that is hit high above the opponent's head.

Love Zero.

Match point The point that, if won, will give a player the match.

Move into the net To move quickly forward, in the hope of volleying the opposition's return.

Net point A ball that hits the net and goes over; it remains in play except on the serve.

Seeding The ranking of competitors by actual or potential ability.

Service court The two subdivisions of each forecourt; a server must place the ball within the opponent's crosscourt service court.

Set A unit of a match; to win a set, a player must win at least six games with a margin of at least two games.

Smash A ball hit hard with an overhand motion.

Volley To hit a return before the ball touches the ground.

Tennis rackets

• Before you buy a tennis racket, try it out for grip size and weight. Some sports shops have a board set up against which you can hit tennis balls to get the feel of a racket.

• When you buy a new racket, get it strung to the tension that suits your playing style. The tighter the tension on the strings, the less energy they absorb and the greater the power and control. If you're not satisfied with your racket tension, ask the sports shop to make the necessary adjustments.

• Check the tiny plastic grommets in the racket head. A cracked or broken one will cut into the string that goes through it, causing the string to snap. Get faulty grommets replaced when your racket is restrung.

• At the end of every game, examine your racket strings and adjust them with your fingers if they are out of line. Strings that aren't properly aligned are more likely to break than ones which are correctly positioned.

• If you're a beginner, look for an old wooden racket at a jumble sale to start playing tennis with; it will give you better ball control than a metal or composite framed one.

Tent pegs

• Carry pegs in a separate bag to avoid damaging the tent.

• For lightweight, inexpensive pegs, use 6in/150mm meat skewers.

• To anchor lines in snow or sand, tie them around sticks, rocks or sacks of sand. Then bury them.

• To reduce wind stress on a flysheet, tie elastic cord between the pegs and the

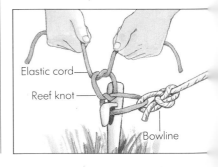

Elastic cord

Reef knot

Bowline

guy lines. If your tent has rubber rings fitted to the flysheet, wind stress will be sufficiently reduced and the elastic cord is not necessary.

Tents

• Before taking a new tent on a camping trip, practise putting it up and taking it down. You may arrive at your campsite at night and you will need to know how to assemble it.

• Check your old tent for tears before setting out. Mend them with a patch of ready-proofed nylon, sewn on with polyester thread. Cut the patch about 2in/50mm bigger than the hole and stitch it to the inside of the tent. Do not pin the patch to the tent first, because this will puncture the fabric more than you need to. On the outside, cut the corners of the excess material diagonally, no more than 1in/25mm, turn the fabric under to make a hem and stitch it all round. Treat the stitches with wax and seal the edges of the patch with seam sealant.

• When you go camping, carry nylon repair tape, seam sealant and patches of ready-proofed material with you for temporary repairs. Beeswax or a stick of lip salve will seal small leaky areas where the hole is not visible. Patch any holes from the inside, except near or over seams – these should be patched from the outside.

• If your tent has a multi-section frame or poles, devise a system of marking the ends that fit together with coloured adhesive PVC tape. Either use the same colours on matching sections, or wrap the same number of tape strips around the ends that go together.

• Every 3 years or so, reproof your tent with a waterproofing product. Spread out the tent, outside up. Dip a brush into water and then into the reproofer and brush on the solution. Allow it to dry and then finally work wax sealant into the outside seams.

• Avoid mildew or mould by folding up your tent only when it is completely dry. If this is not possible, make sure you put up the tent within the next 2 days and let it dry out.

Improvising a tent You can improvise a fairweather tent with a 10 × 10ft/3 × 3m waterproof groundsheet, a 10ft/3m rope, and a couple of poles, waterproof capes and shoe laces. Remember that this tent will be fragile and unable to withstand high winds or heavy rain.

• Drive a pole (a straight, sturdy 5-6ft/ 1.5-1.8m stick will do) into the ground so that it stands erect. Centre the groundsheet over the pole and lash a shoelace around the top.

Weigh down one edge of the groundsheet with rocks. Place the other pole under the opposite edge of the groundsheet to form a door; lash it with the other shoelace.

Guy the top of the front pole to the ground with the rope. (If you don't have a peg to secure the guy rope, tie the end to a stick and bury it.)

• Secure the sides of the groundsheet with more rocks.

• Drape both capes over the door, hanging them by their hoods from the pole.

Theatre tickets

• It is always better to buy your tickets in person from the theatre concerned. That way you can make sure you get the seats you want. Always book well in advance (as soon as bookings open, if possible) for the best seats.

• Telephone bookings can be made with credit cards. Otherwise you will need to confirm by letter, with a cheque. Most theatres will send you your tickets, or will arrange for you to collect them from the box office on the night, in which case take some identification and your credit card with you.

• Only use a ticket agent as a last resort. Some London theatres allow agents to sell excess tickets cheaply, but many agents charge high prices. Be sure that such a ticket is genuine and that it is what you want.

• Never buy tickets from ticket touts outside a very popular show – forgeries are rife and prices high.

• Once you've bought tickets, theatres do not give refunds (unless the show closes). Sell unwanted tickets yourself, ask the box office to sell them if they can or simply give them away.

Thin walls

• The easy way to reduce noise coming through thin walls is to line the wall with built-in wardrobes or books on shelves. If the wall is just a thin partition, these will probably have to be freestanding.

• A more permanent solution is to build a new wall with battens and plasterboard. Fill the gap between the two walls with glass-fibre blanket and line the timber at the floor and ceiling level with foam or expanded polystyrene. This should reduce noise by about 20 per cent.

Threats

• A verbal threat or abuse that distresses or alarms you, or makes you fear some sort of violence against you, should be reported to the police. If the case is considered strong enough it will go to court. If it is the first time that the offender has

threatened you, he or she may simply be bound over to keep the peace; if the offender persists, a fine may be imposed.

• Written threats should also be taken to the police, who will investigate the case.

• If someone threatens to use force against you, this is an assault. If he or she threatens to use a weapon or fist against you, this is assault without battery. Again, notify the police and identify any witnesses, if possible.

Thunderstorms

• Are you, your children or your pets scared of thunderstorms? Try the following tips to get over the fear.

• Get out a drum or saucepan for your toddler and tell him to bang it every time a thunderclap sounds. It soon becomes a game.

• Older children might lose their fear if they understand the scientific cause of thunder. Explain the connection between lightning and thunder. Help them calculate how far away the storm is, by counting (see p.125).

• If your dog is afraid of thunder, the following routine may calm its fears. First, make the dog sit or lie down and give it a treat. Then very softly play a tape recording of thunder and give it another treat. Increase the volume gradually, rewarding the dog with a treat or praise every time you raise the volume. Finally, slowly turn down the volume. Repeat the artificial storms often.

• When a real thunderstorm occurs, make the dog sit or lie down and reward it with treats for brave behaviour, just as you did in the practice sessions. If it shows signs of anxiety, don't discipline it; just ignore it completely.

Ties

• Don't throw away a tie just because its width is no longer in style; fashions are fickle, and your old tie is bound to make a comeback sooner or later. Meanwhile, old ties can also come in useful as dressing-gown belts, hair accessories and curtain tiebacks.

• Are you having trouble tying your bow

tie? It may be easier to practise tying it around your lower thigh. Once you get used to doing this, tying a bow tie around your neck should no longer be a problem.

• To keep the narrow end of your tie in place, slide it through the label at the back of the wide end. If there's no label, attach a strip of cloth tape. Or make a loop of masking or transparent tape.

• If a restaurant requires a tie and you lack one, borrow a scarf and wear it as a cravat. Wrap it around your neck, one end shorter than the other; cross the long end over and bring it up behind, so that it comes out on top.

• When packing ties, fold them over thick cardboard and wrap a rubber band around the middle. Or cut out a piece of card to the tie shape and slip it into the widest end.

• If you don't have a tie rack, tie a piece of string or tape between two cup hooks on the cupboard door or wall. Or use a wire coathanger.

Tights

• To prevent snags, soften rough hands with lotion before handling tights, or wear cotton gloves to put them on.

• Tie the ankles of tights that have laddered so that you can quickly recognise them as 'for wear with trousers only'.

• If a new pair of tights seem a bit short as you put them on, wet your hands and smooth the legs upwards. Always stretch the legs first before putting them on.

• Do your tights tend to tear at the toe? Before putting them on, stretch out the toe area. Or spray it with hair spray after each washing.

• Tights tend to last longer if you hand-wash them; for an extra-thorough cleaning, add two tablespoons of ammonia to the water and detergent in the basin. When machine-washing, put hosiery in a string bag and use the Gentle setting. It's best to let hosiery drip-dry, but if you must use the dryer, set it on Low and remove the tights as soon as the legs and top are dry; the elastic may still be damp, but it will dry quickly.

Tiles

Ceramic tiles

• Before cleaning bathroom tiles, run a hot shower for 5 minutes to steam the dirt loose.

• For stubborn stains, apply a paste of scouring powder and water and leave it for 5 minutes. Scrub with a nylon scourer, rinse and wipe dry.

• To keep the grouting on tiled worktops clean for longer, wash with a solution of 1 to 2 tablespoons chlorine bleach in 2 pints/1 litre of water. Use an old toothbrush to scrub with. Dry thoroughly, then apply an acrylic sealer.

• Remove mildew and make tiles sparkle by sponging with neat white vinegar. Rinse off.

• Remove soot from fireplace tiles with malt vinegar, then wash.

Plastic tiles

• If bathroom tiles are dull, wash them with a solution of vinegar and water; polish with a towel.

• Has a tile come loose? For a quick fix, put a little piece of putty on each corner and press it back in place.

Soundproofing tiles

• Clean with the dusting ring attachment of your vacuum cleaner if it has one.

• Remove stains and dirt with mild soap and water; don't let the tiles get too wet.

Mirror wall tiles

• Apply a solution of 1 tablespoon of white vinegar and 1 pint/570ml of warm water with a chamois leather or soft cloth.

Timers

If you haven't got a timer and your watch is broken, don't give up; as long as you have a television, VCR, radio, record or cassette player or telephone, you have plenty of substitutes around the house for measuring blocks of time.

• Keep an eye on the recording timer on your VCR, if you have one. It's as good as a watch.

• Most commercials on television and radio are 30 seconds long, with an occasional 15 or 60-second one. Many programme breaks are four commercials, or 2 minutes, long.

- Music videos and popular songs usually last 3 to 4 minutes; an album or tape side, about 20 minutes.
- Ring 123 on the telephone. See also ALARM CLOCK, p.10.

Timeshares

These schemes allow you to part-own a property, usually a holiday home, which you can occupy for a week or a specified number of weeks a year. It does have its pitfalls, however, which you should be aware of.

- The United Kingdom Timeshare Act of 1992 entitles you to 14 days (minimum) to reconsider, and a full refund, including deposit, if you do change your mind.
- Timeshare selling can be very aggressive and intimidating, and you may feel coerced into buying something you're not sure what you want. When you visit a timeshare presentation, take a friend along with you. Don't sign anything on the spot, and don't pay anything, even a small deposit, until you've shown the contract to a solicitor. Take detailed notes, especially of maintenance charges and the cost of an exchange scheme, should you not be able to take a holiday at the time your share falls due.
- Don't accept any verbal promises about the deal – make sure they are all in the contract.
- Shop around for timeshare schemes before you commit yourself and compare prices, location and quality.
- Make sure the scheme allows you to sell your shares or lease. This will be easier to do if the lease has a relatively long term to run, that is, more than 20 years. Even so, it is notoriously difficult to sell timeshares on.
- Make sure that the sum you agree for service and maintenance of the property is fixed. Otherwise you may find yourself paying charges that escalate every year.
- If you buy a timeshare property outside England and Wales you are bound by the local property laws, which may impose heavy taxes or prevent you from taking your money out of the country if you sell your timeshare.
- Buying from a distance means that you have no idea of the quality of the property or even if it really exists. If you can, check the property and preferably with a surveyor, before buying.

Tiredness

- Are you tired all the time? See your doctor for a checkup; there may be a medical reason for your fatigue.
- Give aerobic exercise a try. It can combat the tiredness caused by insomnia, anxiety, stress, hormonal changes and – believe it or not – inactivity. It tones up your body, pumps oxygen to your brain and revs up the production of certain positive body chemicals.
- Cut down on caffeine and alcohol by refusing both after dinner. Caffeine may appear to give you energy, but the lift is short-lived; it will also keep you awake. Alcohol makes you drowsy but interferes with normal sleep patterns.
- Review your eating habits; crash diets cause tiredness by producing nutritional deficiencies. The cure is a well-balanced diet.
- Check your drugs. Antihistamines, diuretics, tranquillisers, pain relievers and antihypertensives can all cause fatigue. So can many drug interactions (see p.68). Discuss the problem with your chemist and doctor.
- If you're one of the many who are prone to mid-afternoon energy slumps, try to tackle the more challenging, creative projects in the morning and save your routine chores for the afternoon. Alcohol-free, carbohydrate-based light lunches will also help to combat afternoon fatigue.

Toasters

- If you can't reach a broken piece of toast in the toaster, use dry wooden chopsticks. Never use a knife, and always unplug the toaster first.
- If your toaster's broken, use the grill on your cooker or hold the bread with tongs over an electric hotplate or heating element.

Toilet-flushing problems

If your toilet doesn't flush properly, the water level may not be correct. The ball valve may need repairing or adjusting (see p.17), or the flap valve may be worn and need replacing. If the bowl fills to the brim or overflows with water, then there is a blockage in the drainage system which must be dealt with.

Replacing a worn flap valve Take off the cistern lid and check the water level. This should be 1in/25mm below the overflow outlet or at the water level mark. If it lies below or above the correct level, the ballcock needs attention. If it is

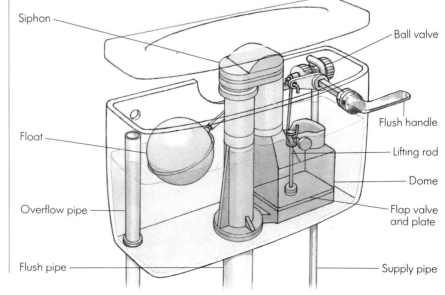

Siphon

Ball valve

Flush handle

Float

Lifting rod

Dome

Overflow pipe

Flap valve and plate

Flush pipe

Supply pipe

at the right level, replace the flap valve. This valve, also known as a siphon washer or cistern diaphragm, is available from a plumber's merchant. If you don't know the size of valve needed, buy the largest one available. You can cut it to fit with a pair of scissors.

If there's no stopcock, place a batten or stick across the cistern. Tie the float arm to it with a piece of string to stop water from flowing into the cistern, and then empty the cistern out.

Use a large pipe wrench to undo the two lowest large nuts under the cistern. Then disconnect the flush pipe.

Put a bucket or large bowl under the cistern and then undo the large siphon-retaining nut under the cistern. Water will flow out as the nut is loosened. If you have a close-coupled toilet suite, the siphon may be held by two or more nuts, or the whole cistern may have to be lifted off to disconnect the siphon.

Detach the lift rod from the flushing lever and remove from the cistern. Remove the lift rod and plate and take off the worn flap valve, which lies just under the plate. Use the old valve as a template for the new one if it's too big: it should touch the sides of the siphon but not be bent by them. Fit the new valve over the lift rod onto the plate and re-assemble the cistern.

Toilet leaks

• If the toilet bowl appears to be leaking, check first that the problem is not condensation. You will see droplets of water glistening on the outside of the bowl. The simplest cure for condensation is improved ventilation while bathing or washing.
• The most likely point for water leaking is where the bowl joins the waste pipe at the rear of the toilet. Drain down the bowl and tank, undo the screws holding the bowl to the floor and ease it forward. Then dig out any old sealant and leave it to dry. For many modern toilets you can get a flexible rubber 'pushfit' connector which bridges the bowl and pipe. These are available at any plumber's merchant. If this is not feasible, use glazing cord or tape to fill the gap between the

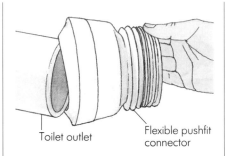

Toilet outlet — Flexible pushfit connector

bowl and the drainpipe. This is highly adhesive and waterproof, but it must be applied to dry surfaces. Do not be tempted to use putty or cement mortar. Both are unsatisfactory as they will set hard and crack easily.

Tomatoes

• Make the most of bland tasting supermarket tomatoes by buying them a few days before you need to use them and then ripening them, stem side up, at room temperature. Never store them in the refrigerator.
• To speed ripening, place a ripe tomato in among your unripe ones. The enzymes in the ripe tomato activate the ripening process in the others.
• You can use your own homegrown tomatoes for cooking right through winter. Just quarter freshly picked washed fruits and freeze them on baking sheets. Then put them in freezer bags and store them until needed. When you defrost the quarters, their skins will peel off.
• To peel ripe tomatoes, make a small slit in the skin at the base and pour boiling water over them in a bowl. Leave for up to 30 seconds, then remove with a slotted spoon. Plunge into cold water and pull the skin away with your fingers.

Tomato purée

• Have you run out of tomato purée? Use a tablespoon of bottled tomato sauce for a tablespoon of purée. Or make 2 fl oz / 60 ml fresh tomato sauce, reducing the amount of other liquids used by 3 tablespoons.
• Buy tomato purée in a tube to avoid the problem of a half-used tin.

• If you do have leftover purée that you know you will not use quickly, spoon it into an ice-cube tray, freeze it and store the cubes in a freezer bag.

Tomato plants

• It is important to choose a reliable disease-resistant variety. Most seed catalogues will indicate which tomatoes have a strong resistance to problems like fusarium wilt, verticillium wilt and tobacco mosaic virus.
• Select varieties that are suited to the growing conditions you are going to provide and to the purpose for which you are growing the fruits. Small-fruited kinds are excellent for salads, giant tomatoes are best for stuffing, and plum-shaped varieties for bottling or canning. There are distinct varieties for warm greenhouse, cold greenhouse and outdoor cultivation.
• When you buy tomato plants at the nursery, look for seedlings with thick stems and large root systems (the clues are a deep container and dark green leaves). Avoid plants that are already in bloom; they've been in pots too long and are stunted.

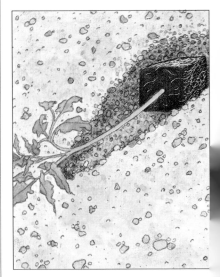

• To help transplants get off to a quick start, trench-plant them. Remove the young plant from its container and pinch off all but the top clump of leaves. Then lay it on its side in a shallow trench and cover the roots and stem with soil, leaving the tuft of leaves exposed. The sun will warm the shallow soil to encourage faster growth, and the heat-loving tomatoes will respond by sprouting roots along the stem.

• Encourage bigger yields by injecting fertiliser around the roots. Use 1½in/ 38mm plastic pipe to stake your tomatoes – a 6ft/1.8m length if you intend to train the plants up a single stake, two 5ft/1.5m lengths to anchor a tomato cage. Fill the pipes with water, adding a soluble fertiliser when the first fruits form. Repeat at 3-week intervals. See also VEGETABLE VARIETIES, p.220.

Tool grips

• To make hand grips for a shovel or spade, slit two pieces of radiator hose lengthwise, slip them over the wooden handle, and hold them in place with insulating tape.

• For a rake or hoe, just slide a couple of 4in/100mm sections of hose over the wooden handle. If it doesn't fit snugly, secure it with insulating tape. Position the hose sections to match your natural hand grip. You'll find raking and hoeing more comfortable, particularly if you also wear work gloves.

Tool storage

• Keep tools organised. Frame a sheet of perforated hardboard with 2 × 1in/50 × 25mm wood and screw it to the garage wall. Then position your tools and put hooks or pegs of the appropriate sizes in

place. Paint a white outline of each tool on the hardboard so that anyone who uses it can put it back where it belongs.

• Put an old metal grill pan with a corrugated bottom in a drawer, to store files and chisels. The vertical bumps keep each type of tool in neat sections. Or glue lengths of D-shape moulding to the bottom of a drawer to create areas for the different tools.

• To separate small items, groove the sides of an open-ended wooden box and slide in patty pans to serve as storage drawers for nails, screws, washers, bolts and other small items. Or re-use small jars with screw-on lids. Nail the lids to the underside of a shelf and then screw on the jars. Label them for easy identification.

• To prevent the engine of your motor mower from rusting during off-season storage, rid the tank and fuel lines of petrol by running the engine until it stops. Brush off any debris, then coat bare metal parts with motor oil. Remove the spark plug and pour in a spoonful of motor oil. Hand-crank the engine to get oil into the cylinder. Cover, but do not seal, the engine.

Toothache

• Saturate a small piece of cotton wool with oil of cloves or make yourself a thick paste of powdered cloves and water; pack the cotton wool or paste in the sore tooth's cavity or place it on the surface. But be warned. The cloves may do more than just numb your toothache; they may also sting your lips and tongue.

• If your tooth has only just begun to ache, drink hot liquids. For an ongoing ache, suck on ice.

• Gargle hourly with warm salt water and take aspirin or paracetamol (see p.13) every 4 hours.

• Try trigger-point pressure. With your index finger, press gently all over your face, neck and head. When you find an especially sensitive area, press hard for 10 seconds and then release.

• Any injury to teeth through an accident, knock or fight should be immediately checked by a dentist.

Toothbrush

• If you don't have a toothbrush, use a clean cotton-wool ball, a bit of towel or your finger as a substitute. Rub in toothpaste, salt or bicarbonate of soda with your tongue.

Tooth filling

• For a temporary replacement for a lost filling, pack the cavity with cotton wool soaked in oil of cloves. Push the cotton wool into the hole and then bite down hard to press it in and shape it.
Caution This measure is strictly temporary. Go to a dentist as soon as possible for proper treatment.

Tooth stains

• Lighten stains by rubbing your teeth with bicarbonate of soda. Then rinse them thoroughly.

• If your teeth stain easily, avoid consuming quantities of tea, coffee, red wine, grape juice, blackberries, curried foods and cigarettes.

Torches for camping

• A torch that throws a short, wide beam is adequate for most camping needs. Long beams use up battery power faster.

• To keep your torch from being turned on accidentally in your rucksack or the glove compartment of your car, reverse one battery; reinsert it when needed. Or place a strip of electrical tape over the switch.

• Attach a loop of string to your torch so that it can be hung inside a tent or from a branch.

• Head torches, of the sort that potholers wear, are often more useful than hand-held torches. They leave your hands free, and you are far less likely to drop them. In addition, they automatically illuminate the area at which you are looking.

• Batteries work better when they are warm, so if the light beam fades in cold weather, warm the batteries next to your skin. Keep your torch warm by carrying it inside your jacket; at night keep it in your sleeping bag.

• Even if your torch is waterproof, always carry a spare one, with spare batteries and spare bulbs, wrapped up in a plastic bag.

Towel rails

• If the bar of your towel rail is broken or missing, use an adjustable curtain rod as a substitute.

• If the bar is hollow, try this remedy. Find a piece of wooden dowel wide enough to almost fill the hollow of the

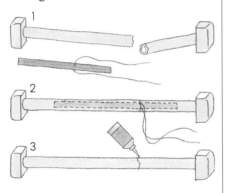

broken bar. Cut it slightly shorter than the longer piece of broken bar. Drill a hole in the middle and hang a length of cotton thread through it (1).

Put the long piece of the bar in its holder and slip the dowel inside, keeping the thread ends out of the bar. Then put the other piece of the bar in place and pull on the thread, sliding the dowel over to bridge the break (2).

Keeping the thread out, apply epoxy resin adhesive to the broken bar ends (3). Leave them to dry for 24 hours, then cut off the thread.

Toys

Are you tired of buying expensive toys for your children? Teach them how to amuse themselves more economically.

• Most schoolchildren love playing with magnifying glasses, torches, magnets, bells, wooden beads and other such items. Pre-schoolers enjoy playing in empty cardboard boxes or in tents made by throwing a sheet over a table.

• Make a 'tunnel' by lining up two rows

of straight-backed dining room chairs and covering them with sheets or blankets. Or sew a piece of canvas all the way around the edge of a beach umbrella to convert it into a special hideaway for your youngsters and their friends to play in.

• Make a life-size doll. To make the pattern for the doll, ask your child to lie on a large piece of paper while you draw her outline on it. Cut out the pattern on a double layer of fabric. Sew the fabric together, and stuff it with old tights or fabric scraps; draw a face or appliqué features onto the doll and then dress it up in your child's clothes.

• If plastic toys become misshapen, plunge them into hot water for several minutes, then work them back to their original form.

• Vacuum stuffed toys, using the upholstery-brush attachment.

• To extend the life of cardboard games, coat them with lacquer.

• To prevent rust and keep colours bright on metal and painted toys, coat them with clear varnish or lacquer.

Transplant shock

• Transplanting damages the fine root hairs that take up a plant's water and nutrients. Give them time to recover by moving trees and shrubs when the plants don't need much water – before the leaves appear in spring or after they drop in autumn.

• If the soil is dry, water the yet-to-be-transplanted tree or shrub thoroughly

several days ahead of time; the moisture will help to keep the earth intact around the roots. When replanting, use a root stimulant (available at most garden centres). Applying the stimulant directly to the root will encourage new growth. Spray evergreen foliage with an anti-transpirant, which retards dehydration.

• To help flower and vegetable seedlings survive transplanting, turn the plants upside-down and slip them out of their containers, keeping the soil intact around the roots. Dip the stems and leaves in a bucket of antitranspirant before planting.

Spray newly laid turf with antitranspirant, too, to keep the grass from browning before it can send roots down into the soil.

Travel for the elderly

• Most hotel chains and some airlines, rail companies and tour operators offer discounts to people of pensionable age. Some tours are specifically designed for the elderly. These discounts are sometimes restricted to certain days of the week and times of year. Ask your travel agent. Also, entrance to tourist attractions is usually at a reduced rate – often half price.

• You may find that associations or organisations of elderly people can arrange discounted travel.

• British Rail do not automatically offer any discount, but with a Senior Citizen's Railcard you can obtain discounts of about one-third off most tickets.

• Many bus companies offer some discount to the elderly. In some cases, evidence of age may be required.

• Most local authorities offer forms of travel discount to people of pensionable age living in their area. Details vary, but commonly this is a card giving reduced bus fares and/or a free or discounted Senior Citizen's rail card.

Taking care of yourself

• Careful preparation can ensure that age does not hinder the fun of travelling. Carry extra sets of glasses and dentures and copies of your prescriptions (written with generic names) to remedy the occasional breakage or loss. Pack all medicines in your hand luggage or bag.

• Consult your doctor about vaccinations at least 2 months before you plan to leave. If you have any doubts about your health or your teeth see your doctor or dentist before you set off. Always take out medical insurance before travelling abroad.

• Designate at least one contact at home: a trusted friend, a colleague or a relative. Give him your itinerary and the numbers on your traveller's cheques; ask him to cancel lost or stolen documents, transfer funds or notify your family in case of an emergency.

• Avoid overtaxing yourself; plan meals, naps and bedtime as close to your normal times as possible. A leisurely pace and occasional rest stops increase endurance while touring; plan short outings rather than long day trips.

Travel insurance

When you're planning to go on holiday, there are several precautions you can take to make sure that things run smoothly and that you don't end up losing money.

• If you book your ticket through your credit-card company, you may get free travel insurance to and from your destination. And if something goes wrong it's often easier to get your money back if you've paid by credit card.

• Take out travel and health insurance if it is not offered by your credit card. Make sure you buy cancellation insurance in case, for some reason, you have to cancel the ticket at the last minute.

Travelling abroad

• Do some research before making travel reservations. Get information about foreign destinations from the public library, a travel agent or a country's tourist board (located in major cities such as London and Edinburgh); buy or rent a travel video to preview a country's sights.

• Buy a good guidebook and a foreign dictionary or phrase book (see FOREIGN PHRASES, p.91).

• Make sure that the travel agent you

book with is registered with ABTA before you make your booking.

• Book your holiday with a travel agent who operates a 'money-back guarantee'. Then, in the event of an airline or travel organisation going out of business, you are guaranteed to get your money back or the offer of a similar holiday.

• Check that your passport is valid (see p.150) and ask a country's consulate, its embassy or your travel agent about applying for a visa or tourist card. Arrange these in plenty of time before departure. If you plan to drive, get an international driver's licence from your automobile association.

• If you are travelling outside Europe, check with your doctor whether you need any vaccinations.

• Make a hotel reservation (see p.109) for your first night and confirm it before departure; take any confirmation letters with you.

• If you're going to Europe, consider buying an Interail pass; it gives you discount rail fares across most of Europe. You can buy one only in this country, so get it before you depart.

• Order your foreign exchange and travellers' cheques in advance. When buying travellers' cheques, make sure that a prompt and efficient refund service is available, 24 hours a day, 365 days a year.

• Pack lightly; then make a list of everything in your case and carry it with your passport. It will be invaluable if you have to make a claim for lost luggage (see p.127).

• If you are taking any electrical appliances with you, carry a travel adapter. In very few other countries can you use the plugs with three flat prongs, common in Britain.

• Before visiting a country that is politically unstable, check with the Foreign Office, Tel. 0171-270 1500.

• Try to fit unobtrusively into any country's culture. Smile and show appreciation or enthusiasm; don't make negative comparisons.

• Find out what is taboo for picture-taking; always ask permission before photographing anyone.

• Keep the receipts for your purchases to show customs (see p.58) and to reclaim any value-added tax when you leave the country.

• If you plan to stay in any country longer than a month, register on arrival with the nearest British Consulate. In any case, carry the address and phone number of the local British diplomatic office; if you have any trouble, contact officials there.

• Remember, however, that while you are in another country you are subject to its laws. Learn the local laws and make sure you obey them.

• Reconfirm return travel arrangements with your airline at least 72 hours before departure. See also EXCHANGING CURRENCY, p.73; ILLNESS AWAY FROM HOME, p.122.

Travelling alone

• Before setting out on a trip, read about your destination and map out a tentative itinerary; without plans you might have too much time on your hands and get lonely.

• Always carry full identification; don't forget to include the name and telephone number of a friend or family member and the address of your hotel.

• To discourage unwanted advances, wear a decorative ring on the third finger of your left hand so that you can slip it around to resemble a wedding ring.

• Before tipping the hotel porter, be sure your hotel room is suitable – in a safe location (preferably near the lift or stairs) and with functional locks on door and windows.

• Always double-bolt your door locks. If there is a peephole, use it before opening the door. Never sleep with balcony doors open. If you hang the Do Not Disturb sign outside your door when you are not there, this may discourage thieves but will also keep the maid from entering your room to clean it.

• When you arrive at your destination, take a city tour to familiarise yourself and, if you want to, to take advantage of the opportunity to meet friendly people who may also be looking for companionship.

• If you want company, look for the local

branch of any professional or social organisations you belong to; or stay at a bed-and-breakfast place where you'll be likely to meet congenial people.

Dining alone

• Make sure the hotel you stay in has a dining room. If you get cold feet about going out alone at night, at least you won't have to eat in your room.

• It is always a good idea to bring along an immersible water heater and tea bags or instant coffee so that you can make an early morning drink. You might even carry a few packets of freeze-dried meals, available from camping supply shops.

• If you want to eat at a popular restaurant, make a reservation for before or after peak time. If you're given a tiny table near the kitchen, firmly ask for a better location. However, an out-of-the-way table does give you a good chance to observe the local scene without drawing attention to yourself.

Children travelling alone

• Most airlines have provisions for unaccompanied children over 5 years old. Children younger than 5 are generally not allowed to travel alone; check with your travel agent. Coach and rail services do not advise it.

• Airlines must always be advised ahead of time when a child will be travelling alone. The child should board the plane early and be escorted from it by airline personnel; someone must be present to meet her on arrival. Whatever the mode of travel, don't leave the terminal until you've seen the bus, train or plane depart with the child aboard.

Travelling with children

• Always carry a bag with snacks, drinking straws, a night light, paper towels and first-aid supplies.

• Give each older child a rucksack and let him carry whatever he needs to amuse himself: books, paper and crayons, games and so forth. However, if travelling by air, some airlines provide special packs containing amusements such as stickers, models and colouring and puzzle books.

• Avoid highly salted foods if you are

travelling by car – they make children drink more, which will mean more stops to visit the toilet.

• Ask restaurants to bring young children's dinners out as soon as they're ready. The children will stay occupied, and you'll probably have their food cut up by the time your meal arrives.

• Instead of expensive souvenirs, encourage children to collect shells or stones. Arrange them in a nice display when you get home.

• Childproof your hotel or motel room as soon as you arrive: tape bathroom locks open, remove any breakables or hazards and lock dangerous windows. Don't ever leave children alone in a hotel room.

By air

• If you are flying with an infant, call the airline ahead of time; it may provide a carrycot and assign you a bulkhead seat with room to put it at your feet. Ask to board early.

• Tell the airline ahead of time that you are travelling with children. It allows them to prepare special meals for children, although not all do this.

• Always try to book night flights; children are more likely to sleep through the flight.

• Give your infant a bottle just before the plane takes off and lands; the sucking will ease the pressure in the baby's ears. Give older children boiled sweets to suck on.

• If your child has a cold, consult your doctor before flying – the pressure of takeoff and landing can sometimes damage eardrums.

By car

• Tie toys to your child's car seat so that they don't fall to the floor.

• On a long car trip, take an extra map and a coloured pencil and let the children mark your progress. Then they won't ask 'Are we nearly there?' every few minutes.

• Take a tape recorder and cassettes with favourite stories or songs. Include blank tapes so that the children can make up their own stories.

• If your toddler is teething, tie a teething ring to a string and pin it to her bib. It will keep her occupied, and it may stop her

from putting undesirable objects into her mouth.

• Try these car games:

Dog catcher One player counts all the dogs on the left side of the road; the other counts dogs on the right. Spotting a white horse doubles your score. If you spot a graveyard on your opponent's side, he loses all his points.

Special cars Tell younger children to look for yellow moving vans, horse trailers, cement mixers and so on. Award 1 point to the first child who spots a special car.

Alphabet game Older children can try to find the first letter on signs, town names, pubs or car number plates for an alphabet race. Start with the letter A and the one who gets to Z first wins.

Travelling without your children

Before you go away, even on a short trip, and leave your small child behind, take steps to ease his anxiety.

• Include the child in discussions about the trip so that he understands why it is necessary.

• Act out the departure and the return home. Stage a little drama in which everyone says goodbye with hugs and kisses and smiles. Then go out of the door with a suitcase, wait a while, ring the bell, open the door, and cry, 'I'm home!' Again, hugs, kisses and smiles.

• Prepare a travelogue in advance, using illustrations cut from magazines (let the

child help) to show where you'll be, how you'll get there, and what you'll do. Make the trip sound interesting and safe.
• Mark the calendar to show when you'll leave and when you'll return. Let the child mark off the days. Leave an envelope for each day you'll be gone, with stories, little notes, jokes, riddles and gifts.

Travelling with pets

Travelling is stressful for pets, but sometimes it can't be avoided. Here are some tips to help them relax.
• Never leave a dog in a car on a hot day. Within a very short time it can become seriously overheated, even to the point of collapse. Should your dog be in distress from overheating, get it into a cool place and soak it in cold water, or wrap wet towels around its body and head.
• Before going on a long car journey, help your pet overcome motion sickness by taking short trips in the weeks before departure. If this fails, ask your vet about the possibility of giving your pet a tranquilliser.
• Use a comfortable, well-ventilated carrier or cage to transport small dogs and all cats. Cats feel more secure travelling in a cage – white mesh cages are the best since they allow the cat to see out while keeping it enclosed. Sit the carrier on a wad of newspaper on the car's back seat. Install a large metal grille to keep a large dog in the back.
• Wicker pet carriers are draughty. In cold weather line the bottom and sides with newspaper.
• Prepare a travel kit with your pet's feeding dish and water bowl, flea spray, a brush, a blanket and a toy. Take the pet's usual food to reduce the risk of diarrhoea that can result from a sudden change of diet.
• In hot weather, put a cool damp cloth on top of a small pet's cage.
• Withhold food for several hours (3 for cats, and 6 for dogs) before departure. On arrival, wait for an hour before feeding your pet. During a car journey, provide water as needed. Exercise your dog (on a leash) often.

• Before taking your pet on any form of public transport, check that pets are allowed.
• When travelling by air, check airline policies about pets. Arrive at the departure desk at the recommended time. If you arrive late, the airline may send your pet on another flight. When flying abroad, check with the airline about animal health requirements in foreign countries and about quarantine requirements on your return. Ask your vet to provide a certificate of good health and proof of vaccinations.

Leaving the pet behind
• If you're leaving an animal with friends or in a kennel, supply its own bedding, toys and dishes and leave it with a toy or blanket that has your scent on it.
• In case of emergency, leave the vet's name and number with the person looking after your pet.
• Cats usually do best in their own homes with someone coming in to feed them. Make sure you keep the cat locked up while you're packing – they often panic and run away if they see signs of your leaving.
• If you plan to leave a pet in kennels, make sure well ahead of time that it has all its vaccinations or it may not be accepted by the kennel owners.

Treasury bonds

Treasury bonds are issued by the government and are one of many different types of securities generally known as gilts. Gilts are divided into short-term (up to 5 years), medium-term (5-15 years) and long-term bonds. Gilts are all different, having various interest rates and redemption dates. They are bought and sold on the Stock Exchange and the price depends on the rate of interest payable and the time to redemption. There is no minimum or maximum holding.
• The interest on gilts is payable half-yearly and tax is deducted at the basic rate. If you are liable for tax at the higher rate you pay the extra tax after the end of the tax year.
• To buy gilts you must contact your bank or stockbroker, although some

gilts can be purchased through the National Savings Stock Register operated by the Department of National Savings. The interest on gilts purchased through National Savings is payable in gross terms.

Tree blights

Fireblight This incurable disease affects a wide range of trees and shrubs including rowan, whitebeam, cotoneaster, crab apples and firethorn. It makes the tree or shrub look as if it has been seared by fire, its leaves still attached but appearing brown and crisp. The twigs have a sticky ooze on them. If there is no ooze then the problem is not fireblight, but drought or some other disorder. Trees or shrubs affected by fireblight should be burned.

Honey fungus This disease is also known as the bootlace fungus because of its creeping black rhizomorphs which invade the internal tissue of trunks and branches. The disease is indiscriminate, attacking all trees and shrubs with impunity. It produces golden fruiting bodies, rather like toadstools, in dense

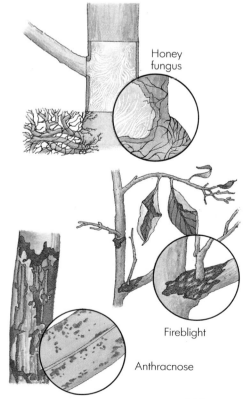

Honey fungus

Fireblight

Anthracnose

clusters during the autumn. Often this is the first indication that the disease is present. There is no cure, although professional tree surgeons can inoculate trees against the disease, with varying degrees of success.

Anthracnose Willows are commonly affected by this fungal disorder, which kills their twigs and then advances to the lower branches, causing extensive dieback. All infected branches and twigs should be pruned away and burned, to slow the blight's progress. It is advisable in the autumn to clean up all fallen twigs and leaves and consign them to the bonfire. Do not add the twigs and leaves to the compost heap because they may spread the fungal spores there. Regular spraying of infected trees with a systemic fungicide in which the active ingredient is benomyl helps to keep the disease under control.

Tripod

Blurred pictures commonly occur in dull light conditions, when the camera's automatic exposure selects a slow shutter speed, and the camera is moved slightly.

• To keep your photographs from blurring, use a beanbag as a substitute tripod. It moulds itself perfectly to uneven surfaces, such as rocks, tree branches or the rim of a car window while the camera or a long lens rests firmly on top. Use it for timed exposures, low-light shots and for the interiors of buildings.

• Buy a beanbag or make your own out

of two pieces of strong fabric measuring 10 × 12 in / 250 × 300mm each. Sew them together on three sides and then fill the bag with 2oz / 60g dried kidney beans. Secure the open end.

Trousers

• If you're away from home and you find yourself without an iron, keep your trouser legs smooth by laying them between the mattress and the base of your bed; press them as you sleep. Allow time in the morning for any spring marks to drop out.

Or hang them in a steamy bathroom over a clothes hanger, the damp air will help the creases to fall out.

• Before buying a new pair of trousers, make sure they fit properly. If they wrinkle up at the crotch, the crotch length is too short; if they wrinkle horizontally, they're too tight across the front.

• To keep knees from wearing out, put iron-on patches on the insides before wearing trousers for the first time.

• Iron-on tape will secure a split seam or shorten trouser legs temporarily.

• When hemming trousers, finish one leg completely, then use it to mark the length of the other. Double check by measuring the length along the inside seam.

Tulips

• To keep cut tulips from drooping, add a couple of spoonfuls of sugar to the water in the vase.

• Spotted petals and foliage are signs of a fungus called tulip fire (*Botrytis tulipae*). Destroy all diseased and adjacent plants.

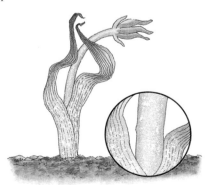

• When dividing your tulip bulbs, plant the smallest ones in an out-of-the-way place; they'll take a few years to become flowering-sized bulbs.

Tumble dryers

• If your dryer won't work, check the door. The safety switch, usually located in the rim of the opening, prevents the dryer from operating when the door is open. Jiggle it around and then see if the dryer will run.

• If it still won't work, check the fuse in the plug, then the circuit breaker or fuse in your fuse box. Next, make sure that the electricity or gas haven't been turned off. If the problem is restricted to your dryer, call the manufacturers for a service.

Dryer fires A tumble dryer fire is usually caused by a build-up of dust in the filter, a dirty exhaust duct or by drying inappropriate or unsafe items such as foam-rubber pillows.

• If a fire starts in your dryer, keep the dryer door closed and shut the door to the room where it's located. Turn off the gas or electricity at the mains if possible. Call the fire brigade right away. See also ELECTRICAL APPLIANCE FIRES, p.71.

If all else fails If you are stuck with wet clothes and a dryer that isn't working, try some of these other drying methods on your washing.

• Speed up line-drying with a fan. Or use a hair dryer on thin fabrics and lingerie. If you have a hose-type hair dryer with a cool setting, slip a plastic dry-cleaner bag over the garment, put the hose in the bottom, and tie the bag around it. See also HANGING LAUNDRY, p.102.

Turkey

• For a tender, juicy bird, choose a young turkey hen. The younger and fleshier the turkey, the better its texture and taste. Allow about ¾lb / 340g per person unstuffed, 1lb / 450g stuffed.

• You can keep a turkey for up to a year in the freezer, but a fresh turkey should be cooked within a day of buying it.

• When home-freezing turkey, freeze the giblets separately. They can be kept frozen for 3 months at the maximum.

• Before cooking, a frozen turkey must be thawed thoroughly. Defrost for 2-3 hours per pound/450g at room temperature, or for 5-6 hours per pound/450g in the refrigerator.

• To defrost a small turkey quickly, submerge it completely in a pot of cold water. Check that the wrapping is not torn and change the water often. Allow 4 to 5 hours for an 8-12lb/3.6-5.4kg

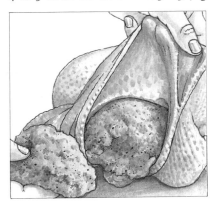

bird; 11 to 12 hours for a bird weighing 20-24lb/9-11kg.

• Plain turkey can be dull, so liven up a small bird by filling it with sage and onion or apple and chestnut stuffing. Create your own or buy it ready mixed.

• Always make sure to remove any giblets that have been packed inside a bird before cooking.

Tweezers

• If it hurts to pluck your eyebrows, stretch the skin between your fingers and then pluck. Or numb the area first by rubbing it with an ice cube. Choose chisel-edged tweezers rather than points so as not to prick your skin.

• When your tweezers don't grip, you can tighten them by putting a pencil between them and bending the tips together. Or just twist a small rubber band around the tips.

Twine

If you need to tie something in a hurry and have run out of twine:

• Make about 4ft/1.2m of cord by knotting your shoe or trainer laces together.

• Prevent your garden twine from becoming tangled by storing it in an old jam jar. Poke a hole in the jar's lid and thread the twine through it.

• Use heavy leather laces or a leather belt to tie up a car's damaged silencer until you can get to a garage. Or, if your car has a 6 or 8-cylinder engine, turn the engine off and remove a long spark plug wire (the engine will still run) and use it as an emergency cord.

Twins and triplets

Before the birth of twins and triplets, get advice on the equipment you'll need for them, how to manage breastfeeding, and how to cope emotionally. Contact the Twins and Multiple Births Association (TAMBA), PO BOX 30, Little Sutton, South Wirral L66 1TH, Tel. 0732 868000.

• Give them very different names (Ann and Rachel, for example, rather than Karen and Corinne), and refer to them by name, not as 'the twins' or 'the triplets'.

• Don't dress them alike. If they're given matching outfits, don't make them wear them on the same day. If they want to dress alike, however, don't prevent them from doing so, but provide each with a varied, separate wardrobe, particularly when they're older.

• Give each child its own toys.

• Bake separate birthday cakes for them.

• Try to spend some special time alone with each child every day.

• When you send them to school, ask for them to be placed in separate classes, unless that would upset them too much.

• Find ways of encouraging a healthy sense of individuality in your children – allow them to develop their separate interests, such as sport, music or art.

Tyre changing

• If you can't loosen frozen or rusted wheel bolts, apply penetrating oil, vinegar or lemon juice. The next time you rotate the tyres or change one, coat the threads with an anti-seize compound, such as copper grease.

• If one wheel has lost its bolts, borrow one bolt from each of the other wheels; replace them as soon as possible.

• Be sure to turn the wheelbrace in the proper direction. In most cars they undo anticlockwise. In some cars, however, the bolts on the driver's side are left-threaded. These are usually marked with an L and are loosened by turning them clockwise.

• More force can be applied by pushing a brace down, not pulling it up. If possible, try using your foot to apply extra turning force to the wrench.

• A cross-shaft wheelbrace, available at motor accessory shops, gives more leverage than a single-shaft brace. For additional leverage, fit a piece of pipe over one arm of the brace.

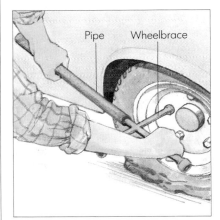

Pipe   Wheelbrace

U

Ulcers

Duodenal ulcers

• Instead of big meals with long gaps in between, take frequent, small meals.

• Avoid coffee, alcohol and highly spiced,

fried or greasy foods wherever possible.

• Check with your doctor whether you should use antacids, available from chemists, to relieve the pain. Do not take aspirin or ibuprofen (Nurofen). If you need a painkiller, use paracetamol.

• Stop smoking.

• Ulcers are often caused by stress. Try to find ways of coping with stress that put less emotional pressure on your body.

• See your doctor, who may suggest a barium X-ray or examination with an endoscope – a fibre-optic device that is passed through the mouth to enable the doctor to see inside your stomach and duodenum.

• Your doctor may prescribe a course of an ulcer-healing drug. With a range of such treatments now available to sufferers, operations for ulcers are rarely necessary.

Mouth ulcers

• Use a mouthwash such as glycerine and thymol or benzocaine lozenges to relieve pain.

• If the ulcers are getting worse they may be infected. Get an antiseptic mouthwash from a chemist.

• If the ulcers are severe, see your doctor, who may prescribe a steroid paste to apply or lozenges to dissolve in your mouth. The doctor can also check that you are not suffering from any other disorders, such as oral thrush or blood problems.

Skin ulcers

• Skin ulcers may be a sign of poor circulation – because of varicose veins, for example. They often heal very slowly. You should always see a doctor or nurse for advice.

Umbrellas

• When buying an umbrella, check for sturdiness by pressing on the ribs when the umbrella is fully opened out – they shouldn't give. Or ask for a specially made windproof umbrella.

• If the fabric has come loose from the tip of a rib, make a temporary repair by inserting a paper clip or safety pin through the cloth and then through the hole in the tip. When you get home, stitch the cloth to the hole.

When is an umbrella more than an umbrella?

The Egyptian pharaohs sat under ceremonial umbrellas, which were said to bring them power from heaven, and in ancient Greece, China and Africa, parasols were used in religious ceremonies. In Japan, the emperor was followed by an attendant with a red sunshade, symbolising absolute power. And in Europe in the 16th century, the Pope decided that the umbrella was a symbol of honour.

Umbrellas were not used in Europe for rain cover until some 300 years ago, when they were called 'parapluies', a French word meaning 'against the rain'. They were carried only by women. Men wore hats and got drenched.

Robert Louis Stevenson felt that an umbrella displayed too much concern about getting wet, and therefore a lack of character. Carrying an umbrella also betrayed a lack of social status; it suggested that you did not own a carriage. Another reason not to carry one was that the early models weighed some 10lb/4.5kg and even then the oil-soaked cotton wasn't very waterproof.

The first Englishman to carry a rain shield was the philanthropist Jonas Hanway in the late 18th century. He suffered public ridicule, and coachmen steered through puddles in order to splash him with mud.

When 'Beau' MacDonald, a fashionable gentleman's servant, began carrying a silk umbrella in 1778, his sister refused to be seen with him. But he persisted, and others soon followed suit, quickly realising that an umbrella cost a lot less than catching a horse-drawn cab every time it rained.

• If the rib is bent, bend it back very gradually so that you don't break it. And don't straighten it too much – it's supposed to be curved.

• To fix a loose handle, remove it and apply epoxy glue to the shaft. Quickly replace the handle; leave it to dry for at least 24 hours.

• To repair a broken umbrella rib, tape a small piece of wire coathanger across the broken part with masking or insulating tape.

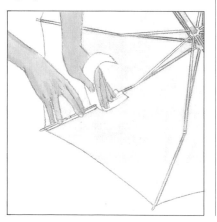

Unsafe goods

• Always examine goods carefully before you buy them and think of the safety aspects. This is particularly true of toys and other items used by children. Make sure that they won't fall apart into easily swallowed bits, or into parts with sharp metal pieces. Check that painted objects state that the paint used is non-toxic.

• Very strict regulations exist as to the safety of consumer items. If something you have bought injures you, or if something you have bought is unsafe, report the matter to your local Trading Standards Department and take the item along to them. They can prosecute the retailer, manufacturer or importer and can have stocks of dangerous goods seized and destroyed. They may also get you compensation.

• In cases of any serious injury, see a solicitor as soon as possible. Even if it was not you who bought the goods, you can win compensation if you can prove they were responsible for your injuries.

Unwanted visitors

• Don't be afraid of telling the truth. If someone arrives unexpectedly and you are tired or busy, say so and suggest that you get together at a more convenient time.

• If you don't enjoy the person's company, however, don't feel obliged to encourage another visit – cutting the relationship short will save wear and tear on both parties in the long run.

• Since considerate people would be embarrassed to overstay their welcome, the nicest thing to say to dinner guests who linger too long is, 'I wish I weren't so tired so we could talk more'. If that doesn't work, you can always resort to doing the dishes or making an important phone call.

• Discourage work colleagues from dropping in to see you when you're busy by arranging to get together after work or in the lunch hour, when you are not under pressure.

Upholstery

• Don't let zips on chair and sofa cushions fool you into thinking that the covers are washable – the fabric will probably shrink unless it's cleaned in place. If the fabric is washable, you can sponge it with a solution of mild detergent and warm water. Work on one section at a time, removing the suds with a clean wet cloth. If you do remove covers for washing, put them back on the furniture while still damp to ensure a good fit.

• Repair a cigarette burn by darning it with matching thread or wool.

• Mend a tear by placing adhesive or iron-on tape on the underside of the fabric, sticky side up. Press the edges closed; trim off stray threads.

• If you can't afford new upholstery, drape your chair or sofa with fabric, quilting, an attractive tablecloth or a bedspread. Secure it to the underside of the frame with upholstery tacks. See also LOOSE COVERS, p.120; RENEWING A SOFA, p.369.

• Is your wooden chair uncomfortable? Wrap the arms and the slats on the back

with fire-resistant foam and then cover with material. Trim the edges with strips of contrasting fabric or ribbon.

• To prevent upholstery from becoming soiled and developing worn spots, get matching covers made for the back and armrests, which can be removed and washed or dry-cleaned.

• Plump up a flattened cushion by turning it in a tumble dryer for 5 minutes on Low. Include a few bath towels to balance the drum.

• Make seat pads by cutting a piece of 1½in/38mm fire-resistant foam to size and covering it with fabric.

• Keep seat pads in place by sewing ties onto the back corners. Or use Velcro strips: sew one side to the cushions and glue the opposing side to the seat.

• Before stuffing a cushion with shredded fire-resistant foam, put the material in an old pillowcase. Then stuff the whole thing into the cushion cover.

Vacuum cleaners

• Never pick up cigarette ends with your vacuum cleaner. Not only could they block up the machine, but a smouldering one could be dangerous.

• If your cleaner isn't picking up dirt as well as it used to, see if the hose is clogged. Look through both ends; if you

can't reach the obstruction with your hand, use a ruler, bamboo cane or the end of a straightened wire hanger.

• Before replacing a torn, fabric, dust-bag jacket on an upright cleaner, try to repair it with iron-on patches.

• If the hose attachment sticks to the cleaner when you're taking it off, rub the join with waxed paper.

• A rule of thumb for vacuuming is to pass over a carpet three times for light cleaning and seven times for heavy cleaning.

Valuables

• To enable you to identify your property if it's ever stolen, mark each item indelibly with your postcode. Then, to make it unique to you, add the number of your house or flat, or the first two letters of your house name. Use invisible, fluo-

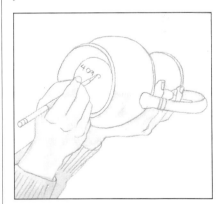

rescent ink pens, ceramic markers or diamond-tipped engravers. These can be bought individually or in kits at art supply or craft shops.

• Ask a professional valuer to assess the value of your jewellery, antiques and rare objects. Then make sure that your contents insurance covers the full replacement value of what you own. Remember, it will probably cost you far more to replace your old oak kitchen table than you originally paid for it.

Making a household inventory

• Compile a complete written inventory of your most valuable household belongings; keep one copy at home, another with your bank or your solicitor and a third with your insurance company. Although making the inventory may be tedious, it will be extremely valuable if you're ever the victim of theft, fire, flood or any other disaster and have to make a claim.

• Catalogue each room thoroughly; open every drawer and cupboard and carefully list anything of value. Write a description of each piece (including its serial number and brand name), the date you bought it and its price. Keep receipts and valuations for any very valuable items.

• Photograph each item against a plain background with a ruler by the side of it to give some idea of scale. Make a careful note of any distinguishing marks such as crests or initials. Small items are often difficult to mark and the photograph is a useful supplement to other precautions. See also HOMEOWNERS' INSURANCE, p.107; INSURANCE CLAIMS, p.114; SAFE-DEPOSIT BOXES, p.173.

Varicose veins

Knotted veins visible just under the skin are common from the late teens on, and in women they can begin with pregnancy. If your veins do swell during pregnancy, they may go down again after the child is born, but they may persist. Here are some do's and don'ts to help you avoid varicose veins in the first place.

• Exercise your legs regularly: jog, walk, cycle or swim. Walk reasonable distances rather than take the bus or car.

• Don't sit or stand for long periods. If you do have to, then make sure you move around as much as possible or flex your calf muscles. When you are sitting down, try to avoid crossing your legs at the thighs.

• Lie down with your legs raised above your heart level whenever you have some time.

• Avoid wearing overly tight boots, jeans, socks or tights. Both men and women in danger of developing varicose veins should wear support stockings, but especially pregnant women.

• Women should wear sturdy-soled shoes with 1in/25mm heels, rather than trainers, high heels or thin-soled shoes.

• If your legs feel especially tired, give them a gentle, soothing massage, starting at the ankles.

• Keep your weight down; eat a balanced diet that is high in fibre, so as to avoid constipation.

• Ask your doctor about ways to remove varicose veins without surgery. One method involves chemical injections into the veins.

Vases

• If there's a whitish film on the inside of your vase, fill it with vinegar or a weak solution of chlorine bleach and water.

• To remove water rings, rub them with salt. If the vase is narrow and you can't reach them, fill it with a strong salt water solution and shake until clean.

• Coat the inside of a leaky vase with hot wax and leave it to harden. Or, if the vase is opaque, put a glass inside it to hold the water.

• Many household items make pretty vases. Teapots, carafes, copper kettles and pitchers are especially attractive. Put single stems in a wineglass or goblet. Let wild flowers or daisies spill out of a basket (first put them in a small waterproof container that won't show). For dinner parties, put a tiny bunch of violets or lilies of the valley in a small bottle at each place setting.

• If your vase has a wide mouth and the flowers need support for a neat arrangement, crisscross the opening with transparent tape – it will hold your arrangement in place.

Vegetable peelers

• For the most efficient peeling, push the blade away from you when using a peeler with a swivel blade; pull it towards you if the blade doesn't move.

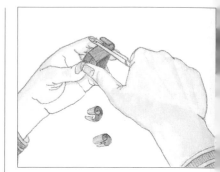

• Use a vegetable peeler to make neat chocolate curls to garnish desserts. Leave the chocolate in a warm place to soften slightly. Or place it on a plate in the microwave on 50 per cent power for 15 to 20 seconds. Then simply draw the peeler across the edge or bottom of the chocolate to make a curl.

• When removing the peel from citrus fruits, it is better to use a stainless-steel peeler rather than a knife.

Vegetable steamers

• To create a makeshift steamer, use a large saucepan with its lid and a metal colander or sieve which fits inside it. Place about 1in/25mm of boiling water in the saucepan, and add the colander or sieve containing your prepared vegetables. Cover the pan tightly and steam the vegetables until they are ready.

• Or make a steamer from a double thickness of foil. Bring an inch or two of water to the boil in a saucepan, jab small holes in the foil with a sharp pencil and tightly crimp the edges over the rim of the saucepan. Place the food inside, cover, and steam until ready.

Vegetable varieties

If your homegrown vegetables aren't up to scratch, you may be planting the wrong varieties. Look for those few varieties that are best suited to your conditions or ask neighbours for the names of successful varieties.

• Note whether the variety is specified as early, mid-season or late and how long they take to grow. If you live in the north and your growing season is short, choose early varieties that can be har vested before the first frost puts an end to the season.

• If you want to save seeds for next year, choose standard (sometimes listed as open-pollinated) varieties instead of hybrids; vegetables grown from hybrid seeds lose their desirable qualities after the first generation.

• Beware of commercial varieties, tailored to the needs of large-scale growers and packers. Their characteristics, such as tough skin and long shelf life, are pointless in the home garden and usually take precedence over taste and texture. Choose varieties that are described as 'for the home garden' or look for clues that the variety is intended for commercial growers: 'excellent for shipping' and 'suitable for processing' are warnings that you should steer clear of these varieties.

• To put old-fashioned flavour back into your garden, plant traditional varieties. Keep dandelion out of your lawn but cultivate it in a vegetable bed, to be used for salad. Blanch it for 10 days before eating by cutting out the light with soil or a cardboard box. Plant Egyptian, or tree, onion, which has its tiny bulbs at the top of its stalk. Or sow Good King Henry, a spinach-like plant, the first leaves of which are suitable for salads. The older leaves cook like spinach, and the shoots of the plants can be boiled and eaten like asparagus. Seakale is an easily grown delicacy once served 'on sippets of toasted bread drenched in white sauce or melted butter'. It has silvery-grey foliage in summer, but the plant is forced on for eating by Christmas. For information on traditional vegetable varieties, contact the Royal Horticultural Society, 80 Vincent Square, London SW1P 2PE, Tel. 071-834 4333.

Velvet

• Check the label of a velvet or velveteen item before washing it. If it does not say that it is washable, get it dry-cleaned professionally.

• To clean washable velvet, use a soft brush to brush dirty spots. Then wash it and rinse in lukewarm water. Spin dry for a brief time, just to get rid of excess

water, and hang it up to dry. When the velvet is absolutely dry, brush it in one direction with a soft brush.

• To restore the nap of crushed velvet, steam it. Tie a piece of muslin over the spout of a kettle and bring the kettle to the boil. Pass the reverse side of the velvet through the steam, then hang to dry and brush as before.

• When you are storing velvet items, pad the inside of the garment with layers of white tissue paper, then fold and cover with tissue paper or muslin. If you are hanging up velvet garments, line them with tissue paper and hang them on a padded hanger.

Veneers

If the veneer on a table top has chipped, smarten it up with an easy repair.

• Find a piece of veneer that matches the original as closely as possible. Cut out a patch slightly larger than the damaged area and lay it over it, matching the grain. Fix it in position with tape.

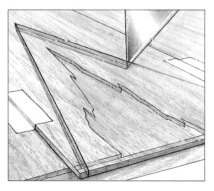

Using a craft knife, cut a triangular shape out of the new veneer over the damaged area. Press hard so that you cut through both the new and old layers. Remove the patch, then lift out the piece of damaged veneer. Using a chisel, scrape off the old glue on the wood and clean the surface.

With PVA adhesive, stick the new patch in position and press it down with a veneer hammer. Cover the repaired area with paper and a piece of board and weight or clamp the board down until the glue has hardened. Trim the edge.

Repairing loose veneer

• Lift any loose veneer and remove the

old glue with a chisel. Then put a water-soluble adhesive on the wood and veneer and stick it back in place. Cover with a weight or clamp it down until the glue has set.

• If the loose area is a small one, try heating the area with a hair dryer or by ironing over a cloth to melt the glue. Then press down the veneer and weight it as before until it sets again.

Videos

Most video care is simply preventive maintenance; once a problem occurs, there are no do-it-yourself remedies – you'll have to take the VCR to an authorised repair centre.

• Record on high-quality videotapes only. Cheap tapes harm the recording heads – as will any tape after about 100 hours of use.

• Cover your VCR when not in use to keep dust and debris out of the vents and to prevent children from putting things into the cassette slot.

• Moisture can ruin a VCR. Don't rest a container of coffee, soft drink or any other liquid on the machine and don't use liquid cleaning products on its exterior. If you live in a damp building, or a caravan in which the condensation is high, buy small packages of silica gel from an electronics supply store and put them on top of the VCR to absorb moisture. When the packages are damp, you can bake them dry in the oven and reuse them.

• If your picture is snowy and the sound is fuzzy, it's time to clean the tape heads; follow the manufacturer's instructions. If you use many rented tapes, you may need to clean the heads fairly often. See also TELEVISIONS, p.205.

Videotaping

• To make homemade videos with a professional touch, take a few minutes to plan your shots. Better yet, jot down a rough shooting script. It should tell a story. Show preparations for a holiday, for example, and then the departure. After filming holiday highlights, attach an ending – perhaps something humorous about arriving home exhausted.

• When shooting, do what the pros do: hold the camera as steady as possible, then pan slowly and smoothly.

• Don't overdo zooms; too many are visually disturbing. Use them to emphasise something important, such as a close-up of a child's face blowing out birthday candles or her reaction when she opens a birthday present.

• Don't make scenes interminably long. Linger on one angle for only 8 to 10 seconds before you switch to another view.

Vines and climbers

Growing grape vines for wine production is increasingly popular in Britain, although grapes for eating are hard to ripen in our climate without protection. Vines do best in areas of low rainfall and poor soils. If you are worried that you'll plant a vine or climber in the wrong place, first find out how it grows.

Twining types Wisteria and honeysuckle wrap their stems around their host. They are best confined to a trellis, arch or fence, or supported up a wall, on a south or west-facing side.

Tendril types Clematis, sweet peas and grape vines pull themselves aloft with delicate tendrils. They clamber up a tree or shrub harmlessly if thinned by periodic pruning and provide the host with a bonus period of bloom or a colourful autumn foliage display. You can also grow them up stakes, on a trellis or supported against a wall.

Holdfast types Wall climbers such as ivy, Virginia creeper and climbing hydrangea stick themselves to a wall with resinous suckers. Contrary to popular belief, they won't damage the mortar; they protect it by insulating the masonry from heat and frost.

Vision loss

• See your doctor without delay if you experience sudden loss of vision, even if things suddenly look blurred.

• Poor vision need not mean doing without books and other reading matter. Large-print books and periodicals are available in most public libraries and day care centres, and from some bookshops and mail-order catalogues. Or try cassette recordings: for magazines and newspapers, contact the Talking Newspaper Association, National Recording Centre, Heathfield, East Sussex TN21 8DB; Tel. 0435 866102; for books, contact the Royal National Institute for the Blind, 224-228 Great Portland Street, London W1N 6AA, Tel. 071-388 1266.

• Many household items are now designed with large print: watches, telephone buttons and dials, thermometers, clocks, typewriter keys, even software for personal computers. Magnifying devices, range from a simple glass with a light attached, which doubles the size of an object, to a closed-circuit television that enlarges up to 60 times.

• Your local social services department or optician can put you in touch with a social worker for blind or visually handicapped people. Also contact the Association for the Education and Welfare of the Visually Handicapped, 24 Vicarage Road, Harborne, Birmingham B17 0SP, Tel. 021-426 6815.

• Your mobility need not be restricted because your eyesight is impaired. Guide dogs will enable you to negotiate public transport and busy roads in safety. Contact the Guide Dogs for the Blind Association, Hillfields, Burghfield, Reading, Berks RG7 3YG, Tel. 0734 835555. The association trains guide dogs and also teaches visually impaired people how to use them.

Voice loss

Hoarseness or voice loss, accompanied by a sore throat and a temperature, are symptoms of laryngitis. There are two forms of this illness: acute laryngitis which is caused by a virus and is

Passion flower

Virginia creeper

Wisteria

The vine is a hardy climber but needs a long, hot summer to produce edible grapes. It is ofen successful in greenhouses and conservatories, planted in a pot or a border.

Alexander's unique technique

The Australian actor Frederick Matthias Alexander (1869-1955) developed his method of improving posture when he found that he was losing his voice on stage. Although rest improved his condition, he wondered if something he was doing on stage affected his voice.

When he acted out his stage part in front of the mirror, he was amazed to see that as he was about to speak he shortened visibly, and at the same time he had difficulty breathing. The stress of having to remember his lines and project them to an audience made him drop his head, which constricted his vocal cords and tightened his throat, making breathing difficult and his body tense.

With constant observation and correction of his reaction, which he called the 'startle reflex pattern', he recovered his voice and developed his posture technique. He started to teach it and was soon highly sought after by the acting profession and people involved in public speaking.

Alexander suffered a stroke at the age of 78, but using his method he surprised his doctors by regaining all his faculties and the entire use of his body.

The Alexander Technique is still much in demand today as a means of improving posture and thereby helping numerous medical conditions ranging from voice loss to high blood pressure, headaches and back pain.

---

infectious, short-lived and affects adults and children; and chronic laryngitis, which is caused by stress, excessive singing or shouting, smoking, dust or irritants, and affects adults only.
• Treat both by resting your voice until it returns to its normal state.
• Drink plenty of fluids.
• Take a painkiller such as aspirin or paracetamol if necessary to ease your sore throat.
• Avoid smoke, dust and irritants.
• If the high temperature lasts for more than 3 or 4 days, see your doctor. Consult him, too, if the voice loss persists for more than 3 weeks, or if you cough up blood or coloured phlegm.

Voluntary work

Do you want to get down to some worthwhile voluntary work but don't know where to start? Try the following places to get some ideas.

Check with your local public library and at the information desk of your own hall, where voluntary agencies often leave pamphlets describing their activities. You can also ask to consult the register of charitable and voluntary organisations in the area. All local authorities keep one.
• Your local churches are also likely to have contact with voluntary bodies working in your area.
• Scan the classified section of your local newspaper. Non-profit organisations often advertise for helpers and workers in small display ads.

Vomiting

• To prevent dehydration after a bout of vomiting, drink as much fluid as you can keep down. Avoid drinks that contain caffeine such as coffee or tea; they may irritate your stomach. Once the liquids stay down, ease back into eating solid foods, beginning with dry toast, clear soup, puréed fruit and rice.
• Support a child's body and forehead while he vomits, then wipe his face with a cool, moist cloth and help him rinse his mouth and brush his teeth. If he's frightened, explain that his stomach is just getting rid of something it dislikes.
• Call a doctor if there is abdominal pain, bloating or constipation, or if vomiting persists for more than a day in a child or adult or 12 hours in a baby.

W

Walking frames

• To make carrying odds and ends easier while using a walking frame, attach a small wicker bicycle basket to the front of the walker. Run an elastic loop or a sturdy rubber band through the wicker to hold a plastic beaker of liquid firmly inside. (For maximum safety, use a covered beaker or a cyclist's plastic water bottle.)
• Tie a plastic supermarket bag to one side of the frame to hold tissues and other light items; a second one on the other side can serve as a rubbish bag.
• Do you have problems closing doors? Get someone to run a cord from the knob to a screw eye on the hinge side; then just pull on the cord to close the door behind you.
• Carry a pair of long tongs, hung from the walking frame with string, to get hold of something that is beyond your reach.
• For comfort and to prevent your hands from slipping, wrap tape around the top bar of the walking frame.

Wallflowers

• Ask a shy guest to help you serve the hors d'oeuvres or the drinks – you'll get a helping hand and he'll have a good reason to circulate among the other guests.
• Introduce the timid soul to another person who looks lost; be sure to give them both some useful information about each other so that they can start a conversation: 'Robert, I'd like you to meet John Smith. He's here for a week from Manchester, where he practises law. John, this is our neighbour Robert Jones, who teaches at our local school.'
• If you are having a small party, take the trouble to brief your guests ahead of time on who else is coming. It will help to break the ice. If one person isn't participating, ask her something she knows

plenty about so that she can have the spotlight for a while.

• You can help to keep people mingling at a cocktail party by arranging the room to encourage movement. Place drinks at one end and the food at the other. And don't provide too many chairs; if potential wallflowers have to stand, they'll be more likely to move around and chat with other guests.

Wallpaper

• To keep the wallpaper around a baby's cot clean, staple clear non-adhesive vinyl over it.

• To dust papered walls, tie a duster over your soft broom and work from the top down.

• To remove pencil marks and other non-greasy spots from non-washable papers, use a putty rubber (from an art shop) or the soft part of a slice of fresh white bread moulded into a ball.

• To remove greasy spots, crayon marks and food stains, use a light application of a solvent such as lighter fuel.

• Wipe off fingerprints with a damp cloth, then sprinkle the moist area with fuller's earth (available in garden centres or builders' merchants). Leave it to dry and then brush it off.

• To prevent splash marks when you're washing skirting boards or other woodwork, mask wallpaper with a wide ruler, a venetian blind slat or a piece of rigid plastic.

• When you save scraps of wallpaper for patching, pin them to a wall in the attic or cupboard. When you use them for repairs, they won't stand out as brand-new.

• Patches that have cut edges tend to show, so don't cut the paper – tear it instead. The feathered edges won't be so noticeable.

• If you don't have any wallpaper left for making patches, just touch up the damaged spots on plain papers with a matching coloured paint.

Hanging wallpaper

• Make a resting and wiping place for the sticky paste brush by slipping a length of coathanger wire through the handle holes on your bucket. Then rest the

bristles on the wire and the handle on the side of the bucket.

• To smooth out air bubbles under freshly applied paper, use a paint roller. Be sure to let the paper expand fully by letting it stand after pasting before putting it on the wall, or you'll get bubbles that won't go away.

• If you're papering over old wallpaper, cover any grease spots with a dab of clear lacquer so that they won't bleed through.

• Use lengths of leftover wallpaper as wrapping paper, book covers or drawer liners (see p.25).

Wallpaper removal

• To make wallpaper easier to remove, rub it down first with coarse abrasive paper. Use nothing metal or you may get rust spots in the plaster.

• Or mix a handful of wallpaper paste into a bucket of water containing a little washing-up liquid. The paste will hold the water in place while the washing-up liquid acts as a wetting agent. Then wipe the walls down with the solution.

• The ideal tool for stubborn papers is a steam wallpaper stripper. Either buy a domestic model, or hire an industrial one from your local hire shop. The combination of heat and steam will move the thickest materials.

• If you're lucky, the wallpaper could be an easy-strip type. Try lifting a corner of the patterned surface and pulling it. If it is easy-strip, the paper will come away in a sheet, leaving the backing paper behind. If the backing paper is well stuck down and in good condition, you can leave it in place and use it as lining for the next covering.

Warming up and cooling down exercises

If you exercise strenuously without warming up, you can injure muscles. If you stop exercising without cooling down, your blood pressure can drop suddenly and cause dizziness, nausea and an irregular heartbeat; this can be life-threatening to someone with a heart problem. Check with your doctor before starting any exercise regime.

• The first step in warming up is to raise your body temperature and increase

Warm up by running on the spot, slowly at first, raising your arms to get your shoulders moving. Before stopping, let your heart and pulse rate return to normal with less strenuous exercises.

your muscle flexibility. Jogging in place and slow aerobic activities are both good. So is a fast walk. Walk briskly, heel first; swing your arms and shake them vigorously as you walk to stimulate circulation. Lengthen your stride and increase your speed as you warm up.

• Once your muscles have warmed up, do at least 5 minutes of stretching exercises (see p.197). If you're warming up to run, choose exercises that will stretch your groin, hamstrings, calves and thigh muscles. If you're preparing to lift weights, concentrate on the muscles of your upper body, particularly those of your shoulders. A good book on your sport should include some specific suggestions for stretching exercises.

• After a workout, the best way to cool down is to stay in motion while gradually reducing your effort; walk briskly or jog slowly for 5 to 15 minutes in order to stabilise your blood pressure and steadily slow your heart rate.

Warped wood

• To prevent a board from warping, saw two $1/4$in/6mm slits along the board's length in the bottom or back surface. Space the slits 2in/50mm apart; they act as stress-release gaps and allow the board to expand and contract without warping.

• To correct a warped board, place it concave side up on a stack of wet towels near (but not on) a radiator or another source of heat. Put heavy weights on each end of the board and let it sit for several days, rewetting the towels as necessary. (Make sure you sand any

scaled boards beforehand so that they can absorb the moisture.)

• If warping causes a board to pull its nails free, replace them with screws; clamp the board back in place before driving in the screws.

• For even greater holding power, drill holes through the board and bolt it down.

Warts and moles

Although they may look similar, warts and moles are unrelated skin conditions. If you are worried about a growth, consult your doctor to make sure which you have.

• Warts vary in size, shape, roughness and colour and grow mainly on the face, neck, hands, forearms, legs and feet. They are almost always harmless, and may disappear by themselves within 6 to 24 months. See box p.226.

To treat a wart that has been diagnosed, soften it overnight with a bandage moistened with a 30 per cent salicylic acid solution; then soak the wart for 30 minutes in Epsom salts and hot water and file it gently with an emery board or a pumice stone.

• Moles, which are small dark spots, can occur anywhere on the body. If you are subject to moles, examine your skin monthly in a hand-held and a full-length mirror. Look for growths larger than a pencil eraser and those that have an irregular raised surface, an asymmetrical outline, and a mottled colour; also look for colour changes, scaliness, oozing, bleeding, itching, tenderness and a bump or nodule. If you spot any of these, see your doctor.

Washing machines

If your washing machine doesn't work, check the plug first, then the socket outlet. Next, see if both the hot and cold taps are turned on. (Turn them off when the machine is not in use; constant pressure on the hoses eventually makes them leak.) Check that the control switches are properly set.

Drainage problems

• If the machine isn't draining, the hose

The hazards of exercising

Exercise is not always a good thing. Too much too soon can cause injuries.

Running injuries are most frequent in people who run more than 30 miles/48km a week. Sports doctors say 20-25 miles/32-40km is quite enough to keep you in top condition.

No pain, no gain — so goes the aerobics refrain. But this is wrong. Strenuous exercise may cause some discomfort, but pain is a warning to stop what you're doing before you injure yourself.

Never take salt tablets before exercising — they can cause nausea and vomiting. To counter salt loss, drink salty liquids or add a little extra table salt to your food.

Many people are seriously injured working out on weight machines because they don't use them properly. Always get advice on how to use the equipment from a qualified instructor before you

begin. Don't guess — it's too risky.

The myth that you shouldn't drink water while exercising is not only wrong but dangerous. Working out when you're dehydrated puts extra strain on your heart and muscles. Drink a glass of water before you start and have more if you feel thirsty.

Don't proceed as usual in very hot, humid weather — you could get heatstroke. Ask your doctor for guidelines for your age and fitness level.

If you haven't played sport for a long time, don't start up at your former intensity. Start slowly to build up strength and endurance.

Exercise can be addictive. Beware if you continue to exercise despite injuries, if you find it hard to sleep even though you're exhausted, if exercise is interfering with your work or social life, or if you feel guilty or out of control when you miss a workout.

Warts and all

Contrary to folklore, warts are not caused by frogs, toads or the water used to boil eggs. The ugly lumps come from viruses that are passed from person to person.

Perhaps because many warts simply disappear in time, an air of mystery has always surrounded them. People have tried to make them vanish by covering them with spider webs, raw potatoes or dandelion sap. Some have believed that they could give their warts to an enemy by rubbing the blemishes with a pebble, wrapping the pebble in a piece of paper with the person's name on it, and then throwing it away. Others thought that their parents or friends could 'buy' warts for a penny, yet not be afflicted.

The folk remedies for getting rid of warts are legion. The more bizarre ones include tying a hair from the tail of a piebald pony or the mane of a grown horse around each wart. Or washing the wart in a blacksmith's trough (in which he plunges horseshoes) every day for a week.

At least there is logic in the remedy that suggests rubbing bacon or raw meat onto the wart and then burying it, in the belief that by the time the meat has decomposed and been absorbed by the ground, the wart will have gone. Since the decomposition and absorption process would take some time, it is quite likely that the wart would have disappeared by the time the meat became rotten.

may be kinked or clogged – perhaps a sock has worked its way into the line. Refer to the manufacturer's instructions to see if you can correct the problem yourself.

Otherwise, disconnect the electricity supply, open the lid if possible, wring out the clothes and bail or siphon out the water. If you have a front-loading machine full of water, it may not be possible to open the door. Call a service man.

Noisy vibrations

• Loud shaking during a spin cycle is usually a sign that the load is unbalanced, probably with bulky items. Stop the washer, rearrange the load, and continue the cycle.
• Too much soap powder can also cause such vibrations to occur. Use less detergent next time or switch to a low-suds soap.
• Check that the adjustable feet are properly set. If not, readjust them.
• The drain hose may not be secured. If not, tighten the clamp.
• Inspect the floor under the machine; it may be uneven, or not sturdy enough to give solid support.
• If a new machine is noisy, look inside

for packing materials that may have been left around the drum.

If all else fails

• Fill a sink or bath with water and washing powder and hand-wash your clothes. Use a plunger to imitate the washing machine's churning action.
• Check the instructions on the care label. If items are suitable for soaking, use the bath to soak them overnight in a warm solution of washing powder. Then just rinse and dry.
• To remove excess water, wring out the clothes or place them on a towel on a firm surface after squeezing gently. Then run a rolling pin over them. Roll delicate garments in a towel.

Clothing problems

• Undiluted chlorine bleach may damage fabric. Use it only as recommended on the container and the fabric care label.
• If there's fluff all over your freshly washed clothes, you may be overloading your machine or misusing it in some other way. Fluff can also result from poor drainage (see above), too little liquid detergent, undissolved washing powder or the incorrect use of a fabric softener.

Wasps

• To minimise the risk of a wasp sting, don't wear perfume or brightly coloured clothing on hot, summer days.
• Don't try swatting a wasp if it lands on you; simply blow it off instead.
• Protect yourself against wasps by covering exposed skin surfaces with insect repellent. For extra protection, keep arms and legs covered with long sleeves and long trousers. Wearing loose-fitting clothing reduces the chances of penetration by the insect's sting.
• If several wasps attack you at once, you've probably disturbed their nest; run through shrubs or hedges – it's harder for the insects to follow you there than in an open area.
• If an insect flies in a car window, slow down, open all the windows, and let it find its own way out.

Waste disposal unit

• *Never* put your hand in a disposal unit to free a jam. If it is blocked, try switching it into reverse, if possible. This may free the blade.
• If this doesn't work, or your unit has no reverse function, use the release tool that comes with the unit. First switch off the electricity at the fuse box or consumer unit. Then push the tool into the plughole and fit it over the blade spindle. Move the tool back and forth several times to free the blade. Take the tool out and switch on the electricity again, and turn on the waste disposal motor.

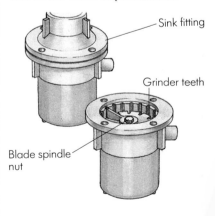

Sink fitting
Grinder teeth
Blade spindle nut

• If this still doesn't solve the problem, switch off the power again. Undo the fittings that clamp the grinder to the sink and take out the motor and grinder. Clear the blockage by hand, and then put the unit back.

• 'Sweeten' your disposal unit by running lemon or orange peels through it from time to time.

• To sharpen the blades and remove grime at the same time, make vinegar ice cubes and run them through the machine every now and then.

Water bottle

An easy-to-clean plastic bottle makes an inexpensive, lightweight water bottle or flask for use in the house or while out walking or camping. Use a distinctive container, such as those that contain dried milk, to prevent mistakenly grabbing detergent or some other liquid when you want a quick drink.

• Provide children with a straw and a small screw-top plastic bottle of juice on long journeys.

• A cord handle tied to the bottle neck helps to prevent the water bottle from slipping from your hands as you fill it in rushing streams.

Water companies

• If you have a mains water supply from a water company, the company has a statutory obligation to maintain the water it supplies you with to a drinkable standard. If the smell, taste or colour of your water seems odd, or seems to change, get in touch with your water company, which will test it free of charge.

Your water may become slightly cloudy or discoloured after the mains have been repaired; this is normal. In this case, or if you have been having plumbing work done, then run your water for a short while to clear any potential contamination. Check it by pouring a glassful and holding it up to the light.

• Water companies do not have an absolute obligation to supply you with water. They may cut it off at any time, for example to make repairs, or in extreme drought or if you do not pay your water bills. Compensation will not normally be payable.

• You will probably pay for your water through the 'rates' system at so many pence in the pound based on the value of your home. Most water companies will install a water meter as an alternative. If you live alone in a large house, consider having a meter installed. It may save you money.

• Water companies have to abide by codes of practice agreed with the Office of Water Regulation (OFWAT). If you have a complaint about your service, get in touch with the company first. If you get no satisfaction, complain to OFWAT (see the phone book or the back of your bills for the address), who have a consumer complaints panel.

Water conservation

• The most wasteful domestic appliance as far as water is concerned is the bath. Try to use less water per bath or, better still, switch to a shower for daily washing. It uses about one-fifth of the amount of water which is required to run an average bath.

• Bath water is quite suitable for garden watering – as long as it doesn't contain oils. Arrange to siphon water from the bath into a butt, using a garden hose.

• Arrange to collect at least some of the rainwater that falls but usually drains away. A large water butt with a lid can be connected to a downpipe, with an overflow to take away any surplus.

• The toilet also uses considerable amounts of water – about 4 gallons/18 litres per flush. To reduce the amount of water used, place a clean brick or

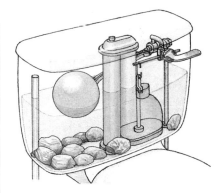

smooth large stones into the base of the cistern. A little experimenting is called for to ensure you have an adequate flush.

• If you are having a new toilet installed, look for the dual-flush models. They use only about 1 gallon/4.5 litres per flush but will flush more – 2 gallons/9 litres – if needed.

• Wash dirty dishes in a washing-up bowl full of water instead of under running water.

Water leaks

The first essential thing to do when you have any form of domestic water leak is to turn off the water supply at the mains. Teach the whole family how to do this – and make sure that the mains stopcock is easy to turn. It can seize up due to lack of use – use penetrating oil if the tap is tight. See STOPCOCK JAMMED, p.195.

• If a cistern in the loft leaks, turn off the

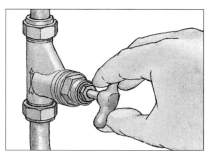

mains supply. Then run all taps and flush toilets to reduce the water level in the cistern as quickly as possible.

• If a ceiling bulges because water has flooded onto it from above, collect as many buckets and bowls as possible, then bore a hole in the ceiling at a convenient spot and let the water out. You will most probably need help with this.

• Ideally, there should be stop valves on all major pipe runs in and around your home so that areas of pipe can be isolated when trouble strikes. It is worth spending time locating and marking these against future use. If you don't have valves, it would be a good investment to get some installed. They are not difficult for a plumber to fit.

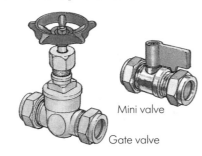

Mini valve

Gate valve

Water purification

• To purify water, first filter it. Your children can make their own filter as an experiment by filling a clean sock with successive 1in/25mm layers of fine gravel, crushed charcoal and sand. Pour water into the sock and let it drain into a cup. Then boil the water for 5 minutes (1 minute longer for every 1000ft/300m in altitude) to make it safe to drink.

• If you use purification tablets, allow 1 hour for them to take effect. Follow the directions on the bottle carefully; dosage can vary significantly with temperature.

Solar still In sunny or hot weather, show your children how to make a solar still that produces 1-3 pints/0.5-1.7 litres of pure water a day.

• Dig a bowl-shaped hole 3ft/1m in diameter and 20in/510mm deep. Set a clean bucket or bowl in the centre of the hole.

• Secure a large piece of clear plastic over the hole with earth or rocks. Then place a stone in the middle of the plastic so that the sheet's lowest point is directly above the container. Solar heat will penetrate the plastic and bake moisture out of the soil. The water will condense on the lower side of the plastic and run down to drip into the container; night cuts accumulation in half.

• Delay collecting the water for as long as possible; opening the still lets out moisture-laden air, which takes some 30 minutes to resaturate.

• When the soil in the still is baked dry, rebuild the still in another spot. Hollows and ditches are likely to have wetter soil than high ground.

• You can use the same method to purify salty or polluted water, and even urine, or to extract moisture from plant materials. Just put the water source off-centre in the hole and let the sun do its work.

Water retention

If bloating and swelling, especially round the feet and ankles, are recurring problems for you, consult your doctor to see if there is cause for concern. If not, consider taking the following measures.

• Cut down your salt intake; avoid all tinned and processed foods, from soup and salami to salted nuts and potato crisps (see LOW-SALT DIET, p.128). It may help to cut back sugar and caffeine too.

• Eat foods that are natural diuretics: cucumber, parsley, beetroot, watercress, asparagus, dandelion leaves, strawberries, apples and grapes, for example.

• Exercise regularly – swim, bicycle, jog, walk briskly – to improve your circulation.

• Wear support stockings.

• Try to take your feet off the ground for 20 minutes during the day and an hour or two before going to bed.

• Temporary swelling may be caused by sitting or standing still for long periods. Try to move regularly.

• If water retention is severe, your doctor may prescribe a diuretic to increase the amount of urine you produce. However, when you stop taking diuretic tablets the water retention will return. Diuretics can also lead to gout, diabetes and potassium deficiency, and over a long period can cause kidney problems.

Water softening

• A built-in water softener, plumbed into the rising main beyond the kitchen cold-water tap, supplies softened water for washing purposes while leaving hard, low-sodium water from the tap for drinking and cooking, which most people prefer.

• Eliminate 'telltale grey' from your laundry by using a heavy-duty liquid detergent and adding 4fl oz/115ml borax or washing soda to the water. Put 4fl oz/115ml of white vinegar in the final rinse water to help remove the last traces of soap scum. Don't do this too often, however, because the washing machine drum is not acid-resistant.

• To rid your washing machine of hard-water build-up, or limescale, add 8fl oz/225ml of citric acid and let it run – without any clothes in it – through a complete cycle.

Water stains

• If the fabric is nonwashable, gently scratch off a water stain (which is made up of mineral deposits) with your fingernail.

• If the stain persists, hold the spot over a steaming kettle until well dampened. As it dries, rub the stain, working from its outer edges towards the centre. However, do not try this treatment on silk or very delicate fabrics.

• Remove hard-water stains from glasses and bottles by rubbing them with a nylon scourer dipped in vinegar.

• Cover hard-water stains on bathroom fittings with a paste of bicarbonate of soda and vinegar. Leave for about an hour, then wipe off, rinse and dry.

• Keep the lavatory bowl stain-free by pouring 4 pints/2.3 litres of vinegar into it once a month. Let it sit overnight before flushing.

Weather forecasting

Despite a highly complex system of collecting information on weather systems around the world – which includes reports from thousands of weather stations, ships, aeroplanes and satellites

– weather forecasting is still an uncertain science.

• If you are going on holiday and want to know what sort of weather you might be in for, check newspapers and weather reports for daily and medium-range forecasts (for up to 3 days in Europe). These are generally accurate.

• Don't rely on weather predictions for a period of 10 days or more. Although forecasters can use the information they have to anticipate certain weather conditions, these are almost impossible to guarantee. Even the smallest change in temperature can alter weather patterns.

Weddings

If you're planning a wedding and are worried about the cost, here are some ways to keep down the expense and still have a day to remember.

• The ceremony doesn't have to be expensive. You could have it at a local approved site, such as a park, or at the local borough town hall, or, of course, in a church or synagogue.

• Instead of hiring a hall or hotel suite, hold the reception at home. Make a festive marquee by sewing strips of brightly coloured fabric or parachute silk together. Then tie it to the trees. Or lash flysheets or canopies to poles and set them up in clusters or against the side of the house. String the garden with a gala canopy of tiny white lights for an evening reception.

• Ask a music student to play at the ceremony. For the reception, make your own dance tapes.

• Rather than arranging an elaborate sit-down meal, set out a cold buffet, or plan an afternoon wedding and serve white wine and hors d'oeuvres. Offer the guests a special punch made with sparkling wine – it will cost less than serving champagne.

• Look for someone who makes wedding cakes at home; the cake will probably cost less than one from a bakery and should taste just as good – and could even be a lot better.

• Ask friends who are photo buffs to take the formal and candid shots at the reception. Get the film developed and printed yourself.

• Make your own floral arrangements and bouquets with flowers from your garden or with wild flowers and ivy. (Pick wild flowers the same day you want to use them; they wilt quickly. And be careful not to pick protected species.)

• Decorate the food table, if you have one, with a good-quality paper table-cloth, or a plain-coloured fabric remnant, ribbons and ivy.

• Hire crockery, cutlery and glasses, if you don't have enough. Buy alcohol in bulk from a discount warehouse.

• Scout around antique and charity shops for the wedding dress and groom's outfit. You can often find beautiful secondhand gowns and good-quality suits that are relatively inexpensive. Or hire them. Remember, the dress doesn't have to be traditional.

• Instead of engraved invitations, ask someone who does calligraphy to write them by hand. Or ask an artistic friend to design an invitation and have it printed at your local print shop. See also YOUR WEDDING CHECKLIST, p.263.

Weeds

• Do you want to get rid of weeds without using herbicides? Thoroughly dig over and fertilise the soil in early spring, and then cover it with a sheet of black plastic. The plastic will absorb sunlight to warm the soil; when weed seeds germinate, the plastic will smother the unwelcome seedlings. Some 6 to 8 weeks later (in late May or early June), the bed will be ready to uncover and sow with flowers or vegetables.

• Make sure you don't sow weeds in your garden. Compost horse and cow manure before adding it to your soil (see p.50); in the process you'll destroy any seeds the animal may have ingested or which are in straw bedding.

• When you're weeding, separate the perennial weeds from the rest. Don't add these to your compost heap but burn them instead.

• Weed every 10 days. Till the soil 10 days before planting and hoe out any seedlings that appear in the interval

---

Weather wisdom

Most adages about the weather – many of them in rhyme – are grounded in centuries of observation by farmers and seafarers who were finely tuned to their environment. We still take some of the old verses seriously today:

Red sky in the morning
Is a shepherd's warning;
Red sky at night
A shepherd's delight.

Dry air supports more dust than humid air and hence reddens the light. When the sky is red to the west – just after sunset – you can suppose that fair weather is on its way, since air currents in the Northern Hemisphere move from west to east. But when the dawn sky looks red to the east, the dry weather has already passed you by, and rain may well be on its way to your part of the world.

Swallows fly high,
Clean blue sky;
Swallows fly low,
Rain we shall know.

Low atmospheric pressure and high humidity, both harbingers of rain, make it difficult for insects to fly high; so swallows fly closer to the earth to prey on them. Other signs of low pressure and probable rain are smoke that curls down from a chimney, soot that falls into the fireplace, clouds forming at low altitudes and a strong smell of earth rising from ditches and marshes.

At night, ice crystals in high cirrostratus clouds refract the moonlight, creating what appears to be a halo around the moon. This indicates that there is an advancing cold front, which brings storms.

A circle round the moon,
'Twill rain soon.

before you sow your plants. Cultivate again 10 days after planting, when the weeds are still small and easy to uproot. Ten days later work the soil yet again. For fast-growing and late-season plants, this should be all the weeding you'll need to do.

• Grow ground-cover plants such as ivy and aubrieta. They will cut out the sunlight needed for weeds to grow.

Weevils

These small beetles, of which there are more than 500 species in Britain, feed at night, eating leaves, buds and new shoots and the roots of pot plants. Their larvae burrow into seeds and fruit and invade potting compost. They are best eradicated with a pesticide.

• Make up a solution of derris and then stand any affected pot plants in the liquid.

• If the leaves of peas and broad beans are perforated with U-shaped notches, the culprit is likely to be pea or bean weevils. They don't really damage the plants, but a dusting of derris will kill them off.

• An alternative to derris is a pesticide containing gamma HCH, but this also kills the parasitic wasps that live on weevils.

• If you don't want to use a pesticide, lay sacking or corrugated paper near the affected plants. The weevils will hide in it during the day. Shake them into soapy water, or burn the material.

Wheelbarrows

If you take care of your wheelbarrow, it will last you for years.

• Clean it after every use, and keep it in a dry place.

• Don't leave anything in it that will rust or rot.

• Don't overload a lightweight wheelbarrow. If you are moving heavy materials around the garden, hire a more substantial one.

• If your barrow has pneumatic tyres, try not to bump it up and down steps or kerbs, or the tyre could burst.

• If the wheel bearings have worn down,

fit new ones. Turn the wheelbarrow upside-down. Undo the wheel nuts and take the wheel out of the frame. Then remove the spindle and hub centre. Using a screwdriver, push the bearings out of the hub centre. Tap in new ones with a soft-headed mallet.

Wheelchair access

• Make a ramp from 4 × 2in/100 × 50mm timber covered with ¾in/19mm marine ply. Store it in the garage and use it to cover stairs, rough ground or sand when you need wheelchair access.

• To make it easy for a wheelchair to pass through narrow interior doorways, use rising butt hinges so that you can remove the doors. Keep the area behind other doors clear of wastepaper baskets, furniture and other items that might impede easy opening.

• Tape down the latches on doorknobs so that doors can be pushed open and closed.

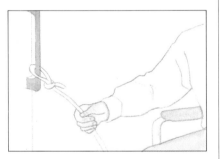

• Tie short lengths of rope to the handles of sliding doors and refrigerators so that they can be pulled open easily.

• Take up all rugs and hallway carpet runners to provide a smooth surface.

Wheezing

Wheezing may be caused by croup in children (see p.56), respiratory infection, laryngitis (see p.121) or choking (see p.44). It may also be a sign of asthma (see p.13).

• Rest in a warm, well-ventilated room.

• Steam inhalations can ease breathing difficulties. If you're treating a child, get her to sit on your knee to breathe the steam from a sinkful of hot water. Do not let her get too close to the water or she

could well be scalded by the steam.

• Feed the sufferer cold drinks.

• See a doctor as soon as possible if your baby under six months wheezes; your child has difficulty swallowing; the steam doesn't ease the breathing; the breathing becomes rapid with the ribs drawn in on each breath; the face turns grey; the sufferer has a history of heart disease; or if you think a blockage in the nose or throat is the cause.

Whipped cream

• As an alternative to whipped cream use a creamy topping.

• Overwhipped cream can be salvaged by adding a little extra cream or milk and stirring it in carefully.

• If the whipped cream is for pouring only, you can substitute it with whipped evaporated milk, adding a little vanilla essence for extra flavour.

Whitefly

These small, triangular white insects cluster on the undersides of the leaves of green vegetables, houseplants and greenhouse plants. The larvae suck the sap from the leaves, which mottles them and turns them yellow.

• Wash the insects and larvae off the leaves with a strong jet of diluted insecticidal soap or soapy water.

• Or treat them with a spray of derris three times in the day at five-day intervals.

• Or you could introduce the parasitic wasp *Encarsia formosa*, which feeds on whitefly.

• In the greenhouse, hang up a square of yellow plastic smeared thinly with grease. Whitefly are attracted to yellow and will trap themselves in the grease.

Wicker

• Remove dust from wicker by vacuuming it with the dusting-brush ring attachment. To remove grime, wash with a solution of diluted washing-up liquid; use a paintbrush or a toothbrush to get at hard-to-reach places. Rinse well; leave to dry in the shade.

- To prevent wicker from drying out, wet it down with a cloth at least once a year. Don't leave it outdoors when not in use – sunshine dehydrates wicker, and water rots it.
- Never strip paint from wicker or it will get brittle. Repaint it instead, using a spray paint. Apply several light coats rather than one heavy one that may clog up the wickerwork. Work outside or in a well-ventilated shed or garage and wear protective clothing and a mask. Brush on a liquid varnish to protect the finish.
- If paint is caked on the weave, remove it with a rigid plastic spatula.

Wigs and hairpieces

- A long plait or hairpiece can be an attractive addition to your hairstyle 'wardrobe'. Tie your hair back with a hair band first, and neaten the end by curling it under or into a small chignon; then secure it with hair clips and pins. Then pin on the hair piece. Hide the join with a ribbon or scarf, or a piece of your own hair wound round the join and clipped in place.
- For a perfect match, why not save your long hair when you have it cut? Ask your hairdresser to keep the hair she cuts off and put it in a bag for you. When you get home, secure one end of the cuttings with a rubber band, and make a plait.
- These days, hairdressers can weave several little plaits or sections of loose wavy hair into short hair, to give you a different look. This is quite fiddly to do and is best left to a professional rather than trying to do it yourself.
- To get a wig of the right style, buy one with long hair and take it to a salon to have it custom-cut.
- If you need a wig stand, use a soft drinks bottle with a roll of toilet paper fitted over its neck.
- If you have a wobbly wig stand, glue the bottom to a square of hardboard.
- The easiest way to hide baldness is with a hairpiece. Ask a friend who has one that looks good where he got it, or consult a hair stylist or dermatologist. Most people need at least two so that one can be worn while the other is being cleaned and restored.

Wilting plants

- Is the foliage in your garden wilting? It's not necessarily a sign of dry soil; it may just be a reaction to a hot summer wind. If the plants revive at sunset, everything's fine. But if the foliage still droops in the morning, water the plants at once. Don't flood the garden; sprinkle only until the soil is moist to a depth of 5-6in/125-150mm. Then stretch some wet canvas between stakes to shade the wilted plants until they revive.
- To revive a wilted houseplant, plunge its pot into a bucket of tepid water. Let it soak until bubbles stop rising from the soil. Drain off the excess water and set the plant in a humid spot such as a bathroom or greenhouse. Or cover the plant with a transparent plastic bag, supporting the plastic with a frame of stakes or coat hanger wire so that it doesn't touch the plant. Secure the bag to the pot's rim with string or a large rubber band. Keep the plant out of direct sunlight while it recovers.

Window boxes

Window boxes can be placed on windowsills, if the sill is wide enough or supported by brackets, or can be fixed to the wall or to a railing.
- Make sure that the pots you put into the box and the box itself have drainage holes to stop the plants from becoming waterlogged.
- Wooden flower boxes provide far better insulation than plastic or metal planters. Cedar is the best material, if you can find it, because it is the most rot-resistant. Less expensive pine must be treated after the box is assembled. Avoid commercial wood preservatives and especially creosote, and char the interior of the box by painting it with paraffin and setting it alight for 30 seconds instead. Smother the flames by turning the box over or covering it with a piece of plywood.
- Make a window box out of ¾in/19mm timber. You will need two pieces for the length, two for the width and one piece for the base.
  Measure the length of the windowsill

and subtract 1in/25mm, and then measure the width. A box for a sill 6in/150mm wide will hold pots up to 4½in/115mm across. Make the box deep enough to hide the tops of the pots.
  The base needs to be 1½in/38mm narrower and shorter than the front and back pieces. Drill ½in/13mm holes through the base for drainage, and screw holes for the joints.
  Char the wood to preserve it, as described, then glue the surfaces together with a waterproof wood glue, and screw them in place with brass or rustless screws. If you want, attach two cross-battens to the bottom of the window box to provide better drainage. Fix the window box to the window frame with angle brackets.

Windows

- Don't clean windows when direct sunlight is shining on them – they'll dry too quickly and streak.
- Clean windows with tepid water. If they're very dirty, add washing-up liquid or methylated spirits to the water, but remember to rinse them afterwards with clean, cold water.
- Chamois or chamois-substitute cloths are the best for cleaning windows. Use one for cleaning and one for wiping the windows dry.
- Clean windows from the outside edges inwards.
- For large panes of glass, use a squeegee on a long wooden pole. Work from the top down, and wipe the blade after each stroke with a dry cloth.
- To keep windows from icing up during winter, sponge them with salt water and then wipe them dry.
- If your windows tend to fog up, wipe them with soap rubbed onto a moist cloth; rinse and dry, then go over them with a glycerine-dampened cloth.

• Hold a cracked window pane together temporarily with sticky tape.

• For more privacy in a room, try frosting the window. Brush it with a solution of 1 tablespoon Epsom salts in 8 fl oz / 225 ml of beer. 'Defrost' your window with concentrated ammonia.

• To loosen windows that stick, lubricate the channels with silicone spray, a bar of soap or a candle.

• When painting or varnishing windows, leave the outer frames until last. When the windows are dry, slide them up and down a few times, or open and shut the casements, to make sure that they haven't stuck.

• To break a paint seal, force the blade of a putty knife between the sash and the frame; slide the blade up and down the length of the window and across the top and bottom as necessary.

Window treatments

• Create a festive look for your windows by draping fabric across the top of them. Screw two large cup hooks into the top corners of the window frame and festoon a length of fabric, such as sheeting, across them. Pull the middle section down slightly to create a swag. You could hide the hooks with fabric bows or ribbons. By using special curtain drape hooks, you can twist a length of fabric through them to produce an elegant hang on either side of a window.

• Small, narrow, louvred panels from DIY shops can be hinged together to make neat, free-standing window screens, which you can place on a windowsill. Apart from providing privacy, they shield the interior from direct sunlight.

• Transform windows without a view with 'stained glass'. Kits are available from DIY and craft shops. Some involve drawing the design with liquid lead on the glass and then filling it in with special glass paints. Others use coloured acetate sheets that are held in place with a self-adhesive leading strip.

• Get children to decorate windows at Christmas with plastic doilies and spray-on snow. Cut-out snowflakes also look festive. Take a square sheet of paper, fold it in half lengthways and then into quarters. Fold again into thirds and trim off the irregular corners at the bottom. To create the snowflake pattern, make cuts in one of the folded edges – the closer you cut to the opposite edge, the more delicate the design will be. Unfold and tape to the window.

Windscreens in cold weather

• Although salt is often used to get rid of ice on windscreens, it may damage paintwork and chrome. Buy a de-icing spray specially designed for the job, instead.

• Use a phone card or piece of old credit card to scrape ice off your windscreen.

• A blackboard rubber works better than cloth for demisting a windscreen.

• Or rub the inside of your windscreen with a soft cloth dipped in a solution made up of 1 tablespoon surgical spirit and 1¼ pints / 725 ml water; it will help to prevent the surface misting in the first place.

Windscreen washers

• Check the water level in the reservoir and refill it if necessary. Always top it up before you embark on a long trip.

• Don't use washing-up liquid in the water, because it may clog up the jets. Use a windscreen-washer detergent instead.

• If the jets are blocked, clean them out with a pin. If they are impossible to clear, fit new ones.

• Check the hose is not bent, and straighten it if necessary. If it is blocked, disconnect it from the pump and blow or pump air through it to free the blockage. If the hose is damaged, fit a new one.

• The bottom end of the pipe in the reservoir should have a filter and non-return valve. Check these and clear of any sediment or blockage. If the filter is gummed up, replace it.

Changing the pump

If you've checked the above and the washer still won't work, the pump may need replacing. Buy a second-hand model if possible, or a new one, from a car accessory shop.

• Disconnect the car's battery. Remove

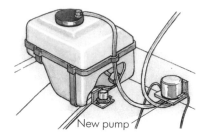
New pump

the wiring from the old pump. Undo the water outlet pipe and push it aside, and then block up the outlet stub with a brass woodscrew.

• Fit the pump according to the manufacturer's instructions. Then attach the outlet pipe to the outlet stub on the new pump. Connect a new length of pipe from the pump's inlet stub to the reservoir. The end of the pipe in the reservoir must have a filter and a non-return valve.

• Reconnect the wiring and then the battery. Fill up the reservoir and then test the washer pump to see that it works.

Windscreen wipers

Are your wipers not working properly? Before buying new ones, clean both the glass and blades thoroughly. If you've had your car cleaned at the car wash, you may have to use a mild household abrasive cleaner to remove any silicone wax. If that still doesn't do the trick, try the following.

• Water beads are the result of grease or silicone build-up. Clean the windscreen with the solvent used for removing grease or silicone from bodywork.

• If the wipers are smearing in only one direction or if they chatter, the blades may be frozen. Warm them between your hands or use a hair dryer; if that doesn't help, dip them in warm water.

• Chattering may also be caused by a bent wiper arm. In this case, stop the wipers in midstroke to see if they are parallel to the windscreen. If an arm is bent, straighten it with two pairs of pliers until it remains parallel to the glass when released. If the tip of the arm is bent, remove the blade before you straighten the arm. The problem may also be corroded joints. Free them up with penetrating solvent.

• Streaking may occur when the nozzle of the windscreen washer is blocked; insert a pin to clear it. Or the washer fluid may not be spraying in the wiper's path; adjust the position of the nozzle with a pin and keep checking until the spray pattern is on target. Some nozzles aren't adjustable; don't force them.

• Before driving in the rain, rub your wiper blades with bicarbonate of soda – you'll see better.

• If the blade on the driver's side isn't working, swap it with the one on the passenger's side. This is a temporary measure only. Get the faulty blade fixed as soon as you can.

• If you need to change your blades, check your car manual for details of the right size to use; it will also advise on how often you should replace them.

Wine

• To decide how many bottles you'll need for a dinner, follow this rule: a standard bottle is generally ample for three people, a half-bottle for two.

• If you're serving two dinner wines, remember this simple protocol: white before red, young wine before old. And a dry wine always precedes a sweet one; the sweet taste will linger. Save your sweet wines to serve with dessert. For this reason it is often a good idea to serve assorted cheeses before dessert.

• Uncork red wines an hour before drinking them so that they can 'breathe' and develop their flavour; then serve at room temperature. Chill whites and rosés but don't uncork them until you're ready to serve.

• Don't throw out wine left in the bottle. Recorked, it will keep in the refrigerator for a few days. And if you don't drink it within that time, it will keep to be used later in cooking. Eventually you can use it instead of vinegar.

• Even if you don't have a cellar, any dark, cool corner with some humidity and no vibration can be turned into a wine storage area. A dark cupboard, an unused fireplace with a blocked-off chimney or a corner of a well-insulated garage will all do. Keep the temperature as close to 10°C/50°F as possible. Store the bottles horizontally so that the corks remain moist.

• If you don't have a wine rack, use empty cardboard boxes with dividers; off licences sometimes give them away.

Wine stains

• If you spill wine on your clothing or a tablecloth, blot it up immediately with an absorbent cloth, and then sponge it with carbonated or warm water. If the fabric is washable, stretch the stained area over a small saucepan (hold it in place with a rubber band), and pour hot water through it. Wash normally, as soon as possible.

• On non-washable fabrics, sponge the stain with a cloth wrung out in warm detergent solution, followed by clean water. Dry-clean as soon as possible.

• If red wine is spilled on your carpet, sponge it with carbonated water. Blot well, then dab with a cloth wrung out in warm detergent solution, followed by clean water. If a stain remains, a 50-50 solution of glycerine and water can be left on the stain for up to an hour, then rinse it off and blot well.

Winter clothing

• Keep warm in winter with thermal underwear. Silk or synthetic thermal underwear comes in flattering styles these days and gives the warmth of several layers of thick clothing, so you can wear lightweight clothing over it and still be warm.

• Wear several layers of clothes rather than relying on one thick garment to keep you warm. T-shirts under a shirt, covered by a thick pure wool sweater is effective.

• Keep your extremities covered at all times. Thermal mittens, socks and wool mix tights make a great difference. Tie a silk scarf at your neck and wear a hat that pulls down well past your ears.

• Wear boots and fingerless gloves when working outside or in cold, unheated rooms.

• If your jacket isn't windproof and you need to go out into the cold, you can, at a pinch, use a large plastic rubbish bag as a windcheater. Cut head and arm holes and wear it under your jacket. Small bags over your socks and gloves will also keep out wind. (However, plastic will make you sweat, so don't rely on these measures for too long, or the moisture will cool you down.) If you don't have plastic bags, put newspaper or foam under your coat or shirt, and inside your boots and hat.

• If your child gets a rash from his wool or wool-mix winter hat, attach a cotton liner to the inside of the hat.

In vino veritas

According to an old wives' tale, the cure for rabies was to drink a glass of wine containing a few hairs taken from a rabid dog. This is the origin of the phrase that suggests taking a drink to cure a hangover – 'the hair of the dog that bit you'.

Dom Perignon, a Benedictine monk, discovered in the 17th century how to create and retain the natural sparkle in champagne. On his first sip he is said to have called out to his brother 'Come quickly! I am drinking stars!'

Legend has it that the shape of the first wine chalice was inspired by the breast of Helen of Troy. Centuries later, the buxom Marie Antoinette of France had champagne glasses made in the shape of her breasts. Today the narrower tulip-shaped and flute glasses are preferred for champagne because they prevent it from losing its bubbles as quickly.

The per capita consumption of wine in Britain in 1990 was just over 20 pints/11.36 litres. This makes Britain 26th in the league table of wine drinkers. Not surprisingly, France is in the lead, with 128 pints/73 litres of wine drunk per head in the same year.

Winter snowstorms

• Listen regularly to the radio for warnings about weather conditions in rural areas that easily become snowbound – advance warning of even a few hours can be a lifesaver.

• Always keep some extra blankets and an emergency heat source (enough to warm at least one room) at the ready.

• Make sure you have a battery-operated radio; candles, lanterns or torches; and extra batteries.

• Store a week's supply of food and water and, if your cooker is electric, a camp stove or burner with fuel. See also CAR STUCK IN SNOW OR MUD, p.37; POWER CUT, p.160; WINTER CLOTHING, p.233.

Wire cutter

• One blow of a hammer on a cold chisel pressed onto ordinary electrical wire will sever it. Cutting cable the same way will take two or three strikes.

• If you don't have a cold chisel to hand, wrap the wire over the corner of a metal file and saw through it.

• Slice wire with the spinning edge of an abrasive wheel in an electric drill. But make sure that you wear eye protection.

• Remember the wire-cutting bite on the side of your pliers. It's designed to cut thin wire.

• At a pinch, pruning shears will cut thin wire, but the edge of the shears will be damaged. Be sure to resharpen the shears before using them on your roses or other shrubs.

Wires and cables

• There is always the danger of drilling into hidden cables in walls and under floors. So invest in a pocket cable-finder which will seek out metallic objects and indicate whether a current is flowing where you want to drill.

• Straighten kinks in thin electrical wire by drawing it between your thumb and a screwdriver handle as though you were combing long hair. After a few passes, the wire will take on a long, uniform curve and will be much easier to roll neatly into coils.

Witnessing a crime

• When you see – or suspect you see – a crime being committed, call the police at once. Don't assume someone else already has. And don't feel intimidated – there's no legal obligation to give your name and address to the police (even if asked) when you describe what you've seen. But you may be the one witness with a vital piece of evidence, so the police may need to know who you are and where they can find you.

• Don't linger near the scene of a crime. Wait for the arrival of the police at a safe distance.

• If you see a street crime from indoors, call the police, but don't put yourself at risk unnecessarily by shouting out from a window or going outside before the police arrive.

• To help the police, write down a description of the criminal or criminals while your memory is still fresh (height? build? hair and skin colour? clothing?) and the make, model, colour and registration number of the vehicle if you know them. Jot down exactly what happened from beginning to end.

• If you hear screams or other loud or unusual noises coming from a neighbour's home, telephone the police. Don't investigate or interfere yourself.

Wobbly furniture

• First, check to see that all screws and bolts are tight.

• To fix a glued joint, such as where a chair rung fits into the frame, pull the dowel out of the socket as far as you can

(take care not to break another joint). Soften the old glue (see p.97) and scrape it off both the dowel and its socket. Apply carpenter's glue all around the dowel and push it back into the socket, wiggling it to spread the glue. Wipe off any excess with a damp cloth and then bind the dowel in place until the glue is dry with a strip of cloth or rag.

• If a table or chair leg is shorter than the others, force it into a piece of wood putty placed on a piece of waxed paper. When it's the same height as the other legs (check with a spirit level), use a craft knife to scrape away excess putty. Then let the putty dry, sand it smooth, and finish the surface as you wish.

• If a screw or dowel is loose because the wood has dried out and the hole is too big, push glue-dipped flat toothpicks in beside it to tighten the fit. Or take out the dowel and wrap the end with a paper shim before pushing it into the joint. Or cut two strips of cloth a bit narrower than the dowel's tip and hold them over it before inserting in the glue-primed hole; use a craft knife to trim off any visible cloth.

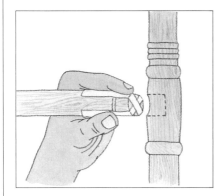

Wood filler

• Save the sawdust when you're doing heavy sanding on a woodworking project. Mixed with PVA glue, it makes a good wood filler.

• If you do buy a wood filler, or stopping, you have a choice of interior and exterior-grade fillers. Be sure to choose the correct one.

• If the wood to be filled is coloured, you can either buy one of a limited range of coloured fillers, or tint the filler with a matching wood stain after it has dried to get a closer match.

• Some modern fillers are epoxy-based, which ensures very fast setting and a tough repair. But some are not compatible with stains. So, if you have staining to do, make sure the filler you choose will absorb the stain and match the surrounding wood.

Wood floors

• Remove food or dried milk stains from waxed floors with a damp cloth, water stains with fine (No.oo) steel wool, and heel marks with steel wool dipped in floor cleaner or methylated spirits. For alcohol spots use boiled linseed oil, silver polish or a cloth dampened with ammonia. Harden wax crayon marks, chewing gum or candle wax with an ice cube in a plastic bag, then scrape off with a dull knife or your fingernail. Or pour cleaning fluid around the spot to loosen it. Then when the floor has dried thoroughly, rewax if necessary and polish.

• Fill wide cracks between floorboards with a paste of lacquer and fine sawdust stained to match. Or make a papier mâché filler, press it into the cracks, leave it to dry and then stain it. See also FLOORS, p.86.

Workbench

A proper workbench, normally sold with a vice attached and compartments for various woodworking tools, can be expensive. A simple and much cheaper alternative is to make your own from two pieces of standard-size timber boards, sold by DIY shops and builders' merchants.

• Simply screw a sheet of $\frac{1}{4}$in/6mm hardboard onto a 3×8ft/0.9 × 2.4m piece of $\frac{3}{4}$in/18mm plywood, then screw through both leaves onto two sawhorses.

• For additional stability and to prevent the worktop from swaying (while planing lengthwise, for example), screw at least two steel angle brackets to the plywood underside and fix these to wall studs in the workshop.

Wrapping packages

• If you want to tie up a package very tightly, moisten the string before you tie it; it will shrink as it dries.

• If you have documents to post that you don't want to fold, wrap them around the cardboard tube from a box of aluminium foil. Cover them with paper or foil, place them back in the aluminium foil box, wrap, address and post.

• If you are not sure how much paper you need to wrap a package, wind a piece of string around it and add 2in/50mm. Measure the length the same way.

• To cushion an object in its packing box, use balls of newspaper, wool, old clothes or fabric remnants, or polystyrene chips.

Wrench

• When possible, pull rather than push a wrench handle; it's easier and more efficient.

• The longer a wrench handle, the more leverage it gives. To add muscle, slip a piece of pipe over it. (But use commonsense – too much pipe breaks tools.)

• A series of sharp tugs works better than an extended pull in loosening a tight nut. For a really hard case, tap the wrench handle with a mallet or piece of wood.

• Protect the finish of plumbing fixtures by putting layers of leather or cloth tape over the teeth of a pipe wrench.

• If you don't have a wrench to hand, try a pair of locking-grip pliers. The next alternative is offset pliers, then standard slip-joint pliers.

• To turn a large nut or secure a bolt head, try a G-cramp.

• If you can move the object, lock the stiff nut in a vice and turn the object until it loosens.

Wrinkles

Premature lines are undoubtedly caused by sun damage. If you look at the skin on parts of your body that are never exposed to sunlight, you will see the difference.

• Always use a sunscreen (see p.198) to protect your skin in the sun, even if you never burn, in hotter climes. Apply a sunscreen whenever you go out; put sunscreen on children, too.

• Don't avoid sunscreens because you want to tan. It is possible to get a light tan if you use a high-protection sunscreen.

• Apply sunscreen to your hands and neck as well as your face – these areas tend to show signs of ageing first.

• Use a moisturiser both morning and evening, every day, especially if your skin tends to be fine and dry.

• Protect your skin from harsh winds, intense cold and biting salt sprays with a moisturiser or skin cream.

• Make a short-term antiwrinkle mask: apply a beaten egg white to your face for 10 minutes, then rinse off. Your face should look smoother for a few hours afterwards.

• Apply a cloth soaked in witch hazel to frown lines for 5 minutes at a time.

• Rub a light eye cream on outer-eye lines. Then open your eyes wide, press the heels of your hands against the areas, and hold for a minute; repeat daily. See also DRY SKIN, p.68.

X-rays

X-rays are invaluable in the early detection and diagnosis of many diseases, but too much exposure to them can be harmful. Here are some tips to help you make the right decisions involving such a vital aspect of your health care.

• Excessive radiation may lead to cancer and leukaemia. Medical and dental X-rays account for more than 80 per cent of the population's exposure to man-made radiation, including nuclear tests, accidents and power stations. Before you have an X-ray, discuss possible alternatives with your dentist, general practitioner or specialist. The Royal College of Radiologists recommends that X-rays should only be given when really necessary.

• Unless you have symptoms of lung or heart disease, a chest X-ray prior to employment or to screen you for lung cancer or tuberculosis is usually unnecessary.

• You should not have a routine skull X-ray after a head injury unless there are special circumstances. For example, if you were knocked out, if a foreign body may have penetrated your skull, if there is evidence of a fractured skull, such as bleeding from the ear, or if you have multiple injuries.

• Back and neck pain are usually caused by conditions that do not show on X-rays, so lumbar spine and cervical spine X-rays, particularly if you are over the age of 40, are usually not worth the risk of excess radiation.

• Unless you have a breast lump, routine mammography has only been shown to be of value in women aged 50 to 64.

• Isotope scans are often more effective and safer than X-rays if bone cancer is a possibility.

• Ultrasound scans are far safer than X-rays for detecting gallstones or enlarged kidneys.

• Unless your doctor suspects kidney disease, routine kidney X-rays for high blood pressure are not usually necessary.

• If you are pregnant, tell your dentist or specialist. They should use a specially heavy lead apron to cover your stomach when X-raying you.

Xylophone

Once you have made an ingenious substitute for a xylophone with eight kitchen glasses filled with water (see also MUSICAL INSTRUMENTS, p.138), adjust the water levels to make a scale.

Line up the glasses and fill the first one nearly to the top; tap the rim with a pencil and think of the note produced as Doh. Put a little less water in the next glass and adjust the level until a tap produces Ray. Continue in this fashion, putting a little less water in each glass, until you've created a complete scale: Doh-Ray-Me-Fah-Soh-Lah-Te-Doh. Then use these tunes to get started playing (the low Doh is 1):

Mary Had a Little Lamb:
3-2-1-2-3-3-3; 2-2-2; 3-5-5;
3-2-1-2-3-3-3; 3-2-2-3-2-1.

Row, Row, Row Your Boat:
1-1-1-2-3; 3-2-3-4-5; 8-8-8-
5-5-5-3-3-3-1-1-1; 5-4-3-2-1.

Yoga

This spiritual, mental and physical training of the mind and body can be beneficial to many ailments, especially those caused by stress-related problems.

• Enquire at your library, health shop or doctor to find a local evening class run by a qualified teacher.

• Different schools of yoga place an emphasis on different aspects of the training, which covers posture, breathing, deep relaxation and meditation. To choose the class that best suits your needs, contact the Yoga Biomedical Trust, PO BOX 140, Cambridge CB4 3SY, Tel. 0223 67301.

• Teachings start with a series of basic posture exercises which limber you up both physically and mentally. Practice the postures regularly, preferably daily. They can take as little as 10-15 minutes once or twice a day, but you should wait for three hours after a heavy meal or one hour after a snack.

• Common ailments that can respond to regular yoga exercises include those associated with heart disorders, such as high blood pressure, asthma, back pain, headaches, migraines and arthritis.

Yoghurt

Try one of these methods to incubate homemade yoghurt (see p.421).

• Pour the yoghurt into a preserving jar and wrap the jar in a wool blanket, down jacket or sheet of bubble plastic.

• Or put the jar in a box along with a hot-water bottle and pack crumpled newspapers loosely around both.

• Or turn an electric heating pad to its lowest setting and wrap it round the jar.

• Or put the jar into a gas oven turned onto the lowest possible setting.

• Or pour the yoghurt into a warmed-up flask and leave to set over several hours.

Youth hostels

Despite the name, anyone can become a member of the Youth Hostels Associations (YHA), although the small membership fees do vary according to age.

• For a full list of places to stay, and for membership details, contact the YHA in England and Wales (Tel. 0727 855215, Scotland (Tel. 0786 451181) and Northern Ireland (Tel. 0232 324733).

• The YHA keeps the costs of overnight stays down by asking guests to carry out some task, such as helping with the washing up. But it's a small price to pay for the chance to stay in historic castles and cottages around Britain.

Zips

• To make a zip work smoothly, run a candle up and down the teeth. If it's really sticky, rub with a lead pencil.

• If you've lost or broken the tab of your zip, use a safety pin or a paper clip.

• Has your zip pulled apart at the bottom? Undo the stitching, remove the stop, and separate the zip completely. Put the sides back into the tab and zip it up then stitch across the bottom of the zip, creating a new stop.

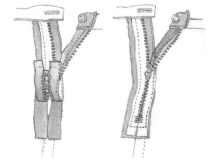

• Before replacing a zip, remove the old stitches from the fabric – but don't press the fabric until you've tacked the new zip in place – you might lose track of the folds and seam allowances.

• Before sewing in a zip, press the underside of the tape to smooth out the folds; if the teeth are plastic, be careful not to iron over them.

• Preshrink any tape that is not 100 per cent polyester by submerging the zip in hot water for 3 minutes; then let the tape dry before pressing it flat.

CHARTS & CHECKLISTS

This useful selection of charts and checklists provides essential basic facts on a variety of subjects that could be important to you, from selling your house to choosing a pension. Where relevant, the text also advises you on where you can go for more detailed information.

237

The paper chase

ORGANISING IMPORTANT PAPERS

Financial documents	Stocks and shares	Bonds	Bank book & pension book	Cancelled cheques	Income tax returns
Insurance policies	Life	Health	Buildings	Household	Car
Certificates	Birth & adoption	Marriage	Divorce	Firearms	Death
Numbers	Social Security & National Insurance	Credit cards	Driver's licence	Employee & student ID's	Bank accounts
Legal documents	Will (copy)*	Power of attorney	Contracts	Deeds or lease	Mortgage
Personal documents	National Health card	Pension plans	Academic diplomas	Passports	Personal property inventory

* Leave original with your lawyer   **Safe-deposit box**   **Personal file**   **Fireproof strongbox**

A foolproof filing system

For your own files, an alphabetical system will suffice. For a family file, use a colour-coded system. Or you can combine the two.

★ Gather all the papers to be filed and make a list of general categories, such as receipts, contracts, correspondence and insurance.

★ Make a separate folder for each category and label it. File each document in its appropriate folder.

★ If an item falls under more than one category, make copies. Or note its location on index cards for other relevant folders.

★ If any misfits remain that don't deserve their own folders, store them in a 'Miscellaneous' file.

★ Within each folder, place items in chronological order, with the most recent item in front.

★ Review the contents of a folder periodically; toss obsolete material into the 'round file' – the wastepaper basket.

★ Staple material together – paper clips snag, or come off, and rubber bands snap.

★ If you don't have time to file regularly, keep items in a To File folder so that they don't get lost.

★ If you are going to remove material for an extended period, leave a note in its folder to remind you where it is.

★ File business cards separately in a handy business card holder.

★ Establish weekly and monthly notes in your diary to remind you of important deadlines.

Cures for the chronic procrastinator

★ Break the chronic procrastinator's habit: whenever you catch yourself thinking 'I can do it later', stop and make a point of doing it now.

★ Tell others about your goals so that you'll have extra motivation to accomplish them.

★ Eliminate distractions, even if it means locking the door, taking the telephone off the hook or switching on your answering machine.

★ Make plans that require you to complete your chores by a certain date.

★ If a project is large or complex, break it down into smaller, more manageable parts.

★ Take time to ask yourself: 'Is there an easier way to do this?'

★ Don't wait until you have time to finish an entire task. Do as much as you can whenever you can.

★ Set firm but realistic deadlines for yourself.

★ Start with the simplest or the most enjoyable part of a job, even if it's not the first logical step. The rest will be easier once you have gained momentum.

★ Or try the opposite strategy: tackle the toughest part of the project first so that you can coast if your energy or enthusiasm run out later on.

★ Deal with smaller projects or problems as soon as possible, but in order of priority.

★ Make a list of everything you have to do, and don't stop until you've checked off every item.

★ Don't be a perfectionist; you can polish your work as much as you wish after you've made some headway.

★ Don't interrupt yourself by starting another task before you've completed the first one.

★ Remember that knuckling down to a task, although it seems hard at first, really makes your life easier in the long run.

★ Treat yourself to a small reward for each deadline you meet.

Protecting personal time

★ Ask friends, relatives or colleagues to ring before they drop in.

★ Put up a list of where everything in the house is stored, and train family members to look at it and help themselves.

★ Teach children that a closed door means 'Do Not Disturb'. If necessary stick or hang the message on the door.

★ Invest in a telephone answering machine. You don't have to answer it while you're at home and you can deal with the message when you have time.

★ If you don't want to cut a telephone conversation short, keep small, undemanding projects nearby and complete them while you're talking.

★ If you can't concentrate at home, take your work to the library and don't tell anyone where you're going.

★ If you don't have a receptionist at work, ask a willing colleague to take your calls and offer to return the favour when she's busy.

How to get out of the house on time

★ Put your keys in the same place every night.

★ Prepare the next day's lunch before bedtime.

★ Set the table for breakfast right after dinner.

★ Take your bath or shower before you go to bed.

★ Lay out your clothes the night before.

★ Put a clock in every room, including the bathroom.

★ Schedule bathroom time for each family member.

★ Air the bed while you are getting dressed and having breakfast. Make it after you have eaten.

★ Turn on the radio instead of the television.

★ Save the newspaper for later in the day.

★ Allow extra time for unexpected delays.

Investing in your future

TYPE	EXPLANATION	SOURCES	ADVANTAGES	DISADVANTAGES
Annuity	Lump sum payment in return for guaranteed income	Life insurance companies	Lower taxation; lifetime income; low risk; can be collateral	Sales charges vary; overall yield depends on age and interest rates
Certificate of deposit	Money deposited for specified period and interest rate	Commercial and savings banks	Low risk; often higher yield than savings accounts	Penalty for early withdrawal
Ordinary shares	Shares owned in a company	Brokerage firms; financial services companies	Potentially high profit on sale	High risk; value fluctuates daily; brokerage fees
Individual retirement plan	Long-term savings for retirement age	Mutual funds; banks; insurance companies	Fund untaxed until retirement; contributions may be tax-deductible	May not be withdrawn before retirement age
Personal equity plans	Managed fund for small equity investor	Banks; brokers; financial services companies	Income and gains totally tax free	No guaranteed return; management fees; small amounts only
Money market	Funds pooled and invested in the market	Banks; brokers; insurance companies	High short-term interest	Fixed interest; penalties for early withdrawal
Local authority bond	Loans to local authorities to fund public facilities	Commercial banks; brokers	Low risk; interest can be high	Long maturities common; broker required
Mutual fund	Pooled funds invested in various common stocks or bonds	Mutual fund companies; brokerage firms; insurance companies	Low risk; diverse securities at low cost; many types of funds	Not insured; values fluctuate; management and sales fees
Preference shares	Shares in a company that yield a fixed dividend	Brokers; financial services companies, including bank subsidiaries	Low risk; dividends stable, paid before those of ordinary shares	Low appreciation potential. Dividend not guaranteed
National savings	Government savings organisation	Post Office; banks; Department of National Savings	Low risk; tax-free yield; wide variety of products	Mainly fixed term investments for small amounts
TESSA	Tax exempt special savings plan	Banks; building societies	Tax-free interest if held to maturity (5 years)	Max £9000 investment over 5 years; tax payable if withdrawn early
Treasury stock	Short and long-term securities of the UK Government	Brokerage firms; banks; National Savings Stock Register	Wide variety of maturity dates; profit on sale tax free	Capital value fluctuates with interest rates; service charge with banks and brokers

Although the national economy and market conditions fluctuate, financial experts still agree on two basic rules: never buy medium or high-risk securities before you have the equivalent of at least 6 months' income in safe, liquid assets. When you can set aside money for investment, aim for diversity.

Your annual budget planner

INCOME
Your take-home pay _____
Spouse/partner's
    take-home pay _____
Bonuses _____
Part-time work _____
Interest _____
Dividends _____
Pension _____
Tenant's rent _____
State benefits _____
Other _____
TOTAL INCOME £ _____

EXPENSES
Housing
Rent _____
Mortgage _____
Maintenance _____
Repair _____
Improvement _____

Utilities
Telephone _____
Gas _____
Water _____
Fuel _____
Electricity _____

Taxes (not withheld)
Income tax _____
Capital Gains tax _____
Council tax _____

Car
Maintenance,
    repairs _____
Fuel _____
Tax _____

Insurance
Life _____
Household _____
Building _____
Car _____
Health _____

Service contracts
Washing machine/
    tumble dryer _____
Central heating _____
Dishwasher _____

Medical
Doctor _____
Dentist _____
Prescription drugs _____
Spectacles/contact lenses _____

Clothing
New clothes _____
Laundry, dry cleaning _____

Transport
Commuting _____
Parking fees _____
Taxis _____
Public transport _____

Recreation
Dining out _____
Books, magazines _____
Films, theatres, concerts _____
Holidays _____
Hobbies _____
TV licence _____

Gifts
Birthday _____
Anniversary _____
Christmas/New Year _____
Wedding _____

Tuition _____
Furnishings, appliances _____
Food, drink _____
Loan payments _____
Regular savings _____
Other _____
TOTAL EXPENSES _____

Total income minus total
expenses = £.... to save or invest

TEST YOURSELF
Do you overspend?

Do you spend money on the assumption that your income will rise?

Do you fail to keep an accurate record of your purchases?

Do you hide your purchases from your family?

Do you often fail to pay your monthly bills on time?

Do you own more than five credit cards?

Does having several credit cards make you feel richer?

Do you spend more than 20 per cent of your income on credit card bills?

Do you tend to make only the minimum payment on your credit card bills?

Do you take cash advances on one credit card to pay the balance on another?

Do you often pay for groceries with a credit card?

When you eat in a restaurant, do you collect cash from friends and then pay the bill with your credit card?

Do you have trouble imagining how you would survive without credit?

If you answered yes to four or fewer questions, you're probably not an overspender.

If you answered yes to five to eight questions, it's time to rein yourself in, pay your debts and follow a strict budget.

If you answered yes to nine or more questions, consult a credit counsellor or financial planner for help in changing your spending habits.

Income Tax countdown

What could be more satisfying than to have your income tax return form completed and signed well before the new September 30th deadline? And what feels worse than hunting around at the last minute, desperately trying to find missing records? You can make things much easier for yourself by taking a number of simple steps during the year and following these general guidelines.

• First, set up a system by which you file, in one place, all the relevant certificates and details as they come in, throughout the year. This saves hunting through all your domestic files when you have to complete the return form.

• If you keep your records on computer, do not destroy vouchers which prove you have paid tax on interest received.

APRIL

• You should receive your tax return this month. If you do not receive it, contact your tax office and request one. The new-look form helps you to work out all your taxable income from April 6th of one year to April 5th of the next. It will be accompanied by one or more forms called schedules, which cover different areas relevant to your circumstances.

• Start checking that you have all the records of your personal income and expenses for the year ended on April 5th.

• If you have not received certificates from your bank or building society, showing interest paid on your mortgage and details of all interest paid on deposit or savings accounts, write or call and ask for them. They are usually sent to all account-holders automatically.

• Make sure you have information about dividends received from any company in which you have shares.

• Check that you have all details relating to sales and purchases of investments during the past year.

MAY

• By the end of May your employer should have given you a P-60 form, which shows how much you have earned in the past tax year and how much tax you have paid on it.

• Read through the tax return and make sure that you understand it and have all the required schedules.

• Contact your tax office if any of the relevant schedules is missing or you do not understand the form.

JULY

• In the first week of July your employer should give you details of your expenses and benefits for the past tax year. Unless there is some sort of dispensation covering these amounts, they will be taxable.

• If you need help completing the return, see an accountant who will help you to complete it. You will need to make sure that he or she has all the relevant information in order to complete your return.

• If you are self-employed, you must make the first of your payments on account for the previous year's income. For more details, get a copy of *Self-Assessment: A guide for the self-employed* from Inland Revenue, Tel. 0345-161514.

SEPTEMBER

• September 30th is an important date in the year. By this date you should have completed your tax form and returned it to your tax office, if you wish the Inland Revenue department to assess your tax for you. If you intend calculating your own tax, you have until January.

• However, if you have done your own assessment and know that you will have to pay extra tax (over and above the PAYE which you have already paid) and wish the amount to be collected over the coming year through PAYE payments, you should send in your completed form now and not wait until January.

• Before sending off your return, check that you have filled the forms in correctly and double check all your calculations.

NOVEMBER

• If you use an accountant, make an appointment before the Christmas rush to check on the completed return and find out whether you will have to make any payment at the end of January. Make sure you will have the necessary funds.

JANUARY

• By January 31st you must have sent in your completed tax return and paid the tax which you and your accountant have estimated is due. A fixed penalty of £100 will be applied if your return and payment are not received by January 31st.

• A further surcharge of £100 will be made if the amount payable is still outstanding six months later.

• Self-employed people must make the second payment on account.

At-a-glance countdown

Date or deadline	Who is affected	What should have happened
6th April	Everyone who gets a return	Tax return received
31st May	Employees	P60 supplied by employer
6th July	Employees who get benefits	Details of expenses and benefits supplied by employer
30th September	People who want their tax calculated	Tax return sent in
31st January	People who calculate their own tax	Tax return and payment sent in
	Self-employed people who make payments on account	First payment on account made
31st July	Self-employed (as above)	Second payment on account made

Where to complain

★ **Salesperson or supervisor.** Talk calmly, but firmly; avoid anger; never shout; be friendly, but insistent.
CONSULT: *A Handbook on Consumer Law* - National Federation of Consumer Groups.

★ **Company 0800 telephone line.** Ask for the name of the person you are speaking to; state your problem clearly; if necessary ask to be transferred to someone who can help you. 0800 calls are free; otherwise be aware of the potentially high cost of telephone calls. If they promise to ring you back and don't, ring again.
CONSULT: the product label for the company's address and telephone number; telephone directories/Yellow Pages/Thomson's directories – your local library will have them if you don't, and using them is free, whereas you are charged for calls to Directory Enquiries.

★ **Write to the owner.** Or write to the regional manager, managing director or complaints department, if the company has one. Write to a named individual, if possible. State your name, address and telephone number very clearly. Keep it short. Send your letter by recorded delivery and keep the receipt. Enclosing a S.A.E. often pays dividends. State purchase/service/date/make and model; problem/steps taken so far; resolution wanted; reply expected by . . .
CONSULT: company directories in your local library, such as *Kelly's Business Directory*; *Sell's Directory*.

★ **Citizens Advice Bureau.** They may be prepared to deal with a trader on your behalf; will give advice on legal rights, arbitration schemes and small claims.
CONSULT: the telephone directory, or write to National Association of Citizens Advice Bureaux, Myddelton House, 115-123 Pentonville Road, London N1 9LZ.

★ **Local Authority Trading Standards Department.** They may be prepared to pursue a matter under criminal law. Will usually offer you advice on civil matters.
CONSULT: the telephone directory, listed under the County or Metropolitan Borough entry.

★ **Consumer Advice Centre or Legal Advice Centre.** Will advise you of your legal rights. May take a matter up with a trader for you. Will check your ability to get legal aid.
CONSULT: The Law Society, 113 Chancery Lane, London WC2A 1PL.

★ **A regulatory agency.** For complaints against gas (Gas Consumers' Council), electricity (OFFER), water (OFWAT), and coal companies (Domestic Coal Consumers' Council), British Telecom (OFTEL) and British Rail (Transport Users' Consultative Committee).
CONSULT: the back of bills, and notices in showrooms and railway stations.

* **Ombudsman.** Will deal with complaints about insurance, banking services and building societies.
CONSULT: the Office of the Banking Ombudsman, 70 Gray's Inn Road, London WC1X 8NB, Tel. 0171-404 9944; the Building Societies Ombudsman, Millbank Tower, Millbank, London SW1P 4XS, Tel. 0171-931 0044; or the Insurance Ombudsman Bureau, City Gate One, 135 Park Street, London SE1 9EA, Tel. 0171-928 7600.

★ **Professional and trade associations.** Will usually deal with complaints against their members. Some run arbitration schemes.
CONSULT: your membership documents.

* **Consumer watchdogs.** Contact local newspapers, radio or TV stations, or *Which?* magazine.

* **Arbitration schemes.** CONSULT: trade associations or Chartered Institute of Arbitrators, 24 Angel Gate, City Road, London EC1V 2RS, Tel. 0171-837 4483.

★ **Small claims** (see p.186).
CONSULT: *How to sue in the County Court*, available from County Court offices.

★ **Solicitor.** To sue for amounts beyond the small claims limit of £1000. Look for the legal aid sign in the window.

Ten consumer caveats

Do patronise local businesses; never buy from one-day sales or door-to-door sellers who will not be there when something goes wrong; use mail-order with discretion.

Do ask your friends about a trader's reputation; check with your Citizens Advice Bureau or trading standards department about traders before entering large contracts.

Do use such magazines as *Which?* to check comparative product quality.

Do read all the fine print on the front and back of a contract. Ask for an explanation of anything you don't understand. Don't be pressured by assurances: if you don't like it, don't sign until the seller has changed it in writing and initialled the changes.

Do keep all contracts, receipts and warranties or guarantees.

Don't pay cash for large items. Use a cheque or credit card. Credit cards may give you additional rights and free insurance. Make cheques payable to the company – never an individual. Get a receipt.

Don't forget to shop around, comparing prices and terms. Ask about extra charges for delivery or installation. Look for the APR to compare credit terms.

Don't accept oral promises; get it in writing.

Don't sign anything unless it is properly and fully filled in.

Don't be pressured. If 'this great offer expires today', let it!

Are you a workaholic?

Work can be like a drug for some people – addictive, possibly damaging and out of control. People who (to the exclusion of family concerns, social pleasures and other interests) allow work to manage their lives, are often called 'workaholics'.

Psychologists have discovered that most workaholics have a definite personality type, called 'Type A'. To find out how much you resemble this type, answer the following questions, quickly but honestly.

* Do you always feel there is never enough time to get everything done?
* Do you walk everywhere fast – other people seem to dawdle along the pavement, getting in your way?
* Do you compete for everything, have to be the best at whatever you do?
* Does your impatience become unbearable when other people waste your time?
* Do you have few or no interests outside your work?
* Has starting work early and finishing late become a habit?
* Do you get anxious about delegating work to your staff?
* Do you hide your feelings?
* Do you talk so fast that people have to ask you to repeat things?
* Do you often try to do more than one thing at a time?
* Do you drive your car to its limits? Get impatient with other drivers?
* Do you interrupt when others are talking, or finish their sentences?
* Do you finish eating before everyone else? Do you regularly eat your lunch while working at your desk?
* Do you have to be busy all the time? Are you unable to relax doing nothing?
* Are you always thinking about the next task before this one is completed?
* Do you lose sleep worrying about problems at work?
* Do you badly need approval from others at work, worrying if your achievements go unnoticed?
* Do you regularly not get round to taking your leave?

If you answered yes to 12 or more questions, your personality resembles Type A. On the good side, Type As are usually mentally and physically alert. They tend to work hard and be self-motivated. They often carry others along with their enthusiasm and drive. On the less positive side, Type As can be demanding, impulsive, critical, hostile, blame others when frustrated and are often not aware of these characteristics.

As long as you are aware of the interpersonal problems that may arise, and maintain a positive attitude to life, being a Type A is not unhealthy. But, if work has taken charge of your life and it makes you unhappy, you need to find ways of regaining control. You could plan short breaks from work, or arrange to do something new that challenges you, like learning a language. You might also find it helpful to ask close friends to tell you when you are going 'over the top' in your critical or hostile reactions.

Is your job right for you?

* Are your colleagues warm, friendly and courteous?
* Is your job so enjoyable that you do extra work?
* Does your work challenge your imagination?
* If you inherited a large sum of money, would you still want to keep doing your job?
* Are your efforts appreciated?
* Are you fairly paid?
* Does your day go by quickly?
* Is your journey to and from work convenient?
* Are you allowed to take time off when personal emergencies arise?
* Are people promoted from within your organisation?
* Is your work area pleasant?
* Are your special talents and skills utilised?
* Is your boss helpful, capable and encouraging?
* Does the benefits package match your needs?
* Could you transfer to another department if it made sense to do so?
* Is your company concerned about the health and well-being of its staff?
* Is your routine varied enough to forestall boredom?
* Are your work hours right for you and your family?
* Does your work make a difference to the company?

If you answered yes to 15 or more of these questions, the chances are you are well suited to your chosen career.

If you answered yes to fewer than 15 questions, you might consider changing your job or career, returning to college or taking early retirement or voluntary redundancy. Seek the advice of your local authority Careers Office, who will give it free. For a fee you can get advice from several agencies: people in middle management, for example, can consult the Independent Assessment Research Centre (IARC), 17 Portland Place, London WIN 3AF, Tel. 0171-255 2505.

Evaluating a company's benefits package

Give careful thought to your needs and those of your family when assessing a company's benefits.

Medical benefits
* Are you offered a group health insurance plan?
* How much is the premium?
* Is major medical insurance for catastrophic illness included?
* Are mental health costs paid for?
* At what age do dependants cease to be covered?
* Will a pre-existing illness preclude you from coverage?
* What doesn't the plan cover?

Holidays
* How much paid annual holiday will you receive?
* Can it be taken any time during the year, and staggered?
* Can you carry forward unused holidays to the next year?

Disability benefits
* What percentage of your earnings would you receive if you became disabled, and for how long?
* How much of the disability insurance premium would you pay?

Health maintenance programmes
* Are exercise facilities available?
* Is the cost of sports and health club activities reimbursed?
* Are there health management programmes?

Maternity/paternity benefits
* How much maternity/paternity leave would you get?
* How much leave would be on full pay?

Child care
* Do child care facilities exist on the premises?
* Are any child care costs reimbursed?

Education
* Are education expenses reimbursed?
* Is there on-the-job training?

Financial savings plans
* Is there group life insurance, and who pays the premium?
* Is there a profit-sharing plan?
* Can you purchase company shares?

Pension plan
* Is there one, and can you make contributions to it?
* How long must you be employed before being able to join?
* At what age can you start receiving your pension?
* If you retire early, what percentage of your pension will you receive, and when will payments begin?
* Will your pension include cost-of-living increases?
* Will you have lifetime medical coverage for yourself and your spouse/partner?
* If your spouse/partner outlives you, how much of your pension will he/she receive?
* Under what circumstances could you lose your pension?

Company car
* Is a company car provided, and of what size and value?
* Will you have to make a contribution for private use?
* Will you have to pay for private fuel?

Home loans
* Is there a subsidised mortgage scheme?
* How much can you borrow and at what rate of interest?
* In what circumstances would the loan be repayable?

CURRICULUM VITAE of Georgina Bury
22, Church Street Solihull West Midlands B92 2PQ
Tel: 021-257-3228 (Home) 021-837-6529 (Office)

CAREER SUMMARY An experienced bank clerk with a sound track record in National City Bank in cashier work, securities and lending at Branch level. Experience of managing office staff in current post as a Branch Administrator. Now seeking to move into a specialised product area, such as mortgages. Age: 36 Qualifications: 5 "O" levels and Stage 2 Institute of Banking passed. Salary £15,400.

WORK EXPERIENCE

1988 TO PRESENT   **National City Bank**
Administrative Officer, Shirley Branch, West Midlands

Reporting to the Branch Manager, with overall responsibility for the management of office staff in the Branch. Achievements include successful introduction of flexitime working and reduction in office administration costs by job redesign.

1987-88   **National City Bank**
Senior Loans Officer, Stratford-upon-Avon Branch

Heading a team of three Branch staff responsible to the Deputy Branch Manager for personal loans. Achievements included expansion of unsecured loan facilities to home owners without increasing default rate and training of two assistants in loan management.

1984-87   **National City Bank**
Senior Securities Clerk, Solihull Branch

1982-84   **National City Bank**
Securities Clerk, Stratford-upon-Avon Branch

1981-82   **National City Bank**
Cashier, Stratford-upon-Avon Branch

1980   Year off whilst having child

1975-80   **National City Bank**
Junior Cashier, Stratford-upon-Avon Branch

1973-75   **Warwickshire County Council, Borough Engineer's Dept.**
Clerical Officer

Writing a curriculum vitae (CV)

EDUCATION AND QUALIFICATIONS

Institution	Dates	Qualifications
National City Bank Training College Westfield Business Park Coventry	1989	Branch Office Procedures
	1987	Principles of Lending
	1985	Securities Management
	1984	Institute of Bankers Part 2
	1982	Institute of Bankers Part 1
Acocks Green Comprehensive School	1968-73	GCE "O" levels Pure Maths 3 English Lang 3 English Lit 4 French 5 Art 3

PERSONAL DETAILS

Date of Birth: 12th April 1957
Health: Excellent
Status: Married, 1 child, Sandra aged 12 yrs
Nationality: British

ADDITIONAL INFORMATION

Member of Solihull District Badminton Club - Second Team Captain 1990-present
Member of World Wildlife Fund 1984-present
Chairperson, St Clement's Primary School (Solihull) Governors 1987-89
Coordinator - Neighbourhood Watch Scheme 1990-present

Planning your retirement

Like a second career, a rewarding retirement requires advance planning and some important choices. But this time you're the boss. There are no right or wrong answers in the following checklist. It's designed to help you decide which issues are most important to you:

For my continued well-being, I will
★ follow a nutritious diet.
★ exercise a little every day.
★ develop activities and hobbies.

My savings programme can most use
★ diversification.
★ regular contributions.
★ professional advice.

If I remain in my home, I'll
★ replace old appliances now.
★ fix dim lighting, frayed carpets.
★ rent part of it for income.

My ideal place for retirement would be

★ the city / country / small town.
★ nonstop sunshine / four seasons.
★ the seaside / hilly countryside.

After I retire, I plan to get around
★ by public transport.
★ by driving the family car.
★ with the help of the children and neighbours.

The most important legal documents I'll need will be
★ a contract to buy / sell my home.
★ an up-to-date, valid will.
★ power of attorney for myself and my spouse / partner.

If I leave my community, I'll
★ travel for a while.
★ sell my house and move for good.
★ rent for 6 months or so before I decide to move permanently.

Other than my spouse / partner, the relationships that matter most will be

★ the children.
★ old friends and neighbours.
★ a new and different social circle.

When I take a trip, I'll opt for
★ independent travel / group tours.
★ Europe / the USA / the Caribbean.
★ cruises / going by car / camping.

If I volunteer my time, I may want to work for
★ the elderly / children / minorities.
★ my favourite political cause.
★ my church / synagogue / mosque.

I'll work until I'm 65 because
★ I want full pension benefits.
★ I enjoy working.
★ I don't want to stay at home all day.

I want to retire early because
★ I don't like my job.
★ my spouse / partner wants us to move.
★ I have lots of other things to do.

Building your nest egg

According to financial experts, after retirement the average family can live comfortably on about two-thirds of their pre-retirement income. But inflation can play cruel tricks with this formula. For example, if you're 65 and plan to retire soon on an income of £15,000 a year, you probably expect to spend roughly £300,000 over a 20 year retirement. But given a 6% annual inflation rate, the same lifestyle will cost some £585,000! By the same token, a 58-year-old planning to retire in 7 years on £20,000 (in today's terms) will need not £400,000 (£20,000 × 20 years) to maintain the same standard of living, but £1,106,000. Fortunately, your assets can grow at roughly the same – or an even faster – rate.

To make a rough projection of your retirement income, add the pension and Social Security income you expect to receive to any income from your investments and savings. Deduct 25% (or whatever figure most closely approximates your tax bracket). If the

result is about two-thirds of what you now spend and you can handle some annual inflation, you are financially prepared to retire.

If your nest egg is smaller than you would like it to be, remember that you may be adding to it by selling your home and that many families are able to live on their capital in carefully planned annual instalments. If there is a substantial gap between your projected income and your anticipated needs, here are some things that you can do about it now.
★ Plan to retire later.
★ Save more money now.

★ Try for a higher return on your present investments. (For example, could you move money from a savings account yielding 5.5% interest into tax-free National Savings Certificates, which pay a higher rate.)
★ If you rent, make every effort to buy a house. The money you're spending on rent could go towards paying off a mortgage on property that is likely to appreciate in value.
★ Consider a second job; or perhaps your nonworking spouse / partner can get a full or part-time job and earmark the income for a retirement fund.

COST OF A 20 YEAR RETIREMENT (assuming 6% inflation)					
Projected annual expenses beginning at age 65					
Age now	£10,000	£15,000	£20,000	£25,000	£30,000
48	£990,000	£1,485,000	£1,980,000	£2,475,000	£2,970,000
53	£740,000	£1,110,000	£1,480,000	£1,850,000	£2,220,000
58	£553,000	£830,000	£1,106,000	£1,383,000	£1,659,000
65	£390,000	£585,000	£780,000	£975,000	£1,170,000

Enjoying your time

Once you stop working, you may be surprised at how much leisure you have. What are you going to do with all that time?

Before you retire, make a list of all the activities – hobbies, voluntary work, travel, club membership, recreation, social gatherings and the like – that you enjoy or that you'd like to try for the first time. Ask the following questions about each activity and give it one point for every 'yes' answer.

* Is it healthy?
* Is it mentally stimulating?
* Is it worthwhile and satisfying?
* Is it relaxing, refreshing, fun?

Not only do the scores on your list tell you which activities are apt to be the most (and least) rewarding, but they also show you whether all four important aspects of retirement living have been included in your plans for your new life.

Retirement housing options

Type	Advantages	Pitfalls	Precautions
Caravan	Low cost	Small space; noisy campsites; depreciation	Check construction quality; visit caravan site
Mobile home	Must meet building code; most parks have recreational facilities	Can't be moved without special equipment; banned in some places	Build installation and site rental into cost; check rules on resale
Purchased freehold house	Privacy, possibility of adapting it to your needs; extra space; can be willed	May have been unsoundly built; you bear all maintenance costs; ties up capital	Check other work done by builder; have the house surveyed; ask your solicitor to investigate water rights, local by-laws and do a local search

Type	Advantages	Pitfalls	Precautions
Rented flat or house	Can move relatively easily; landlord does maintenance	Rents go up; possible surcharges for fuel, cable TV, general service charge	Ask your solicitor to negotiate written lease carefully; check appliances
Purchased flat in a purpose-built block	Can be willed, like a house; outside maintenance done by association	Common charges escalate; look out for loopholes in contracts; shoddy or unfinished construction	Ask a solicitor specialising in property management to check lease
Retirement community and sheltered housing	Services for retirees; some have medical facilities or resident warden	If private, may have high initial cost; may be too far from family; may restrict pet ownership	Check credit and reputation of owners except if council-run

Considering a move

Reasons to stay . . .
* the crime rate in your community is not as bad as in others.
* you enjoy the climate where you presently live.
* you enjoy the friends and neighbours you have now.
* the cost of living is affordable where you are.
* you like your current doctor and hospital.
* the children and grandchildren can visit you.
* a holiday trip or a weekend away now and then will satisfy any need to see new places.

Reasons to go . . .
* council tax and prices are lower in another place that attracts you.
* your doctor recommends a different climate.
* you fear that your neighbourhood is deteriorating.
* you want to move closer to your children.
* you'd like a new lifestyle, new friends.
* you want to be closer to modern health care facilities.
* another area has more chances for part-time work in your field.
* you want to be closer to public transport or better shopping facilities.

TEST YOURSELF

How long will you live?

The average life expectancy for people in the United Kingdom is at best a very general statistic. Individual life spans vary greatly; the reasons are sometimes genetic, but some are to do with smoking, diet and general fitness, and are under a person's control.

To get a more precise idea of how long you may expect to live – and what you can do about it – find the average life expectancy for someone your age in the chart above, then answer the questions below.

Average life expectancy

AGE NOW	MEN	WOMEN
25	72	78
35	73	78
45	73	78
55	75	80
65	78	84

★ For every 5 years that your father lived past 70, add 1 year. Add 1 year for every 5 years your mother lived past 78. ....

★ If you are single, deduct 1 year for each decade you are on your own after the age of 25. ....

★ If you are married, add 5 years. If there is an unusual amount of family strife, subtract 2 years. ....

★ If you live in a city, subtract 2 years. If you live in a small town or on a farm, add 2 years. ....

★ If you have been either poor or wealthy most of your life, subtract 3 years. ....

★ If you're over 40, subtract a year for every 5 pounds above your best weight (p.252). Men only: deduct 2 years per inch that your waist measurement exceeds your chest measurement. ....

★ If you exercise moderately but regularly, add 3 years. If you regularly do vigorous exercise, add 5 years. ....

★ If you think you have a hard-driving, competitive personality or are often tense, deduct 5 years. Add 5 years if you're usually cheerful and easygoing. ....

★ If you drink heavily, subtract 5 years; very heavily, 10 years. If you take recreational drugs, subtract 5 years. ....

★ If you smoke 10-20 cigarettes daily, subtract 3 years. If you smoke 20-30, subtract 5 years; 40, 10 years. ....

★ If you have regular medical and dental checkups, add 3 years. If you're often ill, subtract 2 years. ....

★ If your diet is high in fats, salt and sweets, deduct 4 years. If you eat a balanced diet with plenty of fruit, vegetables, low-fat proteins and complex carbohydrates, add 4 years. ....

Your life expectancy ....

Stress in your life

Scientists rank the causes of stress by severity in Life Change Units (LCUS). Although some stress (up to 150 LCUS) is normal, too much can lower your body's resistance to infection, aggravate allergies and raise your blood pressure, increasing your risk of heart disease or a stroke. More than 300 LCUS in a given year is considered a threat to health. For ways to cope with stress, see also STRESS, p.198.

Christmas **12**
Going on holiday **13**
Trouble with in-laws **29**
Child leaving home **29**
Mortgage over £40,000 **31**
Career change **35**
Death of a close friend **36**
Change in finances **37**
Sexual difficulties or birth of a child **39**
Pregnancy **40**
Retirement **45**
Loss of your job **47**
Marriage **50**
Personal injury or illness **53**
Death of a family member **63**
Marital separation **65**
Divorce **73**
Death of a spouse **100**

The well-stocked medicine cabinet

Don't keep medicines in the bathroom; warmth and humidity shorten their life. And you don't want to reach for nose drops in the night and use mouthwash or something even more harmful by mistake.

What you throw away is important too. Since children get into wastebaskets, flush these medicines away or return them to your chemist:
* Any medicine without a label or not in its original container

* Aspirin that smells vinegary
* Prescription medicines from a former illness
* Over-the-counter medicines you no longer need and any medicine older than its expiry date

Activated charcoal
Antacid
Antiseptic ointment
Antidiarrhoeal medicine with kaolin
Antihistamine cream
Anti-itch lotion or spray, such as
    calamine lotion
Paracetamol tablets
Hydrocortisone cream
Burn ointment
Cough syrup with expectorant
Epsom salts
Eyewash
Eye cup
Foot powder
Mild laxative (bulk-forming, not
    stimulant type)
Petroleum jelly

Oral thermometer
Surgical spirit
Syrup of ipecac (for children)
Oral decongestant (for children)
Paracetamol elixir (for children)
Disposable torch
Plasters
First-aid kit
Sterile gauze dressings
Crêpe or stretch bandages
Cotton wool
Antiseptic lotion
Plasters
Blunt-ended scissors
Triangular bandages
Tubular gauze bandages
Tweezers
Sterile eye dressing

Health records to keep

For yourself and your partner
* Any adverse reaction to an over-the-counter drug or prescription
* Allergies
* Medicines you take regularly
* Date and diagnosis of any illness requiring a doctor's attention
* Frequent or chronic illnesses
* Date of last eye examination

* Date and reasons for any hospital admission or surgery
* Last cervical smear and mammogram
* Dates of immunisations
* Appointment for next dental checkup
For each child
* Birth date and weight

* Allergies and any adverse reactions to medicines
* Types and dates of immunisations
* Dates of childhood illness, such as measles and chicken pox
* Any serious injury or accident
* Next appointments with doctor, dentist and optician
* Reports of school medicals

Dealing with common ailments

PROBLEM	HOME CARE	CALL THE DOCTOR FOR
Fever	Shake oral thermometer, leave under tongue for 3 minutes No extra clothing or blankets, even if body is chilly Lukewarm sponge baths to lower body temperature Extra fluids, given little and often	Dehydration: dry, tight skin; lightheadedness; dry mouth; thirst; dark, frequent or infrequent urine Rash, headache, stiff neck, with irritability or confusion Fever over 38.5°C/101°F lasting 3 days or more (except for a child). Vomiting or seizures Fever after new medication. Respiratory distress Cough with brown or green sputum, severe earache or ear drainage
Back pain	For prevention and self-help, see BACKACHE, p.15	Pain resulting from injury, especially at work Abdominal pain; painful or bloody urination Severe pain that travels down leg; weakness or numbness in legs or feet No improvement in 7 days. Fever over 38.5°C/101°F Any severe pain during pregnancy
Headaches	Paracetamol, massage, cold compresses for muscle-tension headache Decongestant, hot showers for sinus headache (hurts more when chin is lowered to chest)	Fever over 38.5°C/101°F or neck stiffness. Pain worse in morning Recent head injury, slurred speech, visual disturbance, numbness, weakness in arms or legs. Vomiting or convulsions Recurrent, unusually intense or persistent (3 days or more) pain
Heartburn, indigestion	Elevate head of bed No aspirin, caffeine, smoking, irritating foods Take antacid	Severe chest pain; shortness of breath; pain felt through to back; heavy perspiration; sharp pains in arms and shoulders Bloody, black vomit or black stool Severe abdominal pain Abdominal pain that increases or is worse after meals Symptoms lasting more than 3 days; not relieved by antacids
Sprains	Elevate limb. Apply ice once an hour for 15 minutes, up to 24 hours Paracetamol or ibuprofen for pain as needed Apply heat for soreness after 24 hours While limb heals, use elastic bandage	Unsteady, misshapen, cold, blue or numb limb Sprain that resulted from serious accident, such as a car crash or high fall Tenderness in particular area of bone (possible fracture) Pain lasting more than 4 days or requiring large doses of painkiller
Cuts	Control bleeding by pressure (10-15 minutes) Soap and water cleansing; rinse thoroughly Clean again with sterile gauze wet with antiseptic solution or spray Butterfly bandage (p.18), then adhesive strip Change dressing in 24 hours	Uncontrolled bleeding; unclosable wound Cut more than skin deep, more than 1in/25mm long; deep cut on torso Loss of motion or numbness of digits. No tetanus vaccination for 10 years. Infection (pus, swelling, fever, redness) Cut not healing. Persistent numbness
Cough, stuffy nose	Fluids, steam (see LARYNGITIS, p.121) Don't smoke. Suck cough drops. Try nasal spray or antihistamine Family members should wash hands often	Difficulty breathing or swallowing Chest pain, wheezing or shortness of breath Brown, green, bloody or purulent mucus Cough that lasts 10 days. Nasal congestion for 2 weeks
Vomiting, diarrhoea	Flat fruit drinks or water, suck ice No aspirin products No antidiarrhoeal product for 5-6 hours after onset (let bacteria flush out) After nausea subsides, slowly begin bland diet	Vomiting after head injury or accompanied by severe headache Yellow skin or whites of eyes Abdominal pain, tenderness or distension; fever Dehydration (see FEVER, above). Severe thirst Stools that are black or bloody, or vomit with 'coffee grounds' look Symptoms that last 3 days or recur
Sore throat	Drink fluids. Don't smoke. Limit taking paracetamol 6 hourly. Saltwater gargle or over-the-counter anaesthetic solution Lozenges	Fever of 38.5°C/101°F or more, with no other cold symptoms Breathing difficulty, almost impossible to swallow Earache, chest pain, skin rash Severe headache; difficulty bending head White spots on tonsils or large, ulcerated tonsils Hoarseness. Swollen lymph nodes on neck for longer than 3 weeks

How to talk to your doctor

Seeing your general practitioner

⋆ Prepare for your visit. Be clear in your mind what it is that you want to discuss.

⋆ Read your doctor's practice information leaflet so that you know how the appointments system works. You may need to make your appointment well in advance if you wish to see a particularly popular doctor.

⋆ Remember that the doctor only has a limited amount of time to spend with you. Ask the receptionist how long your appointment will last. If necessary, ask for a longer appointment.

⋆ Be aware of your rights, but be courteous and avoid alienating your doctor. If you foster a good relationship, your GP can be your adviser, ally and advocate.

⋆ Organise what you want to tell your doctor in your mind. If necessary, write notes.

⋆ Describe your symptoms in plain language. Don't use medical jargon or emphasise those symptoms that fit in with your theory of what is wrong with you.

⋆ Tell the doctor about your ideas and concerns. What are you worried about?

⋆ Tell the doctor about your expectations of the consultation. Do you want to know the doctor's diagnosis, or do you want reassurance? Are you hoping that the doctor will refer you to a hospital specialist?

⋆ Concentrate on the problem in hand and do not waste time. If you are long-winded, stray from the point or repeat yourself you will not make best use of the time available.

⋆ Be prepared to answer questions about your lifestyle, such as your smoking and drinking habits. Lifestyle affects health and it may be important for your doctor to know such details.

⋆ Be prepared for the doctor or nurse to discuss health promotion and prevention, including blood pressure, weight, cervical smears and tetanus immunisation.

⋆ Make sure that you understand any instructions about treatment or plans for future management. Ask for a leaflet or other written information to take home.

⋆ If the doctor is going to arrange for you to see a specialist, tell him if you have any requests, such as a particular surgeon or hospital, a private appointment or holiday dates to avoid.

Seeing a specialist

⋆ Before you go, find out something about your problem, for example from a medical book.

⋆ When you arrive, report to the reception desk and be prepared to give details such as your name, date of birth, address, post code and telephone number.

⋆ Be prepared to wait!

⋆ Prepare for your visit. Go over your story in your mind and, if necessary, on paper.

⋆ Tell the specialist about any medicines you may be taking, including 'over the counter' medicines from a pharmacist.

⋆ Mention any allergies to medicines that you might have.

⋆ If necessary, take someone else with you. If you do, you must be prepared for him or her to find out confidential details about you. Ask your companion to listen carefully but to allow you and the doctor to consult without interruption.

⋆ Be prepared to see a member of the specialist's team instead of the specialist. Junior doctors report back to the consultant in charge, who remains responsible for your care.

⋆ If you go to a teaching hospital, there may be medical students present during your consultation. They have to gain experience and you can help them to learn. However, you are perfectly entitled to refuse to have a student present, and if you don't want one there, say so!

⋆ Don't be afraid to ask questions.

What should you weigh?

Slimmer people are generally healthier than those who carry extra weight. And the closer you are to your ideal weight as set out in the chart below, the better you will feel generally. If you lead quite an athletic life you will probably be on the heavy side of your weight band. This does not necessarily mean that you are fat, just that the muscle on your body is making you heavier. The fitter you are, the slimmer you will look, even though you may weigh more when you stand on the scales.

To judge whether you are over or underweight, you should know your height and your build. There are several ways of measuring your build. One is to measure the width of your shoulders against the length of your upper arm. If your shoulder width measures less than the length of your upper arm, you have a small build. If they measure the same, you have a medium build. And if your shoulder width is greater than the length of your upper arm, you have a large build.

WOMEN

Height		Small build		Medium build		Large build	
ft in	m	st lb	kg	st lb	kg	st lb	kg
4 10	1.47	7 2- 7 12	45.4-50.0	7 10- 8 8	49.0-54.4	8 5- 9 5	53.1-59.4
4 11	1.50	7 3- 8 0	45.8-50.8	7 12- 8 11	50.0-55.8	8 7- 9 8	54.0-60.8
5 0	1.52	7 5- 8 3	46.7-52.2	8 0- 9 0	50.8-57.1	8 10- 9 11	55.3-62.1
5 1	1.55	7 7- 8 6	47.6-53.5	8 3- 9 3	52.2-58.5	8 13-10 0	56.7-63.5
5 2	1.57	7 10- 8 9	49.0-54.9	8 6- 9 6	53.5-60.0	9 2-10 4	58.1-65.3
5 3	1.60	7 13- 8 12	50.3-56.2	8 9- 9 9	54.9-61.2	9 5-10 8	59.4-67.1
5 4	1.63	8 2- 9 1	51.7-57.6	8 12- 9 12	56.2-62.6	9 8-10 12	60.8-68.9
5 5	1.65	8 5- 9 4	53.1-59.0	9 1-10 1	57.6-64.0	9 11-11 2	62.1-70.8
5 6	1.68	8 8- 9 7	54.4-60.3	9 4-10 4	59.0-65.3	10 0-11 6	63.5-72.6
5 7	1.70	8 11- 9 10	55.8-61.7	9 7-10 7	60.3-66.7	10 3-11 10	64.9-74.4
5 8	1.73	9 0- 9 13	57.1-63.0	9 10-10 10	61.7-68.0	10 6-11 13	66.2-75.7
5 9	1.75	9 3-10 2	58.5-64.4	9 13-10 13	63.0-69.4	10 9-12 2	67.6-77.1
5 10	1.78	9 6-10 5	60.0-65.8	10 2-11 2	64.4-70.8	10 12-12 5	69.0-78.5
5 11	1.80	9 9-10 8	61.2-67.1	10 5-11 5	65.8-72.1	11 1-12 8	70.3-79.8
6 0	1.83	9 12-10 11	62.6-68.5	10 8-11 8	67.2-73.5	11 4-12 11	71.7-81.2

MEN

Height		Small build		Medium build		Large build	
ft in	m	st lb	kg	st lb	kg	st lb	kg
5 2	1.57	8 13- 9 5	56.7-59.4	9 2- 9 12	58.1-62.6	9 9-10 8	61.2-67.1
5 3	1.60	9 1- 9 7	57.6-60.3	9 4-10 0	59.0-63.5	9 11-10 11	62.1-68.5
5 4	1.63	9 3- 9 9	58.5-61.2	9 6-10 3	60.0-64.9	9 13-11 1	63.0-70.3
5 5	1.65	9 5- 9 11	59.4-62.1	9 8-10 6	60.8-66.2	10 1-11 5	64.0-72.1
5 6	1.68	9 7-10 0	60.3-63.5	9 11-10 9	62.1-67.6	10 4-11 9	65.3-73.9
5 7	1.70	9 9-10 3	61.2-64.9	10 0-10 12	63.5-68.9	10 7-11 13	66.7-75.7
5 8	1.73	9 11-10 6	62.1-66.2	10 3-11 1	64.9-70.3	10 10-12 3	68.0-77.6
5 9	1.75	9 13-10 9	63.0-67.6	10 6-11 4	66.2-71.7	10 13-12 7	69.4-79.4
5 10	1.78	10 1-10 12	64.0-68.9	10 9-11 7	67.6-73.0	11 2-12 11	70.8-81.2
5 11	1.80	10 4-11 1	65.3-70.3	10 12-11 11	68.9-74.8	11 5-13 1	72.1-83.0
6 0	1.83	10 7-11 5	66.7-72.1	11 1-12 1	70.3-76.7	11 9-13 5	73.9-84.8
6 1	1.85	10 10-11 9	68.0-73.9	11 5-12 5	72.1-78.5	11 13-13 10	75.7-87.1
6 2	1.88	10 13-11 13	69.4-75.7	11 8-12 9	73.5-80.3	12 3-14 1	77.6-89.4
6 3	1.91	11 3-12 3	71.2-77.6	11 12-13 0	75.3-82.5	12 8-14 6	79.8-91.6
6 4	1.93	11 7-12 7	73.0-79.4	12 2-13 5	77.0-84.7	13 0-14 12	82.5-94.3

TRUE OR FALSE?
Your fitness IQ

1 *Pregnant women should not exercise.*

2 *For most people, exercise is a better way to slim than dieting.*

3 *You can gain weight on an exercise programme.*

4 *If you're sweating profusely, you've had a good workout.*

5 *Eating a bar of chocolate just before you exercise will give you extra energy.*

6 *It's natural to be out of breath after exercise.*

1 False. If you are pregnant it is better not to overexert yourself, particularly in the first three months, but moderate exercise is beneficial. Swimming and yoga are especially recommended. However, consult your doctor.

2 True. It's slower but better. Regular exercise controls appetite and improves muscle tone, bone strength and cardiovascular fitness. Low-calorie diets and appetite suppressants do none of these things.

3 Often true, because muscle weighs more than fat. But, paradoxically, you'll look thinner and your dress size or trousers size will go down.

4 False. Sweating simply means you are too hot and your body is trying to cool off. It can be caused by humidity or warm clothes as well as exercise.

5 False. It will trigger your pancreas to produce insulin, and you'll soon feel tired and thirsty. Instead, try a complex carbohydrate, such as wholegrain bread or pasta, about two hours before you exercise.

6 False. Gasping for breath is a sign of overexertion. You should be able to talk while you exercise.

What's the right sport for you?

The chart below is a guide to the benefits of a number of popular sports and pastimes. These benefits largely depend on how strenuously you work at each activity. The calories used when you swim gently to relax and unwind will be fewer than if you swim lengths fast for fitness training. Similarly, you will burn more calories by digging a garden trench than by pruning roses. The intensity of each exercise is reflected in the range of calories given in the chart.

A sport must appeal to you as well. To find the sport that you will be happiest doing, ask yourself:

★ Does this sport require equipment? Do I have room for it? Can I afford it?
★ Is this exercise appropriate for my age and fitness level? Does my doctor approve of it?
★ Is it fun only now and then, or can I see myself doing it regularly six months from now?
★ Do I prefer a competitive group sport or exercising by myself?
★ Where will I fit this into my daily or weekly schedule?
★ Must I travel to do it? Is the travel time manageable?
★ Can I get better at this and develop my skills, as time goes on?

Activity	Aerobic fitness	Muscular strength	Co-ordination	Relaxation	Sociability	Calories used per minute
Aerobic dancing	★★★★	★★★★	★★★★★	★★★★★	★★★★	8-12
Badminton	★★★★	★★★	★★★★★	★★★	★★★	9-18
Bowls	★	★★	★★★	★★★	★★★★	3-4
Cricket	★★	★★★	★★★★	★★★	★★★★★	3-6
Cycling (13mph/21km/h)	★★★★★	★★★★★	★★★★	★★★	★★	5-11
Football	★★★★★	★★★★★	★★★★	★★★	★★★★★	10-20
Gardening	★★★	★★★	★★★	★★★★★	★	4-10
Golf	★★	★★	★★★★	★★★	★★★★★	5
Hill walking	★★★	★★	★★	★★★	★★★	8-15
Horse riding	★	★★★★	★★★★	★★★★	★★★	3-10
Netball	★★★★	★★★	★★★★★	★★	★★★	6-9
Rowing (110yds/100m min)	★★★★	★★★★★	★★★★	★★	★★★	4-11
Rugby	★★★	★★★★★	★★★	★★	★★★★★	6-12
Running (5mph/8km/h)	★★★★	★★★★	★★	★★★	★★	9-10
Running (10mph/16km/h)	★★★★★	★★★★★	★★	★★★	★★	9-20
Skiing (downhill)	★★★	★★★★	★★★★★	★★★★	★★★★	10-20
Squash	★★★★★	★★★★	★★★★★	★★	★★★★	10-20
Swimming	★★★★★	★★★★★	★★★★	★★★★★	★★★★	11-14
Tennis	★★★	★★★★	★★★★★	★★★	★★★★	8-10
Walking	★★	★★	★	★★★★	★★	3-5
Weight training	★★	★★★★★	★★★★	★	★	3-5

Nutritional values of food

For optimum health, choose a wide variety of different foods. Aim to eat more vegetables, fruit and cereal products (such as bread, rice and pasta) and less fat, particularly saturated fat. Go easy on sugary foods, alcohol and sodium (found mainly in salt). Listed below are the quantities of nutrients in average servings of a wide range of foods (see also CALORIE COUNTING p.30). Helpful nutrition information is included on most food labels.

FOOD	Calories	Protein Grams	Carbohydrate Grams	Fat Grams	Saturated Fat Grams	Fibre Grams	Sodium Milligrams	Potassium Milligrams	Calcium Milligrams	Iron Milligrams	Vitamin C Milligrams	Folate Micrograms
Fruits, vegetables and nuts												
Apple, one medium	50	★	12	★	★	1.8	2	120	4	0.1	6	1
Apricots, three fresh	35	1	9	★	★	2.0	2	325	20	0.6	7	6
Avocado, medium, half	145	1	1	15	3	2.6	5	340	8	0.3	5	8
Banana, medium	95	1	23	★	★	1.1	1	400	6	0.3	10	15
Grapefruit, medium, half	25	1	5	★	★	1.0	2	160	20	0.1	30	20
Grapes, medium serving	60	★	15	★	★	0.7	2	210	15	0.3	3	2
Melon, honeydew, one slice	55	1	13	★	★	1.2	65	420	20	0.2	20	4
Orange, medium	60	2	14	★	★	2.7	8	240	75	0.2	85	50
Peach, medium	35	1	8	★	★	1.7	1	175	8	0.4	35	3
Pear, medium	70	1	18	★	★	4.0	6	280	20	0.4	10	4
Pineapple, fresh, one slice	35	★	8	★	★	1.0	2	130	15	1.6	10	4
Raisins, one tablespoonful	80	1	21	★	★	0.6	20	305	15	1.1	★	3
Asparagus, boiled medium portion	30	4	2	1	★	1.6	1	250	30	0.7	10	175
Beans, red kidney, canned 7oz/200g	200	14	36	1	★	12.4	780	560	140	4.0	★	15
Beetroot, boiled, four slices	20	1	4	★	★	0.6	35	205	10	0.3	2	45
Broccoli, boiled, medium portion	25	3	1	1	★	2.3	15	170	40	1.0	45	65
Brussels sprouts, boiled, eight	30	2	3	1	★	2.5	2	250	15	0.4	50	90
Cabbage, boiled, medium portion	15	1	2	★	★	1.8	8	120	35	0.3	20	30
Carrots, boiled, medium portion	15	★	3	★	★	1.5	30	70	15	0.2	1	10
Cauliflower, boiled, medium portion	30	3	2	1	★	1.6	4	120	15	0.4	25	50
Celery, one stick	2	★	1	★	★	0.3	20	95	15	0.1	2	5
Courgette, boiled, medium portion	15	2	2	★	★	1.1	1	190	15	0.5	10	30
Cucumber with skin, five slices	3	★	1	★	★	0.3	1	35	5	0.1	2	4
Curly kale, boiled, medium portion	20	2	1	1	★	2.5	60	145	135	1.8	65	75
Lentils, red, cooked 7oz/200g	200	15	35	1	★	3.8	15	440	30	4.8	★	10
Lettuce, soft round, medium serving	4	★	1	★	★	0.4	1	105	15	0.5	2	15
Lettuce, iceberg, medium serving	10	1	2	★	★	0.5	2	130	15	0.3	2	40
Mushrooms, fried in oil, medium portion	70	1	★	7	1	0.7	7	155	4	0.5	★	5
Okra, boiled, five	10	1	1	★	★	0.9	1	80	30	0.2	4	10
Onion, raw, three slices	20	1	4	★	★	0.7	2	80	15	0.2	3	9
Peas, boiled, medium portion	50	4	7	1	★	3.6	2	105	25	1.1	8	35
Pepper, green, raw, three slices	5	★	1	★	★	0.5	1	35	2	0.1	35	10
Potato, boiled, medium	245	7	55	★	★	4.9	20	1135	20	1.3	25	80
Potato chips, fried in oil, medium portion	395	5	50	20	2	3.6	60	1090	20	1.5	15	50
Radishes, four	5	★	1	★	★	0.3	3	70	6	0.2	5	10
Spinach, boiled, medium portion	20	2	1	1	★	1.9	110	205	145	1.4	7	80
Sweetcorn (frozen), boiled, medium	100	3	19	1	★	1.9	2	190	3	0.5	7	30
Tomato, raw, one medium	15	1	1	★	★	0.9	8	215	6	0.4	15	15
Brazil nuts, three	70	1	★	7	2	0.4	★	65	15	0.3	0	2
Peanuts, roasted, salted, small bag, 50g	300	12	4	27	1	3.0	200	405	20	0.7	0	25
Sunflower seeds, one tablespoonful	95	3	3	8	1	1.0	★	115	20	1.0	0	N
Walnuts, six halves	140	3	1	14	1	0.7	1	90	20	0.6	0	15

FOOD	Calories	Protein Grams	Carbohydrate Grams	Fat Grams	Saturated Fat Grams	Fibre Grams	Sodium Milligrams	Potassium Milligrams	Calcium Milligrams	Iron Milligrams	Vitamin C Milligrams	Folate Micrograms
Cereals and cereal products												
Bread, wholemeal, one slice	75	3	15	1	★	2.1	200	85	20	1.0	0	15
Bread roll, white, crusty, one	140	5	24	1	★	0.8	320	65	70	1.6	0	15
Pasta, boiled, medium portion	200	7	43	1	★	2.1	2	60	15	1.2	0	7
Rice, boiled, medium portion	250	5	56	2	1	0.2	2	100	30	0.4	0	7
Pizza, medium serving	500	15	66	21	9	3.0	1080	340	360	2.0	N	40
Cornflakes, medium portion	110	2	26	★	★	0.3	335	30	5	2.0	0	75
Muesli, medium portion	185	5	34	4	1	3.8	25	265	25	1.8	0	N
Biscuit, plain, one	35	1	6	1	1	0.1	35	10	10	0.2	0	1
Biscuit, chocolate digestive, one	75	1	10	4	2	0.3	70	30	15	0.3	0	N
Cake, plain jam sponge, medium slice	185	3	39	3	1	1.1	250	85	25	1.0	0	N
Chocolate eclair (frozen), one	140	2	9	11	6	0.3	25	55	30	0.4	★	4
Danish pastry, medium	410	6	56	19	6	1.8	210	185	100	1.4	0	20
Fruit pie, individual	200	2	31	8	3	0.9	115	65	30	0.6	2	2
Dairy products and margarine												
Butter, average on one slice bread	75	★	★	8	5	0	75	2	2	★	★	★
Cheese, Camembert, individual	120	8	★	9	6	0	260	40	140	0.1	★	40
Cheese, Cheddar, 1oz/30g	115	7	★	10	6	0	190	20	205	0.1	★	9
Cheese, cottage, small tub	110	15	2	4	3	0	425	100	80	0.1	★	30
Cheese, Parmesan, one tablespoonful	45	4	★	3	2	0	110	10	120	0.1	★	1
Margarine, polyunsaturated, average on one slice bread	75	★	★	8	2	0	80	1	★	★	0	★
Milk, whole, ½ pint/285ml	185	9	14	11	7	0	155	400	325	0.1	3	15
Milk, skimmed, ½ pint/285ml	95	9	14	★	★	0	155	425	340	0.1	3	15
Yogurt, full-fat, natural, 5floz/150ml	120	9	12	5	3	0	120	420	300	0.2	2	25
Fish, meat, poultry and eggs												
Cod, poached, medium portion	90	21	0	1	★	0	90	385	20	0.4	★	15
Cod in batter, fried in oil, large portion	450	44	17	23	2	0.7	225	835	180	1.1	★	N
Herring, grilled, medium	240	24	0	16	4	0	205	445	40	1.2	★	10
Prawns, boiled, shelled, 2oz/60g	65	14	0	1	★	0	955	155	90	0.7	★	N
Trout, grilled, medium	210	36	0	7	2	0	135	575	55	1.6	★	N
Tuna, canned in brine, medium portion	95	22	0	1	★	0	305	220	8	1.0	★	15
Beef, roast, lean only, medium portion	140	26	0	4	1	0	45	335	5	2.5	0	15
Lamb, roast, lean only, medium portion	170	26	0	7	4	0	60	305	7	2.4	0	4
Lamb's kidney, fried in oil, one	55	9	0	2	1	0	95	120	5	4.2	3	30
Lamb's liver, fried in oil, medium portion	220	23	1	14	4	0	80	300	8	10.0	10	240
Pork chop, grilled, lean only, medium	225	32	0	11	4	0	85	420	9	1.2	0	7
Pork pie, individual	525	14	35	38	14	1.3	1008	210	65	2.0	0	4
Pork sausage, fried in oil, one	125	6	4	10	4	0.3	420	80	20	0.6	N	1
Scotch egg, one	300	14	16	21	5	1.8	805	155	60	2.2	★	50
Veal escalope in breadcrumbs, fried in oil	195	28	4	7	1	0.1	110	380	9	1.4	0	N
Chicken, roast, medium, skinless	150	25	0	5	2	0	80	310	9	0.8	0	10
Chicken drumstick, roast, skinless	80	14	0	3	1	0	45	170	5	0.5	0	5
Egg, size 2, boiled or poached, one	90	8	★	6	2	0	85	80	35	1.1	0	30
Egg, size 2, fried in oil, one	110	8	★	8	2	0	85	80	35	1.1	0	25
Alcoholic drinks												
Beer, bitter, ½ pint/285ml	90	1	7	★	★	0	35	110	30	★	0	25
Wine, dry white, one glass	85	★	1	0	0	0	5	75	10	0.6	0	★

N = no reliable data available.   ★ = negligible (or trace).

Getting more for your pound

Do you get nervous at the supermarket as you watch your receipt flowing from the till? Are you always wondering how you manage to spend so much money on so little? Here are some simple ways to stretch your food budget without sacrificing quality.

★ Leave the children at home whenever you can. They may prompt you to buy items you don't want.

★ Don't go shopping on an empty stomach. You'll buy more than you meant to.

★ Make a list to prevent impulse buying.

★ Buy sale items only when needed and if you have ample storage space.

★ Shop in supermarkets that discount your favourite products.

★ Cut out coupons and use them. Every bit saved helps.

★ Compare brand prices.

★ Try store brands and products.

★ Think small. Buy only what you will use. Throwing out food and unused household products is throwing out money.

★ Buy unwrapped seasonal fruits and vegetables – they are cheaper than wrapped or tinned ones.

★ Don't buy prepacked meals – they are always more expensive than those you could make yourself, and often contain preservatives or extra sugar or salt.

★ Dried lentils, peas and beans are cheaper than tinned ones and don't contain sugar or preservatives.

★ Use protein chunks or meat substitutes occasionally. They are less expensive than meat and go further.

★ If you find yourself throwing away unused vegetables often, buy frozen vegetables. Even though they are more expensive, they last longer and are just as nutritious as fresh ones.

★ Bone chicken and cut up or mince less expensive cuts of beef, lamb and pork for stews and pies.

★ Season your own rice, make your own sauces, bake your own cakes and create your own desserts.

★ Use leftovers to make tasty meals instead of tossing them out.

Food-borne illness

Food poisoning is unpleasant at best and can be life-threatening. Here are some tips to help you eliminate the risk of illness.

★ Discard any food that smells or looks spoiled.

★ Don't keep food for longer than specified in the chart opposite.

★ Keep food hot or cold. Bacteria thrive at room temperature.

★ Scrub your hands with soap and warm water before preparing food, and after handling raw fish, meat or poultry.

★ Wash utensils and scrub cutting boards after each use. If a cutting board develops a crack it is advisable to throw it away.

★ Replace sponges and dishcloths, and wash drying-up cloths, as soon as they smell musty.

★ If you're going to sneeze or cough, turn away from food. Cover your mouth, then wash your hands.

★ If you have broken skin or an infection on your hands, wear thin rubber or plastic gloves in the kitchen.

★ Don't eat very rare meat, fish or poultry unless you are sure it is fresh.

★ Don't let food stand on a worktop to defrost. Thaw it in a microwave oven, the refrigerator or cold water. Cook immediately.

★ Discard bulging or leaking tins.

★ Cool leftovers in their containers in a bowl of iced water before putting them in the refrigerator. When reheating leftovers, do so thoroughly and boil leftover sauces and gravies.

★ Refrigerate perishables as soon as possible.

★ Freeze food in small, shallow, closed containers. Never refreeze frozen food that has thawed.

★ Take the 'use by' date on packaged food seriously.

★ Keep pets away from food and off the table.

★ Don't feed young children or elderly adults soft unpasteurised cheese or food made with raw or lightly cooked eggs.

Microwave do's and don'ts

* Use ceramic and glass ovenware. If you buy new ovenware, check that it's labelled 'microwave safe'.
* Never cook in metal containers. Aluminium foil is safe in some ovens but not others. Check your user's manual.
* Be sure that your microwave ovenware is tall enough to accommodate boiling foods.
* To avoid explosions, loosen the lids of frozen food containers, slit plastic food pouches and pierce food with skin so that steam can escape during cooking.
* Do not deep-fry.
* Place food in the centre of the oven and have the thicker, denser parts facing out, towards the oven walls.
* Follow the recipe and let food stand after you take it out of the oven; it's still cooking.
* Keep the oven turned off when not in use. It should close tightly. If it seems loose, have it checked by a qualified engineer.

Perishable food storage

Most vegetables, except salad vegetables with a high water content, should be blanched before they are frozen, and will keep for 12 months. Cauliflower is an exception to this rule, and only keeps for 6 months. Raw potatoes don't freeze well and should be boiled whole or mashed before freezing.

When frozen, single cream, whipping cream, sour cream and most yoghurts separate but can still be used for cooking. Milk also separates but is still fine for coffee or tea. Soft cheeses tend to lose their texture and flavour.

Most fruits need some preparation before freezing, such as washing, hulling, pitting or peeling, and packing with sugar or syrup. Never freeze bananas.

FREEZER -18°C/0°F or lower			REFRIGERATOR 5°C/40°F or less	
Months cooked	Months uncooked	Items	Days cooked	Days uncooked
		Meat and poultry		
		Bacon (opened		
2-3	3	package)	3-4	5-7
		Chicken,		
1	12	whole/pieces	2-3	1-2
		Eggs		7-14
	2	Cold meats		2-5
		Beef		
3	9-12	Joint	3-5	3-5
3	1-2	Mince	3-4	1-2
3	9-12	Steaks	2-3	2-4
3	3	Sausages	3-4	3-5
		Lamb		
3	9-12	Joint	3-5	3-5
3	3-4	Chops	1-2	2-4
3	1	Mince	3-4	1-2
		Pork		
3	9	Joint	3-4	1-2
3	3-4	Chops	3-4	1-2
1	3	Sausage	2-3	1-2
		Turkey,		
3	3-6	whole/pieces	2-3	1-2
		Fish		
		Lean white fish		
2	3-6	Cod, plaice, sole	2-3	1-2
		Oily fish		
2	3	Mackerel, tuna	2-3	1-2
1	1	Prawns	1-2	1
		Dairy products		
	6-12	Butter		7-14
	2-6	Cheese, hard		7-14
	4	Cream, double		2-4

Handy substitutes when supplies run short

FOOD	SUBSTITUTES	STRETCHERS
Baking powder 1tsp	¼tsp bicarbonate of soda, plus ½tsp cream of tartar, plus ½tsp ground rice. Sift together well	
Beer		Ginger ale, lemonade, tonic water
Bolognese sauce		Extra meat, shellfish, vegetables, olives, soya granules
Bread crumbs (for coating)	Crushed water biscuits, or cornflakes	
Cake		Ice cream, fruit topping; mix broken pieces with custard; trifle base
Self-raising flour 4oz/115g	4oz/115g plain flour, plus 1 level tsp baking powder. Sift together well	
Champagne	White or rosé wine	Fruit juices, soda water
Chicken	Veal, turkey	Onion, celery, rice, pasta
Chilli		Bulgur, beans, rice, spaghetti, sweetcorn
Cornflour 1tbsp (as thickener)	2 level tbsp plain flour	
Cream, single, ½pt/285ml	8fl oz/225ml milk, plus 2fl oz/60ml melted unsalted butter	
Creamed corn		Milk or stock and onion (for soup)
Egg		Omelette or scrambled, with vegetables, cheese, poultry
Egg salad		Celery, potatoes, tofu, rice and pasta
Fish		Cut up, stir-fry with vegetables, or mix with spicy rice
Fruit juice, fruit punch		Soda water, mineral water
Gravy	Condensed tinned soup, or packet soup made up with half quantity of water	Puréed vegetables, tomato sauce, mushrooms
Green pepper	Red or yellow pepper	Stuffing of rice, leftovers

FOOD	SUBSTITUTES	STRETCHERS
Minced beef	Minced pork, veal or lamb	Grated courgette, carrot or marrow, rice, pasta, onion, green pepper, dried peas and beans, lentils
Honey 8fl oz/225ml	8oz/225g sugar plus 4tbsp water, or golden syrup	
Ice cream	Frozen yoghurt	Fruit, sauce, cereal topping
Iced tea		Orange or lemon juice, herb teas, soda or mineral water
Lemon juice 1tsp	½tsp vinegar; lime juice	
Meat loaf		Breadcrumbs, rice, rolled oats, shredded carrots, hard-boiled eggs
Milk, whole ½pt/285ml	½pt/285ml skimmed milk plus 3tsp melted butter	Instant dried milk
Noodles	Spaghetti	Leftover vegetables, diced meats
Salad		Meat, fish, pulses, pasta, vegetables, hard-boiled eggs
Soups		Vegetables, pasta, pulses, tofu, sour cream, barley, yoghurt
Sour cream	Natural yoghurt, smetana	
Steak		Dice and stir-fry with vegetables; grill on skewer with vegetables
Stews		Creamed corn, vegetables, dried peas, and lentils, vegetable protein products
Sauce tartare 4fl oz/115ml	7tbsp mayonnaise plus 2tbsp chopped sweet mixed pickles	
Tomato ketchup or chilli sauce 4fl oz/115ml	4fl oz/115ml tomato sauce plus 2tbsp sugar	
Tomato sauce ½pt/285ml	Condensed tomato soup, or packet tomato soup made up with half quantity of water	Carrots, broccoli, celery, green pepper, olives

Spices and seasonings

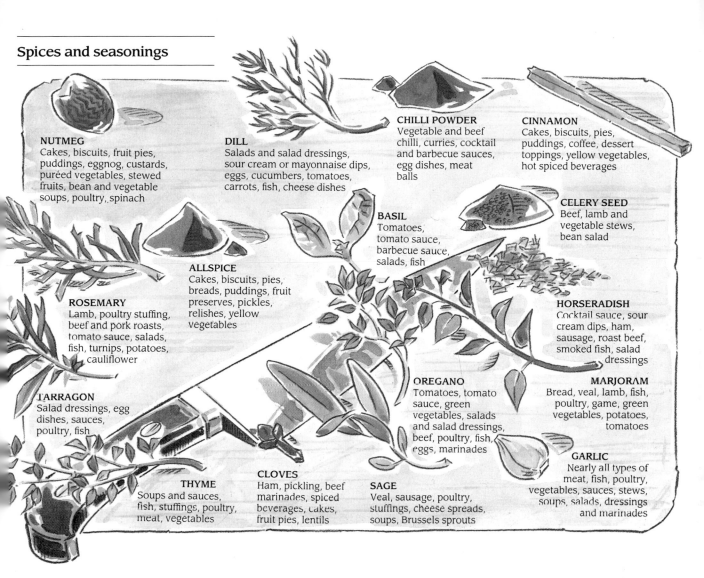

NUTMEG
Cakes, biscuits, fruit pies, puddings, eggnog, custards, puréed vegetables, stewed fruits, bean and vegetable soups, poultry, spinach

DILL
Salads and salad dressings, sour cream or mayonnaise dips, eggs, cucumbers, tomatoes, carrots, fish, cheese dishes

CHILLI POWDER
Vegetable and beef chilli, curries, cocktail and barbecue sauces, egg dishes, meat balls

CINNAMON
Cakes, biscuits, pies, puddings, coffee, dessert toppings, yellow vegetables, hot spiced beverages

BASIL
Tomatoes, tomato sauce, barbecue sauce, salads, fish

CELERY SEED
Beef, lamb and vegetable stews, bean salad

ALLSPICE
Cakes, biscuits, pies, breads, puddings, fruit preserves, pickles, relishes, yellow vegetables

ROSEMARY
Lamb, poultry stuffing, beef and pork roasts, tomato sauce, salads, fish, turnips, potatoes, cauliflower

HORSERADISH
Cocktail sauce, sour cream dips, ham, sausage, roast beef, smoked fish, salad dressings

TARRAGON
Salad dressings, egg dishes, sauces, poultry, fish

OREGANO
Tomatoes, tomato sauce, green vegetables, salads and salad dressings, beef, poultry, fish, eggs, marinades

MARJORAM
Bread, veal, lamb, fish, poultry, game, green vegetables, potatoes, tomatoes

GARLIC
Nearly all types of meat, fish, poultry, vegetables, sauces, stews, soups, salads, dressings and marinades

THYME
Soups and sauces, fish, stuffings, poultry, meat, vegetables

CLOVES
Ham, pickling, beef marinades, spiced beverages, cakes, fruit pies, lentils

SAGE
Veal, sausage, poultry, stuffings, cheese spreads, soups, Brussels sprouts

---

Equivalents for common cooking ingredients

1lb/450g	**Apples**	3 or 4 medium	2-3tbsp juice	**Lemon**	1½tsp grated rind
1lb/450g	**Bananas**	3 or 4 medium	2oz/60g	**Macaroni**	5oz/150g cooked
8oz/225g	**Beans, dried**	1lb/450g cooked	2oz/60g	**Nuts, shelled**	6tbsp chopped
1lb/450g	**Berries**	8-10fl oz/225-285ml purée	1 medium	**Onion**	4oz/115g
1 slice	**Bread**	1oz/30g crumbs	6-8tbsp juice	**Orange**	4fl oz/115ml cup
4oz/115g	**Cheese, grated**	12tbsp	3-4 medium	**Potatoes**	1lb/450g
1oz/30g	**Chocolate, 1 square**	1tbsp melted	2oz/60g	**Rice, uncooked**	6½oz/190g cooked
½pt/285ml	**Double cream**	16fl oz/460ml whipped	2oz/60g	**Spaghetti, uncooked**	6½oz/190g cooked
4oz/115g	**Flour**	13 level tbsp	4oz/115g	**Sugar**	11 level tbsp icing
1 envelope	**Gelatine**	1tbsp	4oz/115g	**Sugar**	9 level tbsp caster
1tsp	**Herbs, dried**	1tbsp fresh	1lb/450g	**Tomatoes**	3 or 4 medium
			1lb/450g	**Walnuts, in shell**	7-8oz/200-225g shelled

Party checklist

Three to four weeks before
* Decide on the type of party.
* Set the budget.
* Draw up the guest list. Post invitations or ring up guests. (Written confirmation of a phone call is usually a good idea.)
* Book hired help if needed.
* Rent equipment.
* Arrange entertainment.

Two weeks before
* Decide on food and drink.
* Plan set-up: bar, buffet, decorations.
* Choose dishes, glassware, table linen, candles and other supplies.

One week before
* Shop for non-perishable foods, drinks and supplies.
* Order flowers.
* Prepare dishes that can be frozen.

Two to five days before
* Polish silver.
* Clean house.
* Make or buy ice and store in freezer.
* Arrange seating plan and write out place cards.
* Clean and press party clothes.
* Choose music (if there's no entertainment).

One day before
* Buy perishable food.
* Set up the bar and buffet table.
* Put out ashtrays and matches.
* Check bathroom supplies.
* Determine area for coats.

Day of party
* Arrange decorations.
* Set out uncooked foods as late as possible.
* Prepare cooked foods.
* Set table (if a dinner party).
* Chill white wine.
* Do last-minute tidying up.
* One hour before: put ice, water, garnishes at bar; open red wine.

How much do you need?

It could be disastrous to run out of supplies during a party and a nuisance to have to cope with too many leftovers afterwards. The amounts given here are meant for 20 guests for a drinks party, buffet or sit-down dinner. If you have invited more or fewer people, simply multiply or divide the quantities we've given by the appropriate number taking into account the likely appetites of your guests.

Drinks
1¾ pints/1 litre each vodka, gin, whisky, brandy
2 barrels beer
5 bottles white wine
3 bottles red wine
5 pints/3 litres mineral water (still and sparkling)
1¾ pints/1 litre each soda water, tonic, orange juice, tomato juice, cola, ginger ale
6 lemons
10lb/4.5kg ice cubes

Hors d'oeuvres
2lb/1kg assorted cheeses
4 French breads
2 packets biscuits for cheese
40 cheese straws
20 mini-quiches
3 large bags crisps
2lb/1kg nuts
4½lb/2kg raw vegetables, and
1¼ pints/700ml dip, *or*
60-100 other assorted finger foods (cocktail sausages, vol-au-vents, sausage rolls, tiny sandwiches)

Dinner
(Choose one meat or fish quantity)
10lb/4.5kg meat with bone
5lb/2.25kg boned meat
15lb/6.8kg poultry on bone
8lb/3.6kg fish fillets
2½lb/1.1kg pasta or rice
5lb/2.25kg any vegetable
4 heads lettuce
6lb/2.75kg fruit for fruit salad
2 cakes or 3 pies
40 wafers or dessert biscuits
3½ pints/2 litres ice cream

Setting a place at your table

These days people have fewer formal dinner parties. The diagram below illustrates where all the elements go in an informal place setting. You may want to leave out a soup spoon or wineglass from the arrangement, depending on the menu you are serving.

White wine glass

Water glass

Napkin

Dessert fork

Dessert spoon

Red wine glass

Soup spoon

Side plate

Dinner fork

Dinner plate

Dinner knife

Butter knife

Cheese choices

Cheese is an excellent protein food to have on hand when people are drinking alcohol and is easy to store and serve. Go to a specialist shop or the cheese counter in your supermarket, where it is sold to order. Ask to sample a small piece of the cheese you want to buy.

★ Store cheeses in the door or salad compartment of the refrigerator, or on a plate in a cold pantry. Wrap leftover pieces tightly in non-toxic plastic film or aluminium foil.

★ Remove cheese from the refrigerator at least an hour before serving (except for cottage or cream cheese).

★ For dessert, combine apples, grapes and pears with Brie, Gorgonzola, Cheddar, Stilton, Wensleydale, Münster, Port Salut or goat cheese.

★ Oranges and tangerines go well with Stilton, cream cheese or cottage cheese. Peaches complement the flavour of Bel Paese, blue cheese, Camembert and Mascarpone.

★ A red Bordeaux or a good white dessert wine, such as a Sauternes or Beaumes de Venise, complement most cheese and fruit combinations. Save Burgundy for strong cheeses.

★ Serve at least one pungent cheese for adventurous diners: Danish blue, ripe goat cheese, Stilton Münster, Bresse Bleu or Roquefort.

★ Aromatic cheeses should be served on a separate board so that they don't overwhelm milder cheeses.

★ Use a wire cutter for blue cheeses to keep them from falling apart.

★ To satisfy everyone's taste, serve a varied selection with an assortment of cheese biscuits and dark bread.

Soft and semisoft cheeses Bel Paese, Boursin, Bresse Bleu, goat cheese, Camembert, Feta, Gorgonzola, Livarot, Mascarpone and Münster.

Hard and semihard cheeses Caerphilly, Cheddar, Edam, Emmental, Esrom, Gouda, Gruyère, Jarlsberg and Stilton.

Tips on tippling

No one wants an inebriated guest, particularly one who is driving after the party.

If you're the host

★ Never urge drinks on guests.

★ Keep a good supply of ice on hand and put plenty of ice into drinks.

★ When you make cocktails for your guests, or serve them spirits, measure the alcohol exactly with a jigger.

★ Have plenty of non-alcoholic refreshments available.

★ Set out plenty of food near the bar or drinks table.

★ If you think a guest is getting tipsy, stop serving him or her alcohol.

★ If someone is obviously drunk, either call a taxi or drive him or her home yourself. Remove a guest's car keys if necessary.

If you're a guest

★ Drink milk or have a snack before you go to a party; eat when you get there as well.

★ Sip your drinks slowly. Keep replenishing the ice in your drink.

★ Ask for diluted drinks.

★ Alternate your drinks with non-alcoholic beverages (but not carbonated drinks, which enhance the effects of alcohol). Make every other drink fruit juice or water.

★ Stop when you've had enough.

Are you in love?

★ Do you think about her every day, and sometimes call, just to ask her what she's doing?

★ Do you have roughly the same standards, laugh at the same things?

★ Are you fond of his physical features, which other people might consider unattractive – like that gap between his teeth?

★ Do you buy things you think she'd like, or give her something important to you, such as a family heirloom?

★ Do you want to know as much as you can about his family, background, interests and work? Do you want to show him things you're proud of?

★ Do you feel the need to discuss every important issue with her?

★ Does he always feature in your plans for the future?

★ Do you want to become a better person for her sake?

★ Do you go to the theatre – or other places – because he enjoys it even

though you don't?

★ Do you feel a strong emotional and mental attraction to her? Do you like being affectionate?

★ Do you no longer feel attracted to other people?

★ Do you feel young, bubbly, glad to be alive? Do people keep asking you why you're so happy?

If you've answered 'yes' to all or most of these questions, it may be time to move on to the WEDDING CHECKLIST.

Ten tips for a happy marriage

Argue, but within limits. Express your feelings, but don't explode. Encourage your partner to tell you what's wrong. Tactfully try to reach the root of problems and resolve them.

Keep your own interests If your life is centred only on your partner, you might make him feel pressurised, apart from restricting yourself. Keep in touch with friends; keep up activities you enjoy; join organisations and enrol for classes ('Floodlight', in your local library, or your local education authority will have details). It all helps to make you a more interesting – and intriguing – 'other half'.

Support your partner If she's worried about an important occasion, such as giving a speech or making a presentation, show her you care, even if you can't really help. Be proud of her achievements without feeling jealous. Don't see her as a rival.

Be affectionate Keep holding hands or taking his arm, no matter how long you've been married. Show him he's still attractive to you after all these years. Don't forget to say 'I love you' –

they're three of the sweetest words in the English language. He won't get tired of hearing them.

Make time for each other No matter how busy you are, find time to be alone with your partner. It might be a couple of hours on Sunday afternoon or even a weekend break, if a friend / granny will have the children. Inject 'excitement' by making a date with each other – such as visiting that new Chinese restaurant on Wednesday evening.

Appreciate each other Do you thank her when she cooks you dinner or does you a favour like picking up your dry cleaning? Do you treat him as considerately as you would a friend?

Do you compliment her enough? It's easy to forget these basic courtesies when we live with someone. But don't let familiarity breed contempt.

Remember the good times When life is tough, make an effort to recall wonderful memories from the past. Sharing them will reinforce the bond between you and remind you why you fell in love in the first place.

Forgive and forget Don't sulk or keep going over old arguments. If your partner has said sorry, resist the temptation to bring it up again. If it keeps bothering you, ask yourself why. And if you really can't break destructive patterns, see a counsellor, either with your partner or on your own. (Contact Relate Marriage Guidance, Herbert Gray College, Little Church Street, Rugby, Warwickshire CV21 3AP. Tel. 01788-573241.)

Communicate your feelings If something is wrong, explain your reactions rather than directly criticise your man's behaviour. Try saying 'When you do that, I feel hurt / humiliated / angry', instead of 'Don't do that!' Praise his good points too. If you say 'I love it when you do that', it encourages you both to feel happy.

Give in occasionally Go on – watch the film that he wants to, even if you don't. If she wants to try out that Italian restaurant, take her. Loving compromises are the key to happy marriages.

Your wedding checklist

Planning a formal wedding can test the fortitude of even the most organised person. Here's a chronological checklist to minimise any last-minute crises on the day.

Six months before
★ Decide date, time and place for ceremony and reception if you haven't already done so.
★ Set a budget.
★ Determine number of guests and make invitation list.
★ Choose a caterer.
★ Discuss ceremony plans with the person who will officiate.
★ Select who will be your wedding attendants and ask them.
★ Bride orders wedding dress, accessories and attire for bridesmaids.
★ Register wedding list at a department store.
★ Order stationery for invitations, announcements, thank-you notes.
★ Choose wedding rings.
★ Hire musicians/DJ and photographer.

Three months before
★ Order flowers for wedding and reception.
★ Arrange honeymoon travel and hotel.
★ Groom orders his wedding attire.
★ Mothers select their dresses.
★ Announce engagement in papers.
★ Order wedding cake.
★ Plan the recording of gifts and their display.

Two months before
★ Plan reception seating, bar, menu, decor.
★ Post invitations. Arrange rehearsal dinner.
★ Arrange transport for wedding party.
★ Select and order gifts for attendants.

One month before
★ Arrange lodging for out-of-town guests.
★ Final fitting for bride's, bridesmaids' dresses.
★ Address announcements. Assign person to post them after the wedding.
★ Arrange your own wedding-day transport.

Two weeks before
★ Make date with hairdresser.
★ Call people who haven't answered their invitations.
★ Tell caterer final number of guests.
★ Arrange a wedding rehearsal if it's needed.
★ Recheck honeymoon reservations.

The wedding day
★ Best man gives minister a fee.
★ Relax, take a bath, eat something.
★ Get to the wedding on time!

A wedding in a week

Six days before
★ Arrange a time and place for the ceremony (registry office or some other designated official location).
★ Find someone qualified to officiate, if necessary.
★ Telephone people you want to invite (not too many).

Five days before
★ If you want a reception at a friend's home, get your friend's consent, and plan it.
★ Buy the marriage licence from the registry office.

Four days before
★ Decide on wedding attire. Order flowers if desired.

Three days before
★ Buy the rings.

Two days before
★ Buy food, drink and any decorations for the reception.

One day before
★ Check final details.

The day
★ Get married.

Games in the car

* Keep young children amused with a surprise bag of goodies like crayons and drawing paper. Bring trays to balance on knees.
* Make glove puppets out of socks (stick on felt circles for eyes), and play out stories, or 'peek-a-boo'.
* Set competitions to spot things, such as a yellow car or a motorbike.
* Encourage children to count the number of lorries going past: the first one up to 50 wins.
* Play 'I spy', stating whether the object is in or outside the car. (If outside, it has to be continually in view, such as hedges, rather than something which flashes past.)
* Draw up a checklist of sights for children to spot, such as a farm, traffic lights or level crossing. They have to tick off each sight as they spot it.
* Make up a sentence with the letters of the car's numberplate in front of you, such as BAB - 'Boys are best'.
* Bring a portable tape recorder and record your own songs on it.
* Draw up a list of general knowledge questions and put the children into teams.

A babysitter's checklist

* What time you expect to return home
* Children's bedtimes
* What television programmes and snacks are allowed
* Whether to answer the door
* How to answer the telephone (it may not be wise for the sitter to say that you're out)
* Special instructions for babies or sick children
* Where things are: nappies, toys, food, books, fire extinguishers, torch, telephone, first-aid supplies, fire exits, children's rooms
* How to lock and unlock windows and doors

Telephone numbers
* Where you can be reached:
* Neighbour:
* Doctor:
* Police:
* Fire:
* Ambulance:

Provisions for the sitter
* Soft drinks, snacks
* Magazines, cushions
* Television, radio

Finding the right day care

* Contact your local social services department. By law it has to license all nurseries, day centres and child-minders, so will have a list of what's in your area. The National Childminding Association (8 Masons Hill, Bromley, Kent BR2 9EY, Tel. 0181-464 6164) has local information. Visit as many nurseries/childminders as possible.
Check the following points:
* What qualifications do the staff have? If you're employing a childminder, ask for two references. If you're dealing with a nursery, ask to talk to other parents for feedback.
* What is the child/staff ratio in the nursery? Under the Children's Act, it should be no fewer than one adult to three children up to 2 years; one adult

per four children aged 2 to 3 years; and one adult per eight children aged 3 to 5 years.
* Do the staff communicate with the children? Can they control them? Does everyone seem happy?
* Does the building seem clean and safe – for example, is there a chain on the door, window bars so that children can't fall out and soap in the lavatory?
* Is there enough heat and light in the building? Is it big enough? The Children's Act decrees that there should be at least 40 sq ft / 4 sq m for children between 0 and 2 years; 30 sq ft / 2.8 sq m for children aged 1 to 4 years; and 25 sq ft / 2.32 sq m for children aged 3 to 5 years.
* Is there enough equipment, and is it

clean and in good condition?
* Ask what happens if a child is naughty. Your idea of discipline might not coincide with theirs.
* What is the children's daily routine? Are there any special activities or outings?
* Look for evidence of children's work, such as drawings on walls.
* What emergency arrangements are made if the child is sick (a good nursery will ask for your doctor's phone number to put on its records).
* What are the fees and do they include food and insurance? Is the money payable in advance? Is there a registration fee? Are you entitled to a refund if your child is ill? How much withdrawal notice must you give?

Games for a rainy day

* Cut out pictures from magazines and glue them onto stiff paper to make greeting cards for a child's friends or relatives.
* You can create a picture storybook on pages of coloured paper in the same way.
* If you have childproof musical instruments, such as maracas, a tambourine or a drum, put on a record and let them play along.
* Invent your own musical instruments. Give children a tin with a lid, such as a cake or biscuit tin, or a shoebox, as a drum; chopsticks can become drumsticks. Put beans or buttons inside two foil plates, and stick them together with sticky tape to make a tambourine.
* Hold a cooking class: make some simple dishes together, which the family can enjoy at dinner.
* Act out a familiar fairy tale, or start making up your own story and let each child add a section in turn.
* Make necklaces by painting cotton reels or pasta with acrylic or poster paints. String them together with wool or coloured cord or ribbon. Make sure that no one swallows anything.
* Put together a gift box for a favourite friend or relative; it could include the child's photo, poems or stories.
* Paint faces on paper bags and cut holes for the eyes and mouth; the children can then act out stories wearing these masks.
Caution Use paper bags only.

You and your teenager

* Remember your own feelings as a teenager. It will help you understand that your own child's emotional highs and lows are perfectly normal. So try not to overreact.
* Don't take it personally if your child isn't as willing to talk as he used to be. Respect his privacy if he wants to be alone.
* Listen seriously to your child's opinions. If you disagree, argue back as courteously and logically as you would with another adult, say, at a party or in the office. Dismissing her views will discourage her from thinking for herself and knock her confidence in her own ideas.
* Give him total responsibility in certain areas – for example, his room or appearance. Teenagers need to learn to make decisions and live with the consequences, whether good or bad.
* Avoid comparisons – either with her friends or yourself, in the belief that you were more reasonable at her age. Your own parents might not have thought so!
* When arguments start, try not to lay the blame on him or attack too fast. Stick to your basic principles but be open to negotiation and be prepared to compromise on less important points.
* Always praise good behaviour and admire his achievements. Constant criticism could make him feel worthless.
* All teenagers want to be accepted by their own age group. Don't constantly criticise her friends, and try to make them feel welcome when they come to the house.
* Talk openly about alcohol, drugs and sex. Encourage him to come to you or another trusted adult if he needs to talk.
* If you feel you can't cope with a particular problem, talk to your GP, a family friend or self-help groups run by professionals and parents, such as 'Exploring Parenthood' (4 Ivory Place, Treadgold Street, London W11 4BP, Tel. 0171-221 4471) or Parent Network (44-46 Caversham Road, Kentish Town, London NW5 2DS, Tel. 0171-485 8535).

Seasonal home checkups

IN THE SPRING
Outside
* Use binoculars to check the roof for loose or damaged slates or tiles. Pay particular attention to ridge tiles.
* Check all flashing (the seals between two surfaces, such as chimney stack and roof). Repair with self-adhesive flashing tape where necessary.
* Clean winter debris from gutters, and check that water flows away through downpipes. Check gutters and pipes for winter damage.
* Examine all exterior paintwork, and repair any damage.
* Check for gaps around window and door frames where damp could get in.
* Have the chimneys swept if solid fuel fires have been used during the winter.
* Check flat roof areas for damage. Seal cracks and gaps with bitumen rubber roofing compound.
* Check exterior cladding and coat with a stain preservative if it has a natural wood effect, or repaint.
* Check all pointing between brickwork. Rake out and replace if soft or damaged.
* Check that doors and windows open easily. Replace any damaged draught-proofing strips.
Inside
* Open up windows of rooms not used during the winter months to ventilate.
* Have the central heating system and boiler checked as soon as regular heating is no longer needed.
* Plan which rooms will need decorating.
* Put garden furniture out, and check to see if it needs painting.
* Check whether carpets, curtains or upholstery need cleaning.

IN THE AUTUMN
Outside
* Check the outside to ensure all windows and doors are weatherproof.
* Ensure that all painted surfaces are sound. Make temporary repairs if bare wood or metal is found.
* Inspect the roof for loose slates or tiles, and chimney stacks for cracked mortar.
* Once the leaves are off the trees, clear debris from gutters and downpipes.
* Prune trees and bushes growing too close to the house.
* Get the lawnmower serviced as soon as the season is over. Don't wait for the spring rush!
* Coat all metal garden tools and equipment with a protective oil, and store in a dry place.
* Rake debris from the lawn.
* Lift delicate plants and tubers. Store these, and tubbed plants which cannot stand frost, indoors.
* Drain outside taps so that they don't freeze in winter.
* Check all draught-proofing strips on doors and windows.
Inside
* Check the central heating system and ensure that the boiler is clean and the pump is running freely. Bleed all radiators to ensure no air is trapped in the system.
* Check the double glazing, and clean between panes where possible.
* Store away all garden furniture after making any necessary repairs. Don't leave this until spring!
* Have the chimney swept if it was not done in spring.
* Check all lighting, and get in a stock of spare bulbs to suit all fittings.
* Check that you have spare fuses for all circuits.
* Ensure that smoke alarms have fresh batteries.

Selecting and working with contractors

* Decide exactly what it is that you want to do. Once you proceed it will be very costly to change your mind.
* First make a clear set of plans for your project. Remember that unethical contractors will put in a low bid, knowing that they will more than make up the difference in the price on extras and changes.
* For small jobs and jobs that are essentially repairs or very minor improvements, give the contractor a list of specific materials, colours, textures and finishes you would like in writing. Where appropriate, add

drawings and detailed measurements.
* Any job that amounts to a change in the structure of the building, or involves any change of use, or any job that is within a conservation or other designated area will require planning permission from the local authority. This must be obtained before the work is started. Allow plenty of time for the granting of permission.
* For any work that requires planning permission, have detailed drawings done by a qualified architect.
* Never hire a contractor who 'happens to be in the area' and offers

you a bargain price because he wants to keep his people busy or for some other reason. Good contractors do not have to solicit new business.
* Find work that you like locally and ask the homeowner who did it. Ask your friends for recommendations.
* Other good sources of information on a contractor's reputation are local estate agents, architects and timber yards.
* Get a financial reference from his bank. If he becomes insolvent your rights will disappear.
* Ask for a few quotations (fixed price

agreements). Do not accept estimates. Make sure all the quotations are on the same basis.

★ Obtain a copy of the contract form 'JCT Minor Works' from your architect or the Royal Institute of Architects (RIBA). Use this as the basis of your contract. Make sure it spells out everything the contractor is to do (including weights, sizes and grades of materials; brand names and model numbers of appliances, etc; the time allowed for doing the work; penalties for late completion). Do not allow amendment to the contract form. If the contractor won't sign it, go elsewhere.

★ Include a provision limiting the cost of the overrun you will accept: up to 10 per cent should be allowed.

★ The contract should specify who does the cleaning up, where things may be stored and whether you want old appliances or materials saved.

★ The contractor must agree to install all items according to the manufacturer's instructions. Manufacturer's warranties, which should be in writing, may be void unless this is done. If the contractor has to be accredited, check his certificate and don't take his word for it.

★ Do not agree to any subcontractors that you have not personally vetted.

★ Check that you have proper insurance cover for any property damage, and for personal and occupier's liability to the contractor. If in doubt, ask your insurance company.

★ Once the contract has started, it is expensive to change your mind. If you do, make sure that all changes are written and get a fixed price.

★ Your contractor will certainly demand some money in advance to purchase materials. Keep this to a minimum and make it a contract term that materials become your property as soon as they come on site.

★ For larger jobs it is not unreasonable to schedule payments at intervals through the contract.

★ Always withhold 15 per cent until 5 days before completion date. Insist that any faults are put right before making the final payment.

The basic home tool kit

The secret of success with jobs around the house lies in having the right tools. They allow you to produce good work in the easiest way possible. Below are the most essential tools to include in your tool kit, but you can add tools and accessories as special jobs are undertaken. Always buy the best, even if you have to assemble your tool kit in stages. Cheap tools may fall apart and often need to be replaced.

It's a good idea to have a range of sizes of certain tools, such as chisels (¼in/6mm, ½in/13mm and ⅝in/16mm), and a variety of screwdrivers (cross-slot, single-slot and insulated electrician's screwdriver). You'll also need accessories for your power tools, such as a drum sander, flapwheel sander, masonry and twist drills, screwdriver bits and jigsaw blades for various materials. Keep an assortment of abrasive papers and a sanding block handy, too.

Sandpaper

Hardpoint handsaw

Electric drill and drill bits

Claw hammer

Pin hammer

Power jigsaw

Chisels

Hacksaw and blades

Hardpoint tenon saw

Screwdrivers

G cramps

Craft knife and blades

Wood glue

Combination square

Fine-nose pliers

Adjustable spanner

Steel tape measure

Pincers

Insulated pliers

Screws and Rawlplugs

Jars for nails

Extension lead in drum

Tool box

Universal saw

Safety tips for your home

Although many people are unaware of the fact, the majority of accidents occur in the home, and it is where you and your family run the greatest risk of being hurt. Most of these domestic incidents are preventable, however (see FIRE SAFETY, p.81). These pages illustrate many of the danger spots in an average British home and suggest how to avoid the avoidable with commonsense precautions. Note that safety tips in one room may apply to other rooms as well.

In Britain, about 6000 people a year die in household accidents and at least 3 million need medical treatment following accidents and fires in the home. Take these simple steps to lessen your chances of being one of them.

Bedroom
★ Keep the bulb wattage to that of lamp and light fixtures. If not known, limit it to 40 watts.
★ Keep electric blankets smooth and flat. Don't tuck them under the mattress. Always switch off an underblanket when you get into bed.
★ Space heaters are dangerous. Keep them away from paper items, curtains, rugs, furniture, traffic paths. Keep children and pets away. Check stability.
★ Have a lamp and telephone accessible from the bed.
★ Avoid clutter on the floor near the bed.

Hallways, stairs and landings
★ Ensure good lighting with a switch on the ground floor and each landing.
★ Fit a smoke detector on each floor, near the bedrooms.
★ Keep stairs and landings clear of clutter or furniture with sharp or protruding parts.
★ Stair treads should have nonslip surfaces. For visibility on dark cellar or attic stairs use 2 in (50mm) white tape on stair edges.
★ Never leave anything on the stairs.
★ Install safety gates across the bottom of the stair and at each landing if you have small children or elderly people.
★ Tack carpeting down.
★ Make sure stair rails are sturdy. If old people are living in the home, fit a rail on each side of the staircase.

Child's room
★ Make sure all paint in your house is lead-free (it may not be in old houses).
★ Don't allow a space heater in a

child's room. The risk is too great.
★ Keep windows locked and install window guards if you have young children who might open them.

Kitchen
★ Install good lighting over the cooker and worktops.
★ Have a fire blanket fitted near the cooker for minor fires.
★ Lock household cleaning fluids out of children's reach.
★ Always read labels. Never mix different cleaning products.
★ Keep matches, lighters, sharp utensils, electrical appliances and cords out of children's reach.
★ Use kitchen steps, a tall stool or a short step ladder to reach high places.
★ Don't store anything attractive to

children, such as snacks, above or near the cooker.
★ Turn pot handles inwards when cooking. Cover frying pans with frying screens or lids. Fit a hobguard.
★ Keep electrical cords and appliances away from the sink and cooker. Repair or throw them away if even a slight shock is felt when you use them.

safety glass or heavy-duty plastic.

★ Attach a grab bar to the wall or side of the bath.

★ Always run cold water before hot if you have young children as they may fall in and scald themselves.

★ Always check the water temperature before getting into the bath.

★ Use non-slip strips on the bath bottom.

★ Never leave young children alone in the bath, even for a moment.

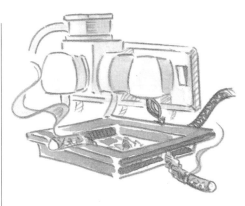

★ When cooking, tie back long hair and avoid loose sleeves.

★ Keep paper items, curtains, drying-up towels, pot holders and plastic utensils away from the cooker.

★ If you smell gas, put out cigarettes and turn off the main gas tap next to the meter. Don't use a torch or candles. Open windows to disperse the gas. When the smell has gone, check the gas burner or pilot light and relight if necessary. If the smell of gas still persists, call the local gas board office.

Bathroom

★ Install a night light.

★ Fit pull-cord switches.

★ Lock up all medicines in a cabinet that is beyond children's reach.

★ Keep breakable items and electrical appliances – such as hair dryers, shavers, radios or the telephone – away from the bath or basin.

★ Shower doors should be made from

Living room

★ Check that the fuses are suitable for appliances and lamps. Overloaded extension cords or plugs cause fires.

★ Install cover plates on all your plugs and switches. Call an electrician if any plug or plate is warm to the touch.

★ Provide wide-rimmed ashtrays; don't empty them into wastebaskets.

★ Shield the fireplace with a screen or heat-resistant glass doors. (Keep the area clear of newspapers.) Make sure your chimney is clean; check often for cracks with a torch.

★ Leave an air space around the television and stereo to avoid overheating.

★ Keep fire, police and doctor's numbers near the telephone.

★ Don't run electrical flexes under rugs or furniture, or in traffic areas. Replace frayed, cracked or pinched flexes.

★ Tack down carpets: back rugs with nonslip coating or pads. Use non-slip polish on waxed floors.

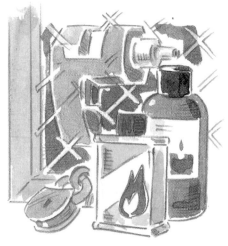

Garage or cellar

★ Throw away paint or oil-stained rags, or store in metal containers.

★ Dispose of combustibles such as newspapers, magazines, boxes and old furniture.

★ Keep flammable and volatile liquids in tightly capped containers. Never store petrol in the home.

★ Power tools should have double insulation. Lock them away when they're not in use.

★ Install extra lighting in work areas, especially where power tools are used.

★ Make sure ladders are sturdy and have nonslip treads on rungs.

★ Check that each fuse is of the proper amperage; never use any substitute for the proper fuse.

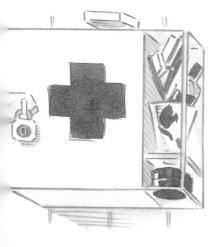

POLICE
HOSPITAL
EMERGENCY
DOCTOR

Protecting your home

One of the most effective ways to protect your home is with an alarm system. You can install some systems yourself, but others are best left to professionals. Ask the crime prevention officer at your local police station for information. Here are some other ways to safeguard your home.

Windows

* Stick adhesive-backed foil tape (window alarm tape) or beware-of-dog signs on windows – whether or not you have an alarm system or a dog.
* Install key locks on windows.
* To substitute for a lock in a sash-window, drill holes at the top corners of the lower window, through the inside of the sash at a slightly downward angle and about three-quarters of the way into the outside sash. Insert nails into the holes.
* Close curtains or blinds and lock all the windows if you're going out
* Place televisions, VCRS and other illuminated screens facing away from the window.
* If you have air conditioning, fasten it securely to the window frame or sill so that it can't be pulled outwards.
* Set timers to turn certain lights and the radio on and off when you're away at night.
* Leave the radio on during the day when you're out.

Drainpipes

* Plastic drainpipes are less likely than metal ones to support a climber.
* Apply anticlimb paint or grease above a height of 8ft/2.4m
* Surround the bottom of drainpipes with prickly plants.

Doors

* Solid wood or metal doors should fit snugly into frames, which should be tightly secured to the brickwork.
* Give a set of keys to trusted neighbours. Don't hide or hang them outside.
* External doors should be fitted with a mortise deadlock with a 5-lever mechanism conforming to BS3621

(look for the kite mark on the box) for Thief Resistant locks.
* External door with glass or lightweight panels should be fitted with a 5-lever mortise deadlock and the glass protected by internal metal grilles. Lightweight panels can be strengthened on the inside by a metal lining. Hinge bolts should be added on the hinged side of the door. A solid iron bar across the inside of the door, is also a good deterrent.
* If you have no alarm system, hang battery-operated doorknob alarms on inside doorknobs.
* Install lights over doorways. Have your house number lit and visible from the street.
* Install a wide-angle peephole and chain lock on the front door.
* Never leave notes on your door that indicate you're out.
* Don't install a pet door; a thief may be small

enough to get through, or have a child accomplice.

Sliding glass doors

* Secure the opening section with special key-operated locking bolts at the top and bottom fixed at opposite corners. Or cut a broom handle to fit in

the track so that the doors won't slide.

★ Secure the door frame to the brickwork and fit special anti-lift devices so that sliding doors can't be lifted out of their tracks.

Porch

★ Keep the porch lit at night.

★ Remove doorstep deliveries promptly. If you are going away, ask a trusted neighbour to do this for you.

Ground-floor windows

★ Consider laminated glass for ground-floor windows or iron grilles with safety gates secured by top-quality, close shackle padlocks.

Basement windows

★ Fix metal bars securely into the brickwork. Or install metal grilles with safety gates secured by top-quality, close shackle padlocks.

Bell

★ Use only your last name on the bell if you live alone.

Shrubs and trees

★ Don't grow trees where they obscure windows or doors.

★ Keep shrub height below windows and use prickly plants, such as pyracantha, roses and holly.

Garage

★ Fit a switch inside your house that can turn garage lights on and off.

★ Fit doors between the house and garage with a peephole and secure with a 5-lever mortise deadlock.

★ Fit doors with a heavy-duty chain with close shackle padlock that prevents the door from being lifted.

★ Padlock the roller bracket on the garage door to the track or place an obstruction in the track to prevent an intruder from lifting the door.

Other precautions

★ Install lampposts or floodlights to illuminate the garden at night.

★ Place floodlights too high for burglars to reach. Infrared sensors will turn the lights on when someone approaches.

★ Put ladders away or padlock them to something immovable.

★ Keep trellises away from the house and garden tables stored away.

★ Walls and fences should be kept low at the front so a thief can be seen.

★ Put Neighbourhood Watch stickers in your windows.

★ Dogs are deterrents to burglars.

Caring for your houseplants

★ Always ensure that houseplants have sufficient light. Foliage plants will tolerate much gloomier conditions than flowering plants. If the ratio of warmth to light is unequal, then the plants will start to become leggy.
★ It is better to have a consistent moderate temperature than a high one which fluctuates. Temperatures which vary cause growth to be checked, often resulting in brown-edged foliage, flowers dropping off and, in severe cases, complete leaf loss.
★ All houseplants require consistently moist compost. Fluctuations in watering result in both leaf and flower drop. You can tell whether the compost is sufficiently moist for most plants by pressing a finger on the surface of the compost. If it is damp to the touch it is all right; if moisture oozes out, it is too wet.
★ If a plant has been overwatered, remove it from its pot, shake it free of compost, and repot in fresh compost. The compost is moist enough when, if you squeeze a handful, it slowly crumbles as you open your hand.
★ Avoid draughts and never shut houseplants behind curtains at night. The temperature drop in the window area at night can be sudden and considerable. Plants chill easily, and this causes their leaves to flag and brown at the edges.
★ A dry atmosphere often causes the leaves to brown and crack at the edges. To overcome this, create a humid microclimate around the plant. Place the plant in its pot in a slightly larger container and fill the gap with damp peat or sphagnum moss.
★ The foliage of houseplants collects dust in the same way as furniture does. Wipe shiny leaves with a cloth that has been dipped in warm milk. This brings a shine to leaves of plants such as rubber plants, Swiss cheese plants and philodendrons. Regularly sponge the leaves of other foliage plants with warm water.
★ Protect plants from fungal diseases

and insect pests like greenfly by spraying them every third week during the growing season with a systemic fungicide and insecticide. The chemicals dry on the leaves and are absorbed through them into the sap stream, where they protect the plant. Any that falls on the compost is immediately inactivated.
★ Give houseplants a liquid feed as soon as you see flower buds and until blossoming is over. Feed foliage house plants regularly from spring until autumn, but not during winter.
★ To encourage flowering, remove fading blossoms regularly and also yellowing and unsightly leaves.

Tips for safe mowing

★ Read and follow carefully the manufacturer's safety instructions.
★ Fill a petrol-fuelled mower outdoors and keep it away from any heat sources, including cigarettes. Wipe up any spills and replace the tank cap securely.
★ If using an electric mower, make sure it is fitted with a circuit breaker.
★ Before mowing, clear the lawn of stones and any objects that could be picked up and spun out by the blades. Set the blade at 2-3in/50-75mm above ground. Never run a mower over gravel.
★ Wear heavy shoes or boots when mowing. Avoid loose clothing and jewellery, and tie back long hair.
★ Mow dry grass only; you can slip on wet grass and it can clog the machine.
★ Mow across, rather than up or down, a slope. You'll have better control of the mower, and you'll be less likely to fall towards the mower. Never make a sharp turn on a slope.
★ Turn the engine off if you're leaving it unattended, even for a few minutes.

Tips for easy gardening

★ Grow varieties of plants that require little or no staking, and plant sufficiently close so that they support one another.
★ Grow vegetables together that have the same growth requirements, such as brassicas. They have the same nutrient requirements, which makes fertilising them more efficient.
★ Spray weeds which are well established in a rock garden and paving with a glyphosate herbicide. This kills entire plants without the need to dig them out.
★ For patio planters and hanging baskets, mix perlite in with the potting compost. It absorbs moisture when water is plentiful and releases it when the compost is dry.
★ Buy plants grown as plugs. These just need growing on in a seed tray.

Seasonal care for the garden

Spring

★ Sow vegetables in the open ground as soon as the soil is workable. The same applies for annual flowers.
★ Plant summer-flowering bulbs and corms such as gladioli, galtonia and acidanthera.
★ Tidy rock garden plants and fertilise immediately flowering is over.
★ Apply a weed and feed dressing to the lawn.
★ Prune spring-flowering shrubs and climbers immediately after flowering. Next season's blossoms are produced

on wood that is made during the coming summer.
★ If lawn edges have become damaged during the winter, cut off the turf at the edge and reverse the chunks so that the rough edge faces inwards.
★ Mulch permanent plantings with well-rotted compost or bark to suppress weeds and conserve moisture.
★ As herbaceous plants with fleshy shoots, like lupins and delphiniums, start to sprout, thin to three or four shoots per plant and use those removed as cuttings.
★ Divide aquatic plants as necessary. If you want to make a pool, this is the best time to plant it up.
★ Apply shading to the greenhouse and ensure adequate ventilation before temperatures start to rise.
★ Attend to houseplants that need repotting. Use a soil-less compost for short-term plants. More permanent plants, such as palms and rubber plants, benefit from a soil-based compost.

Autumn

★ Remove leaves from the rock garden and lawn as soon as they fall. If left on the grass, it will turn yellow.
★ Sow broad beans and round-seeded peas for an early crop next year.
★ Plant spring-flowering bulbs such as daffodils, tulips, snowdrops, hyacinths and crocuses.
★ Plant spring-flowering bedding plants, including wallflowers, polyanthus and pansies.
★ Trees, shrubs and fruit bushes can be planted as soon as their leaves fall.
★ Lift and divide herbaceous plants if they have become congested.

★ Prepare the garden pond for winter. Remove the pump and replace it with a pool heater. Remove dead and dying vegetation from the waterside.
★ Cut back the stems of roses and other tall shrubby plants so that they do not blow about in the winter. Wind-rock, which results from the swirling movement of the wind on tall plants, can cause a severe check in growth by disturbing the roots.
★ Prune soft fruit canes, such as black and redcurrants. Tie in new raspberry canes and remove old fruiting wood.
★ Protect grey or hairy-leafed rock garden plants from winter dampness by raising a small sheet of glass on four pegs or a couple of bricks above each plant. This keeps off the wet but allows air to circulate.

Before you look for a home

Determine your price range

★ Shop for finance first. The amount of your loan will determine which houses or flats you can consider.

Consider the neighbourhood

★ Do planning and other laws prohibit any changes you might wish to make? For example, is it a conservation area? Remember also that there may be legal restrictions such as covenants, which will affect your use of a property.

★ Is there any proposed development you might not want to live close to?

★ Are schools, public transport and shopping nearby?

★ What is the local council tax?

Interview solicitors/licensed conveyancers and estate agents

★ What services will the solicitor or conveyancer provide?

★ What is his or her charge?

★ Will there be additional costs?

★ Remember that the agent represents the seller, and while he or she is not obliged to point out any defects in the property, anything the agent does state must be true.

Hidden costs of home buying

Many first-time buyers are not aware of all the expenses involved in purchasing property. Ask your banker, agent and solicitor about the following, which can add to what you expected to pay.

★ Legal charges for your solicitor or licensed conveyancer, usually 0.5 - 1.5% of purchase price, plus VAT.

★ Arrangement fee for your mortgage.

★ Points on your mortgage.

★ Mortgage valuation fee on the house.

★ Survey of the property.

★ Rot and woodwork infestation inspection.

★ Land Registry and search fees.

★ Stamp duty (if payable) – normally 1% of purchase price on properties costing £60,000 or more.

★ Property insurance.

★ Removal expenses.

★ Connection of essential services.

★ Decoration and repair.

★ Furnishings.

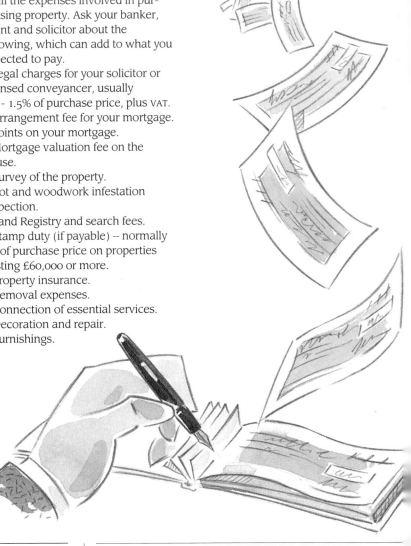

Paying for your house

Shopping for a mortgage is the most crucial step in the home-buying process. Talk to several banks and building societies and take the list of hidden costs (above) with you. Ask which of them the bank or building society will charge. Most of the loans in the United Kingdom are at a variable rate, and those that are fixed rate are for a short term only. The figures shown in the chart (right) therefore illustrate initial monthly payments. The chart relates to endowment mortgages, which account for many new mortgages at present. The figures would be slightly higher for a repayment mortgage.

Interest rate %	£30,000	£40,000	£50,000	£60,000	£80,000	£100,000
12	225	325	425	525	725	925
11	206	298	390	481	665	848
10	188	271	354	438	604	771
9	169	244	319	394	544	694
8	150	217	283	350	483	617
7	131	190	248	306	423	540
6	112	162	212	262	362	462
5	94	135	177	219	302	385
4	75	108	142	175	242	308

INITIAL MONTHLY PAYMENTS ON 25-YEAR ENDOWMENT MORTGAGE

ASSUMES MIRAS ceiling of £30,000 and basic rate of income tax of 25%. Figures shown in table do not include endowment premiums.

Choosing a home

Once you know what you can afford and have found a neighbourhood you like, you can narrow the field to two or three houses or flats.

⋆ Ask yourself. Do I want a home this new (or this old)?

⋆ Determine that the house or flat meets your basic space requirements – for example, if you plan a family, or want a downstairs bedroom for an elderly parent.

⋆ Have a surveyor check the structural soundness of the property and the heating and plumbing systems.

⋆ Ask to see the owner's utility bills for the last 12 months.

⋆ Ask to see the owner's local council tax bills.

⋆ Have a rot and woodwork infestation inspection done if the owner has not.

⋆ In rural areas, have a plumber inspect any septic system. Have well water tested for quality and for flow.

⋆ Before negotiating the price, find out how much comparable property in the neighbourhood has fetched recently.

If you put up your home for sale

⋆ First decide whether you want to do the work of selling your property yourself or whether you'd rather pay an agent to screen buyers and advertise and show your home.

⋆ If you interview an agent, ask: How does he / she plan to advertise your house? What price does he / she suggest for your home?

⋆ Your contract with your agent should specify your asking price and the agent's charges.

⋆ You or a professional valuer must determine what the market is doing and set the right price for your home.

⋆ You or your agent should check with a local lawyer, banks and building societies on types of available finance so that you can advise potential buyers.

⋆ Have your agent or solicitor or licensed conveyancer prepare a contract that can be offered to a serious buyer on request.

⋆ Even after you accept an offer 'subject to contract', go on showing your home until the buyer gets finance and signs a contract. If your deal falls through, you'll have other buyers waiting.

Sprucing up

After you decide to sell your property, make it as attractive as possible to potential buyers. Avoid expensive or unusual renovations. Your goal is to make your home look bright, neat, cheerful and problem-free, at the least possible cost to you.

Outdoors

⋆ Get rid of any clutter in your garden.

⋆ Mow the lawn, weed flowerbeds, prune shrubs, and sweep paths and front and back steps.

⋆ Plant colourful flowers or shrubs where they can be seen from the street.

⋆ See that outdoor lighting works.

⋆ Have gates and fences painted and repaired.

⋆ Touch up exterior paint where needed. Give special attention to the front door, garage door and woodwork around windows.

⋆ See that the roof is in good condition.

Indoors

⋆ Put away any clutter. Storing away extra furniture makes rooms look more spacious.

⋆ Arrange storage areas and cupboards neatly.

⋆ Fix leaky taps. Remove water or rust stains from basins and baths.

⋆ Be sure the central heating system is working smoothly.

⋆ Have a spring cleaning session: shampoo rugs, wax floors, wash walls and windows, wipe away fingerprints, smudges, dust, mildew.

⋆ Replace burned-out or dim bulbs with higher-wattage light bulbs.

⋆ Replace tired-looking shower curtains or kitchen curtains.

⋆ Stick down any loose wallpaper and repair any tears.

⋆ In the kitchen, clear worktops, wax cabinets and clean the oven. Replace flooring if it's in very bad condition.

⋆ Give your house the 'sniff test'. To disguise food and pet smells, bake an apple or sprinkle vanilla or coffee beans in a warm oven on days when you're expecting buyers.

Shopping for a used car

Because the depreciation of used cars is much less than that of new ones, they can cost half as much to run as new cars. These tips will help you tell the bargains from the rip-offs that will be more trouble than they are worth.
Shop for your car loan first. You will save time by knowing which cars you can afford.
Check inexpensive guides that list the values of most used cars. They are available from most newsagents and should be referred to before you accept the price of a car for sale.
Don't confine your shopping to used car dealers. Check trade-ins at new car dealers' showrooms as well as owners' ads, especially those from affluent suburbs.
Best buys are usually cars 3 years old or newer, which have been driven no more than 10,000-15,000 miles/ 16,000-24,000km annually.
Avoid convertibles and luxury cars, which won't be bargains. Small and medium saloons and hatchbacks are easier to maintain and repair.

Inspecting a used car

Bodywork The bodywork can be the most expensive area of the car to put right. Only inspect a car's bodywork on a bright day – never in poor light. The first thing to look for is corrosion, or rust. Surface blisters can be relatively harmless and easily treated, but corrosion coming from the inside of the body panels is more serious.
★ It is usually not worth repairing rust that has perforated the bottoms of doors, the bodywork around the front and rear screen rubbers, on trailing edges of bootlids or tailgates and leading edges of bonnets, and on rear wing panels. These can only be repaired expensively by specialists, and subsequent painting is costly.
★ Treat any cosmetic paint job with suspicion since it may conceal bad repairs. Check for plastic filler by tapping the bodywork.
★ Water stains in the boot, around windows, on carpets and around the sunroof opening may indicate leaks.
Structural bodywork Look for rust perforation on inner wings, the bulkhead, and any cross members and chassis members visible under the bonnet. If you see any, reject the car.
★ Beneath the car, look at side-sills, chassis legs, cross members and subframes. Tap suspicious areas with a lightweight hammer, or push hard with your hand to detect the 'give' of weakened metal. Be wary of freshly applied underseal – it probably hides weakened metal.
★ While underneath, check the floorpan for corrosion. Also look at brake pipes, which are dangerous if they are crusty or pitted with rust.
★ Check suspension and steering mounting points for serious corrosion – especially under the bonnet.
Collision damage A car that has had its suspension and steering damaged in an accident is no good to anyone. Examine under the bonnet for inner wings that have been creased and straightened or even replaced (unsightly welds are a give-away). Also inspect the engine bay forward panels and forward chassis-legs for repairs or creases.
★ Excessively worn inner or outer tread shoulders on the tyres indicate uneven tyre wear which may be due to suspension misalignment. However, it could also be due to incorrect tracking, which is easily rectified.
★ When you test-drive the car the steering should be consistent to the left and right, with no tendency to pull one way.
Inside the car Check the odometer: if the digits are out of line, the mileage may well have been altered.
★ A good guide to the genuineness of a claimed mileage can be given by the condition of the driver's seat, pedal rubbers, driver's carpet, and controls such as steering wheel rim, gear lever knob and stalk switches.
Engine Before starting the engine, remove the dipstick and check the colour of the oil. If it's very black, the car has probably not been recently, or regularly, serviced. Also check for beige 'mayonnaise' on the dipstick, a possible symptom of head gasket leakage.
★ Check that there is sufficient coolant and that it is the bright colour of anti-freeze, rather than rusty red; an engine that has been run without anti-freeze may develop problems.
★ Listen to the engine starting up from cold. The oil light should go out soon after the engine starts, and if it doesn't there may be engine wear. Initial heavy rattling or knocking noises indicate wear of the crankshaft and big-end bearings. Listen for clattering or light knocking noises from the top of the engine, which indicate camshaft wear.

★ Turn the ignition on and open the throttle sharply. Check for black or blue smoke from the exhaust. Blue smoke comes from burning oil and shows engine wear, whereas black smoke is unburnt fuel and has many possible causes. Check for smooth idling when warm.

★ Never buy a car without test-driving it yourself. First make sure you are insured to drive the car. Then, if possible, take it on a drive that covers a mixture of conditions – fast motorway driving, slow urban driving and twisting roads, for example.

★ Check that the engine pulls strongly and cleanly, with no misfires, and that it doesn't pink (this is the metallic rattling sound that occurs when the throttle is opened). If the car does misfire and the engine has electronic fuel or ignition control, only buy it if the misfire is first put right.

★ Keep an eye on the temperature gauge or temperature warning light, which may indicate overheating.

★ Finally, check for engine oil leaks.

Transmission If the car has a manual gearbox, check that the clutch operates smoothly and all gears engage easily. If the gear change stiffens as revs increase, the clutch may be worn. Check for clutch slip by driving the car up a hill in top gear.

★ When driving, change down into each gear from a higher speed than normal to test the syncromesh. If the gears baulk or 'crunch', or if the gearbox whines excessively, gearbox overhaul or replacement are the only solutions.

★ If the car has automatic transmission, check the transmission dipstick for correct fluid level – this is best done with the engine hot and idling. Also smell the dipstick – if it smells burnt, steer clear of the car!

★ When driving, check that the transmission changes down into each gear properly under full acceleration, and at the right time.

Suspension Listen for knocks from the suspension over poor road surfaces, which may indicate worn bushes, joints and dampers. Take note of the car's handling: if it's vague, 'floaty' or bouncy, suspect worn dampers.

★ Test dampers by applying your full weight on each wing, pushing down and seeing if it springs up and settles quickly when released – the sign of a good damper.

★ Check for fluid leakage from the dampers or struts. Slight weeping is acceptable, any more is not.

Steering If the steering is vague and heavy, the tyres may be underpressurised or worn.

★ Rock the steering wheel gently while watching the front wheel – there shouldn't be any noticeable delay between steering wheel and road wheel movement. Free play, accompanied by a knock, will fail the MoT test.

★ Check for wheel wobble at speed; this is often attributable to unbalanced front wheels. Steering wheel shimmy at low speeds indicates distorted wheel rims.

Brakes The brake pedal should offer good resistance, and not sink most of the way to the floor when applied.

★ If a servo is fitted, check that it works by pumping the brake pedal several times, holding the pedal down and starting the engine. You should feel the pedal creep down as it operates.

★ The car shouldn't swerve when the brakes are applied hard at speed. If it does, it may have seized or leaking wheel cylinders or calipers.

★ If the car judders when you apply the brakes, this implies distorted front brake discs. Inspect discs for heavy scoring or unpolished or corroded areas: they may need renewing.

★ Check the brake hoses under the wheel arches for cracking, chafing or swelling or leaks.

Before you make an offer

If a car has passed your inspection and test drive and you want to make an offer, here are some final steps to take.

★ If the car is anything but a banger, ask to see its service and repair history, as well as repair receipts. Treat a denial that these receipts exist with suspicion.

★ See whether the mileage on the odometer tallies with service and repair records.

★ Insist on an MoT that has at least 6 months to run, but preferably 12 months.

★ Check that the car's registration and chassis numbers match those on the registration document.

★ If the vendor is not the person named on the registration document, have him produce a note signed by the registered keeper (who is usually the owner). This should state either that the vendor is the owner, or that the vendor is authorised by the owner to sell it on his behalf.

★ Ask if it is permissible to have the car further investigated by independent, qualified mechanic. If it is, ask the mechanic to carry out a cylinder compresson test to assess the condition of the engine, and also to estimate the cost of any repairs that he thinks may be warranted. You can ask for the cost of these repairs to be deducted from the asking price of the car.

★ If you have a car to trade in to a dealer, don't mention the fact until you have negotiated a discount for the one you want to buy.

★ If you are buying from a trader, depending on the value of the car it may be worth investing in a warranty for it. Read the warranty small print carefully though, because some warranties exclude more than they cover!

If you're in an accident

1 Stop as soon as you safely can. Check for injuries to yourself and to any passengers or pedestrians. Do not admit any possible liability for the accident.

2 Call an ambulance and the police if anyone has been hurt.

3 Make a note of the names, addresses and telephone numbers of all those involved, including passengers and witnesses. Note if anyone was injured.

4 In addition, take the other car's registration number, the driver's licence number, the name and address of his insurance company and his insurance policy number.

5 Make a note of the time, weather and road conditions.

6 Take photos or make a diagram of the accident scene. Be sure to show the cars involved, the direction in which they were moving, any skid marks, and nearby road signs or traffic lights.

7 When a police officer arrives, take his name and number. Make every effort to cooperate, but try to limit your remarks about how the accident occurred.

8 Don't sign any statements.

9 Even if you don't think you're hurt, it is a good idea to go to your own doctor for an examination.

10 Write down your impressions of the event as soon as you get home. Keep a journal afterwards to note any additional recollections or medical symptoms that you develop, in case you ever need to go to court.

11 Notify your insurance company as soon as possible; ask how to proceed with making out a claim, and especially how to fill in the accident report form.

Don't get taken for a ride

★ Shop around for a reliable local mechanic and repair facility before the car fails you.

★ Ask your friends and neighbours, especially those with older cars that run well, for recommendations.

★ Having small problems taken care of before they become big problems is a good practice and helps you assess the general reliability of a workshop and its mechanics.

★ Make a written list of your car's symptoms and give it to the service receptionist or, preferably, direct to the mechanic. Keep a copy for your own reference.

★ Don't ask for a specific repair unless you're absolutely sure about the nature of the problem. You may end up paying for a repair you didn't need.

★ If you don't feel that you can accurately describe what's wrong, ask the mechanic to go with you for a test drive.

★ Insist on a detailed written estimate before you leave your car at a garage, and a guarantee that no additional work will be done without your permission. Leave a phone number where you can be reached.

★ When you pick up the repaired car, it's a good idea to test-drive it before you take it home to make sure it is running smoothly.

★ Ask for an itemised bill and a receipt in case the problem is not solved and you have to return the car for further adjustment.

Coping with car noises

SOUND	POSSIBLE PROBLEM	SOLUTION	SOUND	POSSIBLE PROBLEM	SOLUTION
Backfiring	Incorrect ignition timing, faulty ignition or leaking valves	Have ignition and/or valves checked	**Screech under acceleration**	Slipping auxiliary drive belt	Check/adjust belt
Clatter from engine	Insufficient engine oil Worn or badly adjusted valves	Add oil Refer to mechanic	**Screech when steering**	Power steering belt slipping	Check/adjust belt
Whining or chattering from engine	Incorrectly tensioned camshaft drive belt	Refer to mechanic	**Moan from engine when steering**	Power steering fluid level too low	Top up power steering fluid level
Rattle under acceleration	Wrong grade of fuel, engine overheating, engine needs decoke, incorrect ignition timing, ignition system fault	Use higher grade fuel Refer to mechanic	**Roar or rasp under acceleration**	Blown exhaust	Have exhaust checked
			Squeal or groan when braking	Worn or defective brake components	Refer to mechanic
			Hiss from engine	Leak from coolant or air/vacuum hoses	Refer to mechanic
Knocking from engine increasing with engine speed	Worn camshaft or cam followers	Refer to mechanic	**Clicking from wheel(s)**	Loose hubcap, stone in hubcap, or stone lodged in tyre tread	Tighten hubcap, remove stone

Keeping your car on the road

★ It is vitally important to follow the maintenance schedule provided by the car's manufacturer, so that it remains reliable and that it does not suffer premature wear in any area.

★ Be alert at all times for unusual noises, vibrations, steering wheel pull, brake pedal softness, strange smells (such as exhaust gases or fuel) and abnormal readings on gauges or warning lights.

★ Whenever you fill the petrol tank, or at least once a week, check the levels of engine oil, coolant, brake fluid, battery electrolyte (if it's not a sealed-for-life battery), power steering fluid and windscreen/rear screen washer fluid.

★ At the same time inspect the engine bay and underneath the car for any fluid leaks.

★ Regularly check the tyre pressures and inspect the tyres for cuts, sidewall bulges and tread wear.

★ Regularly test all lights, the horn and the windscreen wipers to see that they work properly.

Packing light

If you want to avoid long waits for your suitcases – or worse still, lost luggage – when you are flying, try to pack everything into bags that you can carry with you on the plane. Wear your heaviest clothes and plenty of layers, unless it's too hot. Here's a checklist to help you choose the items you really need.

Clothes
- ★ Walking shoes
- ★ Smart shoes
- ★ Sweater
- ★ Waterproof jacket or raincoat
- ★ Socks (which can double as slippers)
- ★ Nightwear that can double as a dressing gown
- ★ Two skirts and/or two pairs of trousers
- ★ Jeans or shorts
- ★ Three shirts or blouses (a T-shirt can double as a vest and beachwear)
- ★ Bathing suit
- ★ Underwear
- ★ Folding umbrella

Toiletries and other items
- ★ Medications and prescriptions
- ★ Extra spectacles or contact lenses, or a prescription
- ★ Sunglasses
- ★ First-aid items
- ★ Toothpaste and toothbrush
- ★ Dental floss
- ★ Shampoo, soap, deodorant, cosmetics, razor and sunscreen, all in small plastic containers

Optional
- ★ Washing powder and stain remover in travel-size packets
- ★ Paperbacks and magazines
- ★ Camera and film
- ★ Travel alarm
- ★ Small cassette player or radio
- ★ Travel-sized hair dryer
- ★ Travel-sized iron
- ★ A pack of cards
- ★ Writing and painting equipment – pens, paper, pencils and paints
- ★ Water-heating element

A car survival kit

When you've planned an extensive journey by car, make sure that you pack all that the car will need to keep going through thick and thin. The following items should ensure that you and your family are safe and comfortable on long trips.

In the glove compartment
- ★ Owner's handbook
- ★ Repair manual
- ★ Motor insurance particulars
- ★ Motoring organisation documents
- ★ Emergency telephone numbers
- ★ Coins and phonecard
- ★ Paper and pen
- ★ Maps
- ★ First-aid kit

For your comfort
- ★ Tissues
- ★ Bag for rubbish
- ★ Bottle opener
- ★ Sunglasses
- ★ Cushions and blankets

For breakdowns/repairs
- ★ Jump leads
- ★ Towrope
- ★ Spare wheel and tyre
- ★ Wheel brace
- ★ Tyre pressure gauge
- ★ Tyre pump
- ★ Small fire extinguisher
- ★ Tool kit – including spanners, sockets, screwdrivers, pliers, 12-volt circuit tester, small hammer, adjustable wrench and wire cutters
- ★ Electrical insulating tape
- ★ Torch
- ★ Container of water
- ★ Explosion-proof fuel container
- ★ Paper towels and or rags

In severe winter conditions
- ★ Blankets
- ★ Non-perishable snacks
- ★ Self-heating food packs
- ★ Ice scraper
- ★ Can of de-icer
- ★ Windscreen washer fluid
- ★ Shovel
- ★ Bag of sand or road salt
- ★ Snow chains or traction clamps
- ★ Rugs or mats to aid traction
- ★ Empty fuel can

For long/remote trips
- ★ Brake fluid
- ★ Engine oil
- ★ Pre-mixed coolant
- ★ Gearbox/automatic transmission fluid
- ★ Power steering fluid
- ★ External drive belts (for alternator, water pump, power steering, etc.)
- ★ Fuses
- ★ Bulbs
- ★ Container of drinking water
- ★ Cup holders
- ★ Hot-drinks maker

Extras for travelling abroad
- ★ Reflective warning triangle
- ★ Driving licence
- ★ Insurance certificate and 'green card' (bail bond for Spain)
- ★ Continental motoring insurance (for repatriation of car in event of illness or accident)
- ★ Foreign language phrasebook

Travelling on a budget

Travelling costs and hotel bills are not the only major expenses an average traveller encounters. Here are a few ideas for saving money on your next trip.

★ The tourist information office should be able to give you information on package deals and discount tickets to various events.

★ Cinemas and theatres often sell tickets at a discount on certain days and at certain hours; so do many museums that charge admission fees.

★ Check local newspapers or magazine listings to find free or inexpensive museums, concerts, walking tours and other attractions. Local events are also an enjoyable way to meet people.

★ Avoid restaurant bills by preparing delicious picnics. Explore local markets and buy bread, cheese, vegetables, fruit and regional delicacies. Then have a meal in your room or in a park.

★ Pack an immersion heater for making soups and hot drinks.

★ When you do eat at a restaurant, make lunch your main meal – it's usually cheaper than dinner. Have a snack or picnic for supper.

★ Department stores often have inexpensive lunch counters.

★ Look for popular local cafés rather than dining at hotel restaurants, which tend to be more expensive and less interesting.

★ Avoid making telephone calls from your hotel, which will often add exorbitant surcharges. Whenever possible, call only to give your number and have the person call you back.

★ Never touch the mini bar in your hotel room – the prices will be very high.

★ When shopping abroad, it is often appropriate – even expected – to haggle with a vendor. If you're unsure, offer to pay about half the stated price and see how the vendor reacts. Keep your receipts and present them at the airport to claim back the VAT.

Tipping guidelines

AUSTRIA Widespread, but large amounts are not expected. On restaurant bills, 10-15 per cent is added and it is usual to leave a further 5 per cent. Theatre, cloakroom, petrol pump attendants and similar officials expect to be tipped Sch2-3. Railways and airports have fixed charges for portering. Taxi drivers expect Sch 4 for a short trip and 10 per cent for a longer one.

BELGIUM A 16 per cent service charge is included in hotel and restaurant bills. Cloakroom attendants generally expect Bfr 5-10. A tip is usually already included in any taxi fares.

CYPRUS Hotels add a 5-10 per cent government tax and a 10 per cent service charge. Barmen, waiters and doormen expect a 10 per cent tip.

DENMARK Hotels, restaurants and taxi drivers quote fully inclusive prices and tipping is not necessary. Railway porters and washroom attendants receive tips.

FINLAND Hotels include a 15 per cent service charge in the bill. Restaurants and bars have a 14 per cent service charge on weekdays and 15 per cent on weekends and holidays. The obligatory cloakroom attendant or doorman fee is usually clearly indicated. Taxi drivers and hairdressers are not tipped.

FRANCE A service charge is added to hotel, restaurant and bar bills, but small change is often left with the payment. Taxi drivers expect 10-15 per cent, and tips are paid to hairdressers and porters.

GERMANY A service charge is added on hotel bills. Restaurant bills include 10 per cent service charge. Also tip taxi drivers, hairdressers and cloakroom attendants.

GIBRALTAR Normally 10-15 per cent for waiters, taxi drivers, etc.

GREECE 10 per cent is usual.

HUNGARY Not obligatory, but 10-15 per cent is normal for most services.

ITALY Service charges and state taxes are included in all hotel bills, but give the waiter/waitress 5 per cent of a restaurant bill.

LUXEMBOURG A 15 per cent service charge is included in hotel, restaurant and bar bills. Taxi drivers expect 15 per cent of meter charge.

MALTA 10 per cent is expected in hotels and restaurants if not on the bill. Tip taxi drivers 10 per cent.

MONACO Hotel and restaurant bills generally include a 15 per cent service charge; if they don't, leave a 15 per cent tip. Taxi drivers are usually tipped 15 per cent of the fare.

NETHERLANDS All hotels and restaurants include 15 per cent service charge and VAT. It is customary to leave small change when paying a bill. Gld 1-2 is usual for porters, doormen and taxi drivers.

NORWAY Tipping is not common outside main centres. Service charges and VAT are added to the bill in hotels, restaurants and bars; extra tips are optional. Taxi drivers are tipped.

POLAND A service charge is usually added to restaurant bills.

PORTUGAL Generally 10-15 per cent. Taxi drivers are tipped 10 per cent.

ROMANIA A 12 per cent service charge is added in most restaurants. Porters and taxi drivers expect tips.

SPAIN Service charges and taxes are usually included in hotel bills, but tips should be left for the chambermaid and for the porter per bag. It is also customary to tip the waiter/waitress. Most restaurants bills do not include service and 5-10 per cent should be left. In cafés and bars it is usual to leave loose change. Tip taxis 5-10 per cent when metered.

SWEDEN Hotel and restaurant prices include a service charge, although in restaurants late at night service is higher. Tip taxi drivers at least 10 per cent of the metered fare.

SWITZERLAND By law, a 15 per cent service charge is included in all hotel, restaurant, cafe, bar, taxi and hairdressing bills.

Misused words and phrases

Some words are easy to confuse with others, often because of similar spellings or pronunciations. The following may help you to use *le mot juste* (see A FEAST OF WORDS AND PHRASES, opposite).

Aggravate, irritate A bad situation is made worse, or aggravated. The situation may irritate you.

All right is the correct form, not alright.

All together, altogether All together means all at the same time. Altogether means entirely.

Between you and me Never 'between you and I'. The preposition between requires an object – hence, 'me' and not 'I'.

Canvas, canvass Canvas is the heavy fabric; to solicit votes is to canvass.

Climactic, climatic Climactic refers to a climax. If you're talking about the weather, it's climatic.

Cohort, consort A cohort is a band of people; an individual companion is a consort.

Differ from, differ with One thing differs from another. Two people who disagree about something differ with each other.

Disinterested, uninterested A disinterested person is unbiased, impartial. An uninterested person is unconcerned, bored.

Gibe, gybe To gibe is to ridicule. To gybe is to move a sail or boom to the other side of the boat, or to change the direction of a boat. And what's more, you can spell both 'jibe'.

Incredible, incredulous Something that's incredible is not believable; a person who's incredulous is disbelieving or sceptical.

Lay, lie You lay something on the table, but you lie down on the floor.

Noisome, noisy Noisome means offensive; it has nothing to do with the words noisy or loud.

Prone, supine If you're lying with your face down, you're prone, but if your face is up, you're supine.

Prostate, prostrate The prostate is a reproductive gland in male mammals. Prostrate means lying down full-length, or growing along the ground.

Regrettably, regretfully 'Regrettably, your application has been refused.' But, she admitted regretfully to breaking the vase.

Stationary, stationery The train is stationary at the platform. Stationery refers to writing paper, pencils, etc.

Tortuous, torturous Tortuous means winding, like a tortuous road. Torturous means painful, like torture.

Troop, troupe A troop is a group; a troupe is a company, usually referring to actors ('troupers').

Commonly misspelled words

If you see that you have been spelling a word or two on this list incorrectly, you have plenty of company. Lots of people forget that there's only one n in inoculate, and shouldn't be embarrassed (two r's).

accommodate	fulfil	parallel
address	guerrilla	plebeian
advantageous	haemorrhage	privilege
anonymous	harass	pursue
appalling	heighten	receipt
believe	hygienic	recipe
committee	icicle	recommend
conscience	icily	restaurateur
contemporary	incandescent	rhythm
corroborate	independent	seize
counterfeit	inoculate	separate
definitely	irascible	sergeant
diarrhoea	iridescent	siege
dilemma	liaison	subtle
disappoint	manoeuvre	supersede
ecstasy	mantelpiece	tranquillity
embarrass	minuscule	translucent
esoteric	misspell	usable
excerpt	necessary	vacuous
exhilarate	noticeable	vacuum
existence	occasion	vilify
exorbitant	occurrence	yield

A feast of words and phrases

Words and phrases from different cultural sources flavour our everyday conversation and writing. Below are some often used examples from French, German, Italian, Irish, Latin and Hindi. Can you match them with their definitions on the right?

1. ad lib
2. ad nauseam
3. al fresco
4. au courant
5. blitzkrieg
6. bona fide
7. bon vivant
8. carte blanche
9. cause célèbre
10. caveat emptor
11. c'est la vie
12. chef-d'oeuvre
13. cognoscente
14. comme il faut
15. compos mentis
16. coup de grâce
17. crème de la crème
18. cri de coeur
19. de rigueur
20. de trop
21. dilettante
22. ersatz
23. fait accompli
24. guru
25. idée fixe
26. infra dig
27. in toto
28. je ne sais quoi
29. kitsch
30. mise-en-scène
31. modus operandi
32. mot juste
33. per capita
34. pièce de résistance
35. pied-à-terre
36. prima donna
37. pro forma
38. pundit

39. raison d'être
40. roman à clef
41. schmalz
42. shebeen
43. sotto voce
44. status quo
45. succès fou
46. tant pis
47. tour de force
48. trompe l'oeil
49. wunderkind
50. Zeitgeist

1. A free hand
2. The blow bringing death to one who is mortally wounded; any finishing stroke
3. Excessive sentimentality
4. An illusion created so that the viewer may think the representation is reality, such as a view through a window painted on a brick wall
5. Inferior, a substitute
6. Something already done and probably irreversible
7. Illegal drinking house
8. Chief dish at a meal; most outstanding item in a group or series, especially in art
9. Controversial, public issue
10. The spirit of the time
11. An obsession, a firmly lodged idea not subject to modification

12. Lightning attack
13. The word or phrase that is precisely correct
14. Up-to-date, aware of current events
15. By head of population, per person
16. Required by fashion, social code
17. A person who enjoys living well and to the full
18. The existing state of affairs
19. Spiritual leader or teacher
20. Appropriate or proper; applies especially to behaviour or dress
21. Sentimental bad taste
22. A heartfelt plea or protest
23. Excessive, superfluous
24. Hard to define or describe
25. Of sound mind
26. Arrangement of actors in a play or film; an environment
27. Beneath dignity, vulgar
28. An authority in a particular field
29. Way of working
30. According to or as a matter of form
31. In good faith, genuine and sincere
32. Speaking in a soft voice or an undertone
33. The purpose of a thing or action
34. A novel with real persons or events thinly disguised
35. A second or temporary home
36. An exceptionally skilful act
37. Improvised
38. Let the buyer beware
39. An unusual, total success
40. That's life!
41. So much the worse, too bad
42. To the point of disgust
43. Temperamental performer
44. In the open air
45. The best of its kind
46. Connoisseur
47. Child prodigy
48. Masterpiece
49. As a whole
50. A dabbler, one who is not serious or professional about a subject

ANSWERS: **1**-37; **2**-42; **3**-44; **4**-14; **5**-12; **6**-31; **7**-17; **8**-1; **9**-9; **10**-38; **11**-40; **12**-48; **13**-46; **14**-20; **15**-25; **16**-2; **17**-45; **18**-22; **19**-16; **20**-23; **21**-50; **22**-5; **23**-6; **24**-19; **25**-11; **26**-27; **27**-49; **28**-24; **29**-21; **30**-26; **31**-29; **32**-13; **33**-15; **34**-8; **35**-35; **36**-43; **37**-30; **38**-28; **39**-33; **40**-34; **41**-3; **42**-7; **43**-32; **44**-18; **45**-39; **46**-41; **47**-36; **48**-4; **49**-47; **50**-10.

Personal letters

Congratulations Enhance a friend's enjoyment of an important event – such as an engagement, a wedding, the birth of a baby or a career move – with a note expressing your goodwill.

Thank you To convey your appreciation of a gift, a dinner or a stay at someone's home, mention something specific about it that shows its value to you.

Dear Aunt Joan and Uncle Tony,
Cecilia and I want to thank you for the lovely house-warming present. We had been wanting a rocking chair, so your choice was perfect. It will get plenty of use in the corner we've picked for it, especially after the baby is born!
We look forward to seeing you soon.

Yours,
Patrick

Dear Laura
I heard from Sidney about your promotion. Congratulations! It is, of course, well deserved, and your company is lucky to have someone so creative and dedicated for the position. I should know, from our five-year stint together at Harringtons.
I'll call you soon to arrange a lunch to celebrate.

With best wishes

Paul

Dear Sean,
I understand from Nancy that you are doing well but can't yet have visitors. We miss you at our weekly chess games! Perhaps when you're up to it, I'll bring a set to your room. In the meantime, concentrate on getting your rest and building up your strength. I told Nancy to call if you or she should need anything.

Best regards,
Chris

Dear Martha,
I was very saddened to hear of the death of your father. I remember how friendly he was to me and my brother when we were children. Once, when we visited you, he let us into his workshop and showed us a table he was building. We were thrilled! I'm sure he will be greatly missed.
I know this is a difficult time, and if there is something I can do, please let me know. I would like to have you over for dinner whenever you feel ready.

Much love,

Sharon.

Condolences Any letter of sympathy offers welcome support to someone who is bereaved. It's helpful to mention something personal about the deceased and to offer some small practical assistance when possible.

Get well Illness can be a lonely time. A short note can express your concern and cheer up someone who is convalescing.

COMMON THINGS WITH UNCOMMON USES

If you hate throwing things away, you'll welcome these practical suggestions for making the most of household objects, no matter how humble. Our list is by no means complete, so look around your home for other bits and pieces which you might have dismissed as useless.

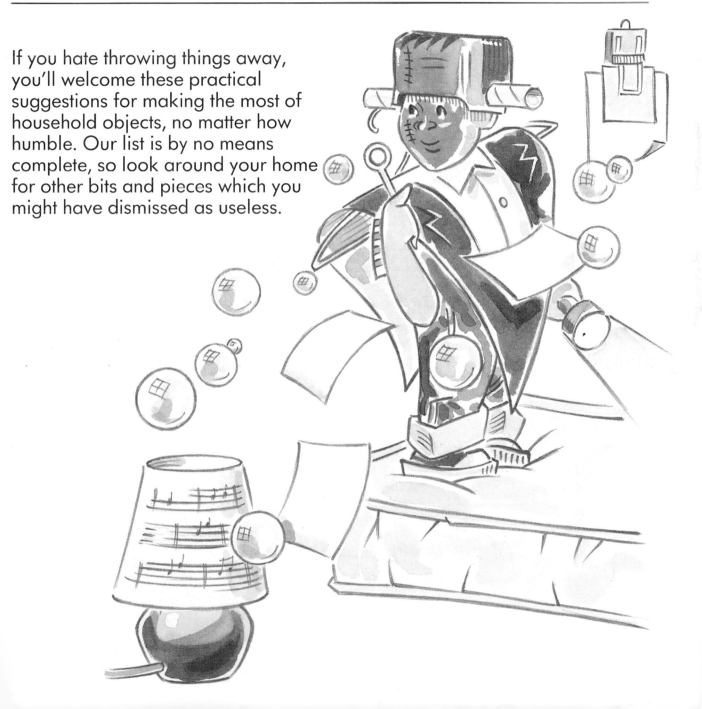

Adhesive tape

Bicycle safety For safer night-time cycling, attach a piece of reflective tape to the edges of your bike's pedals and along the bottom ends of mudguards.

Anti-frost measure If you know there's a good chance of snow, cover the locks of your car doors with masking tape. (This is also a good idea before going through a car wash in winter.)

Label To label jams, freezer containers or DIY storage jars, cut a piece of masking tape to the desired length, stick it on, and write the information with a ballpoint pen. Caption the back of photographs in the same way.

Comb cleaner Remove any old hairs by pressing adhesive or transparent tape along the teeth of a dirty comb and then lifting it off. Then clean the comb in surgical spirit or an ammonia solution.

Court marker Mark up your driveway, path or patio for outdoor games such as hopscotch with adhesive tape.

Gripper Wrap insulating or masking tape around the handle of a knife, tennis racket or tool to improve your grip.

Key finder If you tend to lose your keys or glasses case, make them easier to find with a strip of luminous tape; that way, they will glow in the dark.

Sign letters Make the letters or numbers on a large sign out of masking tape. Use reflective tape if you want the sign to be seen at night.

Wax crayon preserver Wrap masking tape around your children's crayons; it will prevent their breaking in half.

Nail holder If you are doing a job that requires a number of nails or tacks, place them between two layers of masking tape; they'll be easy to find and ready to use.

Castor cover Reduce marks appearing on your vinyl or linoleum flooring by wrapping the castors under chairs and tables in adhesive tape.

Tube hanger To store sticky tubes of household filler or sealant, cut a strip of adhesive or insulating tape several inches long and fold it over the bottom of the tube, leaving a flap at the end. Pierce a hole in the flap and hang the tube on a nail or hook.

Parking aid To help you park the car right in the centre of your garage, stick reflective tape down the middle of the rear wall. Highlight anything else in the garage that you might bump into at night.

Hand protector To remove a broken window without cutting yourself, crisscross the pane of glass on both sides with adhesive or masking tape. Then gently tap the inside edges of the window with a hammer until the pane breaks free. Peel off the tape to remove any shards. Be sure to protect your eyes and hands.

Linoleum fix Repair a piece of cracked linoleum by covering it with strips of see-through sticky tape, and then coating the tape with a layer or two of polyurethane clear varnish.

Glass collector Remove hard-to-spot slivers of broken glass from carpet with a ball of sticky tape.

Animal hair collector To remove pet hairs from an upholstered chair or sofa, wrap a length of tape around your hand, sticky side outwards, and run it over the upholstery you want to clean.

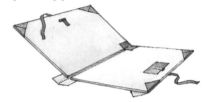

Drawing store Make a portfolio for your drawings and artwork with two pieces of heavy card of the same size. Tape them together along one side with sturdy carpet or masking tape. Protect the corners with tape too.

Aluminium foil

Sun box If your indoor plants need a dose of sunshine, or are growing in the wrong direction, try using a sun box to revive them. Remove the top and one side of a cardboard box and line the remaining sides with foil. Place your plants in the box and leave it near a window which gets plenty of sun – the foil will reflect the light, helping the stems to grow straight instead of bending towards the sun.

Heat reflector You can make the most of your energy supplies by covering sheets of insulation board with thick foil and placing them behind your radiators; less heat will be lost through the wall.

Novelty cake tins If you want to make a novelty cake but don't have the right shaped tin, make an inner lining for a cake tin with a double thickness of heavy-duty foil and shape it accordingly. Teddy-bear birthday cakes, a romantic Valentine heart-shaped cake or a decorative Christmas-tree cake are all easy to make. Just place the lining in a large tin before filling it with the cake mixture – the lining should be as tall as the tin.

Fishing lure Wrap foil around a hook or safety pin, leaving a flap of foil at one side. Then fringe the foil flap with scissors so that the lure wiggles as the line is reeled in.

Foot warmer Cold-weather campers can often do with some extra warmth. Heat several large stones in a campfire and then cover them with foil and wrap them in a towel. Place them at the bottom of your sleeping bag to keep your feet warm as you fall asleep.

Funnel Roll a double thickness of heavy-duty foil into a cone shape and snip off the pointed end to create an impromptu funnel for filling bottles.

Temporary piping bag Roll a double thickness of heavy-duty foil into a pointed cone shape, leaving a small hole at the pointed end. Fill with icing which is not too thick, and then twist to close. If necessary, fold down the top of the cone to prevent the icing coming out of the top.

Pastry support To bake pastry blind without beans, make a foil sausage and press it gently into the pastry around the sides of the quiche dish. It will stop the pastry falling inwards while cooking without a filling.

Soap saver Attach a small piece of foil to the underside of a bar of soap. It will stop it sticking to the basin and make it last longer.

Reflector Glue foil to heavy cardboard to make a light reflector for photography. If you make three identical panels, you can hinge or tape them together; the reflector will then stand upright by itself.

Ammonia

Furniture renewer If an old piece of furniture is heavily stained, rub it with a cloth dampened with full-strength ammonia; when the cloth gets dirty, rinse it in water and reuse.

Do not treat valuable pieces in this way, however, as the ammonia will also remove the finish on a polished surface.

Wax remover Before waxing a very hard floor covering, remove the old polish with a solution of 2 tablespoons household ammonia in 1 pint/570ml water.

Jewellery cleaner Soak pieces of gold jewellery in a solution made up of equal parts ammonia and lukewarm water for 10 minutes. Then rub with a soft brush and leave them to dry without rinsing.

Tableware polish Here's a quick way to brighten up your cutlery. Add a little ammonia to your usual paste polish and apply it to silver-plated and stainless-steel cutlery with a soft cloth. Rub with a clean cloth to finish.

Brass tarnish remover Remove tarnish from solid brass by scrubbing it lightly with a soft brush dampened with a little ammonia – but take care – brighter brass looks nice, but old pieces could be worth more with their aged surfaces intact.

Oil remover When washing sheets, towels and clothes, remove absorbed body oils by adding 8fl oz/225ml ammonia to the usual amount of washing powder.

Caution Do not use ammonia with chlorine bleach.

Aprons

Bib Tie an apron around your young child's neck for an instant bib.

Portable cash box If you're planning on selling bits and bobs at a car boot sale, make yourself a money holder with an old apron. Turn up the bottom and then stitch downwards to create five pockets; that way, you can wear your cash box around your waist, keeping

your coins and notes separated and safe from theft. Or sew some extra pockets into a carpenter's apron.

Ladder tool pocket An efficient way to hold your tools while working on a ladder is to tack or staple a carpenter's apron to the top step of the ladder.

Ashes

Pewter brightener You can bring out the gentle shine of pewter by rubbing it with a paste made of sifted ashes moistened with water; apply them with a soft cloth.

Grease cutter When camping or barbecuing, soak greasy pans and utensils in ashes mixed with water, or make a thick ash-and-water paste for scrubbing them with.

Pest repellent To discourage slugs and snails, build low ridges of wood ash around plants and between rows of vegetables.

Path reinforcer Build up a soggy garden path with your fireplace ashes. Tip them onto the path and then tread them into the ground.

Baking tins

Water bowl Does your dog overturn its water bowl in the garden? You can stop this happening if you use a ring mould to hold the water. Prevent your dog spilling it by driving a stake into the ground through the centre hole to keep the 'bowl' upright.

Plant holder Place a ring mould in the centre of your umbrella table and use it to hold cut flowers or decorative plants that grow happily in the shade. Colourful annuals are especially suitable.

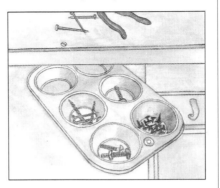

Workroom storage Create a storage space for nuts, bolts, nails, screws and other workshop bits and pieces by attaching a baking tin with a lip to the underside of a workbench. Do this by drilling a hole in one corner of the tin and using a screw, with a washer as a spacer, to make it secure. Or attach cleats under your workbench or shelf to serve as runners for the rim of the tin.

Serving tray A flat baking tin makes a good emergency tray for drinks. You can make it more presentable by covering it in foil or with a pretty cloth.

Balloons

Party invitations Blow up brightly coloured balloons and then carefully write out your invitations with a felt-tip pen of a contrasting colour. Deflate the

balloons, place them in envelopes and post them to your guests. When they blow up the balloon, they will get the message.

Papier-mâché mould A balloon makes an excellent base for a papier-mâché mask or dish. When the paper strips have dried, just remove the balloon by bursting it.

Banana skins

Fertiliser Add any banana skins to your garden's compost pile; they are an excellent source of phosphorus and potassium. Or bury the skins just under the surface of the flower bed around rose bushes.

Emergency shoe shine For a spur-of-the-moment shine, rub your leather shoes with the soft inside of a banana skin, and then clean and buff the shoe's surface with a paper towel or napkin.

Beer

Setting lotion Comb a few spoonfuls of beer through your hair before styling; it will hold it in place.

Insect lure Place several almost empty beer cans around a picnic area; they can draw most stinging insects, such as wasps or bees, away from the food and guests.

Marinade Beer is an effective marinade for cheaper cuts of meat, increasing the flavour and making them more tender. Cover the meat with beer and leave for an hour or so before cooking.

Belts

Luggage guard Before travelling, secure a small suitcase with an old belt: wrap it around the middle of the case and through the handle, buckling it to protect the case against rough handling or a faulty catch.

Strop Keep a leather belt in the kitchen for sharpening knives. When you need to use it, place the buckle over a hook in the wall and hold the belt taut with your free hand.

Book carrier Use an old belt to lash books together and provide a carrying handle as well. If required, punch new holes in the belt with a hole punch or skewer.

Pet collar Cut a belt to the correct length, punch new holes as needed, and add a metal ring to the buckle to attach an identification tag.

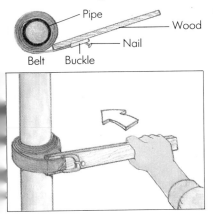

Pipe — Wood — Nail
Belt — Buckle

Strap wrench To give you more effective leverage on a stubborn pipe or handle, wrap a belt around it as shown. Drive a nail securely into a piece of wood and then hook the belt buckle over the nail. Push the wood in the direction that you wish the pipe to move.

Tool holder Nail a belt to the wall in several places, making sure that you leave large enough loops between them to hold the tools or utensils you want to store.

Sling For hand and finger injuries, make a double loop around the wrist of the injured hand with a soft belt. Holding the injured hand in such a way that the finger tips are on a level with the collar bone, pass the belt around the back of the neck and then tie it or fasten it in front.

Bicarbonate of soda (baking soda)

Dishwasher deodorant If you use your dishwasher less than once a day, toss a handful of bicarbonate of soda into the bottom between washes; it will keep it smelling fresh.

Wallpaper washer Remove resistant smudges from washable wallpaper by rubbing them with a thick paste made of baking powder and water. (Test it first on an inconspicuous patch of wallpaper.)

Furniture blancher To take marks off white painted furniture, wash it down with a solution of 1 tablespoon bicarbonate of soda mixed with 2 pints/ 1.15 litres warm water.

Grill scourer To remove grease and encrusted food from grill and oven racks, soak them in a solution of 4 tablespoons of bicarbonate of soda in 2 pints/1.15 litres of warm water. For tough stains, put some bicarbonate of soda on a damp sponge and scrub.

Dog shampoo To add softness and lustre to your pet's coat, put 2 tablespoons bicarbonate of soda in its bath water. It also works well as a dry shampoo for dogs.

Skin soother For sunburn and overheated or irritated skin, add a handful of bicarbonate of soda to a warm bath.

Stain remover Clean stained white socks by rubbing them with a paste of bicarbonate and water before washing.

Shower curtain scrubber Clean stubborn mildew stains off shower curtains by scrubbing them with a thick paste of bicarbonate of soda mixed with water.

Teapot cleaner Clean the inside of a teapot stained with tannin by rubbing it with a paste of bicarbonate of soda on a piece of cloth.

Blankets

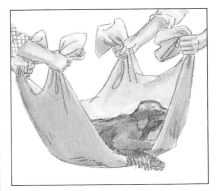

Lightweight pet stretcher Place an injured pet in the centre of a blanket; ask someone to lift two corners at one end while you lift the other two.

Underblanket To stop your underblanket slipping, cut a blanket to the same size as your mattress. Sew two strips of 1in/13mm elastic from corner to corner at each end and then slip these under the mattress to keep the underblanket secure.

Poncho Keep yourself warm by making a simple poncho. Fold a blanket in half, and then cut a slit large enough to go over your head in the centre. Hem the edge to prevent the blanket fraying.

Heat proofing Make your own place mats with a double thickness of blanket cut to the right size. Cover the blanket pieces with attractive fabric.

Curtain padding Sew a blanket between the curtain fabric and lining for insulation and to cut out light.

Homemade duvet Make your own duvet by inserting a thin layer of cotton or wool fibre between two blankets and then stitching the three together.

Hammock Attach four long pieces of a sturdy rope to an old blanket by threading the rope through metal eyelets stitched into each corner of the blanket. Pair off the ropes at each end of the blanket and tie them securely around two trees in the garden. Make sure the blanket can hold a heavy weight before using it.

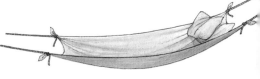

Bleach

Vase preserver Keep a flower vase free from slime and stagnant water by adding a few drops of bleach to the water – it won't harm the flowers.

Bacteria killer If you have a humidifier, add a few drops of chlorine bleach to each gallon (4.5 litres) of water when you refill it. It will prevent bacteria growth.

Freshener Remove any smells lingering in cool boxes and other closed containers by wiping them with diluted chlorine bleach.

Mould exterminator Apply bleach directly to the bath and shower base to rid them of mould and mildew. Then rinse them well.

Blinds

Play mat Put a blind down for children to play on – it will protect the floor and give them a boundary for their activities. When playtime is over, roll up the blind for easy storage.

Canvas Use an unrolled blind for an oil or pastel painting. Then roll it up to store your work.

Craft cloth Cover the table with a waterproofed blind to protect its surface.

Projection screen View your home films or slides on a white blind pulled down over the window or hung from a wall.

Ground cloth Keep an old window blind in the boot of your car. Unroll it when doing emergency work under the car to protect your clothes.

Dust cover Drape a blind over your drawing table or workbench to keep off the dust.

Disappearing door Conceal clutter by hanging blinds in walk-in cupboards and wardrobes.

Room divider Roller blinds with their mechanism intact can be fixed to blocks screwed to joists above a basement workshop. Drill holes in the blocks into which the rods of the blind mechanism can be inserted. Pull down the shades to keep sawdust from flying around the room.

Books

Insulation Book-filled shelves on exterior walls help to keep heat in and the cold out; and they will also muffle sound between one room and the next.

Clamp Hold freshly-glued surfaces together by weighing them down with heavy books, such as dictionaries or atlases.

Flower press Use a large book to press summer flowers prior to placing them in an album or making cards with them. Put the flowers between two sheets of blotting paper in the centre of the book, and then put a heavy weight, such as an iron doorstop, on top of the book.

Booster cushion Raise visiting children up to the height of the kitchen table with a couple of thick books or directories.

Boots

Umbrella stand Stuff the bottom of an attractive old leather boot (a riding boot, perhaps) or a tall rubber boot with newspaper and then pebbles or marbles. Place it next to your front or back door for wet umbrellas. Change the newspaper from time to time.

Nesting box Hang an old boot upside-down on a tree; small birds such as wrens or robins find the toe area ideal places in which to build their nests.

Doorstop Fill a short boot with golf balls or pebbles and then use it to prop open doors around the house.

Borax

Fertiliser Fill a cup with borax (available from chemists) and sprinkle it around your beetroot plants.

Nappy freshener Add 8 tablespoons borax to the recommended amount of soap powder or detergent for a hot-water wash; it will eliminate smells and stains and make reusable nappies more absorbent.

China shiner For a brilliant shine, rinse your fine china in a sinkful of warm water to which 8 tablespoons of borax has been added. Then rinse it once more in clear water. Or add 1 tablespoon of borax to your dishwasher.

Flower preserver To dry flowers, place one or two in an airtight container with a layer of borax and cornmeal mixed together (1 part borax to 2 of cornmeal) in the bottom. Leave the container in a cool, dry place. After 7 to 10 days, remove the flowers and dust them with a soft artist's brush.

Cat litter smells Blend 6 parts cat litter with 1 part borax before you fill the cat tray. It will reduce the smell of the litter box.

Drain cleaner A sink that drains slowly may be clogged up with congealed fat. You can usually ease it with a strong solution of borax and boiling water.

Bottle boxes

Decoration storage Wrap Christmas decorations in newspaper, individually if necessary, and then place them in each of the carton's segments.

Workshop organiser Use a sectioned box to store strips of wood, mouldings, draught excluder and metal rods.

Glass protector Keep fine crystal glassware or light bulbs, sorted by wattage, in sections of a bottle box.

Ball game Place a box at an angle (by leaning it on a cushion, for example) and erect a small ramp leading up to the front – a rubber mat or chopping board resting on a pile of books will do. Assign numbered values to each section of the box. To play, roll golf, tennis or table-tennis balls up the ramp and into the box; the winner is the one with the highest score.

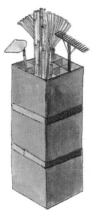

Tool keeper Attach three bottle boxes to each other (only the bottom one keeps its base) with insulating or masking tape, stacking them so the dividers match up. Store a long-handled garden tool in each divider.

Sports caddy Keep one in your child's room for neat storage of tennis rackets, cricket bats, fishing rods and other sporting paraphernalia. Get them to decorate the box with stickers, paintings or adhesive-backed plastic. See also CARDBOARD BOXES, p.294.

Art preserver A clean bottle box with its partitions intact is a great place to store rolled-up drawings, plans and canvases – in or out of cardboard tubes.

Bottle caps

Christmas decorations Spray paint bottle caps gold or silver and then punch a hole in each one. You can hang them on the Christmas tree with string or a hook, or knot each one onto a string to make a garland.

Mini paint holder Mix small amounts of touch-up paint in a bottle cap.

Bottle-top necklace On a rainy day, let a child punch a hole in the centre of a selection of plastic bottle tops, and string them together on a piece of thin elastic or ribbon.

Bird deterrent String bottle tops together and hang them in the garden to keep the birds off your vegetable patch.

Fish descaler Nail several metal bottle caps to a small block of wood, close together and fluted side up. Run the block up and down the sides and back of a fish to rid it of scales. It's best to do this outside, as the scales tend to scatter.

Pest trap If you need to put down poison, place a small amount in a bottle top and leave somewhere out of reach of pets or children – behind cupboards or under chests of drawers, for example.

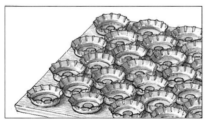

Mud scraper Make a 'doormat' out of bottle tops that will scrape off even the stubbornest mud and can be used outside your back door. Glue or nail the smooth side of bottle caps to a piece of plywood in several rows.

Bottles

Mole and rabbit repellent You may find that bottles set into the ground leaving ½ in / 13 mm of their necks exposed will scare off moles as the wind whistles across the top of them. Place them near any molehills. Bottles which are half filled with water or sand and then placed around the garden may do the same for rabbits.

Rolling pin Fill a smooth-sided glass bottle with water and screw the top on tightly. Dust the sides of the bottle with a sprinkling of flour before rolling out the dough.

Bud vase Remove the spray section from an empty perfume bottle, wash it thoroughly and use it to display small flowers such as violets or primroses.

Bowling pins Paint ten clean plastic bottles of the same size – such as mineral water bottles – with the numbers 1 to 10 and use them as skittles. Play indoors on a rainy day with a rubber ball.

Bellows When thoroughly cleaned and dried, a squeezable washing-up liquid or ketchup bottle with a hole in its spout can serve as a bellows for encouraging a slow fire.

Drill holster To make a portable carrier for a cordless drill or screwdriver, cut the neck off a plastic bottle. Then cut it again about halfway down the bottle on the diagonal. You can either screw the carrier to the wall above your workbench or cut two slits in the taller side and thread it onto a belt.

Bottle openers

Grout remover Use the pointed tip of a bottle opener to gouge out the old grout between ceramic tiles. But take care not to chip the tile edges.

Plumb bob To check whether a shelf is straight, suspend a bottle opener from a string so that it hangs freely with its point down. You should be able to see whether the shelf bracket is straight or not.

Screwdriver Use the side of a bottle opener to turn a large-slotted screw such as those found on waste pipes.

Bread

Bread bowl Cut off the top of a round, crusty loaf and scoop out the centre. Fill the 'bowl' with a dip. Use the inside of the loaf to make fresh breadcrumbs.

Moisturiser A slice of bread kept in a storage container of soft light or dark brown sugar will prevent it from drying out and becoming hard.

Place markers Write the names of your guests on slips of paper and attach them to toothpicks like miniature flags. Then stand each one in a bread roll.

Cake crust Line a greased cake tin with fine breadcrumbs before adding the cake mixture. The cooked cake will turn easily out of the tin, with a delicious crust around the edges.

Mincer cleaner Before using an old hand mincer, run a piece of bread through the mincer to clear out any dust. Do the same when you have finished. It will pick up any fat left inside the machine, making it easier to clean.

Hand saver Pick up slivers of broken glass with a piece of bread and then wrap it all in newspaper.

Flower brightener A good way to clean artificial flowers made of velvet is to brush them with a shaving brush and then rub them lightly with fresh bread. Finally, rebrush.

Instant rubber Bread will make a good substitute for a pencil rubber in an emergency, and works particularly well on wallpaper (try those grubby marks around the light switch) and on old books and prints. Roll the soft part of a slice of fresh bread into a ball and use as you would a rubber.

Microwave tester Check whether your microwave is defrosting or heating your food evenly with a few slices of bread. Cover the floor of the microwave with white bread slices and then heat on High for 3 minutes, watching through the glass door. The bread should brown evenly, not in patches.

Bricks

Desk organiser Glue a scrap of felt to the bottom of a hollow airbrick with epoxy resin and stick pencils and scissors in the holes.

Barbecue base Place an old oven rack over four even stacks of bricks to make an impromptu fireplace with grill.

Garden border Use bricks around the edges of flower beds to separate them from the lawn. Set the bottom edge slightly into the ground.

Book end Cover bricks with fabric or heavy wallpaper and use them to keep your books in place. A fabric-covered brick also works well as a doorstop for an internal door.

Bookshelves Lay a piece of wood or glass between two stacks of household bricks for easy-to-build, attractive shelving.

Brooms

Textured paintbrush Dip an old broom head in paint to create special effects and textures on a canvas or a wall.

Bird guide If a bird has somehow got indoors, open all the windows, leave the room and wait for it to fly away. If it doesn't manage to find its own way out, use a broom to guide it; don't let it batter itself against any glass windows.

Window washer To reach upper windows without a ladder, tie a large sponge or a squeegee to the end of a broom handle.

Garden stake Support a tall, top-heavy plant, such as a tomato, with a broom handle; sharpen one end for easy insertion into the ground.

Painting aid Attach a broom handle to a paintbrush with insulating tape.

Rolling pin Cut a section of a clean broom handle to a size that is suitable for rolling out pieces of dough.

Reach extender Attach a screw hook to one end of a broom handle to lengthen your reach – you will finally be able to reach socks that have dropped down behind the radiator, or get the basket on the top shelf.

Clothes rail Screw large screw hooks into joists in the ceiling of your attic or basement and rest a broom handle on them to create extra hanging space for your clothes.

Curtain rod Cut a broomstick to the desired length and drill holes at both ends. Thread on your curtain rings and then hang the pole from L-hooks fitted through the holes.

Pivot bolt

Stoopless scoop Prevent backache – pick up leaves and rubbish with an extended dustpan made from two broom handles and a plastic planter tray cut in half.

Wall-hanging support Display wall hangings by threading a handle through loops of string along the top of the hanging. Rest the handle on large screw eyes attached to the wall at either end.

Weeding aid Take the strain out of weeding by attaching a small garden fork to the end of a broom stick. Remove the fork's handle and fix the longer one in its place.

Bubble pack

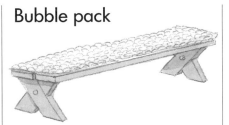

Bench upholstery Soften hard garden benches with a layer or two of bubble pack. And take some with you on outings – bubble pack will make picnic benches more comfortable, too.

Table pad When repairing pieces of glass or china, lessen the chance of breaking something by covering the work surface with bubble pack.

Rain bonnet Keep a square of bubble pack folded up in your handbag for unexpected showers – it makes a good waterproof scarf, or seat cover, in an emergency.

Cooler Wrap ice cream and other frozen or chilled foods in bubble pack if you're going on a picnic – they will stay frozen longer.

Insulation Gluing bubble pack to the inside walls of a kennel will help to keep your dog warm on a chilly night – but don't try it if your dog tends to chew everything; it could be dangerous.

Buckets

Christmas tree stand Stand the tree in a bucket and then pour in wet sand or gravel to support it. Make the bucket look more festive by covering it with Christmas wrapping paper or foil.

Lobster cooker If you don't have a large fish kettle, boil a lobster in an old metal bucket.

Shower Cool off on hot days by dipping a perforated bucket into a stream and hanging it from a tree for a cold shower.

Buckles

Scarf clasp Pass a colourful scarf through a pretty buckle to hold it around your neck over a plain sweater or dress.

Curtain ornament Finish a curtain tie-back with an unusual buckle as an added decoration.

Bulldog clips

Music holder Keep sheet music in place by clipping it to a music stand with a bulldog clip. It will keep songbooks open at the right page too.

Workshop tidy Attach a clip to paintbrushes, gloves or safety goggles, for example, and then hang them on a hook or nail on the wall with the hole in the top of the clip.

Hair clip Use to section off hair while cutting or styling.

Exerciser Squeeze a large one again and again to strengthen your grip and release tension.

Buttons

Doll's house decorations Use buttons as plates and wall hangings in your child's doll's house.

Beanbag filler Use small buttons instead of dried beans to fill homemade juggling bags.

Game pieces Substitute buttons for lost backgammon or draughts pieces. Or use them for a game of tiddlywinks.

Christmas tree garland Knot buttons onto a sturdy length of string to give your Christmas tree an old-fashioned look.

Child's necklace Get your child to string attractive buttons, alternating large and small, onto a double thickness of strong cotton.

Calendars

Drawer liners Take apart an old calendar, especially one with nice pictures, and use the pages to line your desk drawers.

Jigsaw puzzle Glue a favourite calendar page on to a heavy piece of cardboard, and then cut it into large pieces to make a child's jigsaw.

Place mats Back the pages from an illustrated calendar with thick cardboard or cork, varnish front and back or cover with sticky-backed plastic and then use them as place mats.

Collage Glue the cut-out pages of a calendar on to ¼in/6mm plywood to make an attractive picture, or use them to cover an old wooden or metal box.

Greetings card Glue a favourite old calendar picture on to thin poster board for an inexpensive but attractive greetings card.

Wallpaper Use calendar art to paper a small room, such as the toilet; protect and 'antique' it with a coat of shellac varnish.

New Year's tablecloth Pull apart the outgoing year's calendar and glue the months randomly to a large piece of freezer paper for a topical table covering at the year-end celebration.

Candles

Envelope sealer If you have to reopen an envelope after you have stuck the flap down, don't despair. You can reuse it by sealing it with a few drops of melted wax from a lighted candle.

Sledge lubricant Rub candles along the runners of a sledge to cut resistance, for a smoother, faster ride.

Shovel lubricant Snow will slide straight off your shovel if you rub it down with a candle stub before use.

Egg decorator Drip melted wax onto hard-boiled Easter eggs and then dye the eggs by placing them in water which contains food colouring. Peel off the wax to reveal an intricate pattern.

Cardboard boxes

Dust cover Make a dust cover for a small appliance such as a power tool or typewriter by cutting off the top flaps of a box and placing it over the object. If you want, decorate it with adhesive-backed plastic.

Table guard Open out a large box and use it to protect work surfaces and table tops from ink, paint, glue or knife and scissor nicks.

Mechanic's helper Keep the floor of your garage clean by placing a piece of cardboard under your car. It will catch any drips of oil and will also help a mechanic to identify potential problems with the engine or elsewhere.

Gift of suspense Place a friend's gift inside a series of increasingly bigger cardboard boxes, each one specially wrapped, for an extended surprise.

Nail holder When knocking in a small nail or tack, push it through a piece of stiff card to hold it in position. It will prevent you banging your fingers.

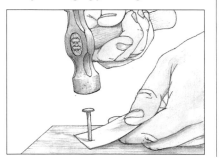

Paint protection Cut a piece of stiff card and hold it at the base of the skirting board to prevent a paintbrush coming into contact with carpet or a dusty floor. And exposed pipework at the base of radiators can be painted cleanly and easily if you hold a piece of flexible card behind the radiator pipe.

Filing tray Remove the top and the front from a cereal box. Lying it on its back, angle the ends of the short sides.

Place mats Cut several pieces of cardboard to the same size and cover them with colourful adhesive-backed plastic. Or get your children to paint pictures on them before covering with plastic. See also BOTTLE BOXES, p.290.

Puppet theatre Stand a large cardboard box on end; cut a big hole in the back for puppeteers to put their hands through and create a platform with a smaller box for the puppets to perform on.

Magazine holder Remove the top of a detergent or cereal box, then cut the front and back of the box at an angle, from the top of one side to the bottom third of the other.

Cardboard tubes

Megaphone When you need to amplify your voice, talk through a cardboard tube.

Knitting-needle case Prevent bending and breaking – store plastic needles in an empty cardboard tube.

Light tidy For easy decorating next year, wrap your Christmas tree lights around an old toilet-roll tube and secure them with a piece of masking tape.

Fluorescent light storage Prevent breakage by keeping unused fluorescent lamps in long cardboard tubes.

Document holder Store diplomas, marriage licences and other certificates by rolling them tightly and slipping them inside a paper towel tube. This prevents creases and will keep the documents clean and dry.

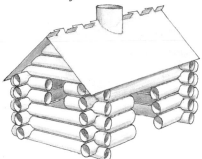

Play logs Notch the ends of several long tubes with a craft knife and then help your children to construct fences or huts with them.

Linen press Wrap tablecloths and napkins around long cardboard tubes after washing. It will prevent creases appearing where they were folded. First cover the tubes with adhesive-backed plastic or plastic film, though, to prevent stains.

Fabric keeper Store leftover fabric scraps, tightly rolled, inside a tube. For easy identification, staple a sample of each fabric to the outside of the tube.

Kazoo Cut three finger holes in the middle of a kitchen towel tube and then cover one end with wax paper held on with a rubber band. Hum into the other end, plugging different holes to alter the pitch.

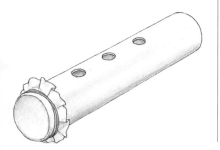

Car mirrors

Monitor Car mirrors that still have their fixing brackets attached can be screwed to the wall on the side of the house so that you can watch the children playing in both the front and back gardens at the same time.

Organist's friend Screw a car mirror complete with its fixing bracket to a wood block to enable an organist to keep an eye on the congregation, or on the choir director, while reading the music.

Signal To signal fellow walkers on distant hilltops, carry a sturdy car mirror in your rucksack. See also LOST IN THE WILDS, p.127.

Carpet scraps

Noise dampener Cut out pieces of unused carpet or underfelt of the right size to fit under typewriters and sewing machines, on cabinet shelves and inside toolboxes.

Bed bumper Pad the corners of a sharp bed frame with small pieces of carpet to prevent scraping the paintwork or gouging out plaster walls.

Foot warmers Trace your feet on a piece of paper; use this as a pattern to cut a piece of thin carpeting to fit inside boots or work shoes.

Buffer Glue an old piece of carpet or felt to a block of wood with epoxy resin; use it to buff shoes or as a blackboard wiper.

Floor protection When doing messy repairs, protect the floor with old carpeting or underlay; if you're using a stepladder, make sure the piece is large enough to take all four of its legs.

Exercise mat Cut a length of old carpet approximately 3 ft / 1 m wide and as long as you are tall. Roll it up and store it under a bed when you are not using it.

Knee pad To protect your knees when you are washing the floor or weeding, cut out two pieces of carpet about 10 in / 250 mm square. Make two parallel slits or holes towards the sides of each piece, and then run an old tie or scarf through the slits and use it to tie the pad to your knee.

Car seats

Dog bed Cut the foam-rubber padding from an old car seat to the right size for your dog's basket.

Furniture Use old car seats as furniture in playrooms or children's bedrooms – then you don't have to worry about what might happen to them.

Castor oil

Eyelash treatment Apply a light smear of castor oil to your eyelashes at bedtime – it keeps them shiny.

Lubricant Use castor oil instead of lubricating oil on kitchen scissors and other utensils that touch food.

Cuticle softener Rub castor oil around your nails before going to bed.

Skin preparation If you've run out of moisturiser for your skin, use castor oil in an emergency. But watch out: it can be messy.

Hair conditioner Rub castor oil into your dry hair, cover it with a bath cap and leave for 30 minutes. Then shampoo your hair as normal.

Cat litter

Drying agent Preserve fresh flowers by placing them on a bed of clean cat litter in an airtight container for 7 to 10 days. See also FLOWER DRYING, p.87.

Smell remover To remove unpleasant smells, sprinkle cat litter granules in dustbins, fireplaces or on the floors of musty rooms. Before packing a suitcase or a trunk, leave an open-top tin filled with litter inside overnight.

Oil absorber Sprinkle cat litter over oil puddles and other spills on the garage floor. Leave until the fluids have been absorbed, and then sweep it up.

Chalk

Rust preventer Place several pieces of chalk in your toolbox; they will collect moisture and help to prevent rust.

Marble polish Wipe clean marble with a damp soft cloth dipped in powdered chalk; rinse with clear water and dry thoroughly.

Grease remover Rub chalk onto a grease spot on clothing or table linens. Let it absorb the oil, and then brush it off. If the stain lingers, rub chalk into it again just before putting it into the wash.

Metal polish Wipe metal with chalk dust on a damp cloth.

Repellent Scatter powdered chalk around lime-loving garden plants to repel ants and slugs.

Chamois leather

Photographer's helper Wipe dusty photographs and camera lenses with a clean chamois.

Glove patch Use hide glue to attach pieces of chamois leather to worn areas on work gloves.

Chewing gum

Valuables retriever To recover a coin or piece of jewellery that's fallen down the drain, moisten a stick of chewing gum and attach it to the bottom of a fishing weight. Dangle the weight from a string in the hole until it sticks to the lost object, let it take hold, and then pull it up to safety.

Crab lure Attach a stick of gum which is moist but still has flavour to a crab line. Lower the line and wait for the crabs to go for the gum.

Filler Fill a crack in a clay flowerpot or dog's water bowl with a piece of well-chewed gum.

Window putty Temporarily hold a loose pane of glass in place with a wad of chewing gum.

Radiator repair You can put a temporary stop to a leaking radiator or the hose to it by applying a piece of softened chewing gum to the crack. But get the problem area properly repaired as soon as you can.

Chicken wire

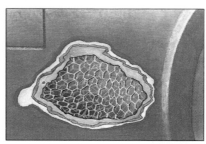

Rust hole repair Push some wire into a cleaned-out rust patch on your car; it will form a backing for the body filler.

Bulb protectors Prevent rodent damage to your spring bulbs by lining the bottom of a prepared bed with wire. Then plant the bulbs and cover them with soil as normal.

Frog Provide a firm base for an arrangement of cut flowers by placing a ball of chicken wire in the bottom of a vase before you add the blooms.

Fence setter To hold a fence post more firmly in place, wrap the base of the post with chicken wire and nail it to a wooden framework before setting the post in concrete.

Insulation holder After placing fibre blanket between the roof and floor joists, staple chicken wire to the joist edges to secure it.

Christmas trees

Plant protector Cut off the branches of an unwanted tree and cover flowerbeds with them; they may not look very attractive, but they will help to keep animals off the beds.

Outdoor lighting Keep your Christmas tree in a garden tub throughout the year, and decorate it with lights for a party.

Bird shelter When you've finished with your Christmas tree, replant it at the bottom of your garden as a shelter for birds. They'll be especially grateful if you keep the tree festooned throughout the cold winter months with bird treats such as sunflower or sesame seeds (see p.382), popcorn or whole peanuts.

Dog repellent Cut off the branches of an old Christmas tree and position them vertically around young tree trunks. It may help to discourage dogs from fouling them.

Citrus fruit rinds

Suet bowl Place a suet-birdseed mixture in an empty orange or grapefruit half; suspend the rind cup from a tree in the garden with string.

Saucepan cleaner Clean a blackened aluminium saucepan by boiling water and citrus rinds in it. If it is still discoloured, rub it with a steel-wool pad.

Tea flavouring Add citrus peel to tea leaves while they're brewing, or put several small strips in a cup of just-boiled water with a tea bag.

Nail groomer Press nail tips into the pithy side of a lemon rind to clean them after doing dirty chores.

Potpourri Add rinds to simmering cinnamon and cloves to fill your home with a wonderful aroma.

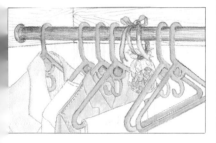

Aromatic bags Put small string bags filled with orange or lemon peel in drawers and cupboards.

Cutting board freshener Rub a lemon rind over your cutting board to clean and deodorise it.

Fireplace freshener Add some dried citrus rinds to the fire; they will give off a spicy fragrance.

Clay

Anchor When repairing broken china or pottery, hold the pieces together on a bed of clay until the epoxy resin glue sets. When the pieces have joined together, remove the clay.

Book cleaner To clean a book's soiled edges, press a lump of clay over the dirty area. Knead it frequently to get a fresh surface and clean one small area at a time, being careful not to rub.

Clipboards

Place mat holder Hang a clipboard inside a kitchen cabinet door and use the clamp as a convenient place to store your mats.

Recipe retainer To make it easier to follow a recipe cut from a magazine or newspaper, attach a clipboard to the kitchen wall at eye level to hold the cutting.

Travel aid Before starting on a long car journey, fold the map so it shows the area you are going to visit. Attach the map, folded area upwards, to a clipboard and keep it near the front seat.

Music holder To keep flimsy pages upright, in place and invulnerable to draughts, attach sheet music to a clipboard.

Clothes pegs

Clamps When gluing two thin objects together, or a thin one to a thick one, hold them in place with a clothes peg until the glue sets.

Nail holder Spare your fingers – use a clothes peg to grip a nail when hammering in hard-to-reach places.

Clipboard Make a rack for small tools, toothbrushes or kitchen utensils by screwing several clothes pegs on to a piece of wood.

Cord holder Prevent the flex of your vacuum cleaner from retracting while in use by clipping a clothes peg to it once it is the length you need.

Fastener Keep packages of biscuits, snacks, cereal or seeds fresh and crisp by fastening open packaging with a clothes peg.

Jumbo paper clips Clothes pegs hold more than paper clips and are handier.

Bag holder Nail two clothes pegs to your garden fence and then use them to hold open a plastic rubbish bag when collecting leaves or other rubbish.

Pair uniter Clip pairs of shoes and boots together with a clothes peg; it saves hunting after one of them.

Note holder Glue or screw a clothes peg onto the kitchen wall. It can hold recipe cards or messages for members of your family.

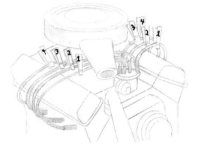

Spark plug reminder Number clothes pegs and attach them to your spark plug cables before disconnecting them. Number from the front of the engine, adding D if it's on the driver's side, P for the passenger side.

Christmas decorations Make angels or toy soldiers by decorating clothes pegs; use the clips as legs.

Memory jogger Clip a note onto the sun visor or the steering wheel of your car to remind you to turn off the headlights or get something out of the boot.

Laundry help Weigh down sheets, pillowcases, shirts and other lightweight items on your washing line by attaching several pegs to the hem along the bottom. It will stop them getting tangled up in a breeze.

Paintbrush Clamp a clothes peg over a small square of foam rubber which can be used for touching up your paintwork.

Paintbrush saver Stop your brushes from sinking into white spirit when you clean them. Clamp them to the side of the container with a clothes peg.

Wooden spoon saver Attach a peg to the handle of a wooden spoon when making jam or chutney. It will stop the spoon slipping into the saucepan.

Hem pins There's no need to baste; hold a new hemline in place with clothes pegs before you press it.

Toothpaste stretcher Clip the bottom of a toothpaste tube with a clothes peg and then roll it up to avoid wastage.

Coffee

Fertiliser Work coffee grounds into the topsoil in your garden; it will help to bring your plants on.

Dye An inexpensive way to dye fabric brown is to soak it in strong black coffee – without sugar. But remember, it won't be colourfast.

Bait carrier Transport your fishing bait – worms or maggots – in a tin or paper cup half-full of moist coffee grounds; they'll be easier to get hold of when needed.

Combs

Washboard After immersing fabric with a stain in soap and water, gently rub the stained section across the teeth of a comb.

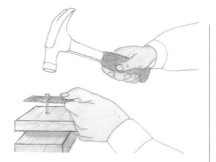

Nail holder Avoid hammering your fingers – hold a small nail in place between the teeth of a comb.

Music maker Fold a piece of wax paper over the teeth of a comb, hold it up to your lips and hum.

Wallet guard To make your wallet less accessible to a pickpocket, put a small comb, teeth up, in your pocket; the teeth will catch on the pocket edges and help secure your wallet.

Vacuum cleaner cleaner Save an old comb to clean off the heads of vacuum brushes.

Back scratcher Clip a comb to the end of a ruler with paper clips or a bulldog clip.

Concrete screen blocks

Anchor Attach a rope or chain to a concrete block and use it as an anchor for a rowing boat while fishing.

Flower box Make a plant holder for a windowsill that drains well and is guaranteed not to tip over – fill the holes of a hollow concrete block with soil and plant it with flowers.

Child's step Wrap a block in a piece of thick foam rubber or an old towel, and then cover it with waterproofed fabric for your child to use in the bathroom.

Corks

Jewellery Punch holes through the centre of several corks and string them together; for variety, use corks of different sizes and paint them.

Pincushion Needles won't prick you or get lost so easily stored in a cork.

Make-up Burn the end of a cork and then use it for make-up at Halloween.

Table guard Use a general purpose epoxy to glue together several wine bottle corks to make a hot pad which will protect the table.

Key ring Attach your boat key to a large painted cork; if it falls overboard, it will stay afloat and be easy to find.

Sailboat Cut a cork in half, and shape one half to resemble the front of a boat. Fit a flat stone in between the two pieces as a keel, and then add toothpicks for masts and sails cut from a yoghurt carton.

Stamp Draw a design on the end of a cork, cut away the material around the outline and ink the cork on a pad. Children can make their own stamps with some supervision.

Safety marker String large corks on a stretch of yellow nylon rope to define a special swimming area for small children.

Knife cleaner Dip a dampened cork in scouring powder and pass it along the edges of a carbon-steel kitchen knife.

Scratch guard Glue thin slices of cork to the bottoms of ashtrays, vases and lamps to reduce the noise and danger of scratching.

Recipe holder Cut a slit in a cork and glue it to the lid of a recipe file box; place a card upright in it so that you can easily refer to it while cooking.

Rust preventer Rub kitchen utensils and garden tools with a cork dipped in cooking oil.

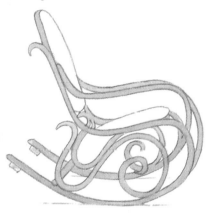

Rocker guard To prevent a rocking chair from tipping too far, use an epoxy resin glue to attach a cork under each end of the two rockers.

Cornflour

Pet shampoo To remove dirt and fluff-up your dog's coat without having to give it a bath, rub cornflour into its coat and then comb or brush it out.

Window cleaner To give a final polish to your windows, mix a little cornflour with ammonia and water.

Knot detangler To help untie a stubborn knot in a piece of string or a shoe lace, sprinkle it with a little cornflour.

Glove easer Sprinkle cornflour inside your rubber gloves – they'll be much easier to put on and take off.

Pastry aid Before rolling out pastry dough, sprinkle the board and rolling pin with cornflour – it's tasteless and cleans up easily.

Baby powder Use cornflour sparingly when changing a baby's nappy.

Cotton wool

Arm guard To keep water from running down your arms when washing walls, wrap a wad of cotton wool around your wrists and secure it loosely with rubber bands.

Glove extender Protect the fingertips of your gloves by stuffing them with little pieces of cotton wool. It will stop long nails from damaging the glove.

Stuffing Use cotton-wool balls as stuffing for dolls, toys or pin cushions.

Cleaning aid Wrap a wisp of cotton wool around the tip of a matchstick or toothpick to make your own cotton-wool bud; use it to remove grit from mouldings, filigree and carving.

Air freshener Saturate a ball of cotton wool with cologne and place it in the bag of your vacuum cleaner; it will sweeten the air as you vacuum.

Smell absorber Get rid of sour smells in your refrigerator by dampening a handful of cotton wool with vanilla extract and putting it on the middle shelf.

Cotton-wool buds

Paint swab Use a bud to touch-up paint jobs around the house and on the car. They also make good paintbrushes for children – use one for each colour and then throw them all away at the end of the painting session.

Tape cleaner Dip a cotton-wool bud in head cleaner (available at electronics supply stores) to clean the heads on tape recorders.

Crevice cleaner Clean between telephone buttons, in sewing machine and camera crevices and in shower-door runners with a cotton-wool bud.

Make-up applicator Use buds to apply eyeshadow and remove any make-up smudges around the eyes.

Credit cards

Scraper When nothing else is handy, use a credit card to scrape frost from your windshield – but avoid scratching the magnetic strip on the back or the card won't work again.

Guitar pick The corner of a old credit card makes a good substitute pick if yours has gone missing.

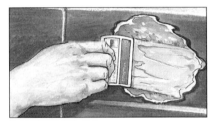

Repair tool A piece of out-of-date credit card makes an ideal instant tool for smoothing down wood filler around the house, or for similar bodywork repairs to the car.

Cup hooks

Place-mat hangers Place a series of hooks inside a cabinet door or behind the dining room door and hang up your mats between meals.

Supports Hang tools and utensils from cup hooks – if necessary, attach a screw-eye to the end of a hammer or spoon handle.

All-purpose hooks Use magnetic cup hooks in your kitchen, bathroom or car as a temporary place to hang your keys, glasses or other small but essential everyday items.

Curtain rails

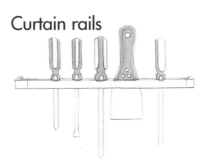

Workshop organiser Fasten a short length of curtain rail to shallow mounts on your workshop wall. Slip screwdrivers, chisels and other tools with handles between the rod and the wall, blades downwards. Be sure to cover the ends of the chisels with plastic caps first.
Garden stakes Use an old curtain rail to support vegetable plants in the garden.

Drying rack Use three or four curtain rails to make your own adjustable laundry dryer; attach them at each end to a cross piece of wood and use a pulley to raise and lower the drying rack as required.

Dandelions

Caution Do not use dandelions that have been treated with herbicides, as may be the case with roadside growth. Pick only those that are at least 25 ft / 7.6 m from sprayed areas.
Natural drink Clean and dry a handful of dandelion roots and then roast them in a warm oven until they turn dark brown. Grind them up and brew into a coffee-like drink. You can percolate the grounds in the same way as you would coffee, using 1 teaspoon per 8 fl oz / 225 ml of water.
Salad greens Use tender young dandelion shoots for vitamin-rich salads; after the flowers form, the greens become too bitter to eat.
Dye Boil dandelion flowers in a small amount of water to give a yellow dye. Do the same with the roots to get a deep purple dye.
Tonic Infuse 2 teaspoons dried dandelion leaves in 8 fl oz / 225 ml boiling water; strain and sip the tonic slowly before a meal. It can work as an appetite stimulant.

Dental floss

Umbrella salvager Attach a loose umbrella to its ribs with dental floss – it's stronger than cotton.
Cooking aid Use a length of unwaxed floss to truss poultry or to tie up a rolled roast.
Jewellery string In an emergency, use floss to restring beads and pearls.

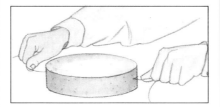

Cake knife Split a cake layer horizontally with clean floss instead of cotton thread or a knife.
Picture wire Hang lightweight pictures with dental floss – it's nearly invisible on white walls.
Moccasin saver Replace worn stitching on soft leather shoes with dental floss (use a large needle), then colour the floss to match the shoes.
Decoration hanger Use dental floss with or without hooks to hang up your Christmas tree decorations.
Photo separator When two photographs are stuck together, work a piece of dental floss between them, gently pulling it from top to bottom.

Dishwasher powder

Surface cleaner Dissolve 4 tablespoons dishwasher powder in 1 gallon / 4.5 litres of hot water. Use the solution to wipe down floors, walls, stoves, fridges, glass or porcelain and then wipe off any residue with a dry cloth.
Stain remover Make a thick paste by adding water to a small amount of dishwasher powder. Apply the paste to a crockery stain and leave for 5 to 10 minutes. Rinse and wash as usual.
Caution Always wear gloves when using dishwasher powder.

Doors

Folding screen Make a useful screen by hinging three lightweight, narrow, plain or louvre doors together, and then decorate it with paint or wallpaper as desired.
Emergency bench Lay a solid door on top of concrete blocks or trestles to make emergency seating or a simple, outdoor table.
Desktop Flat, solid doors provide a sturdy surface for computers, typewriters and other large or bulky equipment. Set the door on top of two filing cabinets of matching height. Placed on a pair of trestles, it works well for pasting up wallpaper.
Table extender Enlarge a small dining table by placing a flat door on top. Put a pair of thin rubber gloves on the table first to keep the door from sliding off its base.
Temporary path After a heavy rainstorm, lay old doors over soggy ground for easy walking.
Tree house If you have a large garden with a suitable tree, nail together several old doors to make a tree house for the children. Or you could make a smaller, freestanding Wendy house if you have no trees.

Dowels

Pencil holder Drill a circle of ¼ in / 6mm holes close together in a board, and then fill them with dowels held in place with a strong wood glue.

Shelf extender Attach a ½ in / 13mm piece of dowelling to the front edge of a shelf; it will catch any rolling toys such as miniature cars and marbles before they hit the ground.

Draught excluder

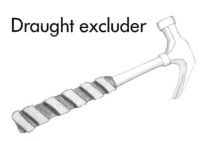

Gripper Wrap self-adhesive foam weatherstripping around handles of your woodworking tools for a better and more comfortable grip. It works on tennis rackets, too.

Scratch guard Attach a strip of draught excluder to the bottom of the rockers on a rocking chair, chair legs or sofa feet to prevent the furniture marking the floor.

Skid preventer Attach strips of draught excluder to the bottoms of telephones and other lightweight appliances; it will stop them sliding off desktops.

Leak fixer Using the end of a screwdriver, force slivers of draught excluder into sagging weatherstripping around the doors of a car to prevent wind whistles. Or force it into any gaps in the seal around the car's boot.

Drawers

Sliding storage Fit old mismatched drawers with castors and slide them under your workbench or bed for extra storage.

Shadow box Paint or paper the interior of a drawer. Fix it to the wall by screwing

through the base of the drawer, inserting metal washers onto the screws, to display trailing plants or ornaments.

Dried peas and beans

Perfect pastry Bake pastry blind by lining a pastry case with a sheet of greaseproof paper and then filling it with dried peas or beans.

Juggling ball stuffing Fill juggling balls made out of scraps of fabric with dried peas or rice.

Baby's rattle Place a few dried peas inside a plastic film case to make a baby's rattle. Make sure that the lid cannot be opened by the child.

Dustbin lids

Birdbath Place a lid upside-down on a slightly smaller dustbin and fill it with water.

Sledge A dustbin lid with handles on either side makes an excellent sledding disc.

Cymbal Let your children use a pair of metal lids as cymbals.

Drip tray If your car is leaking oil or other fluids, leave an upside-down plastic dustbin lid under the engine overnight. In the morning you'll be able to see how bad the problem is.

Eating utensils

Nail holder Protect your fingers when hammering in a nail; hold it steady between the prongs of an old fork.

Multipurpose tool Keep old table knives in the workshop; they're ideal tools for filling in plasterwork.

Egg and spoon race Keep your children occupied during the summer holidays with an egg and spoon race. Give each one a hard-boiled egg in a tablespoon; the first person to cross the finishing line with their egg intact and still in the spoon is the winner.

Houseplant hoe Bend the prongs of an old fork at a right angle and use it to aerate the soil of your potted plants.

Eggs and egg boxes

Shine restorer Beat two egg yolks and work them into your hair with a sponge. Leave them for 20 minutes, and then rinse in warm water.

Wood protector Use any leftover egg whites to make glair (see p.399), a non-toxic, waterproof varnish that is ideal for protecting the raw wood surface of children's toys.

Desk organiser Remove the top of an egg box and place the base inside a desk drawer; it can hold paper clips, rubber bands and other small desk items.

Coin toss Number each section of an egg box and then use it as a game for the children. Place the box at a suitable distance and give them each a few coins to throw into it. The child with the highest score is the winner.

Jewellery box Store rings, earrings and chains in the individual cups.

Easter decorations Carefully blow several chicken or duck eggs (make a hole in each end with a pin, one slightly larger than the other, and blow hard to push out the liquid egg), then get the children to paint or draw Easter designs on them.

Toy 'centipede' Cut 2 or 3 boxes into individual segments and then string them together with thread. Glue on legs and antennae made from pipe cleaners and then paint the resulting centipede in bright primary colours.

Christmas storage Store fragile Christmas tree decorations in empty egg cartons; one glass ball per segment.

Seed starter Punch a hole in the bottom of each cup, and then fill it with potting soil and water. Leave to drain overnight, then sow one or two seeds per cup and cover with plastic wrap. Uncover the cups when the seeds begin to sprout.

Palette Children can mix paints neatly in an empty plastic egg carton.

Game storage Keep track of the small items in your children's games: use one egg box per game, label it with the name of the game, and keep it closed with a sturdy rubber band.

Ice cube tray When you need extra ice for parties, fill plastic egg boxes with water and place in the freezer. Store the frozen blocks in a plastic bag.

Eggshells

Mini funnel Poke a hole in half an eggshell, then pour the liquid through it into a container.

Blown eggs Poke a small hole in both ends of an egg (the hole at one end should be slightly larger than the other). Then with your lips at the smaller hole,

gently but firmly blow out the contents. Leave the shell to dry, and then paint and decorate it with scraps of material or sequins. To use as a Christmas tree decoration, attach a ribbon or string to one end.

Planter Fill half an eggshell with soil, moisten it with water and then plant a seed. Support the shell in an egg box.

Fertiliser Sprinkle crushed eggshells around garden plants to discourage slugs. Toss any extra eggshells into the compost heap for the same reason.

Pot scrubber When cleaning pots and pans while camping, a handful of broken eggshells is a good substitute for steel wool.

Mosaic Paint the inside and outside of eggshells a variety of colours, and then crush them in a paper bag. Draw a picture on cloth or paper and spread slightly diluted white glue over it; sprinkle appropriately coloured shells over the glue. Protect your picture with several coats of acrylic sealer.

Garden aid Sprinkle freshly planted seeds with crushed eggshells to mark the rows; they may also help to keep the birds away.

Emery boards

Glass restorer File away any rough edges on glassware with the fine-grit side of a damp emery board.

Pencil pointer Use an epoxy resin to glue an emery board to the edge of your workbench or desk and use it to put a needle-sharp point on pencils.

Eyedroppers

Glue dispenser If the top of a glue container becomes clogged, you can use an eyedropper instead; this only works with thin, runny glue, however.

Quicksilver catcher Use an eyedropper to pick up the mercury from a broken thermometer.

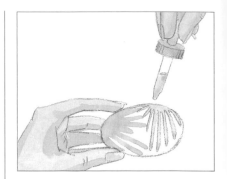

Egg decorator Decorate the outside of Easter eggs with food colouring carefully positioned with an eyedropper.

Fabric scraps

Shelf brightener Brighten up dull storage shelves by keeping fabric scraps rolled up in glass jars. Sort them into similar colours first.

Bean bags Make bean bags out of rectangular scraps of fabric measuring about 7 × 6in/180 × 150mm. Fold them in half, sew up three sides, turn the bags inside-out and fill them with rice or dried peas. Then sew up the open end.

Jam jar decoration Finish off a gift of homemade jam with a circle of fabric cut to size with a pair of pinking shears. Slip it over the rim of the jar and secure it with an elastic band.

Fabric softener sheets

Shoe shiner Buff shoes to a high gloss with a fabric softener sheet.

Air sweetener Line drawers and cupboard shelves with fresh sheets.

Car freshener Place several sheets under the front seat of your car to mask stale smells.

Screen cleaner Save used sheets of fabric softener to remove dust and static from television and computer screens.

Static cutter To reduce static electricity in your hair, rub a sheet over your hairbrush.

Glasses cleaner Wipe lenses with a fabric softener sheet to clean them and prevent them misting up.

Sewing aid Run your threaded needle through a fabric softener sheet before beginning to sew; it can prevent the cotton from tangling.

Fat

Cleanser If your hands need heavy-duty cleaning, rub them with shortening – such as lard – before using soap.

Bird food Combine melted fat, breadcrumbs and sunflower seeds in a paper cup. When the mixture hardens, peel away the cup and hang the contents from a tree in a string bag.

Feathers

Quill pen You can make your own quill pen out of a large bird feather – goose feathers are the best. Cut the horny, hollow barrel of the feather into the shape of a nib with a sharp knife or pair of nail scissors (see picture), and then cut a small slit in the centre of the nib. Then you just dip the nib into ink to write.

Duster Use a large soft feather to clean the dust off delicate bric-a-brac and paintings.

Instrument cleaner Use a peacock or pheasant feather to clean out the insides of straight-bodied wind instruments, such as recorders, flutes, clarinets and oboes.

Felt

Rug Cover the floor of a playroom with a sturdy layer of felt; it is warm and inexpensive to replace.

Lining Cut a piece of felt to fit the inside of your cutlery drawer – it will soundproof and scratchproof the interior.

Place mat Using an old mat as a pattern, cut a piece of thick felt to the right size and then trim the edges with bias tape of a matching or contrasting colour to go with your tablecloth.

Dish separators Cut pieces of felt the size of your good china with pinking shears and place between the stacked plates for protection.

Film canisters

Toolbox Store small nails, screws, fuses and nuts and bolts inside plastic-capped film canisters.

Paperweight Decorate the outside of a canister with enamel paints and then fill it with sand – an ideal present for your children to make for their relatives.

Dry box On camping and boating trips, film canisters will keep your paper money, matches and pills dry.

Spice storage Similarly, use old canisters for small quantities of salt, pepper, herbs or oil that might be needed on an outing or short camping trip.

Fly deterrent If you don't finish your bottle of wine at one sitting, cover the opening and neck with a film canister. It will keep out fruit flies and other small flying insects.

Pillbox Keep aspirin, pills and vitamins in separate canisters when travelling; label each one clearly with masking tape.

Sewing kit Put two needles, black and white cotton wrapped around a piece of toothpick, a couple of buttons and several safety pins in a canister. Pack it in your suitcase for emergency repairs.

Organiser Put paper clips, rubber bands and safety pins in individual canisters.

Coin holder Keep some small change for telephones, buses, parking meters or the laundrette in your bag.

Jewellery box Store earrings and rings in a canister; put chains in individual canisters to keep them tangle-free.

Swimmer's helper Carry your earplugs to the beach in a film canister. Then make a swap – put your small valuables inside the canister while you have a swim so they'll be protected from moisture and sand.

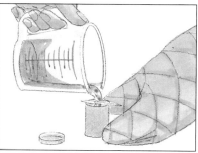

Candle mould Tape a wick to the bottom of the canister and tie it to a toothpick across the top. Pour in hot wax and leave it to harden overnight. To use the candle, remove it from the canister and place in a candle holder.

Stamp saver Keep stamps unstuck and all in one place.

'Dry' ice cubes Partially fill a canister with water. Let it freeze and then cap it tightly. Place several in a pitcher of iced coffee, lemonade or martinis to keep the drink cool without diluting it.

Flowers

Wreath Dry a selection of your garden's prettiest flowers and then wrap clusters of three to five stems together with wire. Attach these to a straw wreath.

Potpourri Dry some scented flowers from your garden, and mix them with a few crushed fragrant leaves, spices and a drop or two of aromatic oil. Leave some out in a decorative bowl, and store the rest in an airtight container.

Salad additions In summer, put the flowers of pansies, nasturtiums and violets in your salads, or carnation leaves.

Cake decorations Dip edible flowers in egg white and then place them in a saucer of caster sugar. Shake the saucer until coated, then leave them to dry on a wire rack. Finally, arrange them decoratively on your cake icing.

Foam rubber

Clothes retainer If your lightweight clothes slip off wooden coat hangers, stick a small patch of foam rubber on each end of the hanger with adhesive.

Soap sponge Sew two 6in/150mm squares of thin foam rubber together, leaving a small slit in the top. Slip slivers of old soap inside the rubber casing to make a bath mitt. You can also cut the foam into a decorative shape, such as an animal or fruit, if you want.

Hair remover Pick animal hairs off upholstered seats by wiping them with a piece of damp foam rubber.

Mat retainer Stick small, flat pieces of foam rubber to the underside of each corner of a rug or mat. It will stop it slipping.

Weeding aid Stuff an old hot water bottle with pieces of foam rubber and use it as a kneeling pad when working in the garden.

Frisbees

Pet dish When you're camping with your dog, a Frisbee works well as a makeshift food or water dish.

Birdbath Punch three holes in a Fris-

bee's edge at equal distances apart and insert wire plant hangers. Then hang the birdbath from a tree.

Biscuit tray Turn a Frisbee upside-down and fill it with biscuits for your child's birthday party.

Furniture polish

Tile saver To prevent water spots and soap scum on shower walls, coat them with furniture polish.

Lubricating oil Use furniture polish to oil a squeaky door if no other lubricant is available.

Garden hoses

Tree protector Slip a section of old hose around the trunk of a very young tree to protect it from support ropes. Or alternatively, pad the ropes themselves with sections of hose.

Blade guard Protect the blades on your lawnmower by cutting an old hose into sections, slitting them open and slipping one over each blade when not in use. This is also a sensible precaution when storing an axe or saw; it will protect the tool's cutting edge and could prevent an accident.

Bucket handle To make carrying a

heavy bucketful more comfortable, slit open a 4in/100mm length of old garden hose and slip it along the length of the bucket handle.

Gloves

Toy antlers Stuff a pair of brown or beige gloves with cotton wool and use them as antlers for Halloween costumes or on Christmas decorations.

Hand insulation Keep an old pair of gloves handy for removing hot light bulbs.

Finger puppets Create faces on glove fingertips by sewing on buttons and wool, or just paint them on. Insert your fingers to work the puppets.

Salvage Cut up a pair of old leather gloves to make elbow patches and knee pads, or to re-cover leather buttons.

Venetian blind cleaner Put on a pair of soft cotton gloves and spray them with furniture polish. Then wipe each slat with one long stroke.

Greaseproof paper

Tracing Fine greaseproof paper is so translucent that it makes ideal tracing paper.

Finger painting There's no need to buy special paper for finger painting – just paint on waxed greaseproof paper. (Make finger paints by mixing dry wallpaper paste with liquid poster paint.)

Shelf paper Line cupboard and kitchen cabinet shelves with a layer of fine greaseproof paper.

Chopping board Dice, mince and chop vegetables on the waxy side of a sheet of greaseproof paper, but make sure you protect the surface underneath first.

Pastry bag Twist the paper into a cone, waxy side inwards, and fill with icing or jam. Fold down the top of the cone and use as you would a fabric piping bag.

Greetings cards

Recipe tag When giving home-baked biscuits or cakes as a present, write the recipe on the back of an old greetings card illustration.

Picture frame Cut a rectangle, oval or circle frame from a piece of card, making the inner section of the frame ¼in/6mm smaller on all sides than your picture. Attach the picture to the back of the frame with masking tape. Make the frame from card of a suitable colour.

Place mat Glue a selection of greetings card pictures onto a 12 × 18in (300 × 450mm) piece of cardboard. Then coat them with several layers of clear acrylic to make the mat heatproof, or cover it with transparent sticky-backed plastic.

Christmas decorations Punch a tiny hole in the top of a decorative card, and insert a length of ribbon which you can use to hang the decoration with. Write a favourite verse on the back of the card.

Hair dryers

Wax remover If candle wax drips onto a table, allow it to harden and then scrape off as much as possible with a spoon or blunt knife blade. Soften the remainder with warm air from a hair dryer, and then lift it off with a paper towel or blotting paper.

Invisible ink revealer After writing a message on a piece of paper with lemon or onion juice, make it invisible by drying it with the hair dryer on Low. Make the writing visible again with a dryer set on High.

Traveller's aid Hang just-washed garments on a towel rack or shower curtain rod and blow-dry.

Bandage remover Ease an adhesive bandage off a wound by blowing warm air onto the plaster.

Trainer dryer If the toes of your trainers never seem to dry, aim the nozzle of a dryer set on Low into each shoe for about 5 minutes.

Duster Blow dust off a high shelf or out from underneath an electrical appliance – such as a stereo or computer – with a dryer.

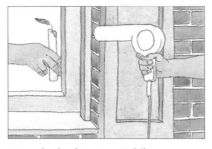

Heat leak detector While someone holds a lit candle just inside a window, go outside with a hair dryer and blow air around the frame; if the flame wavers, the window is leaking heat. Repeat this procedure around every exterior door and window. Draughtproof if necessary.

Barbecue starter Fan the charcoal briquettes in a barbeque with a hair dryer set on Low.

Hairpins

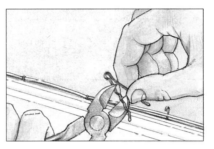

Wire holder Clip the ends off hairpins so they slide easily into cracks; you can then use them to secure speaker or telephone wires to the skirting board or moulding.

Ornament hanger Slip a hairpin through the loop at the top of any fragile Christmas decorations. They'll be easier to hang on the tree.

Apple bobbing Let your guests bob for apples without getting wet. Insert hair-

pins into the tops of a dozen apples, leaving part of each pin exposed. Then thread a string through the hairpin loops and hang the apples from a broomstick suspended between two chairs.

Zip pull Replace a broken zip handle with a hairpin.

Cuff links Insert a hairpin through the cuff-link holes on a shirt to make a temporary cuff link. Secure the cuffs by twisting the pin together.

Bookmark Use a hairpin to mark your place in a book.

Peg When propagating plants by layering, hold their stems down with wire hairpins or pieces of bent wire.

Paper clip Hold several pieces of paper together with a hairpin.

Nail holder Spare your fingers – use a hairpin to grip a nail when hammering in tight spaces.

Invisible tie holder Run the rear apron of your tie through the loop on the back of the front section, then clip it to your shirt with a hairpin to keep it in place.

Hair spray

Caution Do not use hair spray near an open flame.

Artist's fixative Protect a child's pastel and pencil drawings with a coating of hair spray.

Run stopper If you get a run in your tights, spray it immediately to prevent it from spreading further.

Flower extender To make your cut flowers last longer, give them a dash of hair spray. Stand about 1ft/300mm away and direct the spray at the undersides of the leaves and petals.

Needle threader Stiffen a piece of cotton by lying it on a piece of newspaper and spraying it with hair spray.

Hammocks

Utility tarpaulin Cover roof racks or truck loads with an old hammock made of solid canvas. Or use it to gather up autumn leaves.

Storage Tie a hammock up in the basement or loft to hold sleeping bags, out-of-season clothes and other lightweight items.

Garden canopy Make a simple wooden frame to the size you want and then cover the top with a hammock.

Handbags

Needlework carrier Keep your embroidery in an old handbag, but make sure it's clean first. Store needles, cotton or wool, scissors and other supplies in its various compartments.

Clothespeg holder Slip the bag's handle over the line to keep your pegs handy, or attach the handbag to the line with a clothespeg.
Tool carrier Keep a handbag filled with emergency tools in the boot of your car; choose a bag which is light and easy to carry, and wrap the tools in fabric to stop them rattling.

Handkerchiefs

Emergency sun hat Tie knots in all four corners of a large handkerchief or bandanna and use it to shield your head from strong sun.
Smoke mask If you're ever caught in a burning building, tie a handkerchief around your nose and mouth to filter out harmful smoke and gas. It will be more effective if you can dampen it with water first.
Bouquet garni Tie a couple of bay leaves and a few sprigs of parsley and thyme into a small muslin handkerchief and drop it into soup or a stew while cooking. Remove it from the dish before serving.

Hangers

Plant marker Insert a section of straightened wire hanger tagged with the plant's name and the planting date at the end of each row of seedlings.
Green box To convert a window box into a mini greenhouse, bend three or four small pieces of hanger into a U-shape and place the ends in the soil. Punch small holes in a dry-cleaner bag, wrap it around the box, and then place in bright sunlight.
Sealant tube stopper Here's a way to prevent oozing from the tube once a job is done. Cut a 3in/75mm piece of hanger and shape one end into a hook. Insert the other into the tube. Use the hook to pull out the stopper when the sealant is needed again.
Christmas trim Cut lengths of wire from a hanger and bend them into star and angel shapes. Decorate them with spray paint and then hang on the tree.

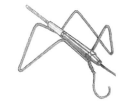

Soldering iron rest Prevent a hot soldering iron from rolling away by placing it in a coat hanger rest as shown.
Croquet hoop Replace a lost hoop in your croquet set with one made out of a coat hanger.
Bubble maker To make extra-big bubbles, shape a length of hanger wire into a hoop with a handle and dip into an extra-strong bubble solution (see p.333). Then wave it through the air.
Wings Use wire coat hangers to make wings for Halloween and Christmas costumes.
Boot dryer To speed the drying of wet boots and other footwear, form two loops in a hanger, and hang it up with the boots, inverted, in the loops.

Plant display Wrap a straightened hanger around a 6-8in/150-200mm pot just below the lip; twist the hanger wire back on itself to secure it, then suspend the plant from a wall or fence.
Arm extender If a utensil has fallen behind the refrigerator or you want to reach a plastic cup or jug on a high shelf, straighten out a coathanger except for the hook at the end, and use it to retrieve the object.

Hatpins

Drawing pins Use striking or unusual hatpins instead of drawing pins on a notice board.
Stick pin File down the point of a decorative antique hatpin and attach it to your lapel.

Ice

Taste remover Give your child an ice cube to suck on before getting him to take a spoonful of unpleasant-tasting medicine. The cold will help to numb his taste buds.
Carpet smoother If there are dents in your carpets which have been left by furniture legs, you can smooth them out with an ice cube. Place it on the indentation and leave it – the moisture will plump up the carpet fibres.
Compress Make a cooling compress for swellings or muscle strain by placing several ice cubes in a plastic bag and then breaking them up with a rolling pin. Leave the bag of ice chips on the sore area for 10 minutes or so, then replace in the freezer. Repeat again after 15 minutes. This treatment will also help to ease a sore back.
Pet cooler During a very hot spell, keep animals such as hamsters or rabbits cool by placing a few ice cubes in their water bowls. Dogs and cats will appreciate it too.

Ice cream scoops

Beach toy Give one to your child for making castles in the sand (or in his sandpit).

Trowel When you are transplanting seedlings, use an ice-cream scoop to make equal-sized planting holes.

Soil scoop To repot a plant with as little mess as possible, use an ice cream scoop to add soil to the container.

Melon scoop Use an ice cream scoop to make extra-large melon balls.

Ice lolly sticks

Stirrer A wooden ice lolly stick is useful for mixing small amounts of paint, putty and glue – just throw it away when you have finished.

Ruler Use a stick as an emergency ruler.

Shim Use wood glue to attach a small section of stick to the bottom corner or leg of a piece of furniture to make it stand level on the floor.

File Glue a piece of fine sandpaper to one end of a stick with wood glue and use it for sanding tricky corners and intricate mouldings.

Index file marker Make a stick slightly longer than the height of an index card. Attach it to the back of the card with strong paper or wood adhesive, and then letter the top of the stick with a marker pen. Repeat for each letter of the alphabet.

Splint In an emergency, carefully put an ice lolly stick along the side of an injured finger. Tape the finger and 'splint' to a neighbouring uninjured finger, or tie the two together with strips of cloth, and keep them elevated to avoid swelling.

Garden marker Mark your vegetable rows by writing the name and date of planting on a stick in indelible ink; then push it into the soil at the end of the row.

Putty trowel Use an ice lolly stick to spread freshly applied putty evenly around window and door frames. Dampen the stick with water first to prevent the putty sticking to it.

Ice scrapers

Paint remover Use an ice scraper to remove paint splatters off acrylic baths or other non-metallic surfaces that would be scratched by a razor blade.

Filling knife The smooth side of an ice scraper is perfect for minor repairs with wood filler.

Freezer cleaner Scrape away the frost without damaging the inside of your freezer.

Wax remover Use an ice scraper to take old wax off the bottom of your skis.

Worktop cleaner Scrape up sticky bits of bread or pastry dough from a worktop or breadboard.

Iron-on fabric bonding

Stickers Show your children how to cut out their own designs from iron-on tape. Then they can iron them onto sweatshirts and trousers.

Camping aid Patch tears in a tent or tarpaulin with iron-on tape.

Identification To mark your child's sports shirt with their position on the soccer or netball team, cut the number out of iron-on tape and then press them into place.

Decoration Make a hatband from tape or adorn T-shirts with cut-out and pressed-on flowers.

T-shirt decoration Cut flowers out of pretty or striking printed fabrics and appliqué them to plain T-shirts.

Jar lids

Reflectors Cover a number of jar lids with reflective paint and press them into the ground in an upright position along paths and driveways. They will help you find your way at night. Short lengths of wood can be attached to the back of the lids with an epoxy resin glue to make the reflectors easier to insert into the ground.

Biscuit cutter Use a deep lid to cut out shallow biscuits. Dip it in flour first, and then press it into the dough.

Food saver To keep the remaining half of an apple or orange fresh for a day or so, place it face down on a paper-lined lid and refrigerate. To save a partially consumed glass of milk, cover it with a large lid and refrigerate.

Coaster Glue felt or cork to the inside of a lid with a general purpose expoxy then rest your cold drink in it.

Candle holder Take a supply of old lids with you when you go camping, and use them to hold candles.

Photo frame Paint a large lid or cover it with a scrap of decorative fabric; glue a photograph cut to fit inside the lid.

Paint palette For quick touch-ups around the house, pour a small quantity of paint into a lid and dip into it with an artist's brush.

Jars

Dressing maker Put all the ingredients for a vinaigrette dressing into a jar, screw the lid on tightly and then shake well. You can keep the jar of dressing in the refrigerator.

Terrarium Place a 1in/25mm layer of pebbles and charcoal chips in a large jar, and then 3in/75mm of sterilised potting compost. Add the plants of your choice. After planting, moisten the compost slightly and place the open terrarium in a bright spot for a day before covering.

Cocktail shaker Use a glass jam jar for mixing daiquiris or margaritas.

Savings jar Punch a slit in the metal lid of a jam jar with an old screwdriver or chisel, and then flatten the rough edges on the underside of the slit with a hammer. Use the jar to collect all your loose change, or decorate a small round jar as a piggy bank for a child to keep pocket money in.

Mitten dryer Pull a wet mitten over the bottom of a small jar, and then stand the open end on a radiator; your gloves or mittens will be dry in a trice.

Workshop storage Nail the lids of several jam or coffee jars to the underside of a workshop shelf. Use the jars to store nails, screws, nuts and bolts.

Boat storage Keep paper money or matches dry on board by storing them in screw-top jars. Nail the lids of the jars to the underside of one of the seats.

Insect collector Punch a few holes in the metal lid of a jam jar and give it to your children to collect caterpillars or ants. Show them how to put some leaves in with the insects so the caterpillars have something to eat.

Glue pot Drill a hole big enough to take the handle of an old paintbrush in the metal lid of a preserving jar. To let the brush hang in the pot, rest the lid on top of the screw-on ring. Wipe off excess glue on the ring.

Jeans

Draught excluder Cut off both legs and then cut each in half lengthwise. Make all four halves into tubes and then stuff them with rags or kapok. Sew up the ends and use the tubes to block out winter draughts.

Shoe bag Cut 18in/460mm off the bottom of one leg. Sew up one end of this piece and hem the other so it can take a drawstring (or simply cut holes to hold a string). Thread a piece of cord around the top with a safety pin and pull tight.

Patches Save pieces of tattered jeans to use as patches on a pair that's still worth saving.

Cushion Cut off one leg, hem the raw edges and then tie one end tightly with decorative cord. Stuff the leg with old tights or some other filler, and then close the other end with a matching piece of cord.

Tripod holder Cut one leg off a pair of jeans and then sew up the bottom and attach a shoulder strap.

Keys

Fishing sinker Don't throw out any old keys you have lying about the house – you can use them as weights for your fishing line.

Curtain weight To ensure that a pair of curtains hang properly, slip a number of old keys into the hem of each one at regular intervals.

Knife holders

Fishing box organiser There's no need to poke around in your tackle box for lures. Using an epoxy resin glue, mount a magnetic strip on the inside of the lid to keep them all together.

Sewing box organiser Attach a magnetic knife holder to the inside of your sewing box with epoxy resin glue. It will hold scissors, loose needles and pins in one place.

Medicine chest neatener Use a magnetic knife holder to keep nail clippers, scissors and tweezers close at hand.

Tool holder Mount one on the wall of your workshop or office and use it to hold scissors, screwdrivers, pliers and other small metal tools.

Ladders

Decorative arch Make a covered archway through a garden path by placing two ladders opposite each other, screwing them to posts that have been fixed firmly into the ground. Place a third ladder across the top, binding it securely to the two upright ladders with a strong cord.

Trellis Or use an old ladder (preferably one with rounded rungs) as a trellis to support climbing plants.

Emergency workmate To make yourself a sturdy sawhorse, just lay an open stepladder on its side.

Utensil holder Tie a thin but sturdy rope around the rungs of a short length of ladder. Screw two metal eyes into the ceiling, using expanded Rawlplugs to ensure a firm fit, and thread the rope through them to hang the ladder from the ceiling. Suspend your pots and pans from the ladder, placing them on hooks attached to the various rungs.

Planting guide To ensure your rows of vegetables are straight, lie a ladder with parallel sides flat on the prepared soil and press it down. Repeat until you have marked enough rows for all the vegetables you wish to plant.

Loading ramp Place a ladder against your front doorstep or the boot of your car and cover it with board.

Painting shelf Make yourself a secure place to stand when painting the tops of walls and doors by laying planks across the rungs of two stepladders placed opposite each other. Adjust the height as required.

Laundry basket

Sledge Use a laundry basket to make spur-of-the-moment toboggan for snow-covered hills.

Carrier Keep spare baskets handy at the top and the bottom of the stairs for transporting odds and ends from one floor to the other.

Toy box Store children's toys in brightly coloured laundry baskets.

Log store A plastic laundry basket is ideal for transporting and storing logs for the fire; it is light, and the holes in the sides allow plenty of ventilation.

Leaves

Autumn collage Encourage your young children to collect a selection of leaves of varying colours, sizes and shapes. Then they can stick them onto sheets of coloured paper using a thick flour and water paste.

Doily When entertaining guests, serve cheeses, hors d'oeuvres or individual pastries on plates covered with clean, shiny leaves.

Place mat Dry and press several leaves and arrange them between two sheets of clear adhesive plastic as a lightweight table mat.

Lemon juice

Fingernail treatment Soak your fingertips for 5 minutes in 8 fl oz / 225 ml warm water and the juice of half a lemon. Gently push back the cuticles on each fingernail and then rub the nail all over with lemon peel.

Hair lightener Comb lemon juice evenly through your hair, and then let it dry in the sun. Repeat the treatment once a day for at least a week.

Bathroom cleanser Rub stained enamel fixtures with a cut lemon. Use a thick paste made of lemon juice and borax on stubborn stains.

Lettuce crisper Soak soggy lettuce in a bowl of cold water to which you've added the juice of half a lemon; refrigerate for 1 hour before serving.

Blemish healer Dab a pimple with lemon juice several times a day.

Pore cleanser In a bowl, combine 2

pints / 1.15 litres boiling water, the juice of ½ lemon and 1-2 tablespoons dried thyme or mint. Place your face about 12 in / 300 mm above the mixture and steam for 15 minutes. Then rinse your face off with very cold water.

Sponge renewer To salvage a soured sponge, saturate it with lemon juice, then rinse it thoroughly.

Fruit preservative Keep sliced apples, bananas, pears, peaches and avocado pears from turning brown by coating the cut surfaces with lemon juice.

Piano cleaner Rub a paste of 2 parts salt and 1 part lemon juice onto dirty piano keys. Then wipe it off with a damp cloth, and buff the keys with a dry one.

Air freshener If fish smells linger in the oven long after you've finished cooking, place a pierced lemon in a Gas Mark 2, 150°C / 300°F oven for 15 minutes, leaving the oven door slightly open.

Hand cleanser Remove a fishy smell on your hands by sprinkling them with powdered mustard and then adding enough lemon juice to make a paste. Rub the paste in well, and then wash it off with soap and water.

Fish freshener Rub fresh fish all over with lemon juice or half a lemon before cooking. The lemon will remove any lingering fish smells as well as adding to the flavour.

Lip balm

Moisturiser Rub a small amount of colourless lip balm onto your face when exposed to very cold weather – such as while skiing, or at sea.

Face saver Dabbing some lip balm onto a shaving nick will help it to stop bleeding.

Zip lubricant Place a small amount on a zip and run it up and down the teeth to ease any sticking.

Styling wax Use lip balm to groom moustaches or eyebrows.

Liquid starch

Threader Dampen the end of a piece of cotton with a little liquid starch before threading your sewing machine. It will hold the cotton straight.

Papier-mâché Blow up a balloon and use it as the base for making papier-mâché masks. Cover it with strips of newspaper soaked in a stiffening agent (see p.408), and then leave it to dry thoroughly overnight.

Magazines

Bench softener Wrap several thick magazines in a heavy-duty plastic bag and use the package as a cushion at football matches.

Funnel Roll a large magazine into a cone, tape it into shape and then use it to funnel dry substances.

Boot trees Roll up a magazine or two and place them inside a pair of damp boots. It will help the boots to keep their shape as they dry.

Magnets

Drawer organiser Place a magnet in your catch-all drawer to keep pins and paper clips together.

Tidying mate Use a magnet to pick up spilled pins, needles, tacks or staples.

Margarine tubs

Paint can Pour paint into an empty margarine tub for small touch-up jobs around the house.

Ice cream containers Use small tubs to freeze individual portions of ice cream.

Mould Make individual jellies to serve at children's tea parties, salads or mousse desserts.

Pet dish Remember to take several lightweight disposable containers with you when you're travelling with your pet to use as feeding bowls.

Baby bowl Store leftover baby food in them. Or use them for feeding the baby away from home – you can even carry the food in them.

Piggy bank Cut a slit in the lid and decorate the sides to make a piggy bank for a child.

Starter pot Poke holes in the bottom of a tub and add potting compost; then sow the seeds as recommended on the packet.

Storage bin Clean and use to store odds and ends in the kitchen, garage, workshop or children's rooms; they're ideal for jigsaw puzzle pieces.

Freezer storage Store leftovers, soups and stock in the freezer in sturdy tubs which are not cracked.

Lunch box aids Keep a supply of tubs for your children's lunchboxes – that way, they don't have to have sandwiches every day. They could even take a salad from time to time.

Mattresses

Trampoline Small children love bouncing on an old mattress, but make sure they take their shoes off first and that there are no sharp objects nearby.

Crash pad Surround a child's climbing frame with thin mattresses to prevent injuries if someone should fall.

Truckle bed Keep an old mattress under the bed. When unexpected guests spend the night, pull it out and make it up – it will be much more comfortable than sleeping on a blanket on the floor.

Door protector If it is a tight squeeze to park in your garage, nail a mattress to the wall to prevent damaging the car door as you open it.

Party accessory Put out an old mattress indoors or in the garden for children to bounce on; they can use it as seating when they eat their tea, too.

Mayonnaise

Ring loosener If you can't shift your ring, smear some mayonnaise onto your finger and then try to slide it off.

Hair and scalp conditioner Apply a good quality mayonnaise to your hair after washing and leave for 30 minutes. Remove with lemon or vinegar solution.

Microwave ovens

Raisin plumper Place 4oz/115g dry raisins in a glass measuring cup with 1 teaspoon of water. Cover the cup with plastic film and microwave on High for 30 seconds; stir, and then leave the raisins to stand for 1 minute before use.

Crisper Freshen soggy crisps, cheese biscuits or rolls by microwaving them on High for 10 to 30 seconds; leave them to stand for 2 minutes before eating.

Hot hand towel Microwave a dampened flannel or napkin wrapped in plastic for 15-30 seconds on High or until it's warm to the touch.

Milk cartons

Paint holder Pour paint into the bottom half of a cut-off carton; just throw it all away when the job is finished.

Weight Weigh down a tarpaulin by attaching milk cartons half-filled with sand or stones to its edges. Punch holes in opposite sides of the cartons; thread through a piece of string and tie to the holes around the tarpaulin's edge.

Candle mould Coat the inside of a clean carton with cooking oil then anchor a candle taper to the centre of the base with melted wax. Fill the carton with hot wax. When the wax cools, peel off the carton to reveal a square candle.

Toe guard When camping, avoid stubbing your toes in the dark by covering tent pegs with cut-off carton tops.

Bird feeder Combine melted fat or suet and birdseed in a saucepan and then pour it into a clean carton. Insert a loop of string into the top of the mixture. Leave it to cool, and then after it hardens, tear away the carton and hang from a branch.

Seed starter Cut the top off a carton, punch holes in the bottom and fill it with potting mix. Then sow your seeds according to the instructions on the back of the packet.

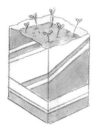

Scrap collector Keep an empty milk carton next to the kitchen sink to hold food scraps. These can then be thrown onto the compost heap.

Vegetable collar Cut off the top and bottom of several cartons and push them into the ground around your tomato and pepper plants; they will discourage grubs and cutworms from attacking the plants.

Mirrors

Handkerchief presser Stick a wet, just-washed cotton handkerchief onto a steamy bathroom mirror; as it dries in place, it will press itself.

Reflector Place mirrors along paths and driveways; they will catch the light from a torch in the dark.

Shelf Mirrors on the bottom and back of your glass-fronted cabinet will make your glassware sparkle and show off both sides of your ornaments.

Tray Use double-sided tape to fix a piece of mirror cut to size to the inside of a plain tray. Smooth the mirror edges first. Or make your own tray by attaching the mirror to a piece of medium density fibreboard.

Compact Use two-sided tape to fit a small rectangular mirror inside the lid of a pastille tin.

Signal mirror Use the sun's rays to send messages in Morse code or the International Distress Signal – six flashes per minute, then pause for a minute. The sos signal is three short flashes, three long flashes, then a further three short flashes.

Basement detective If your basement seems damp, stand a mirror against one wall. Check it the next day; if it's moist or misted over, the problem is condensation; if the mirror is dry but the wall is damp, the problem is seepage.

Flush enhancer Check under the rim of your toilet bowl with a small mirror; if the openings are clogged up, clean them out with a piece of wire coat hanger.

Mothballs

Bin freshener Keep your kitchen rubbish bin fragrant by putting a couple of mothballs between the bin and its plastic liner.

Pest deterrent Place mothballs around any holes or air vents in your outer walls. They will discourage squirrels, rats and other animals from coming into the house. This also works for moles if placed in mole runs.

Plant protector Sprinkle a few crushed mothballs around your flower beds to deter cats from scratching up your plants or new seedlings.

Tarnish inhibitor Place a few mothballs in your silver chest or cutlery drawer to prevent discoloration.

Motor oil

Caution Don't let motor oil touch your skin; it is carcinogenic.

Tool cleaner Add used motor oil to a bucket of sand, then thrust the metal parts of garden tools into the mixture to clean them after use and help keep them rust-free.

Body protector To prevent corrosion on your car from salted roads in winter, brush the underside of your car with used motor oil.

Concrete release agent To prevent concrete sticking to where it is not wanted, brush wooden shuttering with motor oil before pouring in the concrete.

Mousetraps

Wall clamp Fasten a spring trap to your workshop or kitchen wall to hold frequently used but easily misplaced items such as gloves, cloths or recipes.

Bulldog clip If you're short of a large paper clip, a mousetrap makes a good substitute. Keep several on your desk for organising bills, receipts, business cards and other loose papers.

Mugs

Utensil container Keep spoons, spatulas and other kitchen utensils in an attractive mug that has cracked or has lost its handle.

Planter Even if it's chipped, a mug still makes a good kitchen windowsill container for small plants.

Pencil holder Keep one next to the telephone to hold pens or pencils for any messages.

Muslin

Food tents Protect your food from dust and insects at outdoor parties by wrapping a piece of muslin around an old wire umbrella frame. Use it to cover food and plates when not in use. You can remove the handle of an umbrella with a hacksaw.

Paint strainer Remove the skin from an old tin of paint by straining it through a piece of muslin, an old cheesecloth skirt or a clean nylon stocking.

Pressing cloth When ironing delicate fabrics, press them through a damp piece of muslin – it leaves no fluff and won't overwet your clothes.

Minnow catcher Muslin makes a good net for catching small fishing bait.

Digital drape If the light from your digital clock keeps you awake at night, veil it with a piece of muslin – you'll still be able to see the numbers, but they won't be so bright.

Seed protection To protect newly sown grass seed from wind and birds, cover the seeded area with a layer of coarse-mesh muslin and weigh it down at the edges with heavy stones.

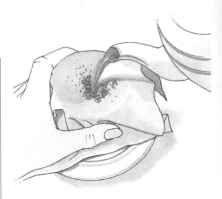

Tea strainer Strain freshly brewed tea into a cup or mug through a piece of muslin.

Jelly strainer Before using muslin to make fruit jams and jellies, scald it in boiling water, rinse it in cold water and then allow it to dry. To use, pour the cooked fruit through three layers of muslin to strain out seeds and skins.

Frost protection Drape muslin over stakes to shield transplants from frost.

Fat remover To skim fat from soups or stews, wrap two or three ice cubes in a piece of muslin and draw them across the surface of the saucepan.

Vacuum attachment Instead of removing the contents of a drawer to dust it, cover the nozzle of your vacuum with muslin so that small objects aren't sucked in but the dirt is removed.

Nail polish

Organiser Label metal storage boxes with a brightly coloured nail polish, printing the name of the contents (nails or screws, for example) on the outside of the tin. If you change the contents, just remove the name with remover.

Decorative paint Touch up Christmas decorations with a drop of nail polish.

Run stopper Dab clear nail polish onto the top of a run in a stocking or pair of tights; it will stop it from growing.

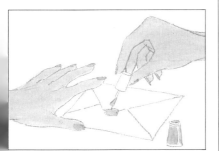

Sealing wax Seal letters with a dab of fingernail polish; it sticks to paper just as well as wax and doesn't need to be melted first.

Measure marker Highlight the liquid measurements on baby bottles or measuring cups by marking them with bright red nail polish.

Brand Paint your initials on the handles of wooden tools with nail polish. Before it dries, hold a lighted match to the polish – it will burn, leaving your brand in the wood. But do this outside.

Sealant Keep a bottle or jar from leaking while you're travelling; apply a light coat of nail polish around the base of the cap to seal it.

Shell varnish Retain the shiny sparkle of seaside shells and stones by painting them with clear varnish once they dry.

Nails

Post strengthener If you are setting a tall, wooden fence post in concrete, you will get a more solid result if you hammer a few long or bent nails half-way into its base. Then set it in place and pour the concrete around it.

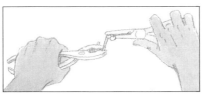

S-hook Hold a thin nail with one pair of pliers and then bend it into an S-shape with another. With a larger nail, clamp it in a vice and hammer it into an S-shape.

Nappies

Bed protector Sew several towelling nappies together to form a thick, absorbent mattress pad. It's useful if your child is still wetting the bed.

Compress Use a towelling nappy as a hot compress for aching muscles, or as a cold compress for bruises and strains.

Cover Wrap a hot-water bottle in a towelling nappy to protect your skin.

Car waxer Use a washable nappy to apply and buff wax and polish.

Drip catcher If your roof has sprung a leak, put disposable nappies under the hole to catch the drips; they're an absorbent, quieter alternative to saucepans. Or place the nappy in a baking tray; it will absorb the sound while the tin holds any excess water.

Newspapers

Fire lighters Lie two or three sheets of newspaper together, form them into a tight roll and then tie them into a simple knot. Half a dozen of these will start even the stubbornest of logs.

Duster For reaching those hard-to-dust places, or as a substitute feather duster, roll a sheet of newspaper into a tube and fringe one end with a pair of scissors.

Cleaner Use crumpled-up balls of newspaper to remove heavy grease from the inside of an oven, or a frying pan, before wiping with a damp cloth.

Glass cleaner After washing windows or mirrors with soap and water, crumple up a sheet of newspaper and wipe the glass dry; it will leave it sparkling and streak-free.

Cat litter If you've run out of cat litter granules, shred a newspaper and use it to fill the cat tray.

Draught blocker Keep out the cold in winter by stuffing newspapers under doors and in window cracks; they will help stop the draughts.

Boot dryer Stuff crumpled newspaper into wet boots or shoes to absorb any moisture. Leave it overnight.

Moplets Keep a supply of newspapers in your workshop for cleaning up grease or sopping up paint remover. Pile them into a stack and then cut them into quarters with a sharp knife. Drill a hole in one corner of the wad of squares with an electric drill, run a wire through the hole, and hang them from a hook.

Odour eater Stuff wads of newspaper into shoes or boots overnight to remove unpleasant foot smells.

Plastic container freshener A piece of crumpled black and white printed newspaper placed in an airtight plastic container overnight will remove most lingering smells.

Luggage airer If your trunks and suitcases haven't been used in a while, place several crumpled newspapers inside them and leave for a couple of weeks before packing.

Tablecloth For messy meals, set the table with newspapers.

Draught remover Spread several layers of newspaper under rugs and carpets to cut out draughts and save on wear.

Trench liner Spread papers out flat, or tear them into strips, and place in the bottom of a trench for potatoes or beans. Water thoroughly to hold in place.

Nylon thread

Necklace cord Restring beads or pearls without a needle.

Heavy-duty thread Sew or repair dog leads, straps on rucksacks, outdoor deckchairs or window screens with nylon thread. (Don't use it on anything that needs ironing – it may melt.)

Invisible trellis Attach strong nylon thread to the outside garage walls and to pegs set in the ground and then train your climbing plants up the string.

Picture wire Use it to hang pictures, wind chimes, mobiles and Christmas decorations; the thread is almost invisible at a distance.

Olive oil

Chamois softener To renew an old piece of chamois leather, soak it for 15 minutes in a bucket of warm water to which you've added 1 teaspoon olive oil. It is important to stir the water every few minutes.

Eye make-up remover Moisten a

cotton-wool ball with olive oil, dab it onto the eye area, and then remove any excess oil with a tissue. Wash your face to remove the smell of the oil.

Leather treatment Rub olive oil into dry leather bags, shoes or upholstery with a soft, clean cloth; it will make old leather more supple. Then wipe off the excess with a tissue.

Paint remover If you get paint in your hair, dip a piece of cotton wool in olive oil and draw it gently over the unwanted spot until it has gone.

Hand softener To give your hands a treat, immerse them in a bowl of warm olive oil for about 10 minutes, then wipe off the excess with tissues. It will help your fingernails to counter dryness and brittleness.

White ring remover Remove ring stains from wooden furniture (but not valuable pieces) by rubbing a paste of equal parts olive oil and salt gently over the mark with your finger. Wipe it off with a dry cloth after 2 hours. Rewax if necessary.

Overflow inhibitor Before boiling a saucepan of water for cooking pasta, add a little olive oil.

Dry hair repair Heat enough oil in a cup over hot water, and then apply it liberally to your hair. Cover with a plastic bath cap, wrap in a hot towel and leave for 30 to 40 minutes. Then shampoo as normal and rinse thoroughly.

Onions

Eyewash If there is a speck of dust or small insect in your eye that you just can't get rid of, chop up an onion and let your tears wash it out. See also EYE PROBLEMS, p.75.

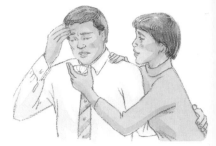

Smelling salts Hold a cut onion under the nose of a person who is feeling faint.

Smell remover Eliminate the smell of paint from inside a cupboard or kitchen cabinet by leaving a sliced onion inside it for several hours.

Dye Boil red onion skins in water to make red dye, yellow skins for yellow.

Knife renewer Plunge a rusty knife into an onion two or three times; it will clean off the discoloration.

Windscreen de-mister Rub a cut onion on the inside of your windscreen to prevent it from misting up on a chilly morning.

Athlete's foot soother To relieve the itch that often comes with athlete's foot rub onion juice on the affected area.

Wart remover Rub a stubborn wart with a raw onion dipped in salt; repeat until the wart disappears. See also WARTS AND MOLES, p.225.

Oven gloves

Waxing cloth Use one side of the glove for applying wax, the other for buffing.

Egg warmer Keep boiled eggs warm for half an hour underneath an oven glove.

Drink cover If you're called away to the telephone or front door, cover your mug of tea, coffee or soup with an oven glove to keep it warm until you return.

Bulb changer There's no need to wait for the bulb to cool down when replacing a burned-out light bulb – protect your hand with an oven glove.

Paddling pools

Crumb catcher To prevent spills on the carpet, let small children sit in an empty paddling pool while watching television and eating snacks. It's a good idea for a children's tea party, too.

Storage bin Put toys, craft items and out-of-season clothing in a plastic paddling pool and slide it under a bed.

Cooler Chill drinks for an outdoor party in a paddling pool half-filled with water and lumps of ice.

Paintbrushes

Pastry brush Keep a clean, small paintbrush in the kitchen and use it to brush pie crusts with milk or egg white for a shiny golden finish. But make sure the brush is used only in the kitchen.

Baster Use a similar brush to brush a marinade or meat juices over a chicken or meat when roasting.

Puppet Paint the base and handle of a paintbrush, and then draw a face just below the bristles, or hairline; glue on a bow tie for men and a collar or necklace for women.

Toaster cleaner Disconnect your toaster at the mains and then use a fine paintbrush to get to the more inaccessible parts of your toaster.

Paper bags

Apple saver Protect ripening apples from insects or birds by placing a paper bag over each one until they are ready to pick.

Fish cooker Prevent fish from drying out in the oven – bake it in a tin which is then covered with an oiled bag.

Brown paper If you want to send a small parcel through the post, cut up an old grocery bag and use that as wrapping.

Paper clips

Decoration hanger Bend a paper clip into an S-shape and carefully hook one looped end through the opening of a decorative Christmas glass ball; hang the other loop over a branch of the tree.

Money clip Fold your £5, £10 and £20 notes in half and then hold them together with a large-size paper clip.

Tack holder Avoid banging your fingers when hammering in tacks. Wedge them between the two parts of a paper clip.

Watch setter Use the tip of a straightened paper clip to press the tiny time-setting controls on your digital watch.

Bra-strap repair If the adjustable buckle on your bra strap breaks, use a paper clip as a temporary measure.

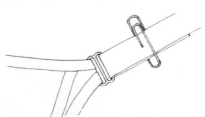

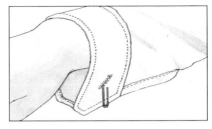

Emergency cuff links Partially straighten a paper clip and insert a looped end into each of the two cuff holes; then reshape the paper clip.

Bookmark Use a paper clip to hold together three or four pages of your book at the spot which you last reached.

Soap bubble frame Shape a large paper clip into an S-shape, and then pinch the larger loop to make a closed circle with needle-nose pliers.

Collar stiffener If you lose a stiffener, replace it with a paper clip; it will keep the tip of your shirt collar neatly in place. But make sure you remove it before the next wash.

Unclogger Clear the clogged holes of a shower head, a salt cellar or an aerosol nozzle with the tip of an opened paper clip.

Packet clip Keep bags of cereal, crisps and other snacks fresh by closing them with a large paper clip.

Coin retriever Reach coins that have fallen between the windscreen and dashboard with a large paper clip reshaped into a hook.

Pipe cleaner Straighten a large paper clip, cover it with a strip of tissue or paper towel and run it through the length of the pipe stem.

Paper cups

Ice mould Freeze water in cups, then peel the paper off as required.

Funnel Poke a hole in the bottom of a paper cup close to the sides and use as required. To make an oil funnel for your car, cut off the bottom of a paper cup, squash the sides until they fit into your car's oil filler and then pour oil into the top of the cup.

Pouring cup Squash the rim of a cup enough to create a spout but without cracking or tearing it.

Wind vane Remove the bottom of a sturdy paper cup and then suspend it from a piece of string attached to the centre of one side. The wide end will usually turn to face the wind.

Freezer container Use small cups as containers for individual portions of ice cream. Or freeze puréed baby food or meat stock in them.

Paint holders Mix up powder paints in individual cups and put a paintbrush in each one – that way small children won't mix the colours together.

Paper towels

Corn cleaner Husk an ear of corn, then wipe it down from tip to base with a dampened paper towel – the silky threads will come off in a single stroke.

Tea strainer If your tea bag breaks in the cup, carefully pour the tea through two layers of paper towel into another cup – the towel will act as a filter, catching the tea leaves.

Wax remover Place a paper towel over melted wax on the carpet, then press an iron on a low setting onto it – the wax will melt and be absorbed by the towel.

Oil saver When you have finished deep frying, allow the oil to cool and then pour it through a paper towel into a container. Then it can be used again.

Coffee filter Strong paper towel can be used as an emergency filter if you run out of coffee filters.

Pastille and sweet tins

Sewing box organiser Save all small tins to store sewing equipment such as hooks and eyes, poppers, sequins, buttons and beads. Label the lids clearly, or stick a sample of the contents onto the top for easy identification.

Stamp tidier If you are always searching around for a stamp, make life easier for yourself by keeping them in an old pastille tin on your desk or in a kitchen drawer.

Emergency sewing kit Keep a tin fitted out with a needle and thread, fold-away scissors, thimble and a button or two for on-the-spot repairs. It's small enough to fit into a handbag or pocket.

Small presents Save any tins for your children to decorate as Christmas presents for their relatives and friends. They can line the inside with felt or silk, and decorate the outside with enamel paints, scraps of fabric, stickers and stars or coloured paper.

Workshop storage Use larger tins for workshop and tool cupboard items such as screws, fuses, Rawlplugs and washers.

Broken-jewellery box Keep all the little pieces of a broken necklace safe and together in a tin.

Earring keeper Prevent pairs of small earrings from straying; store them together in tins.

Practising aid Help children to practise their scales on a musical instrument by writing all the scales down on strips of paper. Encourage them to pick 3 or 4 out of the tin to practise every day.

Mini safe Hide the keys to desks and doors in an innocent-looking tin in your first aid box.

Car fuse cache Make sure you always know where your spare car fuses are. Store a supply of them in an empty tin in the glove compartment of your car.

Pencils

Play logs Slice the rubber and tapered ends off a bundle of old pencils. Glue them together to build a miniature log cabin; cut up a foil freezer tray to make a tin roof.

Plant stake To keep a small plant upright, insert a pencil into the soil next to it and loosely tie them together.

Moth repellent Many pencils are made of fragrant cedarwood. Put the shavings from a pencil sharpener in lightweight bags to make sachets for your cupboards, wardrobes and chests of drawers.

Petroleum jelly

Cuticle softener Massage petroleum jelly into the cuticles of your fingertips every morning and night.

Body insulator If you don't want to wear bulky clothes while exercising out of doors, cover your exposed skin with petroleum jelly; it will keep you warm.

Easy wheeler To ease rolling and eliminate squeaking, lubricate the axles of trolleys, skateboards and roller-skate wheels with a layer of petroleum jelly.

Rust preventer Protect the metal parts of tools, fishing rods, cooking utensils, skates and skis by coating them with petroleum jelly.

Nail polish saver If the top of your nail polish tends to stick to the jar, smear the inside of the lid with a thin layer of petroleum jelly.

Thread easer If you find it hard to unscrew the U-bend under your sink, cover the thread with a thin film of petroleum jelly before you replace it. It will be much easier next time.

Santa brows Apply a light coat of jelly to your eyebrows, then dust with cornflour or ordinary flour as part of your Father Christmas disguise.

Glider If your windows are hard to open, apply a small dab of jelly to the tracks. It also works on a drawer that sticks.

Ring remover Get a tight ring off your finger by smearing the skin around it with petroleum jelly.

Photographs

Paperweight Make a cube out of a milk carton and fill it with sand. Decorate it by sticking photographs onto each side with a general purpose glue and then protect and seal them by spraying with varnish.

Wall hanging Mount an assortment of various-size prints on a clean window blind with a latex adhesive.

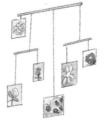

Mobile Using a contact adhesive, glue 12 photographs back to back onto 6 pieces of cardboard, and then darken the edges of each decorated card with a felt-tip marker. Thread a piece of nylon thread through the centre of the top edge of each one, and suspend them from either end of three pieces of wire coathanger.

Headboard Enlarge a favourite photograph and mount it on a semicircle of ¾ in/19mm plywood the same width as the bed (see p.103) with a solvent-based adhesive.

Piggy banks

Paperweight A piggy bank full of pennies will keep any number of papers from flying away.

Doorstop A coin-filled metal piggy bank in front of a door will prevent it from blowing shut.

String dispenser Place a small ball of string inside a piggy bank and slip the end of the string through the slot.

Pillowcases

Sheets Use standard-size pillowcases as sheets for a baby's carry cot.

Defroster Cover short tomato plants with a pillowcase made of light cotton whenever frost threatens.

Sweater saver To prevent the wool balling up when washing sweaters, put them inside a pillowcase and tie the top

with string before placing in the machine. (This also works well when machine-washing lingerie.)

Strainer When making jelly, separate the fruit juices from the seeds and pulp by pouring through an old pillowcase which can be stained. Be sure to scald the case in boiling water first, though, then leave to dry before use.

Pipe cleaners

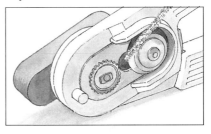

Mini scrubber Remove the dirt from the wheel of a tin opener or clean the bobbin area of a sewing machine with a pipe cleaner.

Gift decorator Shape into a bow or a heart or whatever is appropriate, poke one end through a hole in the name tag, and fix it to the package with transparent tape or a dab of general purpose glue.

Twist tie Use a pipe cleaner to seal the top of a rubbish bag.

Unclogger Open up and clear the vents in steam irons with a pipe cleaner.

Napkin ring Shape them into circles, squares or hearts and use to keep your napkins tidy.

Plant tie Secure small plants to stakes or climbers to trellises or other supports.

Pipe men Provide your children with a selection of pipe cleaners on a rainy afternoon and show them how to fashion a family of people.

Stitch holder Use a pipe cleaner to hold stitches when you are knitting. They are easy to pick up later.

Plastic bags

Paintbrush protector If you're interrupted while painting, prevent the brush from drying out by slipping it into a plastic bag and wrapping it tightly.

Liner Tape pieces of plastic bag into the bottom of wicker picnic baskets to prevent the wicker being spoiled if something spills.

Piping bag Fill a small but sturdy plastic bag with icing or whipped cream, then snip a tiny hole in one corner and squeeze, holding the top tightly together.

Meat seasoner Coat meat in flour before casseroling by tossing the two together in a plastic bag.

Packing aid Instead of folding delicate items over tissue paper when packing, use plastic bags – they are cheaper and your clothes will crease less.

Biscuit crusher If you are making a biscuit base for a dessert, place the biscuits in a plastic bag and then crush them with a rolling pin.

Plant ties Cut a plastic bag into 1in/25mm strips and use them to secure climbing plants to a pole or trellis.

Filler Or use plastic bag strips to stuff outdoor cushions, bathtub toys and other items likely to get wet.

Plastic containers

Clothespeg holder Cut off the top of a large plastic container with a handle, punch holes in the bottom to let out the rainwater, and then hang the peg holder from the clothes line by its handle.

Weight Fill 1 gallon/4.5 litre containers three-quarters full of water and attach them to the reinforced holes around the edge of a tarpaulin or pool cover to hold it down on windy days.

Scoop Cut diagonally across the bottom of a plastic container (from the base of the handle to the bottom of the opposite edge) and use it to scoop up dog food, sand, fertiliser or potting compost.

Hip bucket Keep your hands free for picking fruit. Cut the top off a large container and string your belt through the handle.

Boat bailer Cut off the bottom half of a large plastic water bottle at an angle. Don't forget to keep the cap on so that the water doesn't run straight through.

Funnel Cut a bottle in half; remove the cap and turn upside-down to use as an emergency funnel for motor oil, antifreeze or just about anything.

Buoy Tightly close the caps of several containers and string them together to define swimming and boating areas.

Toss-and-catch game Cut a plastic water container as shown. Using a tennis ball, you can play toss and catch on your own or with a group of friends with their own containers.

Plastic lids

Sink stopper Place a plastic lid, its rim facing down, over the outlet hole if you're short of a plug.

Scraper Cut a lid in half and use the straight edge to scrape batter from bowls or leftovers from plates.

Lens cap Keep your eyes open for plastic lids that are just the right size to fit snugly over camera, binocular or telescope lenses.

Water tray Place large plastic lids under your houseplants to protect the furniture from water leakage.

Frisbee Toss a large lid with a flip of the wrist (see FRISBEES, p.304).

Hand shield To keep paint from dripping onto your hand, slit an X in the centre of a lid and push the paintbrush handle through it.

Hair clip To keep your hair out of your face while cooking or cleaning, cut a large X in the centre of a plastic lid and poke your hair through it in a pony tail.

Dust catcher When making holes in plasterboard or plaster ceilings, drill through a plastic lid. The lid won't catch all the dust but it will protect your eyes and minimise the mess.

Coaster Protect table surfaces on hot, humid days by placing plastic lids under icy drinks.

Stencil Cut numbers, letters or shapes into thin plastic lids; your children can then draw around them.

Drawer organiser Store small nails, screws and other supplies in the tops of aerosol cans; attach them with contact cement to a piece of hardboard cut to fit your workshop drawers.

Pastry cutter In an emergency use the cleaned lid from an aerosol can for cutting out biscuit rounds or scones from dough rolled out to a thickness of approximately ½in/13mm.

Plastic tablecloths

Travelling games board Take a tablecloth with large checks with you on long journeys or picnics – it can double up as a draughts or chess board.

Shower curtain Punch a series of holes 6in/150mm apart and ½in/13mm from one edge of a hemmed tablecloth. Insert shower curtain rings or loop strings through the holes and loosely tie to the curtain rod.

Floor cover Spread a plastic tablecloth underneath a baby's high chair to save on floor cleaning.

Leaf collector Rake autumn leaves onto an old plastic tablecloth, then grab the corners and tie them firmly together. You'll then be able to dispose of the leaves easily.

Window blind Remove the rollers and slats from an old blind. Cut a tablecloth to the size of the blind; hem one end of the cloth to hold the slat and glue or staple the other end to the roller.

Drop cloth Use plastic tablecloths to protect rugs and floors when doing touch-up paint jobs or messy chores such as cleaning a chandelier.

Party table Spread a large tablecloth on the floor for children's birthday parties; get the guests to sit on the floor with the food in the centre.

Plastic trays

Plate Save the plastic foam trays from packages of meat and other foods to clean and reuse as plates when camping.

Plant saucer Place trays under houseplants to catch any excess water.

Palette Use plastic foam trays for mixing small amounts of paint.

Padding Slip foam trays between plates or around other breakables when packing your china in tea chests.

Plastic film

Book cover Protect the dust jacket of a book with a layer of plastic film.

Seal Place a scrap of plastic film between the neck and screw top of a bottle; it will keep the fizz in a bottle of soft drink.

Window repair As a temporary measure, tape plastic film over a small hole to keep out the wind and rain.

Paint saver To prevent a skin from forming in an old tin of paint, place a layer of plastic film over the paint's surface before tapping its lid back in place.

Screw setter To hold a screw in position, push its threads through a piece of plastic wrap. Then fit the screwdriver into the slot in the head and pull the plastic film back over the blade of the screwdriver.

Draught remover Keep warm in winter by making your own 'double glazing' with plastic wrap. Stick it to the window frame with double sided tape, then heat it with a hairdryer until all the wrinkles disappear.

Map preserver Cover a map with a piece of plastic wrap; then you'll be able to mark your route on it in felt tip pen without harming the map itself.

Conditioning aid When colouring or treating your hair with henna or another type of conditioner, cover your wet hair with plastic wrap. It will keep the conditioner warm and moist, and will protect the towel you are using.

Invisible tablecloth Protect wooden table tops from liquid spillage with plastic wrap before covering it with a tablecloth.

Plungers

Chip catcher When using a drill or chisel overhead, catch falling chunks of plaster, cement or brick by placing a plunger cup over the shank. Cut a hole in the rubber which is small enough to make a tight, slip-proof fit over the drill handle.

Dent remover Try pulling out a shallow dent in a car door, boot or bonnet by pushing a wet plunger over the dent and pulling out sharply.

Outdoor candle holder Insert the plunger's handle into the ground and fix an aromatic candle into the cup with melted wax.

Potatoes

Shoe restorer If your badly scuffed shoes won't take polish, rub them first with a raw potato.

Stain remover Rub away vegetable stains from your hands with a slice of raw potato.

Potato stamp Keep your children happy on a wet afternoon by making potato stamps with them. Cut a potato in half, then carve out relief designs on the flat sides. Dip the design into a plateful of paint and print on plain paper. Older children can make their own stamps.

Itch reliever Rub a thin slice of salted raw potato onto an allergic reaction or insect bites.

Blackhead remover Put warm mashed potatoes inside a muslin pouch and apply to a stubborn blackhead several times a day; it should soften it, making it easier to remove.

Hair darkener Dip a comb into potato water (in which potatoes have been boiled) and run it several times through blonde or brown hair. To speed up the darkening and help set the colour, dry your hair in the sun.

Pots and pans

Oil catcher Save a large discarded saucepan to place underneath the drain plug when you change your car's oil.

Caddy Leave heavy sacks of fertiliser or grass seed in the garden shed and use a pot to carry what you need to the place you're tending.

Birdbath Set an old frying pan on top of a flower pot in the garden and keep it filled with water.

Barbecue Build your charcoal fire in a large discarded pot and cook on a wire cake rack placed over it. After you're finished, cover the pot with its lid to put out the fire and save the charcoal for another barbecue.

Scoop A light saucepan with a handle works well as a boat bailer, dog food dipper or compost shovel.

Preserving jar rings

Bath mat Lash a number of rubber jar rings together with strong nylon thread so that they lie flat, making a non-slip bath mat.

Skid guard Sew one or more rubber rings to each corner of a loose rug; it will prevent it from slipping around on a polished floor.

Quoits For a rainy-day indoor game, small children can try to toss rubber jar rings over an upright post (perhaps the leg of an upside-down stool). Smaller children should stand closer to the post.

Table protectors Place rubber jar rings under lamps, vases, ornaments and other household objects to protect the surface of furniture from marks and scratches.

Punnets

Bulb cage Foil hungry rabbits by setting planting bulbs inside a plastic punnet covered with soil.

Sweet bowls Weave colourful ribbons through the sides of a plastic punnet to make a decorative container. Use it to hold a selection of sweets at a party.

Easter basket Make a handle for the Easter basket out of a pipe cleaner, and fill it with shredded paper 'grass' and small, foil-wrapped chocolate Easter eggs.

Bread basket Cover the inside of a fruit punnet with foil or a napkin and use it to serve bread or rolls in when you have guests.

Bow saver When sending a beautifully wrapped present through the post, protect the bow with an inverted basket taped in place.

Colander Drain pasta or wash fruits and vegetables under cold running water in a plastic punnet.

String dispenser Place twine inside two baskets, tie them together, and then pull the end of the twine through a hole.

Frog Turn a basket upside-down and place it in the bottom of a vase; it will hold flower stems in place as you arrange them.

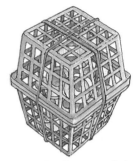

Dishwasher basket Put baby bottle caps and teats into a plastic punnet, and secure another on top with rubber bands. Place the basket in the upper rack of the dishwasher.

Portable cage Line two punnets with brown paper, tape them together and use to carry small pets (mice, toads or gerbils, for example) to school.

Mobile Suspend a colourful punnet upside-down over an infant's crib and tie bells, scraps of ribbon or fabric to it – but make sure it is out of reach.

Quoits

Furniture bumper Before you begin to vacuum, put these flat plastic or wooden rings around furniture legs to protect them.

Coaster Cut a piece of cork to glue inside a quoit. Use it to protect table tops and side tables from ring marks.

Razor blades

Scraper Remove paint or stickers from windows with a single-edge blade set in a holder, or a double-edge blade gripped in a bulldog clip.

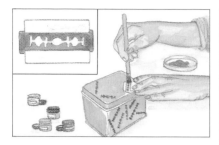

Stencil Use the design of the cut-out in a double-edge blade to decorate small boxes or plaques. Tape the edges of the blade for safety's sake and apply the pattern with a felt-tip marker or a stiff-bristled brush, using a small amount of paint or ink. This is not a suitable stencil for children to use.

Refrigerators

Dryer Suspend an old refrigerator rack from the garage ceiling with a rope and use it to hang laundry out to dry.

Tool chest Remove the door of an old refrigerator and store tools and other workshop equipment inside it.

Rubber bands

Table stabiliser Create a large table by fastening two or more card tables together with sturdy rubber bands around adjacent legs.

Clamp When gluing something small, hold the parts together with a rubber band.

Gripper Stretch rubber bands around doorknobs, jar lids or tools in order to give yourself a better grip.

Roll guard Wrap one or more rubber bands around a flashlight or screwdriver handle to prevent it from rolling off a flat or sloping surface.

Toilet roll saver Wrap an elastic band around the holder for your toilet paper. It will stop the toilet roll spinning round too quickly.

Rubber gloves

Hand warmer When doing wet work on cold days, put an old pair of rubber gloves over your garden gloves; they will keep your hands dry and warm.

Jar grip Put on dry rubber gloves, hold the container in one hand, and twist the stubborn lid anticlockwise with the other.

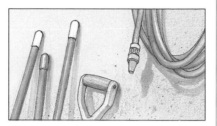

Broom stabiliser Slip a finger from an old glove over the end of a broom so that it won't fall down when propped against a wall.

Pliers guard To prevent ugly marks and scrapes, cover the jaws of a pair of pliers with fingers from a ripped glove.

Piping bag Tie off all but one finger of an unused, unlined rubber glove; fill it with icing, snip the tip to make a small hole, and squeeze.

Ice pack Fill a rubber glove with crushed ice cubes, and then tie up the wrist. Place on muscle strains for 10 minutes at a time.

Rubbers

Page turner Use the rubber end of a pencil for turning the pages of catalogues or telephone directories.

Table stabiliser Cut a thick slice of rubber to the same size as the bottom of your table legs; attach the rubber with a contact adhesive or countersunk nails.

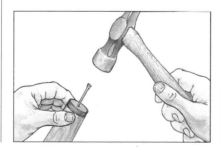

Diviner Insert a pencil rubber into a houseplant's soil; if it comes out dry, get out your watering can.

Calculator punch The rubber end of a pencil is ideal for pushing the small buttons of a pocket calculator.

Key cleaner Remove finger marks from piano keys with a rubber; choose a size that fits easily between the black keys and gets into all the corners. For extra-tough spots, wrap it in a cloth soaked in cleaning fluid.

Wall saver Glue two rubbers to the bottom edge of a picture frame at the back; the frame will hang straighter, and it won't mark the wall.

Rug fixer Glue thin slices of a rubber to the underside of a mat or rug to keep it from slipping. Put a piece in each corner.

Household cleaner Rub scuff marks from floors and fingerprints from woodwork with a rubber or gum eraser.

Blade protector Protect your craft knife – and yourself – by storing the tip in a rubber when not in use.

Rubber stamp Draw a design on the flat side of a soft rubber, outline it with the tip of a craft knife to a depth of about ¼ in/6mm and then carve away the waste, leaving the design.

Golf ball cleaner On your next golf outing, take a rubber with you to clean the ball at holes where there's no bucket.

Pincushion Keep safety pins from drifting to the bottom of the dresser drawer; stick the points into a rubber.

Upholstery cleaner Rub lightly soiled cotton upholstery with a gum eraser.

Bit cushion Store small drill bits, point first, in a large rubber.

Rubbish bags

Disposable apron Cut holes in a rubbish bag for your head and arms and wear it to protect your clothes while doing grubby chores. When you've finished, throw it away.

Weed killer You can get rid of the weeds in a flower bed you want to dig over by covering them with several black plastic bags.

Strawberry protector Keep your strawberries off the damp ground by surrounding each of your strawberry plants with an opened-out rubbish bag.

Windscreen de-icer Before leaving the car on an icy day, cut open a heavy-duty rubbish bag and place it over the windscreen underneath the wipers. Trap the bag's edges in the car doors.

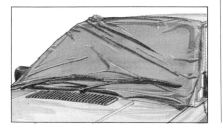

Barbecue cover When it's not in use, protect your outdoor grill with a large plastic rubbish bag.

Summer storage Add a few mothballs to a bag filled with your winter woollens; squeeze out the excess air and seal with a twist tie.

Clothing protector In case of an emergency on the road, keep several large rubbish bags in the boot. Spread them out on the ground and stay clean if you have to work under the car.

Ground sheet When camping, place your sleeping bag on several large rubbish bags to prevent moisture from seeping in.

Safety pins

Stitch counter When knitting, use a safety pin to mark or hold stitches.

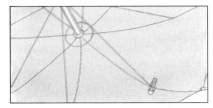

Rivet If a rivet connecting a rib and stretcher on your umbrella has broken, remove the stub with a pair of pliers or wire cutters and substitute a safety pin.

Missing link Use a small safety pin as a temporary replacement for a broken clasp, a link on a necklace or a mislaid cufflink.

Salt

Stain remover Combined with lemon juice, salt will remove fruit stains from your hands.

Flower cleaner Clean artificial flowers by shaking them in a large paper bag with 8oz/225g fine table salt.

Spill container Cover fresh oven spills with salt, leave it for 15 to 20 minutes and then wipe it up. (Follow the same procedure when you drop grease or a raw egg on the floor.) Never put salt on a carpet stain, however.

Ice defroster Sprinkle your paths and steps with salt if there's a chance of snow; it will stop a layer of ice forming.

Scarves

Belt Liven up a plain-coloured dress or make an old outfit look like new by twisting a scarf of a contrasting colour around your waist.

Sarong Wrap a large scarf under your arms, at your waist or low on your hips; pull the fabric taut, then knot the top ends where you want the opening to fall.

Sling You can support an injured arm, or an arm where the shoulder, collar bone or chest is injured, with a scarf that is about 3ft/1m square, folded in half diagonally at the neck.

Bandage Make an instant bandage with a 3ft/1m square scarf. Fold the scarf in half diagonally, and then fold twice more in on itself. The emergency bandage can be used to secure dressings on wounds and tying injured limbs together.

Bag sling If your shopping bag starts to give way, take off your scarf and loop it under the bottom of the bag to stop it splitting open.

Choker Fold a 24in/610mm scarf in thirds on the bias and knot several times around your throat.

Shawl If you're going to the seaside, wrap a scarf around your shoulders; use it as a cover-up when travelling or on the beach.

Sealant

Gasket If the seal is torn on your refrigerator or dishwasher, repair it with silicone rubber sealant.

Shoe gum Temporarily fill a hole in your sole with a dab of sealant; let it dry thoroughly before walking on it.

Seeds

Artwork 'Paint' a design on heavy paper with white glue, then drop seeds onto the glue and let them dry. Use different types of seeds for colour and texture.

Jewellery String large fresh seeds onto nylon thread with a heavy-duty needle. Then leave them to dry.

Snack Coat fresh sunflower, melon or pumpkin seeds with oil, spread them in a shallow pan, season them, and bake in a Gas Mark ½, 120°C/250°F oven for an hour, or until they're dry.

Shampoo

Shaving cream If you're out of shaving foam, apply a small amount of shampoo to your wet skin and work up a lather.

Detergent If you've run out of a gentle soap for hand-washables, use your shampoo instead.

Shaving cream

Lubricant Spray both sides of the joint of a squeaky door hinge with some foamy shaving cream. Then wipe off any excess.

Upholstery cleaner Rub a fresh stain on upholstered furniture with a small amount of shaving cream, wipe with a damp cloth, then dry. (Test first in an inconspicuous corner.)

De-mister To prevent your bathroom mirror from misting up during cold weather, spread a little shaving cream over it, and then wipe the mirror clean with a tissue.

Sheet music

Lampshade Attach sheet music to a lampshade frame, then brush it with linseed oil or varnish and leave to dry thoroughly before turning on the light. (Be sure to use a low-wattage bulb.)

Wrapping paper Wrap a music lover's birthday gift in sheet music.

Wallpaper Paper a small room with sheet music, using mildew-resistant wallpaper paste.

Book cover If you've lost the jacket to a book, cover it with sheet music.

Sheets

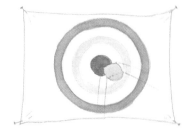

Bull's-eye Hang an old sheet on the wall and draw a target on it; let young children try to score bull's-eyes by throwing beanbags at it.

Tablecloth Convert a patterned sheet into an attractive table covering.

Leaf scoop Rake leaves onto an old sheet, gather the four corners together, and haul it over to your compost heap.

Drop cloth Place old sheets over the furniture before decorating, or under the table when having a children's party.

Christmas wrap-up After removing holiday decorations, wrap an old sheet around the tree so that you can carry or pull it out of the house without leaving a trail of pine needles.

Banner Advertise your garage sale or wish a neighbour 'Happy Birthday' by painting the message on an old white sheet and hanging it up on your fence.

Shells

Gravel Crushed cockleshells make an excellent pathway or flowerbed border.

Paint palette Use large commonplace shells as disposable paint containers for small projects.

Jewellery holder Glue small shells onto a large shell and use it as a decorative container for pins, chains and earrings.

Plant drain Crush shells and use the fragments for drainage when repotting a houseplant; put a small layer in the base of the flowerpot before filling with compost. This is not suitable for azaleas and other lime-haters, however.

Seafood casserole Cook and serve miniature seafood casseroles, prawn cocktails or devilled crab in well-cleaned scallop shells.

Wind chimes Drill holes in a number of attractive shells and then run nylon thread through them, knotting it to keep them apart. Attach several strings of shells to a small piece of wood and hang it where they will catch the breeze.

Shoe bags

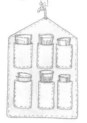

Magazine rack Hang a shoe bag from a hook on the toilet door to hold magazines, paperbacks and other types of reading material.

Toy bag Attach a shoe bag to the back of your car seat to provide storage space for travelling toys, games, books and snacks for those in the back.

Kitchen caddy Fasten a shoe bag to the back of the kitchen door to keep cleaning supplies all in one place.

Shoe boxes

Carry box Paint a sturdy old box a bright colour and then seal it with varnish; keep it closed with a length of twine or a belt.

Doll's bed Build a bed for your child's favourite doll by placing the base of the box inside the top, which is standing up. She can make miniature blankets and pillows out of fabric scraps to keep her doll warm.

Play bricks Children can use shoe boxes to build play houses and forts; they can decorate them by painting on the scenery they require.

Animal transport Punch a few holes in the lid of a shoe box and you have an excellent way of transporting your small pets or birds to the vet. The darkness tends to keep them quiet.

Safekeeping Store mementos, cancelled cheques and other items in one or more labelled shoe boxes.

Kitchen store Use a shoe box to keep small baking tins, such as tartlet tins, neat and tidy.

Gift box Decorate the outside of a shoe box and use it to protect a delicate present before you wrap it in gift paper. Children, particularly, will enjoy this.

Filing system Use a shoe box to store address cards, cookery cards or old photographs.

Shoe polish

Wood stain Mix polishes of two or more colours together until you get just the right shade, and then apply the mixture to the wood with a dry cloth. Buff the surface with a clean cloth.

Paint Touch up scratches and picture hook holes in stripped woodwork with a dab of polish.

Shower caps

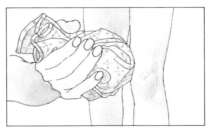

Ice pack Half-fill a cap with ice cubes or pieces of ice, then twist it shut and apply the compress to the injury. Make sure you hold the cap securely shut.

Hair preserver Wear a shower cap when you paint the ceiling; or put one over your hair when you are dyeing or deep-conditioning it.

Bowl cover Use a clean cap to cover any leftovers in the refrigerator.

Shower curtain hangers

Wardrobe organisers Slip several of them over the end of your clothes rail and use them for hanging up bags, umbrellas and belts.

Key ring Keep rarely used keys together by threading them onto a shower ring.

Shower curtains

Apron Make an old shower curtain into an apron by cutting it with a pair of pinking shears, and then glue or sew ties to the top and the middle.

Groundsheet Place an old shower curtain under a tent or sleeping bag.

Waterproof poncho Fold a curtain in half, snip an opening for your head, then trim to the length required.

Weed guard When landscaping with gravel or bark chips, place old shower curtains beneath the material to prevent weeds from growing through.

Rain cover Toss a shower curtain over the barbecue grill (if it's out) and any outdoor furniture during sudden summer storms.

Baby proofer Cut a large square out of a shower curtain to protect the floor beneath a high chair. Use any leftover scraps to make bibs; sew ties to the two top corners.

Tablecloth Use a shower curtain to cover the picnic table.

Tarpaulin Throw a shower curtain over your wood pile to protect it from rain, snow and dew.

Defroster On wintry nights, cover your windscreen with a plastic shower curtain. A magnetic hem, made by sticking a few magnets along the bottom of the curtain, will hold it in place on the car.

Skirt hangers

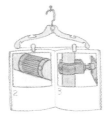

Place keeper When working from printed plans, hold the page in place with a hanger; hang it from a nail or wire in a convenient spot.

Mat keeper Hang place mats from a hanger on the inside of a kitchen cabinet door.

Dryer Use a spring hanger to dry your children's artwork.

Soap

Pomander Place soap scraps in drawers or luggage to keep their contents smelling fresh.

Magnetic hammer When banging in carpet tacks, rub the face of your hammer over a bar of soap and your tacks will cling to it.

Water softener Shave or grate leftover pieces of soap to make flakes; store them in a container by the bath.

Collar-mark remover Put odd bits of soap in a string bag and use it to scrub collar stains.

Shoe softener Rub the backs of new leather shoes with a bar of soap. It will help to soften the leather.

Pin cushion Stick pins and needles into a wrapped bar of soap to keep them all in one place with their points lubricated.

Tailor's chalk Store a few dry slivers of soap in your sewing box and use them to mark darts and hems on clothes made of washable fabrics.

Flea trap If you are cleaning your pet to get rid of fleas, collect individual fleas that fall off with a wet bar of soap before they hop away.

Socks

Pet bandage If your dog or cat has a wound on its leg, pull a clean old sock over the dressing to help hold it in place and prevent the animal scratching.

Scratch preventer Before moving a piece of heavy furniture, slip socks over the base of the legs. Do the same on ladder tops so that you won't mark the walls.

Cosy When interrupted, slip a thick, clean sock over a baby bottle or a mug of coffee, tea or cocoa to help keep the contents warm.

Shoe keeper Pull an old pair of socks over your shoes while painting; remove them before leaving the room.

Bath fragrance Put potpourri into a cotton sock and add it to the bath water while it is running; remove the mixture before you get in and dry it for reuse.

Arm guard Cut the feet off old socks, hem the raw edge and use the leg portions as sleeve protectors for messy eaters.

Soda water

Soft drink Add to fruit juice for a healthful and inexpensive beverage.

Carpet saver To save a stain developing on your carpet if it is marked with urine, douse the area with soda water.

Tummy tamer Cold club soda with a dash of bitters works wonders on an upset stomach brought on by indigestion or a hangover.

Spectacle cases

Fishing companion Keep hooks and lures in a safe, convenient place – fasten them to the inside of an old spectacle case.

Pocket protector Prevent pens and pencils from damaging your clothing by keeping them in an empty spectacle case in your pocket.

Sponges

Sound soother Push a dry sponge between large appliances (such as a dishwasher or fridge) and the wall. It will reduce vibration and eliminate rattling sounds.

Sealer Before posting a stack of greetings cards, 'lick' the envelopes and stamps by whisking them over a damp sponge in a jar lid filled with water.

Soaper Make a sudsy scrubber for bathing or cleaning by slitting a sponge and inserting soap scraps. Or cut two thin slices of sponge into the shape of a fish, and stitch them together most of the way round, leaving a space for soap slivers to be inserted.

Pin cushion Push pins and needles into a dry sponge.

Paint applicator Use a sponge to add an unusual texture to walls and other surfaces (see p.357).

Knee pad Sew pockets onto the knees of old trousers used for handiwork around the house and garden and fill them with small soft sponges. It will make weeding and floor washing much more comfortable.

Blocks Cut large colourful sponges into wedges and cubes and give them to the children to use as basic building blocks.

Squeeze bottles

Fire controller Use a water-filled squeeze bottle to damp down flames when barbecuing outdoors.

Ice pack Fill an empty bottle three-quarters full of water and freeze.

Spotter Put liquid laundry detergent in a squeeze bottle and use it to treat grimy collars, cuffs and stains.

Water gun Fill and use old squeeze bottles for water fights – outside the home. Make sure they are thoroughly cleaned out first, though.

Stools

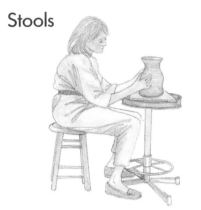

Modelling stand When painting or working with clay, place your piece of work on a swivelling bar stool – it gives you access to all sides. If you are dressmaking, stand your model on a rigid stool to pin up the hem; it will now be at eye level.

Barber's chair Seat your child on a tall stool to cut his hair.

Tomato cage Remove the seat of an old stool and then push the tops of the legs into the soil of your vegetable patch. Plant a small tomato plant at the base of each leg, and then wrap strong garden twine round the legs. As the plants grow, tie the shoots to the twine and legs, for support.

Side table Drape a circular tablecloth over a stool, or top it with a circle of toughened Perspex. It makes an excellent lamp stand or small table.

Lazy Susan Place small serving bowls filled with snacks, starters or dips on a revolving bar stool next to a buffet.

Plant display Feature a favoured indoor plant by sitting it on a stool; you could paint the stool in striking colours to draw the eye.

Jack rest The seat of a broken stool makes a good jack rest when your car is on soft ground. Detach the seat from the legs and keep it in the boot.

Straws

Stem stretcher If you want to arrange short-stemmed flowers in a tall (preferably opaque) vase, slip the ends of the stems into drinking straws before placing them in the container.

Liquid release If your tomato ketchup refuses to budge, insert a straw into the bottle to break the surface tension and get the contents flowing.

Dropper Insert a straw into any liquid that you wish to transfer in small quantities. Place your finger over the open end of the straw and lift. The liquid will stay in the straw until you move your finger.

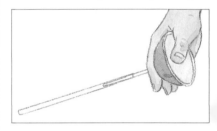

Spout extension When lubricating hard-to-reach spots, extend an oil can spout with a plastic straw. Secure the straw in place with masking or insulating tape if necessary.

String

Door preserver Loop a piece of thick string around both doorknobs, avoiding the catch; that way, the door won't bang shut.

Handle grip To improve the grip on a walking stick or tennis racket, wind a length of string tightly and neatly around the area which you hold.

Information guard Attach any important pieces of information (a weekly television guide or railway timetable, for example) to a noticeboard by punching a hole in one corner and threading a piece of string through it. Then tie the string where convenient – next to the television or on an office noticeboard.

Clothes line Make it a habit to carry a length of string when you travel; then you can hang hand-washables over a bath or sink to dry.

Temporary drip silencer Stop the tom-tom effect of a dripping tap by tying a piece of string around the tap opening and letting the end fall into the drain – the water will silently slide down the string and drain away. But replace the washer as soon as possible.

Brush support Tie a piece of string tightly across the top of a tin of paint or bucket of wallpaper paste. You can use it to scrape off any excess on an over-loaded brush and also as a place to rest the brush on.

Airing cupboard enlarger Create more space in your airing cupboard by stretching pieces of string across it at varying heights. Use the string for drying lightweight items of clothing.

String bags

Soap on a string When going on a camping trip, put a bar of soap in a string bag and use it as it is. Then simply hang the bag on a tree to dry when you've finished with it.

Bird feeder Make some bird feed out of melted fat and birdseed (see p.311) and then place the mixture in a string bag and hang it from the branch of a tree. The holes in the bag give bird beaks easy access.

Keep net Secure any fish you catch by putting them in a bag; hang it in the water until you're ready to go home. For a more sophisticated net, bend a wire hanger into a ring as large as the bag's mouth and stitch the open edge of the mesh bag to it.

Salad spinner Place washed lettuce leaves in a string bag, then whirl it around outdoors for several seconds.

Frog Crumple up a small string bag and place it in the base of a vase before arranging flowers.

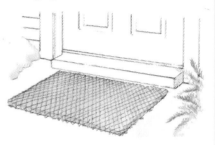

Shoe scraper In autumn and winter, put a string bag over your doormat to give it a rough surface.

Lingerie wash bag Place delicate underwear in a string bag so that it doesn't tangle with other clothes in the washing machine.

Dishwasher basket Put baby bottle caps and teats in a string bag to prevent them from flying all over the dishwasher while being washed.

Vegetable picker Save yourself time and energy by picking vegetables such as leeks or potatoes directly into a string bag with a drawstring top. Then pull the string tight and wash off the vegetables with a hose or bucket of water while they are still in the bag.

Drain filter Stop your shower drain from blocking up by placing a scrunched-up string bag over the plug-hole drain; it will help to catch any stray hairs.

Scrubbing pad Place a sponge inside a string bag, dampen them both, and use the pad for gentle but effective scrubbing on pots and pans. If you don't have a sponge, simply bunch up the string bag and use it as a scrubbing pad.

Soap holder Fold a small plastic string bag and put it in the bottom of the kitchen soap dish; it will keep the soap dry and also serve as an emergency pot scrubber.

Letter holder If you have a bad back, attach a string bag to the inside of your letter box to catch the letters as they come through the door. Then you won't have to bend down to pick them up.

Beach bag Before leaving the beach, put all the children's toys in a string bag. You can then dip them in water to wash off any excess sand.

Surgical spirit

Pepper neutraliser If your hands burn after handling hot chilli peppers, rub surgical spirit into them to take the sting away.

Windowsill cleaner If your wooden windowsills are rain spotted or have become discoloured, brighten them up by wiping with a little surgical spirit diluted with water on a soft cloth.

Bathroom cleaner Keep a bottle of surgical spirit handy; it will bring up the shine on chrome taps and handles, and remove hair spray from mirrors.

Ornament polish Carefully clean delicate crystal and porcelain objects with a cloth dampened with surgical spirit.

Tea

Facial Keep used herbal tea bags to make fragrant steam treatments for your face. Empty the contents of the bag into a saucepan of boiling water, put a towel over your head and lean over the saucepan for 5-10 minutes.

Hair brightener For golden highlights in red or brown hair, rinse your hair with orange pekoe tea after a shampoo.

Plant tonic Help ferns and other house-plants to thrive by watering them once a week with a weak solution of tepid tea.

Pet soother If your dog has wet, red skin eruptions, soothe the sore spots by putting cold, damp tea bags on them; consult the vet as soon as possible.

Lacquer shine Wash black lacquer pieces with strong tea and then wipe them dry with a soft cloth to bring out their deep shine.

Dust damper Keep dust down when you clean out a fireplace by sprinkling moist tea leaves over the ashes first.

Dental aid A cool moist tea bag pressed against a bleeding gum with your finger will help to stop the blood after an extraction.

Eye relaxer Save the moist tea bag after making a cup of tea and place it in the refrigerator. Then, when you have a spare moment, squeeze out the excess liquid and lay the bag over hot, itchy or tired eyes for 15 minutes or so.

Telephone directories

Origami Remove the pages from an old directory, cut them into squares and then fold them into original pieces of art.

Confetti Cut through several pages at a time with a craft knife, or run a few pages through the office shredder.

Insulation Lay several discarded directories side by side to create a 'floor' for your young children's tent or the bottom of the kennel.

Towel Use the pages of an old telephone book to remove the first layer of grime from your hands after gardening or working with oil.

Booster seat Slip a cover over an outdated telephone book so your child can reach the table when sitting on a chair.

Tennis balls

Garden fork guard As a safety measure when storing garden forks or other sharp-pointed tools, push old tennis balls onto their tips.

Massager Put several tennis balls in a long sock, tie up the open end and use it to massage your back and shoulders.

Safe Make a small slit along one seam of a tennis ball, then place jewellery and spare cash inside. Store it with other sports equipment to prevent detection.

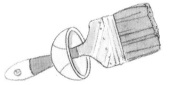

Drip catcher Before beginning a paint job, cut a tennis ball in half. Make a slit in the top of one of the halves and push the brush handle through it; the ball cup will prevent paint from dripping onto your hand.

Christmas wreath Paint a number of tennis balls green and leave them to dry. Then drill holes at the same height on

opposite sides of each one and thread them onto a hanger shaped into a circle. Fill the spaces in between with greenery and attach a bow.

Doorstop Cut a tennis ball in half and then nail or screw it into the wall behind a swinging door.

Clown nose Spray paint a tennis ball red and then cut a hole that is big enough to fit over your nose. If necessary, thread a piece of elastic through each side (knotted on the inside of the ball to prevent it pulling out) and tie it at the back of your head.

Parking aid Attach a tennis ball to a length of string to hang from the garage ceiling; position it in such a way that when the ball touches the windscreen, the car is the right distance from the garage entrance.

Ties

Belt Wrap a colourful tie around your waist to liven up a solid-colour outfit. Or make a narrow belt and set of matching buttons covered in tie fabric as an accessory to everyday work clothes.

Hair band Use a bright, decorative tie to hold back long hair.

Crazy quilt Unpick the stitching on plenty of ties and press them flat with a warm iron. Arrange the ties into the pattern you want on a flat surface, and then sew them together along the outer edges. If you need more ties, try looking out for them at jumble sales.

Stuffed snake Stuff the inside of a tie with fabric scraps or small pieces of foam, and then sew up both ends. Decorate the head end with buttons for eyes and a forked tongue cut out of a piece of red felt.

Tights and stockings

Stuffing Make a sturdy, washable filler for cushions and toys by cutting up your old pairs of tights or stockings which have been laddered.

Paint saver If you're reusing an old tin of paint which has become lumpy, get rid of the lumps by straining the paint through a clean nylon stocking into another tin or bowl.

Stretch tie Cut the legs off a pair of tights and use them to tie bundles of old newspapers or firewood together.

Scrubbing pad Moisten scrunched-up tights with warm water and sprinkle with dishwasher powder. Use the pad to clean nonstick cookware.

Photo enhancer To add a misty, soft-focus quality to a photograph, fasten a piece of stocking over the camera lens with a rubber band.

Timers

Prod Set a timer to remind you to make a telephone call, or to call again if the line is engaged.

Organiser When working in blocks of time, set a timer to prompt you to move on to the next task at the right moment.

Memory jogger Use a timer to remember to turn off the garden sprinkler, or to set the video to record a television programme.

Mediator When youngsters can't resolve whose turn it is to play with a toy, give each one 15 minutes with the desired object. When the buzzer sounds, their turn is ended.

Tin cans

Caution Beware of sharp edges. Only use tins opened with a rotary cutter for the following ideas.

Plant protector Remove both ends of a tin, place it over the top of a young seedling and push it into the earth as a collar; it will protect garden plants from cutworms.

Bird feeder Wedge a small, open tin filled with suet between tree branches or posts. Make sure it's out of the reach of cats, however.

Egg poacher Remove the top and bottom of an empty tuna tin, and then carefully oil the inside of the tin circle. Place it in a shallow frying pan containing enough simmering water to just reach the top of the tin, and then crack an egg into it. Leave until poached and then remove the tin and egg together.

Outdoor candle holder Remove the label from an empty tin, punch holes in its sides, place a candle in the bottom, and light.

Seeder Perforate the bottom of a tin, fill it with grass seed, and shake it over any bare patches on your lawn.

Rain gauge Keep an eye on how much water is falling in your garden with a rain gauge made out of an open tin.

Reflectors Remove the bottom of an empty tin and cut it in half lengthwise with wire cutters to make two reflectors for a campsite, or around the edge of your garden.

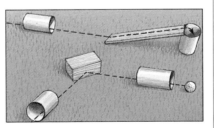

Miniature golf Use several tins with both ends removed to create miniature indoor or outdoor golf. Arrange them as obstacles, so that the ball has to go through the tins, or up a ramp and into them, or ricochet off a piece of wood through them, to make the course more difficult. File the rough edges of the tins to prevent anyone getting hurt.

Miniature basketball Attach a large tin, with its top and bottom removed, to a garage or garden wall with nails; then

play with a tennis ball as a basketball.

Bread tin Bake or steam bread in large, empty fruit tins. Make sure they are clean and then greased before you add the dough.

Ash spreader Punch holes in the bottom of a large tin. Fill with wood ashes and shake over the garden soil.

Pigeonholes Paint 6 or more tins of the same size with bright enamels and then glue them together with an epoxy adhesive. You can use them to store office supplies, or other odds and ends. Smooth all rough edges first.

Tissue paper

Biscuit keeper Crumple up a piece of tissue paper and place it in the bottom of your biscuit tin. It will keep newly baked biscuits fresh.

Glass protector If you are leaning several panes of glass against each other, separate them with sheets of tissue paper – it will prevent moisture from sealing the panes together and will help lessen the chances of breakage.

Candle stabiliser If your candle holder is too large for the candles you have, fill any excess space with crumpled strips of tissue paper.

Sound effect If your children are creating a homemade radio drama, and taping it, tissue paper can sound like wind in the trees, a breaking wave or footsteps in a leafy forest when crumpled up.

Tracing paper Tape a piece of white tissue paper tightly over the drawing you are copying and work under a good light, or on a sheet of strong glass placed over a light source.

Antique preserver Wrap cleaned silver in acid-free tissue paper to prevent tarnishing. Store old and delicate fabrics by laying them on acid-free tissue; then roll around a foil-covered cardboard tube.

Toothbrushes

Mini scrubber Unblock the vents on small appliances, such as vacuum cleaners, and clean tile grout, grimy combs and dirty typewriter keys with an old toothbrush.

Crevice cleaner Put a small amount of silver polish onto a toothbrush to remove tarnish from filigree pieces or intricate decoration, or furniture polish to remove dust in carved wood.

Manicure implement Clean fingernails and toenails with a soft toothbrush and soapy water.

Motor cleaner A toothbrush dipped in paraffin is great for getting oil out of hard-to-reach nooks and crannies.

Facial scrub Use a toothbrush on greasy but unblemished skin to scrub the face gently with soapy lather, avoiding eyes and lips.

Toothpaste

Surface restorer Cover a stain or scratch on an acrylic or plastic surface with toothpaste. Leave it to dry, and then rub it with a soft cloth.

Jewellery cleaner Work a tiny amount of toothpaste into pieces of costume jewellery with a toothbrush, then rinse well and polish dry with a soft cloth.

Caution Do not try this cleaning method on valuable antique or modern pieces.

Christmas decoration Write holiday messages or draw festive pictures on your window with toothpaste. Afterwards, clean the window, first with a wet cloth, and then with a dry one.

Toothpicks

Plug Dip the end of a toothpick into glue, then force it into tiny holes in wood which need filling. Trim off the top of the toothpick with a craft knife, sand the area smooth and finish or stain the wood to match if necessary.

Bookmark Save your place in a book or magazine with a toothpick.

Glue applicator Dip one end of a toothpick into glue or epoxy to apply just a drop for small jobs.

Buffet accessory Cover your buffet dishes prepared ahead of time with plastic film, kept off the surface of the food with toothpicks in the corners of each tray. It prevents any harm coming to the food's appearance.

Wall markers When repapering a wall, push toothpicks into the holes left by screws for plug and light fittings. Leave about $1/8$in/3mm of the toothpicks exposed. They will pierce the new paper and show you where to replace the fittings when the wall is repapered.

DIY stopgap Use toothpicks as a makeshift Rawlplug in an emergency.

Button check Ensure that you don't sew your buttons on too tightly by pushing a toothpick or cocktail stick between the button and fabric and holding it there as you sew.

Towel rail

Spread hanger Screw a sturdy rail to the back of a solid-wood bedroom door; then you can use it to store a bedspread overnight.

Garage organiser Mount one on a garage wall to store rags, rubbish bags or a dust cloth.

Reading rack Place one on the wall next to the toilet to hold newspapers and magazines.

Storage Attach a towel rail to the inside of a wardrobe or kitchen cabinet door to store extra table leaves out of sight.

Broom holder Attach a towel rail to one wall of your utility room and use it to support long-handled household equipment such as a broom or mop.

Shed tidier A towel rail attached to the wall of a garden shed could keep your bamboo sticks, rakes, pieces of trellis and other tall items tidy.

Towels

Neck support pillow Keep your hair free of sand on the beach by rolling up a hand towel and wrapping it in a large scarf. Tie each end with a length of ribbon or wool.

Beach dress Stitch the long sides of two bath towels together to make a simple swimsuit covering. Allow for armholes at one end, then sew up one of the short sides, leaving enough room for your head to pass through. See also BEACH TOWEL, p.339.

Anti-locking precaution Drape a towel over the top of the bathroom door to prevent small children from locking themselves in.

Sink cushion When you are washing your most valuable or delicate crystal and china, line the bottom of your kitchen sink with terry-cloth towelling; it will protect them from cracking against the stainless steel.

T-shirts

Duster Old cotton T-shirts are soft and washable, and since dust clings to them they make ideal dusters. Keep a stack in your cleaning cupboard.

Filler Cut discarded T-shirts into strips and use them to stuff pillows, beanbags and toys.

Rope Unpick the hem of an old T-shirt and then cut it into a 1in/25mm continuous strip until you get to the sleeves. Use the strips to tie up parcels, or knit a rag rug with it (see p.349).

First aid In an emergency, use a clean shirt as a bandage to control heavy bleeding or as padding for splints.

Plant tie Cut old T-shirts into strips and keep these in the garden shed. Use them to tie climbers and top-heavy plants to garden stakes.

Twist ties

Shoelace If your child's shoelace breaks, keep the shoe on by putting twist ties in the eyelets.

Key coder Twist a different colour twist tie through the holes in each of your keys; then you'll be able to pick out the one you want in a hurry.

Emergency cufflinks Pull the tie through the holes in the cuff in such a way that you can secure it inside.

Craft aid Use twist ties as stitch markers, or to hold a knitted or crocheted project in place while you sew it up.

Binder Hold sheets of loose-leaf paper together by inserting twist ties in the holes.

Cable tidies To prevent electrical wires from making contact with (and being damaged by) hot engine parts, use twist ties to keep them in place under the bonnet.

Decoration hanger Use them to secure balls and other ornaments to the Christmas tree.

Reminder Tie one around your finger if you're out of string.

Tyres

Cold frame Lay a tyre on its side out of the reach of hot sun and plant it with seedlings. Cover the top with plastic film, leaving ventilation holes on each side.

Bumper barrier Nail sections of tyre to the back wall of the garage at the level of your car's bumper.

Paddling pool Drape a shower curtain over the centre of a large truck tyre and fill it with water to make your small children an instant pool.

Doormat Cut tyres into short strips with a hacksaw and then drill a small hole on each of the sides and at each of the ends of the strips. Thread individual lengths of wire through the holes and attach the strips together. Depending on the number of strips you've cut, you can make the doormat as small or as large as you wish.

Swing Drill holes in a tyre so that rainwater can escape and bolt two chains to it. Then hang it from a tree as a sturdy swing for the children to play with.

Fish playground Weigh down a tyre with rocks, stones or bricks and toss it into a homemade pond for the fish to hide in. Make sure your pond is deep enough first.

Skid preventer Nail strips of old tyres to ramps, jetties and stairways to prevent slipping.

Planter Plant tomatoes, potatoes, aubergines and peppers inside tyres laid on the ground – they'll protect the plants from the wind, and the dark rubber will warm the surrounding soil, so helping the plants to thrive.

Buoy Drill drainage holes in a tyre, paint it white (it will stop it getting so hot) and then anchor it with a chain to a concrete block.

Retaining wall Fill a number of old tyres with soil and embed them in a hillside which is being gradually washed away. Grow ground cover in between to hold the earth.

Umbrellas

Drying rack Remove the waterproof fabric from an umbrella frame and hang the frame upside-down.

Seedling shield Use a hacksaw to remove the handle from an old open umbrella and place the frame over young seedlings to protect them from unexpected winter frosts.

Wall saver Put an open umbrella behind your houseplants when you spray them.

Stake Use the ribs from a broken, dismantled umbrella as supports for top-heavy plants such as flowering daffodils.

Picnic cover Keep flies off your food by removing the handle from an old umbrella and using the open frame to cover the plates of food.

Vegetable oil

Hair conditioner Massage lukewarm vegetable oil into dry hair. Cover it with a plastic bath cap for 30 to 60 minutes and then shampoo and rinse thoroughly.

Lubricant Give your snow shovel a heavy coating of vegetable oil to prevent snow from sticking to it and weighing it down.

Skin smoother Apply sparingly to dry skin only. Or add a tablespoon or two to your bath, and then pat yourself dry when you get out. But be careful – the oil can make your bath slippery.

Venetian blinds

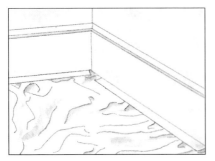

Carpet protector If you have to repaint a room leaving the carpet in place, spread a dust sheet over the entire floor. Then slide slats taken from an old blind under the skirting board and over the edges of the cloth – they're just broad enough to catch errant drips.

Room divider Hang a row of blinds from a board attached to the ceiling to

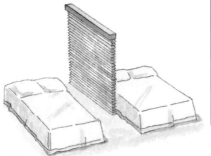

divide off a dining area or den in your living room. Or if your children share a bedroom, use the blinds to partition off a private area for each one.

Vinegar

Pain reliever If ice doesn't seem to ease the discomfort of a strain or sprain, apply hot vinegar compresses. If the injury is still hurting 24 hours later, you should consult your doctor – it could be a fracture.

Ironing aid Remove mineral deposits from an old steam iron by filling it with a solution of equal parts white vinegar and water and letting it steam until dry. Rinse the tank with plain water, then refill it and shake the water out through the steam holes.

Sticker detacher Give stickers an extra-heavy dose of vinegar and leave it to sink in. Then peel them off.

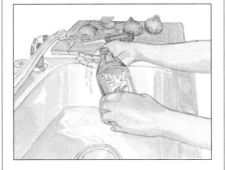

Hand deodorant Remove the smell of onions or fish on your hands by rinsing them with vinegar. Wash thoroughly with soap and water afterwards.

Kettle cleaner Lime deposits in your kettle can sometimes be removed by filling it with equal parts vinegar and water. Bring it to the boil, then leave it to stand overnight.

Egg substitute If you are baking but find that you are short of an egg, replace it with 1 tablespoon of white wine vinegar, as long as the recipe contains another rising agent or uses self-raising flour.

Shoe smartener Remove winter salt stains from your shoes by wiping them with a cloth dampened in a vinegar solution of 1 tablespoon of vinegar to a cupful of water.

Pre-spotter Get rid of collar grime by rubbing a thick paste of baking soda and vinegar onto the stains before your normal wash. Eliminate perspiration marks by saturating them with vinegar before washing as usual.

Rust remover Soak a corroded bolt in a small container of vinegar for several days, or until the rust begins to dissolve.

Bath additive Relieve aching muscles or itching skin by adding 8fl oz / 225ml cider vinegar to a bath of warm water. Then have a relaxing soak for at least 15 minutes.

Egg container To poach an egg without having the white spread out too far, add 1 tablespoon vinegar to a shallow pan of boiling water.

Laundry rinse To brighten white clothes and get rid of detergent residue soak them in 1 gallon / 4.5 litres warm water with 8fl oz / 225ml white vinegar follow with a clear-water rinse.

Hair treatment Make dark and greasy hair extra shiny by adding a couple of tablespoons of vinegar to your last rinsing water.

Dishcloth restorer If a dishcloth, bathroom sponge or flannel becomes slimy or begins to smell, soak it overnight in a vinegar solution (half vinegar, half water) and then rinse in clear water Leave it to dry.

Window washer Clean windows with a solution of 2 tablespoons vinegar in a pints / 1 litre warm water. Wash from top to bottom when cleaning the inside of the window, and from side to side on the outside.

Vodka

Astringent Close your pores and give your face a fresh, clean feeling by wiping it with cotton wool dampened with a little vodka.

Pipe cleaner Soak a pipe cleaner in some vodka to clean and freshen the interior of a pipe stem. (Do not, however, use it on the bowl or exterior of the pipe.)

Wallpaper

Jigsaw puzzle Cover a piece of cardboard with wallpaper and cut it into intricate shapes with a pair of scissors.

Liner Use wallpaper strips in drawers or on shelves – but not ready-pasted vinyl in food cupboards.

Place mat Cut a piece of leftover wallpaper into a rectangle or an oval of a suitable size and cover it with adhesive-backed plastic.

Screen Match a folding screen to your decor by covering it with wallpaper.

Room coordinator Use leftovers from repapering the walls as covers for plant holders and wastepaper bins.

Wrapping paper Use an attractive or decorative wallpaper to wrap up presents.

Book cover Protect school books by covering them with a sheet of leftover wallpaper.

Washers

Weight Sew several washers into the hem of a pair of curtains to give them some weight and help them to hang properly.

Jewellery Knot graduated sizes of washer onto a length of nylon thread for a child's necklace.

Sinker Loop one or more metal washers onto the end of your fishing line; change the weight depending on the current and depth of the water.

Surface protector When drilling holes on a glazed surface, slip a rubber washer over the bit; it will protect the finish if you drill too far.

Washing-up bowls

Cupboard organiser Store clothing, towels, sheets and pillowcases in square, plastic washing-up bowls. Label them on the side with their contents.

Seed-starter tray Spread a layer of moist potting compost on the bottom of the bowl, sow your seeds and then cover with clear plastic film.

Oil pan Place a washing-up bowl underneath the drain plug when changing your car's oil; make sure the container is large enough to hold at least 1.1 gallons / 5 litres of liquid.

Baby's bathtub Fill a plastic bowl with enough lukewarm water to make a shallow bath and lower the baby gently into the water, supporting his head and shoulders.

Birdbath Set a washing-up bowl on or into the ground and surround it with rocks and foliage.

Washing-up liquid

Shampoo In an emergency, you can use well-diluted washing-up liquid to get a clean head of hair.

Lubricant Squirt a little washing-up liquid on vinyl tiles to help when moving heavy objects such as a dishwasher or washing machine. It will help them slide.

Car cleaner Add some water to a nearly empty washing-up liquid bottle to keep in your glove compartment. Use it for wiping up spilled drinks or ice cream.

Puncture finder Mix with a little warm water and brush on a leaky tyre or tube; the bubbles will indicate the exact location of the puncture.

Bubble solution Dilute the concentrate slightly and dip a bubble blower into it. For longer-lasting bubbles, add a few drops of glycerine to the solution.

Wastepaper baskets

Basketball goal Remove the bottom of a metal wastepaper bin and attach it to a garage wall. Use foam balls to play a game of lightweight basketball.

Umbrella stand Line a tall wastepaper basket with a plastic rubbish bag and keep it near the front or back door.

Plant holder Display a big plant in an attractive wastepaper basket.

Magazine rack Keep reading material in a metal bin.

Vase Use an attractive bin to hold tall dried-flower or catkin arrangements.

Wax

Cotton strengthener Pull the cotton of a threaded needle over a piece of wax before sewing on a button.

Drawer glider Remove a drawer that is sticking from its frame and rub a candle stub up and down the edges and sides, especially where they seem rough.

Lubricant Rub wax onto the shaft of a nail or screw; it will make it easier to insert in wood.

Window aid Rub a stub of wax along window sash tracks to prevent sticking. Also rub it onto rails so that curtain rings or hooks slide easily.

Rainproofer After writing identifying details on garden markers, dip them in a pan of melted wax to protect them against wet weather.

Toboggan speeder Rub a candle stub along the bottom of your toboggan runners to make it run more smoothly over snow and ice.

Wax crayons

Candle dye Save stubs to melt with wax when making coloured candles.

Sealing wax Melt the remnants and use to seal envelopes.

Wax paper

Leaf preserver Assemble colourful autumn leaves in a pleasing pattern on wax paper, cover with another sheet and then iron to seal. Trim the paper around the leaves in any desired shape.

Super sealer Place a piece of wax paper over the opening of a jar before closing it.

Kitchen buffer For a nice shine, rub appliance exteriors and other surfaces with wax paper.

Wood scraps

Door stop Make a practical door stop for a door that always swings shut by cutting a scrap of wood into a triangular shape.

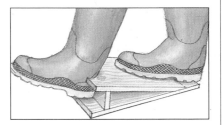

Boot jack Assemble with nails or screws as shown. Hold the baseboard flat on the floor with one foot and pull the other back into the semicircular cut to catch it just above the heel; pull up.

Chessboard Cut a 16in/400mm square of wood and divide it into 64 equal squares of 2in/50mm each (8 squares along each side). Paint them alternately black and white and then coat the chessboard with varnish.

Kitchen aid Turn clean pieces into bread, cheese or pastry boards.

Jigsaw puzzle Glue a photograph onto a piece of ¼in/6mm plywood. When completely dry, cut it into a puzzle with a fretsaw.

Leveller Place scraps of wood under cupboards, tables and appliances to level them out where the floor is uneven. Use two overlapping pieces for bad dips.

Cleat Screw 4-6in/100-150mm strips of wood to the backs and/or undersides of chests, desks and other pieces of heavy furniture. These 'handles' will make the furniture easier to move when you are spring cleaning.

Wooden planks

Garden edging Cut three boards 10, 12 and 14in (250, 300 and 360mm) high and sink them 6in/150mm into the ground. Repeat the sequence for an undulating border.

Makeshift lock Jam one end of a board under the doorknob and the other end tight against a carpeted floor. No-one will be able to open the door from the outside if it opens inwards.

Wool

Pom-pom Wrap a length of wool at least 20 times around a small piece of cardboard, a rolled-up magazine or other mould. Tie the loops together at one end, then remove the mould and cut through the loops at the other end.

Ribbon Use a piece of wool to tie up birthday or Christmas presents.

Yoghurt

Facial toner Spread a thick coat of natural, unflavoured yoghurt all over your face; leave it for 15-20 minutes before removing it with plenty of tepid water.

Hair conditioner Apply natural yoghurt to your hair after shampooing. Leave it on for 10 minutes and then rinse off.

Sunburn soother Smear a thick coat of plain, low-fat yoghurt onto mild sunburn before going to bed and then wash it off in the morning. Be prepared for a dirty pillowcase, though.

Zips

Valuables securer Sew a zip across the inside pocket of a jacket to keep your passport, traveller's cheques and other valuables safe.

Puppet mouth Make a puppet out of an old sock by sewing on buttons for the eyes and nose and a small zip for the mouth.

Convertible jeans Make cut-offs by carefully removing most of the legs from a pair of jeans and then reattaching them with zips. Wear the cut-offs when you are walking or cycling on a hot day; zip on the legs in the evening or when it gets chilly.

RECYCLING & RENEWING

Those keen to use obsolete everyday wares can find a wealth of ideas in among these practical projects. Transform an old car tyre into an attractive garden planter, spruce up an old sofa with flamboyant loose covers, or rejuvenate functional but tired-looking wooden furniture with one of the simple renewal techniques.

Baby blankets Bath mat

You can turn a few old baby blankets into a super-absorbent colourful bath mat with the aid of an easy-to-make loom. Use five or six flannel or wool blankets and don't worry about coordinating their colours – a rag-rug look is what you're after.

To make the loom, you need two 33in/840mm and two 23in/580mm lengths of 1 × 3in/25 × 75mm pine. Cut lap joints at the corners, and make sure they're square. Glue the pieces and secure them further with ¾in/19mm nails driven from both sides. Alternatively, use artists' stretcher bars which slot together at the corners.

On the face of the frame, trace a pencil line along the centre of each length of wood. Then hammer a number of 1in/25mm galvanised nails about ½in/13mm deep along the lines, spacing them 1in/25mm apart on the long sides of the frame and 1½in/38mm apart on the short sides. Make sure that the nails align with those on the opposite side and that they're secure enough to hold the strips of fabric you'll be weaving around them.

Now cut the baby blankets into 3in/75mm wide strips and sew several strips together end to end. Iron the seams flat. Have a sewing machine or needle and thread handy so that you can sew on more strips as you weave. Use your least stretchy blankets for the warp strips (the ones that you'll be attaching first, running lengthwise on the loom) because they'll form the base through which the other strips are woven.

Begin by folding the end of your long strip in half lengthwise (unfinished seams inward) and knotting it to the second nail on a 23in/580mm side of the loom (ignore the corner nails; you won't use them). Now stretch it to the nail on the opposite side, creasing the strip down the centre as you go. Loop it around and back to the next nail on the other side. Continue, keeping the fabric tight and sewing on more strips as you need them, until you've reached the end. Tie off the strip on the last nail and knot it tightly.

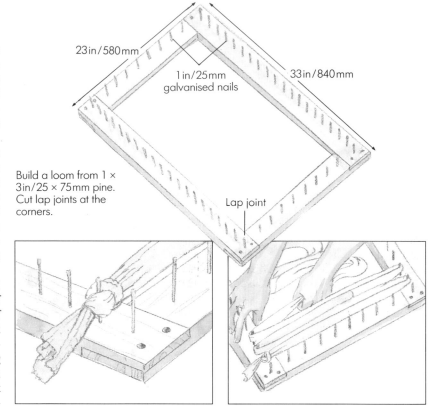

23in/580mm
1in/25mm galvanised nails
33in/840mm

Build a loom from 1 × 3in/25 × 75mm pine. Cut lap joints at the corners.

Lap joint

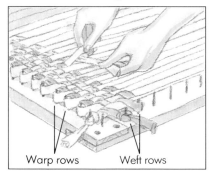

Warp rows   Weft rows

3 Weave the weft rows over and under the warp rows, using strips from stretchy blankets to make the job easier.

1 Fold blanket strips, sewn end to end, in half lengthwise and tie one end to the second nail on the long side of the loom.

2 Loop the strip around the opposite nail, then continue working back and forth until you tie it on the last nail.

4 Untie the knots at the corner of the rug and trim the excess fabric. Hand-stitch the edges onto the underside of the rug.

Now start weaving. Use strips cut from stretchy blankets – they'll be easier to work through the warp. As before, fold the strip in half lengthwise; this time, knot it to the second nail on the 33in/840mm side. Weave it through the warp strips to the nail on the opposite side, creasing it as you go. Loop it around and start back, adding more strips as you need them.

As you work, push the strips as close as possible against one another. If the last few rows are hard to weave, use the end of a spoon to push and pull them through. Tie the strip to the last nail.

Gently work the rug off the nails. Turn it over and untie the knots at the corners. Trim the excess fabric, turn the cut edges under, and hand-stitch them onto the underside of the rug.

Balusters Table base

If you replace the balustrade on your stairs, save four of the balusters to make handsome supports for an occasional table. Use plywood or timber as a base and whatever you like as a table top – a large metal tray, a marble slab, the top of an old desk or a cut-to-order wooden top that you finish yourself.

Most balusters are 24in/610mm long. Since occasional tables should stand 17-22in/430-560mm high, the length of your balusters should be ample. Cut the balusters to size, then paint or stain them. After sawing, check that the height and cuts are even with a spirit level.

You can make a base from a circle of ¾in/19mm plywood. Use an electric jigsaw to cut it about 12in/300mm in diameter. Stain or paint the base to match the balusters and then finish the edge with an adhesive veneer.

Cut an 8in/200mm square of ¼in/6mm plywood to support the table top and draw a 4½in/115mm square in the centre. Draw another 4½in/115mm

square in the centre of the base. Then drill and countersink for No. 12 screws at each corner of both squares. Use 4in/100mm screws to attach the base and 2in/50mm screws to attach the support.

For the sake of stability, don't choose a table top longer or wider than about 28in/710mm. Centre it on the support and attach it with screws, carriage bolts or epoxy glue.

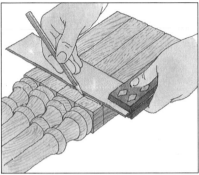

1 Using a straightedge, mark the cutting level on the balusters, about 2in/50mm shorter than the height of your table.

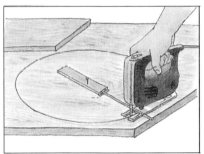

2 Cut an 8in/200mm square from a piece of ¼in/6mm plywood. Then cut a 12in/300mm circle from ¾in/19mm plywood.

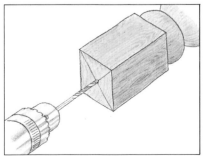

4 Use a straightedge to draw an X on the bottom and top of each baluster and drill a pilot hole exactly in the centre.

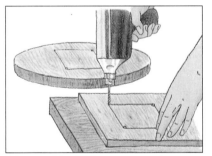

3 Draw a 4½in/115mm square in the centre of both pieces; drill at each corner for No. 12 screws.

5 To assemble, drive No. 12 countersunk screws through the plywood pieces and into the balusters. Then attach the top.

Weathering wood

Here's an instant, inexpensive way to disguise or dress up old pine floorboards, kitchen units, wooden furniture and wall claddings. Use a thinned-down coat of gloss paint to create a fashionably 'distressed' or 'weathered' look. Cream, white and pale greens and blues are the most effective colours.

Wear rubber gloves and protective clothing such as an apron or overalls when applying the paint, because the thinned paint is liable to drip everywhere. Mix 2 parts gloss paint to 1 part white spirit.

1 Working in a 3ft/1m area at a time, strip the paint off the wood. Sand any rough surfaces. Then apply the paint with a wide brush.

2 Allow the paint to sink into the wood (around 5 minutes). Soak a rag in white spirit and wring it out. Use to rub off excess paint.

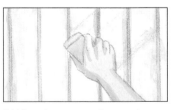

3 When the paint is dry, sand any uneven paint streaks and patches so that the paint has a pleasingly uniform look.

Barrel Garden irrigator

Collecting rainwater is an excellent way of providing controlled irrigation for the garden. You can buy ready-made water butts, but you may also be able to find an old plastic drum or container to convert.

The barrel will need a tap at its base and an overflow outlet at the top. A ready-made water butt may already have these. You will have to drill a hole at the bottom and the top of the barrel with a hole cutter. Fit a bibcock tap at the bottom of the barrel and an elbow pipe at the top to direct the overflow back into the rainwater drain.

The barrel will need to be sited next to a downpipe to collect rainwater and to redirect the overflow. It should be raised off the ground on concrete blocks to allow a watering can to be filled, or to increase the water pressure for a hose. Cut the downpipe just above the barrel level and fix an angled elbow to it to position over the barrel.

If you do not have a ready-made lid, cut one from exterior grade plywood, using a jigsaw. Cut a hole in the lid for the downpipe. Seal the pipe to the lid with mastic sealant so that insects won't be able to breed in the stored water.

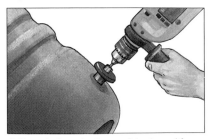

1 Place the barrel on concrete blocks. Cut the downpipe and remove a section slightly shorter than the elbow pipe.

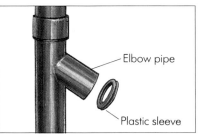

Elbow pipe

Plastic sleeve

2 Fit the elbow pipe onto the downpipe. Twist it round to fit against the barrel and keep the plastic sleeve aside.

3 Cut a hole in the top of the barrel for the elbow pipe and fit the plastic sleeve inside the hole.

4 Cut a hole in the base of the barrel for the bibcock. This will need to be smaller than the hole at the top.

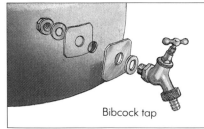

Bibcock tap

5 Fit a nut, washer and holding plate on either side of the barrel and fix the tap in position.

6 Reposition the barrel on the blocks and fit it to the elbow pipe. Make a lid for the barrel, position it and seal the edges.

Beach towel Wrap

With a few strips of Velcro, you can make a beach towel double as a towelling wrap to wear over your bathing suit, while also still being able to use it as a towel.

Any large towel, with any design – from a solid colour to a gaudy map of Hawaii – will do, although thin ones work better than those with a thick pile.

To get the proper fit, wrap the towel around you so that it's snug under the arms and overlaps in front. With tailor's chalk, mark three 4in/100mm strips along the outer top edge of the inner layer and along the inner top edge of the outer layer. Then cut three pairs of 4in/100mm from 1in/25mm Velcro and stitch them onto the marks. Your beach wrap is now ready to wear.

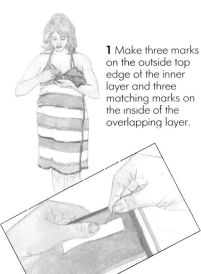

1 Make three marks on the outside top edge of the inner layer and three matching marks on the inside of the overlapping layer.

2 Sew the Velcro strips over the marks, with the 'loop' strips on one side and 'hook' strips on the other.

3 The three pairs of Velcro strips should now line up and stick together to hold the towel securely in place.

Bedspread Wall hanging

Don't toss out that old, worn bedspread. An undamaged section with a complete design can be mounted on plywood as a wall hanging, sewn onto backing material and stuffed as a cushion or used as place mats, a table runner or a cloth for a dressing table. If the bedspread is totally beyond repair, store it in the garage to use as a dust sheet or a furniture pad for moving.

You'll need a piece of ½in/13mm plywood slightly smaller than the area of the hanging, drawing pins, a staple gun, and screw eyes and picture wire for hanging. Use drawing pins to keep the fabric straight as you staple it to the plywood. Staple one side first, then the opposite side, then the remaining two sides. Do the corners last, pulling them tight and folding them with diagonal folds before stapling them.

1 Measure off and mark a section of bedspread that contains the complete picture or design that you want to mount and display. Add 3½in/90mm to all four sides and cut out the section.

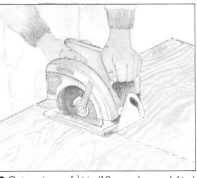

2 Cut a piece of ½in/13mm plywood 6in/150mm shorter and narrower than the fabric. The corners must be square.

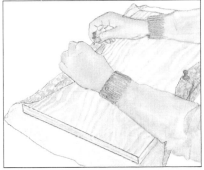

3 Lay the fabric face down and centre the plywood on it. Pull the fabric over the edges and secure with drawing pins.

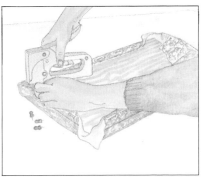

4 Staple the fabric to the back of the board, leaving the corners open. Pull the corners tight, fold them flat, and staple.

5 Attach two screw eyes just below the top edge of the fabric, then thread with picture wire for hanging.

Birdhouse Clock

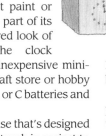

If the birds have abandoned your birdhouse, bring it indoors and convert it into a wall clock. For the best effect, don't paint or stain the birdhouse – part of its charm is the weathered look of the wood. For the clock mechanism, buy an inexpensive mini-quartz type from a craft store or hobby shop. They run on AA or C batteries and are easy to install.

The kind of birdhouse that's designed to be nailed to a tree trunk is easiest to convert. If you have the two-sided hanging type, you can make two clocks from it – just saw it in half and mount each half on a board cut to size. If the birdhouse doesn't have a removable roof, hinge the back or bottom so that you can install the clock mechanism and change the battery. You may need to reduce the thickness of the timber around the clock face to accommodate the thickness of the mechanism. Plane down the outer face of the birdhouse or chisel a recess inside it.

To mark the hour positions, make a paper template as shown. Trace around the rim of a glass; make a mark at the 12, 3, 6 and 9 positions, then place two equidistant marks between each pair of numbers. To mark the hours on the clock itself, you could use shiny copper rivets. As a finishing touch, why not glue a colourful carved bird to the perch?

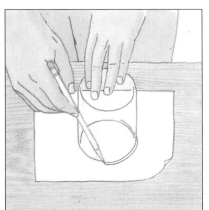

1 Draw a circle on paper for your clock face, using a glass or compass. Mark the hour positions on it.

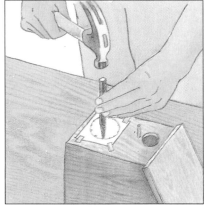

2 Stick the template on the birdhouse. Use a nail punch to mark the positions of the centre hole and each hour.

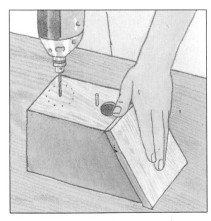

3 Drill the centre hole large enough to accept the clock shaft. Drill holes for the rivets being used as hour markers.

4 Mount the clock in the birdhouse and glue the rivets in place. Insert a battery and hang the clock on the wall.

Blue jeans Bag

When the legs of your jeans wear out but the top part still has strong seams, transform the jeans into a handy denim bag. Just cut off the legs and stitch the holes closed. Then add the kind of handle or straps that will turn the bag into a clothespeg or tool bag, sewing bag, shoulder bag or child's backpack. See also JEANS, p.308.

1 Turn the jeans inside out and mark them for cutting about 2in/50mm below the crotch. Cut off the legs on the mark.

2 Sew across the leg openings with two or three lines of straight stitches. Turn the jeans right side out and press.

3 For a handle, cut a 3in/75mm wide strip from one of the legs. Crease, stitch on the wrong side, and turn inside out.

4 Sew ½in/13m of the handle to the inside of the waistband at both sides. Use a zigzag stitch for extra strength.

Sewing bag Use to hold thread, wool and pincushions; scissors, needles and thimbles fit in the pockets. A measuring tape runs through the belt as a drawstring.

Shoulder bag
Use a strip of colourful fabric, heavy ribbon, or cording for the handle. Make the drawstring from the same fabric.

Child's backpack
Attach the straps as shown and make an easy-to-operate drawstring with cord and a piece of leather.

To turn the bag into a child's backpack, first measure it against your child to determine the length of the straps. Hold the bag to the child's back and loop your measuring tape from the top of the bag, over the shoulders and back to the bottom of the bag.

Allow an extra 3 in / 75 mm so that you can stitch the straps to the inside of the waistband and the bottom of the back pockets with a zigzag stitch. Rip open a few stitches in the bottom of the back pockets and tuck the straps inside, then sew them in place.

To make a drawstring that even a toddler can operate, cut a 1 in / 25 mm square of heavy leather and drill or punch a ⅛ in / 3 mm hole in each corner. Run a long piece of strong cord through the belt loops in the backpack, then through the top set of holes in the leather. Cross the cords to make an X, then thread them through the bottom holes. Knot the cord ends.

To close the bag, just pull on the cords; to open it, hold the leather patch and tug at the part of the cord that runs through the belt loops.

Book Jewellery safe

Delay thieves in their search for your valuables by turning a book into a small safe and hiding it among the other books on your shelf.

Choose a hardcover book at least 1½ in / 38 mm thick. Glue all but the first few pages together with a mixture of 3 parts PVA adhesive to 1 part water. Insert a sheet of waxed paper between the first glued page and the loose ones; insert another between the last page and the back cover. Close the book, weigh it down with several heavy volumes or some concrete blocks (don't skimp on the weight or the pages may wrinkle), and let it dry overnight.

When the glue is dry, score the section to be cut; leave at least a 1 in / 25 mm margin at the edges. Drill starter holes in the corners and use a coping saw to remove the section. Glue the back cover in place and weigh the book down again. For a finishing touch, line the cutout with satin or felt.

1 With a wide brush, apply glue sparingly to all the pages except the first few.

2 Leave a margin of at least 1 in / 25 mm all around when you score the section to be cut out.

3 Drill starter holes in the corner and cut out the book section with a coping saw.

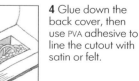

4 Glue down the back cover, then use PVA adhesive to line the cutout with satin or felt.

Cable spools Child's table

The big wooden spools that hold telephone cable or nylon rope can make unusual and attractive furniture for children. Turn a 24in/610mm spool and two 16in/400mm ones into a table and stools. (The spools can be obtained from a builder's merchant.)

If the spool ends are secured with protruding round-head screws, countersink them. Attach three rubber feet to the bottom of each spool to steady it on the floor and to prevent it from slipping.

Paint the spool ends with a bright colour and decorate the reels with thin rope. Spread a suitable adhesive randomly around the reel, nail down the end of the rope at the inside base of the reel, and wrap it round, pushing each coil down tightly against the previous one. If you need more than one piece of rope, secure the ends with tacks and remove them when the glue has dried.

For comfort, fit the two small spools with padded seats of foam rubber and fabric. Cut the fabric 4in/100mm larger than the foam all around and staple it under the spool ends. If there are holes in the centre of the table top, glue on a piece of hardboard or plastic laminate the size of the table top.

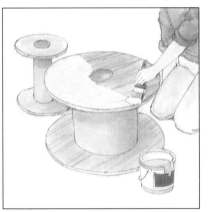

1 Lightly sand the spool ends and paint with semi-gloss paint. Apply an extra coat to the table top.

2 Spread glue onto the reel of each spool and wrap rope around it, securing the ends with tacks.

3 Trace the shape of the small spool ends on a sheet of foam rubber and cut out two pieces. Cut out the fabric.

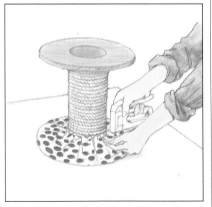

4 Place the spools on the fabric and foam, and fold and staple the fabric over the spool ends.

Candles Lanterns

Save large tin cans and candle stubs to turn into your own decorative lanterns. You can place them along your garden path during summer evenings and festival days. You could also position a few of these lanterns in rock gardens or flower beds to light them up at night.

Melt the candle stubs in a double boiler and use a slotted spoon to skim off the wicks that float to the surface. If you need more wax, buy it from a craft or hobby shop and add it to the stubs. Use

1 Melt the candle stubs in a pan set in a larger pan filled with at least 2in/50mm of simmering water. Cut the milk cartons down to 3in/75mm.

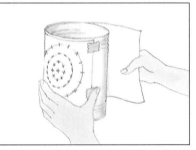

3 With the aid of compasses and a ruler, draw a series of geometric dot patterns on a piece of paper and tape the paper all the way around the tin.

5 Peel the milk cartons from the candles, place a candle in each decorated tin and line up the tins at the edge of the path to your front door.

clean ½ pint/285ml or 1 pint/570ml milk cartons for the moulds and pour the molten wax into them. You will need 3in/75mm lengths of new candles to stand in the molten wax. For each lantern case you'll need a 1lb/450g tin with the label removed. With a nail punch or chisel, punch holes in circular patterns into the tin for the candlelight to shine through.

When the wax has cooled, remove it from the carton, and place in the tin.

2 Pour ¼in/6mm of wax into the bottom of each carton. Then hold a 3in/75mm candle stub upright in the middle until it stands by itself. Fill the carton to the top.

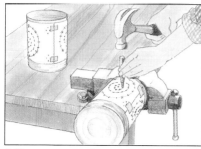

4 Clamp a piece of 2 x 4in/50 x 100mm wood in a vice and slip the tin over it. Use a nail punch and hammer to punch out the design on all sides of the tin.

Car tyre Planter

A car wheel and tyre can be transformed with a knife and a little physical effort into an attractive garden planter. With a coat of paint and filled with a few flowering plants it will grace any patio, path or porch.

You need a car tyre on a wheelrim, preferably a tubeless tyre. Deflate the tyre if it is not already flat. You will also need a sharp craft knife to cut the rubber. The cut is made around the circumference of the tyre where the tyre wall meets the tread. You then turn the tyre over and pull the rubber upwards, so turning the tyre inside out. The base of the resulting cup shape can be lined with 2in/50mm of gravel, covered with potting compost and filled with plants.

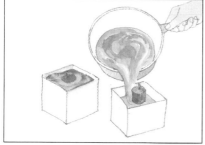

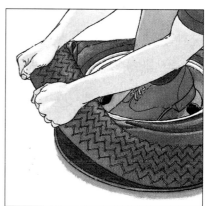

1 Lay the wheel on its side. Using a craft knife, carefully cut through the rubber, where the tyre wall meets the tread.

2 Turn the tyre over. Slip your fingers inside the cut rubber and pull the rubber towards you.

3 Using your foot to hold the tyre down, pull the bulk of the rubber up to turn the tyre inside out.

4 Paint the cup shape with a special tyre paint – dark green, white and black look attractive. It is now ready for planting.

Transforming cardboard boxes

With the help of a decorative adhesive plastic, you can turn a plain cardboard box into an attractive storage container.

The material comes in 18in/460mm wide rolls. To determine how much plastic you'll need, measure the five sides of the box (six if you're covering the lid) and add them together. Then double the amount for covering the inside, too.

Cover the inside bottom of the box first, cutting the plastic an extra ¼in/6mm all round. Mitre the corners of the plastic by making a cut from the corner of the box inwards, then again at a 45° angle.

Next, use a single sheet to cover the outside bottom and both sides of both ends. Cut the plastic to the exact length and add 2in/50mm to the width so that you'll have an edge to fold over on each side. Fold the sheet in half and crease it

across the middle so that you can find the centre when you align the adhesive plastic on the box.

Peel off two-thirds of the backing and lay the plastic down, adhesive side up. Centre the box on the crease and press down; then smooth the plastic up one end, slit the extra plastic at each side and smooth it down the inside. Peel off the remaining backing and repeat the process on the other end. Press down the overlaps.

Cover the other two sides of the box in the same way (the bottom will have another thickness of plastic for extra strength), but don't add any extra width; you won't need to fold over edges this time.

Always smooth the plastic from the centre out. If the surface still has air bubbles, just puncture them with a straight pin and flatten the bumps with your fingers.

1 Cover the inside bottom, cutting the plastic with an extra ¼in/6mm all the way round. Mitre the corners.

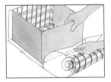

2 Cut a sheet for the outside base and two sides, inside and out. Add 2in/50mm to the width.

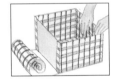

3 Unpeel most of backing, centre box on plastic, and cover one side. Unpeel the rest and cover.

4 Slit the corners and fold the edges over. Cut a second sheet and cover the remaining sides.

Cavity brick Birdhouse

After a house has been built or extended, or on an abandoned building site, you occasionally find an air brick cavity duct lying around. It makes an ideal birdhouse.

Chisel a hole in the block to create an instant house for birds. If you want to attract small birds, be sure not to make the hole larger than 1½in/38mm or you'll attract starlings, which keep away smaller birds. And chisel carefully to keep the hole neat and round.

Use a piece of pipe or a stout wooden pole as a stake to support the block 4-5ft/1.2-1.5m off the ground. Or try a shapely tree branch or an attractive piece of driftwood. Plant the stake at least 24in/610mm deep so that it won't blow over in the wind.

A piece of slate makes an attractive roof for the birdhouse. If the piece you have is too big, such as a roofing slate, have it cut down to the right size – slate shatters very easily.

Position the birdhouse on the base with the hole facing east. After each family of birds leaves, lift it up and clean it out to attract others.

2 Slowly drill through the punch marks with a ³⁄₁₆in/5mm masonry bit. Then punch or chisel the hole and enlarge it to no more than 1½in/38mm.

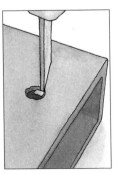

1 Use a felt-tip pen to draw a 1in/25mm circle centred about 2in/50mm from the top of the block. Make punch marks all the way around the circle with a sharp punch, chisel or large masonry nail.

3 Cut a roof and base from ¼in/6mm exterior grade plywood about 1in/25mm larger than the block. Use epoxy or mastic adhesive to glue the roof to the block. Nail the base to the top of the stake.

Ceramic tiles Trivet and table top

Left-over ceramic tiles can make a decorative surface for a trivet or even a table top. Because food is likely to come into contact with the trivet you should use an epoxy grout, which is not absorbent. A trivet could even be used as a pastry board, as the tiles provide an appropriately cool and smooth surface.

Making a trivet

Glue some tiles to a piece of ½ in / 13 mm plywood with a hardwood border, and you have a trivet that looks as good as expensive ready made ones.

Before spreading the adhesive on the plywood, seal the wood with PVA sealer. To ensure that the tile joints are even, use ready-made plastic tile spacers between the tiles.

To gauge the thickness of the border so that it will be flush with the tiled surface, add the thickness of the plywood and the tile plus the thickness of the adhesive indicated by the manufacturer's instructions.

Tiling a table top

If you have some spare tiles in good condition, you can set them on a board, fit a hardwood edging and make an attractive and hardwearing table top for an occasional table.

There are several ways of making a table top, which depend on the table. You could tile straight onto the table top, after having sanded it with coarse abrasive paper to create a roughened surface. Or you could increase the size of the table top by nailing a board with a larger surface area onto the table and tiling over that. Before laying the tile adhesive, seal the table top or board with PVA sealer and let it dry.

You will probably need to lay a wood fillet around the tiles because it is unlikely that they will fit right to the table edge. The fillet can be any width, because it can extend over the table edge. But to determine its thickness so that it lies flush with the tiles, add the thickness of the tile to the thickness of the adhesive as shown in the manufacturer's instructions.

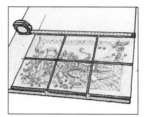

1 Lay the tiles on the plywood with the plastic spacers. Allow the same space around the border and mark for cutting.

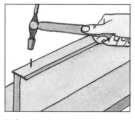

2 Cut the hardwood border to size and mitre the edges. Glue and pin to the plywood edge, using PVA adhesive.

3 Seal the border with polyurethane varnish. When dry, spread wall tile adhesive on the plywood with a spreader.

4 Lay the tiles onto the adhesive putting the plastic spacers between them and between the tiles and the border.

5 Remove any surface adhesive. Once it has set, push epoxy grout into the joints. Smooth the grout with a grouting tool.

6 Remove all surplus grout and clean the tiles with a damp cloth. When dry, polish the tiles with a dry cloth.

! Centre all the tiles on the table. Measure the space between the tiles and the table edge for a wood fillet.

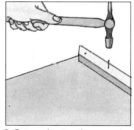

2 Cut and mitre the wood fillets to fit. Seal them with polyurethane varnish. When dry, nail them in place.

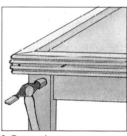

3 Cut and mitre hardwood mouldings to cover fillets. Glue and nail in place, wiping off any excess adhesive.

4 Varnish the dry mouldings, then use an adhesive spreader to cover table surface with tile adhesive.

5 Position tiles using plastic spacers, wiping off excess adhesive. Grout dried tiles with flat side of spreader.

6 Wipe off excess grout with a dry cloth and leave overnight. Polish the table with a clean cloth to finish.

Chair Rocker

Create a new piece of furniture by fitting two hardwood rockers onto the legs of an old straight chair.

First, enlarge the rocker pattern shown here, using 1in/25mm grid paper for an average chair which measures 12-14in/300-360mm between the front and back legs. Cut around the paper pattern to make a template. Check to see that your rocker shape is long enough for the chair. You need 2in/50mm at the front and at least 9in/230mm protruding at the back.

Draw round the template onto two lengths of hardwood a little thicker than the legs. You could also tape two A3 sheets of carbon paper to the wood, tape the pattern over them, and draw over the pattern to transfer it onto the wood. You may be able to clamp the two pieces of hardwood together and cut them simultaneously if you have a bandsaw or powered jigsaw. Otherwise, cut out the two pieces using a coping saw.

To join the legs of the chair to the rocker use a mortise and tenon joint. If you have straight section legs, make a rectangular mortise and tenon. With round chair legs you may be able to drill a hole to accept the legs. Before you make the tenons on the bottom of the chair legs, make sure the chair will tilt back by cutting about ½in/13mm off the back legs. Experiment with the angle by trimming the legs a little at a time. Cut a tenon in the bottom of each leg with a tenon saw. It should be long enough to fit at least three-quarters of the way into the rocker.

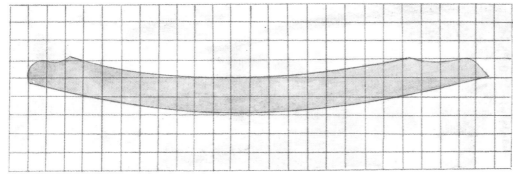

To make rockers for an average-size chair measuring 12-14in/300-360mm from the front to back legs, transfer this pattern to 1in/25mm grid paper. (You could draw this grid yourself using a ruler.) For larger chairs, use a 1¼in/32mm grid; for smaller ones, use a ¾in/19mm grid.

1 Clamp the two pieces of wood together. Mark the pattern on the top piece, and cut them out with a jigsaw.

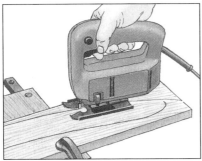

2 Clamp the rockers together and shape them with a plane or rasp before sanding them smooth.

3 Put the chair on the rockers and mark the mortise positions. Cut them out with a drill and a chisel. Chisel out the tenons.

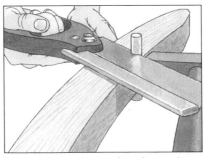

4 Fit the rockers to the chair legs. Drill holes through the rockers and tenons to take a dowel of about ⅜in/10mm.

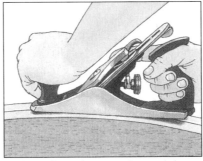

5 Detach the rockers and apply wood adhesive to the joints and dowels. Refit the rockers. Drive dowels into the holes.

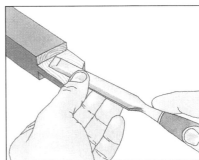

6 Wipe off any excess adhesive. Trim the dowels flush with the rockers and sand them. Then paint or stain the rockers.

Chest of drawers Bookcase

If you find an old chest of drawers that's missing a drawer or two, don't dismiss it as worthless. With some pine shelves and a lick of paint, it can be transformed into an attractive free-standing, two-sided bookcase.

If the vertical space between the drawer supports is less than 8in/200mm, you'll have to prise out every other support to make the shelves tall enough for books. Leave one or two of the smaller spaces for magazines or oversize books, which can be laid on their sides.

Fill any holes with wood filler, then paint the back of the chest and the shelves to match the front. You could also stencil on a design (see below).

1 Remove the drawers and carefully prise the backing from the chest.

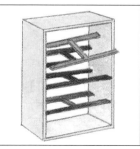

2 If necessary, remove every second support. Prise out the centre drawer rail.

3 Measure the inside and cut shelves of ¾in/19mm pine to size.

4 Drill and countersink for screws in shelf corners. Secure to the supports.

Stencilling a traditional design

Shabby tables, chairs and chests are the best candidates for stencilling. Paint them in matt white, ivory, soft turquoise or grey-greens, then stencil on any design, from Scandinavian hearts and flowers to Greek key borders.

Ready made stencils are sold in craft shops, but you can make your own by tracing a design and enlarging it. Make sure you leave enough uncut sections, or 'bridges', to hold the stencil together.

Cut the stencils from non-absorbent waxed stencil paper or photocopied motifs, and cover them with clear, self-adhesive laminate. Or decorate with a quick drying acrylic, or poster or emulsion paint. Felt pens also work well on stained wood surfaces. Use a stencil brush with stiff bristles and dryish paint.

If you're grouping several designs together, work out your overall pattern on a piece of paper cut to the same size as your work surface. Then use it to position the stencils when you're ready to paint.

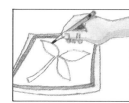

1 Choose a simple design from a stencil pattern book. Use a sheet of carbon paper to trace the design onto non-absorbent waxed stencil board. Then draw an evenly spaced grid on top of the tracing.

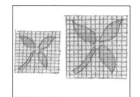

2 To enlarge your design to the desired size, use a ruler to draw a larger grid on a separate piece of paper and draw the design on it by carefully duplicating the pattern in each square of the smaller grid.

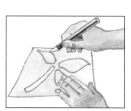

3 Using a sheet of carbon paper, transfer the design to the stencil board. Then cut out the design with a sharp craft knife, being sure to leave bridges of at least ⅛in/3mm. Trim any ragged edges.

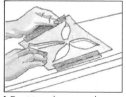

4 Position the stencil on the work surface and tape down the outside edges with masking tape. If you plan to use more than one colour, use more tape to cover those cutouts that will be painted later.

5 Dip your brush in the paint and blot it well on a paper towel so that it holds only a little dryish paint. Working from the sides to the centre, paint each cutout with a quick up-and-down movement.

6 Let the paint dry before lifting the stencil off. Paint over any fuzzy outlines with a fine brush and some background paint colour. Protect the design with a clear, matt craft varnish.

Christmas cards Decorations

Recycle your Christmas cards as seasonal decorations for the following year. Make them into little baskets for the tree or festive place mats.

Paper baskets

These colourful baskets make unusual tree ornaments. Before gluing the paper strips together, fold each strip in half, unfold, and use the crease as a centre mark to make the top of the basket even. The handle could be hung onto the end of a tree branch or secured with a hook.

1 For each basket, cut cards into nine ½ × 8 in/13 × 200 mm strips. Then cut one ½ × 11 in/13 × 280 mm strip, or make one by gluing together two strips.

2 Glue eight 8 in/ 200 mm strips at the centre, using paper adhesive. Stack them colour side down in a circle; weigh them down until the glue dries.

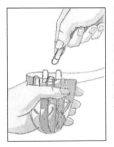

3 Cup the strips in your hand. Stick the remaining 8 in/ 200 mm strip around the top edge and secure each strip to it with a paper clip until the glue dries.

4 Stick on the 11 in/ 280 mm strip as a handle and let the glue dry. Fill the basket with holly sprigs or tiny gifts for children, before hanging on the tree.

Place mats

Twenty to 25 cards are enough to make one 13 × 18 in/330 × 460 mm oval place mat with scalloped edges. The place mats are covered with a protective layer of adhesive plastic, which is easy to wipe clean.

1 Use compasses or a glass to trace 28 circles, each about 3½ in/90 mm across, on the fronts of the cards. Cut them out.

2 Overlap 16 to 18 cutouts to form the outline of an oval on the sticky side of a 13 × 18 in/330 × 460 mm sheet of adhesive plastic. Fill in the centre with the remaining cutouts.

3 Place clear adhesive plastic on top of the cards, sticky side down, and smooth from the middle out to the edges.

4 With sharp scissors, trim away the excess adhesive plastic – both backing and top sheet – to finish the place mat.

Cistern and hopper Planters

Discarded ironware, such as a cast-iron cistern or a drainpipe head, or hopper, can be used imaginatively in the garden, with a little cleaning up and a coat of paint. It is best to treat the ironwork before planting or hanging it. Old paint can be removed with a chemical paint stripper. Loose flaking paint and rust can be removed using a wire brush or a wire brush attachment on an electric drill. If the casting is particularly decorative, valuable or fragile, it may be worth taking it to a specialist to get it shot blasted.

Once down to the bare metal, treat the container inside and out with a proprietary brand of anti-corrosive metal primer, followed by a top coat of a suitable paint. You may be able to pick out some of the fine detail in the casting in a different colour.

These planters look most effective against or hung on a wall, supported by decorative cast-iron brackets.

Clothing Rag rug

Instead of throwing away old clothes, cut them into strips to create a highly individual rug. Any lightweight fabric will do, from old shirts, skirts and shorts to ties, ribbons, and shoelaces.

Apart from the fabric strips, you'll need a 3-count rug canvas, a latch hook to knot the strips onto the canvas, and some 2 in/50mm binding for the edges.

Start by cutting the canvas to the desired size for your rug, adding an extra 1 in/25mm all around. Then press masking tape over the edges to keep them from fraying as you work.

Cut your fabric into ½ in/13mm strips 5 in/125mm long (don't cut on the bias or the strips will tend to fray). Then use the latch hook to knot them onto the rug canvas as shown, mixing the colours, textures and patterns for the most interesting effect.

When you've finished the rug, remove the masking tape, fold and pin the binding over the margin of canvas, and sew it on as close to the knots as possible.

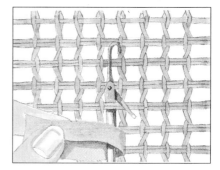

1 Slip the fabric strip around the latch hook and push the curved tip under a strand of canvas. Flip the latch back.

1 Remove light rust with wire wool. For heavily rusted iron, use a wire brush or wire brush attachment in a drill. Wear protective goggles while wire brushing.

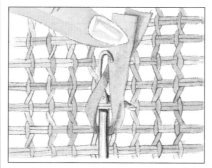

2 Still holding the fabric strip, and with the latch open, bring the ends of the strip up and into the open hook as shown.

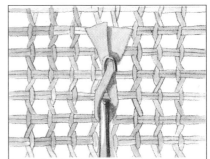

3 Carefully pull the hook across and under the strand. When the latch closes, release the fabric strip.

2 Paint the bare metal with a rust inhibitor, following the maker's instructions. When dry apply a primer inside and out and then a metal paint.

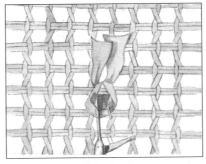

4 Continue to pull the hook across and under. It will pull the ends of the fabric strip through the loop to form a knot.

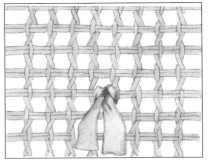

5 Tug on the ends of the fabric strip to tighten the knot and to bring both ends even with each other.

Copper pipes Wind chime

An attractive and decorative wind chime can be made easily from household scraps and is the sort of project to keep children busy during school holidays. With a little experimentation you can hang different materials from bits of nylon fishing line to see which make the best sounds. We used short lengths of copper tubing cut to varying lengths, but the ideas are endless – shells, stones, even scraps of wood.

Suspend the chimes from a wooden disc, or use a small upturned basket or metal dish. To support the disc and hold the chimes, use nylon fishing line. You can drill very small holes right through the disc and tie knots in the line or use small steel screw eyes to hold the line.

1 Draw a 6in/150mm diameter circle on a piece of ½in/13mm thick timber. The chimes will be hung from this disc.

2 Cut out the circle using an electric jigsaw or coping saw. Sand down the rough edges or smooth them with a rasp.

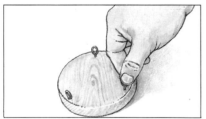

3 With a bradawl, make three equidistant small holes near the edge, and screw steel screw eyes into them.

4 Turn the disc over, make several, evenly spaced holes with the bradawl, and screw in screw eyes. These will hold the chimes.

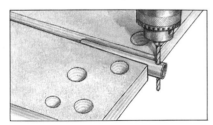

5 Cut varying lengths of tubing using a hacksaw or tube cutter. Remove any burrs. Drill a hole through the top of each tube. Knot fishing line through it.

6 Cut equal lengths of line and tie them onto the three screw eyes. Tie the other ends to an old key ring. Attach the pipes to the screw eyes on the other side.

Corks Pin board

Old wine corks stuck in rows on a thin board can make a useful and attractive pin board. The board is screwed to the wall at the corners and four corks are fixed over the screws to cover them.

First mark up a piece of ¼in/6mm plywood to the size you want your panel to be. Lay the corks on it loosely and adjust the measurements to suit the number and size of corks you have available. After cutting the plywood to size, drill and countersink a hole at each corner to suit the screws for wall mounting.

1 Starting at one corner, avoiding the screw holes, apply PVA wood adhesive to a cork and lay it on the board.

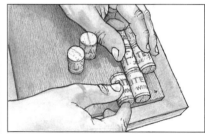

2 Continue gluing the rest of the corks, sticking each cork to the board and to each adjoining cork.

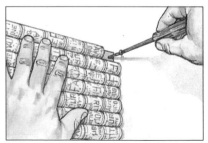

3 When all the corks are glued on, leave the adhesive to dry overnight. Screw the pin board to the wall with countersunk screws, using wall plugs where necessary. Glue the four remaining corks to the board to cover the screw heads.

Curtain Roller blind

If you are replacing old curtains, or even a bedspread, instead of throwing away the old material you could consider using a good section of it for a roller blind. If the material is faded, dye it a bright colour. Alternatively, once the blind is made, you could paint patterns or appliqué shapes onto it.

First wash or dryclean the old fabric and then iron it thoroughly to make sure there are no creases which may prevent it from rolling up smoothly. The best fabric for a roller blind is firm and closely woven. To give the fabric more body if needed, spray the wrong side with an aerosol blind stiffener.

You will need to buy a blind-making kit, available from furnishing shops and department stores or DIY shops. The kit should contain a spring-loaded roller, batten, pull cord, cord cover and knob (or acorn), wall brackets and glue or screws.

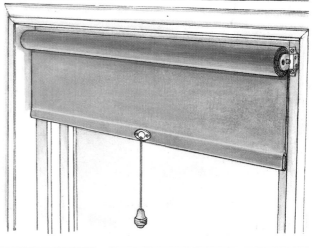

1 First screw the bracket with a slot for the spring-loaded end of the roller either to the side of or above the window recess. The bracket should be on the left as you face the window.

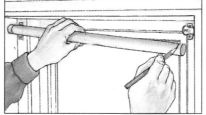

2 Hold the roller with the spring loaded end in the bracket, and mark the length to cut the roller to. Or, measure the window width and mark this on the roller, allowing for the thickness of the other end cap.

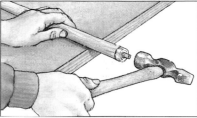

3 Cut the roller to length with a tenon saw, and smooth the end with sandpaper. With the roller laid on a flat surface, so as not to damage the spring mechanism, tap the end cap onto the cut end with a hammer.

4 Cut the fabric to size, adding 1½in/38mm to each side and about 10in/250mm to the length. Use the right angle of a sheet of paper to check that the edges are square. Snip off the selvedges.

5 Trim the sides with pinking shears and turn over 1in/25mm on both edges. Pin in place and check that the width is correct. Press the hem flat and fix with iron-on tape, as shown, or stitch in place.

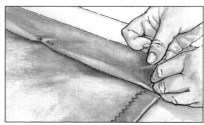

6 Turn up 2in/50mm of the bottom of the fabric, turn in the edge, pin and press. Make sure that the corners are right-angled. Stitch or fix with iron-on tape. Cut the batten to length and slip into the hem.

7 Stitch the sides of the hem. Measure and mark the centre of the bottom edge. Knot the cord into the cord cover and screw it to the centre of the batten. Attach the knob to the end of the cord.

8 Lay the roller on the top edge of the fabric right side up. If the roller does not have a marker line as a guide to laying it straight, draw one on it. Glue the fabric to the line and staple at intervals.

9 Put up the second bracket in line with the first. Roll up the blind and fix it into the brackets. Adjust the spring tension by pulling the blind halfway down the window and re-rolling it.

Renewing deck chairs

Deck chairs that have suffered from exposure to rain and sun can be revived with a stain finish or paint and some bright new fabric.

An upholstery tack remover, available from most DIY shops, makes short work of removing tacks. Then sand the wood with medium-grade abrasive paper, paying special attention to any dark or rusty marks left by old tacks. Paint or stain the frames, as you prefer. If you will

be using the chairs outdoors, finish with a coat of exterior polyurethane varnish.

Choose deck-chair-weight canvas, or double lengths of tough furnishing cottons stitched together. When you cut the fabric, allow 3in/75mm or so extra to wrap around the back rails and seat frame; trim it to the exact size just before hemming and stapling. Pull the fabric as tight as you can when you tack.

1 Remove the old tacks with an upholstery tack remover. Or prise them out with a screwdriver.

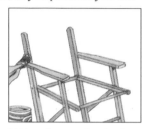

2 Wipe the wood with white spirit. If necessary, sand and finish with paint or stain and polyurethane varnish.

3 Measure the new fabric using the old canvas as a template. Add 3in/75mm for the rails.

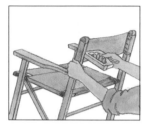

4 Wrap the fabric over the rails and stretch. Hammer tacks or staple into the rails at 2in/50mm intervals.

Desk Workbench

An old desk is a perfect base for a workbench, complete with storage drawers. Instead of lifting it up on blocks to raise the work surface to a comfortable level, build a new top of ³⁄₄in/19mm plywood and 4 × 2in/100 × 50mm softwood, and cover it with a sheet of ¹⁄₈in/3mm hardboard, which will fit snugly into a recess at the top.

Finish the edges all around with pine, making it ¹⁄₈in/3mm higher than the plywood surface to create a recess for the hardboard. Two lengths of 8 × 1in/200 × 25mm pine, 1¹⁄₂in/38mm longer than the width of the plywood, provide the side trim, or end pieces. The front and back trim consists of two pieces of 3 × 1in/75 × 25mm pine for the bottom, and two pieces of 1 × 1in/25 × 25mm pine for the top all cut to the same length as the plywood top.

1 Measure the desk top and cut two pieces of ³⁄₄in/19mm plywood and one piece of ¹⁄₈in/3mm hardboard to match. Cut four pieces of 4 × 2in/100 × 50mm softwood to the width of the desk and two more to the length of the cross braces.

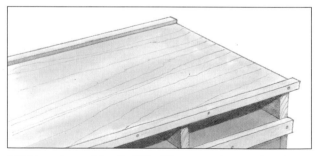

4 Cut two pieces of 1 × 1in/25 × 25mm pine the same length as the desk top. Glue and nail them to the edges of the plywood so that they stand ¹⁄₈in/3mm above the surface, creating a recess for the hardboard.

Doilies Bowls

You can turn crocheted doilies into delicate, lacy bowls by simply stiffening them with a sugar-and-water solution. Use the smallest bowls for sweets or potpourri; larger ones make good centrepieces or bowls for lightweight fruit such as grapes.

This recipe is enough to convert one 9in/230mm doily. Mix up a fresh solution for each bowl.

As you dip a doily into the solution, squeeze it gently with your fingertips for even distribution; repeat two or three times and squeeze out the excess. Use a bowl of the desired size as a mould, turned upside-down on a heavy towel. Leave the doily over it until it is dry.

When you want to restore the doily to its original form, just hold it under warm running water and knead it until it's no longer sticky. Then wash it with a mild detergent.

1 To make the stiffening solution, place 4fl oz/115ml sugar in a large bowl and stir in 2fl oz/60ml boiling water. Stir for 3 minutes or until almost opaque.

2 Dip a dry doily into the solution until it's thoroughly soaked. Squeeze out the excess and stretch it over the mould. Pin the edges to the towel with rustproof pins.

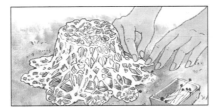

3 Let the doily dry for at least 6 hours. Then unpin it. Loosen it by wedging your fingers between the mould and the doily and working slowly around the perimeter.

4 Gently pull the loosened doily and the mould apart. To prevent small objects from falling through the holes in the bowl, line it with plastic film.

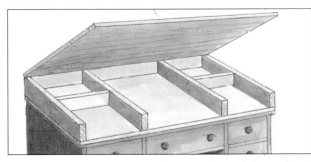

2 Set the 4 × 2in/100 × 50mm timbers on edge and glue and nail them to one of the plywood panels as shown. Then glue and nail the other panel on top so that the 4 × 2in/100 × 50mm pieces are sandwiched between the plywood panels.

3 Cut two lengths of 3 × 1in/75 × 25mm pine the same length as the desk top. These will make the front and back bottom trim for the plywood. Hold the front piece in place before nailing to make sure that it doesn't hinder opening drawers; trim if necessary.

5 To make the end pieces, cut two lengths of 8 × 1in/200 × 25mm pine equal to the width of the plywood plus the trim. Glue and nail them in place so that they extend 1/8in/3mm above the top of the desk.

6 Tidy up the exposed ends of the 4 × 2in/100 × 50mm pieces so that they are flush with the rest of the trim. Insert the hardboard top in the recess and then attach a vice to the corner of the plywood top.

Door Table top

An old door need not be left out in the back yard to rot but could be put to good use as a table top. A flat door is more suitable, but a panelled door could be covered with a sheet of plywood to provide a smooth surface.

There are several ways of covering a table top, from simply painting or staining it, to decorating it with a large photographic print or even fabric glued onto it to provide a permanent surface, as this project shows. The final surface could be several layers of polyurethane varnish sanded down and reapplied or a sheet of toughened or reinforced glass approximately ⅜in/10mm thick, but this then makes the project very expensive. These methods of decoration could also be used to cover an existing table top which may be badly stained or scored.

Fill any holes in the door's upper surface and sand it down. Then prime the surface with a white emulsion, which does not detract from the colour of the fabric laid onto it and gives it maximum luminosity. When the surface is dry, coat it with a diluted PVA adhesive before laying the decorative covering over it. If the covering is fabric, cut it slightly larger than the table top, dampen it thoroughly by dipping it into a bath and then stretch it over the adhesive. Smooth out air bubbles with a clean paintbrush or a wooden ruler. When the fabric is absolutely dry, start applying the layers of varnish.

If you are gluing fabric to the surface it is worth testing out the suitability of the fabric first. The best fabric to use in this way is a medium-weight cotton with a close weave. Stick a small piece of the chosen material onto a painted scrap of wood and brush on some adhesive to make sure that the dyes in the fabric do not run, that there is no reaction between the glue and the varnish, and that the overall finish is what you desire.

Once the table top has been made, you could mount it on trestles or an existing table frame. Neaten the edges by nailing or screwing strips of wooden or aluminium moulding to them.

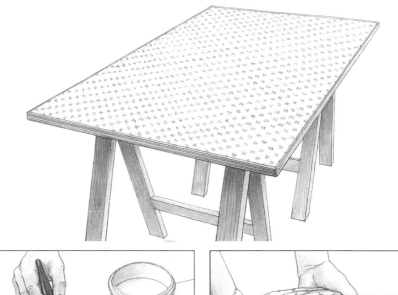

1 Prepare the surface with a white emulsion. Then coat it evenly with a diluted PVA adhesive/sealer.

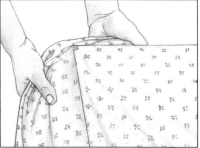

2 Dampen the cloth thoroughly, lay it on top of the still sticky glued surface and stretch it flat.

3 Sweep the cloth with a clean brush to smooth it out. Hammer tacks into the edges to hold the cloth taut while it dries.

4 When dry, remove tacks and trim the material, leaving a little over the edges. Apply 3 or 4 coats of varnish.

5 To build up a glassy finish, rub down each dry coat of varnish with fine wet and dry abrasive paper.

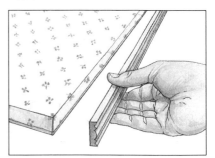

6 When you are happy with the surface, nail or screw a hardwood or aluminium edging strip all round.

Marbling to give an antique finish

Give walls, woodwork, mantelpieces and furniture the look of fine marble with this simple painting technique.

First, find a picture or sample of the marble that you want to imitate. You will need four or five colours of emulsion paint, including white, as well as dark brown or black poster paint. Soft white, pale grey or warm beige are good background colours to form the base paint. Darker paints should be used to paint in the marble streaks or veins, and they will need to be feathered with the very dark poster paints.

When dry, protect the finish with a coat of clear craft varnish.

 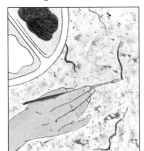 

1 Apply the base paint to the surface. When it is dry, pour the paints for the streaks onto a couple of paper plates. You will need a darker colour than the base, such as ochre and dark grey. Sponge on the colour lightly in diagonal stripes. Then take a rag and a damp sponge and smooth out the colour in places. You may need to use some white paint or the base coat colour to blend the colours smoothly.

2 When the paint is dry, take a feather or a fine 00 artist's brush. Dip it into the dark brown or black poster colour, and paint rough lines over the veins. Then 'fidget' in the colour with the brush tip. While the paint is still wet, use a damp sponge to lightly dab the veins in different places to soften any harsh lines.

3 To add a speckled effect over a marbled surface, dip an old toothbrush into dark brown or black poster paint or a contrasting colour as shown here, and flick a knife or your thumb across the bristles. Be careful not to overdo it – a few well-placed splatters should be enough. When the paint is completely dry, apply a couple of coats of matt finish craft varnish to seal and protect the surface.

Doors Folding screen

Hinge two or three old doors together for a folding screen that can divide a room or shield a corner. Then try your hand at marbling (above), sponging (p.357) or stencilling (p.347), to turn your screen into a true original. Buy steel or brass butt hinges which are the appropriate width for the doors. You'll also need to fill holes and cracks with wood filler.

First sand or strip the doors. Then remove the old hinges. Make a wooden fillet to fill the hinge recess and a wooden plug to fill the lock or door handle hole. Tidy up the remaining gaps with wood filler.

If, once you have hinged the doors together, the tops of the doors are out of alignment, place the unfolded screen across two sawhorses or trestles. Clamp a board all the way across the top, flush with the lowest door, as a guide. Then trim the protruding tops with a circular saw or plane them off to make them all level.

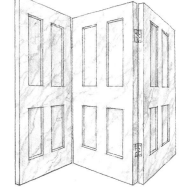

1 Remove the old hinges and fill the recesses with a wooden fillet glued into place. Fill any gaps with wood filler.

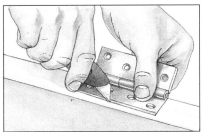

2 Align the doors at the bottom and mark the position of the new hinges 6in/150mm from the top and bottom.

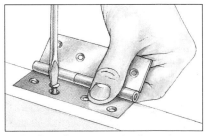

3 Chisel out the recesses for the new hinges and screw them into place. For heavy doors, fit a third, central hinge.

Drainpipe Uplighter

A lamp that shines up from the floor creates dramatic light and shadows, especially if it's placed indoors among potted plants. For an uplighter that's as attractive as it is simple, you can easily convert a round clay drainpipe.

All you need apart from the drainpipe is a piece of ½in/13mm plywood and a lamp kit (sold in DIY shops) that contains a socket, a threaded brass nipple, nuts and washers and a lamp cord with the plug attached.

Cut a plywood disc to fit inside the pipe, attach the lamp parts and screw in a bulb. Simply plug in the lamp or fit it with a switch. For safety, don't bed the lamp in earth, and if it is placed near plants, remove them for watering.

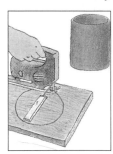

1 Cut a circle of ½in/13mm plywood about ¹⁄₁₆in/2mm smaller than the inside diameter of the pipe.

2 Drill a ⅜in/10mm hole in the centre of the disc. Then drill a ¼in/6mm hole near the base of the pipe.

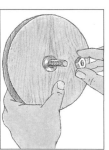

3 Fit a 1½in/38mm brass nipple into the hole in the plywood and secure a washer and nut on each side.

4 Thread the bare end of the lamp cord through the hole in the bottom of the pipe, then up through the nipple.

5 Wrap the two wires clockwise round the appropriate terminal screws of the socket. Screw the socket onto the nipple.

6 Turn the plywood disc on edge and wedge it into the bottom of the pipe. Screw in a bulb and plug in the lamp.

Drawers Bookcase

By joining a few old wooden drawers together an attractive bookcase can be easily constructed. Select the number of drawers and decide how you wish to arrange them. You could stack them one on top of another to make a tall, narrow bookcase, or place them side by side, or arrange them in steps.

First remove any fittings such as handles or knobs. The drawer front may be able to be removed by unscrewing it from the inside of the drawer. But before you remove the drawer fronts, consider whether you would like one or several to form a top for the bookcase. Some have a lip which extends beyond the drawer and forms an attractive gable. If the drawers are big you can subdivide them or add a shelf to take small books.

1 Cut pieces of 1 × 1in/25 × 25mm softwood to fit the depth of the drawer. Screw them in halfway up each side. Cut a shelf to fit. Glue it in with PVA wood adhesive.

2 Fill any old screw holes with wood filler and use a fillet of wood to plug any grooves in the drawer sides. Glue it in with wood adhesive and fix with pins.

3 To fasten the drawers together, drill and countersink one of the sides. Screw the drawers together, making a pilot hole for the screw with a bradawl.

4 Finally, lightly sand down the bookcase and paint, stain or varnish it to match the furniture in the room. You could also sponge the wood for a textured effect.

Sponge patterns

All it takes is a sponge and emulsion paints to give an attractive stippled pattern to anything from a bookcase to living-room walls. Inexpensive, tiny, natural sea sponges are excellent for sponging small objects; a bath-size sponge is best for walls; latex sponges are effective over large areas.

Pick two or three harmonious colours, such as creams and whites with a pale turquoise, beige, greys and peach. Try out colour combinations on a 'dab board' first. Once you've decided, brush on the lightest colour and let it dry thoroughly.

1 Dip a damp sponge into the second colour and wipe off any excess on absorbent paper.

2 'Pounce' or dab the paint on with firm, swift movements. When dry, repeat with the third colour.

3 When the paint is dry, brush on a couple of protective coats of clear, matt craft varnish.

Drying rack Tie rack

The top of an old drying rack makes a space-saving tie holder for your cupboard door. All you need are a couple of brass hinges and lightweight chains to fix it in place. Then add a screw eye and hook to keep it up out of the way. Just make sure the rack is wide enough to attach to the stiles or side panels of your door; the centre section may be too flimsy to support the hardware.

Start by removing the rack from the legs. Measure between the arms of the rack and cut a section of leg to size to use as an end piece. Cut the ends of the arms square if they are rounded or notched, then screw the end piece in place or join it with dowel pins. Sand and paint the rack or finish it to match the door.

Once you've screwed brass hinges into the end piece, attach a chain near the end of each arm of the rack and mount the rack at eye level on the back

of the cupboard door. Fold the rack up and mark the positions of the chains on the door; then level the rack and hold the chains to the marks. Cut them to the appropriate length and fix them to the door with screws.

Put a screw eye in the centre of the front dowel, then fold up the rack to position the hook. Clip the rack to the hook when closing the cupboard door.

1 Free the top section of the drying rack from the folding legs by removing the small brads or prising out the nails that hold it in place.

3 Attach hinges about 1 in/ 25mm from each end of the end piece. Then secure chains near the other ends of the arms with No. 4 screws.

5 Fold the rack against the door and mark the position of the chains. Use a spirit level to adjust the rack. Cut the chains to the correct length.

2 Cut a section from one of the rack legs. Drill and countersink for two No. 8 screws and attach it to the end of the arms as an end piece.

4 Fit a screw eye into the front dowel. Draw a level line on the cupboard door and place the rack against it, screwing the hinges into the side panels of the door.

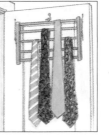

6 Fold the rack flat against the door to mark the position for a screw hook. Then install it so that it engages the screw eye on the rack.

Fabric scraps Napkins and gift decorations

Fabric left over from sewing projects can be used to decorate jars of homemade preserves and dress up the bottles of spirits or liqueurs you're giving as presents. Large scraps can be cut with pinking shears – and left unhemmed – to make pretty fabric napkins for parties and gifts. These projects are easy enough for children to do.

Jar lid covers

These handmade fabric tops give your jars of homemade chutneys and preserves the professional finish of those sold in specialist food shops. Use traditional checked gingham or a pretty paisley for a country look or choose a solid colour and trim it with lace or rickrack. If you're passing on the jars as gifts, why not combine them in a basket with a few napkins that match the lid covers?

1 Trace the jar lid on the wrong side of the fabric, add 2in/50mm all round, and cut out with pinking shears.

2 Use latex glue to fix the trim. Secure the cover on the lid with a rubber band, then tie with ribbon.

Napkins

Use these to complement your gifts of homemade treats. Or make several from different fabrics to use at a party or buffet. Cut large remnants of material into squares of 10in/250mm, using pinking shears. The napkins will stand up to four or five trips through the washing machine, because the pinked edges will not fray easily.

Cut out a 10in/250mm square of cardboard and trace round it with chalk on the wrong side of the fabric. Cut out with pinking shears and fold.

Bottle bag

With a sewing machine, you can make one of these clever little gift bags in less than 5 minutes. Use a running stitch to sew a seam on the wrong side of the fabric and then turn the piece inside out so that the seam won't show.

Your finished product doesn't have to be used just for a bottle of Christmas cheer. Make bags of different sizes for other gifts – toys for a child's birthday or assorted kitchen gadgets for a bride-to-be. You could decorate the bags by gluing on a few felt cutouts or sequins, felt letters to form a name or greeting, or embroider a pattern or picture on it. Tie with a bow of ribbon or wool.

1 Cut a piece of fabric 13 × 15in/330 × 380mm. Hem a short side by folding over ½in/13mm of material.

2 Fold in half lengthwise, wrong side out. Press, then sew the long side and bottom with a running stitch.

3 Turn right side out and press the seam flat. Put the bottle inside and tie at the neck with ribbon or wool.

Printing with potatoes

Carve a simple motif on a cut potato, dip it into poster, emulsion or fabric paints or press it on a stamp pad. Your prints will have that attractive, uneven, handmade look redolent of stencilling and naive folk art.

Potato prints also give individual style to gift wrappings. Use decorator's white lining paper, available from DIY shops. You can also print flat surfaces, such as table tops, chests, bedheads, trays and boxes. Protect designs with a coat of clear craft varnish.

If you're printing a row of the same design, cut a notch in the potato skin at the top of the design so that you can keep the prints aligned.

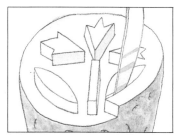

1 Cut a large potato in half and use a pencil to sketch your design on the surface. With a paring knife or artist's knife, carve ¼in/6mm into the pulp to remove the sections that are not part of the design.

2 Wipe off any moisture on the potato surface with kitchen paper. For printing on paper, ink pads provide ideal, instant colour. When decorating fabrics and furniture, brush paint onto the cut potato.

Fence Headboard

To give your plain bed the look of a handsome antique, attach a section of decorative iron fence to the frame as a headboard. Two gates can be bolted together to serve the purpose as well. Ensure that the iron struts are not more than 4 in / 100mm apart and that the gap between the bed and a horizontal strut is not more than 4 in / 100mm. This is to prevent a child from getting its head stuck in the gaps.

A hacksaw will probably be strong enough to cut the fencing to size; be sure to have several coarse blades on hand – they'll dull quickly. Alternatively, an angle grinder with a cutting disc will do the job. If the metal is too heavy to cut, take the fence to a professional metal-worker and have it trimmed.

1 Choose an attractive section of fence and cut it to the width of your bed frame with a hacksaw equipped with a coarse blade or angle grinder with a cutting disc.

2 Strip the railings down to bare metal by sandblasting them, sanding thoroughly or using paint stripper. Prime with metal primer and spray-paint to match your bedroom.

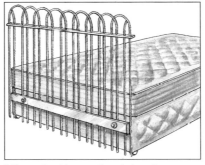

3 If your bed frame already has flanges for mounting a headboard, use a long steel, aluminium or wooden strip with two fixing holes to clamp it onto the bed.

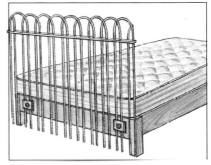

4 For a pine bed frame without flanges, use two large steel or aluminium washers and bolts to fix the fence onto the bed. Tighten well.

Fish tank Herb garden

An old fish tank, cleaned and shining, can become a striking indoor garden in a few easy steps and with little effort.

Herbs are a practical choice for this window garden, but the idea works just as well for ornamental purposes. Consider planting crocuses or tulips, flowering cacti or even ornamental grasses. Cacti need a different compost from other plants, and should be planted in separate pots within the tank if you wish to display them together with other sorts of plants.

To start, tip out any remaining gravel and keep it aside. Fill the tank with water to check for leaks. If you find any, seal them with mastic sealant or transparent waterproof tape. (You can turn the repaired side of the finished garden to the window so that it won't show.) Wash the glass with warm soapy water and rinse several times.

Polish away fingerprints with a dry cloth (but don't use window cleaner on the inside since it may harm the plants).

If you plan to keep the garden on a wood table, line the bottom of the tank with felt to protect the table's finish.

If you wish to, you can reuse the gravel which you kept to one side as a drainage base for the soil. First wash the gravel well to remove any slime and chemicals. If your tank did not hold any gravel, buy some or get hold of some small, chipped stones. Spread a 1 in / 25mm layer of gravel or stones over the bottom of the tank. Then cover the base with a 1 in / 25mm layer of charcoal chips, which will provide some nutrients.

Fill the tank to within about 5 in / 125mm of the top with sterilised potting soil. Transplant some healthy herbs, bulbs or other flowering plants from your local nursery and water them well so that the soil is moist but not soggy. Cacti will need less water.

Place the garden on a table or portable TV stand next to a sunny window. Keep the soil moist but don't overwater it.

Floorboards Dolly

If you're replacing old floorboards, don't chop them all up for firewood – a couple will come in handy as a dolly to make light work of heavy loads.

First remove any nails from the boards and sand down any splintered edges. Cut two lengths of about 30in/760mm.

Place the two boards side by side on your workbench and measure their total width. Then cut two pieces of 2 × 1 in/50 × 25 mm softwood to this length and screw them onto each end of the floorboards. Attach 4 castors. Then drill holes in one end of the floorboards for a rope to pull the dolly with.

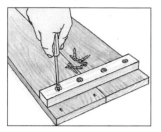

1 Treat the cut wood with preservative. Drill four holes through the 2 × 1 in/50 × 25mm pieces and countersink them. Screw onto the boards 2in/50mm from each end.

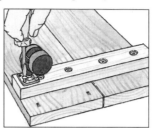

2 Screw a castor onto each end of the 2 × 1 in/50 × 25mm pieces. Choose the correct type of castor for the weight you intend to carry and the terrain it will be travelling over.

3 Drill two holes into one end of the boards. Thread the rope through one hole. Fit a piece of hose pipe onto the rope and thread the rope through the other hole. Knot.

4 The finished dolly will be sturdy enough to pull a fully loaded crate. If you are going to pull very heavy loads over uneven terrain, fit the dolly with large castors.

Rejuvenating a folding table and chairs

Give a card or garden table set a face-lift by painting the frames and re-covering the top and seats with some bright, waterproof PVC fabric and they'll look like new.

Start by removing the old fabric and wadding from the chair seats and tabletop. Lever out staples or tacks with a screwdriver. Wipe down the frames with white spirit and sand off any blemishes. Treat rust on metal frames with metal primer after first sanding the rusted areas. Spray paints are good for this project, but use them in a well-ventilated area, preferably outside. Prevent drips by applying two light coats instead of one heavy one.

For upholstering wooden-seat frames, a heavy-duty staple gun or an adhesive gun make the job quicker. Otherwise attach the waterproof fabric with upholstery tacks. Metal chair seats can be made more comfortable with tie-on cushions.

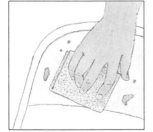

1 Sand the frames and check the metal for any blemishes. Treat rust spots on metal frames with primer.

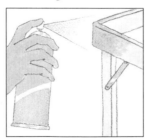

2 Working in a ventilated area, wipe over the chair frames with white spirit. Spray-paint with two coats.

3 Cut thin foam sheet to fit the table top and seats. Cut PVC to the same size plus 2in/50mm all round.

4 Centre the wadding and PVC on the tabletop and seats. Staple, glue or tack in position. Trim excess fabric.

Garden hose Soaker hose

That leaky old garden hose can be a boon to your garden. Just drill more holes in it and use it as a soaker hose. It waters more deeply and gently than the usual spray or sprinkler – and more efficiently, as less water is lost to evaporation. It is important that the tap end of the hose attached to the soaker hose is fitted with a non-return valve to prevent backflow into the mains. Place the hose next to plants – or, for an invisible watering system, bury it in a trench alongside them. If you plan to use it to water shrubs or trees, save still more water by drilling holes only in the sections adjacent to the plants.

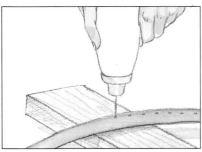

1 Place the hose on some scrap wood and drill ¹⁄₁₆in/2mm holes all the way through, spaced about 1in/25mm apart.

2 Attach the soaker hose to a new piece of hose, without holes, with a brass or plastic coupling.

3 Seal off the loose end of the soaker hose with a plastic or metal plug and a hose clip. Place the hose next to the plants or bury it near them, taking care not to damage the roots as you dig. Adjust the water to a trickle and leave it on for 30 to 40 minutes.

Renewing hangers

Old wooden hangers – the kind with a single bar – can be transformed into luxurious and colourful padded ones with quilting and a silk cover.

Cut the quilting to 10 × 18in/250 × 460mm. Sew three pieces of fabric together to make the cover, gathering two of them to form decorative gathers. Finish off the hanger with a ribbon bow. You might want to tie on a small pot pourri sachet as well, which will lightly perfume the cupboard.

The directions given here are for a standard 16in/400mm hanger.

1 Snip a hole in the centre for the hanger hook, and wrap the quilting around the hanger, cutting a hole for the hook in each layer. Tack along the edge.

2 Cut fabric into two 5 × 12in/125 × 300mm top pieces and a 5 × 19in/125 × 480mm bottom piece. Sew a gathering stitch along the long sides of the top pieces.

3 Lay the top pieces on the bottom piece, wrong side out. Arrange the gathers until the pieces fit together. Sew one of the top pieces to the bottom piece.

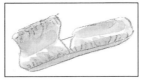

4 Sew the second top piece to the bottom, leaving most of one side open so that you can fit it over the hanger. Then turn this fabric sleeve right side out.

5 Gently pull the sleeve over both ends of the hanger. Hand-stitch the open side of the sleeve together. Stitch the top pieces together at the hook.

6 Tie a ribbon bow of a contrasting colour to the hook to decorate the hanger. Or, if you like, attach a small, lightly scented sachet with ribbon.

Jars and bottles Vases

Make unusual and attractive vases from old jars and bottles simply with spray-paint or felt pens and some imagination. Car spray-paints are ideal. But always work in a well-ventilated area and wear a mask, rubber gloves and an apron. Spray over shapes cut from masking tape, and peel them off later to reveal the colour of the glass. Or spray over dry paint with a second colour. You could also draw patterns or write on the glass with waterproof felt pens. Glass paints thinned with methylated spirits are suitable for simple motifs on small jars. When drawing or painting on clear glass slip a roll of white paper inside the jar to make the motif easier to see. You could trace a pattern onto the paper and use it as a guide. Coat the dried paint with a clear craft varnish to protect it.

Using a thin paintbrush, brush glass paint onto the glass with single strokes. Don't try to work over the paint. It's easier if you work with a pattern in front of you.

Stick irregular strips of masking tape onto the bottle. Spray-paint and wait for the paint to dry. Then spatter with a second colour. When dry, peel off the masking tape.

Spray the jar, rotating it to get a uniform colour. When dry, sand any drips. Draw over the jar with waterproof felt pens. You could use several colours for the pattern.

Spray-painting

Spray-painting with gloss paints can give a very professional finish both on irregular surfaces such as wicker, or smooth surfaces such as ceramic and glass. Car spray-paints come in a huge variety of colours, as do modelling paints, which come in 40ml mini spray cans and are good for painting small objects. Spray in a well-ventilated area and wear a protective mask, rubber gloves and apron. Shake the can well for at least 2 minutes before spraying. Hold the can at 90° to the items you are spraying.

Bed of nails

Tap finishing nails into a ceiling tile to act as little poles to support small objects. If the bottom of an object already has a recess – as a drawer knob has – it will stay on the head of the nail without a problem. If there's no recess, you'll need to drive the nail through the tile, pointed end up, and stick the sharp point into the underside of the object to keep it from moving around in the force of the spray.

Supporting an object on a nail allows you to spray all round the object and under it at the same time. Spray only one object at a time.

Wire mesh platform

Choose a piece of wire mesh 12-24in/300-610mm long. Cut 4in/100mm squares from each corner, then bend the edges over to form a rough box shape. The wire is stiff enough to hold its shape by itself. The raised mesh makes a handy platform for spraying wooden and cardboard cutouts. Spray-paint lightly; when one side is almost dry, turn the objects over and spray them on the other.

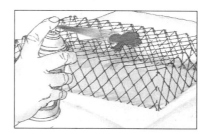

A wire mesh platform makes it easy to spray flat and cutout objects without having them stick to the surface or having to handle them too much.

Cardboard spraying booth

Make a nifty little spraying booth from an old cardboard box, a wooden dowel and some clothes-pegs. Use a sharp craft knife to cut the box as shown. Cut two notches for the dowel near the top of the box, then glue the top ends of the clothespegs (the ends that you pinch) to the dowel with epoxy adhesive. Clamp small objects in the clothespegs and spray with a couple of light coats. To spray the other side, simply turn the dowel round.

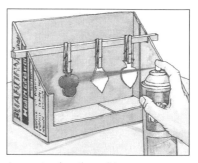

A spraying booth enables you to spray small objects from several angles and also contains the overspray. Use in an open, well-ventilated area.

Renewing a lampshade

If an old lampshade is discoloured and stained, give it a face-lift with a new fabric cover.

Leave the old shade on and sew the new cover on top of it. Measure the bottom diameter of the shade and multiply by 3 ½ to get the length of fabric you'll need, then measure the height of the shade and add 2 ¼ in / 57 mm to get the width. Cut the fabric, sew the ends together, then pleat and stitch it. Trim the edges of the new shade with a decorative trim.

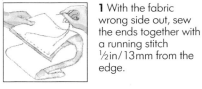

1 With the fabric wrong side out, sew the ends together with a running stitch ½ in / 13 mm from the edge.

2 Place the cover right side out over the shade and fold the top edge into pleats, securing them with a straight pin.

3 Remove the cover from the shade and stitch the pleats with a continuous running stitch, 1 in / 25 mm from the top edge. Unpin.

4 Peg the cover to the shade aligning the top stitch and the top edge. Pleat the bottom and pin. Remove and stitch 1 in / 25 mm from the bottom edge.

5 Replace the cover, align the stitches with the edges of the shade, and sew the cover to the shade frame with an overcast stitch.

6 Cut off excess fabric. Trim the edges of the shade with double-fold bias binding, ribbon or braid fixed with latex glue.

Packing crate Table

A rough, weather-beaten crate makes an interesting side table that fits perfectly with country-style decor. If weathered wood is not to your taste, sand and prime the crate and paint it. You could also stain or sponge it for a more unusual effect or even paint it with thinned paint for a fashionably faded, 'distressed' look (see p.337).

Set the crate on its side. Drive in any loose nails and pull out rusty ones and replace them. Then cut a piece of ½ in / 13 mm plywood to fit the top of the crate and nail four small plywood blocks to the underside to keep the top from shifting (place them just close enough to the edge to fit inside the crate).

Use a piece of canvas as a cover to complement your rustic table. Then, depending on its height and shape, top the table with a lamp and use it as a side table or place it in front of a sofa as a coffee table with an arrangement of dried flowers.

3 Cut a piece of canvas or country print heavy cotton fabric to throw over the crate, and place it at an angle for the best effect. For a more rustic look, pull several threads off the edges of the fabric to create a fringe on all four sides.

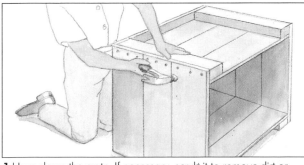

1 Hose down the crate. If necessary, scrub it to remove dirt or peeling paint. Drive any raised nailheads into the wood and sand any rough corners.

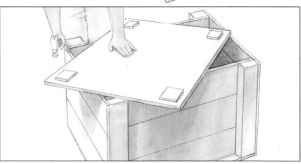

2 Cut a piece of ½ in / 13 mm plywood to fit the outside dimensions of the top of the crate. Then glue and nail small plywood blocks to the underside of the top.

Paper towel tubes
Napkin rings

For some fun napkin rings, cut up paper towel tubes with a craft knife and cover them with gathered sleeves of fabric, or raffia bias binding wound round the tubes. Children love to make the simpler napkin rings, embellishing them with discarded costume jewellery or dried flowers. When you cut the tubes, take care not to push the cylinder out of shape.

Gathered fabric Cut a 4 × 9in/100 × 230mm piece of fabric, fold it in half lengthwise, and iron flat. Cut a 1½in/38mm section of paper towel tube with a craft knife and insert it into the fold. Hand-sew the cut edges of the fabric, gathering it as you go. Trim excess fabric.

Raffia Wind a strip of 50in/1.25m raffia to the inside of the ring and let dry. Wind over the top and up again. At each top turn, tuck the raffia under the previous loop and pull it out all the way. Continue until the ring is covered. Stitch the last few loops in place.

Bias binding Glue a 50in/1.25m strip of binding inside the ring at an angle. Wind the binding around the ring, slanting it slightly and overlapping half of each previous turn. Secure the last turn with a few stitches.

Picket fence Garden trellis

When you replace an old picket fence, keep aside a section or two to use as a garden trellis. Bolted together to form an A-frame, two sections provide climbing space – and in hot weather, welcome shade – for beans, peas and tomatoes. Use two equal sections of fencing to construct this simple trellis. If you don't want to bolt them together, try securing them with wire.

Alternatively, you could attach a section of fence to a planter box and fix it to a patio or balcony wall for climbing roses or jasmine. Use an existing planter or make your own from any 12 × 1in/300 × 25mm timber (waterproof the wood first with a PVA varnish). Just be sure that the box is slightly longer than the section of fence you plan to use for the trellis.

A-frame trellis

1 Cut two sections of fence (4-8ft/1.2-2.4m), so that the rails are about 2in/50mm longer than the pickets at each end. Then position the two sections to form an A-frame, with the rails flush against each other.

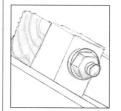

2 Drill a ¼in/6mm hole through the joined rails and fasten together with ¼in/6mm bolts; secure with nuts and washers.

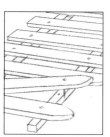

3 If your trellis is higher than 6ft/1.8m, anchor it by driving four stakes into the ground and nailing the four rails to them.

Planter trellis

1 Cut a section of fence and prise off two pickets. For a uniform look, saw the pointed ends off. Sand rough areas and paint with several coats of exterior paint.

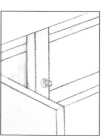

2 Position the exposed rails at the back of the box and drill ¼in/6mm holes. Attach the fence with ¼in/6mm bolts and fill the box with soil to keep it from tipping over.

Lightening wood

Stripping a piece of furniture will lighten it, but using special wood lighteners or bleachers will create more dramatic and even paler colours. Lightening heavy, dark carved oak furniture and picture frames enhances the wood grain, gives it a contemporary look and makes it a shade or two lighter than its original colour. Bleaching, however, actually whitens wood.

Most wood bleaching and lightening kits contain hydrogen peroxide. Some of these solutions are self-neutralising, but others may need an application of vinegar and water to neutralise them.

Always read the manufacturer's instructions carefully, work in a well-ventilated area and wear rubber gloves and protective clothing. Successful results depend largely on thorough removal of all the old finishes beforehand, as lightening products will work only on bare wood. Wet the wood with water after you've stripped it. If it darkens evenly, it will bleach to a uniform colour; any light areas must be stripped again.

Once the wood dries after the first application, it should be lighter. To make it lighter still, apply the solution two or three more times. But don't overdo it – after four or five applications the wood may start to look grey and lifeless. If this happens, wipe on a light stain to highlight the grain and add definition.

1 Protect the work area with newspapers and a plastic sheet. Apply the first part of the bleach or lightener, and leave it to dry.

2 Apply the second part of the lightening solution. If further lightening is needed, use spot applications to touch up areas of uneven colour.

3 Let the treated wood dry out at least overnight. Then sand twice, first with medium-grade abrasive paper, then with a fine grade.

4 Finish the wood with an oil or wax, or a wood stain. Pastel colours take well on whitened woods. Coat with a clear, matt craft varnish.

Picture frame Mirror frame

An old picture frame can be revitalised as a mirror frame and painted or stained. If it still contains a picture, remove the back and the picture, and carefully lift out the glass. If the glass is intact, use it as a template for your mirror. If not, measure the recess. Get a piece of mirror glass cut to size. When fitting the mirror into the frame try not to touch the silvered backing, which lifts off easily. A large frame will need a hardboard backing nailed and taped to the back of the frame to support the mirror.

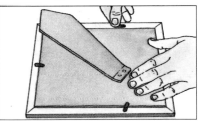

1 Remove the backing from the frame. This may involve twisting the retaining tabs to release the backing, or mean peeling off tape and removing staples.

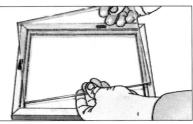

2 Take out any backing paper and the picture. Then carefully lift out the glass. Use the measurements of the glass for the mirror to be cut.

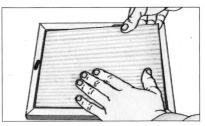

3 Carefully fit the mirror into the glass rebate, and then pack the back with corrugated cardboard. Secure the original backing in place or fit a new one.

Quilt Place mats

When an old quilt is worn beyond repair, cut out the undamaged sections and use them as place mats and pot holders. You simply stitch extra-wide double-band bias binding around the edges.

For a set of place mats, you'll need quilted sections of about 12 × 18 in/300 × 460mm. To determine the length of bias binding you need for the edging, measure the outside edges of the piece, add them together and add 3 in/75mm to the total. Make pot holders 10 in/250mm square; add 8 in/200mm to the binding so that you'll have enough to make a loop from which to hang each pot holder.

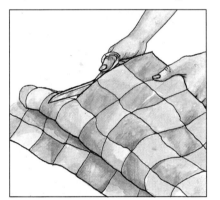

1 Cut out a good section of quilt. Measure the edges. Cut the binding to the measurement. Add 3 in/75mm for place mats, 8 in/200mm for pot holders.

2 Unfold the bias binding at one end and stitch a ½ in/13mm hem. Pin the outside edge of the unfolded tape to the edge of the fabric. Stitch along the first crease.

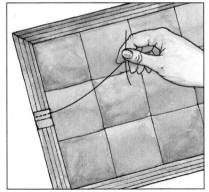

3 Pin and stitch the binding to the other three sides. Mitre the corners as you go. Then fold the end of the tape under and stitch a ½ in/13mm hem. Remove the pins.

4 Fold the binding over the edge of the fabric so that there is a double fold of binding on the wrong side. Sew it to the wrong side with a running stitch.

Ribbons Clutch bag

Weave some old ribbons together to create a colourful piece of silky material. Then, after lining the back, turn it into an eye-catching clutch bag.

Hardly any sewing is involved. You weave the ribbons directly onto a 12 × 19 in/300 × 480mm piece of fusible interfacing, pinning the ends as you

1 Cut 18 in/460mm lengths of ribbon to measure 11 in/280mm across when pinned side by side to the interfacing.

3 Remove the pins and fuse the ribbons to the interfacing with a hot iron. Then trim the material to 10 × 17 in/250 × 430mm.

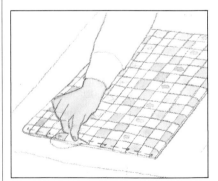

5 Turn the piece right side out, turn in the open lining edge, pin it in place and hem stitch it closed.

work. Then press with a hot iron. The work will go even more smoothly if you place the interfacing on a padded surface, such as a folded towel or a clean rug. Once you've lined the material and folded it into a bag shape, attach a fastener and a decorative tassel, a catch, or button and loop to close it.

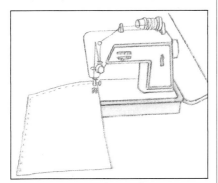

2 Cut several 11in/280mm ribbons and weave them through, pushing them tight and pinning each end as you go.

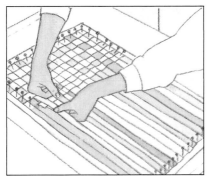

4 Pin lining fabric 10¾ × 17¾in/269 × 449mm to the ribbon side of the piece and stitch around three sides.

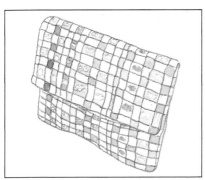

6 Fold one end up 5½in/140mm and hem stitch the edges together. Fold the top flap over and sew on a catch.

Road maps Paper trim

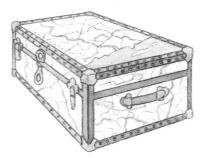

In your cupboard you may already have stashed away the most eye-catching paper for covering boxes, trunks or small wall areas – old road maps! Once you've bought some wallpaper paste, you'll find the paper is almost as easy to apply as the adhesive plastic sold in DIY stores, especially if you let it lie flat for a while and press out the creases with a warm iron.

Road maps aren't the only material you can use for this decorative technique. Be imaginative and try navigation charts, vintage magazine covers – even sheet music. Remember, however, that some paper is so thin that even a new razor blade can't trim it without fraying the edges. If this is the case, paste the paper down and let it dry before trimming (before the paste dries, use your fingernail to make an outline of the area to be cut).

If the surface you're covering has a bold pattern that might show through, give it a coat of white paint and let it dry. Then prime the surface with some diluted paste.

1 Thoroughly clean the surface to be covered and use a wide brush to prime it with diluted wallpaper paste. Let the paste dry for at least 3 hours.

2 Spread ready-prepared wallpaper paste onto the back of the paper with a small roller or paste brush. Fold the pasted sides together until you need them.

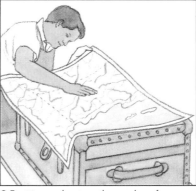

3 Position a sheet on the work surface, paste side down, and use your hands to slowly smooth it from the centre towards the edges to prevent air bubbles.

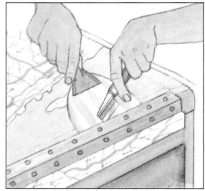

4 Trim the paper with a craft knife, using a wide putty knife as a guide. If the paper tears easily, wait until it is dry before trimming.

Rolling pin Key keeper

What do you do with an old wooden rolling pin? Make a bracket from scrap wood and fit the rolling pin into it, creating a revolving bulletin board. Mounted on the wall and adorned with a few cup hooks and crocodile clips, it makes an ingenious holder for your various keys, business cards, and messages. You need never again turn the house upside down looking for your car keys!

The bracket consists of a baseboard and two arms with holes for the rolling-pin handles. Use any scrap wood you have on hand and make it as decorative as you like. Bevel the front edges of the arms with a rasp or a saw and incorporate a few scrolls and turns – or even some hand carving – into the entire piece. Drill and countersink for four screws to hold the pieces together.

Another idea is to saw slits into the rolling pin itself. The slits should be

angled downwards to hold business or calling cards. They can be sawn both horizontally and vertically on the pin to form a decorative pattern of squares in which you can centre the cup hooks and other holders.

Before you assemble the unit, stain or paint the bracket – and the rolling pin if you like (be aware, however, that the stains are not likely to match, since the wood of the rolling pin and the bracket is likely to be different). Then apply two light coats of matt-finish polyurethane varnish. Or try sponging colour onto the rolling pin or lightening it and the bracket (see pp.356-7, 364-5) for a still more interesting look.

Use No. 8 screws and suitable wall plugs to mount the unit to the wall in a place where it will be seen often – near the front or back door or next to the kitchen phone.

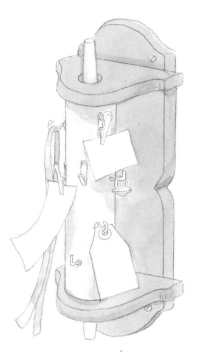

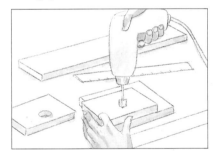

1 From a piece of ¾in/19mm pine, cut a baseboard about 1in/25mm longer than the length of your rolling pin. From the same wood, cut two arms and drill a central hole in each, large enough to hold the rolling-pin handles.

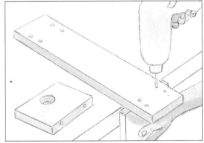

2 Drill and countersink two holes at each end of the baseboard for the No. 8 screws that will attach the unit to a wall. Position the arms underneath and drill two holes for No. 4 screws in the baseboard and the arms.

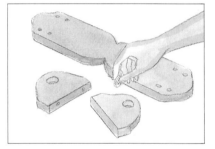

3 Bevel the edges of the wood, and shape as you like. Sand and stain, then apply two coats of polyurethane varnish, sanding lightly between coats. Glue a fibre washer to the hole in the lower arm to make the rolling pin rotate more easily.

4 Pre-drill several holes for cup hooks, and screws to hold the crocodile clips, on all sides of the rolling pin. Screw in the cup hooks and screws and attach the crocodile clips. Saw slits into the surface to hold cards.

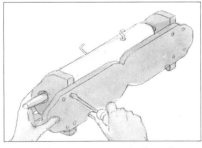

5 Attach the upper arm to the base from behind with countersunk No. 4 screws. Insert the top handle of the rolling pin through the hole, then place the lower arm over the bottom handle and attach with screws as shown.

6 Choose a spot in the kitchen or near the back door. Hold the unit against the wall at eye level and mark the positions of the holes on the wall, then drill for No. 8 screws. Mount the unit and hang it with keys, cards and messages.

Salad bowls Bird feeder

Plastic or wooden salad bowls of two different sizes make a clever bird feeder that has the added advantage of discouraging squirrels. No feeder is entirely squirrel-proof, of course, but the slippery roof of this one makes it harder for the furry thieves to reach the seed.

Choose a large bowl as a roof and another about half the size as a feeder. The two bowls, one of them upside-down, are joined with a threaded rod and secured with nuts and washers. To hang the feeder, bend the top of the rod into a hook (allow a few inches for the hook when you put the first nut in place) or attach a lamp hook or ceiling hook for a hanging plant, with a nut.

The birds you attract will depend on the positions of the bowls. Leave plenty of space between the bowls to attract large birds, or place them close together to limit the feed to smaller birds. If you use transparent plastic bowls you will have the added pleasure of being able to see the birds while they feed, especially if you hang the feeder near a window.

1 Drill a hole through the centre of each bowl to accommodate your threaded rod, using scrap wood as a backing as you drill through the bowls.

2 Place a nut near the end of a threaded rod, add a flat washer and insert the rod inside the large bowl. Secure with another washer and nut on top.

3 Place another nut and washer at the other end of the rod and secure the small bowl so that the insides of the two bowls face each other.

4 Bend the rod above the large bowl to form a hanging hook. Fill the small bowl with bird seed and hang the feeder from a tree branch.

Renewing a sofa with loose covers

Reupholster a sofa cheaply and quickly by fitting loose covers. You will need three pieces of fabric, one for the back and seats, and two for the arms and sides. To fix the folds of fabric down the front and back edges of the sofa, punch eyelets into the fabric and thread them with coloured silk cord, or pin them with ribbons or rosettes, or use Velcro or ties.

For the back piece, measure from the floor to the top of the sofa back, the width of the top, the depth of the back down to the seat, the seat width and from the front of the seat to the floor. Add 6-8in/150-200mm for pushing inside the back seat and 1in/25mm at each end for a hem at the front and back. Measure the width of the sofa and add 2in/50mm on either side.

For each side piece, measure from the floor to the top of the sofa arm, the width of the arm and from the top of the arm to the seat. Add 1in/25mm for a hem at the side and 4-6in/100-150mm to tuck inside the seat.

Hem the outside edges of the fabric pieces, with machine seams or iron-on webbing. If the back is to be visible, hang curtain weights in the back hem to weigh it down and give it a professional finish.

1 Drape the side pieces over the arms and adjust so that they touch the floor. Push the excess down into the sides.

2 Similarly, drape the back piece so that it touches the floor. Push the excess fabric down into the seat.

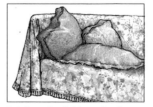

3 Fold the material at the back corners and down the edges. Tack with stitches to hold in place, if necessary.

4 Adjust the folds at the front of the arms to suit and fix with tacking, Velcro, ties or threaded cord, as you wish.

Tablecloth Runner and napkins

Don't consign a stained or torn tablecloth to the rag bag. Instead, cut out an unmarred panel and hem it for use as a table runner; then cut out some smaller sections to turn into matching place mats or napkins. If the fabric is free of fluff you can make tea towels from it, too.

First cut your runner to a width of 15in/380mm. Cut place mats to 15 × 18in/380 × 460mm and napkins in 16in/400mm squares (use coloured tailor's chalk as your marker for a white tablecloth, white chalk for dark fabric). After hemming, this will yield a 14in/360mm runner, 14 × 17in/360 × 430mm mats and 15in/380mm square napkins. As you stitch the hems, mitre all corners as shown.

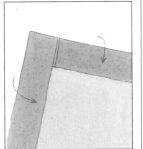

1 Cut a clean section of cloth. Fold the right side over ½in/13mm on all four sides and press.

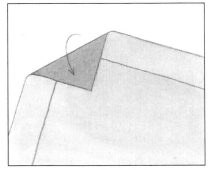

2 To mitre a corner, first fold the point back on itself and press with an iron to make a crease.

3 Unfold the corner, place the unfolded hem flaps together wrong side out, and stitch along the diagonal crease.

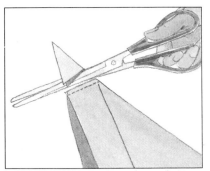

4 Trim the fabric just above the stitch. Turn the hem flaps right side out and straighten to form a neat corner.

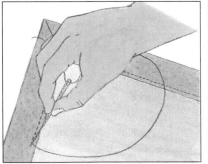

5 Stitch the adjoining hem flap down the edge and mitre the next corner when you come to it.

Timber Planter

You can easily create a rustic planter which will blend into your garden, with timber offcuts and solid logs. The logs can be retrieved from a tree you may have chopped down or from a timber yard at very little expense. Select the straightest, most uniform pieces.

Measure the width of the pieces and plan the dimensions of your planter to suit. Use galvanised nails to fix the timbers together. First make the base from 3 × 2in/75 × 50mm timber.

Treat the finished planter with wood preservative.

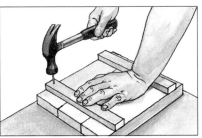

1 Measure the total width of the base pieces. Cut two pieces of 2 x 1in/50 × 25mm section to this length and nail them to the base.

3 Drill the ends of the timber to make starter holes for the nails to prevent the wood from splitting. Nail the frame together using galvanised nails.

5 Stand the base and frame on edge and nail the rough-edged timber to them with the frame at one end of the timber and the base at the other.

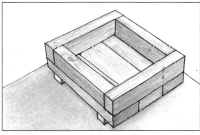

2 Cut four pieces of 3 × 2in/75 x 50mm or 2 × 2in/50 × 50mm section to make a frame the same size as the base. This will sit at the top of the planter.

4 Cut enough pieces of rough timber to clad one side of the planter without overlapping. Cut them approximately 12in/300mm long with a saw.

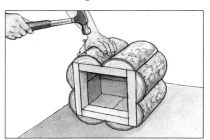

6 Selecting pieces of timber that best fit the sides, cut them to size and continue nailing them around the planter. Trim the width of the timber where necessary.

Brightening up clothes with fabric paints

Fabric paints, sold at craft and hobby shops, enable you to give new life to old clothes you might otherwise throw away. Use them to paint colourful designs or emblazon your name on jeans, sweatshirts, T-shirts and plimsolls. Or give your own touch to a roller blind (see p.35) or a table runner and napkins (see opposite). To decorate canvas shoes, make cardboard patterns of your designs and trace round them on the shoes with a pencil. Then fill in the designs with the fabric paints.

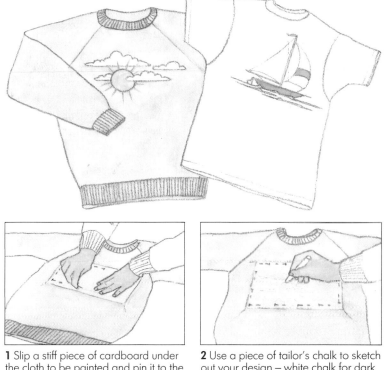

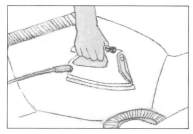

1 Slip a stiff piece of cardboard under the cloth to be painted and pin it to the cloth. Leave the cardboard in as you sketch and paint. It will protect the second layer of fabric and provide a firm surface to work on.

2 Use a piece of tailor's chalk to sketch out your design – white chalk for dark fabrics and coloured chalk for lighter colours and whites. If you make any mistakes, lightly rub them out with a damp cloth.

3 Paint your design with the fabric paints, using brushes of several different sizes for variety in strokes and shapes. Apply the paint sparingly and let it dry for at least 12 hours before preparing to set it with an iron.

4 Unpin and remove the cardboard, turn the fabric wrong side out and place a towel under the painted area. Press the wrong side of the painting with an iron set at the hottest setting for that particular fabric.

Tins Containers

Here's the simplest recycling project of all – save tins and decorate them. Then use them as attractive containers for fudge, sweets and other treats. Or convert those with plastic lids into coin banks – a simple and entertaining project which children can do by themselves.

For an interesting look, try using a spray-paint to create a spatter effect. Use car paints, which come in bright colours. These should be used only in a well-ventilated area, preferably outside, and you should wear a protective mask and clothing. Press the spray button lightly, varying the pressure to produce paint droplets. Let the paint dry before spraying with a second colour.

Desk organiser

Glue a few painted tins together to make an organiser for your odds and ends.

Choose tins of different sizes, spray-paint them as ·shown on the right, and then arrange as you choose. Use a glue gun to attach the cans to one another with hot glue. Fill your holders with pens, paper clips and other equipment.

Coin bank

Use a tin that has a plastic lid. Spray-paint as above; then, with a sharp craft knife, cut a ⅛in/3mm slit in the centre of the lid. Let your child decorate the bank with stickers or transfers once the paint is dry – either arranging a few figures or shapes in a ring around the can or covering most of the surface with a colourful collage.

Gift holders

Use tins with plastic lids. Or make your own cover by cutting a piece of fabric with pinking shears and securing it with ribbon or wool. Even plastic film is fine, especially if you dress it up with stick-on stars or other designs.

To make your gift tins look even neater, leave the metal rims unpainted (do the same with the desk organiser and coin bank if you like). Just mask the top and bottom rims with masking tape. The bottom circle of tape will keep the tin lifted off the surface and make freeing it after painting easier.

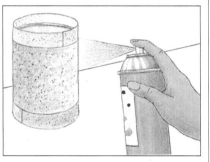

1 To give your painted tins a professional look, protect the shiny metal top and bottom rims with masking tape before spraying them with a car spray-paint.

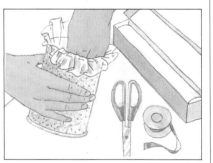

2 When the paint is dry, line the inside of the tin with plastic film. Once you've filled it, press on the lid or secure a cover on top with a piece of ribbon.

Tree branch Post and door handle

Recycle fallen tree branches – as rustic signposts, birdbath supports or door handles.

When you go to a wooded area to find your material, choose a branch that's a little heavier than you think you'll need. Check it thoroughly to see that it has no signs of decay or insect damage.

For a signpost, look for a large, straight branch and a couple of smaller

Signpost

Choose a sturdy branch measuring 5-6ft/1.5-1.8m in length and then select two smaller branches to make the arm for your sign to hang from. Drill a 1-2in/ 25-50mm hole near the top of the post and whittle the end

of one straight small branch to fit snugly into the hole. Then brace the joint with a branch that has a natural curve; hold it in place with large brass screws and reinforce it by tying a loop of rope around it. Attach two small chains to the branch, and screw two hooks into the top of the sign to fix onto the chains.

Installing the post

1 Dig a hole three times the diameter of the branch. Add about 2in/50mm of stones to the hole and insert the post. Prop it up with two timber stays.

ones to form a right-angle arm. An irregular board sawn from another branch can provide the sign that you'll hang from the post.

For a support for a birdbath, choose a heavy branch with a natural crook at the top. The crook should fit the diameter of your birdbath.

For a door handle, use a sharply curved branch that is thin enough to fit in your hand but thick enough to be sturdy.

Bird table

Start with a table top from exterior grade plywood, 18 × 12 in / 460 × 300mm in size, with a rim of 1 × 1 in / 25 × 25mm softwood around the edges. Cut one of the rim pieces 2 in / 50mm shorter than the others to leave a gap for drainage and cleaning. Paint the completed table top with non-toxic wood preservative.

Find a forked branch that will fit within the length of the table top and cut it so that the two forks are even. Set the post into the ground, as detailed below. Then nail the table top onto it with galvanised nails.

If you plan to leave the bark on, make sure it is smooth enough to be comfortable to the touch.

Use galvanised nails or brass screws for all three of these projects. And lengthen the life of the posts by treating the ends with wood preservative before you place them in the ground.

Measure the diameter of the tree branch. Multiply the diameter by 3 and dig a hole to at least that depth.

Door handle

Start with a nicely curved branch thin enough to get your hand around and cut an 18 in / 460mm section out of it. Saw or plane the end to make a flat surface suitable for mounting the branch on a door. You can leave the bark as it is, but sand down any rough or splintered areas, or strip off the bark; either way, the branch will eventually develop a smooth patina simply from being handled.

Pre-drill two holes about 2 in / 50mm from each end. Position the branch on the door and mark for drilling, then attach with brass screws.

Tyre rim Planter

Many hollow metal objects, once they've been given a coat of paint, can make attractive planters to hold groups of plants in pots – and tyre rims are no exception. The steel rim needs to be cleaned thoroughly to remove any rust or loose paint before being painted with anti-rust primer and car paint.

1 Using a wire brush or wire brush attachment for an electric drill, remove any rust or loose paint from the inside and outside of the wheel rim.

2 Prepare a small bag of dry-mix concrete and fill the hole with it, forcing it around the post and the edges of the hole and packing it just above ground level.

3 Using a trowel, smooth the concrete around the base of the post so that it tapers to the ground at an angle to allow rainwater to fall off.

2 Once the metal has been thoroughly cleaned, paint it with a good-quality anti-rust primer and spray or brush on car paint. Arrange your plants within the rim.

Repairing wicker and cane work

Cane furniture

The most common repair to cane furniture is replacing broken or missing binding cane. Binding cane can be found in specialist or craft shops. Take a piece of the cane from your furniture with you to be sure that you buy the same thickness. Estimate the length you will need and buy at least 6in/150mm more to allow for folding it under at each end. Remove broken or unravelled binding cane. Soak the new piece in hot water for 15-20 minutes to make it pliable. You need a staple gun with staples of about ¼-⅓in/6-8mm, or ½in/13mm panel pins, to hold the binding cane at its start and finish.

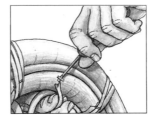

1 Remove any damaged staples or pins holding the binding cane. Or loosen good staples for use later.

2 Twist the end of the softened cane and fold it back on itself. Staple or pin to the back of the chair.

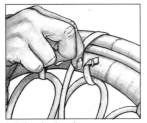

3 Take the binding cane under the chair arch and wrap it tightly round to cover the starting point.

4 Wrap the cane around the chair arch two or three times. At the back of the chair, cut the strip to 4in/100mm.

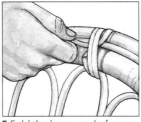

5 Fold the loose end of cane back on itself. Push the reversed end under the cane to the other side.

6 Staple or pin through the cane and the piece tucked under it. Trim the cane close to the binding.

Baskets

Wicker work can be repaired simply by soaking a replacement reed in warm water and then weaving it in place. This applies to a chair back or seat, or a basket. But one of the most frustrating mishaps can be a broken basket handle, particularly when the rest of the basket is in perfect condition. You'll need a thick piece of cane for the bow (the stout cane that forms the handle), and binding cane to wrap around it. The bow will need to soak for at least an hour; the binding cane needs only 15-20 minutes. Strip off the old binding, pull out the broken bow and use it as a guide to the length of the new bow.

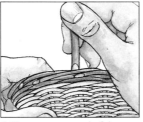

1 Sharpen one end of the new bow. Push it down through the basketweave next to a stave, if there is one, to about 2in/50mm.

2 Bend the bow. Cut it to length, allowing 2in/50mm extra to push into the weave. Sharpen the end and insert it opposite the first end.

3 Insert the binding to the left of the bow. Bend it across the bow to the right and push it through the basket to the inside just below the rim.

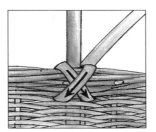

4 Pull the binding over the rim to the outside and across the left of the bow. Push it through inside.

5 Wrap the binding tightly around the bow. Then wind the binding round the rim as in 3 and 4.

6 Push the loose end through the weave to the outside just below the rim. Cut close to the rim.

Wine bottle Lamp

A plain wine bottle makes a simple lamp base with clean lines. All you need to convert it is a bottle adapter lamp kit (sold at hardware and lighting shops) and a lamp shade.

The base of the bottle adapter kit is made to fit most sizes of bottle mouth. You may also want to fit a cable click switch – this allows the lamp to be turned on and off nearby, without requiring you to go to the wall plug every time.

Because the lamp cord runs from the lamp holder instead of being concealed in the base, this lamp is best used in an informal setting.

If the bottle is tall and slender (as some commemorative or decorative containers are), it may need ballast. In that case, fill it with small stones, shells or sand. If the bottle glass is clear, you might want to use the coloured fish-tank gravel sold at pet shops or coloured marbles.

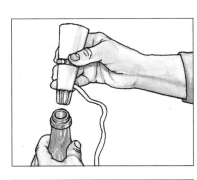

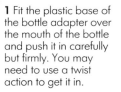

1 Fit the plastic base of the bottle adapter over the mouth of the bottle and push it in carefully but firmly. You may need to use a twist action to get it in.

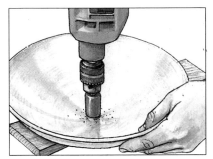

2 Splice the cord and attach the wires to the appropriate screws in a cable click switch. By fitting this you don't have to move far to switch the lamp on and off.

Wok lid Hanging lamp

The shiny aluminium lid of a Chinese wok makes a contemporary-style shade for a hanging lamp. All you have to do is remove the handle, which will probably be wooden and fixed with a screw, drill a hole in the centre and fit a lampholder connected to a flex. Lampholders and flex are sold at hardware and lighting shops. You could also spiral flex for a more decorative look.

It is best to use a lid that has not seen much wear and has therefore not absorbed a lot of oil. If you are using an old lid, scrub it and soak it thoroughly several times to remove all traces of grease. If you do not do this, the grease will smoke when it is heated by the bulb.

To diffuse the glare of the light, use a half-silvered reflector bulb, and you could paint the inside of the lid white. Flattened bulbs suit the shape of the lamp and also help to diffuse the light.

It is essential that the lamp is secured to the ceiling hook from which the flex is suspended, to prevent it from falling if the plug is taken out of the wall socket. Or use the wok lampshade in place of an existing, unwanted hanging lampshade.

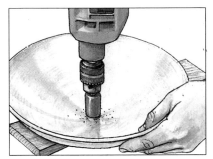

1 Place the inverted lid on some scrap wood. Drill a 1 in/25 mm hole in the centre using a hole saw attached to your electric drill. Check that the lampholder fits.

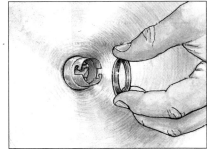

2 Clean up any rough edges with a round file. Insert the lampholder into the hole and make sure it is centred. Then tighten the retaining ring to lock it in place.

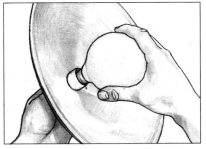

3 Screw a bulb into the socket. Install a hook in the ceiling where you want the fixture to hang and another hook in the ceiling above a socket.

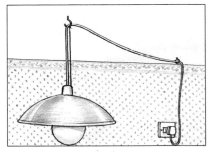

4 Hook the flex over the ceiling hook and adjust the lamp to the desired height. Lead the flex to the second hook and then down to the socket.

Wooden ladder Toy box

To make a handy storage box for toys or other bulky objects, mount an old ladder horizontally on a wall and hang some brightly coloured canvas carrier bags from its rungs. You'll need little more than screws, bolts, and a couple of wooden supports.

A short section of ladder – five or six rungs – should be adequate, but the unit can be as long as you like. Clear pine sections, $3 \times 1\frac{1}{2}$in / 75×38mm in width, will make sturdy supports. Make sure that the vertical supports for the ladder rail are no higher than 18in / 460mm so that the toy-filled bags will be within easy reach of children.

Sand the ladder to remove splinters. Fix the supports onto each end with a coach bolt and washer. If the unit is longer than 4ft / 1.2m, add a third support in the centre. Then use 3in / 75mm screws to attach the ladder to the wall. Before you fix the carrier bags onto the ladder, paint it or stain it a bright colour.

Canvas carrier bags that measure about 16×22in / 400×560mm are big enough to fill the spaces between the rungs. Secure them at each corner with a screw and washer, then screw each side to the centre of a rung. You can either remove the handles of the bags or drape them over the sides.

1 To make the supports for the ladder, saw two pieces of $3 \times 1\frac{1}{2}$in / 75×38mm clear pine to a a length of 18in / 460mm.

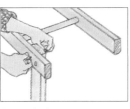

2 Attach the supports near both ends of the ladder rail, using a suitable coach bolt and a washer to secure them.

3 Position the ladder rail against the wall and drill for No. 10 screws. Then attach it to the wall with 3in / 75mm screws.

4 Hold a canvas carrier bag between each set of rungs and drill $\frac{1}{8}$in / 3mm pilot holes in all four corners and at the centre of the rungs on either side.

5 Fix each canvas bag with $\frac{3}{4}$in / 19mm No. 8 round head screws and washers at their corners and at the centre of the rungs.

6 If the bags lose their shape when filled with toys or other items, cut a piece of $\frac{1}{4}$in / 6mm plywood to • fit into each as a solid bottom.

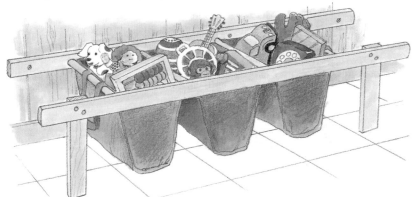

Sanding techniques

Having trouble sanding the curves and crevices on a piece of furniture? Some common household items can become simple sanding aids for those awkward shapes.

Tape To make a sanding strip for sanding round chair legs, balusters and other similar shapes, cut a strip of electrical or masking tape 3in / 75mm longer than the sandpaper. Stick the tape onto the back of the sandpaper along the edge. Fold the extra tape over the grit side as handles, then cut the sandpaper to the width of the tape. Use a gentle backwards and forwards movement for smooth results.

Playing cards For hard-to-reach grooves on picture frames, window frames or drawer tracks, use a deck of playing cards as a sanding block. Wrap the sandpaper around one edge of the deck and grip onto the extra paper on either side of the block. The block will take on the shape of the irregular surface as you push the edge against it.

Sanding block When sanding large flat areas, use a timber or cork block. Wrap the sandpaper around the block and hold along the long edges as you sand the area.

Wood scraps Drawing board and candle holders

The leftover wood on your workshop floor doesn't have to end up as fireplace kindling. Instead, turn some of the end scraps into interesting little candle holders; just cut them to various heights, bore holes in the ends, and glue them together in any design you choose. Or use a piece of shelving and some waist elastic to put together a drawing board with pen or pencil holders for a child. Both projects are easy to make, and both make excellent gifts.

Drawing board

This child's drawing board, complete with handle, has room for four coloured marker pens. The drawing pad is secured by stapling the cardboard backing onto the board (use heavy-duty staples to make sure the pad stays in place).

When you staple down the strips of waist elastic to hold the marker pens, pull them tight before you drive in the second staple, then neatly trim away the excess.

Candle holders

The project shown uses pieces of wood 2 × 2in/50 × 50mm, but you can use wood scraps of any shape and invent your own design.

Caution Don't leave burning candles unattended; a sputtering flame can ignite wood.

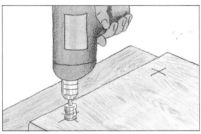

1 Cut pine to 12 × 18 × 1in/300 × 460 × 25mm. Drill a 1in/25mm hole 3in/75mm from one edge and 1½in/38mm from top.

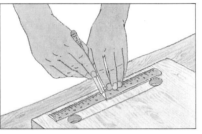

2 Drill another 1in/25mm hole in the same position on the opposite side, then draw horizontal lines to connect the holes.

1 Cut scraps of 2 × 2in/50 × 50mm square section pine into 3in/75mm, 5in/125mm and 7in/180mm lengths.

3 Use a coping or electric jig saw to cut out the area between the holes to make a handle. Sand and apply a finish.

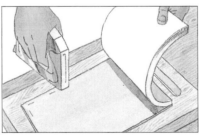

4 When the finish dries, centre an 11 × 8in/280 × 200mm drawing pad below the handle and staple to the board.

2 Check the diameter of the candles you plan to use and bore a hole the same size in the end of each piece of wood.

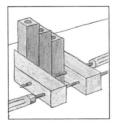

3 Sand the pieces smooth and use wood adhesive to attach them to each other, side by side. Clamp together until the glue dries.

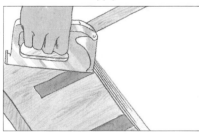

5 Staple the end of a wide piece of waist elastic just beneath the pad. Place a marker pen next to the staple.

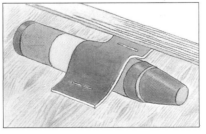

6 Pull the elastic over the marker pen and staple it to the other side. Make holders for three more pens in the same way.

4 Stain with a clear finish or paint as you like. Or, if you choose, leave the wood unfinished. Fit the candles into the holes.

Wrought-iron gate Garden screen

If you have an old wrought-iron gate or panel which is beyond repair, don't just throw it on the scrap heap. By salvaging the good decorative elements and framing them with timber, you can create an attractive screen to hide unsightly dustbins, a trellis or even an indoor room divider. Extra cast-iron rods and decorative pieces of wrought iron are available from ironmongers if you would like to add to what you've salvaged.

Decide how you will arrange the pieces and select timber of a suitable size to make the frame. The vertical sides of the timber frame should be shorter than the length of the metal-work by the thickness of the horizontal sides. Paint the metal before you assemble the frame. If surfaces are badly pitted, a matt black paint conceals blemishes better than shiny gloss. Or you could give it a verdigris finish, as shown below.

1 With a hacksaw, cut off the corroded areas of metal from the gate. These are most likely to be the hinges and the outer frame.

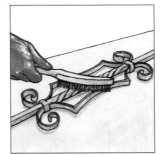

2 Wearing rubber gloves, use a wire brush to remove any rust or flaky paint. Then paint the cleaned iron with a rust inhibitor.

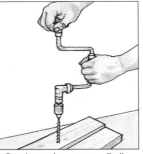

3 Cut the timber to size. Drill holes into the top and bottom pieces to accommodate the metal struts. Chisel them to fit square bars, if needed.

4 Assemble the frame and metalwork and screw the framework together. Fix it to a supporting wall, or fix on timber feet if freestanding.

Creating an antique look with verdigris

Wrought and cast-iron can be given a fashionably 'antique' look by simulating the green colour, or verdigris, of oxidised bronze and copper. The technique can also be used on wood and plastic. Use a picture of an object with verdigris as a colour guide, and test out the technique to get the colour you want. Work in a well-ventilated area, cover your work surface with plastic sheeting and wear a mask and protective clothing. Emulsion paints can be substituted with artist's acrylic paint, which comes in smaller amounts. These are mixed with fast-drying powdered filler, so work quickly in small areas at a time; use old paintbrushes. Coat outdoor objects with matt acrylic varnish.

1 Remove any rust or flaking paint with sandpaper or scrub with a wire brush and water. Leave to dry.

2 Spray with bronze, copper or gold car paint. If the object is made from bronze or copper, leave it plain.

3 Mix one part dark green emulsion paint to four parts water. Brush on, leaving some metallic areas bare.

4 Mix light turquoise emulsion with plaster filler powder to make a dryish paint. Don't add water.

5 Brush on, allowing previous colours to show through in places. Repeat with mint green emulsion.

6 When dry, scrub back the paint on the edges and weathered areas with a nail brush and water.

FORMULAS & RECIPES

Why pay more for your household products and herbal remedies than you have to? Do away with packaging costs with these simple, foolproof formulas for homemade alternatives. And follow the recipes for family favourites — including low-fat coffee cake, strawberry jam and Yorkshire pudding — for a healthy, preservative-free diet.

African violet compost

Also suitable for gesneriads, fibrous begonias, caladiums and most ferns.

To make as much as you need
3 parts peat
2 parts vermiculite
1 part perlite
Balanced potting nutrients, available from garden centres and used as directed on packet

Mix all the ingredients in a bucket. Don't repot African violets in too much space – unless the roots thoroughly penetrate the soil, it will remain wet and the plant will rot. As a rule, the diameter of the pot should be one-third that of the plant.

After-bath splash

A refreshing citrus-scented lotion.

To make 5fl oz/150ml
4fl oz/115ml rubbing alcohol
3 teaspoons lemon essence
Juice of 1 lime

In a small bowl, combine the alcohol, lemon essence and lime juice. Shake well, and then transfer to a covered jar and store in the refrigerator. On dry skin, use a moisturiser after the splash.

Aftershave

To soothe your skin and leave it smelling fresh.

To make about 16fl oz/450ml
16fl oz/450ml rubbing alcohol
1 tablespoon glycerine
1 tablespoon dried lavender
1 teaspoon dried rosemary
1 teaspoon ground cloves

Combine all the ingredients in a medium-size bowl and then transfer to a lidded jar. Refrigerate for 3-4 days, shaking occasionally to mix the ingredients. Strain before using. The aftershave will keep for 1-2 months if tightly covered and refrigerated.

Air freshener

A spicy fragrance that will overpower most strong smells.

To make 8fl oz/225ml
4 tablespoons dried sage
8 tablespoons crumbled bay leaves
8fl oz/225ml witch hazel

Mix all the ingredients together in a jar. Cover and leave to sit in a dark place (but not the fridge) for 3 days. Strain out the herbs and pour the remaining liquid into a spray bottle. Use as necessary.
Eucalyptus variation This fragrant freshener made of 7oz/200g eucalyptus leaves and 1¾ pints/1 litre vinegar will freshen up most rooms. Marinade the eucalyptus leaves in the vinegar for 2 weeks, then strain off the leaves and discard them. Store the freshener in a screw-top jar. To use, place a small amount of the liquid in shallow bowls close to central heating radiators.

Alcohol-free tropical punch

A good way to pamper your teetotal and car-driving guests.

To make 6 servings
7oz/200g creamed coconut
½ pint/285ml water
4 ripe bananas
Juice of 2 lemons
Bottle of lemonade

Dissolve the coconut in the water, purée the bananas with the lemon juice, and mix the two together. Dilute to taste with the lemonade and serve.

All-purpose cleaner

For heavy-duty help when removing tough stains from worktops, woodwork or tiling.

To make 4 pints/2.3 litres concentrated cleaner
8 tablespoons household ammonia
8 tablespoons washing soda
2 pints 8fl oz/1.4 litres warm water

In a large plastic jug with a lid, combine the ammonia, washing soda and 8fl oz/225ml of the warm water. Close the jug, shake vigorously and then add the remaining warm water. Label the jug clearly with the contents.
   To use, mix 4fl oz/115ml of the cleaner with about 12 pints/7 litres of hot water. Before using on delicate surfaces such as wallpaper, test on a small, inconspicuous area.

Almond butter

If you are tired of peanut butter, try this delicious alternative nut paste.

To make 8fl oz/225ml
10oz/275g blanched almonds, whole or slivered
2 tablespoons vegetable oil
½ level teaspoon salt

Preheat the oven to Gas Mark 2, 150°C/300°F. On an ungreased baking sheet, roast the nuts for about 20 minutes or until they are lightly browned. Leave to cool and then transfer them to a blender or food processor. (For a chunkier spread, coarsely chop a quarter of the nuts and set them to one side for later.)
   Add the oil and salt and blend until creamy, working in batches if neces-

sary. (If chopped nuts were set aside, stir them in now.) Transfer the butter to a covered container; it will keep for up to 1 month tightly covered and refrigerated.

Aluminium cleaner

Removes tarnish and greasy film from cookware and surfaces.

To make 8oz/225g cleaner
8 tablespoons cream of tartar
8 tablespoons bicarbonate of soda
4fl oz/115ml white vinegar
4 tablespoons soap flakes

Combine the cream of tartar and bicarbonate of soda in a medium-size bowl. Add the vinegar and mix until the ingredients form a soft paste. Add the soap flakes. Transfer to a jar or bottle with a secure lid and label it clearly.

To use, apply with a steel wool pad, then rinse off with warm water. Store out of the reach of children. It should keep for 1-2 years.

Anti-dandruff scalp massage

This simple remedy can help to clear dandruff problems.

To make 1 treatment
½oz/15g sage leaves
1¾ pints/1 litre water

Place the sage leaves and water in a saucepan and boil over a moderate heat for 5 minutes. Leave it to infuse for another 5 minutes, then strain. Massage into the scalp with the fingertips.

Antiperspirant

This rose-scented spray will keep you fresh and dry.

To make 1 pint/570ml
8fl oz/225ml purified water
8fl oz/225ml rubbing alcohol
2 tablespoons alum
3 tablespoons rose water

In a small bowl, mix the water, alcohol, alum and rose water together. To use, transfer the mixture into a plastic spray bottle.

Antistatic solution

You can prevent carpets made of synthetic fibres from collecting so much dust by spraying them with this homemade preparation.

To make 1¼ pints/725ml
1 pint/570ml water
¼ pint/150ml fabric softener

Mix the water and fabric softener together in a bowl or jug and then transfer the solution to a spray bottle. Spray the liquid lightly and evenly all over the carpet surface.

Aphid spray

Some swear organic insect sprays work, others say they do not. Try this concoction on your garden aphids.

To make 6 pints/3.4 litres spray
1lb/450g elder or rhubarb leaves, or
8oz/225g wormwood leaves
6 pints/3.4 litres water

Chop up the leaves and place in a large saucepan with 2 pints/1.15 litres water. Bring to the boil and simmer for 30 minutes. Strain off the leaves, add the rest of the water and allow to cool. Transfer to a spray bottle, clearly labelled, and use against aphids as required.

Apple butter

The apples used in this spicy low-sugar spread are cooked uncored and with their skins on; the pectin these parts contain adds body to the butter.

To make 1½lb/700g
4lb/1.8kg Granny Smith or Golden Delicious apples, quartered
8oz/225g caster sugar
16fl oz/450ml apple cider
1 vanilla pod, split
2 cinnamon sticks
4 whole cloves

Place the apple quarters in a large saucepan, cover with a lid and cook over a low heat for about 30 minutes, or until soft. (The apples should contain enough moisture to keep them from burning; if they do dry out, add a few tablespoons of water.)

Force the apples through a food mill or sieve into a large saucepan; discard the solids. Add the sugar, cider, vanilla pod, cinnamon sticks and cloves. Cook the mixture over a low heat, uncovered, for about 1½ hours, or until it holds its shape when parted with a spoon.

Let the mixture cool slightly and then remove the vanilla pod, cinnamon and cloves. While still warm, transfer the apple butter to two hot, sterilised 12oz/340g jam jars and cover. If stored in the refrigerator, the apple butter will keep for 1 month.

Astringent

This effective astringent tightens pores and helps remove excess oil from your skin.

To make 6fl oz/175ml
½ lemon, sliced thin
½ orange, sliced thin
6fl oz/175ml rubbing alcohol

Place the lemon and orange slices in a blender and add the rubbing alcohol. Blend until the fruits are well puréed – for about 1 minute – and then strain through a small strainer or cheesecloth into a jar. It will keep for up to 6 months in the refrigerator.

Baby powder

A powder to keep you and your children's skin soft and dry.

To make 3oz/85g
2 tablespoons crumbled, dried
camomile flowers
4 tablespoons cornflour
1 tablespoon orris root
½ teaspoon alum

In a small bowl, mix all the ingredients together. Transfer into old talcum powder boxes to store.
Caution Do not use on a baby's nappy rash.

Barbecue sauce

A delicious sauce good with beef, chicken or pork which contains absolutely no preservatives.

To make about 1 pint/570ml
1 medium onion,
peeled and finely chopped
2fl oz/60ml vegetable oil
8fl oz/225ml ketchup
6fl oz/175ml water
2 tablespoons
Worcestershire sauce
2 tablespoons sugar
2fl oz/60ml cider vinegar
2 tablespoons
prepared English mustard
1 level teaspoon salt
½ level teaspoon black pepper

Combine all the ingredients in a medium-size saucepan. Simmer over a low heat, uncovered, for 20 minutes and then leave to cool. The barbecue sauce

will keep for several days if refrigerated in a clean glass jar with a tight-fitting lid. Or store in the freezer in a plastic container for up to 6 months.

Basic batter

This most adaptable of recipes can be used to make the traditional accompaniment for roast beef or a delicious apple dessert.

To make 4-6 servings
4oz/115g plain flour
Pinch of salt
2 eggs, size 3
½ pint/285ml milk or milk and water

Sieve the flour and salt together into a bowl. Make a well in the centre, add the eggs and ¼ pint/150ml liquid, and beat until smooth. Stir in the remaining liquid and leave for at least 20 minutes.
Pancake variation Place a frying pan over a moderately high heat and oil lightly with sunflower oil and a pastry brush. Spoon in a ladleful of batter, and tip the pan until it covers the base. Cook until the underside is golden, toss or turn with a spatula, and cook the other side. Transfer to a plate and repeat.
Yorkshire pudding variation Heat the oven to Gas Mark 7, 220°C/425°F. Put 1oz/30g fat in a 7 × 11in /180 × 280mm roasting tin and heat the oil in the oven. When very hot, add the batter and cook for 40-50 minutes.
Fruit batter variation Make as if for Yorkshire pudding, using butter in place of the fat. Then add 8oz/225g of apple slices tossed in 1oz/30g of sugar to the batter and pour into the tin. Serve with plain yoghurt, cream or custard.

Bath oil

A soothing skin softener.

To make enough for 1 bath
8fl oz/225ml honey
16fl oz/450ml milk
16 tablespoons sea salt or cooking salt
4 tablespoons bicarbonate of soda
4fl oz/115ml baby oil

In a large bowl, combine the honey, milk, sea salt and bicarbonate of soda; stir well. Pour the mixture into a bathful of warm water and then add the baby oil. Mix well with the water. Make fresh each time of use.

Bath salts

Prepare in advance this refreshing, relaxing concoction for tired muscles.

To make enough for 1 bath
16 tablespoons sea salt
16 tablespoons bicarbonate of soda
8fl oz/225ml inexpensive shampoo

Fill a bath half-full of warm water. Pour the ingredients into the bath, then add more water, swirling it around with your hand to spread out the bubbles.

Bird treats

Keep your garden birds happy this winter.

To make 2lb 3oz/1kg
12oz/340g lard
16 tablespoons sesame seeds
16 tablespoons hulled sunflower seeds
16 tablespoons crushed biscuits
6 tablespoons raisins
4 tablespoons peanut butter

Using a double boiler, melt the lard over a low heat. Leave it to cool down and then transfer to a medium-size bowl. Mix in the sesame and sunflower seeds, biscuit crumbs and raisins, and then add the peanut butter and stir well until combined. Let the mixture harden overnight.

To use, place the mixture in a standard bird feeder or hang it in a piece of coarse netting, which allows the birds to reach it.

Blancmange

For a vanilla blancmange, add a few grains of nutmeg to the milk. For chocolate, add 3 tablespoons cocoa to the blancmange mix and proceed as directed.

To make 4 servings
5 oz / 150g blancmange mix (below)
8 fl oz / 225ml milk
8 fl oz / 225ml water
2 teaspoons vanilla essence
1 egg, lightly beaten
½ oz / 15g unsalted butter or margarine, cut into small pieces

Place the blancmange mix in a medium-size heavy saucepan and gradually whisk in the milk and water. Cook, stirring constantly, over a moderate heat until the mixture thickens – about 3-5 minutes. Cook, still stirring, for a further 1½ minutes. Remove from the heat.

In a small bowl, stir the vanilla into the egg and then whisk in 4 fl oz / 115ml of the hot mixture. Stir, and then whisk in another 4 fl oz / 115ml. Add the egg mixture to the contents of the saucepan and whisk until combined. Finally, whisk in the butter.

Strain the blancmange into a bowl, leave to cool for a few minutes, and then spoon into dessert dishes. Cover with plastic film and refrigerate for several hours before serving. The dessert will keep for 2 days refrigerated.

Blancmange mix

Delicious, and it only takes minutes to make. It is very good to keep on hand for emergencies.

To make 24 servings
10 oz / 280g powdered skimmed milk
10 oz / 280g caster sugar
7 oz / 200g cornflour
¼ level teaspoon salt

Use a whisk to combine all the ingredients in a large bowl. Stored in a tightly closed container or jar, this mix will keep for 3 months in the refrigerator.

Bloody Mary mix

This smooth drink with a bite makes the perfect accompaniment to Sunday brunch.

To make about 1¾ pints / 1 litre, or 6 Bloody Marys
1 pint 12 fl oz / 910ml tomato juice
2 tablespoons lime or lemon juice
2 tablespoons Worcestershire sauce
2 teaspoons prepared horseradish
1 teaspoon salt
¼-½ teaspoon Tabasco sauce
Vodka as required

Mix all the ingredients in a jug and then refrigerate. Before serving, fill a balloon wineglass with ice and add a measure of vodka. Stir the tomato juice well, and then fill the glass to the brim. Add a wedge of lemon or lime and a celery stalk to stir the drink with. The tomato juice mixture will keep for up to 4 days refrigerated.

Blueberry or bilberry syrup

This fruit syrup is delicious poured over freshly made pancakes and waffles.

To make about 28 fl oz / 800ml
1¼ lb / 550g blueberries or bilberries
2 thin strips lemon peel,
1 × 3 in / 25 × 75mm each
1 pint 4 fl oz / 680ml water
1 lb 5 oz / 600g sugar
1 tablespoon lemon juice

In a large saucepan, crush the berries with a wooden spoon. Add the lemon peel and 8 fl oz / 225ml of the water and bring to a simmering boil over a moderate heat. Turn the heat down to low and cook, uncovered, for 5 minutes without simmering. Then leave the liquid to cool slightly.

Strain the berries through in a cheesecloth-lined sieve, squeezing out all the juice – which should come to

Bilberry

Blueberry

about 16 fl oz / 450ml. Discard the pulp but keep the juice to one side.

Boil the sugar and the remaining 16 fl oz / 450ml water in a large saucepan, stirring constantly until the sugar dissolves and the solution is clear. Keep boiling, without stirring, until a sugar thermometer reads 126°C / 260°F when tested in the syrup.

Add the berry mixture, boil uncovered for 1 minute, and then leave to cool. Finally, add the lemon juice. Refrigerated, the syrup will keep for 1 month.

Brass and copper cleaner

Clean your tin-lined brass and copper cookware outside and in with this effective solution.

To make 2 pints / 1.15 litres
2 oz / 60g plain flour
4 oz / 115g salt
8 tablespoons washing powder
6 fl oz / 175ml white vinegar
2 fl oz / 60ml lemon juice
4 fl oz / 115ml warm water

In a large glass bowl, mix the flour, salt and washing powder, then pour in the liquid ingredients and stir. Transfer the mixture to a jam jar, close it tightly, and label clearly. Store out of the reach of children.

To use, shake the jam jar thoroughly and then pour some of the cleaner onto the pot. Rub gently with a dishcloth, or scrub any stubborn stains or spots with an old toothbrush. Rinse with clear water, dry, and then polish with a soft cloth.

Breakfast cereal

A quick meal that is high in protein and an excellent start for the day.

To make about 1¾lb/800g
3oz/85g rolled oats
1½oz/45g whole wheat flakes
or coarsely crumbled
shredded wheat
2oz/60g bran or bran cereal
1oz/30g wheat germ
4oz/115g any combination unsalted
walnuts, almonds, pecans or cashews,
coarsely chopped
3oz/85g pitted dates, chopped
4oz/115g any combination dried
prunes, apricots, pears, apples or
bananas, chopped
5oz/150g sultanas
3½oz/100g powdered skimmed milk

In a large bowl, combine the oats, wheat flakes, bran, wheat germ and nuts. Add the dates and dried fruit and toss to coat with the oats mixture. Add the sultanas and powdered milk and mix thoroughly. The cereal will keep for 2 months in an airtight container, stored in a cool, dry place.

Brown-and-serve rolls

For hot homemade bread in minutes, make a supply of these rolls ahead of time.

To make 2 dozen rolls
½oz/15g active dry yeast
2 tablespoons lukewarm water
2 tablespoons light brown sugar
4oz/115g unsalted butter or
margarine, at room temperature
8fl oz/225g milk, scalded
and cooled to lukewarm
2 large eggs, beaten
1¼lb/550g sifted strong plain flour
1 level teaspoon salt
2oz/60g lightly salted butter or
margarine, melted (optional)

In a small bowl, stir together the yeast, water and 1 tablespoon of the sugar and leave until bubbly – about 5 minutes. Stir until the ingredients are dissolved.

In a food processor or an electric mixer fitted with a dough hook, cream the unsalted butter and the remaining tablespoon of sugar until light and fluffy (about 3 minutes in the mixer or 30 seconds in the food processor). Add the milk, eggs and yeast mixture, and continue beating until very light (about 1 minute in the mixer, 15 seconds in the processor). Sift in the flour and salt and mix until smooth (2 minutes in the mixer, 30 seconds in the processor).

This dough is too soft to knead, so just transfer it into a large, lightly greased bowl and cover with plastic film. Let the dough rise in a warm, draught-free place until doubled in bulk – about 1 hour 15 minutes.

Punch the dough down and, on a lightly floured board, roll out to ⅓in/8mm thick. Cut into 3in/75mm rounds. Brush each round with melted

butter, if desired, and top with a second round. Place 2in/50mm apart on ungreased baking sheets.

Preheat the oven to Gas Mark 6, 200°C/400°F and, if desired, brush the top of each roll with the remaining melted butter. Cover loosely with plastic film and leave to rise in a warm, draught-free place until doubled in size – about 25 minutes. Bake for about 5 minutes or until the rolls begin to brown.

When cooled to room temperature, wrap in aluminium foil and label. Freeze for up to 3 months. When you want to serve the rolls, preheat the oven to Gas Mark 6, 200°C/400°F, remove the aluminium foil and place the rolls on an ungreased baking sheet. Bake for 10-12 minutes or until golden brown, and serve while still hot.

Brownie mix

An indulgent, richly chocolate alternative to shop-bought brownies.

To make 56 brownies
1½lb/700g caster sugar
12oz/340g strong plain flour
6oz/175g unsweetened cocoa
2 level teaspoons baking powder
1½ level teaspoons salt
1lb/450g chilled butter or hard
margarine

In a large bowl, mix together the sugar, flour, cocoa, baking powder and salt. Crumble the fat into the flour with your fingers, a pastry blender or 2 knives until the brownie mix resembles coarse breadcrumbs. Work in batches if you need to.

The mixture will keep for 6 weeks refrigerated in airtight containers, or for 6 months frozen in freezer containers. For cooking instructions, see below.

Brownies

These brownies include chocolate drops for extra richness.

To make 16 brownies
1lb/450g brownie mix (see above)
2 eggs, size 2
1 teaspoon vanilla extract
4oz/115g chocolate drops

Preheat the oven to Gas Mark 4, 175°C/350°F. Place all the ingredients in a bowl and mix thoroughly. Pour into a greased 8in/200mm baking tin, smooth the surface, and bake for 30

minutes or until a knife inserted into the centre comes out clean.

Place the tin on a wire rack and leave it to cool to room temperature. Then cut into squares and serve.

Brown ink

Make your own writing ink with ordinary household tea.

To make 4fl oz/115ml
4fl oz/115ml boiling water
5 tea bags
1 teaspoon gum arabic

In a medium-size bowl, pour the water over the tea bags, stir in the gum arabic and steep until cool.

Then squeeze the tea bags hard to get out all the tannic acid. You can use the ink with a paintbrush, quill pen or any other type of writing implement. See also INK, p.402.

Bubble bath

A long soak in this will leave your skin sweet-smelling and soft.

To make enough for 4 baths
16fl oz/450ml liquid soap (see p.404)
16fl oz/450ml inexpensive shampoo
or washing-up liquid
2fl oz/60ml glycerine
Few drops of scented oil or perfume

In a small bowl, mix the soap with the shampoo, glycerine and scented oil. Transfer the bubbly mixture to a 2 pint/1.15 litre container, cover, and store in the bathroom. Add about 8fl oz/225ml to a bathful of water.

Butterscotch sauce

Pour this sauce over ice cream, sponge pudding or apple pie.

To make 12fl oz/340ml
8oz/225g
dark brown sugar
¼ level teaspoon salt
12oz/340g golden syrup
4fl oz/115ml evaporated milk
1oz/30g butter or margarine
2 teaspoons vanilla essence

In a medium-size saucepan, combine the sugar, salt, syrup and evaporated milk. Bring to a boil over a moderate heat, stirring constantly, and then boil briskly for 5 minutes, stirring occasionally. Remove from the heat and add the butter and vanilla essence.

Either serve immediately or store by leaving to cool slightly and then pouring the sauce into hot, clean, glass jars. When completely cool, cover. It will keep for up to 1 month refrigerated. To reheat, place in the top of a double boiler over hot (but not boiling) water.

Cantaloupe melon ice

Light and refreshing, this ice contains only 136 calories per 4oz/115g.

To make about ¾ pint/425ml
1 envelope powdered gelatine
3 tablespoons cold water
1 cantaloupe or honeydew melon
(2½lb/1.1kg) peeled,
seeded and coarsely chopped
2fl oz/60ml each
orange juice and honey
1 tablespoon lemon juice
2 teaspoons finely grated orange rind

In a small saucepan, soften the gelatine in the cold water for 5 minutes or so. Set over low heat and stir until dissolved.

In a food processor or blender, purée the melon in batches and turn it into a medium-sized bowl. Stir in the gelatine, orange juice, honey, lemon juice and orange rind until well mixed, and then pour the mixture into a 9in/230mm baking dish (it should not be made of aluminium). Cover tightly with plastic film, and freeze until firm – 2-4 hours.

In a food processor or blender, purée the cantaloupe ice in batches until smooth but not liquefied and then refreeze. You can store it in the freezer for up to 1 month.

Watermelon variation Follow the directions above, but eliminate the orange rind and juice and substitute the flesh of a 3lb/1.4kg watermelon, seeded and coarsely chopped, for the cantaloupe melon; use 6oz/175g golden syrup (or to taste) instead of the honey and increase the lemon juice to 2 tablespoons.

Canvas waterproofing

Brush this onto the surfaces of tents, awnings, and car and boat covers to stop rot from setting in.

To make enough for 1 treatment
8fl oz/225ml soya-bean oil
4fl oz/115ml turpentine

In a medium-size bowl, mix the oil and turpentine together. Store in a cool place, clearly labelled, out of the reach of small children and pets.

Caramel corn

Make this treat for the children on a dry day. The sugar may crystallise in damp weather.

To make about 24 popcorn balls
1¼lb/550g unflavoured popped corn
12oz/340g golden syrup
¼ level teaspoon salt
4oz/115g unsalted butter
2 teaspoons cider vinegar
12oz/340g soft
light brown sugar
1 teaspoon natural vanilla essence
½ teaspoon bicarbonate of soda

Spread the popped corn out on a large roasting tin or two shallow 13 × 9in/330 × 230mm cake tins, and put to one side.

In a medium-size saucepan, mix together the golden syrup, salt, butter, vinegar and sugar. Cook over a moderate heat, stirring constantly, until the butter melts and the sugar dissolves. Use a pastry brush dipped in hot water to wipe down the sides of the saucepan.

Increase the heat slightly and place a sugar thermometer in the syrup. Cook, without stirring, until it reaches the hard ball stage (122°C/250°F).

Remove the saucepan from the heat and stir in the vanilla and bicarbonate of soda. Pour the syrup over the popcorn, turning it with a wooden spoon to coat it. Leave to cool and then shape the popcorn into tennis-ball-size clusters with a spoon and place on non-stick baking paper.

Caraway cheese sticks

A tasty snack or hors d'oeuvre. You can make the dough ahead of time and bake the sticks as needed.

To make 6 dozen sticks
8oz/225g unsalted
butter or margarine, at room
temperature
8oz/225g grated Cheddar cheese
¼ level teaspoon cayenne pepper
10oz/275g sifted plain flour
½ level teaspoon salt
2 level tablespoons caraway seed
1½ level teaspoons dry mustard
1oz/30g grated Parmesan cheese
(about 2 tablespoons)
Egg Wash
1 egg beaten with 1 tablespoon water

In a large bowl, cream the butter and Cheddar cheese with an electric mixer. Beat in the cayenne pepper, flour, salt, caraway seed and dry mustard. Shape the dough into a flat patty, cover with plastic film or aluminium foil, and chill for 2 hours. (At this point the dough can be kept for 1 week refrigerated, or for 6 months in the freezer.)

Preheat the oven to Gas Mark 4, 175°C/350°F. On a lightly floured surface, roll out the dough to ¼in/6mm thick. Using a sharp knife, cut into 5 × ½in/125 × 13mm strips. On an ungreased baking sheet, place the strips ½in/13mm apart. Brush each strip with the egg wash, and then sprinkle with the grated Parmesan cheese.

Bake for 10-12 minutes or until golden brown and crisp. Let the sticks cool for 1 minute, and then move to a wire rack. They will keep for 2 days in an airtight container. See also CHEESE CRACKERS, p.388.

Carrot cake

Keeps for 2-3 days in the fridge.

To make an 8in/200mm cake
5oz/150g butter
7oz/200g soft brown sugar
8oz/225g carrots, finely grated
2 eggs
7oz/200g self-raising flour
3 level teaspoons baking powder
1 level teaspoon ground cinnamon
½ teaspoon ground nutmeg
½ teaspoon salt
4oz/115g seedless raisins
2oz/50g walnuts, chopped
3 tablespoons milk

Grease a round cake tin and line the base. Melt the butter in a bowl and add the sugar, carrots and eggs. Beat well. Sieve the dry ingredients and fold them into the carrot mixture, and then add the raisins, walnuts and milk.

Preheat the oven to Gas Mark 4, 175°C/350°F. Turn the mixture into the tin, level it, and bake the cake for about an hour, or until springy to the touch.

Car wash concentrate

This straightforward mixture will leave your car clean and shining.

To make enough for 2 washes
1 cup salt-free washing-up liquid
¾ cup washing powder

Mix the washing-up liquid and washing powder together and store in a clearly labelled bottle. To use, add half a cup of concentrate to a large bucket of water. (Add more, if the car is very dirty.) Then, rinse the car with clean water.

Car wax

To avoid overdrying, wax your car one section at a time.

To make enough for 1 waxing
8oz/225g carnauba wax
2 tablespoons yellow beeswax
16fl oz/450ml turpentine
1 tablespoon pine oil

In a double boiler, heat the carnauba wax and beeswax. Stir, then leave to cool until the mixture just starts to harden. Stir in the turpentine and pine oil. To use, dip a rag into the mixture, rub onto the car's surface and then polish with a soft cloth.

Cat food

A balanced supplement that will provide your cat with all it needs in the way of vitamins and trace minerals (meat alone is not enough).

To make 1¾lb/800g
1lb/450g minced beef, cooked
4oz/115g beef or pork liver,
cooked and diced

8oz/225g cooked rice
(without added salt)
1 teaspoon vegetable oil
1 teaspoon calcium carbonate
(crushed antacid tablets)

Combine the ingredients in a bowl and mix thoroughly. Store in an airtight bowl in the refrigerator for 2-3 days.

Chamomile astringent

This is especially good for oily skin.

To make 1½ pints/850ml
1¾ pint/1 litre purified water
8 tablespoons chopped fresh mint
or 2 tablespoons dried mint
2 tablespoons dried chamomile flowers,
crumbled

Place all the ingredients in a medium-size saucepan and boil for 10 minutes. Remove from the heat and steep for 5 minutes before straining into a screw-topped jar. It will keep for 2 weeks refrigerated. Apply with cotton balls.

Chamomile tea

A relaxing beverage to help you get a good night's sleep.

To make 2 mugfuls
2 tablespoons dried mint, crumbled
2 tablespoons dried chamomile flowers,
crumbled
12fl oz/340ml water
1 teaspoon honey
1 teaspoon lemon juice

In a small saucepan, boil the herbs with the water for 5 minutes. Then remove

from the heat and steep for another 5 minutes. Drain and add the honey and lemon juice. The tea can be reheated if desired, but do not let it boil.

Cheese and walnut balls

An interesting alternative to plain cheese balls. Make them ahead of time for parties and freeze them.

To make around 24 balls
3oz/85g cream cheese
4oz/115g gorgonzola or blue cheese
3oz/85g finely chopped walnuts

In a small mixing bowl, blend together the cream cheese and blue cheese. Roll the mixture into 1in/25mm balls with your hands, using approximately a

teaspoon of mixture to make each one.

Spread the chopped walnuts on a sheet of wax paper and roll the cheese balls in them. They will keep for up to 1 week in the refrigerator, covered with plastic film, or place the balls in a single layer on a plate and cover tightly with aluminium foil to freeze. When frozen, transfer the balls into double plastic bags (one inside the other); they will keep for 1 month.

Cheesecake

Simply scrumptious, right down to the last crumb.

To make 12 servings
6oz/175g crushed digestive biscuits
2oz/60g caster sugar
3oz/85g butter, melted
Filling
2½lb/1.1kg cream cheese,
at room temperature

12oz/340g caster sugar
3 level tablespoons plain flour
¼ teaspoon vanilla essence
Grated rind of 1 lemon
Grated rind of 1 orange
Five size 2 eggs plus 1 egg yolk
2fl oz/60ml double cream

To make the crust, mix the biscuit crumbs, sugar and butter in a small bowl. Stir well to moisten all the crumbs. Press the mixture over the bottom and up the sides of a 10in/250mm spring release cake tin, stopping ½in/13mm from the top. Chill for 10 minutes in the freezer to set the crust.

To make the filling, cream the cheese with an electric mixer in a large bowl. Add the sugar, flour, vanilla essence and lemon and orange rinds, and beat well. Add the eggs and the egg yolk, one at a time, beating lightly after each addition and scraping down the sides of the bowl. Add the double cream, beat lightly, and then pour the filling into the prepared pan.

Bake for 10 minutes at Gas Mark 9, 240°C/475°F. Lower the temperature to Gas Mark ½, 120°C/250°F and continue baking for a further 1 hour 20 minutes. Remove from the oven and leave on a wire rack, in the tin, until cool. Cover and refrigerate for at least 4 hours, or until the filling is set.

With a narrow spatula or knife, loosen the crumb crust from the sides of the tin. Remove the sides but not the bottom of the pan. Slice and serve. The cheese-cake will keep for 2 days refrigerated; frozen, it will keep for 1 month if the sides, but not the bottom, of the tin are removed and the cheesecake is wrapped tightly in foil.

Cheese crackers

A flavourful snack to keep on hand for unexpected guests.

To make 56 crackers
8oz / 225g unsalted butter or margarine, at room temperature
8oz / 225g grated Cheddar cheese
10oz / 275g sifted plain flour
½ level teaspoon salt
¼ level teaspoon cayenne pepper
Egg Wash
1 egg beaten with 1 tablespoon water

In a large bowl, cream the butter and cheese with an electric mixer and then beat in the flour, salt and cayenne pepper. Shape the dough into a flat patty, cover with plastic film and chill for 2 hours. (It can be kept for 3-4 days refrigerated, or for 6 months if frozen.)

Preheat the oven to Gas Mark 4, 175°C / 350°F. On a lightly floured surface, roll out the dough to ¼in / 6mm thick. Cut into any desired shape – a 2½in / 60mm biscuit cutter works well. Place on ungreased baking trays and brush each one with the egg wash.

Bake for 10-12 minutes or until crisp and golden. Let the snacks cool for 1 minute on the baking sheet, and then transfer onto a rack. The crackers will keep for up to 2 weeks in an airtight container.

Cheese soufflé

Hot soufflés are much easier to make than often thought, and can be prepared in advance.

To make 4 servings
1oz / 30g butter
1oz / 30g plain flour
5fl oz / 150ml milk
3oz / 85g grated cheese
3 eggs, size 2, separated
Pinch of salt and black pepper
Dried herbs to taste

Melt the butter in a saucepan over a moderate heat, add the flour and cook for 1-2 minutes. Add the milk gradually, continually stirring with a wooden spoon or wire whisk to prevent lumps forming. Bring to the boil and cook for 2-3 minutes, then leave to one side to cool slightly.

Add the grated cheese and the 3 egg yolks and beat in thoroughly. Season to taste with the salt, pepper and herbs. In a glass bowl, whisk the egg whites until they stand in soft peaks (do not overbeat them), and then fold them into the cheese mixture.

Heat the oven to Gas Mark 6, 200°C / 400°F. Pour the soufflé mix into a greased 7in / 180mm soufflé dish. Place the dish in the centre of the oven and bake for 35 minutes, or until risen and golden-brown.

Chilli sauce

A hot sauce that packs more punch than tomato ketchup.

To make approximately 2 pints/ 1.15 litres
14oz / 400g can tomatoes
Three 11oz / 300g cans tomato purée
1 large onion, peeled and grated
2 cloves garlic, crushed
2fl oz / 60ml cider vinegar
1 level tablespoon chilli powder
2 teaspoons salt
2 teaspoons sugar
⅛ level teaspoon crushed red pepper flakes or ground cayenne pepper
⅛ level teaspoon ground allspice
2 level tablespoons cornflour
2 tablespoons cold water

Purée the tomatoes in a blender or food processor and then transfer to a large saucepan and set over a moderate heat.

Add all the other ingredients except the cornflour and water, and mix them well.

Heat until bubbling, then blend the cornflour with the water and add to the mixture. Cook for 2-3 minutes, stirring constantly, and then reduce the heat and simmer, uncovered, for 20 minutes.

Allow the sauce to cool to room temperature, then transfer to 1 pint / 570ml freezer containers, leaving a space of about ½in / 13mm at the top of each one, and cover. Refrigerated, this sauce will keep for 1 week in a covered jar.

Chocolate sauce

A special blend of rich chocolates.

To make about 1 pint / 570ml
4oz / 115g unsalted butter
2 level tablespoons cocoa
3 tablespoons cold water
6oz / 175g Swiss dark chocolate
4oz / 115g semi-sweet chocolate
8fl oz / 225ml boiling water
8oz / 225g soft light brown sugar
5oz / 150g granulated sugar
6oz / 175g golden syrup
¼ level teaspoon salt
1 teaspoon vanilla essence

Melt the butter in a saucepan over a low heat. Dissolve the cocoa in the water and add it and the dark and semi-sweet chocolate to the butter. Stir in the boiling water, brown sugar, granulated sugar, golden syrup and salt.

Bring the mixture to the boil and boil uncovered for 5 minutes (7 minutes for a thicker sauce that will harden the moment it hits ice cream). Remove the saucepan from the heat and allow the sauce to cool to room temperature, then stir in the vanilla essence.

This sauce is excellent with plain vanilla ice cream, with poached pears or with profiteroles.

Christmas snow

Add a touch of wintry beauty to your Christmas tree by painting the branches with this unusual, attractive 'snowy' mixture.

To make enough for a 4ft/1.2m tree
6fl oz/175ml liquid starch
1lb/450g soap flakes or
washing powder
2-4 tablespoons water
Blue food colouring

In a medium-size bowl, mix together the liquid starch and soap flakes, and then add the water. Beat with an electric whisk until the mixture becomes very thick. Add the food colouring a drop at a time (an eyedropper is a good idea), beating until the 'snow' has an icy-white colour. Put a sheet of polythene, or a dust sheet, under or around the tree base before painting on the snow. Add white glitter last of all to give a crystalline appearance.

Christmas pudding

Prepare these several weeks beforehand and finish them on the day.

To make two large puddings
1lb/450g stoned raisins, chopped
2oz/60g mixed peel, chopped
2oz/60g blanched almonds, chopped
8oz/225g each currants and sultanas
4oz/115g plain or self-raising flour
½ level teaspoon each ground
nutmeg, mixed spice and cinnamon
1 level teaspoon salt
2oz/60g ground almonds
1lb/450g shredded suet
8oz/225g fresh white breadcrumbs
4oz/115g soft brown sugar
6 large eggs, lightly beaten
4 tablespoons brandy
8fl oz/225ml milk

Mix together the fruits, chopped almonds, sifted flour, spices, salt and ground almonds in a large bowl. Add the suet, breadcrumbs and sugar, and then the beaten eggs. Stir in the brandy and milk to make a soft, dropping consistency. Spoon the mixture into two large, well-buttered pudding basins. Cover each with a double layer of buttered greaseproof paper.

Place the basins in a saucepan of water (the water should come two-thirds of the way up the basins' sides)

and boil for 6 hours, topping up the water as required. Then remove the puddings, leave them to cool, and then cover them with fresh greaseproof paper and pieces of cloth. Store in an airtight place until needed. Boil the puddings for a further 4 hours before eating.

Chutney

Quick to make and delicious with beef, curried lamb or chicken.

To make 1lb/450g
1 jar (12oz/340g)
apricot or peach preserve
½ level teaspoon garlic powder
½ level teaspoon ground ginger
½ level teaspoon dry mustard
½ level teaspoon salt
¼ level teaspoon ground coriander
1 tablespoon cider vinegar
2oz/60g sultanas or raisins (optional)

Mix all the ingredients in a small bowl and then transfer to a covered container to store. The chutney will keep for 6 months refrigerated.

Cinnamon tea

A refreshing drink which is good for relieving nausea.

To make 1 drink
1 tablespoon dried chamomile flowers
1 teaspoon whole cloves or
½ teaspoon ground cloves
8fl oz/225ml boiling water
1 tablespoon ground cinnamon
1 teaspoon ground nutmeg

Put the chamomile flowers and whole cloves in a small pan, add the boiling water and steep for 15 minutes. (If you are using ground cloves, do not add at this time.) Strain the flowers from the water with a tea strainer and add the cinnamon, nutmeg and ground cloves

(if using) to the liquid. Stir and reheat, either in a mug in the microwave or in a small pan on the stove.

For use against morning sickness in pregnancy, omit the nutmeg or substitute a pinch of ground ginger.

Cleaning a chamois leather

Wash out your chamois leather after each time of use, and it will remain soft and supple.

To clean a chamois leather
2 pints/1.15 litres warm water
3 tablespoons soapflakes
1 tablespoon olive oil

Place the warm water in a large bowl or bucket, and add the soapflakes. Wash out the chamois leather in this solution, and then rinse it in clean water with the olive oil added to it. The oil will keep the chamois soft.

Cockroach exterminator

Get rid of the pests with this easy-to-make insecticide.

To make 1 treatment
2 tablespoons household borax
1 tablespoon flour
1½ teaspoons cocoa powder

Mix all the ingredients in a small bowl. To use, place a small amount of the mixture in bottle caps or other small, unsealed containers and set them out in areas where the cockroaches are known to congregate.
Caution Keep out of the reach of pets and small children.

Cocktail sauce

Add zest to your seafood meals with this savoury sauce. For a hotter accompaniment, use more horse-radish or Tabasco sauce.

To make about 8fl oz/225ml
8fl oz/225ml tomato ketchup or chilli sauce
1 level tablespoon prepared horseradish
1 tablespoon lemon juice
½ teaspoon Worcestershire sauce
⅛ teaspoon Tabasco sauce

Combine all the ingredients in a small bowl. Cover and chill for 1 hour before serving. This cocktail sauce keeps for about 1 month tightly covered and refrigerated.

Coffee cake

Whip this cake up the night before and pop it in the oven in the morning for breakfast or an 11 o'clock treat.

To make 8-12 servings
10oz/275g sifted plain flour
1 level teaspoon baking powder
1 level teaspoon bicarbonate of soda
1 level teaspoon ground cardamom
¼ level teaspoon salt
4oz/115g butter or margarine at room temperature
7oz/200g caster sugar
2 eggs, size 2
6fl oz/175ml soured cream
4oz/115g soft light brown sugar
2oz/60g chopped walnuts or pecans
¼ teaspoon each ground allspice and cinnamon
Glaze
2oz/60g sifted icing sugar

2 teaspoons lemon juice
½ teaspoon vanilla essence or water

Sift together the flour, baking powder, baking soda, cardamom and salt. In a large bowl, cream the butter with the caster sugar until fluffy. Add the eggs and beat for 1 minute or until well mixed. Then add the soured cream and beat again thoroughly. Fold in the sifted flour and pour the batter into a 9in/230mm square cake tin that has been lightly greased and floured.

Combine the brown sugar, walnuts, allspice and cinnamon and sprinkle evenly over the batter. Cover with plastic film and refrigerate overnight.

Preheat the oven to Gas Mark 4, 175°C/350°F. Bake for 1 hour 10 minutes or until a toothpick inserted in the centre comes out clean. (If the cake browns too quickly, cover it loosely with aluminium foil.) Remove it from the oven and leave to cool for 10 minutes while you make the glaze in a small mixing bowl by combining the sugar, lemon juice and vanilla. Drizzle over the cake after it has cooled slightly.

Coffee liqueur

Serve this easy-to-make liqueur as an accompaniment for ice cream or as an after-dinner drink.

To make about 3 pints/1.7 litres
8oz/225g instant coffee powder
24fl oz/680ml boiling water
2½lb/1.1kg granulated sugar
1 vanilla pod
1 bottle (750ml) vodka

In a large saucepan, dissolve the instant coffee in the water. Add the sugar and vanilla pod and set over a low heat, stirring with a wooden spoon until the mixture becomes syrupy. Remove from

the heat, allow to cool, and then stir in the vodka.

Transfer the mixture into a glass or earthenware jug, seal it tightly, and then leave the liqueur to stand for at least 30 days before serving.

Cold cream

A good, inexpensive moisturiser for dry skin.

To make 8 applications
1 egg yolk, beaten
2 tablespoons lemon juice
4fl oz/115ml olive oil
4fl oz/115ml vegetable oil

Beat the egg yolk and lemon juice together in a small mixing bowl. Gradually add both oils, stirring constantly with a wire whisk, until the mixture thickens. If it gets too thick, add more lemon juice. The cream will keep for 2 weeks if refrigerated if tightly sealed.

Cold remedy

You can relieve cold symptoms if you drink plenty of fluids and encourage your body to sweat.

To make 1 drink
⅛ teaspoon cayenne pepper
Juice of 1 lemon
1 clove garlic, crushed
1 tablet Vitamin C
4fl oz/115ml hot water

Mix all the ingredients together in a cup which already holds the water and then sip slowly. The garlic and cayenne pepper will make you sweat, while the lemon juice and Vitamin C tablet provide extra Vitamin C.

Cologne

A lovely, light scent which is quick and economical to make.

To make around 1 pint/570ml
8fl oz/225ml rubbing alcohol
8 tablespoons dried lavender flowers
1 tablespoon olive oil
8fl oz/225ml purified water
3 drops oil of bergamot

Pour the alcohol into a screw-top jar and add the lavender and olive oil. Cover tightly for 2 days, shaking occasionally. Strain and discard the lavender flowers, then add the water and oil of bergamot. Close tightly.

Comb and brush cleaner

This cleaning solution will remove the oily residue which often clings to the bristles of hair brushes and combs.

To make 1 treatment
8 tablespoons household ammonia
2 pints/1 15 litres water
½ teaspoon shampoo or
mild washing powder

Mix all the ingredients in a shallow bowl. Place combs and brushes in the solution bristle-side down (but check that the brush handles can be safely

immersed in case they get wet) and leave them to soak for 5-10 minutes. Then remove from the solution and clean the comb with the brush, and then vice versa. Rinse the brush and comb with water and leave them to dry on a towel before using.

To keep your brushes and combs in top condition, repeat this treatment at least once a fortnight.

Cornbread mix

A real time-saver. You can have hot muffins on the table in minutes.

To make enough for 2½ lb/1.1 kg
15oz/425g sifted plain flour
12oz/340g yellow cornmeal
5oz/150g powdered skimmed milk
3 tablespoons sugar (optional)
3½ level tablespoons baking powder
2½ level teaspoons salt
6oz/175g solid butter or margarine

Mix together all the dry ingredients in a large bowl. Rub the fat into the flour with your fingers, 2 knives or a pastry blender until the mixture resembles coarse crumbs. This basic mix will keep for up to 6 weeks if tightly sealed and in the refrigerator.

Cornbread

Good with salads, Mexican food or celebration dinners.

To make 8 servings
12oz/340g cornbread mix (above)
3 eggs, lightly beaten
8fl oz/225ml water

Preheat the oven to Gas Mark 7, 220°C/425°F. Place all the ingredients in a large mixing bowl and mix well. Pour into a shallow, greased, 8in/200mm square tin. Bake for about 20 minutes or until a knife inserted in the centre comes out clean. Cut into squares and serve hot with butter or store by covering the tin tightly with aluminium foil. The cornbread will keep for 3 days refrigerated or for 2 months frozen.

Cough drops

An old-fashioned alternative to boiled cough sweets.

To make around 24 pieces
1 handful horehound leaves and
stems, washed and chopped
16fl oz/450ml water
1¼lb/550g lump or

soft brown sugar
2oz/60g butter

In a medium-size saucepan, boil the horehound leaves in the water for 30 minutes. Strain and discard the leaves. Add the sugar and boil for a further 30 minutes, or until a spoonful of the mixture hardens when dropped into cold water. Stir in the butter, remove from the heat, and transfer to a buttered shallow pan. When cool, crack the toffee into pieces and wrap each one in wax paper. Store in a tightly covered jar.

Cough mixture

Simple and effective for soothing a nagging cough.

To make 1 treatment
3 tablespoons lemon juice
8fl oz/225ml honey
2fl oz/60ml warm water

In a medium-size bowl, combine the lemon juice and honey and slowly stir in the water. Store the mixture in a screw-top jar in the refrigerator, and take 1 or 2 tablespoons once every 3 hours.

Courgette bread

This rich, versatile loaf is good for breakfast, afternoon tea or dessert.

To make 2 loaves
15oz/425g sifted plain flour
2 level teaspoons baking powder
1 level teaspoon salt
½ level teaspoon bicarbonate of soda
1 level teaspoon ground cinnamon
½ level teaspoon ground allspice
2 eggs, size 2
8fl oz/225ml vegetable oil
5oz/150g granulated sugar
4oz/115g soft light brown sugar
2 tablespoons orange rind,
finely grated
2 tablespoons crystallised ginger,
chopped
1lb/450g unpeeled courgettes, grated
4oz/115g walnuts or pecans,
coarsely chopped

Preheat the oven to Gas Mark 4, 175°C/350°F. Sift the flour, baking powder, salt, bicarbonate of soda, cinnamon and all-spice onto a sheet of greaseproof paper and set to one side.

In a large bowl, beat the eggs, oil, granulated sugar, brown sugar, orange rind and ginger until well blended. Stir in the flour mixture – it may seem a little stiff at this point – and then mix in the courgettes and nuts.

Divide the mixture between two 8½ × 4½ in/215 × 115mm loaf tins that have been greased and dusted with flour. Bake until a toothpick inserted into the centre of each loaf comes out clean – about 1 hour.

Remove the loaves from the oven and cool for 15 minutes in their tins on a wire rack. Turn the loaves out and leave them to cool. They will keep for 1 week wrapped in foil and refrigerated, or for 3 months in the freezer.

Cradle cap remedy

To soothe a baby's irritated scalp, gently work this rinse into the head with a flannel after a shampoo.

To make 4 rinses
2oz/60g dried comfrey leaves
or root, cut up
1¾ pints/1 litre water

Place the comfrey and water in a medium-size saucepan. Cover, bring to the boil, and simmer for 20 minutes. Strain and discard the comfrey root. Let the remaining liquid cool. It will keep for 4 days in the refrigerator.

To use, warm the solution to skin temperature, apply, and then let it dry naturally on the baby's scalp. Repeat the process nightly until the irritated area clears up.

Caution If the condition does not change within 7 days, consult your doctor.

Cranberry-orange relish

Both tart and sweet, this is a superb accompaniment to roast chicken, turkey or pork, and makes a nice gift.

*To make approximately 2½ pints/
1.4 litres*
3oz/85g halved pecan nuts
10½oz/295g granulated sugar
3fl oz/85ml fresh orange juice
1 cinnamon stick
1 vanilla pod, split, or 1 teaspoon
vanilla essence
1 large orange, peeled and diced into
½in/13mm chunks
1½lb/700g fresh or solidly frozen
cranberrries, picked over
4oz/115g sultanas

Preheat the oven to Gas Mark 4, 175°C/350°F. In a small roasting tin, roast the pecans for about 7 minutes or until lightly fragrant and crispy. Leave them to cool, and then coarsely chop or halve them.

Combine the sugar, orange juice, cinnamon stick and vanilla pod in a large heavy saucepan (if using vanilla essence, do not add now). Over a moderate heat, cook uncovered – stirring occasionally – until the sugar dissolves and begins to turn brown – about 7 minutes.

Add the orange chunks to the mixture and cook, stirring often, until they soften slightly – about 4 minutes. Add all of the cranberries and cook for another 8-10 minutes, or until all the berries pop. Leave the mixture to cool.

Scrape the vanilla pod seeds into the mixture, then discard the vanilla pod and cinnamon stick. (If using vanilla essence, add it now.) Stir in the pecans and sultanas, spoon into clean jars and cover and refrigerate until serving time. It will keep for 2 months refrigerated.

Crème de menthe

This liqueur is surprisingly easy to make and is also delicious in chocolate sauces or poured over ice cream.

To make 1 pint/570ml
16fl oz/450ml vodka
12oz/340g golden syrup
1 teaspoon peppermint essence
40 drops green food colouring

Pour the vodka into a sterilised 2 pint/1.15 litre jar. Add the remaining ingredients, cover, and shake to mix. Store until required.

Crème fraîche

Spoon over fresh summer fruits or use as called for in recipes.

To make 8fl oz/225ml
8fl oz/225ml double cream
2 tablespoons soured cream, plain
yoghurt or buttermilk

Mix the double cream and soured cream together in a medium-size jar and cover loosely with plastic film. Leave it to stand at room temperature overnight or until thickened. Stir again and cover tightly. Refrigerate for at least 2 hours before serving – it will keep for up to 1 week in the refrigerator.

Crumb-coated chicken

Quick, delicious and healthy too.

To make 4 servings
2fl oz/60ml vegetable oil
1 roasting chicken (about 3lb/1.4kg),
cut into 8 pieces
2½oz/70g crumb coating (see below)

Preheat the oven to Gas Mark 4, 175°C/350°F. Use some of the vegetable oil to grease a roasting tin – make sure you choose one that is large enough to hold all the chicken pieces – then use the rest to brush each piece of chicken.

Place the crumb coating in a paper bag, add 2 chicken pieces, and shake until both pieces are evenly coated. Repeat this procedure until all the pieces of chicken are thoroughly coated with the crumb mixture.

Place the chicken pieces in the roasting tin and bake, uncovered, until the chicken is no longer pink on the inside – about 1 hour. You may find that dark pieces of chicken take an extra 5-10 minutes.

Crumb-coated fish

The same coating used on fish fillets or steaks will keep the fish moist.

To make 4 servings
2 fl oz/60ml vegetable oil
or melted butter
2 lb/900g fish fillets or steaks
6 tablespoons crumb coating
for fish (see below)

Preheat the oven to Gas Mark 4, 175°C/375°F. Grease a baking tray with some of the oil and then brush oil on both sides of each piece of fish. Spread the crumb coating on a sheet of greaseproof paper and dredge each of the fish pieces until well covered; shake off any excess. Arrange the fish on the baking tray and cook until it flakes easily – 10-20 minutes, depending on the thickness of each piece.

Crumb-coated pork chops

Great taste without any additives.

To make 4 servings
2 fl oz/60ml vegetable oil
4 pork chops, trimmed
6 tablespoons crumb coating (below)

Preheat the oven to Gas Mark 4, 180°C/350°F. Grease a roasting tin large enough to hold all the chops with some of the oil, and use the rest to brush the chops on both sides. Put the crumb coating in a paper bag and shake each chop in the mixture until evenly coated. Place them in the roasting tin and bake until no longer pink on the inside – 45-75 minutes, depending on the thickness of the chops.

Crumb coating

Healthier and more economical than commercial brands.

To make enough to coat 20 pork chops or 4 chickens (about 3 lb/1.4kg each)
10 oz/275g sifted plain flour
1 level tablespoon paprika
2 teaspoons each dried marjoram and thyme, crumbled
4 level teaspoons onion granules
1 level teaspoon dried rosemary, crumbled
1 level teaspoon salt

Put all the ingredients in a plastic or paper bag. Close it and shake to mix. Pour the mixture into a jar and cover tightly. It will keep for 6 months in a cool, dark place.

Fish variation To coat 30 fish fillets or steaks, use 10 oz/275g plain flour, 2 level teaspoons dried tarragon, 1 level tablespoon dill, 2 level teaspoons black pepper, 2 level teaspoons parsley flakes, 2 level teaspoons salt, 2 level teaspoons onion granules and 1 level teaspoon

paprika. Apply the crumb coating as you would that for chicken or pork. This will also keep for 6 months in a cool, dark place.

Currant jelly sauce

This turns a plain roasted chicken into fare for a celebration.

To make 6 servings
4 fl oz/115ml redcurrant jelly
1 tablespoon lemon juice
1 level teaspoon Dijon mustard
¼ level teaspoon paprika

In a medium-size saucepan, warm the jelly over a moderate heat until it begins to melt. Stir in the lemon juice, then add the mustard and paprika. When heated, transfer the sauce to a medium-size bowl and serve immediately.

Curry powder

Try this basic recipe, and then vary the ingredients to suit your own taste.

To make 2 oz/60g
4 level tablespoons ground coriander
2 level tablespoons ground turmeric
2 level teaspoons each ground cumin, ginger and allspice
1 level teaspoon each ground cinnamon, celery seasoning and black pepper
¼ level teaspoon cayenne pepper

Thoroughly mix all the ingredients in a medium-size bowl, and then transfer to a screw-top jar. The mix will keep for 6 months at room temperature.

Cuticle cream

A cream to soften cuticles and which helps to prevent hangnails.

To make 15 treatments
3 tablespoons melted wax
4 fl oz/115ml mineral oil
1 tablespoon coconut oil
1 tablespoon glycerine

In a double boiler, slowly heat the wax

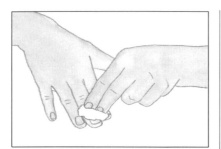

with the mineral and coconut oils until blended. Stir in the glycerine, remove from the heat and leave to cool.

To use, apply directly to the cuticles with cotton balls, or soak your fingertips in the cream for about 5 minutes. Store in the refrigerator, where it will thicken.

Dandruff rinse

This rinse will relieve an itching and flaking scalp.

To make 2 rinses
8 fl oz / 225 ml witch hazel
1 tablespoon dried rosemary
1 tablespoon dried lavender
1 tablespoon ground comfrey root

Combine the witch hazel and the herbs in a medium-size bowl and steep for 2 days. Strain the herbs and discard. To use, massage the rinse into the scalp and allow to dry. Then shampoo your hair. Store refrigerated in a covered jar.

Date and nut balls

Quick and easy to make with no baking required.

To make 36 balls
2 eggs, size 2, lightly beaten

6 oz / 175 g pitted dates, finely chopped
5 oz / 150 g sugar
4 oz / 115 g pecan nuts or walnuts, finely chopped
3 oz / 85 g toasted rice cereal
3½ oz / 100 g coconut flakes

Place the eggs, dates and sugar in a medium-size saucepan and cook over a moderately low heat, stirring constantly, until the mixture thickens – about 5 minutes. Allow to cool for 5 minutes, and then stir in the pecans and cereal. Leave to one side for a further 10 minutes.

Meanwhile, spread out the coconut flakes on a sheet of greaseproof paper. Roll the cooled date mixture in the coconut, a teaspoonful at a time, until each one is well covered and shaped into a ball. The sweets will keep for up to 2 weeks if refrigerated in an airtight container.

Delicate-washables soak

Save on dry-cleaning expenses and keep fine fabrics looking new.

To make 1 soak
8 tablespoons soap flakes
or grated soap ends
16 fl oz / 450 ml soft water (from a filter jug if your tap water is hard)
2 tablespoons borax

Mix all the ingredients in a saucepan and simmer over a low heat, stirring, until the solution develops an even consistency. Strain into a jar or jug, cover and store. To use, add enough soap solution to warm water to make good suds. Use cold water for wool, and only soak delicates for a few minutes.

Deodorant

Stay dry all day without the chemicals or perfume of commercial products.

To make 8 fl oz / 225 ml
4 teaspoons alum
2 teaspoons baking soda
8 fl oz / 225 ml rubbing alcohol

In a small mixing bowl, combine the ingredients. Transfer to a spray bottle and use as an all-over spray after a bath or as an underarm deodorant.

Digestive biscuits

You'll never want to buy them again.

To make 24-28 biscuits
5 oz / 150 g plain flour
7 oz / 200 g wholemeal flour
5 level tablespoons sugar
½ level teaspoon each salt and bicarbonate of soda
1 level teaspoon baking powder
¼ level teaspoon ground cinnamon
1½ oz / 45 g chilled butter or margarine, in small pieces
2 oz / 60 g white vegetable fat
2 tablespoons honey
1 tablespoon black treacle
2 fl oz / 60 ml water
1 teaspoon vanilla essence

In a medium-size bowl, combine the plain and wholemeal flours, sugar, salt, bicarbonate of soda, baking powder and cinnamon. Rub the butter and white fat into the flour until the mixture resembles coarse breadcrumbs.

In a small bowl, mix together the honey, treacle, water and vanilla essence. Sprinkle this mixture slowly over the dry ingredients, then toss the two together with a fork until well blended. Form the dough into a ball, cover with plastic film and chill for several hours.

Preheat the oven to Gas Mark 4, 175°C/350°F. Cut the dough in half and let it sit for 15 minutes at room temperature.

Lightly sprinkle a piece of greaseproof paper with wholemeal flour. Put a piece of the dough on top and flatten it with a rolling pin. Sprinkle the dough with more flour and cover with another sheet of greaseproof paper. Roll out to ⅛ in / 3 mm thick.

Peel off the top piece of greaseproof paper, then use a fork to prick the dough at ½-1 in / 13-25 mm intervals. Cut either into 2½ in / 60 mm squares, or into rounds with a plain round cutter. With a

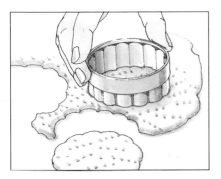

spatula, transfer to a large, ungreased baking sheet. Repeat the process with the remaining piece of dough, then roll out and cut up the scraps.

Bake the biscuits in the centre of the oven for 15 minutes or until lightly browned on the edges. Remove from the oven and let them cool on a rack. Store for at least 24 hours before serving. The digestives will keep for up to 1 month in an airtight container at room temperature, or for 6 months tightly covered in the freezer.

Dog biscuits

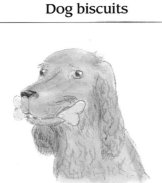

Tasty treats for your pup – and you know what they are made of.

To make 16 medium-size biscuits
14oz/400g dog food (below)
8oz/225g unprocessed bran
8oz/225g old-fashioned oatmeal
4fl oz/115ml vegetable oil

Preheat the oven to Gas Mark ½, 120°C/250°F. Mash the dog food in a medium-size bowl to remove all the lumps, and then mix in the bran and oatmeal. Slowly add the oil, mixing to a consistency that is easy to mould into patties or bone shapes. (You may find it

necessary to use more or less oil than the recipe calls for.)

Bake for 3½ hours, then cool and store in a covered tin. If completely airtight, the biscuits will keep for 1 month refrigerated.

Dog food

A well-balanced diet for your pet.

To make 3lb/1.4kg
1lb/450g minced beef (not lean)
2 eggs, hard-boiled
2lb/900g cooked rice
6 slices white bread, crumbled
2 teaspoons calcium carbonate (crushed antacid tablets)

Cook the meat in a covered pot until no longer pink, retaining the fat. Mix it thoroughly with the other ingredients in a medium-size bowl – the resulting mixture tends to be dry, so add water (not milk) as required.

Drain cleaner

This cleaner helps to clear drains and will also remove a build-up of fat.

To make 5 treatments
16 tablespoons bicarbonate of soda
16 tablespoons salt
4 tablespoons cream of tartar

Place all the ingredients in a jar with a lid, close it tightly and shake until the ingredients are well mixed.

To use, pour 2oz/60g directly down the drain, followed by a kettleful of boiling water. After 1 minute, rinse with warm or cold tap water. Repeat weekly. Store in a dry place in a tightly sealed container.

Drop scones

Quick and easy to make, nothing can beat a batch of freshly made drop scones for tea.

To make 10 drop scones
8oz/225g scone mix (p.415)
2 eggs, size 2, lightly beaten
8fl oz/225ml milk or water

Place the scone mix in a large bowl and stir in the eggs and liquid until just blended; do not overmix. (The batter should be slightly lumpy.) Heat a well-oiled griddle or large frying pan over moderate heat until hot but not smoking. Spoon a large tablespoon of batter per drop scone onto the griddle and cook until bubbles form across the top – about 2 minutes. Turn the drop scone and cook 2 minutes longer. Serve immediately with butter and honey, jam or golden syrup.

Fruit variation If you want to add some variety to a batch of plain drop scones, add 2oz/60g of the fruit of your choice to the batter. Bananas and strawberries work especially well.

Dry carpet cleaner

This brightens up rugs and adds a fresh scent to the room.

To make enough for a small rug
10oz/275g baking powder
2½oz/70g cornflour
5 dried bay leaves, crumbled
1 teaspoon ground cloves or
2oz/60g potpourri (see p.411)

In a covered container, mix all the ingredients thoroughly. Store in a safe place, away from children. To use, shake well and sprinkle generously on the carpet. Leave for several hours (overnight if possible), keeping children and pets off the carpet. Vacuum thoroughly to remove any residue.

Dry shampoo

To avoid making a mess of your floor, apply the shampoo over a sink or bath.

To make enough for 6-8 treatments
2 tablespoons cornmeal
1 tablespoon ground almonds
1½ tablespoons orris root

Combine all the ingredients in a small mixing bowl. Massage 1 teaspoonful of the shampoo into the scalp, and then brush it out thoroughly. Repeat the process at least once if your hair still feels greasy.

Eboniser

Blacken any wood that contains tannin – such as mahogany, walnut, cherry or oak – by sponging it with this vinegar solution.

To make enough to stain a small table
1 fine steel-wool pad
16 fl oz / 450 ml cider vinegar

Put the steel-wool pad in a small plastic or glass bowl and add the vinegar. Leave

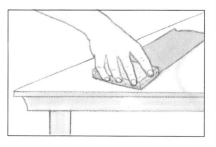

for several days or until the steel wool dissolves.
Caution Leave the bowl uncovered, so as to allow any gases from a reaction between the vinegar and steel wool to escape.
To use the stain, sponge the solution evenly onto a sanded wood surface. If a second coat is desired, wet the wood liberally but evenly with tap water at least 1 hour before re-staining. Then allow the wood to dry naturally overnight – away from direct heat – before applying a finish.

Egg facial mask

Smooth away any wrinkles and moisten dry skin on your face.

To make enough for 1 treatment
1 egg
4 fl oz / 115 ml coconut oil
1 tablespoon honey

Place the egg in a small bowl and beat it thoroughly. Slowly add the coconut oil and honey, beating until the mixture is the consistency of mayonnaise. Place a paper toilet roll upright in a bowl (with plastic wrap sealing the base) and spoon the mixture into it. Place the roll in the freezer.
To use, peel away some of the cardboard and rub the frozen stick over your face and leave for 5-10 minutes. Then rinse off with warm water. After using, cover the exposed end of the stick with plastic film and return to the freezer, where it will keep for several months.

Facial mask

Cleans and revitalises tired skin.

To make enough for 1 treatment
1 tablespoon powdered skimmed milk
½ cucumber, peeled
1 teaspoon plain yoghurt

Purée the ingredients in a blender until smooth. Apply the mask to your face, avoiding the area around the eyes, and leave it to dry for about 20 minutes. Rinse off. It is best to mix a fresh batch of the mask each time of use, although it can be frozen in an ice-cube tray.

Facial scrub

Avoid messing up your floors by applying this over the sink.

To make enough for 1 treatment
6 tablespoons cornmeal
2 tablespoons honey
1 tablespoon ground almonds
or walnuts

Combine the ingredients in a small bowl, adding a little water if the mixture is too dry to apply easily. To use, pack the scrub onto your face and leave for at least 5 minutes. Remove with warm water and a flannel.

Fertiliser

This simple fertiliser will provide general nutrition for most nonflowering houseplants.

To make 1 dose, used monthly
1 tablespoon Epsom salts
1 teaspoon bicarbonate of soda
½ teaspoon saltpetre
¼ teaspoon household ammonia
8 pints / 4.5 litres warm water

Combine the Epsom salts, bicarbonate of soda, saltpetre and ammonia in a small bowl. In a bucket, dissolve the mixture in the warm water. Use once a month in the place of your regular watering. For an acid-loving plant, add 4 drops white vinegar.

Fig bars

Chewy, healthy snacks which are much tastier than commercial brands.

To make about 32 bars
15 oz / 425 g sifted plain flour
½ level teaspoon salt
½ level teaspoon ground cinnamon
6 oz / 175 g butter or margarine
4 oz / 115 g soft light brown sugar
4 oz / 115 g soft dark brown sugar
2 egg whites, size 2
1 teaspoon vanilla essence

8oz/225g dried golden figs,
finely chopped
8fl oz/225ml water
2 tablespoons granulated sugar
2 tablespoons lemon juice

Combine the flour, salt and cinnamon in a small bowl and set to one side. In a

large mixing bowl, cream the butter and light and dark brown sugars until the mixture is fluffy.

Beat in the egg whites and vanilla essence, and then slowly beat in the flour mixture. Shape the dough into a ball. Cover with plastic film and refrigerate for an hour.

Place the figs, water, granulated sugar and lemon juice in a medium-size saucepan. Cook over a moderate heat, stirring constantly, until the mixture is thick – about 7 minutes. Leave it to cool but not to get cold.

Preheat the oven to Gas Mark 4, 175°C/350°F. Place half of the dough between two sheets of greaseproof paper and roll into a 10in/250mm × 12in/300mm rectangle. Cut this into four lengthways, then into four widthways, to make 16 equal-sized rectangles.

At one end of each strip, place 2 level teaspoons of the filling. Roll up the strips and place them 1in/25mm apart on two ungreased baking trays. With a spatula, flatten them to a ½in/13mm thickness. Repeat with remaining pastry and filling.

Bake in batches in the centre of the oven for 15-20 minutes or until the bars are lightly browned. Transfer to a rack to cool.

The fig bars will keep for 1 week wrapped in foil and in an airtight container at room temperature, or for 3 months in the freezer.

Finger paints

A colourful diversion to keep your children occupied – get them to paint outdoors in warm weather.

To make enough for 3 colours
6oz/175g plain flour
8fl oz/225ml water
3 tablespoons glycerine
Assorted food colourings

Mix the flour and water in a medium-size bowl. Divide the mixture equally among 3 small bowls. Add 1 tablespoon glycerine to each batch, stirring constantly, to which you have added the food colouring of your choice.

Make up a fresh batch of paint each time it is needed.

Fireplace cleaner

This cleaning solution will remove soot and grime that attaches itself to the fire surround.

To make ½ bucketful
2 bars (6½oz/185g each)
naphtha soap
5 pints/2.8 litres hot water
1½lb/700g powdered pumice
12oz/340g household ammonia

Shave the naphtha soap into a large pot, pour in the water and heat until the soap dissolves. Remove from the heat and leave to cool. Then add the pumice and the ammonia and stir until the mixture is thoroughly combined.

To use, brush the cleaner onto sooty

areas with a paintbrush and leave it to stand for about 1 hour. Then scrub it off with a stiff brush and soap or washing-up liquid. Rinse it with a sponge and clear water.

Florida water

A delicate toilet water which has a sweet citrus scent.

To make 1 pint 6fl oz/740ml
1 teaspoon lavender oil
1 teaspoon lemon oil
2 teaspoons jasmine oil
3 teaspoons bergamot oil
4 drops each of clove
and cinnamon oil
2 teaspoons tincture of musk
1 pint 2fl oz/625ml vodka
4fl oz/115ml rose water

Mix the oils and tincture of musk with 4fl oz/115ml of the vodka. Gradually add the remaining vodka and the rose water, stirring constantly. Transfer the liquid to a bottle with a secure lid. Leave it to mature for 1-2 months, shaking every few days. If the mixture gets cloudy, strain it through a coffee filter until clear. Store tightly covered.

Flypaper

This helpful summer insect trap is very attractive to flies.

To make six 18in/460mm strips
4fl oz/115g golden syrup
1 tablespoon light or dark brown sugar
1 tablespoon granulated sugar

Combine the ingredients in a small bowl. Place 6 strips of brown paper in a

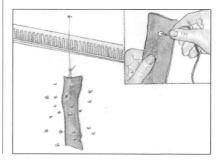

flat container and cover them with the syrup. Leave them to soak overnight. To use, scrape the excess syrup off each strip, poke a hole in one end of it and insert a string. Hang near open windows and doorways.

French toast

Make this the night before and just pop it in the oven in the morning.

To make 4 servings
3 eggs, size 2
12 fl oz / 340 ml milk
1 oz / 30 g unsalted butter or margarine, melted
3 tablespoons soft light or dark brown sugar
½ teaspoon lemon rind, finely grated
⅛ level teaspoon each ground nutmeg and cinnamon
16 slices French bread (about ¾ in / 19 mm thick)
1 tablespoon icing sugar, sifted

In a medium-size bowl, beat together the eggs, milk, butter, brown sugar, lemon rind, nutmeg and cinnamon. Pour half the mixture into a small, greased roasting dish. Lay the bread slices on top of the mixture in a single layer, as close together as possible. Pour the remaining mixture over the bread slices and cover the dish with aluminium foil. Refrigerate overnight or for at least 2 hours.

Preheat the oven to Gas Mark 4, 175°C / 350°F. Bake uncovered until the toast is puffy and golden brown – 50-60 minutes. Sprinkle with the icing sugar. Serve piping hot with golden syrup, honey or fresh fruit, nuts and yoghurt.

Fruit compote

Keep some dried fruit in the store cupboard so you can whip up this delicious dessert in no time.

To make 6 servings
6 oz / 175 g dried pitted prunes
4 oz / 115 g sultanas
3 oz / 85 g dried figs

3 oz / 85 g dried apricots
12 fl oz / 340 ml orange juice
3 fl oz / 85 ml water
2 oz / 60 g caster sugar
1 cinnamon stick, broken
¼ level teaspoon ground ginger
⅛ level teaspoon ground cloves
Pinch of black pepper
¾ teaspoon vanilla essence (optional)

Place all ingredients except the vanilla in a medium-size enamel or stainless-steel saucepan. Set it over a high heat and bring the fruit to the boil. Then reduce the heat to low, cover and simmer for 25-30 minutes, or until the fruit is tender.

Remove the saucepan from the heat. Take out the cinnamon stick and discard. Leave the contents to cool to room temperature before adding the vanilla, if desired. Chill.

Serve with double cream or crème fraîche (see p.392). It will keep for 3 days if tightly covered and refrigerated.

Fruit jelly

More nutritious than commercial brands. Vary the sugar according to the sweetness of the juice.

To make 4 servings
2 envelopes gelatine
6-8 tablespoons caster sugar
16 fl oz / 450 ml grape, cranberry, prune, apple or orange juice
4 oz / 115 g chopped fresh fruit (optional)

Mix the gelatine with the sugar in a small saucepan and slowly stir in 4 fl oz / 115 ml of the juice. Leave it to stand for 5 minutes. Then stir over a moderately low heat until the sugar and gelatine have dissolved. Remove from the heat and stir in the remaining juice.

Pour into a mould or bowl and leave it to cool. Then cover it with a plate or piece of plastic wrap and place it in the refrigerator. If you are using fresh fruit, add it when the jelly has just begun to set.

Chill until firmly set – for about 3 hours. It will keep for up to 2 days refrigerated.

Furniture cleaner

A cleaner to remove surface dirt and grime from finished wood.

To make ¾ pint / 425 ml
8 fl oz / 225 ml boiled linseed oil
5 fl oz / 150 ml turpentine
2½ fl oz / 70 ml white vinegar

Thoroughly mix all the ingredients in a large bowl. Apply to wood surfaces with a soft cloth, rubbing with a circular motion to remove dirt and excess polish. For badly caked-on dirt, use superfine (gauge 0000) steel wool. Store in a tightly covered jar out of the reach of children.

Gargle

How to soothe a sore throat.

To make 1 treatment
8 fl oz / 225 ml warm water
3 tablespoons cider vinegar
2 drops Tabasco sauce
Pinch of salt

Pour the water into a glass and add the remaining ingredients. Gargle as much as necessary and then spit the rinse out. If the mixture is too spicy, add another tablespoon of water. Make only as much as needed at one time. If the sore throat persists, consult your doctor.

Easy breathing variation Help to clear the thick mucus associated with a heavy cold or catarrh with 1 drop each of eucalyptus, lemon and cedarwood essential oils added to 4 fl oz / 115 ml water. Stir well before each mouthful, gargle and spit the liquid into the sink.

Gentian root tonic

Perks up a declining appetite.

To make 2 mugfuls
2-4 teaspoons dried gentian root, chopped
16 fl oz / 450 ml water
2 teaspoons dried peppermint (optional)

In a small saucepan, bring the gentian root and water to a boil. Reduce the heat and simmer for 15 minutes. Remove from the heat and add the peppermint (if desired). Cover and leave to steep for 5 minutes, then transfer to a cup. Sip slowly when lukewarm. The tonic will keep for 2 days if tightly covered and refrigerated.

Gesso

A primer coat to be used on raw wood before applying gold leaf.

To make 1 lb/450g
2 fl oz/60ml rabbitskin glue
12 fl oz/340ml water
1-1½ lb/450-700g gilders' whiting, sifted

In a heatproof glue pot or the top of a double boiler (stainless steel is easiest to clean), mix the glue with 8 fl oz/225ml of the water. Leave it to sit until the glue swells and softens – about 5 minutes – then place the pot over a low heat until the glue melts and runs clear, about 15 minutes.

Meanwhile, mix the gilders' whiting with the remaining 4 fl oz/115ml water in a large jar. Add about 3 oz/85g of the heated glue and stir thoroughly. The gesso should have the consistency of heavy cream. If it is too thick, add more glue. Use as needed – it will keep for 2 days if tightly covered and refrigerated.
Bole variation If more glue is added, the result will be a very thin gesso called bole. Use this variation for the last coat, to give a perfectly smooth ground on which to apply the gold leaf.

Ginseng tea

An ancient Chinese remedy said to increase energy and relieve stress.

To make 1 mugful
8 fl oz/225ml water
2 tablespoons ginseng extract
1 teaspoon honey

Bring the water to a boil in a small saucepan, then add the ginseng and the honey. (For a sweeter tea, add more honey.) The ginseng tea may be reheated, although its flavour will decrease each time. It is preferable to make it fresh as desired. Do not drink for more than 10 consecutive days.

Glair

A light finish for raw wood which repels moisture, dirt and oil and is nontoxic. It is ideal for children's toys.

To make 16 fl oz/450ml
8 fl oz/225ml egg whites
8 fl oz/225ml water
Pinch of sugar
Gum arabic

Mix the egg whites and water in a medium-size bowl, then add the sugar. To use, brush onto the wood surface and then let it dry overnight before sanding. Apply 2 more coats, letting each dry overnight. Because glair tends to be very thin and seeps into wood easily, you might want to thicken it with gum arabic. You may have to recoat the wood occasionally, as this is not a very durable finish.

Glass cleaner

An efficient glass cleaner that will leave your windows sparkling.

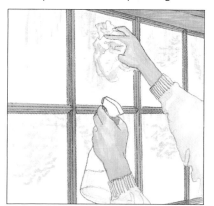

To make 3½ pints/2 litres
4 fl oz/115ml rubbing alcohol
4 fl oz/115ml household ammonia
3 pints/1.75 litres warm water

Pour the alcohol and ammonia into a bucket, add the water and mix well. To use, transfer to a spray bottle and spray the glass with it. Allow it to sit for 30 seconds, then wipe off with newspaper.

Glue

A waterproof binding mixture, good on most fabrics and paper.

To make ¼ pint/150ml
6 tablespoons water
2 envelopes gelatine
2 tablespoons white vinegar
2 teaspoons glycerine

Bring the water to a boil in a small saucepan, then remove it from the heat. Stir in the gelatine until it dissolves, and then add the vinegar and glycerine; stir well. Leave the mixture to cool.

Apply the glue while warm. It will keep for many months in a tightly sealed jar, but will gel after a few days. Heat the jar in hot water before reusing.

Grease solvent

Removes stubborn oil stains from your skin.

To make enough for 1 treatment
2 tablespoons liquid soap gel
(see p.404)
3 tablespoons cornmeal
1 teaspoon glycerine

Combine the ingredients in a small bowl. Pour the mixture onto your hands and scrub until stains disappear; rinse off with warm water.

Gum arabic adhesive

Use this to mend broken crockery.

To make 3½ fl oz/100ml
3 tablespoons gum arabic
1 tablespoon glycerine
½ teaspoon water

In a small mixing bowl, thoroughly combine the ingredients. Apply a thin coating to each surface with a matchstick,

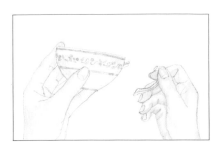

fit the pieces together, and clamp firmly in place until the glue dries – about 1 hour. Leave for at least 24 hours before washing or using the piece.

Hair conditioner

Softens dry hair and helps prevent split ends.

To make 8fl oz/225ml
3fl oz/85ml olive oil
2½fl oz/70ml vegetable oil
2½fl oz/70ml honey

Place all the ingredients in a small saucepan and heat until just boiling. Allow the contents to cool for 5 minutes, then transfer to a 1 pint/570ml plastic spray bottle. Spray some of the conditioner onto your hair and rub it in thoroughly. Wrap your head in a warm, damp towel and leave it for 1 hour. Shampoo to remove the conditioner and then wash your hair as usual.

Ham and cheese bread

A meal in itself. Make it in advance to be used for packed lunches or breakfast.

To make 1 loaf
10oz/275g unsifted plain flour
2oz/60g yellow cornmeal
2¼ level teaspoons baking powder
½ level teaspoon salt
¼ level teaspoon black pepper
4oz/115g ham, coarsely chopped
4oz/115g plus 2 tablespoons grated
Parmesan cheese
8fl oz/225ml milk
2fl oz/60ml olive oil
2 eggs, size 2

Preheat the oven to Gas Mark 5, 190°C/375°F. Sift the flour, cornmeal, baking powder, salt and pepper into a large mixing bowl, and stir in the chopped ham and 4oz/115g of the grated Parmesan cheese.

In a small bowl, whisk together the milk, olive oil and eggs. Add them to the flour mixture and stir until just combined. Spoon the mixture into a greased 9in/230mm bread tin and then sprinkle the top with the remaining Parmesan cheese.

Bake until a fork or toothpick inserted into the centre comes out clean – 1 hour. Leave the tin to cool on a wire rack for 20 minutes, then turn out the loaf. Serve it warm or cool. Wrapped in foil, it will keep for 1 week in the fridge or for 3 months in the freezer.

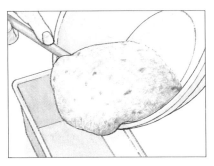

Hand treatment

Moisturises chapped hands.

To make enough for 1 application
3 tablespoons ground almonds
2 tablespoons dried comfrey root
1 tablespoon parsley, chopped
1 egg
1 tablespoon honey
1 tablespoon glycerine

Mix the ground almonds, comfrey root and parsley in a small bowl and put to one side. In another bowl, combine the egg, honey and glycerine. Stir in 3 tablespoons of the almond mixture.

Dip your hands into the concoction and gently massage it in, especially around the nails. Leave for about 30 minutes and then rinse off with warm water. Double quantities will keep for 5 days if refrigerated.

Herbal face mask

Cleans skin and tightens pores.

To make enough for 1 treatment
1 tablespoon honey
1 egg
1 teaspoon dried chamomile flowers, crumbled
1 teaspoon fresh mint, finely chopped

Mix all the ingredients together in a small bowl. Apply the mixture to your face and neck and leave it to dry. Then rinse it off with warm water. Make a fresh batch each time.

Herbal ice cubes

The peppermint and bitters are soothing for an upset stomach, and the ice cubes are easier to keep down than liquids.

To make 50 ice cubes
8fl oz/225ml water
1 peppermint tea bag
16fl oz/450ml cranberry juice
1 teaspoon angostura bitters

Bring the water to a boil in a small saucepan. Add the tea bag, turn off the heat, and leave to steep for 10 minutes. Discard the tea bag, let the tea cool for a further 5 minutes and then stir in the remaining ingredients.

Transfer the mixture to an ice-cube tray and place in the freezer until solidly frozen. To use, suck or chew up to 3 ice cubes each hour or rub on your lips. **Caution** Call your doctor if the vomiting lasts more than 24 hours or is severe.

Herbal shampoo

Makes oily hair shiny and manageable. If your hair needs conditioning, use the egg and milk.

To make enough for 4 washes
2 tablespoons dried peppermint
2 tablespoons dried spearmint
1 tablespoon dried sage
8fl oz/225ml purified water

2½fl oz/70ml baby shampoo
1 egg, beaten (optional)
2½fl oz/70g milk (optional)

Place the herbs in a small saucepan, add the water, and bring to a full boil. Remove the pan from the heat and steep the herbs for 20 minutes. Then strain the liquid and discard the herbs. In a jar, mix the baby shampoo with 2fl oz/60ml of the herbal water. Shampoo as usual. The basic mixture will keep for 6 months, but if using egg and milk, make fresh each time.

Variation for dry hair Substitute 1 tablespoon each of dried comfrey root, rosemary and chamomile for the peppermint, spearmint and sage; proceed as directed.

Herb butters

These butters freeze very well, so the delicate flavour of fresh herbs can be enjoyed through the winter.

To make 8 servings
4oz/115g butter or margarine, at
room temperature
4 tablespoons chopped dill, or
2 tablespoons chopped tarragon, or
3 tablespoons chopped chives, or
1-3 cloves garlic, peeled and crushed
¼ level teaspoon salt

Blend the butter, your chosen herb or garlic and the salt in a small bowl. Refrigerate until firm enough to handle. Make into a log shape and cover with plastic wrap and foil, or spoon the soft butter into a piping bag fitted with a ½in/13mm plain nozzle. Then pipe neat rounds of the butter onto a foil-lined baking sheet. Freeze and then later transfer the butter rounds from the foil into a plastic container. Herb butters will keep for 5 days refrigerated, or for 4 months in the deep freeze.

The dill butter is particularly good on grilled fish or vegetables; the tarragon butter on steaks or poultry; the chive butter on baked potatoes, scrambled eggs or fresh vegetables; and the garlic butter on hamburgers, steaks, lamb chops or bread.

Herb dressing

For a stronger flavour, add ½ teaspoon more of the herb dressing mix to this recipe.

To make 16fl oz/450ml
2 tablespoons herb dressing
mix (below)
12fl oz/340ml warm water
2 tablespoons olive oil
5 tablespoons white vinegar or
tarragon vinegar
2 cloves garlic, peeled and crushed

Add the herb dressing mix to the warm water, olive oil, vinegar and garlic in a small bowl. Whisk the ingredients together and let the dressing sit at room temperature for 30 minutes before using. Whisk again, then pour the desired amount over your salad. The dressing will keep for 1 week if tightly covered and refrigerated.

Herb dressing mix

The fresh taste of this dry mix makes it ideal for the store cupboard.

To make approximately 4oz/115g
8 level tablespoons dried parsley
4 level tablespoons each dried
oregano, basil and marjoram,
crumbled
2oz/60g caster sugar
2 level tablespoons fennel seed,
crushed
2 level tablespoons dry mustard
1 level tablespoon black pepper

Place all the ingredients in a large jar, cover, and shake thoroughly until well blended. The dressing mix will keep for 6 weeks in a cool, dark, dry place.

Herbed cheese spread

As good as commercial brands and less costly.

To make 6oz/175g
6oz/175g cream cheese, softened
1 teaspoon chopped parsley

1 small clove of garlic, peeled
and crushed
¼ level teaspoon salt
¼ level teaspoon black pepper
¼ teaspoon lemon juice

Mix all the ingredients in a small bowl, cover, and refrigerate for at least 2 hours to allow the flavours to blend. The spread will keep for up to 7 days refrigerated in a tightly sealed container, but can also be frozen for 3 months shaped as a log and covered with plastic film and foil.

Herbed rice

This contains less salt than packaged mixes and takes just minutes to prepare.

To make 6 servings
1 pint/570ml water
2 level tablespoons herbed
rice mix (see below)
8oz/225g raw white or brown rice
1oz/30g unsalted butter or margarine

Bring the water to the boil in a large saucepan. Pour in the herbed rice mix and stir to combine. Add the rice and lower the heat until the water just simmers. Cover and cook white rice for 25 minutes or until tender (cook brown rice as directed on the packet). Stir in the butter and serve hot.

Herbed rice mix

Keep this spicy white or brown rice mix in your kitchen cupboard at all times – an instant meal.

To make 7 tablespoons
2½ level tablespoons onion flakes
1¼ level teaspoons salt
1 bay leaf
¾ level teaspoon dried basil, crumbled
¾ level teaspoon celery seasoning
½ level teaspoon paprika
½ level teaspoon garlic granules
1 teaspoon grated lemon peel

Place all the ingredients in a plastic bag and shake to combine. Store in a tightly covered jar or canister.

Hot dog relish

This is also good with beefburgers and sausages.

To make ¾pt/425ml
1 large Spanish onion, finely chopped
2 tablespoons cider vinegar
2 level tablespoons caster sugar
¼ level teaspoon salt
4oz/115g pimentos (mixed peppers), drained and chopped

Mix all the ingredients in a medium-size bowl, and then leave them to stand at room temperature for 30 minutes before serving. The relish will keep for up to 1 week if covered and refrigerated.

Hot pepper jelly

This spicy jelly is delicious served with cold ham or pork.

To make four 12oz/340g jars
2 medium-size sweet red peppers (about 6oz/175g each), cored, seeded and chopped
3 fresh red or green chillies, cored, seeded and finely chopped
16fl oz/450ml cider vinegar
2¾lb/1.25kg sugar with pectin

In a food processor or blender, process the peppers and chillies with half of the vinegar until finely chopped.
Caution Don't touch your eyes until you have washed your hands.
Transfer the mixture to a large stainless-steel saucepan and add the sugar and remaining vinegar. Stir over a moderate heat until the sugar dissolves, then bring the mixture to a rolling boil for 4 minutes.

Remove the pan from the heat and allow to stand for 5 minutes. Then skim any scum off the surface with a large, flat spoon. Pour the jelly into hot, sterilised 12oz/340g jars. Wipe the jar rims and seal tightly. The jelly should keep for 6 months in a cool, dark cupboard.

Household cleaner

Use this efficient cleaner on worktops and floors.

To make 1 pint/570ml
16 tablespoons washing powder
1 pint/570ml hot water
8fl oz/225ml pine oil

Mix the washing powder and water in a bucket and stir slowly until the detergent dissolves. If a foam appears on the surface, stop stirring and skim off the bubbles, or wait until they dissolve. Then gradually add the pine oil, mixing well.

To use, dilute the cleaner with water for floors and surfaces and use neat on areas such as toilet bowls where bacteria flourish. Store in a labelled jar with a tight-fitting lid, out of the reach of small children.

Household duster

An economical way of turning old rags and scraps of material into a duster that polishes as well as dusts.

To make 1 duster
2fl oz/60ml vinegar
2fl oz/60ml paraffin
12in/300mm square piece of cloth

Mix the vinegar and paraffin together in a glass or plastic bowl and add the cloth

square. Leave for 1 hour – until well impregnated – then wring out the cloth and hang it up to dry before using; store in a dry place.

Hyssop cough syrup

A syrup to soothe an irritated throat with a pleasant liquorice taste.

To make ½ pint/285ml
8fl oz/225ml honey
2fl oz/60ml water
2 tablespoons dried flowering hyssop tops or 6 tablespoons fresh hyssop flowers, chopped
1 teaspoon aniseed

Place the honey in a small heavy saucepan and add the water a tablespoon at a time, stirring until the mixture is syrupy. Gradually bring it to a boil, skimming off any scum that surfaces. Use 1-2 tablespoons water to moisten the dried hyssop, then crush the aniseed with a spoon. Add both to the honey and stir. Cover and simmer for 30 minutes.

Remove the lid and leave to cool slightly. Then strain it into a jar with a screw-on lid. When cold, cover tightly.

Ink

Buy lamp black in a tube or make it by holding a plate over a lit candle. Dissolve the resulting blackener in a few drops of water.

To make 4fl oz/115ml
1 egg yolk
1 teaspoon gum arabic
4fl oz/115ml honey
½ teaspoon lamp black
Water to mix

Mix the egg yolk, gum arabic and honey in a small bowl. Add the lamp black, thinning with more water if necessary.

Jewellery cleaner

Use this simple solution to clean your pieces of jewellery every couple of months. It will keep them sparkling.

To make ½ pint/285 ml
½ pint/285 ml warm water
3-4 drops washing-up liquid
1 drop household ammonia

Mix the ingredients together in a small bowl. To clean frequently worn items, soak them in the solution for 1-10 minutes, depending on how heavily tarnished they are. If a piece has an intricate pattern or several cracks or crevices, swish it through the liquid. A toothbrush with soft bristles works especially well for cleaning large items. Wash an old mascara brush and use it to clean small, hard-to-reach spaces. Rinse and dry with a soft clean cloth.

Pour any remaining cleaner into a glass jar, label, cover and store out of children's reach.

Caution Don't soak pearls or other pieces with a closed setting, rub gently with a soft chamois.

Caution Do not combine the cleaner with any substance containing chlorine bleach; together they produce hazardous fumes.

Diamond-cleaning variation Mix together 2 fl oz/60 ml warm water and 2 fl oz/60 ml household ammonia in a small bowl. Rinse afterwards with warm water.

Ketchup

A fresh tasting tomato ketchup which makes a nice gift. Cover the pot as it cooks with a wire mesh shield.

To make 16 fl oz/450 ml
Two 1 lb 12 oz/800 g cans tomatoes, sieved

2 bay leaves
1 level teaspoon celery seasoning
1 level teaspoon mustard seed
1 teaspoon whole allspice
1 stick cinnamon
½ teaspoon peppercorns
1½ level teaspoons salt
8 fl oz/225 ml white vinegar
7 oz/200 g sugar

In a large, deep saucepan over a moderate heat, simmer the tomatoes uncovered for 1 hour, stirring occasionally. Tie the bay leaves, celery seasoning and spices in a piece of muslin and add to the saucepan, then add the salt. Partially cover the saucepan with a lid and simmer for another 30 minutes.

Remove the spice bag and add the vinegar and sugar. Turn up the heat to moderate and cook the ketchup uncovered at a slow boil, stirring often, until very thick – about 1 hour. At the end of the cooking time, you may have to stir constantly to prevent the mixture catching on the bottom of the saucepan.

Ladle the hot tomato ketchup into 2 hot, sterilized 8 oz/225 ml preserving jars, stopping ⅛ in/3 mm below the rim. Clean the jars and seal tightly while still hot – the ketchup will keep for 1 month if refrigerated.

Laundry pre-spotter

Glycerine softens stains on any fabric and colour, making them easier to remove by normal washing. Keep a half glycerine, half water solution handy in the house.

To make 8 fl oz/225 ml
4 fl oz/115 ml glycerine
4 fl oz/115 ml water

Combine the ingredients in a jar and shake thoroughly. Transfer the mixture to a spray bottle, label and store safely away out of the reach of children and pets.

To use, spray the area affected and rub the liquid into the fabric. Leave for 1 hour and then sponge with warm water before washing.

Lawn fertiliser

Use this to encourage a healthy spring growth in your winter-weary lawn.

To make 32 gallons/145 litres
16 tablespoons Epsom salts
8 fl oz/225 ml household ammonia
Water

Combine the Epsom salts and ammonia in a clean jar. To use, mix 2 tablespoons of the mixture with 16 pints/9 litres water in a watering can, and sprinkle over 150-200 sq ft/14-18.6 sq m of turf. For use with a hose attachment, pour into the sprayer container.

Lemonade mix

For pink lemonade, add 6 fl oz/175 ml grenadine syrup. For limeade, substitute lime juice for the lemon juice.

To make 24 servings
1¾ pints/1 litre fresh lemon juice
(about 24 large lemons)
7 oz/200 g caster sugar
1½ lb/700 g golden syrup

Stir all the ingredients together in a large bowl until the sugar dissolves. Pour into a screw-top jar, cover and store in the refrigerator. Each time of use, shake well and add 2 fl oz/60 ml of the mix to 6 fl oz/175 ml water or soda water. Stir well and add ice if desired. The lemonade mix will keep for up to 2 weeks if refrigerated.

Lemon curd

Serve this versatile spread in tart shells, as a filling for sponge cake or on toast. It also makes a nice gift.

To make approximately 1½lb/700g
4oz/115g butter or
margarine
14oz/400g sugar
Grated rind of 2 lemons
Strained juice of 4 lemons
6 eggs, size 2, lightly beaten
Pinch salt

Melt the butter in a double saucepan over a low heat. Then remove from the heat and add the sugar, lemon rind and juice, eggs and salt. Mix thoroughly. Cook over moderate heat, stirring constantly, until the mixture thickens – about 8 minutes. Do not let it boil.

Strain the mixture through a nylon sieve into a bowl and discard the solids. Spoon the lemon curd into clean, warm jars and leave it to cool to room temperature; then cover. You can keep it for 1 month if refrigerated.

Lip balm

An inexpensive way to keep your lips soft in all kinds of weather.

To make 2fl oz/60ml
1 tablespoon olive oil
1 teaspoon glycerine
2 tablespoons honey

Mix all the ingredients together in a small bowl. To use, apply the ointment to dry or sore lips with your finger or a cotton ball. Use as often as necessary for chapped lips until the condition improves. Store it refrigerated in a tightly covered jar.

Liquid soap

Turn leftover bits of soap into a versatile cleaning agent which can be used as hand soap or for general household chores.

To make 7 pints/4 litres
1lb/450g soap flakes or
grated soap
6½ pints/3.7 litres water
2 tablespoons glycerine

Mix the ingredients together in a large pot and place it over a low heat, stirring occasionally. When the soap has dissolved, leave to cool slightly and then transfer the liquid into a storage container such an old ice-cream tub. Cover tightly, label, and store out of the reach of children.

Gel variation For a thicker, more gelatinous soap, use half as much water.

Low-fat coffee cake

A scrumptious, light, spongy cake which is perfect for tea.

To make 8-10 servings
3oz/85g soft dark or
light brown sugar
1½ level teaspoons ground cinnamon
¼ level teaspoon ground nutmeg
1oz/30g chopped pecans or walnuts
2oz/60g margarine
7oz/200g granulated sugar
10oz/275g sifted plain flour
2 level teaspoons baking powder
½ level teaspoon salt
6fl oz/175ml skimmed milk
1 teaspoon vanilla essence
3 egg whites, size 2, stiffly beaten

To make the topping, combine the brown sugar, cinnamon, nutmeg and nuts in a small bowl and put to one side.

Preheat the oven to Gas Mark 5, 190°C/375°F. Cream the margarine in a large bowl, then slowly add the sugar, beating until light and fluffy. Sift the flour, baking powder and salt onto a sheet of greaseproof paper, then add the flour mixture a little at a time to the margarine mixture, alternating with a little milk. Beat well after each addition. Beat in the vanilla essence, then fold in the egg whites.

Pour the mixture into a square, greased cake tin, and sprinkle with the topping. Bake until a toothpick inserted in the centre of the cake comes out clean – about 1 hour. Let the cake cool in the tin on a wire rack until just warm and then turn it out. It can be served warm or cold. It will keep for 2 days in the refrigerator if covered with foil, and for up to 2 months if frozen.

Marigold tea

Herbalists consider marigold tea an excellent way of soothing itchy or blistered skin and eczema.

To make 3 drinks
1 pint/570ml water
1oz/30g marigold flowers or petals

Bring the water to a boil and then remove from the heat. Add the marigold flowers and leave them to infuse for 5-10 minutes. Strain off the liquid and drink as required over the next 24 hours.

Marinade for poultry and fish

This light marinade will bring out the flavour of chicken or fish.

To make enough for 4-6 servings
¼-½ pint/150-285ml olive oil
Juice of half a lemon
2 bay leaves, crumbled
1 teaspoon dried thyme,
oregano or mixed herbs

Mix all the ingredients together in a small bowl. Place the chicken or fish in a plastic bag, pour the marinade over the top and put the bag into a large glass bowl. Leave for 2 hours or longer, turning from time to time.

Marsh mallow cough syrup

The orange juice helps to keep the syrup from crystallising. For a tarter flavour, substitute the juice of 1 lemon for the orange juice.

To make 1¼ pints/725ml
1½-2½ teaspoons chopped dried
marsh mallow root, leaves or flowers
16fl oz/450ml water
12oz/340g brown sugar
2fl oz/60ml orange juice

In a small saucepan, stir the marsh mallow root into the water; bring to a boil over a moderately high heat. Reduce the heat to low and simmer for 20 minutes.

Strain the liquid into another saucepan – there should be about 8fl oz/225ml left – and slowly stir in the sugar over a low heat, making a thick syrup. Simmer for another 5 minutes,

making sure the sugar dissolves completely. If the mixture gets too thick, stir in a little more water.

Remove the pan from the heat and allow to cool slightly, then gradually add the orange juice and mix. Transfer to a lidded container and cover when cool.
Wild cherry variation Simmer 1 teaspoon wild cherry bark or stalks with the marsh mallow root, omit the orange juice and add a scant ½ teaspoon cream of tartar to the sugar.

Meringue

This simple mixture is delicious with fresh fruit and whipped cream, and also makes an excellent topping for pies and puddings.

*To make enough for 1 topping or 8
individual meringues*
2 egg whites
4oz/115g caster sugar

Place the egg whites in a bowl and whisk with an electric or hand beater until stiff. Add half of the sugar and continue to beat until the mixture stands in soft peaks, or holds its shape. Fold in the rest of the sugar with a metal spoon.

To use as a topping, spread the mixture evenly over the filling, sprinkle with caster sugar and bake in the oven. To make individual meringues, preheat the oven to Gas Mark ¼, 110°C/225°F. Spoon or pipe rounds of the mixture onto a baking tray lined with greaseproof paper, and bake for 2 hours or until just beginning to brown.

Minty mouthwash

Keep your breath fresh and fragrant with this healthy mouthwash.

To make 16fl oz/450ml
16fl oz/450ml water
1 tablespoon fresh or dried parsley
2 teaspoons whole cloves
2 teaspoons ground cinnamon
2 teaspoons peppermint extract

Boil the water in a small saucepan and then remove it from the heat. Add the

remaining ingredients and leave them to infuse in the water for 5-10 minutes. Strain off the liquid and keep it tightly covered and refrigerated for up to 2 weeks.

Mock mayonnaise

This creamy salad spread has only 18 calories per tablespoon and no cholesterol. For a little spiciness, add a tablespoon of tomato ketchup or Tabasco sauce.

To make 1 pint/570ml
16fl oz/450ml cold water
3 level tablespoons cornflour
2fl oz/60ml olive oil
2fl oz/60ml white vinegar
2fl oz/60ml plain low-fat yoghurt
2 teaspoons prepared English mustard
1 teaspoon horseradish sauce

Whisk together the water and cornflour in a small saucepan. Set over a moderate heat and cook, stirring continuously, until the mixture comes to the boil. Boil for 1-2 minutes, or until the mixture is clear, and then transfer it to a small bowl.

Whisk in the remaining ingredients in the order listed. If tightly covered, the dressing will keep for up to 2 weeks refrigerated.

Mock sour cream

Just 11 calories per tablespoon and no saturated fat. A delicious topping for fruit, soups and vegetables, but not to be used for cooking.

To make 12fl oz/340ml
8fl oz/225ml milk
4 teaspoons buttermilk powder
(available in health-food stores)
½ level teaspoon gelatine
4fl oz/115ml plain low-fat yoghurt

Combine the milk and buttermilk powder in a medium-size saucepan. Sprinkle the gelatine on top and leave it to soften – about 5 minutes. Place the pan over a low heat and cook uncovered, stirring occasionally, for 5 minutes, or until the gelatine dissolves. Remove the pan from the heat, let the milk cool a little and then whisk in the yoghurt.

Transfer the mixture to a medium-size bowl, cover and refrigerate for 1 hour, or until thickened. If required, it will keep for up to 5 days if tightly covered and refrigerated.

Modelling dough

This is a good modelling dough for children which can also be used to make Christmas tree decorations.

To make 1½lb/700g dough
8 tablespoons table salt
(do not use rock or sea salt)
4fl oz/115ml hot water
4fl oz/115ml cold water
8 tablespoons cornflour
2 drops food colouring (optional)

Mix the salt and hot water in a large saucepan and bring to a boil over high heat. Place the cold water in a small bowl and stir in the cornflour; mix well. Add food colouring if desired.

Add the cornflour mixture to the boiling salt water and stir vigorously to keep it from forming lumps. Cook over a low heat, stirring constantly, until the mixture is stiff. Remove from the heat and, using a large spoon, carefully turn the mixture onto a bread board.

Leave the dough to cool and then knead it until smooth. Use immediately or wrap in plastic wrap and store in an airtight container. If you want to dry the models, leave them standing at room temperature for 3 days, or bake them at Gas Mark ¼, 110°C/225°F for 2 hours.
Christmas tree decorations Roll out the dough to ¼in/6mm thick and then use biscuit cutters to make a variety of shapes. Make a hole at the top of each one with a toothpick (so a string or wire can be inserted later) and bake them as above. Decorate as desired.

Moisturiser

A mixture of oils which softens the skin and also removes make-up.

To make 3fl oz/85ml
1 tablespoon olive oil
1 tablespoon coconut oil
1 tablespoon vegetable oil
2 tablespoons mashed strawberries
1-2 drops vitamin E oil (optional)

Mix together the olive, coconut and vegetable oils in a small bowl, then stir in the strawberries. If desired, add the vitamin E oil. Store in the refrigerator in a covered jar, where it will keep for several weeks.

Mouth ulcer treatment

Minor mouth ulcers may be small but they can be extremely painful. Try using this soothing mouthwash.

To make enough for 1 treatment
2-3 drops of essential oil of lemon, chamomile, sage or fennel
4fl oz/115ml boiling water

Let the water cool slightly in a cup, and then add the drops of your chosen oil. Rinse out your mouth with the concoction several times a day. Consult your doctor after a few days if the condition persists.

Mushroom barley soup

For heartier soup, add sautéed mushrooms or leftover meat or chicken to this broth.

To make 4 servings
2 pints/1.15 litres water
1 recipe mushroom barley soup mix (below)
14 oz/400g whole peeled tomatoes with juice
1 small carrot, peeled, halved lengthwise and thinly sliced

Place the water in a medium-size saucepan and bring to the boil over a moderately high heat. Add the soup mix, tomatoes (breaking them up with a spoon) and carrot. When the mixture returns to the boil, cover it, turn the heat down to low and leave the soup to simmer slowly until the barley is tender – about 30 minutes.

Remove the pan from the heat and leave the soup to cool for 10 minutes. Then take out the bay leaf and serve.

Mushroom barley soup mix

Although unusual, dried mushrooms can be found in supermarkets or delicatessens.

To make 4 servings
1oz/30g dried mushrooms
3½oz/100g pearl barley
2 level tablespoons dried onion
1 tablespoon dried green pepper flakes
1 level teaspoon ground sage
1 level teaspoon dried marjoram, crumbled
1 small bay leaf
1 level teaspoon salt
½ level teaspoon garlic powder
¼ level teaspoon black pepper

Rub the mushrooms with paper towels to remove any surface dirt, then break them into small pieces, discarding any tough stems. Place in a plastic bag or small container and add the remaining ingredients. Close the bag or container tightly and shake well.

This dried soup mix will keep for up to 6 months in a tightly covered container in a cool place.

Mustard

This hot and spicy homemade mustard is good with cold meats or on sandwiches.

To make 8 fl oz / 225 ml
1½ oz / 45 g mustard seeds
3 level tablespoons dry mustard
4 fl oz / 115 ml cider vinegar
4 fl oz / 115 ml dark beer
2 cloves garlic, peeled and
finely chopped
2 oz / 60 g soft light brown sugar
¾ level teaspoon salt
½ level teaspoon ground ginger
¼ level teaspoon ground allspice

Mix the mustard seeds, dry mustard and vinegar in a small bowl. Cover with plastic wrap and leave to stand for 3 hours at room temperature.

Place the remaining ingredients in a small saucepan, add the mustard mixture and stir well. Bring to the boil over a moderate heat, then turn down to low and simmer for 5 minutes, stirring occasionally. Remove from the heat and transfer to a clean, hot preserving jar. Seal tightly and leave to cool. The mustard will keep for up to 1 month if tightly covered and refrigerated.

Mustard plaster

A traditional remedy for relieving the chest congestion that sometimes accompanies a cold.

To make 1 batch of paste
1 tablespoon dry mustard
4 tablespoons flour for adults, or 6 tablespoons flour for children
Lukewarm water

Sift the mustard and flour into a medium-size bowl. Slowly add just enough water to make a paste. Spread the flour paste onto a piece of muslin big enough to cover the chest area. Place another piece of muslin on top.

Make sure the chest is dry, then cover with the mustard plaster. Check frequently; when the skin begins turning red, usually after 10-20 minutes, remove

the plaster. (Do not use for more than 30 minutes at a time.) Rub the area with petroleum jelly or olive oil to hold in the heat. Use the plaster twice a day until the congestion clears up.
Caution Discontinue use immediately in case of allergic reaction.

Nappy rash ointment

Soothe sore patches on your baby's skin with this herbal remedy.

To make 20 applications
1 tablespoon dried chickweed
1 tablespoon dried marsh mallow root
1 tablespoon dried comfrey root
⅛ teaspoon goldenseal powder
8 fl oz / 225 ml sweet almond oil
2 oz / 60 g beeswax

Combine all the ingredients except the beeswax in a medium-size saucepan. Cook over moderately low heat until soft – 5-10 minutes. Add the beeswax and stir over the heat until the beeswax melts completely. Then strain through cheesecloth into a small glass jar. Seal

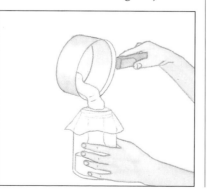

tightly and refrigerate until solid. Apply each time you change the baby's nappy. It will keep for 2 months in a cool place.
Caution If the rash doesn't disappear after 3-4 applications, consult your doctor as to whether or not to continue the treatment.

Natural wool dye

Many dyes made from plants and fruits need the wool to be prepared first, but dark brown and black dyes made from walnuts work with no additional preparation.

To make enough dye for
5 lb / 2.3 kg wool
5 lb / 2.3 kg whole walnuts,
ripe or unripe
Cold water

Place the fresh walnuts in a large saucepan and cover generously with cold water. Bring to the boil over a moderate heat and boil for 30 minutes. Strain off the liquid into another saucepan, allow to cool, and then add the wool. Slowly bring the liquid back to the boil and simmer until the wool has a good colour. Remove it from the dye, squeeze it out gently, rinse thoroughly in cold water and leave to dry.

No-fry chicken

This recipe produces crusty, moist meat without deep frying. For a less spicy dish, omit the Tabasco sauce.

To make 4 servings
¼ level teaspoon dried oregano
¼ level teaspoon ground ginger
½ level teaspoon dried basil
1 clove garlic, peeled and crushed
2 level tablespoons plain flour
½ level teaspoon salt
4 skinless boneless chicken breasts
(about 6 oz / 175 g each)
2 tablespoons milk
⅛ teaspoon
Tabasco sauce
1 oz / 30 g bran flakes or cornflakes,
coarsely crumbled

Preheat the oven to Gas Mark 4, 175°C/350°F. Place the oregano, ginger, basil, garlic, flour and salt in a plastic bag and shake to mix. Put the chicken in the bag and shake until evenly coated.

In a shallow bowl, combine the milk and Tabasco sauce. Place the cereal crumbs on a plate. Dip each chicken breast in the milk mixture, then roll in the crumbs until coated all over.

Oil a wire rack and place the chicken on top. Set the rack on a baking tray and place in the oven. Bake, uncovered, until the breasts are no longer pink on the inside – about 25-30 minutes. Serve hot or cold.

Nose drops

To relieve a stuffed nose. You can replace the distilled water with tap water left in a bowl overnight.

To make 16fl oz/450ml
1 teaspoon salt
16fl oz/450ml distilled water

Mix the salt with the water. Transfer to an atomiser and spray into your nose. Or place a tablespoon in the palm of your hand and inhale. Use alone or before using decongestant drops.

Onion cough mixture

A soothing and aromatic remedy.

To make 12fl oz/340ml
2 medium onions, thinly sliced
8fl oz /225ml honey
4fl oz/115ml warm water
1 tot vodka (optional)
Juice of 1 lemon

Place the onions in a medium-size bowl. Add the honey, water and vodka (if desired) and leave to sit overnight in the refrigerator. Strain off the liquid, discarding the onions, and transfer to a bottle. Cover tightly. Take 2 teaspoons every 3-4 hours. The cough mixture will keep for 1 week if refrigerated.

Oven cleaner

This solution works well on stoves and barbecues.

To make 16fl oz/450ml
2 tablespoons liquid soap (see p.404)
or washing powder
2 teaspoons borax
12fl oz/340ml warm water
4fl oz/115ml household ammonia
Non-chlorine scouring powder

Pour the soap, borax, water and ammonia into a 1 pint/570ml spray bottle. Shake well and then leave to stand until all the crystals have dissolved; otherwise they might clog the sprayer.

To use, put old newspapers on the floor in front of the oven. Make sure the room is well ventilated and wear rubber gloves. Spray the liquid onto the oven surface and leave for about 10 minutes. Spread some scouring powder on one area and rub with a wet kitchen scrubbing pad. Move around the oven surface, using more cleaner, water and scouring powder as required. For tough

spots, rub with a pumice stone or scrape with a razor blade, having tested an inconspicuous area for scratching. Wipe clean with water and a sponge, or with paper towels, and dry.

Caution Check the instruction manual for your oven to check that you should use a cleaner on it. Don't use on continuous-clean ovens or those which clean themselves.

Papier-mâché

A good holiday pastime for the children and suitable for original gifts.

To make enough papier-mâché for
1 small bowl
8 tablespoons flour
¼pint/150ml water
Newspaper strips about
1½in/38mm wide

Mix the flour and water together in a medium-size bowl – it should be the consistency of thick glue. If a thicker mixture is desired, add more flour.

Dip the paper strips into the paste one

at a time and gently pull them through your fingers to remove any excess. Then apply to the surface you want to cover (clay, milk cartons, balloons, bottles or any disposable container make a good base). Repeat until well covered.

When dry, decorate the paper surface with poster paint. For a longer-lasting and harder surface, coat with shellac after the paint dries.

Mash variation Make a mash out of newspaper rather than using strips. Soak pieces in water overnight and then boil, stirring to make a pulp. Cool, strain off any liquid and add 2 tablespoons each of PVA glue and wallpaper paste.

Paste

An all-purpose paste, excellent for papier-mâché projects.

To make 1½lb/700g paste
7 oz/200g plain flour
3 oz/85g white sugar
8fl oz/225ml cold water
16fl oz/450ml boiling water
1 tablespoon alum
1 teaspoon oil of cinnamon

Combine the flour and sugar in a large saucepan and slowly stir in the cold water. Add the boiling water gradually, then bring the mixture to a boil, stirring constantly. When the mixture is stiff, remove from the heat and stir in the alum and oil of cinnamon. Store in a tightly sealed container. When required, thin with boiling water if necessary.

Peach jam

Natural fruit juices act as a sweetener in this low-sugar preserve. It's best made in the summer, when peaches are in season.

To make 1½lb/700g
2½lb/1.1kg ripe peaches
3 strips orange peel
½ × 2in/13 × 25mm each
6fl oz/175ml fresh orange juice
6fl oz/175ml unsweetened white grape juice
6oz/175g soft light brown sugar
1 tablespoon fresh lemon juice
¼ level teaspoon ground ginger

Bring a large saucepan of water to a boil over moderate heat. Drop the peaches in, 2 or 3 at a time, and boil for 30 seconds. Remove with a slotted spoon and rinse with cold water to cool. Peel off the

skins, cut in half and remove the stones. Coarsely chop the flesh.

Transfer the peaches to a large saucepan, add the remaining ingredients and set over moderate heat. Let the mixture boil slowly, stirring frequently, until it thickens and reaches 105°C/220°F on a sugar thermometer – about 30 minutes.

Discard the orange rind and transfer the jam to hot, sterilised 12oz/340g jars. Cover and leave to cool before sealing. The peach preserve will keep for up to 2 months if refrigerated.

Peanut butter

This recipe is easy to make and delicious to eat.

To make approximately 9 oz/250g
10oz/275g salted dry-roasted peanuts
1 tablespoon plus 1 teaspoon vegetable oil

For creamy peanut butter, process the peanuts with the oil in a food processor or blender until smooth, working in batches if necessary. Stop the machine occasionally and scrape down the sides.

To make chunky peanut butter, coarsely chop about 5 tablespoons of the peanuts in a blender or food processor and put to one side. Process the remaining peanuts with the oil until creamy, then stir in the coarsely chopped peanuts. It keeps for 1 month in a covered jar in the refrigerator.

Peanut butter bars

Good for lunchboxes and picnics. For crunch, add the unsalted peanuts.

To make 24 × 2in/50mm bars
3½oz/100g granulated sugar
12oz/340g golden syrup
12oz/340g
crunchy peanut butter
4oz/115g toasted rice cereal
5oz/150g coarsely chopped unsalted peanuts (optional)

In a very large saucepan, bring the sugar, syrup and peanut butter to a boil

over a moderate heat, stirring constantly. (Watch carefully to make sure the mixture does not stick to the bottom of the pan.) Remove from the heat and mix in the remaining ingredients.

Press the peanut mixture into a shallow, well-greased 12 × 8in/300 × 200mm baking tin and leave to cool before cutting into three lengthways and then eight widthways. Place the bars on a plate and serve. Store in tightly covered container and keep for 1 week at room temperature, 2 weeks refrigerated and up to 3 months frozen.

Peppermint lotion

A light lotion which relieves itching.

To make 8fl oz/225ml
4fl oz/15ml water
4fl oz/115ml rubbing alcohol
3-4 drops peppermint oil

Pour the water and alcohol into a bottle and add the oil. Close the bottle tightly and shake well. Apply the lotion to sensitive spots with a clean cloth, but test it on a small patch of your skin before using; dab a little on the inside of your wrist and wait a few hours to see if it causes a reaction. If not, use as needed.

Peppermint tea

Ease a stuffy nose or stimulate a sluggish digestive system with this tea.

To make 1 drink
5 tablespoons dried peppermint
8fl oz/225ml water
1 tablespoon each grated lemon and orange rind
2 teaspoons crème de menthe liqueur
1 teaspoon honey

Bring the peppermint leaves and water to a boil in a small saucepan. Remove the pan from the heat and let the tea steep for 10 minutes. Strain off the liquid and, if needed, add enough boiling water to make it up to 8fl oz/225ml. Add the grated lemon rind, grated orange rind, crème de menthe and honey. Make the tea fresh every time.

Perfume

A nice spicy scent at a bargain price.

To make ¼ pint/150ml
4 fl oz/115 ml rubbing alcohol
4 tablespoons whole cloves
1 teaspoon orris root

Put the alcohol and cloves in a small jar and then add the orris root. Close the jar securely and shake. Leave the contents to sit for 2 days, stirring occasionally. Strain off the liquid, discarding the solids, and transfer it to a clean jar; cover tightly. To use, dab behind the ears or on your wrists. Store out of the reach of small children.

Pesto

An easy-to-prepare sauce that is great on pasta or potatoes. Mixed with mayonnaise, it makes a good dip for raw vegetables, and it freezes well too.

To make 8 fl oz/225 ml
2 oz/60g fresh basil leaves, washed and patted dry with paper towels
4 fl oz/115 ml olive oil
2 cloves garlic, peeled and crushed
3 tablespoons pine nuts or chopped blanched almonds
½ level teaspoon salt
2 oz/60g grated Parmesan cheese

Put all the ingredients except the cheese in a blender or a food processor and purée until smooth; if using a blender, stop frequently and push the mixture down with a rubber spatula. Stir in the cheese (the mixture will be very thick) and then 2-3 tablespoons water; serve on hot vegetables or pasta. The sauce will keep for up to 1 week if refrigerated or for 6 months frozen – leave room for it to expand during freezing.

Parsley variation For a lighter sauce, you can omit the pine nuts and substitute 1 oz/30g fresh Italian parsley for 1 oz/30g of the basil.

Pizza

A quick, low-calorie, low-fat version of the old favourite. For variety, top with sautéed mushrooms, cooked and crumbled sausage or steamed spinach.

To make 2 servings
Base
4 oz/115g plain flour, or 2 oz/60g each plain and wholemeal flours mixed
⅛ level teaspoon salt
1½ level teaspoons baking powder
6 tablespoons water
Topping
8 oz/225g jar pizza sauce
3 oz/85g grated mozzarella cheese
½ large green pepper seeded and sliced
1 tablespoon chopped basil (optional)

Combine the flour, salt and baking powder in a small bowl. Add the water and stir with a fork until the dough comes together, adding a few teaspoons more water if necessary. Knead the dough until smooth – for about 2 minutes. Shape it into a ball, cover with a towel and leave it to rest for 5 minutes. Roll the dough into a

10 in/250mm circle, using flour as needed to stop it sticking.

Preheat the grill. Lightly brush a medium-size non-stick frying pan with vegetable oil and set over a moderate heat until very hot – about 1 minute. Add the dough and cook until the underside is dry and flecked with brown spots – for about 2-3 minutes. (The dough will puff up in spots, but the sauce will cover them.)

Transfer to an ungreased baking sheet and spread the sauce evenly over the dough crust. Sprinkle with the cheese and top with the green pepper rings.

Grill 4 in/100mm from the heat until the sauce is bubbling and the cheese has melted – 2-3 minutes. Before serving, sprinkle with the basil if desired. Serve immediately.

Pomander ball

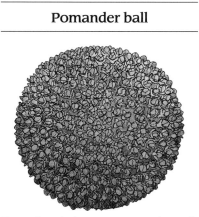

Keep the clothes in your cupboards and drawers fresh-smelling with this attractive pomander ball. It will also make a nice present.

To make 1 ball
1 whole orange or lemon
4 oz/115g whole cloves
1 teaspoon ground cloves
1 tablespoon orris root powder

Press the sharp end of the whole cloves into the orange or lemon until the fruit is completely covered. Mix the ground cloves and orris root together in a plastic bag, add the clove-studded piece of fruit and shake well until the orange is entirely covered with the fragrant, ground spices.

Remove the pomander ball from the bag, wrap it in tissue paper and leave for 2 weeks. Finally, attach a piece of string or ribbon to the top and hang the ball in your cupboard.

Potato sausage

A delicious way to stretch meat and much less fatty than most sausage.

To make 4lb/1.8kg
1½lb/700g potatoes, peeled and sliced
2 tablespoons olive oil
2 large onions, peeled and finely chopped
2 medium-size tart apples (such as Granny Smith), peeled, cored and finely chopped
3 cloves garlic, peeled and finely chopped
1lb/450g minced veal
1lb/450g minced pork
1½ level tablespoons prepared mustard
4 level teaspoons salt
1½ level teaspoons black pepper
1½ level teaspoons ground sage
1 level teaspoon ground allspice
¼ level teaspoon ground nutmeg
1½ tablespoons vegetable oil

Bring a large saucepan of salted water to the boil over a moderate heat and cook the potatoes until tender – for about 20 minutes. Leave them to cool and then mash until smooth; set to one side.

In a large frying pan, heat the olive oil over a moderate heat, and then add the onions, apple and garlic. Cook, stirring occasionally, until soft – 15-20 minutes.

Combine the remaining ingredients (except the vegetable oil) in a large mixing bowl. Add the mashed potatoes and the onion mixture; mix well. Shape the mixture into sausage shapes, or force it into sausage casings if you can get them (try your butcher). Or add 3 eggs to the mixture and form into 2 × 3in/50 × 75mm patties.

To cook, heat the vegetable oil in a large frying pan. Add the sausages and fry over a moderate heat until lightly browned and cooked through – about

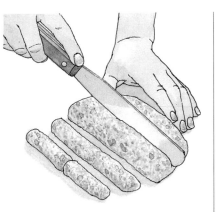

15 minutes for sausage shapes, or 4 minutes each side for the patties. Add more oil if necessary.

Pot mix for chrysanthemums

Use the following recipe for a potting mix which provides good drainage and encourages October and November flowering.

To make 1 bucketful
⅓ bucketful loam (best garden soil)
½ spadeful crumbly garden compost
¼ bucketful coarse peat
½ bucketful coarse sand
Commercial chrysanthemum fertiliser, used as directed on packet

Mix all the ingredients in a large bucket, taking good care with the proportions. Use to plant out new plants in a pot with an 18in/460mm stake.

Potpourri

Bring the wonderful aroma of garden flowers inside your home.

To make 1 bowlful
10 dried marigold blossoms
6 dried geranium leaves
Dried petals from 5 roses
2 teaspoons dried lavender
2 teaspoons orris root
2 drops rose fixative

Combine all the ingredients in a medium-size bowl. Then set out in bathrooms, living rooms or the bedroom for a sweet, flowery scent.

Pine variation This mix re-creates the scent of a forest. Combine 16 tablespoons snipped balsam needles, 20 miniature pine cones, 8 tablespoons rose hips, 2 teaspoons orris root and 2 drops pine-scented fixative.

Poultice

This natural poultice may help to fade bruises and relieve any pain and inflammation.

To make 1 treatment
1oz/30g comfrey root
1oz/30g dried wintergreen leaves
1 pint 12fl oz/910ml water

In a medium-size saucepan, combine the herbs and water and bring to the boil over a high heat. Reduce the heat to low and simmer for 5 minutes. Drain off the water, reserving the herbs.

Dampen a 12in/300mm square towel in warm water and place the herbs in the centre. Fold the towel over the herbs and place the poultice on the bruise. Leave until the herbs have cooled. Reheat and use once a day until symptoms subside.

Pretzels

These soft pretzels are a delicious American speciality, and are excellent as a snack or served with a hearty soup.

To make 12 pretzels
½ pint/285ml warm water
4 level teaspoons caster sugar
½oz/15g active dry yeast
1 level teaspoon salt
4oz/115g strong plain flour
12oz/340g plain flour
2 pints/1.15 litres water
3 tablespoons bicarbonate of soda
1 tablespoon coarse salt

In a small bowl, combine 4fl oz/115ml of the warm water with 1 teaspoon of the sugar and the yeast. Leave until bubbly – about 10 minutes.

Put the remaining 6fl oz/175ml warm water in the bowl of an electric mixer or food processor with the salt, strong plain flour and 5oz/150g of the plain flour. Beat on medium-low speed until well blended – about 1 minute. Add the yeast mixture and beat for a further 4-5 minutes. Then stir in the remaining flour.

On a floured surface, knead the dough until very smooth – about 10 minutes. Add more flour if the dough is too sticky. Form into a ball, place in an ungreased bowl and cover with plastic film. Leave the dough to rise until doubled in bulk – 45 minutes to 1 hour.

Preheat the oven to Gas Mark 7, 220°C/425°F. Punch the dough down, cut it into 12 equal pieces, place them on a baking tray and cover with plastic film. Roll each piece, stretching it as you do so, into a rope about 20in/510mm long. Twist each rope into a pretzel shape (see below) and then place it on a lightly floured surface. Cover them and leave to rise until not quite doubled – about 20 minutes.

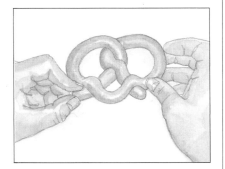

In a medium-size enamelled or stainless-steel frying pan, combine the remaining 2pints/1.15litres water, the bicarbonate of soda and the remaining sugar. Bring to a simmer over a moderately low heat. Place 3 pretzels in the water and cook for 20 seconds on each side, flipping them gently with a large slotted spoon. As you remove each pretzel, let it drain over the pan for a few seconds, then place on a piece of paper towel. Repeat until all the pretzels have been cooked and drained, then transfer them, top side up, onto greased baking sheets and sprinkle with the coarse salt.

Bake in the centre of the oven until nicely browned – about 15 minutes. Serve warm or cold.

Proving a frying pan

A new frying pan or omelette pan – or one that constantly sticks – can easily be treated to prevent foods catching on the bottom.

To prove 1 pan
1-2 tablespoons of olive oil
Salt

Pour the oil into the pan and sprinkle salt liberally all over the inside. Heat over a moderate heat until smoking hot, and then carefully rub the salt and oil well into the pan with paper towel. Remove from the heat and wipe dry.

Repeat this process twice more. Once completed, finally wipe the frying pan dry with paper towel.

Puffed pancake

This impressive-looking soufflé ome-lette is much easier to make than your guests might think.

To make 2 servings
2 eggs, size 2
2½oz/70g sifted plain flour
4fl oz/115ml milk
¼ level teaspoon ground nutmeg
½ level teaspoon salt
2oz/60g butter or margarine, melted
1 tablespoon icing sugar, sifted
½ level teaspoon ground cinnamon

Preheat the oven to Gas Mark 6, 200°C/400°F. Lightly beat the eggs in a medium-size bowl, then add the flour, milk, nutmeg and salt until just blended. Do not overbeat.

Cover the bottom of a 13 × 9 × 2in/330 × 230 × 50mm baking dish with the melted butter, and then pour in the batter. Place in the centre of the oven and bake until puffed and golden brown – about 20 minutes.

Mix the sugar and cinnamon together and sprinkle them over the pancake just before serving. One way of presenting the 'pancake' is to cut it into 2-4 equal pieces and serve it with honey or golden syrup and a small jug of melted butter, if desired.

Raspberry liqueur

This strong flavoured liqueur has a rich, red hue – it's delicious over ices or ice cream.

To make approximately 1¼ pint/725ml
5oz/150g granulated sugar
4fl oz/115ml water
12oz/340g fresh or frozen raspberries
3 strips lemon peel, ½ × 2 in/13 × 50mm each
½ vanilla pod, split
1 teaspoon lemon juice
12fl oz/340ml vodka

Combine the sugar and water in a medium-size heavy saucepan. Add the raspberries, lemon peel and vanilla pod, and cook over a low heat until the sugar dissolves.

Raise the heat to moderate and boil for 3 minutes. Remove from the heat, cover and leave to stand for 30 minutes. Strain the fruit through a muslin-lined sieve – you should be left with about 12fl oz/340ml liquid. Discard the fruit pips, lemon peel and vanilla pod.

Stir in the lemon juice and vodka, pour into a bottle or other container, and cover tightly. The liqueur may be served immediately but will keep for 1 month refrigerated. Serve chilled or at room temperature.

Refrigerator refreshers

These will keep your refrigerator smelling clean and work better and quicker than plain baking powder. Buy regular charcoal briquettes and use a hammer or brick to crush them into small chunks.

To make 9 refreshers
8 tablespoons crushed charcoal
8 tablespoons baking powder
2 tablespoons powdered orange or lemon peel
1 tablespoon ground cloves or cinnamon
2 tablespoons vanilla essence
Old, clean nylon stockings, cut into

2in/50mm squares
18in/460mm porous, bright-coloured fabric (terry cloth, loose-weave cotton, muslin or towelling), cut into 2in/50mm squares
String or ribbon, cut into 8in/200mm lengths for tying and hanging

Combine the charcoal, baking powder, citrus peel and cloves in a glass or enamel bowl. Sprinkle on the vanilla essence, stir to mix and leave for 1 hour.

Put 2 tablespoons of the mixture in the centre of a nylon stocking square and wrap this packet in a fabric square. Tie up the corners with string or ribbon.

To use, tie a packet in an inconspicuous spot in the refrigerator or freezer. For a longer life, add a few more drops of vanilla and 1 teaspoon baking powder after 10-12 weeks.

Rejuvenating skin cream

For smooth, fresher-looking skin.

To make 2fl oz/60ml
2 capsules vitamin E
1 tablespoon honey
1 tablespoon coconut oil
1 tablespoon rose water
(available from chemists)
1 tablespoon olive oil

Remove the vitamin E from the capsules and place with the remaining ingredients in a bowl; mix well. To use, apply to the skin with cotton balls. Store covered in the refrigerator for up to 3 months.

Rose rinse

Use this sweet-smelling rinse to remove any traces of soap after washing your face.

To make 1 pint 12fl oz/910ml
1 tablespoon dried rosemary or 2 tablespoons fresh rosemary
2 tablespoons dried chamomile flowers
1 pint 12fl oz/910ml purified water
2 tablespoons dried or fresh rose petals

Combine all the ingredients in a small stainless steel or enamelled saucepan and boil, uncovered, over a moderate heat for 10 minutes. Leave it to cool down and then strain off the liquid, discarding the herbs. Transfer it into a bottle with a lid. To use, dab on with cotton balls, and then rinse off. The lotion will keep for up to 2 months if tightly covered and refrigerated.

Rose vinegar

A versatile skin freshening lotion. Undiluted, this concoction makes an effective gargle for sore throats, or can be used mixed with an equal quantity of vegetable oil as a salad dressing.

To make 1 pint/570ml
2 large handfuls fresh pink or red rose petals
7 tablespoons white wine vinegar
1 pint/570ml purified water

Place the rose petals in a glass container and add the wine vinegar. Leave in a cool, dark place for 1 week, shaking occasionally. Strain and discard the petals, then dilute the rose vinegar with water to make a refreshing skin lotion.

Rum balls

A sweet you can make without using the oven, and that makes a nice gift.

To make about 42 balls
8oz/225g fine vanilla wafer biscuit crumbs
4oz/115g pecans, finely chopped
4oz/115g unsifted icing sugar
1oz/30g cocoa
3 tablespoons golden syrup
2fl oz/60ml light or dark rum or bourbon whiskey
1½oz/45g sifted icing sugar

Put all the ingredients except the sifted icing sugar in a medium-size bowl and mix well, using your hands if necessary. Roll the mixture into 1in/25mm balls, then dredge in the sifted sugar. The rum balls will keep for as long as 10 days inside an airtight container and at room temperature.

Scented sachet

Put one of these in your cupboards to keep your clothes fresh smelling.

To make 1 sachet
10 dried bay leaves, crumbled
2 tablespoons each dried sage, oregano, basil, thyme and lavender flowers, crumbled
3 tablespoons dried rosemary, crumbled
¼ cup orris root

Place all the ingredients in a bowl and combine well. Then put 3 tablespoons of the mixture on a 4 × 4in/100 × 100mm piece of cheesecloth. Tie the corners together with a ribbon.

Saddle soap

A preparation which both softens leather and removes dirt.

To make around 4 pints/2.3 litres
2 pints 16 fl oz/1.5 litres water
24 tablespoons soap flakes
8 fl oz/225ml melted beeswax
4 fl oz/115ml neat's-foot oil

Bring the water to a boil in a large saucepan, and then reduce to a simmer. Gradually stir in the soap flakes. In the top of a double boiler, heat the wax with the neat's-foot oil and stir to combine. Remove from the heat and add to the soap solution. Stir until thick.

Transfer the soap to small containers (old shoe polish tins are ideal). To use, apply to leather with a wet sponge, then buff until dry with a clean soft cloth.
Caution Neat's-foot oil is flammable; use with care. It might also darken some types of leather or make them less receptive to regular shoe polish, so test on a small patch of leather first.

Salt-free mustard

A healthy alternative to shop-bought mustards.

To make ½lb/225g
1½oz/45g mustard seeds
3 fl oz/85ml dry white wine
4 fl oz/115ml white vinegar
4 fl oz/115ml water
2 tablespoons honey
¼ level teaspoon ground allspice
⅛ level teaspoon each ground
cinnamon and ginger

Mix together the mustard seeds, white wine and vinegar in a medium-size bowl and leave them to stand for 3 hours at room temperature. Then transfer the ingredients to a food processor or blender and add the water, honey, allspice, cinnamon and ginger. Process until fairly smooth.

Place the mixture in the top of a double boiler, or in a bowl over a saucepan containing simmering water. Cook, stirring occasionally, until the mustard

thickens – 10-12 minutes. Pour it into a hot, clean preserving jar and leave it to cool; then cover tightly. This low-salt mustard will keep for up to a year if refrigerated. See also MUSTARD, p.407.

Salt substitute

Use this in place of table salt. You can make your own dried orange and lemon peel by stringing strips onto a piece of string and hanging them up in the kitchen. When quite dry, they can be ground in an electric grinder. Citric acid can be bought at chemists.

To make about 1½oz/45g
4½ level teaspoons cream of tartar
1 level tablespoon each garlic
granules, dried and ground orange
peel, arrowroot and sugar
2 level tablespoons each black pepper,
celery seasoning and onion powder
1½ level teaspoons citric acid
1 level teaspoon each white pepper,
dill weed and dried thyme, crumbled
Dried, ground rind of one lemon
½ level teaspoon cayenne pepper

Put all the ingredients in a small electric spice grinder, coffee grinder or blender. Grind for 10 seconds or until the mixture

is fine. With a funnel, transfer the salt substitute into a glass saltshaker. Store any that is left over in a tightly covered container and keep in a cool, dark, dry place.

Saucepan cleaner

It can be hard to get rid of stains on non-stick saucepans, but this solution usually shifts them.

To clean 1 saucepan
1 pint/570ml water
4 fl oz/115ml liquid bleach
2 tablespoons bicarbonate of soda
Few drops cooking oil

Pour the water and bleach into the stained saucepan and add the bicarbonate of soda. Bring the solution to the boil over a high heat and continue to boil for 5 minutes.

Then pour out the bleach solution, wash, rinse and dry the saucepan as usual and finally rub the surface with a little cooking oil on a paper towel.

Saucy dressing mix

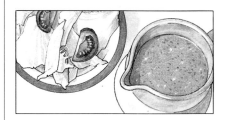

Keep a supply of this mix made up in your store cupboard to use as a tasty instant salad dressing (see opposite).

To make 16 recipe dressings
6oz/175g horseradish sauce
4 tablespoons wholegrain, Dijon or
spicy brown mustard
5 tablespoons honey
2 tablespoons dried minced onion
1½ teaspoons dill weed

Mix all the ingredients in a medium-size bowl until well blended. Transfer to a tightly closing jar; this dry mix will keep in the refrigerator for up to 2 months.

Saucy salad dressing

A sweet dressing with bite which is particularly good in chicken, meat or cheese salads.

To make enough for a 4-person salad
2 tablespoons saucy
dressing mix (see opposite)
4 teaspoons vinegar
3 tablespoons olive or vegetable oil

Combine the dressing mix and vinegar in a small bowl. Whisk in the olive oil. Keep the dressing for up to 2 weeks if tightly covered and refrigerated.

Sausage patties

Hot and spicy taste with less fat than most commercial sausages and none of the preservatives. For a milder sausage, eliminate the cayenne pepper.

To make 1 lb/450g
1 level teaspoon salt
½ level teaspoon cayenne pepper
¼ level teaspoon black pepper
1 level teaspoon dried sage, crumbled
½ level teaspoon each dried marjoram
and summer savoury, crumbled
½ level teaspoon ground coriander
1 lb/450g minced pork (not too lean)

Mix all the herbs and spices in a small bowl. Place the pork in a large bowl, sprinkle the mixture over it and combine.

Shape the pork mixture into an 8in/200mm long roll. Cover with plastic film and then foil. Refrigerate for several hours to allow the seasonings to blend thoroughly.

Cut the sausage into ½in/13mm

slices, place in an ungreased frying pan and sauté over a moderate heat until cooked through and lightly browned – about 10 minutes on each side. You can keep the pork roll slices for 3 days if tightly wrapped in foil and refrigerated, or for 2 months frozen.

Scone mix

Use this to whip up scones, pancakes or waffles in a flash.

To make 3 lb/1.4kg
2 lb/900g plain flour (or
1 lb/450g plain flour and
1 lb/450g wholewheat flour)
3½ level tablespoons baking powder
3½oz/100g powdered skimmed milk
½ level tablespoon salt
8oz/225g margarine or butter

In a large bowl, combine the flour, baking powder, milk powder and salt. Mix well. Rub the fat into the mixture until it resembles coarse breadcrumbs. Refrigerated, this mix will keep for 6 weeks in a closed container. See also SCONES, below; WAFFLES, p.419.

Scones

Quick to prepare and good to eat, you'll want to make them often.

To make 6 scones
8oz/225g scone mix (above)
6 tablespoons water or milk

Preheat the oven to Gas Mark 8, 230°C/450°F. In a medium-size bowl, stir the scone mix and water with a fork until just blended. Then gently knead the dough on a lightly floured surface 10 times. Roll it out to a ½in/13mm thickness, cut it into 2½in/60mm rounds. Bake on an ungreased baking sheet for 10-12 minutes or until golden. Serve hot.

Scratch remover

An effective surface filler on metal or glass surfaces.

To make ¼ pint/150ml
2fl oz/60ml glycerine
4 tablespoons jeweller's rouge
2fl oz/60ml water

Place the ingredients in a medium-size glass or plastic jar and mix into a smooth paste. Apply the mixture to scratched areas with a clean cloth and rub in. Rinse with clean water. To fill deeper scratches, repeat the process several times. Store in a tightly covered jar.

Self-buffing floor polish

Use this polish on resilient floor coverings – it dries to a shine without polishing and isn't as slippery as a waxed floor.

To make around 2 pints/1.15 litres
1 pint 12fl oz/910ml denatured
alcohol
4 tablespoons gum arabic
2fl oz/60ml turpentine
or white spirit
16 tablespoons orange shellac

Place all the ingredients in a bucket and stir until the gum arabic dissolves. To use, wash the floor and then apply the polish with a cloth, sponge or mop. Leave it to dry for ½ hour before walking on it. After 2-3 applications, strip the old layers off with hot water and detergent and start afresh. Store the polish in a tightly covered jar.

Shampoo enhancer

The egg conditions normal or dry hair, while lemon juice makes it shine.

To make 1 application
1 egg
1 teaspoon lemon juice or
cider vinegar
3 tablespoons mild, unscented
shampoo

Mix the ingredients in a small bowl. Shampoo the mixture into your hair and then rinse well with warm water. Make fresh each time of use.

Shellac

Commercial brands of this thin varnish have only a 6-week shelf life, so it makes sense to mix up your own when required.

To make ¾ pint/425ml varnish
12 tablespoons shellac flakes
8fl oz/225ml ethyl alcohol or denatured alcohol

Place the shellac flakes in a 1 pint/570ml jar, then pour in the alcohol. Cover the container and leave the shellac to stand for at least 8 hours. Shake every few hours until all the flakes have dissolved. Stir well, then apply the varnish with a brush. To apply with a rag or spray gun, the mixture will have to be thinned. Add more alcohol until the desired consistency is reached. The shellac will keep for up to 6 weeks if stored in a tightly covered container.
Caution Keep out of children's reach.

Sicilian courgettes

Use up a glut of courgettes at the end of the growing season with this dish.

To make a starter for 4
4fl oz/115ml olive oil
2 onions, finely chopped
1lb/450g courgettes, thinly sliced
1 green pepper, diced
1 aubergine, finely sliced in rounds
6 large tomatoes, skinned and chopped
4oz/115g black olives, stoned
¼ pint/150ml dry white wine
Sugar
Salt and pepper

Heat the oil in a frying pan and fry the onions until golden – 3-5 minutes. Add the courgettes, pepper and aubergine slices and cook for 3 minutes, stirring, until they begin to soften. Turn down the heat to low and add the tomatoes, olives

and half of the wine. Cook until well combined, stirring to prevent sticking, gradually adding the rest of the wine. Season with sugar, salt and pepper. Serve hot or cold with crusty bread.

Silver polish

A good all-purpose mix that contains an abrasive for cleaning and a cushioning agent to reduce scratching.

To make 1¼ pints/725ml
16 tablespoons soap flakes
16 tablespoons whiting
1 tablespoon household ammonia
16fl oz/450ml boiling water

Combine the soap flakes, whiting and ammonia in a small enamelled saucepan. Add the boiling water and stir until all the solid particles have dissolved. Leave the mixture to cool and then transfer it into a clean 2 pint/1.1 litre glass jar. Label, screw on a tight-fitting lid and store out of the reach of children.

Before use, shake the jar well. Wash the silver with soap and warm water, and apply the polish with a sponge. Rub gently with a clean cloth, rinse and dry.

Skin cleaner

Clear out oil-clogged facial pores with this natural skin cleaner.

To make 1 application
1 teaspoon milk
1 teaspoon honey
1 tablespoon ground almonds

Combine all the ingredients in a small bowl. Using your hands or a washcloth, apply the mixture to your face and scrub lightly. Rinse with clean water. Mix up a fresh batch every time of use.

Sloe gin

Liqueurs made from soaking fruit in spirits are extremely easy to prepare, as the alcohol prevents the fruit from going bad. Sloes are generally ready to pick from late August.

To fill 1 large preserving jar
12oz/340g fresh sloes
8oz/225g white sugar
1 bottle (1 pint 6fl oz/750ml) gin

Wash the sloes and prick them each several times with a needle. Half-fill a clean preserving jar with the fruit and then add the sugar. Fill up to the rim with gin, close the jar tightly and shake well. Leave on a shelf, turning twice weekly, for 2 months. Strain off the pink liqueur

and bottle – there will be more liquid than you started with.

Blackberry liqueur Use the same method, substituting blackberries for the sloes and also adding 2 whole cloves and a small piece of cinnamon. Fill the jar with brandy rather than gin. Once the liqueur has been strained off, use the fruit to make a pie or jelly, served with whipped cream.

Snow and ice dissolver

This mixture is very effective on windscreens, icy paths, pavements and garden steps.

To make 4lb/1.8kg
2lb/900g rock salt
2lb/900g magnesium sulphate
2 tablespoons ammonium sulphate

Mix all the ingredients in a large bucket. To use, sprinkle as required on steps, paths and pavements, or water down some of the mixture, transfer to a spray bottle and use on your car windscreen. Store in a tightly covered canister or jar out of the reach of children.

Soap bubbles

An inexpensive, safe and fun diversion for children.

To make 12 fl oz/340 ml
4 fl oz/115 ml washing-up liquid
8 fl oz/225 ml water
2 drops food colouring

Mix all the ingredients together in a glass jar and cover. Use a bubble pipe or make a homemade bubble wand out of an old coat hanger or other wire. Store the bubble mixture in a tightly covered jar.

Soda-water fruit juice

A natural carbonated drink which is filled with vitamins and free of refined sugar.

To make 1 serving
2 fl oz/60 ml frozen orange or grapefruit juice concentrate
6 fl oz/175 ml soda water
Ice cubes

Pour the frozen juice concentrate into a large, tall glass. Add a few tablespoons of soda water and stir until the concentrate has dissolved. Fill the glass with ice cubes, add the remaining soda water, and mix well. Drink before the ice has melted.

Spray starch

A cheap, easy-to-prepare shirt starch. Use 1 tablespoon of the cornflour to make up a light starch, and up to 3 tablespoons for a stiffer finish.

To make 16 fl oz/450 ml
1-3 tablespoons cornflour
Cold water

Mix the cornflour and water in a 1 pint/570 ml spray bottle that gives a fine spray mist. Store out of the reach of children.

To use the spray starch, shake well, spray the area to be stiffened and then iron immediately.

Stainless-steel cleaner

Give your pots an extra sparkle.

To make 8 oz/225 ml
8 tablespoons soap flakes
4 tablespoons whiting
2 tablespoons household ammonia
2 tablespoons water

Combine all the ingredients in a medium-size bowl. Transfer the cleaner into a glass jar, close it tightly, label and store out of the reach of children. To use, spread the cleaner onto the stainless steel pieces with a clean soft cloth and rub. Then rinse and buff to dry.

Starch paste

This recipe is a good homemade glue which can be safely used by children, but is also excellent for the delicate mending of torn pages or prints.

To make 10 fl oz/285 ml paste
1 pint/570 ml de-ionised water
5 teaspoons calcium hydroxide
(available from chemists)
3 oz/85 g wheat flour

Mix together the water and calcium hydroxide and add a little of the liquid to the wheat flour. Blend it into a smooth paste, then add the rest of the liquid. Pour the mixture into a warm saucepan and boil for 5 minutes, stirring continuously. Reduce the heat and simmer for a further 15 minutes.

Transfer the paste to a clean bowl and leave to solidify. It should keep for a few

days in the refrigerator, but discard it if it starts to go mouldy.

To mend a torn print, cover a piece of fine tissue paper slightly wider and longer than the tear with the paste. Place it carefully over the edges at the back of the print, and cover with a piece of greaseproof paper and then blotting paper. Place a weight on top and leave to dry for 24 hours.

Strawberry jam

Not as sweet as commercial brands. For the best flavour, choose firm, ripe strawberries.

To make approximately 2 lb/900 g
3½ oz/100 g sugar
4 fl oz/115 ml fresh orange juice
2 lb/900 g strawberries, washed and hulled
2 large sweet apples (such as Cox's or Golden Delicious), peeled, cored and coarsely chopped

Combine the sugar and orange juice in a large glass or enamel bowl. Add the strawberries and toss to coat. Leave to stand for ½ hour at room temperature.

Transfer the mixture to a large non-aluminium saucepan, add the apples and place over a moderately high heat. Cook uncovered for 45 minutes, or until it is thick and glossy – it should read

106°C/220°F on a sugar thermometer.

Pour the jam into hot, sterilised jam jars. Cover and then leave the jam to cool to room temperature. Then keep the jam in the refrigerator, where it can be stored for up to 2 months.

Sunburn soother

Takes the bite out of a mild burn.

To make enough for 1 bath
4 tea bags
16 tablespoons dried
mint (double if fresh)
1 pint 12 fl oz / 910 ml water

Place all the ingredients in a medium-size saucepan and bring to the boil over a high heat. Reduce the heat to low and simmer for 5 minutes. Remove from the heat and leave the mint to infuse for 15 minutes. To use, strain the liquid into a jar, discarding the tea and mint leaves, and allow it to cool. Dab the mixture onto sunburned areas with cotton balls or a washcloth. Or pour the liquid into warm bath water; you can also add the tea from the bags and the mint tied in a piece of cheesecloth and dropped into the bath. Soak in the mixture for 10-15 minutes. Repeat as necessary.
Caution For severe burns with blistering or crusting, consult your doctor.

Tile and grout cleaner

Get rid of that grimy soap film that forms on and between ceramic bathroom tiles.

To make 3 pints / 1.7 litres
8 tablespoons baking powder
5 tablespoons household ammonia
2 fl oz / 60 ml white vinegar
2 pints 16 fl oz / 1.6 litres warm water

Combine the ingredients in a plastic jug or fruit juice container, cover and shake vigorously. Label the container and store it out of the reach of children. For small jobs, fill a pump-type container with the solution; spray directly onto the tile surface, then wipe with a damp sponge or cloth.
Caution Do not mix this cleaner with anything containing bleach.

Toddy

Many people swear by toddies as a remedy for a bad cold, and it will certainly make you feel better.

To make 1 drink
3-4 lumps of sugar, or 2 teaspoons
granulated sugar
Slice of lemon
4 fl oz / 115 ml boiling water
4 fl oz / 115 ml whisky

Place the sugar and lemon in a cup and add the boiling water. Fill the rest of the cup with whisky, stir, and drink while hot. If you would prefer, use 1 heaped tablespoon honey in place of the sugar, or rum in place of the whisky.

Toffee apples

Children love these sticky treats, but you'll need 8 wooden skewers to make them.

To make 8 toffee apples
8 small, crisp eating apples, washed
and stalks removed
For the toffee
8 oz / 225 g soft brown sugar
1 oz / 30 g unsalted butter
1 tablespoon golden syrup
5 tablespoons water
1 tablespoon vinegar

Push a wooden skewer into the centre of each apple, and set to one side. Put all the toffee ingredients in a heavy-based saucepan and heat gently until the sugar has dissolved.
Bring to the boil and cook until a drop of the toffee mixture separates into threads when dropped into a glass of cold water. Pick up each apple by its stick and thoroughly coat it in the toffee. Leave them to set fully on a greased or non-stick baking tray.

Toilet bowl cleaner

Use regularly to keep your lavatory sparkling clean.

To make 4 pints / 2.3 litres
1 tablespoon household ammonia
8 fl oz / 225 ml hydrogen peroxide
3¼ pints / 1.85 litres water

Mix the ingredients in a bucket, then pour the solution slowly into the toilet. Leave it to stand for at least 30 minutes, then scrub the inside of the bowl and flush. For stubborn stains, allow the solution to remain in the bowl for several hours.

Tomato juice

You won't believe how good your own can be.

To make five 1 pint / 570 ml jars
12 large, ripe tomatoes, cored and cut
into thin wedges
1 large sweet green pepper, cored,
seeded and diced
1 large yellow onion, chopped
1 stalk celery, diced
1 tablespoon salt

Place all the ingredients in a very large, non-aluminium saucepan, cover and bring to a simmer over a moderate heat. Simmer for 35 minutes, stirring occasionally, until the tomatoes have cooked down to a juice.

Purée the mixture in a blender or by pushing through a fine sieve. Discard the solids and return the juice to the saucepan; bring to a full boil over high heat. Pour into 5 hot, sterilised 1 pint/570ml preserving jars, leaving ¼in/6mm headroom below the rim. Close tightly, place in saucepan and fill to half-way with water. Bring to the boil and cook for 20 minutes. Kept on a cool, dark, dry shelf, the juice will keep for up to 1 year. Once opened, the juice will keep for 4 days if refrigerated.

Toothpaste

A fresh-tasting way to start your day.

To make 4oz/115g
4 tablespoons each arrowroot, powdered orris root and purified water
½ teaspoon each oil of cinnamon and oil of cloves
1 teaspoon ground sage

Mix all the ingredients in a small bowl. If the paste is too thick, add more water until the desired consistency is reached. Transfer the paste into a tightly covered jar. Use it as required.

Vegetable dip

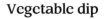

The tangy Oriental flavour of this dip complements the texture of crisp raw vegetables. Serve as a starter or on a buffet.

To make 8fl oz/225ml
8fl oz/225ml mayonnaise
¼ teaspoon Oriental sesame oil
1 teaspoon soy sauce
1 clove garlic, peeled and crushed

Mix all the ingredients together in a small bowl, then transfer the dip to a serving dish. Serve with a plate of raw vegetables such as carrots, celery and courgettes sliced into evenly sized pieces.

Vinyl upholstery cleaner

Never apply leather cleaner to vinyl car upholstery; use this gentle solution instead.

To make 1 pint/570ml
4 tablespoons washing powder
8 tablespoons baking powder
16fl oz/450ml warm water

Mix the washing powder and baking powder together in a bowl and add the water. To use, moisten a soft cloth with the solution and rub the vinyl surface with it, concentrating on the arms, seat and headrest; then rinse well with clean water and wipe dry.

Waffles

Make these up in a minute for a good start to the day.

To make 5 waffles
2 eggs, size 2, separated
7oz/200g scone mix (see p.415)
8fl oz/225ml water or milk
3 tablespoons butter or margarine, melted

Preheat a waffle iron. In a large mixing bowl, lightly beat the egg yolks. Add the scone mix, water and butter and stir just enough to moisten. In a medium-size bowl, beat the egg whites until stiff. Fold into the batter until just blended.

Cook the mixture according to the waffle iron manufacturer's directions. Serve the waffles hot with butter and golden syrup if desired.

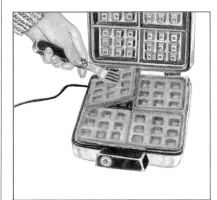

Walnut butter

This nut butter is excellent on biscuits or in sandwiches; combine it with apple butter (see p.381) for a delicious lunchtime snack.

To make approximately 7oz/200g
8oz/225g walnuts
1 teaspoon vegetable oil
½ teaspoon salt

Preheat the oven to Gas Mark 2, 150°C/300°F. Spread the walnuts on an ungreased baking sheet and bake uncovered until lightly browned – about 20 minutes. Leave the nuts to cool. If a chunky texture is desired, coarsely chop ¼ of the nuts and leave them to one side. Transfer the remaining nuts to a blender or food processor, add the oil and salt and process until creamy, working in batches if necessary. Incorporate the chopped nuts, if desired. Walnut butter will keep for 1 month if tightly covered and refrigerated.

Walnut sauce

A superb topping for ice cream.

To make 1 pint/570ml
8oz/225g golden syrup
4fl oz/115g maple or maple-flavoured syrup
2fl oz/60ml water
2oz/60g caster sugar
5oz/150g coarsely chopped walnuts

Place the golden syrup, maple syrup, water and sugar in a small heavy-bottomed saucepan. Bring to the boil over moderately high heat, stirring constantly. Add the walnuts, then turn down the heat to low and simmer, partially covered, for 30 minutes. Do not stir. Leave the sauce to cool and then transfer it into a clean 1 pint/570ml jar. It will keep for 4 months if tightly covered and refrigerated.

Watercolours

A good children's substitute for the commercial product.

To make 2 fl oz/60 ml
1 tablespoon
white or cider vinegar
2 tablespoons baking powder
1 tablespoon cornflour
½ teaspoon glycerine
2 drops food colouring
1 teaspoon water

Mix the vinegar and baking powder together in a small bowl; add the cornflour and glycerine when the baking powder stops foaming. Stir in the food colouring and add water if the solution seems too stiff. Store in a tightly covered jam jar or plastic container.

Wax finish for raw wood

This treatment is for raw wood, such as exposed beams, and should not be used over other finishes (see below).

To make 1 pint 4 fl oz/680 ml
8 fl oz/225 ml turpentine
8 fl oz/225 ml melted beeswax
8 fl oz/225 ml boiled linseed oil

Warm the turpentine in the top of a double boiler; stir in the beeswax until it dissolves, then add the oil. Remove from the heat and brush the warm mixture onto raw wood. Allow to dry and then buff with a clean soft cloth.

Caution Because this recipe uses flammable materials, make sure the mixture does not overheat or spill onto a hot cooking surface.

Wax for finished wood

A highly durable finish that repels water and minimises scratching to the wood surface.

To make 1 pint 8 fl oz/800 ml
8 fl oz/225 ml turpentine
or white spirit
1 lb/450 g white wax shavings

Warm the turpentine in the top of a double boiler; add the wax shavings and stir until melted. Remove from the heat, pour into a container and allow to cool. If the wax becomes too hard to use, soften it in a double boiler and add more turpentine.
Caution Because this recipe uses flammable materials, make sure the mixture does not overheat or spill onto a hot surface.

Wheatless brownies

Chocolate treats for allergy sufferers that are both wheat and milk-free.

To make 16 brownies
2½ oz/70 g margarine, at room temperature
8 oz/225 g soft light brown sugar
2 eggs, size 2, lightly beaten
2 oz/60 g chocolate, melted
1 teaspoon vanilla essence
4 oz/115 g rice flour or ground rice
½ level teaspoon baking powder
¼ level teaspoon salt
2 oz/60 g coarsely chopped pecan nuts or walnuts

Preheat the oven to Gas Mark 4, 175°C/350°F. Cream the margarine and sugar in a large bowl. Add all the remaining ingredients except the nuts and stir until smooth. Stir in the nuts, then pour the batter into a greased, 8 in/200 mm square cake tin.

Bake uncovered until the edges pull away slightly from the sides of the tin and a toothpick inserted into the centre comes out clean – about 40-45 minutes. Leave the brownies to cool in the tin and then cut them into squares. They will keep for 3 days in an airtight container.

Whipped cream substitute

This recipe is much lower in saturated fats than real cream fillings.

To make 4 servings
1 small can evaporated milk
2 tablespoons cold water
1 teaspoon unflavoured gelatine
2 level tablespoons caster sugar
3 tablespoons corn or sunflower oil

Pour the milk into an empty ice-cube tray or a pan and place in the freezer. When crystals form around the edges – about 20 minutes – the milk is cold enough to whip.

Meanwhile, place the water in a small heatproof dish and add the gelatine without stirring. Heat 1 in/25 mm of water in a small saucepan. Take the pan off the fire and place the dish of water and gelatine in it. Heat until the gelatine dissolves – about 2 minutes. Remove the dish from the water, stir the gelatine solution and leave to cool.

In a medium-size bowl, beat the milk until stiff peaks form. Gradually add the sugar, then the oil and then the gelatine mixture. Continue beating until stiff peaks form again. Cover the bowl with foil and place in the freezer for 10 minutes, then transfer to the refrigerator. The mixture will become stiff; stir to soften it before serving. It will keep for 3 days if covered with foil and refrigerated.

White ring remover

The white rings made by hot drinks or water on wood surfaces can be hard to remove. Try the following paste on a waxed surface.

To cover 1 small table top
4 tablespoons salt
3 tablespoons olive oil

Combine the salt and olive oil in a small bowl and mix into a thick paste. Wipe the paste onto the wooden surface with a cloth and leave to stand overnight. The next day, wipe off the paste and re-wax the surface immediately.

White sauce

For a richer sauce, stir in 2 table-spoons butter or margarine during the last minute of cooking.

To make ½ pint/285ml sauce
1oz/30g white sauce mix (below)
½ pint/285ml whole, semi or
skimmed milk

Place the white sauce mix in a medium-size saucepan and gradually whisk in the milk. Set the pan over moderate heat and cook, stirring constantly, for about 2 minutes or until the mixture thickens. Then reduce the heat to low and simmer, stirring constantly, for 2 minutes longer. This sauce is best made fresh as needed.

Cheese variation Add 2oz/60g or more shredded extra sharp Cheddar cheese, a dash or two of Worcestershire sauce, and a pinch of cayenne pepper to the sauce in the last 2 minutes of cooking. Serve on broccoli, cauliflower, potatoes or other vegetables.

Curry variation Add 1 teaspoon curry powder to the white sauce mix and proceed as directed. Serve with roast chicken, poached fish fillets or eggs.

Mushroom variation At the end of the cooking time, add 4oz/115g chopped mushrooms sautéed in butter. Serve with chicken or vegetables.

Mustard variation Stir in 2 tablespoons Dijon or spicy brown mustard and proceed as directed. Serve with boiled ham or pork chops.

Paprika variation Add 1 or more tablespoons paprika to the white sauce mix and proceed as directed. Serve with veal or chicken.

Parsley variation Add 2 tablespoons chopped parsley after adding the milk and proceed as directed. Serve with carrots, fish or boiled ham.

White sauce mix

This low-fat version of the classic recipe you can keep ready prepared in the cupboard. Use for any of the ideas given above.

To make 8oz/225g
5oz/150g plain flour
3½oz/100g powdered skimmed milk
1½ level teaspoons salt

Combine all the ingredients in a jar, cover, and store at room temperature.

Whitewash

A cheap coating that must be re-applied frequently. Excellent for farm buildings because the lime is germ-icidal. For interior use only.

To make 2 gallons/9 litres
5lb/2.3kg hydrated lime
6½ pints/3.7 litres water
at room temperature
1½lb/700g salt
1 pint/570ml warm water

In a large container, mix the lime with the room-temperature water and leave it overnight. The next day, mix the salt with the warm water and leave until dis-solved. Add the salt water to the lime mixture and stir well. For colouring, add powdered pigment if desired. Store tightly covered.

Windscreen cleaner

Remove dirt, general mess and even dried insects with this effective spray.

To make 12oz/340g
8 tablespoons powdered chalk
4 tablespoons baking soda
16 tablespoons Fuller's earth
Enough water to make a paste

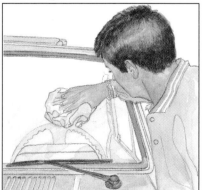

Combine the ingredients in a small pan or other container and stir slowly until a paste is formed. Apply the mixture directly to the dirty windscreen with a sponge, then polish with a dry cloth.

Witch hazel lotion

Use as an astringent or apply in a cold compress to a fevered brow.

To make 1½ pints/850ml
4 tablespoons fresh witch hazel leaves
and/or bark
16fl oz/450ml purified water
8fl oz/225ml rubbing alcohol

Rinse the leaves well, then chop them coarsely. Bring the water to a boil in an enamelled saucepan, add the leaves and simmer for 15 minutes. Leave the witch hazel to infuse until cool, then strain and stir in the alcohol. The lotion will keep for 4-5 days if tightly covered and refrigerated.

Yoghurt

For a rich yoghurt, use a mixture of whole milk and cream. For a healthier substitute, use sour cream and low-fat milk.

To make four 8oz/225g containers
1 pint 12fl oz/910ml milk
2fl oz/60ml plain yoghurt

Pour the milk into a small saucepan and heat to 80°C/180°F – you can check with a sugar thermometer. Remove from the heat and allow the milk to cool to 40°C/105°F. Stir in the yoghurt and pour the mixture into glass jars. Close them tightly and place in a saucepan of warm water (40-45°C/105–112°F). Keep the yoghurt in the water for 5-6 hours, adding hot water as required to main-tain the water temperature. Or set the saucepan on a radiator, check the tem-perature often with the sugar ther-mometer. The yoghurt is ready when it retains the impression of a spoon pressed into the surface. Remove the jars from the water, allow to cool and then refrigerate for up to 1 week.

Useful addresses

The organisations listed on the following pages are just a few of the many groups working around Britain. Additional names and numbers can also be found in the Yellow Pages, Thomson's Directories and the front of your local telephone book. The local library is a good source of information about any community and educational services run by the local authority. It is well worth assembling your own list of numbers (especially those for the emergency services) and keeping it on a noticeboard close to the telephone, or where you and others can reach it in a hurry.

Consumer information and legal advice

BUILDING SOCIETIES OMBUDSMAN
Millbank Tower
Millbank
London SW1P 4XS
Tel. 0171-931 0044
Looks into complaints about building societies.

CHARTERED INSTITUTE OF ARBITRATORS
24 Angel Gate
City Road
London EC1V 2RS
Tel. 0171-837 4483
Arranges for consultation and binding arbitration for settling commercial and consumer legal disputes out of court.

CONSUMERS' ASSOCIATION
2 Marylebone Road
London NW1 4DF
Tel. 0171-486 5544
Publishes books and magazines with information and advice on consumer matters.

THE HOME LAUNDERING CONSULTATIVE COUNCIL
5 Portland Place
London W1N 3AA
Tel. 0171-636 7788
Will answer queries about washcare instructions and how to treat specialist fabrics.

INSURANCE OMBUDSMAN BUREAU
City Gate One
135 Park Street
London SE1 9EA
Tel. 0171-928 7600
Investigates any disputed claims between individuals and insurance companies.

THE LAW CENTRES FEDERATION
Duchess House
18-19 Warren Street
London W1P 5DB
Tel. 0171-387 8570
Provides addresses of centres in cities and towns offering free legal advice and assistance.

THE LAW SOCIETY
113 Chancery Lane
London WC2A 1PL
Tel. 0171-242 1222
Will provide names and addresses of local firms of solicitors.

LEGAL AID BOARD
29-37 Red Lion Street
London WC1R 4PP
Tel. 0171- 813 5300
Gives advice about eligibility for legal aid and help on where and how to apply for it.

NATIONAL ASSOCIATION OF CITIZENS ADVICE BUREAUX
Head Office
Myddleton House
115-123 Pentonville Road
London N1 9LZ
Tel. 0171-833 2181
Provides free confidential and impartial information, guidance, counselling and support on a wide range of subjects to all individuals. Local branches operate throughout the country.

OCCUPATIONAL PENSIONS ADVISORY SERVICE
11 Belgrave Road
London SW1V 1RB
Tel. 0171-233 8080
Will advise on pensions that are available currently and make investigations into relevant complaints.

THE OFFICE OF THE BANKING OMBUDSMAN
70 Gray's Inn Road
London WC1X 8NB
Tel. 0171-404 9944
Looks into complaints about the conduct of banks.

OFFICE FOR THE SUPERVISION OF SOLICITORS
Victoria Court
8 Dormer Place
Leamington Spa
Warickshire CV32 5AE
Tel. 01926-820082
Deals with written complaints about solicitors.

Education and self-help

ALCOHOLICS ANONYMOUS
General Service Office
P O Box 1
Stonebow House
Stonebow
York YO1 2NJ
Tel. 01904-644026
Centres around the country help those who want to stop drinking, with the support of reformed alcoholics.

AL-ANON FAMILY GROUPS
UK AND EIRE
61 Great Dover Street
London SE1 4YF
Tel. 0171-403 0888
Help for the families and friends of problem drinkers. Groups countrywide.

BRITISH DYSLEXIA ASSOCIATION
98 London Road
Reading RG1 5AU
Tel. 01734-668271/2
Provides information and support for people with reading difficulties; has details of local classes and tutors.

BRITISH STAMMERING ASSOCIATION
15 Old Ford Road
Bethnal Green
London E2 9PJ
Tel. 0181-983 1003
Free information service about self-help groups and speech therapists.

CRUSE-BEREAVEMENT CARE
126 Sheen Road
Richmond
Surrey TW9 1UR
Tel. 0181-332 7227 (the Cruse bereavement line)
Offers counselling services and support for the bereaved.

INDEPENDENT ASSESSMENT AND RESEARCH CENTRE (IARC)
Ashridge Management College
17 Portland Place
London W1N 3AF
Tel. 0171-255 2505
Educational charity which gives free advice on career development and counselling.

MENSA
Mensa House
St John's Square
Wolverhampton
West Midlands WV2 4AH
Tel. 01902-772771
Promotes social contact between people of like intelligence, including gifted children. Groups meet regularly, countrywide.

NARCOTICS ANONYMOUS
PO BOX 1980
London N18 3LS
Tel. 0171-351 6794
Counselling for drug victims, modelled along the lines of Alcoholics Anonymous; members provide support for each other to stay free of their addiction.

RELATE
Herbert Gray College
Little Church Street
Rugby
Warwickshire CV21 3AP
Tel. 01788-573241
Can advise on finding a local counsellor to see on your own or with a partner.

UCAS
PO BOX 28
Cheltenham
Gloucestershire GL50 3SA
Tel. 01242-222444
Produces handbook listing all university courses, and processes applications

Confidential helplines

CHILDLINE
2nd Floor
Royal Mail Building
Studd Street
London N1 0QW
Tel. 0800 1111 (free call)
Offers counselling to children and adults who have suffered abuse.

NATIONAL DEBTLINE
Tel. 0121-359 8501
Advises on matters relating to debt.

RAPE CRISIS CENTRE
PO BOX 69
London WC1X 9NJ
Tel. 0171-837 1600 (6-10pm)
Offers counselling and practical advice to victims of sexual attacks.

SALVATION ARMY
101 Queen Victoria Street
London EC4P 4EP
Tel. 0171-236 5222
Maintains hostels for the homeless throughout the country.

THE SAMARITANS
Head Office
10 The Grove
Slough
Berkshire SL1 1QP
Head Office Tel. 01753-532713
Central London Tel. 0171-734 2800
A 24-hour service which listens to those in despair. Countrywide, local numbers are available.

Health and first aid

BRITISH RED CROSS SOCIETY
9 Grosvenor Crescent
London SW1X 7EJ
Tel. 0171- 235 5454
Provides a wide range of services to the sick and elderly or handicapped. Runs

courses of first aid, nursing and welfare services, and will provide first aid at public events.

BRITISH VETERINARY ASSOCIATION
7 Mansfield Street
London W1M 0AT
Tel. 0171-636 6541
Has a register of all vets in Britain and will provide local names.

LONDON LIGHTHOUSE
111-117 Lancaster Road
London W11 1QT
Tel. 0171-792 1200
Fax. 0171-229 1258
A centre offering support for people affected by HIV and AIDS.

ROYAL LIFE SAVING SOCIETY
Mountbatten House
Studley
Warwickshire B80 7NN
Tel. 01527-853943
Branches throughout Britain run courses in water safety, and rescue and resuscitation techniques. Provides lifeguards for certain beaches and some inland waterways.

ST ANDREW'S AMBULANCE ASSOCIATION
St Andrew's House
Milton Street
Glasgow G4 0HR
Tel. 0141-332 4031
Runs courses in Scotland on first aid, nursing and other welfare subjects. Attends public events to provide first aid.

ST JOHN AMBULANCE
1 Grosvenor Crescent
London SW1X 7EF
Tel. 0171-235 5231
Runs courses throughout England and Wales on first aid, nursing and other welfare subjects. Also attends public events to provide first aid.

THE TERRENCE HIGGINS TRUST
52-54 Gray's Inn Road
London WC1X 8JU
Helpline Tel. 0171-242 1010
A registered charity set up to inform, advise and give support on AIDS/HIV-related matters. The trust also provides speakers.

Raising children

ASSOCIATION FOR POST-NATAL ILLNESS
25 Jerdan Place
London SW6 1BE
Tel. 0171-386 0868
Helps mothers to identify and cope with the symptoms of post-natal depression.

THE CHILDREN'S SOCIETY
Edward Rudolf House
69-85 Margery Street
London WC1X 0JL
Tel. 0171-837 4299
Provides care for children in need.

EXPLORING PARENTHOOD
4 Ivory Place
Treadgold Street
London W11 4BP
Tel. 0171-221 4471
Self-help group run by parents and professionals, dealing with teenage-related problems.

FAMILY PLANNING ASSOCIATION
2-12 Pentonville Road
London N1 9FP
Tel. (England) 0171-837 5432
Tel. (Wales) 01222-342766
Tel. (Northern Ireland) 01232-325488
Provides advice and leaflets promoting general sexual health and advice on family planning.

FSID AND COT DEATH RESEARCH AND SUPPORT
14 Halkin Street
London SW1X 7DP
Tel. 0171-235 0965
24-hour helpline 0171-235 1721
FSID (the Foundation for the Study of Infant Deaths) sponsors research into sudden, unexplained infant death, and also counsels bereaved parents.

NATIONAL ASSOCIATION FOR GIFTED CHILDREN
Elder House
Milton Keynes MK9 1LR
Tel. 01908-673677
Provides information on any local social activities and advises on the emotional welfare of gifted children.

NATIONAL CHILDBIRTH TRUST
Alexandra House
Oldham Terrace
London W3 6NH
Tel. 0181-992 8637
Gives help and advice on all aspects of motherhood. Runs pre- and post-natal classes led by trained counsellors nationwide. Can provide literature on preparing for childbirth.

NATIONAL CHILDMINDING ASSOCIATION
8 Masons Hill
Bromley
Kent BR2 9EY
Tel. 0181-464 6164
Provides lists of registered childminders (who take children into their own homes).

PARENT NETWORK
44-46 Caversham Road
Kentish Town
London NW5 2DS
Tel. 0171-485 8535
Self-help group of parents and professionals addressing problems with teenagers.

PARENTS AT WORK
45 Beech Street
London EC2P 2LX
Tel. 0171-628 3578
Emotional and practical support for working mothers.

TWINS AND MULTIPLE BIRTHS ASSOCIATION (TAMBA)
PO BOX 30
Little Sutton
South Wirral L66 1TH
Tel. 01732-868000 (7-11pm)
Provides support to parents of twins and multiple births and promotes public awareness of their needs.

Coping with disability

AGE CONCERN ENGLAND
(National Council on Ageing)
Astral House
1268 London Road
London SW16 4ER
Tel. 0181-679 8000 (see telephone directory for local numbers)
Campaigns for better services for the aged; also provides practical help.

DISABLED DRIVERS' ASSOCIATION
National Headquarters
Ashwellthorpe
Norwich NR16 1EX
Tel. 01508-489449
Offers disabled people information on how to keep mobile. Local groups throughout the country.

GUIDE DOGS FOR THE BLIND ASSOCIATION
Hillfields
Burghfield
Reading RG7 3YG
Tel. 01734-835555
Trains guide dogs and teaches visually handicapped people how to use them.

HELP THE AGED
16-18 St James's Walk
London EC1R OBE
Tel. 0171-253 0253
Provides help and advice on the welfare of the aged. Branches nationwide also run charity shops.

ROYAL NATIONAL INSTITUTE FOR THE BLIND (RNIB)
Head Office and General Enquiries
224-228 Great Portland Street
London W1N 6AA
Tel. 0171-388 1266
Supplements support provided by local councils for the visually handicapped.

ROYAL NATIONAL INSTITUTE FOR THE DEAF (RNID)
19-23 Featherstone Street
London EC1Y 8SL
Tel. 0171-296 8000
Textphone 0171-296 8001
Provides information and services which include interpreting and specialist telephone services.

THE ROYAL SOCIETY FOR MENTALLY HANDICAPPED CHILDREN AND ADULTS (MENCAP)
117-123 Golden Lane
London EC1Y ORT
Tel. 0171-454 0454
Local groups throughout the country offer a range of services to the mentally handicapped and their families.

TALKING NEWSPAPER ASSOCIATION
National Recording Centre
Heathfield
East Sussex TN21 8DB
Tel. 01435-866102
Provides tapes of newspapers and magazines for the visually handicapped.

Gardening and local history

BRITISH ASSOCIATION FOR LOCAL HISTORY
Shopwyke Manor Barn
Chichester
West Sussex PO20 6BG
Tel. 01243-787639
Aims to promote education through study of local history. Provides information and leaflets.

THE SOIL ASSOCIATION
86 Colston Street
Bristol BS15DB
Tel. 0117-9290661
Provides information and advice on organic gardening and pest control.

HENRY DOUBLEDAY RESEARCH ASSOCIATION
National Centre for Organic Gardening
Ryton Gardens
Ryton-on-Dunsmore
Coventry CV8 3LG
Tel. 01203-303517
Answers written queries on organic gardening and supplies predator insects and bacteria for pest control.

ROYAL HORTICULTURAL SOCIETY
80 Vincent Square
London SW1P 2PE
Tel. 0171-834 4333
Provides practical advice on horticultural queries.

Sports and holidays

ASSOCIATION OF BRITISH TRAVEL AGENTS (ABTA)
55-57 Newman Street
London W1P 4AH
Tel. 0171-637 2444

Provides financial safeguards for holidaymakers who have booked package holidays through travel agents who are ABTA members.

AUTOMOBILE ASSOCIATION
Fanum House, Basingstoke
Hampshire RG21 4EA
Tel. 01256-20123
Operates a vehicle breakdown service for members, both at home and on the road. Also offers touring and travel information and insurance benefits.

BRITISH MOUNTAINEERING COUNCIL
177-179 Burton Road
Manchester M20 2BB
Tel. 0161-445 4747
Local climbing clubs throughout Britain run training courses for all levels and give advice on equipment and safety. Also publishes guides and instruction manuals.

BRITISH WATERWAYS
Willow Grange
Church Road
Watford WD1 3QA
Tel. 01923-226422
Administers more than 2000 miles of rivers and canals in Britain. Sells charts and maps and is responsible for issuing licences which allow craft to use its waterways.

THE CAMPING AND CARAVANNING CLUB
Greenfields House
Westwood Way
Coventry CV4 8JH
Tel. 01203-694995
Runs campsites throughout Britain. The organisation also offers members a breakdown and recovery service which operates throughout Europe, as well as worldwide medical insurance cover.

INSTITUTE OF ADVANCED MOTORISTS
359 Chiswick High Road
London W4 4HS
Tel. 0181-994 4403
Runs advanced driving tests. Local volunteer groups run training courses.

RAC MOTORING SERVICES
RAC House
Brent Terrace
London NW2 1LT
Tel. 0181-452 8000
Provides members with a vehicle breakdown service at home and on the road, and touring and travel information.

THE RAMBLERS ASSOCIATION
1-5 Wandsworth Road
London SW8 2XX
Tel. 0171-582 6878
Local groups throughout the country provide information about all aspects of walking.

ROYAL YACHTING ASSOCIATION
RYA House
Romsey Road
Eastleigh
Hampshire SO50 9YA
Tel. 01703-629962
Can supply names of affiliated sailing clubs and recognised training schools throughout Britain. Covers all areas of boating and windsurfing.

THE SKI CLUB OF GREAT BRITAIN
118 Eaton Square
London SW1W 9AF
Tel. 0171-245 1033
Provides information on ski resorts throughout the world, and has representatives in many Alpine resorts. Advises on equipment and skiing courses.

THE YOUTH HOSTELS ASSOCIATION
Trevelyan House
8 St Stephens Hill
St Albans
Hertfordshire AL1 2DY
Tel. 01727-855215
Runs hostels offering members cheap overnight accommodation throughout the world. Publishes handbook and maps for members.

INDEX

B

C

All About
CHILDREN

E

F

All About
FINANCES

All About
FIRST AID

G

H

All About
HOUSEPLANTS

All About
PETS

Aggressive 9
Allergies 152-3
Bandage from old sock
　325
Bedding 20
Fleas 85-86
For the elderly 85
Grooming 153
Holiday care 215
Hypertension 111
Ice cubes in water
　bowls 306
Liability 124
Lost 128
New 141
Odours 153
Parked cars 149
Poisons 159
Positive reinforcement
　160
Quarantine 163
Soother 328
Stretcher 289
Toys 153
Travel 215

All About
PHOTOGRAPHY

Cameras 30
Close-ups 46
Family 154
Films 149, 154
Filters 30
Selling 91-92
Separating prints 178
Slides 185
Snow and sand 154
Soft focus 189
Storing 153
Travelling abroad 213
Tripods 216
Unusual uses for
　photos 317

T

XYZ

CREDITS AND ACKNOWLEDGMENTS

Bantam Doubleday Dell Publishing Group Inc.
The Doubleday Cookbook by Jean Anderson and Elaine Hanna. Copyright © 1975 by Doubleday, a division of the Bantam Doubleday Dell Publishing Group Inc. Used by permission.

Dover Publications, Inc.
The Standard Book of Quilt Making and Collecting by Marguerite Ickis. Copyright © 1949 by Marguerite Ickis. Reprinted by permission.

E P Dutton, A Division of Penguin USA Inc.
Fresh 15-Minute Meals by Emalee Chapman. Copyright © 1986 by Emalee Chapman. Reprinted by permission.

Harmony Books, A Division of Crown Publishers, Inc.
Natural Child Care by Maribeth Riggs. Copyright © 1989 by Maribeth Riggs and Rita Aero. Reprinted by permission.

Harper & Row Publishers, Inc.
Better Than Store-Bought by Helen Witty and Elizabeth Schneider Colchie. Copyright © 1979 by Helen Witty and Elizabeth Schneider Colchie. *Scarne's Encyclopedia of Games* by John Scarne. Copyright © 1973 by John Scarne Games Inc. *Cheaper & Better: Homemade Alternatives to Store-Bought Goods* by Nancy Birnes. Copyright © 1987 by Shadow Lawn Press, Inc. Reprinted by permission.

Little, Brown and Company
The Town & Country Cookbook by James Villas. Copyright © 1985 by James Villas. Reprinted by permission.

Mark Morris Associates, Topeka, Kansas
High Quality Maintenance Diet of Dogs and Cats. Reprinted by permission.

New American Library, A Division of Penguin USA Inc.
Deliciously Simple: Quick and Easy, Low-Sodium, Low-Fat, Low-Cholesterol, Low-Sugar Meals by Harriet Roth. Copyright © 1986 by Harriet Roth.

Deliciously Low: The Gourmet Guide to Low-Sodium, Low-Fat, Low-Cholesterol, Low-Sugar Cooking by Harriet Roth. Copyright © 1983 by Harriet Roth. Reprinted by permission.

The New York Public Library, Picture Collection

Ten Speed Press
The Moosewood Cookbook by Mollie Katzen. Copyright © 1977. Reprinted by permission.

Times Books, A Division of Quadrangle/The New York Times Book Co, Inc.
Check Yourself Out, edited by Craig T Norback. Copyright © 1980 by Craig T Norback. *The Grass Roots Cookbook* by Jean Anderson. Copyright © 1974 by Jean Anderson. Reprinted by permission.

Zondervan Corporation
Play It! by Wayne Rice and Mike Yaconelli. Copyright © 1986 by Youth Specialities, Inc. Reprinted by permission.

Consultants (American edition)
Ron Alford
Jean Anderson
Richard Asa
David A Barnebl, Sr VP, Paine Webber
Jennifer Birckmayer
Walter F Burghardt, Jr DVM, PhD
John J Byrne, MD, FACS
Al Carrell
John T Cavanaugh, MS, PT/ATC
Russell B Clanahan
John L Costa, MD, FAAP
Sheila Danko
Seymour Diamond, MD
Michaell M Dresdner
Ben T Etheridge
Michele C Fisher, PhD, RD
Todd P Forte
Michael S Frank, MD
Jim Fremont
Alan French, MBA, MM
Dora Galitzki
Bernard Gladstone
Leon Grabowski
Ray Greenley
Walter A Grub, Jr
Elizabeth Hall
Wade A Hoyt

Robert E Hueter, PhD
Marjorie Grossman Jaffe
John Karl
Roberta Ann Kaseman
William J Keller, PhD
Carolyn Klass
Steven Lamm, MD
Frances La Rosa
Walter LeStrange, RN, MPH
Scott Lewis
Cynthia J MacKay, MD
Jim McCann
Jean McLean
Janet E Meleney
John Mulligan, Assistant Fire Commissioner, New York Fire Department
Mary E Purchase, PhD
Ruth Raimon-Wilson
Maureen Reardon
Marilyn S Rogers
Gertrude Rowland
Lauren B Scheib
Gerry Schremp
Victor J Selmanowitz, MD
Frances E Shanahan
Leonard A Sipes, Jr, MS
Stanley H Smith
Joanne Tunney Stack, JD
Eric Stand

Marjabelle Young Stewart
Martha Strohl
Valerie Sutton
John Warde
Paul Weissler, SAE
Stephanie Whalen
Thomas A Wilson, DDS
Donald E Witten, National Weather Service

Special Thanks
American Health and Beauty Aids Institute
American Society of Travel Agents, Inc
Carole Collins
Consumer Communications Group
Carol Ennis
Gerald Ferguson
Lester Harrison
Melanie Hulse
Det Bernard Jacobs
Lothian Lynas
National Institute of Aging
Rosemary Nelson
Reynolds Metal Co
Kelly Riley
Ruth Savolaine
Salt Institute
The Soap and Detergent Association
The Softness Group

Separations: J Film Process Co Ltd, Bangkok
Paper: Townsend Hook Ltd, Snodland
Printing and Binding: Arnoldo Mondadori Editore, Verona

40-355-04